# Dictionary of Literary Biography

## Documentary Series

## *Yearbooks*

## *Concise Series*

Dictionary of Literary Biography® • Volume One Hundred Ninety-One

# British Novelists Between
# the Wars

Dictionary of Literary Biography® • Volume One Hundred Ninety-One

# British Novelists Between the Wars

Edited by
George M. Johnson
*University College of the Cariboo*

A Bruccoli Clark Layman Book
Gale Research
Detroit, Washington, D.C., London

**Library of Congress Cataloging-in-Publication Data**

British novelists between the wars / edited by George M. Johnson.
   p. cm.–(Dictionary of literary biography; v. 191)
"A Bruccoli Clark Layman book."
Includes bibliographical references and index.
ISBN 0-7876-1846-2 (alk. paper)
1. English fiction–20th century–Bio-bibliography–Dictionaries. 2. Novelists, English–20th century–Biography–Dictionaries. I. Johnson, George M. II. Series.
PR881.B728 1998
823'.9109–dc21
                                      97-52103
                                          CIP

10 9 8 7 6 5 4 3 2 1

*Dedicated to my parents, F. Eleanor Johnson and George J. Johnson*

# Contents

# Plan of the Series

*. . . Almost the most prodigious asset of a country, and perhaps its most precious possession, is its native literary product — when that product is fine and noble and enduring.*

Mark Twain*

The advisory board, the editors, and the publisher of the *Dictionary of Literary Biography* are joined in endorsing Mark Twain's declaration. The literature of a nation provides an inexhaustible resource of permanent worth. We intend to make literature and its creators better understood and more accessible to students and the reading public, while satisfying the standards of teachers and scholars.

To meet these requirements, *literary biography* has been construed in terms of the author's achievement. The most important thing about a writer is his writing. Accordingly, the entries in *DLB* are career biographies, tracing the development of the author's canon and the evolution of his reputation.

The purpose of *DLB* is not only to provide reliable information in a convenient format but also to place the figures in the larger perspective of literary history and to offer appraisals of their accomplishments by qualified scholars.

The publication plan for *DLB* resulted from two years of preparation. The project was proposed to Bruccoli Clark by Frederick C. Ruffner, president of the Gale Research Company, in November 1975. After specimen entries were prepared and typeset, an advisory board was formed to refine the entry format and develop the series rationale. In meetings held during 1976, the publisher, series editors, and advisory board approved the scheme for a comprehensive biographical dictionary of persons who contributed to North American literature. Editorial work on the first volume began in January 1977, and it was published in 1978. In order to make *DLB* more than a reference tool and to compile volumes that individually have claim to status as literary history, it was decided to organize volumes by

*From an unpublished section of Mark Twain's autobiography, copyright by the Mark Twain Company*

topic, period, or genre. Each of these freestanding volumes provides a biographical-bibliographical guide and overview for a particular area of literature. We are convinced that this organization—as opposed to a single alphabet method—constitutes a valuable innovation in the presentation of reference material. The volume plan necessarily requires many decisions for the placement and treatment of authors who might properly be included in two or three volumes. In some instances a major figure will be included in separate volumes, but with different entries emphasizing the aspect of his career appropriate to each volume. Ernest Hemingway, for example, is represented in *American Writers in Paris, 1920–1939* by an entry focusing on his expatriate apprenticeship; he is also in *American Novelists, 1910–1945* with an entry surveying his entire career, as well as in *American Short-Story Writers, 1910–1945, Second Series* with an entry concentrating on his short stories. Each volume includes a cumulative index of the subject authors and articles. Comprehensive indexes to the entire series are planned.

The series has been further augmented by the *DLB Yearbooks* (since 1981) which update published entries and add new entries to keep the *DLB* current with contemporary activity. There have also been *DLB Documentary Series* volumes which provide biographical and critical source materials for figures whose work is judged to have particular interest for students. One of these companion volumes is entirely devoted to Tennessee Williams.

We define literature as the *intellectual commerce of a nation:* not merely as belles lettres but as that ample and complex process by which ideas are generated, shaped, and transmitted. *DLB* entries are not limited to "creative writers" but extend to other figures who in their time and in their way influenced the mind of a people. Thus the series encompasses historians, journalists, publishers, book collectors, and screenwriters. By this means readers of *DLB* may be aided to perceive literature not as cult scripture in the keeping of intellectual high priests but firmly positioned at the center of a nation's life.

*DLB* includes the major writers appropriate to each volume and those standing in the ranks behind them. Scholarly and critical counsel has been sought in deciding which minor figures to include and how full their entries should be. Wherever possible, useful references are made to figures who do not warrant separate entries.

Each *DLB* volume has an expert volume editor responsible for planning the volume, selecting the figures for inclusion, and assigning the entries. Volume editors are also responsible for preparing, where appropriate, appendices surveying the major periodicals and literary and intellectual movements for their volumes, as well as lists of further readings. Work on the series as a whole is coordinated at the Bruccoli Clark Layman editorial center in Columbia, South Carolina, where the editorial staff is responsible for accuracy and utility of the published volumes.

One feature that distinguishes *DLB* is the illustration policy—its concern with the iconography of literature. Just as an author is influenced by his surroundings, so is the reader's understanding of the author enhanced by a knowledge of his environment. Therefore *DLB* volumes include not only drawings, paintings, and photographs of authors, often depicting them at various stages in their careers, but also illustrations of their families and places where they lived. Title pages are regularly reproduced in facsimile along with dust jackets for modern authors. The dust jackets are a special feature of *DLB* because they often document better than anything else the way in which an author's work was perceived in its own time. Specimens of the writers' manuscripts and letters are included when feasible.

Samuel Johnson rightly decreed that "The chief glory of every people arises from its authors." The purpose of the *Dictionary of Literary Biography* is to compile literary history in the surest way available to us—by accurate and comprehensive treatment of the lives and work of those who contributed to it.

The *DLB* Advisory Board

# Introduction

*Dictionary of Literary Biography* volume 191, *British Novelists Between the Wars,* provides a companion to *DLB 153: Late-Victorian and Edwardian British Novelists, First Series* (1995), and a forthcoming *Second Series* volume. The rationale behind the current volume is similar to that of the *Late-Victorian and Edwardian* volumes. Like them, it moves beyond the established literary canon to deal with writers who are not covered in *DLB 15: British Novelists 1930–1959* (1983), *DLB 34: British Novelists, 1890–1929: Traditionalists* (1985), or *DLB 36: British Novelists 1890–1929: Modernists* (1985). Since those volumes were published, the interwar period and the writers who contributed to its discourses have attracted increasingly wider attention. Especially thought-provoking have been several feminist studies, including Nicola Beauman's *A Very Great Profession: The Woman's Novel 1914–1939* (1983) and Angela Ingram and Daphne Patai's collection of essays, *Rediscovering Forgotten Radicals: British Women Writers 1889–1939* (1993); socialist analyses, notably Andy Croft's *Red Letter Days: British Fiction in the 1930s* (1990); and more-general literary histories, such as John Onions's *English Fiction and Drama of the Great War: 1918–1939* (1990), Samuel Hynes's *A War Imagined: The First World War and English Culture* (1991), and Rosa Maria Bracco's *Merchants of Hope: British Middlebrow Writers and the First World War, 1919–1939* (1993). Most of these works challenge accepted views of the literary history of the period by examining writers excluded from the traditional literary canon, and a few even question the basis of that canon. When one becomes familiar with writers who are not normally given much consideration, one realizes that a great deal more revisionist work needs to be done.

*British Novelists Between the Wars* both responds and contributes to that process of revision. Although interest in the period has also been indicated by recent full-scale biographical or critical treatments of several of the writers in this volume—including H. E. Bates (1987), Vera Brittain (1995), Robert Graves (1986–1997), Charlotte Haldane (1996), Radclyffe Hall (1998), Patrick Hamilton (1993), Georgette Heyer (1984), Naomi Mitchison (1997), Edwin Muir (1993), Beverley Nichols (1991), William Plomer (1989), Edward Sackville-West (1988), Henry Williamson (1995), and Francis Brett Young (1986)—the majority of the authors remain obscure to many readers. This volume attempts to recover those writers.

The novelists treated in *DLB 191* range from those who started to write just as World War I drew to a close in 1918 to those who embarked on their literary careers just prior to the advent of World War II in 1939. The wars have not always demarcated this period in literary histories. In the early years of the period itself, writers and critics began to refer to themselves as Georgians, after the accession to the throne of George V in 1910. In 1912 the first of several collections of Georgian poetry appeared, and the label was solidified by various writers, notably by Virginia Woolf and by that influential man of letters Frank Swinnerton, whose literary history *The Georgian Literary Scene 1910–1935* appeared in 1935. The designation followed a long tradition of naming literary periods after reigning monarchs. The work of these writers was characterized by a reaction against Victorian moral conventions and by a seriousness of purpose that often included an interest in social reform or in psychological probing of character. From within this movement, however, there appeared just prior to World War I a small group of writers who practiced a much more radical experimentation in form than did the majority of their peers. In the genre of the novel the radicalism of these writers—who included Woolf, James Joyce, D. H. Lawrence, and Dorothy Richardson—gained enormous impetus from the feelings of chaos, disillusionment, and disintegration generated by the war, even though most of them had not participated in it. In the postwar decades such younger writers as Aldous Huxley, Rose Macaulay, and Rebecca West followed their lead. By their early critics these writers were variously labeled "avant-garde" or "sophisticates" because of their progressive attitudes and the technical daring and complexity of some of their work, or "post-Freudian" because of their assimilation of some of the findings and techniques of Sigmund Freud's psychoanalytic theory and, perhaps, because of the inward-looking character of their work. Not until the earliest of these writers was in mid career, in the late 1920s, did the label *Modernist* begin to be applied to the poets among them; it has continued to be applied to writers working up to the early 1960s. Though nebulous, *Modernist* has overtaken the other labels and is sometimes used loosely to characterize the entire body of writing of this period.

Neither the time frames nor the character represented by the terms *Georgian* or *Modernist,* however, most appropriately identify the novelists treated in this volume. *Georgian* is not the most apposite term because it was not the reign of the monarch that defined these years or the writing produced during them but the collective traumas of the world wars. And, strictly speaking, *Modernist* accurately describes only a few experimental writers—though they have exerted an impact disproportionate to their numbers—and could only be applied to a few of the writers in this volume, such as Romer Wilson, and to a few individual works, such as Muir's *The Marionette* (1927), Naomi Royde-Smith's *The Lover* (1928), and John Hampson's *Saturday Night at the Greyhound* (1931).

Many writers thought that World War I had opened up a huge gulf in society, and they compared the chaotic postwar world with a prewar one that, in retrospect, seemed Edenic. The novelist J. D. Beresford, who would become a close collaborator of Esmé Wynne-Tyson in the 1940s, reflected in *The Bookman* (May 1930) that "the whole of modern life had been sharply divided into the two incompatible periods of 'before' and 'after' the great event [the war], and it was exceedingly difficult to bridge them and still preserve the nice sense of continuity that was essential to the life-story of hero or heroine." He went on to describe other commonly held feelings: that there was a great divide between combatants and noncombatants and that the latter were at a definite disadvantage with regard to the subject matter of novel writing: "I remember very clearly that in the years immediately following the War I often felt that for such non-combatants as myself there was little left to write about." There can be no doubt that the war and its effects became a major theme in literature, beginning with a trickle of novels that were published in the last two years of the war and continuing with a flood of more-critical and disillusioned novels that started to appear around 1928. Noncombatant novelists added their voices to descriptions of the toll of war, typically on the home front. Not surprisingly, war is the dominant theme that runs through this volume. The war is present in the feelings of absence and loss that characterize many works discussed here that would not usually be considered war novels.

With the signing of the Treaty of Versailles in June 1919, some perceptive people became uneasy about the potential for another conflict. In his war memoir *Good-Bye to All That* (1929) Graves recalled: "The Treaty of Versailles shocked me; it seemed destined to cause another war some day, yet nobody cared." The founding of the League of Nations in 1920 temporarily assuaged the fears of some intellectuals; but the league's authority was challenged in 1923 by the attack on the Greek island of Corfu by Italy under Benito Mussolini. In retrospect, the so-called postwar years seem to have been plagued by armed conflict, from the bloody aftermath of the Bolshevik Revolution in Russia through "the Troubles" in Ireland to a 1926 military coup in Poland and Adolf Hitler's violent rise to power in Germany, though British involvement in and attention to these events varied considerably. By the early 1930s, however, anxiety about another world-level conflict had grown in Britain, at least among more-perceptive people, and the outbreak of the Spanish civil war in July 1936 only exacerbated those fears. The triumph of fascism in Spain seems merely to have been the "curtain-raiser" to World War II. That conflict officially began when Britain and France declared war on Germany on 3 September 1939, although serious fighting did not commence until May 1940.

What kinds of impact did World War I have on British society of the 1920s and 1930s? Volumes have been written on this subject, but a few salient points might usefully be made here. The statistics are well known. Of the six million British men who served in the war, nearly one million were killed in action; five hundred thousand of those remained in unmarked graves at the war's end. These dead are the true lost generation, but, as Hynes points out, the phrase *lost generation* also refers to the disoriented and directionless survivors, some of whom were permanently maimed physically or psychologically or both. In 1920 sixty-five thousand of them were receiving disability pensions for neurasthenia. Many survivors returned home to find themselves displaced from their jobs and unemployment rising at an alarming rate. One group that stands out is the "Temporary Gentlemen," men from the lower-middle and working classes who had been promoted to officer rank during the war but who, after the war, could not maintain the status traditionally associated with that rank. As Martin Petter says in his "'Temporary Gentlemen' in the Aftermath of the Great War: Rank, Status and the Ex-Officer Problem" in *The Historical Journal* (1994): "The figure of the distressed ex-officer was one which came to seize the popular imagination in the years following the Great War. Indeed, it became somewhat of a cliché in the novels and tracts of the period." The social and economic decline these men experienced heightened their class consciousness and increased the tensions between the classes and between combatants and noncombatants. In their survey of the interwar years, *The Long Week-end: A Social History of Great Britain, 1918–1939* (1940), Graves and Alan Hodge drive home the disparity between the latter two groups by referring to them as "two distinct Britains."

Although those who had actually fought in the war often felt the strongest alienation in postwar society, since they were unable or unwilling to convey to noncombatants the horrors they had experienced, few people were not affected by the deaths of friends and loved ones. Women responded in a variety of ways: some mourned; some gave in to despair, bitterness, or cynicism; some developed a certain toughness; and some abandoned themselves to hedonistic pleasures. As Graves and Hodge sardonically report, those who could afford to do so "went on personally conducted tours to the 'Devastated Regions' and ate picnics in the trenches with old ammunition-boxes as makeshift tables." Some threw off social restraints, expressing their newfound freedom through more-revealing dress and by engaging in formerly frowned-on activities such as smoking and ragtime dancing. Male resentment of women was high because most had remained in the relative comfort of the home front, and many had moved into the traditional sphere of the man—the working world—in large numbers: about 1.3 million had done so by the war's end. They were, according to Graves and Hodge, "represented as vampires who deprived men of their rightful jobs." In reality, however, some 750,000 women had been dismissed from their wartime posts by the fall of 1919, and they received no unemployment benefits. Although women had made some other gains, including the right to vote (extended in 1918 to women at least thirty years old who owned their own homes) and entry into professions such as law and government and into at least one of the universities (Oxford), their position in society remained unenviable. The war's toll on the male population left a surplus of 1.75 million women, and for many of them the absence of men would have a long-term effect on their lives.

Many of the writers who had fought in the war returned home to find that during their absence their noncombatant colleagues had secured the most influential positions; Muir is an example of one who benefited in this way. Also, as Hynes points out, a younger generation was already vying for position in the literary limelight. Looking back in 1945 in his *The Nineteen Twenties: A General Survey and Some Personal Memories,* the novelist and literary historian Douglas Goldring, who was thirty-one in 1918, lamented the practice of closed-circle literary reviewing, or "log-rolling," which boycotted iconoclastic authors and led to a decline in their income and status. Writers who were combat veterans did not form a coterie but pursued diverse and, at times, eccentric interests. A few, such as Young and, later, Graves, found that they could not remain in England and, encouraged by the strength of the pound sterling, began to drift to foreign lands.

In immediate postwar Britain, then, relief at the cessation of fighting was overshadowed by a dominant tone of loss, bitterness, disillusionment, alienation, and frustration, though responses to these feelings were diverse. Many felt, as Goldring did, that war had ruined the best people and enriched the worst—the "rising Medicis" who had made their fortunes selling armaments and other war goods.

Britain limped uncertainly into the 1920s, crippled by wartime neglect of its infrastructure, by unemployment, and by debts to the United States. The Americans, who profited enormously from the war, negotiated a settlement of £1,000 million in interest on the war debt of £978 million—a rate twice as high as that later negotiated with France. Despite this "victory," Americans expressed some hostility toward Britain, which went largely unnoticed there—even though American influence pervaded British culture, from fashion to dancing, motion pictures, and fiction.

The decade that became known as the Roaring Twenties and the Careless Twenties has been characterized as a glittery, superficial age of flappers and Bright Young Things. Critics during the period repeatedly comment on the collapse of prewar propriety and morality. The new generation resented and rebelled against the older one that had led England into the catastrophe of war with its false ideals of patriarchal virtue and patriotic honor. Satire was frequently used to expose false rhetoric and ideals; this trend is represented in this volume by A. P. Herbert and Alec Waugh. In his *Children of the Sun: A Narrative of "Decadence" in England after 1918* (1976) Martin Green explores the revival of decadence and aestheticism during these years, a tendency notably reflected in Nichols's novel *Patchwork* (1921). Much of the frenzied hedonism and negativity can be seen as reactions to loss.

But the 1920s can also be seen from a more positive perspective. Goldring fondly recalls the "flood of liberating ideas let loose in the early 20s" and the "outburst of creative energy" that transformed those ideas into art. Male and female intellectuals discussed sexuality and other topics that were formerly shrouded in secrecy with more frankness and less hypocrisy, in spite of the rage for applying to such matters the jargon of Freudian psychoanalysis. Prophets of the new morality, such as Dr. Marie Stopes in her enormously popular *Married Love* (1918), educated people about sexual practices and removed the stigma from birth control, though not without opposition from religious leaders. Living together before marriage, and "companionate" marriages for those who could not afford to marry legally, became more acceptable. The education of children was more enlightened and began to include sex education. Nor was the populace politically apathetic; the demand for change can be seen in the rise of the Labour Party from the election of 1918, when it secured fifty-seven seats in Parliament, to formation of a Labour government in 1924, as well as in the formation of the British Communist Party in 1920. The main organ of socialism was *The Daily Herald,* with a circulation of one hundred thousand and the popular George Lansbury as editor.

Graves and Hodge claim that there were few left-wing intellectuals in the 1920s; but as the decade progressed, the intelligentsia identified more and more closely with the working class. Throughout the 1920s there were many writers who were committed to social and political change, including, among those treated in this volume, Rhys Davies and Naomi Jacob. One of the more notable left-leaning avant-garde publications was *Coterie,* published from Frank "Bomb" Henderson's Left Wing Bookshop in the Charing Cross Road. Davies and L. A. G. Strong, who also appears in the present volume, were among the contributors to that journal. Writers achieved a stronger voice in 1921 through the formation of the P.E.N. Club, the international writers' organization. The event that really galvanized, and polarized, writers' political commitments, however, was the General Strike of 1926. Although there had been strikes earlier in the decade, notably the miners' strike of 1921, this one was different because of its scale, the fear of revolution that it inspired, and the repressive manner in which it was handled by the Conservative government. Under the direction of Chancellor of the Exchequer Winston S. Churchill, the government enlisted upper-middle- and middle-class volunteers to maintain essential services through the ten days of the strike. The allegiance of writers tended to divide along class lines, with members of the privileged classes such as Waugh and John Galsworthy supporting the government and writers from the lower middle class standing with the workers. Goldring asserts that the General Strike "set back the political clock for twenty years" and crushed the hopes of the intelligentsia. From a perspective more distant in time, Hynes observes that the strike marked the end

of the political innocence of many writers and the beginning of the political activism of the 1930s. It is no coincidence that the first recorded use of the term *Leftism*—by H. G. Wells—occurred in the year following the strike.

Britain entered the 1930s reeling from the effects of the Great Depression. In the aftermath of the stock market crash of 24 October 1929 the United States terminated loans to Britain and other countries, capital became scarce, the level of British exports fell, and unemployment increased. By the end of 1931, 23 percent of British workers covered by unemployment insurance, or around 2.5 million, were out of work; but, as Norman Page notes in *The Thirties in Britain* (1990), the total number of unemployed was probably around 3.5 million. Not until 1935 did it drop below 2 million, and it remained well above a million for the rest of the decade. Voices arose in protest, and political consciousness increased dramatically. The solutions proposed were diverse, however, and political polarization was the result. Following the defeat of the Labour Party in 1931, a nationalist party, consisting of a coalition of representatives of the major parties, came to power; with several changes of leadership, it would remain in power until after World War II. In 1932 Sir Oswald Mosley formed the British Union of Fascists, which took Mussolini's and, later, Hitler's governments as models. Its leadership came from the middle class, but it had strong financial backing and claimed a membership of twenty thousand less than two years after its inception. The strongest voices of protest came from the left-wing groups, including socialists and communists, though they were in no sense unified.

Political writing was the dominant form of writing in the 1930s; but its scope has traditionally been restricted by the focus on highbrow literature of the period, and the left-wing W. H. Auden generation of poets, in particular. Their retrospective view of the decade as an embarrassing failure has prevailed; in Auden's words, it was "a low, dishonorable decade" because the "clever hopes" of its leftist writers and idealists were defeated by the triumph of fascism and a second world war. Revisionist literary historians, however, have shown that on the domestic level, at least, literature had a considerable impact on culture. Andy Croft argues in *Red Letter Days: British Fiction in the 1930s* (1990) that leftist writers, novelists in particular, captured the imagination of the public, exposed the failure of political leadership and the grim realities of poverty, and breathed new life into the genres of historical, romantic, and dystopian fiction. The decade opened with a torrent of novels dispelling sentimental illusions about the last war by demonstrating its futility and the incompetence of its leaders. Soon after, the proletarian, or "working-class," novel, with its depictions of the harsh realities of slum life and the social and psychological devastation of economic collapse, came into its own. Political awareness and consciousness of the need for change permeated the middle and upper classes, and many writers from these groups added their voices to the articulation of the plight of the less fortunate.

Important organs for the dissemination of leftist views included the *Left Review,* first published in October 1934. As Croft notes, it was soon selling more than five thousand copies a month, second only to the rather fusty liberal review, the *London Mercury.* The Left Book Club was formed in May 1936, just before the outbreak of the Spanish civil war, and soon had a membership of forty thousand. It provided its members one book a month on a wide variety of contemporary topics from a leftist point of view. Penguin books were also first produced in 1936; although they had a more general scope, they provided inexpensive (sixpence) editions of recent successful books for the masses.

All but three of the Left Book Club titles were nonfiction political works, and political books flooded the general market as anxiety increased about the possibility of another war. The abdication of Edward VIII in December 1936 seemed to be yet another sign that past certainties could no longer be counted on. One response to the feeling of uncertainty early in the decade had been a nostalgia for Victorian culture that found expression in a variety of ways, from dress to drama; Noel Coward's panoramic *Cavalcade* (1932) is a striking example in the latter category.

A more significant response to war anxiety, as well as to the antiwar feeling generated by the war novels of 1929 to 1931, was the growth of a peace movement in the mid 1930s. In October 1934 the pacifist canon "Dick" Sheppard invited people to state their renunciation of war by sending him a postcard; within a year eighty thousand had done so. In 1935 a Peace Ballot was held in Britain, and, as Graves and Hodge record, "out of eleven and a half million voters, ten and a half declared their faith in the League of Nations, and in the use of non-military sanctions against aggressor nations. But a large majority also favored disarmament."

Despite these efforts and the government policy of appeasement of the fascist dictatorships, signs of aggression in Europe increased with the Italian occupation of Abyssinia (Ethiopia) in 1935 and Hitler's occupation of Austria in 1938 and of Czecho-slovakia in 1939. Writers responded with an outpouring of darkly fantastic and dystopian fiction. By the outbreak of war in September 1939, the mood could not have differed more from that at the beginning of World War I. Gone was the exuberance; a desire for glory was replaced by dread and depression. Graves and Hodge refer to the period as "confused and inglorious." Hynes notes that the 1930s generation of poets fell silent at this time, since they believed that their protest against fascism had been made during the Spanish civil war. Novelists, however, such as R. C. Hutchinson in *The Fire and the Wood* (1940), continued to articulate the sinister possibilities of the latest version of fascism, the Third Reich.

Graves and Hodge close their survey of the interwar years by ruefully noting that poetry was in decline and that the "crown had passed to the novelist, who was essayist, dramatist, pamphleteer, prose-poet, historian, all in one." In the process the novel became the servant of powerful commercial forces. One feature of postwar American influence in Britain was the opening of a large American market for British writers. By the mid 1920s the boom was on. The British had adopted the American terms of *highbrow, middlebrow,* and *lowbrow,* based on the type of audience to which a novel would likely appeal. *Highbrow* was reserved for cerebral and often experimental Modernist narratives; *middlebrow* referred to more-conventional narratives that provided some intellectual stimulus; and *lowbrow* designated light "formula" fiction, primarily in the romance, adventure, mystery, and thriller genres. Contemporary highbrows as diverse as Woolf and George Orwell tended to ignore lowbrow fiction and to disparage middlebrow fiction because of its conservatism and lack of literariness. Literary critics and historians have followed this lead, typically focusing on highbrow writers between the wars. From the 1920s the Bright Young People, including Aldous Huxley and Evelyn Waugh, and in the 1930s Auden and his friends have received most of the attention, although in both cases they represent only a handful of the worthy writers who were producing at the time. Similarly, a handful of novelists, including Joyce, Woolf, Orwell, Huxley, and Alec Waugh's brother, Evelyn, constitutes the canon in that genre and is used to represent the period. In an even more extreme case of distortion, Orwell's rather polemical statement that in the 1930s there was "practically no fiction of any value at all" became accepted as dogma. This volume demonstrates the narrowness of conceptions of the interwar period based on canonized writers. Although their particular expression of fragmentation and alienation represents an admittedly important part of the ethos of the period, it does not come close to suggesting the range of attitudes and responses to the times that were expressed in the novel.

If, as Hynes and others have argued, the war made history discontinuous, and the Modernists responded by escaping that history through fragmenting narrative, many of the novelists in this volume help restore a sense of historical context. Although Woolf disparaged "froth of the moment" fiction chronicling the times, she grudgingly provides insight into its importance:

> To know the outside of one's age, its dresses and its dances and its catchwords, has an interest and even a value which the spiritual adventures of a curate, or the aspiration of a high-minded school mistress, solemn as they are, for the most part lack. It might well be claimed, too, that to deal with the crowded dance of modern life so as to produce the illusion of reality needs far higher literary skill than to write a serious essay on the poetry of John Donne or the novels of M. Proust. The novelist, then, who is a slave to life and concocts his books out of the froth of the moment is doing something difficult, something which pleases, something which, if you have a mind that way, may even instruct.

While not all of the novelists treated in this volume are "slaves to life," most provide vivid details about their period. Wynne-Tyson's colorful depictions of the 1920s Noel Coward set come to mind. More important, the novelists represented here reflect the values of their society. Some of the novels discussed in this volume are important for specific historical reasons. Alec Waugh's *The Loom of Youth* (1918), by attacking the public-school system and Victorian conventions, had a scandalous impact on the novel similar to that which Lytton Strachey's *Eminent Victorians* (1918) had on biography. Herbert's *The Secret Battle* (1919) was one of the first and most striking of a new kind of war novel depicting the damaged man, a forerunner of the modern antihero. Wilson's *The Death of Society* (1921), together with Lawrence's *Women in Love* (1920) and E. M. Forster's *A Passage to India* (1924), "helped to establish the unmoral tone of post-war fiction," as William C. Frierson notes in *The English Novel in Transition 1885–1940* (1942). A few novels even helped to change public opinion or government policies: Walter Greenwood's best-selling *Love on the Dole* (1933), for example, was one of the first works of fiction that graphically depicted the miseries of unemployment for a middle-class reading public; and Ernest Raymond's *We, the Accused* (1935) influenced the

commissioners charged with reforming the prison system, all of whom had read the novel.

Some of the novels discussed in this volume provided a strong countertrend to the endemic sense of alienation and fragmentation in postwar society, not by ignoring or providing escape from social ills but by giving hope that these ills could be endured and, in some cases, overcome. Rosa Maria Bracco argues in *Merchants of Hope: British Middlebrow Writers and the First World War, 1919–1939* (1993) for the cultural significance of middlebrow fiction by claiming that

> a whole body of work, 7s 6d novels which formed the staple of publishers' lists, needs to be reopened to reveal a set of evidence concerned not with describing the alienated role of the writer, nor with presenting a reality of irreconcilable fragments, but rather with offering an analysis of their society which would serve as a blueprint for reconstituting the fragments into a familiar picture.

In *A Room of One's Own* (1929) Woolf laments the absence of the quality of romance in the postwar world; but this is a typical highbrow view, since many of the novels discussed in this volume demonstrate that romance continued to flourish, though in slightly altered form, in middlebrow novels between the wars. Not only were middlebrow novels therapeutic for their audience, but they also provided therapy for the writers themselves, notably so in the case of the war novelists. Several of them wrote and rewrote about their war experiences as a means of expunging the powerful emotions and painful memories of that time. But another important role of these novels is alluded to by Woolf: their entertainment value. This volume includes discussions of several classic comic writers, such as the *Punch* contributor Herbert, but many more of these authors provided entertainment in an age when radio was just coming into its own and television was in its infancy.

The biographies of the writers in *DLB 191* provide a composite portrait of what conditions were like for professional, "Grub Street" writers during the era. Goldring, a contemporary of many writers in the volume, reflects:

> Writers of my age and generation have suffered under severe handicaps. Two major wars in one lifetime, apart from their economic consequences for what is humorously regarded as a "luxury profession," have been too much of an emotional strain for any except the major talents or those protected from the harsh winds of adversity by what are called "private means."

Most of these novelists lacked those "private means," as they came from the middle classes; and their biographies well illustrate the emotional and economic struggles of the writers of the period. If many could not afford to be experimental in their work, a few—including Jacob, Wynne-Tyson, and Ethel Mannin—achieved experiments in living, making their biographies intrinsically fascinating.

The works of many of the novelists in this volume achieved best-seller status; thus, these writers typically touched more lives than did their longer-remembered and more critically acclaimed colleagues. A high proportion of them managed the more difficult accomplishment of combining popularity with critical acclaim. Novels that received one or more of the most prestigious British literary awards—the Femina–Vie Heureuse Prize, the James Tait Memorial Award, the Hawthornden Prize, and the Book Guild Gold Medal—during the interwar period include Wilson's *The Death of Society* in 1921, Hall's *Adam's Breed* and Williamson's *Tarka the Otter* in 1927, Siegfried Sassoon's *Memoirs of a Fox-Hunting Man* and Young's *Portrait of Clare* in 1928, Graves's *I, Claudius* and *Claudius the God and His Wife Messalina* and Raymond's *We, the Accused* in 1935, Richard Church's *The Porch* in 1937, and Hutchinson's *Testament* in 1938. Several novels received American prizes, including Elizabeth Goudge's *Green Dolphin Country* (1944), which won an M-G-M Literary Award worth $125,000, and Ann Bridge's *Peking Picnic* (1932), which was awarded the *Atlantic Monthly* Prize. Some of the works of these writers were adapted as motion pictures, thereby reaching an even wider audience.

If these novels both instructed and entertained a whole generation of readers, it seems strange, as Beauman notes, that they have subsequently been dismissed or ignored. Aside from the pervasiveness of a Modernist aesthetic that views this kind of fiction harshly, there are other factors that have helped to relegate these novels to obscurity: some of them are long-winded, have unnecessary plot complications or weak plots, are stylistically uneven, have not assimilated the issues treated, or have characters who fail to come to life. Many, however, suffer from none of these flaws and have been passed over for less-justifiable reasons. In some cases gender bias has contributed to the neglect. Alison Light claims in *Forever England: Femininity, Literature and Conservatism between the Wars* (1991) that "it is extraordinary how much of the literary history of 'the inter-war years' has been rendered almost exclusively in male terms." In the fiction of the 1930s not one female is traditionally included in the canon, although, as Valentine Cunningham notes in *British Writers of the Thirties* (1988), "the novel, in the 1930s as in the whole period since the form established itself in Britain, was the classic medium of the woman writer." Nevertheless, even Cunningham provides in his voluminous survey only the scantiest treatment of a few of the better-known women novelists. *DLB 191* at least begins to rectify that glaring omission, since almost half of the entries are on women novelists. Politics and class also play important roles in the neglect into which these novelists have fallen. Then, too, some of the novelists in this volume, especially those who wrote romances, have been dismissed as genre writers and therefore as unworthy of consideration in the mainstream development of the English novel. Finally, many of these writers were extremely prolific, and one wonders whether the sheer bulk of their work has discouraged scholars from attending to it.

Nevertheless, the novels produced by these writers reveal trends that illuminate the period in question. Through the interwar years the historical novel became more prevalent and, in some cases, prominent. Graves and Hodge claim that by the early 1930s the dominant feeling was against reading books merely for entertainment: "people read a novel to acquire factual knowledge pleasantly. It was expected of an historical novel, for example, that though certain romantic incidents and conversations must be invented, the framework of history should be sound and no major historical fact distorted." Graves himself benefited from this trend with his successful novels of classical civilization, especially *I, Claudius*. Other novelists treated in this volume who wrote historical novels include Goudge, Heyer, Young, C. S. Forester, Doris Leslie, Naomi Mitchison, Adelaide Eden Phillpotts, Naomi Royde-Smith, and D. E. Stevenson. The periods covered range from Old Testament and ancient Roman times in Graves's work through the Regency period (1811 to 1820) in Heyer's to the mid-Victorian period in Royde-Smith's. While a few, such as Mitchison in *The Conquered* (1923), used historical settings to comment indirectly on the woes of their contemporary culture, others provided distant, closed-off, and thus secure worlds for readers attempting to cope with a rapidly and disturbingly changing world.

As Graves and Hodge mention, many of these historical novels included romantic elements; and romance fiction as such, of varying levels of quality, is also featured prominently in this volume. Among the practitioners are Bridge, Goudge, Heyer, Leslie, Jacob, Stevenson, and A. J. Cronin; there is also the odd novel by Haldane (*Melusine; or, Devil Take Her!:*

*A Romantic Novel,* 1936) or by Graves himself, such as his biblical romance *My Head! My Head!* (1925). The tone of this type of work ranges from Sassoon's pastoral *Memoirs of a Fox-Hunting Man* to R. C. Sherriff's sentimental *Greengates* (1936) and the melodrama of Cronin. Women novelists such as Jacobs often adapted the form to explore the emancipation of their heroines.

War novels, probably the dominant type between the wars, might be considered a subgenre of the historical novel as they attempt to grapple with recent history; they also often draw on the romance genre. These works deal with the war on all fronts, from the western through the East African (as in Young's *Marching on Tanga (with General Smuts in East Africa),* 1917) to the home front. The tone of these novels varies from the patriotic and enthusiastic attitudes prevalent at the outset of the war, as in Raymond's *Tell England* (1922), to disenchantment and bitter condemnation of war characteristic of the novels that flooded the market in the late 1920s, such as John Brophy's *The Bitter End* (1928) and George Blake's *The Path of Glory* (1929)—the last of which is considered by Bracco the most realistic and somber portrayal of warfare produced during the period. The earlier patriotic and sentimental novels tended to be written by noncombatants or, at least, by those who had not experienced the front lines. Frequently, as in *Tell England,* they treat war as a game and take their heroes straight from the public school to the battlefield. These novels embody the romantic ideals of youth and courage, although some of them trace the movement from boyish elation to disillusion. In contrast, war veterans produced the later works, which might more accurately be termed antiwar novels. These ironic and realistic novels typically explode the heroic myth, though occasionally they attempt to redefine the notion of heroism, and they probably represent the most lasting contribution of World War I fiction. This volume includes discussions of some of the best-known and most controversial of these novels, including Sassoon's *Memoirs of an Infantry Officer* (1930) and Sherriff's *Journey's End* (1930).

The prominence and thematic significance of the war in these novels varies considerably. In many the war is merely a backdrop for an adventure tale or a sentimental love story. The theme of love between enemies, and particularly the extraordinary Christmas Day Truce of 1914, captured the imagination of some novelists, notably Williamson. More often the war disrupts or destroys romantic relationships. Several novelists deal with the war obliquely or indirectly, while others use the war to bring out the characteristics, including the weaknesses, of an individual under the stress of combat. In the most deeply engaged war novels, such as Wilson's *If All These Young Men* (1919), war can even be considered the protagonist. Some novelists employ the war to prove a thesis, either of the disintegration of values in the postwar world or its opposite, the continuity of prewar values. In middlebrow fiction, as Bracco notes, expressions of human value constantly counter memories of the degradation of war.

Though male authors, such as Williamson, wrote novels depicting the home front, women, for obvious reasons, drew more frequently on such settings. Vera Brittain's experiences as a V.A.D. (Voluntary Aid Detachment) nurse provided the subject matter for her novel *Honourable Estate* (1936). Several women drew on their roles as nurses and ambulance drivers in Europe during the war; among them was Enid Bagnold in *The Happy Foreigner* (1920). A recurring theme in such novels is the contrast between the life-and-death crises of wartime and the trivial problems of civilian life.

The majority of the war novels discussed in this volume deal with World War I, but other wars also receive attention—World War II in novels by Stevenson and Forester; the Spanish civil war, which is foreshadowed in Mannin's political *Cactus* (1935) and detailed in Bridge's *Frontier Passage* (1942); and the Russian and Turkish Revolutions, in Hutchinson's *Testament* and Bridge's *The Dark Moment* (1952), respectively.

Most of the war novels of the 1920s and 1930s attempt to deal with their subject realistically, although the realism ranges from a restrained and circumspect documentation to graphic depictions of ugly or mundane realities that are disparagingly referred to as "the latrine school of fiction." These novels belong to the tradition of realism, which continued as a strong vein in the interwar years and was probably tapped most fully in the 1930s. The immediate postwar years, however, also saw the flourishing of a particular type of realism: psychological realism, under which heading might be placed psychoanalytical fiction and the sex novel—the latter considered by Graves and Hodge "the most popularly compelling fiction of the day." Before the war the psychologist Havelock Ellis's work on dreams and sexuality had achieved notoriety, and Freud's ideas on the same topics had begun to circulate among a select group of medical practitioners. During the war psychoanalysis received an impetus when M. D. Eder and W. H. R. Rivers applied its ideas to identify and treat "shell shock" (what is today referred to as post-traumatic stress disorder). Following the war Freudian, Jungian, and, later, Adlerian insights into such topics as the unconscious and complexes were more widely disseminated and popularized. In 1919 Beresford wrote, in an article titled "Psycho-analysis and the Novel," that "psycho-analysis is becoming at once the craze and the curse of the modern novelist." He praised its potential for providing "material for comparatively unworked complications of motive" and its liberating effect on morality, but he lamented the mechanical application of its materials by opportunists and sensationalists. Although the major exponents of the serious assimilation of the "new" psychology into novels, such as May Sinclair, Dorothy Richardson, and Rebecca West, are not treated in this volume, included are several novelists who employed it to break through the boundaries of conventional morality and its taboo subjects. Wilson in *The Death of Society* depicts a woman fulfilling herself in adultery with the consent of her aging husband, and Wynne-Tyson portrays sexual liberation in *Security* (1926). Royde-Smith probes the taboos of homosexuality and suicide in *The Tortoiseshell Cat* (1924) and *The Housemaid* (1926). Hall aroused the most public controversy of any of these novelists with her lesbian novel *The Well of Loneliness* (1928), which was banned in England until 1949 even though it is a model of reticence. Serious novelists continued to test propriety with frank depictions of sexuality throughout the period, as in Davies's *The Withered Root* (1927) and Mitchison's *We Have Been Warned* (1935).

Some of these psychologically realistic novels brought women's issues to the fore, and the feminist novel made significant progress between the wars. After women attained the vote (the franchise was extended to women aged twenty-one and above in 1928), attention shifted from that issue to self-fulfillment, independence, and equality of opportunity in general. Beauman claims that "The feminist novels that were written between the wars tend to be in the tradition of the 'Old' feminism, being concerned less with the stark realities of either male or political oppression than with women's chances for self-fulfilment in a still unequal society. They were about the importance of the human being when that being happens to be female." Several novelists present strong, independent women fulfilling themselves through unconventional behavior. Bridge's *Peking Picnic* portrays a thirty-seven-year-old married woman's sexual desire for more than one man, while her *Illyrian Spring* (1935) broaches the taboo subject of an older woman's love for a younger man—although the denouement has the woman reconciled with her husband. Mitchison wrote about sex outside marriage and birth control in *We Have Been Warned*. Through the influence of Stopes,

Mitchison had become aware of the importance of contraception to women's independence, and she had even helped to run a birth control clinic in the 1920s. The most courageous novels dealing with the forging of new identities for women, however, such as Hall's *The Well of Loneliness*, show that a price is to be paid in guilt. The strong female protagonists of Phillpotts, Royde-Smith, and Phyllis Bentley are not as unconventional, but they do express dissatisfaction with male-dominated society. Some male novelists, such as Davies, also feature strong-willed female characters. Although most novels of the period do not show women giving up marriage and families for a career, a few have them stepping outside stereotypical roles. In a striking example, Mannin's *Red Rose* (1941) portrays a female revolutionary based on the anarchist Emma Goldman. More often, novels—including Bridge's *Illyrian Spring*—treat the issue of women's work not being taken as seriously as men's.

Most of these types of realism, from the war novel through psychological realism to the feminist novel, were characterized as "unpleasant fiction." The prewar debate about the merits of this type of fiction continued to flare up on occasion, as an April 1925 symposium in *The Bookman* shows.

With the retreat in the postwar years from heroism on a grand scale, another type of fiction, centering on domestic life, came into prominence. Although it overlaps with feminist novels, not all of this type of fiction is feminist. These works include novels that focus on marriage, child rearing, relations with servants, and the house itself as a symbol of security. Many novels, feminist and otherwise, deal with the frustrations and limitations of married life. Children are the focus of adult novels such as Sackville-West's *Simpson: A Life* (1928), about a child and its nanny, and Bagnold's *National Velvet* (1935). Mannin's *Linda Shawn* (1932) is one of several novels that express progressive views on the education of children. The difficulty of finding and paying domestic help after the servant class—particularly women—had tasted the freedom and financial benefits of factory work during the war is a recurring theme; it receives humorous treatment in Bagnold's *The Squire* (1938). As labor-saving devices became more prevalent, they began to appear in fiction, along with the people who marketed them. Joanna Canaan's *The Simple Pass On* (1929), for instance, deals with the trials and tribulations of a vacuum-cleaner salesman. In contrast, Brett Young was one of those who carried on the reassuring tradition of the country-house novel. In his *White Ladies* (1935) the house is the central character, and in several of Stevenson's novels the house embodies emotional and spiritual strength.

With the postwar housing shortage came the building of suburbs, or "garden cities," and along with them the novel of suburban life. The suburban type with his respectable bungalow, wife, and children was often vilified by highbrows such as Orwell, in *Coming Up for Air* (1939), or Goldring, who says that

> during the 'twenties a horrifying sub-human suburban type came into existence which was genially depicted as the "little man," by the [*Daily Express*] cartoonist [Sidney] Strube. This odious homunculus and his revolting wife—ignorant, stupid, a moral craven but easily capable of being infected with mob hysteria—exemplified one of the worst of the economic consequences of the so-called "Peace."

The novelists treated in this volume, however, tended to be less condescending in their depictions of suburban life. Williamson compellingly depicts a fictionalized version of the suburb Brockley in his novel series A Chronicle of Ancient Sunlight (1951–1960). Hutchinson turned his attention to the suburban middle class in *Elephant and Castle* (1949). Young's novel of life in a suburb of Birmingham, *Mr. and Mrs. Pennington* (1931), is more critical, but the story ends happily.

The older cousin of the suburban novel, the novel dealing with life in the city, found a few practitioners in the 1920s, but these novels were not in the mainstream. Blake's rather sensational stories of Glasgow's mean streets, *Mince Collop Close* (1923) and *Young Malcolm* (1926), are examples of this type of novel. This form gained a new focus and urgency following the economic collapse of 1929 through the development of the "industrial novel." Among those who depict life in and around factory settings are Bates in *Charlotte's Row* (1931) and *Spella Ho* (1938) and Bentley, who provides an historical perspective on the textile industry in her generational novel *Inheritance* (1932).

Many of these novels are regional in scope because the Depression hit certain industrial areas harder than others and because novelists felt compelled to bring stories of hardship to the attention of the public. Croft argues that the regional or provincial novel was a major form in 1930s fiction and reflected a sense of social fragmentation and dislocation. The dominance of the regional novel led Walter Allen to claim in his *Tradition and Dream: The English and American Novel from the Twenties to Our Time* (1964) that "novels that take on the whole of society, or express it in any acceptable way are not there." Bentley, however, in *The English Regional*

*Novel* (1941) views the renaissance in regional writing more positively as depicting the rootedness of ordinary people and as "essentially democratic." Among the most distressed areas chronicled by writers discussed in this volume are South Wales (Davies), Lancashire (Greenwood), and the Clydeside area in Scotland (Blake). Other writers who treat distinct regions include Bentley, Jacob, and Winifred Holtby (Yorkshire); James Hanley (Wales); Strong (the western Highlands and Dartmoor); Williamson (Devon); and Young (Worcestershire and the Birmingham area).

Many of the industrial and regional novels depict the working class and cannot easily be distinguished from another significant genre of 1930s writing: the working-class, or proletarian, novel. Most of the portrayals of working-class woes discussed in this volume were written by middle-class observers, such as Cronin (*The Stars Look Down*, 1935), Davies, and Young (*The Black Diamond*, 1920); only a few writers treated here–Bates, Church, Greenwood, and Howard Spring–had working-class backgrounds, and only Greenwood consistently wrote proletarian novels. The working-class novels typically convey graphically the consequences of unemployment, including the breakup of the family, but they were criticized for failing to advocate political action.

Also overlapping with the regional novel were rural novels and animal novels. Some of the former, such as Wilson's *Greenlow* (1927), lament the inroads made on rural life by urbanization; some, such as Adrian Bell's back-to-the-land novels, have pastoral or humorous elements; while still others, such as Bates's *The Fallow Land* (1932) and *The Poacher* (1935), convey the harsh realities of life on the land. The most outstanding wildlife writer treated in this volume is Williamson, whose *Tarka the Otter* was an enormous popular and critical success.

Another response to industrialization and to postwar malaise in general was the exodus of writers from England. A wide variety of writers took part in and described this phenomenon—including William Plomer, who labeled the period "the Age of the Displaced Person"—which gave rise to novels of foreign lands and foreign travel. In contrast to the novels of domesticity, this type has received much more critical attention, although the focus has been almost exclusively on highbrow male writers such as Lawrence, Huxley, and Graham Greene. Though several of the male writers covered in this volume wrote novels set in exotic locales, including Hutchinson and Plomer, more female novelists employed these settings. Bridge's novels stand out in this regard, since foreign leaders actually approached her to write about their countries because the veracity of her representations frequently increased tourism in them. Mannin, Mitchison, and Stevenson were also well known for novels based on their experiences abroad, from the Middle East to the Soviet Union. In the 1930s awareness of political turmoil abroad increased, as did the output of novels about foreign affairs. Themes treated include conflicting national identities, as in Hutchinson's *The Unforgotten Prisoner* (1933), and other consequences of cultural displacement, as in Haldane's *Youth Is a Crime* (1934).

The focus on documentary realistic writing in the 1930s has obfuscated an important contrasting trend: futuristic and fantasy fiction. In the 1920s a few novels discussed in this volume were written in this vein, including the dystopian visions of Young's *The Red Knight* (1921) and Haldane's feminist *Man's World* (1926). But in the 1930s more writers turned their attention to these genres in response to anxiety about the possibility of another war, one that might lead to an apocalypse. These novels include Stevenson's *The Empty World: A Romance of the Future* (1936), Hamilton's *Impromptu in Moribundia* (1939), and Sherriff's *The Hopkins Manuscript* (1939). A trickle of such works continued to be written after World War II by authors such as Graves, in *Watch the North Wind Rise* (1949), and Mitchison, in *Memoirs of a Spacewoman* (1962) and *Solution Three* (1973).

Throughout the disruptive, uncertain interwar period writers expressed their quest for spiritual values and certainty in religious novels; those represented in this volume include works by Cronin, Goudge, Hall, Hutchinson, Spring, and Young. Several writers probed less-conventional topics, such as psychic phenomena, magic, and the occult. Novels in this vein had received an impetus during World War I as people sought solace in stories of connections with loved ones beyond death, and novelists in the 1920s and beyond continued to entertain a fascination with the extrasensory, as demonstrated in Young's *Cold Harbour* (1924), Hall's *A Saturday Life* (1925), Sackville-West's *Mandrake over the Water Carrier* (1928), and Goudge's *The Scent of Water* (1963).

The trends mentioned so far give some idea of the vast range of the fiction produced between the world wars. Unprecedented numbers of writers entered the profession following World War I and were able to survive partly because of the openness to British fiction of American publishers, who commanded a large and lucrative market. With so many novels being written and so many novelists writing

them, this volume could not hope to be comprehensive. Rather, it attempts to be representative, to gather a range of writers from lowbrow to highbrow and from obscure to popular to critically acclaimed. The initial aim was to include as wide a variety as possible of the "lost generation," that is, survivors of the war whether on the western or the home front. All of the novelists treated here experienced the war, whether as combatants, war workers, observers on the home front, or children.

To distinguish this group from those in other volumes of the *DLB,* especially the *Late-Victorian and Edwardian British Novelists* series, it was decided that these writers should not have begun to write earlier than the last years of World War I and that their careers as novelists should have been well under way by the advent of World War II. Writers who wrote only one or two novels during this period or who did not achieve their main impact until after World War II were excluded. This criterion eliminated such writers as Cyril Connolly, Edward Upward, and Antonia White. Since most novelists writing between the wars were middle class and wrote for a middlebrow audience, the majority of those treated here are also middle class and middlebrow. Nevertheless, some working-class novelists have been included, as well as some from the upper classes, such as Sackville-West and Sassoon. The "lowerbrow" novelists are represented by such writers as Leslie and Heyer. Highbrows, or those who wrote at least one highbrow, Modernist work and had not been covered in earlier volumes, also found a place here, including Graves, Muir, Royde-Smith, and Wilson. Also, the volume attempted to cover the full spectrum of political leanings, from communists (Haldane) to socialists (Davies, Hamilton, and Jacob) to liberals (Young) to conservatives (Nichols, Williamson, and Daphne Du Maurier) and even an anarchist (Mannin). In these volatile times, however, many novelists shifted political allegiances. Another consideration in the selection process was the degree of previous critical attention paid to a novelist. An attempt was made to retrieve novelists considered worthy by their contemporaries but subsequently neglected by standard reference works. Among this group are Bell, Bentley, Cronin, Leslie, Hampson, Hanley, Spring, and Stevenson. Although most of those selected produced fiction prodigiously, the editor has tried to include a sprinkling of novelists with small but unusual or significant outputs, such as Muir, Sackville-West, and Wynne-Tyson. Also important to include were those whose novel writing illuminates their writing in other genres on which their reputation stands, such as Brittain, Church, Graves, and Sassoon.

Needless to say, practical considerations also entered into the picture at various stages of the project. Many novelists had to be excluded because they produced only one or two novels or because a paucity of biographical information made their inclusion difficult. Among these are war novelists Vernon Bartlett (*No Man's Land*, 1930), C. R. Benstead (*Retreat*, 1930), F. P. Crozier (*Brass Hat in No Man's Land*, 1930), George Gordon MacFarlane ("Patrick Miller," *The Natural Man,* 1924), and John Oxenham (*1914,* 1916). More information on some of these writers can be obtained in Onions's *English Fiction and Drama of the Great War, 1918–1939.* Working-class novelists falling into this category include Walter Brierley, Alec Brown, Harold Heslop, James C. Welsh, and Amabel Williams-Ellis. Readers interested in these writers might begin by consulting Croft's *Red Letter Days: British Fiction in the 1930s,* Jeremy Hawthorn's *The British Working-Class Novel in the Twentieth Century* (1984), and David Smith's *Socialist Propaganda in the Twentieth-Century British Novel* (1978). Contributors could not be found to complete entries on another set of writers, including Ralph Bates, Richard Blaker, Ethel Boileau, Mary Butts, Stella Gibbons, E. M. Hull, Louis Golding, Norah James, Elizabeth Jenkins, E. B. C. Jones, Molly Keane ("M. J. Farrell"), A. G. Macdonell, Denis Mackail, E. Arnot Robertson, Angela Thirkell, and Sylvia Thompson. These writers will have to wait for a later date to gain the recognition they deserve.

Although the task of eliminating writers from the volume was often difficult, the final selection does succeed in making available the information necessary for constructing a broader view of fiction writing between the wars. Not only does the volume illustrate the diversity of contributions to the novel in this period, but it also highlights significant, though in some cases previously overlooked, trends in interwar fiction. Although these novelists will never be as critically acclaimed or as exhaustively studied as their Modernist contemporaries, they provide a much-needed wider context in which to read those giants. The many biographical connections between the two sets only hint at the degree of intertextual complexity, an issue that needs to be explored further. A few examples will suffice: both Davies and Young became friends of Lawrence, who had a completely opposite effect on the writing of the two. Williamson befriended the other Lawrence—T. E.—and wrote a book on their relationship, *Genius of Friendship: "T. E. Lawrence"* (1941). Williamson also became a friend of that other iconoclast, Wyndham Lewis, who included Mitchison among his many Modernist portraits. Both Mitchi-

son and her sister-in-law, Haldane, were at the center of important literary and intellectual coteries in the 1910s and 1920s.

Novel writers responded not only to their contemporaries and the traditions out of which they worked but also to an increasingly complicated and seemingly chaotic world. Some of them helped destroy illusions, particularly about the glory of war, while others embraced what might be called new illusions, such as the security of domesticity. The political and economic decisions made, and the fictions created in that world, continue to exert an enormous impact on the Western world today. Croft points out the revival of interest in the literature and culture of the 1930s in the economically beleaguered, rapidly—and, some would argue, chaotically—changing Britain of the 1980s. Judging from the spate of recent biographical and critical studies of some of the novelists of the 1920s and 1930s who are included in this volume, that revival seems to be continuing through the 1990s. The editor hopes that this volume will help to make more apparent the complexities of the relationship between the novel writing of the time and the culture that generated it, as well as to facilitate awareness of the relevance of some of these works for our time.

*–George M. Johnson*

## Acknowledgments

This book was produced by Bruccoli Clark Layman, Inc. Karen L. Rood is senior editor for the *Dictionary of Literary Biography* series. Philip B. Dematteis was the in-house editor.

Administrative support was provided by Ann M. Cheschi and Brenda A. Gillie.

Bookkeeper is Joyce Fowler.

Copyediting supervisor is Jeff Miller. The copyediting staff includes Phyllis A. Avant, Patricia Coate, Christine Copeland, Thom Harman, and William L. Thomas Jr. Freelance copyeditor is Rebecca Mayo.

Editorial associate is L. Kay Webster.

Layout and graphics staff includes Janet E. Hill and Mark McEwan.

Office manager is Kathy Lawler Merlette.

Photography editors are Margaret Meriwether and Paul Talbot. Photographic copy work was performed by Joseph M. Bruccoli.

Production manager is Philip B. Dematteis.

Systems manager is Marie L. Parker.

Typesetting supervisor is Kathleen M. Flanagan. The typesetting staff includes Pamela D. Norton and Patricia Flanagan Salisbury. Freelance typesetters include Melody W. Clegg and Delores Plastow.

Walter W. Ross, Steven Gross, and Ronald Aikman did library research. They were assisted by the following librarians at the Thomas Cooper Library of the University of South Carolina: Linda Holderfield and the interlibrary-loan staff; reference-department head Virginia Weathers; reference librarians Marilee Birchfield, Stefanie Buck, Stefanie DuBose, Rebecca Feind, Karen Joseph, Donna Lehman, Charlene Loope, Anthony McKissick, Jean Rhyne, and Kwamine Simpson; circulation-department head Caroline Taylor; and acquisitions-searching supervisor David Haggard.

The editor would like to express his gratitude to Alan Bishop, John Ferns, George J. Johnson, and Alastair Watt for helpful comments on the introduction, and to Ferns for his suggestions about potential contributors. Thanks also to Deborah Morrison for her editorial assistance in the early stages of preparing this volume. Finally, sincere thanks to all of the contributors for their fine entries, their patience, and their suggestions for illustrations.

# British Novelists Between the Wars

# Dictionary of Literary Biography

# Enid Bagnold
*(27 October 1889 – 31 March 1981)*

Lenemaja Friedman
*Columbus College*

See also the Bagnold entries in *DLB 13: British Dramatists Since World War II* and *DLB 160: British Children's Writers, 1914–1960.*

BOOKS: *The Sailing Ships, and Other Poems* (London: Heinemann, 1917);

*A Diary without Dates* (London: Heinemann, 1918; Boston: Luce, 1918);

*The Happy Foreigner* (London: Heinemann, 1920; New York: Century, 1920);

*Serena Blandish; or, The Difficulty of Getting Married,* as A Lady of Quality (London: Heinemann, 1924; New York: Doran, 1925);

*Alice and Thomas and Jane* (London: Heinemann, 1930; New York: Knopf, 1931);

*National Velvet* (London: Heinemann, 1935; New York: Morrow, 1935);

*The Door of Life* (New York: Morrow, 1938); republished as *The Squire* (London: Heinemann, 1938);

*Lottie Dundass* (London: Heinemann, 1941);

*The Loved and Envied* (London: Heinemann, 1951; Garden City, N.Y.: Doubleday, 1951);

*Two Plays* (London: Heinemann, 1951); republished as *Theatre* (Garden City, N.Y.: Doubleday, 1951)—includes *Lottie Dundass* and *Poor Judas*;

*The Girl's Journey,* foreword by Arthur Calder-Marshall (London: Heinemann, 1954; Garden City, N.Y.: Doubleday, 1954)—includes *The Happy Foreigner* and *The Squire*;

*The Chalk Garden* (London: Heinemann, 1956; New York: Random House, 1956);

*The Chinese Prime Minister* (London: French, 1964; New York: Random House, 1964);

*Enid Bagnold (photograph © Jerry Bauer)*

*Autobiography: From 1889* (London: Heinemann, 1969); republished as *Enid Bagnold's Autobiography* (Boston: Little, Brown, 1970);

*Four Plays* (London: Heinemann, 1970; Boston: Little, Brown, 1971)—includes *The Chalk Garden,*

*The Last Joke, The Chinese Prime Minister,* and *Call Me Jacky*;
*A Matter of Gravity* (London: Heinemann, 1978; New York: French, 1978).

PLAY PRODUCTIONS: *Lottie Dundass,* Santa Barbara, California, Santa Barbara Summer Theatre, 21 August 1941;
*National Velvet,* London, Embassy Theatre, 23 April 1946;
*Poor Judas,* Bradford, Bradford Civic Theatre, November 1946;
*Gertie,* New York, Plymouth Theatre, 30 January 1952; retitled *Little Idiot,* London, Q Theatre, 10 November 1953;
*The Chalk Garden,* New York, Ethel Barrymore Theatre, 26 October 1955; London, Haymarket Theatre, 11 April 1956;
*The Last Joke,* London, Phoenix Theatre, 28 September 1960;
*The Chinese Prime Minister,* New York, Royale Theatre, 2 January 1964;
*Call Me Jacky,* Oxford, Oxford Playhouse, 27 February 1968; revised as *A Matter of Gravity,* New York, Broadhurst Theatre, 3 February 1976.

OTHER: *National Velvet* [play], in *Embassy Successes: 1945–46,* volume 2 (London: Low, Marston, 1946).

TRANSLATION: Princess Marthe Bibesco, *Alexander of Asia* (London: Heinemann, 1935).

SELECTED PERIODICAL PUBLICATION—UNCOLLECTED: "The Flop," *Atlantic Monthly,* 4 (October 1952): 53–57.

Enid Bagnold's artistic life began, she says in her *Autobiography: From 1889* (1969), when she and her family moved to Jamaica. "Beauty never hit me until I was nine. . . . This was the first page of my life as someone who can 'see.' It was like a man idly staring at a field suddenly finding he had Picasso's eyes. In the most startling way I never felt young again. I remember myself then just as I feel myself now." Most people know her only for the novel *National Velvet* (1935), which is now considered a classic; but those who appreciate beauty of diction and an understanding of human nature recognize the excellence of her other novels, as well. She began writing poetry at an early age and published a collection, *The Sailing Ships, and Other Poems,* in 1917. For the first years of her literary career she wrote novels; she published her first play when she was fifty-three; and from then on she was dedicated to the theater. Her life was filled with

interesting and unusual people—socialites, artists, writers, actors, directors, foreign dignitaries, and government officials—and her stories and plays grew from these sources.

Enid Algerine Bagnold was born in Rochester, Kent, on 27 October 1889 to Maj. Arthur Henry Bagnold of the Royal Engineers and Ethel Alger Bagnold. Major Bagnold's engineering assignments required the family to move several times, mainly in the south of England. Bagnold's brother, Ralph, was born when she was six.

During the family's three-year residence in Jamaica Bagnold developed a love of horses; as Velvet does in *National Velvet,* she cut out pictures of horses from old magazines and pretended that she was riding one at a gallop through the coffee bushes. Later she was allowed to ride a donkey and to wander freely in the mountains. At night she wrote poems.

The family returned to England in 1902. The following year Bagnold entered Prior's Field, the boarding school run by Julia Frances Arnold Huxley, the mother of the biologist Julian Huxley and the writer Aldous Huxley. At the age of fifteen Bagnold, who until then had been the class clown, received her first literary award in a schoolwide poetry contest. After four years at Prior's Field she briefly attended boarding schools in Germany and Switzerland, then spent a year at a school in Paris.

In 1907 she returned to England, where her father had become chief superintendent of building works at Woolwich Arsenal and had bought a house called Warren Wood. In 1912–1913 Bagnold and Dolly Tylden, the daughter of the commanding general of the arsenal, rented an apartment in London, where Bagnold took art lessons from Walter Sickert and conducted interviews and wrote articles for Frank Harris's periodicals *Hearth and Home* and *The Modern Age.* Her relationship with Harris became intimate but ended after he was sent to prison for contempt of court.

After living in London for less than a year, Bagnold moved back to her parents' home. At the outbreak of World War I, Bagnold took training for a Voluntary Aid Detachment Certificate and worked at the nearby Royal Herbert Hospital. She spent her weekends in London at the home of Baroness Catherine d'Erlanger, who had been a neighbor of her parents in Woolwich. At one of d'Erlanger's parties she met Prince Antoine Bibesco of the Romanian Embassy, with whom she had a brief love affair. She kept a diary of her hospital experiences, which, with Bibesco's encouragement, she published in 1918 as *A Diary without Dates.* The book was critical of the nurses and of the conditions in the wards, and on its publication she was dismissed

*Bagnold riding her donkey, Queenie, during her family's three-year residence in Jamaica*

from the hospital. *A Diary without Dates* is written in an impressionistic style: the narrator is never identified, and names and dates are not given. The book received much acclaim; a reviewer in the *Daily Mail* (26 January 1918) called it "one of the most moving books that the war has evoked" and said that "there are passages in it which by their perfection of expression, and beauty of thought, rise to unaccustomed levels."

Bagnold had a craving for adventure, and at Bibesco's suggestion she volunteered for a six-month stint as a driver for the French army. After taking a course in automobile maintenance she left for France in November 1918. Her experiences there provided the material for her first novel, *The Happy Foreigner* (1920). The narrator, Fanny, is an Englishwoman through whose eyes the reader sees the war-torn country. The novel is divided into four parts, each dealing with an area to which Fanny is assigned. Like *A Diary without Dates,* it is written in an impressionistic style: one learns nothing about Fanny's past other than that her father was in the British army; about Julien, the French army captain with whom she becomes romantically involved, the reader knows only that he may be married; only one of the other women drivers, Stewart, is given a name. As Fanny visits battlefields

almost immediately after the cessation of fighting, the reader sees the devastation of fields and villages. Russian prisoners of war are still in camps abandoned by the Germans; no one seems to know what to do with them. Footloose Americans and other nationalities wander about the countryside; when Fanny's car breaks down one night, her food is stolen by a band of hungry Asians, but she is unharmed. Near the end of the book Julien is released from the army; he promises to visit Fanny, but as the weeks go by he does not come and sends no message. Finally he arrives and asks her to drive him to his family property. She does not tell him that she will be leaving for England in the morning. She loved him, but now it is over. Everyone has seen her as "the happy foreigner"; she has not lost "the astonishment of living," and one is sure that the independent and self-reliant Fanny will recover. The reviews of the book were favorable: in the *Athenaeum* (16 July 1920) Katherine Mansfield said of Fanny that "it is in her nature . . . to find in all things a grain of living beauty."

On 8 July 1920 Bagnold married Sir G. Roderick Jones, owner and director of Reuters News Agency. They had four children: Laurian, born in 1921; Timothy, in 1924; Richard, in 1926; and Do-

*Magazine editor Frank Harris, for whom Bagnold worked in 1911–1912 and with whom she had an affair*

minick, in 1930. As Lady Jones much of her time was taken up with entertaining; but by agreement with her husband, three hours of each day were set aside for her writing.

Bagnold's next novel marks a major change in form and style. *Serena Blandish; or, The Difficulty of Getting Married* (1924) is not impressionistic; the writing is highly stylized, showing linguistic precision and a deft wit. The work is modeled on Voltaire's *Candide* (1759), with the title character as a sort of female Candide. As in Voltaire's work there are cynical pronouncements about life; the style is reminiscent of the eighteenth-century mock-heroic: the extravagant show of the banal. The language sparkles, and Bagnold makes effective use of aphorisms. Countess Flor di Folio, based on Baroness d'Erlanger, acquires things and people for her amusement. Among those she collects is the young and beautiful Serena Blandish, whose family has undergone economic hardship. The countess takes Serena into her household and tries to help the younger woman find a husband. Serena is guileless and innocent; she has slept with many men, not for the pleasure of doing so but for the

pleasure of saying "yes." The countess and Martin, the butler, tell her that to win a husband she must deny her favors, but she is unable to do so. The countess becomes impatient and is about to throw Serena out of the house when the rich, mysterious Portuguese count Montague D'Costa arrives and falls in love with Serena. Because he speaks almost no English, he is unable to seduce Serena; thus, she cannot resort to her usual behavior. He proposes, and the countess arranges a hasty marriage. But when his relatives appear on the wedding day, the countess and Serena discover that he is not a count at all but the illegitimate son of a Nicaraguan Indian woman and her first lover, a Spanish Creole. The ending is bittersweet: Serena's wish to be married has been fulfilled, but the circumstances are not what she expected.

Bagnold did not publish the book under her own name, instead using the pseudonym "A Lady of Quality"; her father had read the manuscript and believed that the book would cause the family embarrassment. On the book's publication the indignant d'Erlanger banished Bagnold from her London home and threatened to sue her. The American playwright S. N. Behrman adapted the novel into a play, which opened in New York in 1929.

Eleven years passed between the publication of *Serena Blandish* and Bagnold's next novel, *National Velvet;* in between she wrote a book for her children, *Alice and Thomas and Jane* (1930). According to her autobiography, Bagnold originally intended *National Velvet* to be a short story, but her enthusiasm for the subject matter led her to expand it into a novel. The Joneses were avid riders at their country home, North End House, in Rottingdean, Sussex; their trainer, Bernard McHardy, became the model for Mi Taylor in the novel.

The story takes place in a village similar to Rottingdean. In contrast to the impressionism of *The Happy Foreigner* and the mock-eighteenth-century style of *Serena Blandish, National Velvet* is written in a realistic, conventional style. Probably the strongest feature of the novel is its characterizations: even the family pets—the old horse, Ada, and the old fox terrier, Jacob—have distinct personalities. Mr. Brown runs a slaughterhouse; Mrs. Brown, in her younger years, had won fame for swimming the English Channel. Fourteen-year-old Velvet is the youngest of the four girls; the only boy, four-year-old Donald, is the source of much of the novel's humor. Mr. Brown's assistant in the slaughterhouse, Mi Taylor, has, in his mysterious past, had experience in the racing world, but he does not ride now; his father had been Mrs. Brown's trainer for the Channel swim. Like her author, Velvet plays with paper horses and dreams of riding: her prayer is "O God, give me horses, give me horses! Let me be the best rider in England!" In a village raffle she wins a piebald horse that has repeatedly escaped from its former owner's farm by jumping the fence. Soon after, she also inherits five horses from an elderly squire who was aware of her love of riding. All of the girls become involved in caring for the horses and begin riding in local races. Velvet especially prizes the piebald horse, whom she calls the Pie and whose abilities she recognizes.

Mi and Velvet decide to enter the Pie in the Grand National; Velvet, disguised as a boy, will ride him. Mi has faith in Velvet: she has the same determination and willpower that her mother must have had. They know that if she wins, she will be disqualified because of the deception; but for the Pie's sake, she wants to try. Mi arranges the details, and Velvet receives her mother's support and her father's permission. On race day Velvet rides the Pie through the rain to victory; but she falls off the horse after crossing the finish line, and it is revealed that a fourteen-year-old girl has won the Grand National. She is besieged by fans and reporters. The National Hunt Committee holds an inquiry but brings no charges after interviewing Velvet and Mi and concluding that money was not their goal. Eventually the excitement dies down, and the Brown family's life returns to normal. This ending is somewhat anticlimactic, but it is satisfying in showing that Velvet has not been affected by the public adulation.

In the *Saturday Review of Literature* (4 May 1935) Christopher Morley called *National Velvet* a "masterpiece," saying that "you can learn more about the mind of childhood from this book than from many volumes of pedagogy. The mind of childhood, zigzag, indolent, unblemished by the subjunctive mood, is the mind of any great artist." The motion-picture version of the novel, starring the twelve-year-old Elizabeth Taylor as Velvet and Mickey Rooney as Mi, appeared in 1944. In 1946 Bagnold's stage adaptation of *National Velvet* opened at the Embassy Theatre in London, but the production did not achieve the success of the novel or of the movie.

Bagnold's next novel, *The Door of Life,* was published in New York in 1938 and republished the same year in London as *The Squire.* The setting is, again, an area like Rottingdean; the main character, called only "the squire," is a forty-four-year-old woman whose fifth child is born while her husband is away on a business trip to India. The events take place in the family home and garden during a six-week period beginning immediately before the birth and are seen through the eyes of several of the characters, mainly the servants. The squire's friend Caroline, a young socialite, comes to visit; her man-centered love life is contrasted to the

*Prince Antoine Bibesco, who was briefly Bagnold's lover and who encouraged her to publish* A Diary without Dates

squire's love of her newborn child. The novel has philosophical overtones, as the squire ruminates on the wonder of birth, the satisfactions of her life at this stage, and the prospect of death. Her qualities are much like those of Mrs. Brown in *National Velvet:* she is optimistic, strong, and self-reliant. She has a sense of humor and acknowledges her imperfections. The servant problem is one of the main sources of humor in the novel, but the work is essentially serious. The midwife is depicted as almost holy.

Of Bagnold's novels, *The Squire* has been the least popular; nevertheless, Heinemann Publishers republished it in 1954, along with *The Happy Foreigner,* in a volume titled *The Girl's Journey.* Noel Coward wrote in his diary for 21 February 1965: "I have read about eight books since I arrived [in Jamaica], including *The*

*Bagnold with her husband, Sir G. Roderick Jones*

*Happy Foreigner* and *The Squire* by Enid Bagnold. Both exquisitely written. She really is an extraordinary writer and her use of English is magical."

After the publication of *The Squire* Bagnold became interested in the theater and wrote three plays—*Lottie Dundass* (1941), *National Velvet,* and *Poor Judas* (1946)—before finishing her final novel, *The Loved and Envied* (1951). *Lottie Dundass* resulted from Bagnold's substituting for the reader of a prologue at a charity production in Brighton; the original reader had become ill, but on the second night she was back in the theater. Bagnold had put much effort into learning the lines and enjoyed performing, and she was disappointed when the first reader returned so soon. *Lottie Dundass* is about a typist and would-be actress who is scheduled to substitute for the star of a play; the star has been stricken with appendicitis, and the understudy is snowbound. When the understudy arrives after all, Lottie kills her backstage and goes on but dies of a heart attack before the performance is over. The play was first produced in Santa Barbara, California, in 1941; it opened in London in 1943 and ran for five months.

*Poor Judas* is another play about a would-be artist—in this case a writer—who feels justified in doing whatever is necessary to accomplish his ends. Edward Walker betrays the trust of an associate by pretending that he is finishing their joint literary project, which was interrupted by World War II. The play was first performed in Bradford, England, in 1946; it had a limited three-week engagement in London in 1951, re-

ceiving the Arts Theatre Prize for a new play of contemporary significance.

The main character of *The Loved and Envied* is Lady Ruby Maclean, a legendary beauty based on Bagnold's friend Diana Manners Cooper, the wife of the former British ambassador to France and a good friend of Coward and Evelyn Waugh. Bagnold had first seen Cooper at one of d'Erlanger's parties in London and had been struck by the way people gravitated toward her. In the novel Lady Ruby has a similar effect on those around her. When the work opens she is fifty-three, still incredibly attractive but on the verge of having to consider the problems of older age. Her husband and her friends, all of whom are somewhat older, are already finding disturbing changes in their lives. This novel has more characters than Bagnold's previous works, and it includes flashbacks that allow the reader to learn about their histories. The story revolves around five well-to-do couples who live in a countrified suburb of Paris. Each character undergoes a crisis, and several experience self-revelations that change their thinking and behavior. Ruby's husband, Sir Gynt, develops the need to explore his spiritual side and to learn more about God. He cannot share this quest with Ruby, who is not religious, so he leaves her to travel to the East; he may or may not return. The rupture in their marriage is devastating to Ruby. She also has to deal with her daughter, Miranda, who has never been able to communicate with her and has envied the admiration bestowed on her. Miranda has made one disastrous marriage, against her parents' wishes, and she is about to make another mistake by marrying a homosexual dress designer. But a young family friend, James, who has worshiped Ruby over the years, suddenly realizes that he loves Miranda and proposes to her. Miranda and James are thus beginning their married life as the other characters are slowly ending theirs. During the course of the novel three of the major characters die; one of them leaves his fortune to Ruby, whom he had always loved. Although World War II takes place during the period covered by the novel, it receives only a brief mention and has no effect on the characters. They seem to exist in an insulated microcosm.

Most critics were enthusiastic about the book, although the Americans seemed to like it more than the English. F. Butcher wrote in the *Chicago Sunday Tribune* (7 January 1951): "If any novelist has ever written more understandingly and more enchantingly about the aged and their long shadows of philosophy than Enid Bagnold has . . . I have not read that story. But Enid Bagnold's latest book is no more the typical story about aging and aged men and women than her delightful 'National Velvet' was a typical story about a horse."

Bagnold's play *Gertie* opened in New York on Wednesday, 30 January 1952, and closed the following Saturday. In her article "The Flop" in the *Atlantic Monthly* (1952) Bagnold recalls the critics' reaction: "My play, they said in effect, was written backwards when it wasn't written sideways. And in any case static. It was the description of a crab frightened at its feast." Her next play, however, *The Chalk Garden,* about a girl, her governess, and her grandmother, was a great success and continues to be popular today. The director Irene Mayer Selznick worked with Bagnold on the script, and it reached Broadway in October 1955; the London production opened the following year, and the film version, with Hayley Mills, Deborah Kerr, and Edith Evans, appeared in 1964. Critics especially noted the brilliance of the dialogue: in *The New York Times* (13 November 1955) Brooks Atkinson called the play witty, in the literary tradition of William Congreve, and Kenneth Tynan said in a review in the London *Observer* (reprinted in his *Curtains,* 1961) that it "may well be the finest artificial comedy to have flowed from an English . . . pen since the death of Congreve."

*The Chalk Garden* marks the peak of Bagnold's career as a playwright; her later plays enjoyed only limited success. *The Last Joke* (1960), based on the lives of Antoine Bibesco and his brother Emmanuel and starring John Gielgud and Ralph Richardson, went through many rewrites; though the dialogue is vivid and the characters are colorful, the three acts do not hold together.

After Bagnold's husband died in 1962, she began to think of simplifying her life and shedding many of her responsibilities. This is, in part, what the major character—a seventy-year-old actress retiring from the stage and seeking a new life—does in her next play, *The Chinese Prime Minister* (1964). The play includes much humor, sparkling dialogue, and elements of fantasy along with a serious undertone. The New York production was a hit; the play did not fare as well in London the next year, partly through the leading actress's misinterpretation of her role. Bagnold's next play, *Call Me Jacky* (1968), another comedy, is about the elderly Mrs. Basil; her crazy cook, Jacky DuBois; and her strange assortment of houseguests. The play did not do well, but eight years later, rewritten as *A Matter of Gravity,* it became a successful starring vehicle for Katharine Hepburn.

For years friends and family had been urging Bagnold to write her autobiography; she was eighty years old when it was published. *Autobiography: From 1889* is a collection of delightful tales written in an impressionistic style, with a scarcity of detail and almost no information about her children or family life. Bagnold died on 31 March 1981. Although she is not considered a major writer, she was a brilliant stylist, a master of dialogue, and a creator of vivid and memorable characters.

**Letters:**

*Letters to Frank Harris and Other Friends,* edited by R. P. Lister (Andoversford, Gloucestershire: Whittington Press/Heinemann, 1980).

**Interviews:**

Keith Harper, "Enid Bagnold Talks to Keith Harper," *Manchester Guardian,* 20 August 1965, p. 9;

John Gale, "Just the type for H. G. Wells," *Observer* (London), 26 October 1969, p. 23.

**Biography:**

Anne Sebba, *Enid Bagnold* (London: Weidenfeld & Nicolson, 1986).

**References:**

Noel Coward, *The Noel Coward Diaries,* edited by Graham Payn and Sheridan Morley (Boston: Little, Brown, 1982), p. 592;

Lenemaja Friedman, *Enid Bagnold* (Boston: G. K. Hall, 1986);

Kenneth Tynan, "'The Chalk Garden,' by Enid Bagnold at the Haymarket," in his *Curtains* (New York: Atheneum, 1961), pp. 127–128.

# H. E. Bates

*(16 May 1905 – 29 January 1974)*

Brian Evenson
*Oklahoma State University*

See also the Bates entry in *DLB 162: British Short-Fiction Writers, 1915–1945.*

BOOKS: *The Two Sisters* (London: Cape, 1926; New York: Viking, 1926);

*The Seekers* (London: Bumpus, 1926);

*The Last Bread: A Play in One Act* (London: Labour Publishing, 1926);

*The Spring Song, and In View of the Fact That: Two Stories* (London: Archer, 1927);

*Day's End, and Other Stories* (London: Cape, 1928; New York: Viking, 1928);

*Catherine Foster* (London: Cape, 1929; New York: Viking, 1929);

*Seven Tales and Alexander* (London: Scholartis, 1929; New York: Viking, 1930);

*The Hessian Prisoner* (London: Jackson, 1930);

*The Tree* (London: Lahr, 1930);

*Charlotte's Row* (London: Cape, 1931; New York: Cape & Smith, 1931);

*Mrs. Esmond's Life* (London: Privately printed, 1931);

*A Threshing Day* (London: Foyle, 1931);

*Holly and Sallow: Blue Moon Poem for Christmas 1931,* broadside (N.p., 1931);

*The Black Boxer: Tales* (London: Pharos Editions, 1932; New York: Ballou, 1932);

*Sally Go round the Moon* (London: White Owl, 1932);

*A German Idyll* (Waltham Saint Lawrence, Berkshire: Golden Cockerel, 1932);

*The Fallow Land* (London: Cape, 1932; New York: Ballou, 1933);

*The Story without an End and The Country Doctor* (London: White Owl, 1932);

*The House with the Apricot, and Two Other Tales* (London: Golden Cockerel, 1933);

*The Woman Who Had Imagination and Other Stories* (London & Toronto: Cape, 1934; New York: Macmillan, 1934);

*Thirty Tales* (London: Cape, 1934);

*Flowers and Faces* (London: Golden Cockerel, 1935);

*The Poacher* (London: Cape, 1935; New York: Macmillan, 1935);

*H. E. Bates (courtesy of Stanley Bates)*

*The Duet* (London: Grayson & Grayson, 1935);

*Cut and Come Again: Fourteen Stories* (London: Cape, 1935);

*Through the Woods: The English Woodland—April to April* (London: Gollancz, 1936; New York: Macmillan, 1936);

*A House of Women* (London: Cape, 1936; New York: Holt, 1936);

*Down the River* (London: Gollancz, 1937; New York: Holt, 1937);

*Something Short and Sweet: Stories* (London: Cape, 1937);

*Spella Ho* (London: Cape, 1938; Boston: Little, Brown, 1938);

*The Flying Goat* (London: Cape, 1939);

*My Uncle Silas: Stories* (London: Cape, 1939);

*Country Tales: Collected Short Stories* (London: Cape, 1940);

*The Seasons and the Gardener: A Book for Children* (Cambridge: Cambridge University Press, 1940);

*The Beauty of the Dead and Other Stories* (London: Cape, 1940);

*The Modern Short Story: A Critical Survey* (London & New York: Nelson, 1941);

*In the Heart of the Country* (London: Country Life, 1942);

*The Greatest People in the World and Other Stories,* as Flying Officer "X" (London: Cape, 1942); republished as *There's Something in the Air* (New York: Knopf, 1943);

*How Sleep the Brave, and Other Stories,* as Flying Officer "X" (London: Cape, 1943);

*The Bride Comes to Evensford* (London: Cape, 1943); enlarged as *The Bride Comes to Evensford and Other Tales* (London: Cape, 1949);

*Country Life* (London & Harmondsworth: Penguin, 1943);

*O More Than Happy Countryman!* (London: Country Life, 1943);

*Fair Stood the Wind for France* (London: M. Joseph, 1944; Boston: Little, Brown, 1944);

*Something in the Air, Comprising The Greatest People in the World, and How Sleep the Brave: Stories,* as Flying Officer "X" (London: Cape, 1944); enlarged as *The Stories of Flying Officer "X"* (London: Cape, 1952);

*There's Freedom in the Air: The Official Story of the Allied Air Forces from the Occupied Countries* (London: His Majesty's Stationery Office, 1944);

*The Day of Glory: A Play in Three Acts* (London: M. Joseph, 1945);

*The Cruise of the Breadwinner* (London: M. Joseph, 1946; Boston: Little, Brown, 1947);

*The Tinkers of Elstow* (London: Bemrose, 1946);

*The Purple Plain* (London: M. Joseph, 1947; Boston: Little, Brown, 1947);

*Thirty-One Selected Tales* (London: Cape, 1947);

*The Jacaranda Tree* (London: M. Joseph, 1949; Boston: Little, Brown, 1949);

*The Country Heart* (London: M. Joseph, 1949)—comprises revised versions of *O More Than Happy Countryman!* and *In the Heart of the Country;*

*Dear Life* (Boston: Little, Brown, 1949; London: Joseph, 1950);

*Edward Garnett* (London: Parrish, 1950);

*The Scarlet Sword* (London: M. Joseph, 1950; Boston: Little, Brown, 1951);

*Colonel Julian, and Other Stories* (London: M. Joseph, 1951; Boston: Little, Brown, 1952);

*Twenty Tales* (London: Cape, 1951);

*The Country of White Clover* (London: M. Joseph, 1952);

*The Face of England* (London: Batsford, 1952);

*Love for Lydia* (London: M. Joseph, 1952; Boston: Little, Brown, 1953);

*The Nature of Love: Three Short Novels* (London: M. Joseph, 1953; Boston: Little, Brown, 1954);

*The Feast of July* (London: M. Joseph, 1954; Boston: Little, Brown, 1954);

*The Daffodil Sky* (London: M. Joseph, 1955; Boston: Little, Brown, 1956);

*The Sleepless Moon* (London: M. Joseph, 1956; Boston: Little, Brown, 1956);

*Death of a Huntsman: Four Short Novels* (London: M. Joseph, 1957); republished as *Summer in Salandar* (Boston: Little, Brown, 1957);

*Sugar for the Horse* (London: M. Joseph, 1957);

*Selected Stories* (Harmondsworth & Baltimore: Penguin, 1957);

*The Darling Buds of May* (London: M. Joseph, 1958; Boston: Little, Brown, 1958);

*A Breath of French Air* (London: M. Joseph, 1959; Boston: Little, Brown, 1959);

*The Watercress Girl, and Other Stories* (London: M. Joseph, 1959; Boston: Little, Brown, 1960);

*An Aspidistra in Babylon: Four Novellas* (London: M. Joseph, 1960); republished as *The Grapes of Paradise: Four Short Novels* (Boston: Little, Brown, 1960);

*When the Green Woods Laugh* (London: M. Joseph, 1960); republished as *Hark, Hark, the Lark!* (Boston: Little, Brown, 1961);

*Now Sleeps the Crimson Petal, and Other Short Stories* (London: M. Joseph, 1961); republished as *The Enchantress, and Other Stories* (Boston: Little, Brown, 1961);

*The Day of the Tortoise* (London: M. Joseph, 1961);

*The Golden Oriole: Five Novellas* (London: M. Joseph, 1962; Boston: Little, Brown, 1962);

*A Crown of Wild Myrtle* (London: M. Joseph, 1962; New York: Farrar, Straus, 1963);

*Achilles the Donkey* (London: Dobson / New York: Watts, 1962);

*Seven by Five: Stories, 1926–1961,* preface by Henry Miller (London: M. Joseph, 1963); republished as *The Best of H. E. Bates* (Boston: Little, Brown, 1963);

*Achilles and Diana* (London: Dobson, 1963; New York: Watts, 1964);

*Oh! To Be in England* (London: M. Joseph, 1963; New York: Farrar, Straus, 1964);

*The Fabulous Mrs. V* (London: M. Joseph, 1964);

*A Moment in Time* (London: M. Joseph, 1964; New York: Farrar, Straus, 1964);

*Achilles and the Twins* (London: Dobson, 1964; New York: Watts, 1965);

*The Wedding Party* (London: M. Joseph, 1965);

*The Distant Horns of Summer* (London: M. Joseph, 1967);

*The Four Beauties: Four Novellas* (London: M. Joseph, 1968);

*The White Admiral* (London: Dobson, 1968);

*The Wild Cherry Tree* (London: M. Joseph, 1968);

*An Autobiography,* 3 volumes—comprises volume 1, *The Vanished World* (London: M. Joseph, 1969; Columbia: University of Missouri Press, 1969); volume 2, *The Blossoming World* (London: M. Joseph, 1971; Columbia: University of Missouri Press, 1971); volume 3, *The World in Ripeness* (London: M. Joseph, 1972; Columbia: University of Missouri Press, 1972);

*A Little of What You Fancy* (London: M. Joseph, 1970);

*The Triple Echo* (London: M. Joseph, 1970);

*A Love of Flowers* (London: M. Joseph, 1971);

*The Song of the Wren* (London: M. Joseph, 1972);

*A Fountain of Flowers* (London: M. Joseph, 1974);

*The Good Corn and Other Stories,* edited by Geoffrey Halson (London: Longman, 1974);

*H. E. Bates,* edited by Alan Cattell (London: Harrap, 1975);

*The Poison Ladies, and Other Stories,* edited by Mike Poulton, introduction by John L. Foster (Exeter: Wheaton, 1976);

*The Yellow Meads of Asphodel* (London: M. Joseph, 1976).

OTHER: David Garnett, *A Terrible Day,* foreword by Bates (London: Jackson, 1932);

"Thomas Hardy and Joseph Conrad," in *The English Novelists: A Survey of the Novel by Twenty Contemporary Novelists,* edited by Derek Verschoyle (London: Chatto & Windus, 1936), pp. 229–244;

W. H. Hudson, *Green Mansions,* introduction by Bates (London: Collins, 1957), pp. 11–16;

*Six Stories,* edited by Bates (London: Oxford University Press, 1965).

SELECTED PERIODICAL PUBLICATIONS – UNCOLLECTED: "Stephen Crane: A Neglected Genius," *Bookman,* 81 (October 1931): 10–11;

"Why I Live in the Country," *Countryman,* 12 (January 1936): 494–499;

"The Novelist's Ear," *Fortnightly,* 145 (March 1936): 277–282.

H. E. Bates was one of the most prolific English writers of his generation. From 1926 to 1972 he published, on average, more than one book of fiction a year as well as many nonfiction and juvenile works. He is best known for the power of his descriptions of nature—he had had an early ambition to be a painter, and he was an avid gardener for most of his life—and his ability to use such descriptions to create mood and to reinforce characterization. His real forte was short fiction; his novels tended to receive either critical or popular acclaim, but rarely both. In his later years critical praise for his work waned, but his popular success reached its height in the last two decades of his career. Widely anthologized, Bates was praised by Graham Greene for his poetic sensibility and lyrical renderings of nature and by Henry Miller for his humor and perceptive treatment of women.

Herbert Ernest Bates was born on 16 May 1905 in Rushden, Northhamptonshire, the first of the three children—two sons and a daughter—of Albert Ernest Bates and Lucy Elizabeth Lucas Bates. His father's boot- and shoemaking shop was soon swallowed up by industrialization, forcing the father to spend his later years working in a factory. Bates's dislike of Rushden, a factory town, informed his fiction with a mistrust of industrial "progress."

Bates's resentment of the strict Methodism of his parents eventually led him to reject organized religion. From his grandfather, William Lucas, who left shoemaking to run a small, barely profitable farm, Bates gained a respect for the simple life and for nature. The bucolic descriptions of nature that are one of the strengths of Bates's fiction stem from his childhood memories of traveling the countryside with his grandfather.

Having attended the local school since age four, in 1916 Bates won a free place at the Kettering Grammar School. There he rapidly acquired a distaste for instruction and for the headmaster and came to regard school as little more than a prison. His attitude changed in 1919 when a shell-shocked soldier-turned-teacher sparked his interest in literature. From then on Bates was one of the best students at the school in literature and composition though his marks in the other areas continued to be mediocre. In 1921 he turned down an opportunity to attend the University of Cambridge, partly from lack of interest and partly because of the financial burden it would have placed on his family. He would receive no further education.

On leaving school Bates became a junior reporter for the *Northhampton Chronicle,* but, out of boredom and a dislike for his boss, he resigned after a few months. He spent the next several months unemployed, enjoying the countryside, and then took a position as a bookkeeper in a warehouse. He was fired after a few years because he was neglecting his duties to read and write.

During 1924 and 1925, after several indifferent attempts at a novel and a few short-story publications, Bates wrote *The Two Sisters* (1926). After he had sent it to nine other publishers, the novel was accepted by Edward Garnett, chief reader at the Jonathan Cape firm. Garnett—who at first believed Bates, who always signed his work with his initials, to be a woman—became Bates's mentor until Garnett's death in 1937. (Bates would publish a memoir of Garnett in 1950.) While awaiting the appearance of his novel, Bates supported himself with scattered periodical publications, odd jobs, and loans from his parents.

*The Two Sisters* depicts the desolate lives of Jenny and Tessie Lee. A young man, Michael Winter, courts each in turn, promising them escape from their tyrannical father. But before he can choose between them he is killed in a flood, leaving the sisters with empty memories. Critics praised Bates's ability to create atmosphere but disparaged the weakness of his plot and characterizations.

In summer of 1926 Bates moved to London, accepting a job that Garnett had arranged for him in a bookstore. Quickly dissatisfied with city life, Bates returned to Rushden after a few months. The following year Bates toured Germany with a group of artists and writers, including Rhys Davies.

A second novel, "The Voyagers," was rejected by Garnett as facile and sentimental and would never be published. The failed novel was followed by *Day's End, and Other Stories* (1928), the first of the many story collections Bates would publish. It is primarily on the stories rather than on his novels that Bates's reputation rests. The most notable of his story collections include *The Black Boxer* (1932), *The Woman Who Had Imagination and Other Stories* (1934), and *The Daffodil Sky* (1955).

Bates's second published novel, *Catherine Foster* (1929), is written in an even harsher and tighter style than *The Two Sisters* and is imbued with a biting realism not found in the earlier work. Catherine Foster, trapped in a loveless marriage, has an affair with her husband's shiftless brother, who abandons her. After a brief moment of joy she is all the more trapped because she is now conscious of the extent of her misery. *Catherine Foster* received better reviews than had *The Two Sisters,* but it did little to improve Bates's financial situation; in 1929 he went on the dole. On 18 July 1931 he married Marjorie (Madge) Helen Cox, whom he had met in 1926; they had postponed their wedding twice because of Bates's financial situation.

*Charlotte's Row* (1931), Bates's third novel, is organized around a place rather than around characters. It chronicles the meager, sometimes desperate existence of the residents of a sordid Rushden street, from a boy's thefts to a mother's realization that her baby is dead.

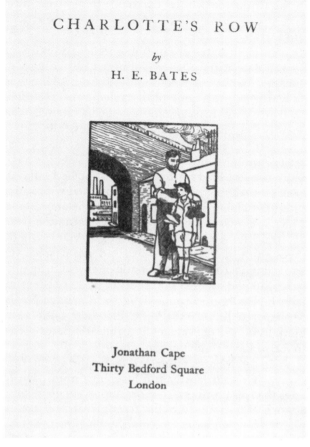

CHARLOTTE'S ROW

*by*

H. E. BATES

Jonathan Cape
Thirty Bedford Square
London

*Title page for Bates's third novel, about the residents of a slum in his hometown of Rushden*

By 1932 Bates and his wife had moved into a converted granary in Kent, paid for by Madge's savings from her work in a shoe factory and by the sale of some of Bates's stories. That year Bates began to review books for such periodicals as *Fortnightly, Bookman,* and the *New Statesman and Nation,* often with a minimum of tact. The same year also brought the birth of the Bateses' first child, Anne Catharine—they would have another daughter, Judith, and then two sons, Richard Lucas and Jonathan—and the appearance of Bates's fourth novel, *The Fallow Land.* Depicting the harsh side of existence on the land, the work concerns a former city girl who raises two boys and tries to cope with her drunken husband, who turns the management of their farm over to her. Her health is broken by the hard work, and she dies. *The Fallow Land* sold well and received enthusiastic reviews.

Near the end of 1933 Bates began writing essays about rural life for periodicals such as *Town and Country* and the *Spectator.* Shortly thereafter he became one of the founders of *New Stories,* a magazine devoted to the publication of experimental fiction.

In the three years of its existence the journal published work by such authors as Stephen Spender and Dylan Thomas.

In 1935 Bates began filling in occasionally for the regular writer of the "Country Life" column in the *Spectator;* he continued to do so until 1940 when he was given full control of the column. He often used it as an instrument for social change, eloquently describing the plight of country folk.

Bates's next novel, *The Poacher* (1935), was praised on both sides of the Atlantic. The title character tries to lead an honest life, but he is driven back to poaching by his well-intentioned wife and is caught and imprisoned. He ends up as an outcast. The novel was followed by another about the woes of rural life, *A House of Women* (1936). Drawing on the themes of *The Fallow Land* and *The Poacher,* the work details the struggle of a farmer's wife against hardship and against persecution by her sisters-in-law. It was highly praised; in the *Christian Science Monitor* (15 July 1936) V. S. Pritchett said: "The book lives, the characters live and Mr. Bates seems to me to have come very much alive."

In 1936 Bates published an important literary essay, "Thomas Hardy and Joseph Conrad." He argues that plot is the third most important element of a work of fiction after characterization and atmosphere. His own works exemplify this thesis: Bates's strength lies in his descriptions of nature and the way he uses such description to reinforce mood and characterization.

*Spella Ho* (1938) is the strongest of Bates's novels of the 1930s. Advance copies of the book were so enthusiastically reviewed in the United States that Bates was invited to serialize and abridge the work for *The Atlantic Monthly.* Bruno Shadbolt is a poor boy who breaks into the mansion Spella Ho to steal some coal; he grows up, mechanizes his farm, rises to financial success, has four unsuccessful love affairs, and ends up as the owner and sole inhabitant of the mansion. *Spella Ho* was a commercial as well as a critical success.

In 1939 Bates began an antiwar novel but abandoned it because of criticism from his friends and his editor. He had held an exemption from the military draft for family reasons, but it expired in 1941; through Garrett's efforts he was offered a special assignment in the Royal Air Force, writing propaganda tales about bomber pilots. The first group of stories was published under the pseudonym Flying Officer "X" as *The Greatest People in the World and Other Stories* (1942). At the request of the Air Ministry the work came out in an edition of 250,000 copies—an extremely large printing, considering the wartime paper shortage. It was repub-

lished in the United States as *There's Something in the Air* (1943) and followed by another such collection, *How Sleep the Brave, and Other Stories* (1943). Bates received little more than his RAF wages for his Flying Officer "X" stories, a situation that added to his growing dissatisfaction with his longtime publisher, Jonathan Cape. The novella *The Bride Comes to Evensford* (1943), about a woman obsessed with material success, was his last work to be published by Cape.

*Fair Stood the Wind for France* (1944) is Bates's first work to be published by the Michael Joseph firm. The novel chronicles the return of the downed British pilot John Franklin through occupied France to England. He loses an arm, narrowly escapes from the Germans, and falls awkwardly in love with Françoise, a member of the Resistance. The novel sold about four hundred thousand copies worldwide, and Bates was finally free from the financial anxiety that had plagued his earlier years.

The novella *The Cruise of the Breadwinner* (1946) is the strongest of the fiction works Bates wrote during and immediately after the war. The *Breadwinner*, a fishing boat, rescues a downed British pilot and an injured German airman and then is attacked by German planes. The events are seen through the eyes of Snowy, a boy who works on the boat and comes to an understanding of the horror of war.

During the late 1940s Bates continued to write the war stories that had made him famous. Three novels of this period draw on a tour of the East he had made in 1945 while reporting for the RAF. All three gratuitously exploit sex and violence, and all were best-sellers. The best of the three, *The Purple Plain* (1947), sold nearly a million copies. The bride of Forrester, an RAF flight commander based at an airstrip in Burma (today Myanmar), has been killed by an explosion, literally blown out of his arms as he held her. Shattered by the loss, he longs for death during each flight until he meets Anna, an educated Burmese woman. Her image sustains him when his plane crashes and he has to endure a hazardous journey through the Burmese desert.

While *The Purple Plain* teeters between popular and literary fiction, *The Jacaranda Tree* (1949) and *The Scarlet Sword* (1950) are strictly popular works. *The Jacaranda Tree,* also set in Burma, focuses on the interactions of a group of English and Burmese fleeing from invading Japanese forces and offers a harsh critique of British colonialism. *The Scarlet Sword* deals with a Catholic mission overrun by troops after the postwar partition of the Subcontinent to form India and Pakistan. It depicts a world rife with violence and terror, prefiguring the even harsher world of Bates's next work of fiction.

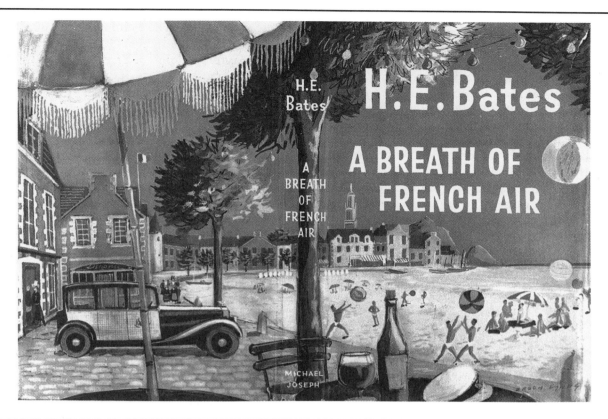

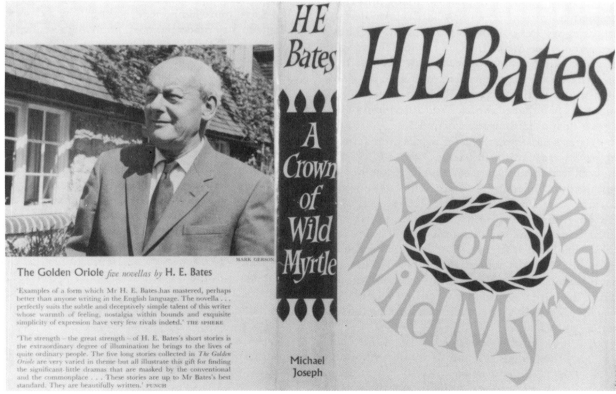

*Dust jackets for two of Bates's comic novels about the Larkins, a family of junk dealers in Kent*

In *Dear Life* (1949) Laura, a teenage girl living in shattered postwar London, turns to a former soldier-turned-criminal for affection. They go on an unreflecting rampage of robbery and murder until he is killed and she is captured. *Dear Life* depicts a soulless world like those of Greene's *Brighton Rock* (1938), William Golding's *Lord of the Flies* (1954), or Anthony Burgess's *A Clockwork Orange* (1962). An anomaly in Bates's career, it may also be his most powerful work of fiction.

Bates's postwar novels seldom reach the literary level of his earlier work although many attained popular success. *Love for Lydia* (1952), about a beautiful but cruel girl who manipulates men for her pleasure, chronicles the destruction of the men who pursue her and provides an intriguing image of England in the 1920s. *The Feast of July* (1954) is about a simple country girl who is seduced, impregnated, and abandoned. As the novel begins, she is traveling, alone and exhausted, in search of her lover. A family of shoemakers takes her in, and the reader sees through their eyes the hardships of industrial life in the late nineteenth century. When the novel ends two years later, she is once again alone and traveling, little having changed.

In 1954 *The Purple Plain* was made into a motion picture, with a screenplay by Eric Ambler and with Gregory Peck in the role of the pilot. Bates's next novel, *The Sleepless Moon* (1956), though initially receiving some praise, is now seen as little more than a weaker rewriting of *Catherine Foster*. Bates wrote to the novelist Richard Church on 3 February 1956 that the work had caused him to lose "a great deal of faith in my capacities."

Bates's most popular later works are a series of five novels recording the antics of the Larkins, a family of junk dealers in Kent who have avoided the "corruptions" of mannered life. The first novel in the series, *The Darling Buds of May* (1958), is the best realized. A tax collector, Mr. Charlton, shows up at the Larkins' home to collect a colossal amount of back taxes. He is at first shocked by the unorthodox family but is finally won over by their simple, joyous approach to life. He gives up his profession to marry the already pregnant Mariette Larkin. *A Breath of French Air* (1959) turns the Larkins loose in France on vacation while *When the Green Woods Laugh* (1960; republished as *Hark, Hark, the Lark!*, 1961) pits them against a pair of snobbish Londoners. In *Oh! To Be in England!* (1963) Ma and Pop Larkin finally get around to baptizing their many children—an idea drawn from Bates's late baptism of his own children. *A Little of What You Fancy* (1970), the last novel both of the Larkin series and of Bates's career, concerns Pop Larkin's fight against

plans for an underground tunnel to connect France and England. The delight of these novels lies in their playful violation of English conventions and manners; they have some of the ribaldry of François Rabelais and Geoffrey Chaucer, as Bates himself suggested. Although critics quickly grew tired of the novels, the public did not.

Meanwhile, 1962 brought *A Crown of Wild Myrtle*, a suspense novel set in Greece and involving a lesbian affair. *A Moment in Time* (1964), which was made into a television series, views the 1940 Battle of Britain through the eyes of a female narrator. *The Distant Horns of Summer* (1967), set on an English country estate after World War II, charts the fantasies of a young boy alongside his naive governess's affair with a more experienced man.

Bates's last novella, *The Triple Echo* (1970), was made into a 1973 film starring Glenda Jackson. Written in a stripped and fast-moving style, the book has the power of Bates's earlier fiction—perhaps because he had been working on it intermittently for twenty-five years. During World War II Mrs. Charlesworth, whose husband has been captured by the Japanese, is desperately lonely. She is joined in her isolation by Barton, a soldier who has deserted, and disguises him as a woman to prevent his discovery. Barton becomes more and more feminine, even attending a dance as a woman. A twisted relationship in which gender roles are reversed develops between the two characters. Finally, rather than allowing Barton to be captured and imprisoned, Mrs. Charlesworth kills him. *The Triple Echo* is a powerful illustration of the desperation of human relationships.

Bates suffered a nervous breakdown in 1963 and a heart attack in 1966. By 1968 his health had improved, and he was able to write a three-volume autobiography. Often playful, occasionally comic, and always entertaining, the autobiography was well received even by critics who had disparaged Bates's later fictional work. *The Vanished World* (1969) covers Bates's youth up to the acceptance of his first novel by Jonathan Cape and chronicles the end of preindustrial England; *The Blossoming World* (1971) traces his career up to his enlistment in the RAF; and *The World in Ripeness* (1972) deals with his wartime experiences and a few later incidents. For some reason Bates did not choose to record events that occurred after 1958.

After 1972 Bates's publications dropped off, but a series of seven television versions of his stories, as well as two films and a radio play, renewed his popularity. In 1973 Queen Elizabeth made him a Commander of the British Empire. He died of kidney failure on 29 January 1974 in Canterbury Hospital.

H. E. Bates was once ranked among the most-talented authors of his time, but his critical reputation has waned. Had he written less and taken more care with what he did write, his work would probably have been stronger. Some of his novels still enjoy popular success, especially the Larkin series. But Bates produced more than a handful of novels, novellas, and short stories that are worthy of serious attention. His neglected novellas, in particular—especially *Dear Life* and *The Triple Echo*—contain literary wealth that has yet to be adequately mined.

**Bibliography:**

Peter Eads, *H. E. Bates: A Biographical Study* (Winchester, Hampshire: St. Paul's Bibliographies, 1990).

**Biography:**

Dean R. Baldwin, *H. E. Bates: A Literary Life* (Selinsgrove, Pa.: Susquehanna University Press, 1987).

**References:**

Frederick Alderson, "Bates Country: A Memoir of H. E. Bates (1905–1974)," *London Magazine,* 19 (July 1979): 31–42;

Dean Baldwin, "Atmosphere in the Stories of H. E. Bates," *Studies in Short Fiction,* 21 (Summer 1984): 215–222;

Baldwin, "H. E. Bates's Festive Comedies," *West Virginia University Philological Papers,* 29 (1983): 77–83;

Baldwin, "H. E. Bates: *The Poacher,*" in Recharting the Thirties, edited by Patrick J. Quinn (Selinsgrove, Pa.: Susquehanna University Press / London: Associated University Presses, 1996), pp. 124–133;

Baldwin, "Uncle Silas: H. E. Bates's Romantic Individualist," *West Virginia University Philological Papers,* 28 (1982): 132–139;

Joseph Braddock, "H. E. Bates: The Man and the Story Teller," *Books and Bookmen* (May 1926): 7, 9;

Braddock, "H. E. Bates's War Stories," *Fortnightly Review,* new series 165 (March 1949): 205–206;

Wilfred De'ath, "The Quiet World of H. E. Bates," *London Illustrated Magazine* (May 1973): 43–44;

David Garnett, *Great Friends: Portraits of Seventeen Writers* (New York: Atheneum, 1980), pp. 204–209;

James Gindin, "A. E. Coppard and H. E. Bates," in *The English Short Story, 1880–1945: A Critical History,* edited by Joseph M. Flora (Boston: Twayne, 1985), pp. 113–141;

Fred Urquhart, "The Work of H. E. Bates," *Life and Letters Today,* 23 (December 1939): 289–293;

Dennis Vannatta, *H. E. Bates* (Boston: G. K. Hall, 1983).

**Papers:**

Most of H. E. Bates's manuscripts and letters are at the Harry Ransom Humanities Research Center at the University of Texas at Austin.

# Adrian Bell
## (4 October 1901 – 5 September 1980)

## Margaret Crosland

BOOKS: *Corduroy* (London: Cobden-Sanderson, 1930);

*Silver Ley* (London: Cobden-Sanderson, 1931; New York: Dodd, Mead, 1931);

*The Cherry Tree* (New York: Dodd, Mead, 1931; London: Cobden-Sanderson, 1932);

*Folly Field* (London: Cobden-Sanderson, 1933);

*The Balcony* (London: Cobden-Sanderson, 1934; New York: Simon & Schuster, 1936);

*Seasons* (London: Centaur, 1934);

*Poems* (London: Centaur, 1935);

*By-Road* (London: Cobden-Sanderson, 1937);

*The Shepherd's Farm* (London: Cobden-Sanderson, 1939);

*Men and the Fields* (London: Batsford, 1939; New York: Scribners, 1939);

*Apple Acre* (London: John Lane, 1942; revised edition, Leicester: Brockhampton, 1964);

*Sunrise to Sunset* (London: John Lane, Bodley Head, 1944);

*The Budding Morrow* (London: John Lane, 1946);

*The Black Donkey* (London: Blandford Press, 1949);

*The Flower and the Wheel* (London: Bodley Head, 1949);

*The Path by the Window* (London: Bodley Head, 1952);

*Music in the Morning* (London: Bodley Head, 1954);

*A Young Man's Fancy* (London: Bodley Head, 1955; New York: Abelard-Schuman, 1956);

*A Suffolk Harvest* (London: Bodley Head, 1956);

*The Mill House: A Novel* (London: Bodley Head, 1958);

*My Own Master* (London: Faber & Faber, 1961);

*A Street in Suffolk* (London: Faber & Faber, 1964);

*A Countryman's Notebook* (Ipswich: Boydell Press, 1975);

*The Green Bond* (Ipswich: Boydell Press, 1976).

OTHER: *The Open Air: An Anthology of English Country Life,* compiled by Bell (London: Faber & Faber, 1936).

No writer has described the everyday practical work of farming and the thoughts of a reflective farmer more convincingly than has Adrian Bell. He wrote in the tradition of Gilbert White, Richard Jefferies, and Thomas Hardy, although his work has a lighter touch and more humor than theirs. He began to write with no literary pretensions, but he quickly achieved critical recognition for the easy pace and constant variety of his work.

Adrian Hanbury Bell was born in London on 4 October 1901 to Robert Bell, a journalist, and Frances Hanbury Bell. After being educated at Uppingham School, he decided in his late teens to take up a career as a farmer in Suffolk. "I have ancestral roots in Suffolk on my mother's side," he wrote, "[her] forbears of a century ago were going about their work in the fields when Gainsborough was painting it." After spending a year as a pupil on a Suffolk farm, he set up his own establishment in the same county. In 1931 he married Marjorie Gibson; they had a son and two daughters.

Bell was consistently modest about his writing, describing himself as "a feckless cockney youth full of baseless fancies" who began to write as a means of passing the "long, lonely and unoccupied" evenings during his student year in the country. His most important works are the autobiographical trilogy *Corduroy* (1930), *Silver Ley* (1931), and *The Cherry Tree* (1931). *Corduroy,* which Bell characterized in *The Cherry Tree* as a "bullheaded account of my year at Farley Hall," was brought to the attention of the publisher Cobden-Sanderson by the poet Edmund Blunden, a neighbor of Bell's for a time, who had encouraged the author to write it. It describes the first year in the career of a young man who has decided to leave London and take up farming, about which he knows virtually nothing. Under the tutelage of a gentleman farmer he learns every aspect of agricultural life. The narrator's descriptions of his experiences with pigs, cows, and horses are lively and amusing; he is never afraid to reveal his ignorance, mistakes, fears, and clumsiness. Occasionally the reader learns something of the narrator's early life in London, where he attended studio parties that form a contrast with the hunts and the gatherings in farmhouses, laborers' cottages, and inns of Suffolk. Bell has a good ear for dialogue but avoids the trap of attempting to reproduce the local dialect—an attempt that is rarely successful and makes parts of Hardy's fiction difficult to read.

In addition to giving a detailed picture of the narrator's daily life, *Corduroy* provides a chapter of vanished social history: though not published until 1930, it was written in 1921, when Britain had barely recovered from World War I. Life in agricultural communities was difficult, and farmers received little help from the government. Although there was some progress in the use of machinery, even in what was regarded as a backward area of Britain, many Victorian traditions remained. Bell's narrator has a deep appreciation of tradition; after enjoying an agricultural show he reflects:

> I found I was at heart a rigid Tory. Yes, the old things were best. When England ceased to have pleasure in them it would surely be the end of her. This show, for instance; why, it was England, her very soul. All that remained of tournaments and the country festivals of old was to be found here. It was the holiday of farmer and labourer alike: the country gentleman's gesture of self-justification, the landed proprietor's answer to Socialism and reformers.

After a year as a student of farming the narrator, who is not yet twenty-one, persuades his parents to help him purchase a small farm of his own. This farm, Silver Ley, is the title and setting of the second volume of the trilogy, which describes the struggles of the beginning farmer. The narrator meets the sophisticated Emily Jarvis, who reads a great deal and plays the piano and thinks it strange that her new acquaintance should have deserted Chelsea, where she longs to go, for a farm in Suffolk. The narrator soon becomes fully integrated into the community, joining the hockey team and the board of managers of the local school. Eventually his family moves from Chelsea to Suffolk, buying a home near Silver Ley; later his younger brother and sister have to move back to London to find work, but the narrator, like Bell himself, will never leave East Anglia. He does not want to lose money, but he is not interested in becoming rich: "Two pounds an acre—that was the average profit to be expected in normal times. It may sound like squalor, but it must be remembered that the farmer half-lives out of his farm" and "can hold out against adversity

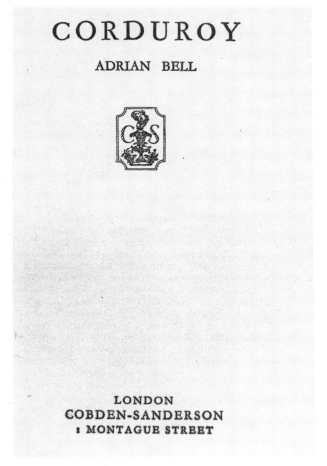

*Title page for Bell's first novel*

longer than 'modernized man,' because his domain is partly provisioned by God. . . . Because I had come to know what I wanted in life I was not afraid of the prospect of two pounds a week. I could achieve it with that—home and its patient pleasures. As to knowledge and company, I preferred the poetic pedestrianism of a Gilbert White to the society of the intellectuals of the twenties." He adds that it would take "several lifetimes" thoroughly to know a single acre of his land. To the narrator "the post-war world appeared . . . ugly and threatening, overpopulated already with high ambitions, and would-be wresters of power. I only wanted to live in peace and earn my bread."

The final work in the trilogy, *The Cherry Tree,* takes the narrator's life an important step forward: "It is good to be a bachelor while freedom has still the bloom on it and is prized for itself alone. . . . However that may be, in time mere freedom became empty of possibility. I wearied of solitude and married a wife." He meets Nora in London and is surprised when the sophisticated

*Adrian Bell* (The Daily Telegraph)

play together; among them are Dick, the farmer's son, and pretty Sally, who lives in the village. Her proud father buys her a dress for the village dance, but when it is revealed that he paid for it with stolen money the family is forced to leave the village. After his father dies suddenly, Dick gives up his dream of a Cambridge education to run the family farm. Sally, who has become an actress, returns and professes her love for Dick; but her career requires her to live in the city, and Dick is unwilling to follow her there. Dick marries the house-proud Muriel; although he still loves Sally, he remains faithful to Muriel. He feels the conflict between the traditional country life and the outside influences that are beginning to affect some of his friends as the nearest town expands ever closer to the village. The story ends with the juxtaposition of two scenes: men with pickaxes start work on a new road, and Dick's son is born.

Bell was the first to admit that he had no natural talent for the "conventional" novel: "I could not invent a plot for the life of me," he told a fellow writer. Critics and the public were pleased when, in 1942, he returned to the style of his trilogy in *Apple Acre,* in which the author-narrator again describes the country life from which his existence is inseparable. That life is now enriched by a daughter, Anthea, and her younger twin brother and sister, Martin and Sylvia. (Martin Bell would become a distinguished radio reporter, especially remembered for his dispatches from the former Yugoslavia.) The account of Anthea's fourth-birthday party is delightful; it is rare to find a father writing of such events and even rarer to find them evoked with the humor and lack of sentimentality that characterize the best of Bell's writing. It is, however, Bell's description of farmwork that gives his prose its lasting quality. His depictions of prosaic activities convey the worker's satisfaction so vividly that the reader can share vicariously in it. Even digging is rewarding: "The freshness of turned earth is comparable to the bloom on a plum; it does not stay rough and crumbly like that for long. . . . Half the beauty of it is that it is so perfectly drained, it lies up light as a newly-made bed above the water-level of a very rainy November." The three-year-old Anthea "immediately recognized the brown squares my spade cut out as chocolate cake."

There is another important dimension to *Apple Acre:* at the time of its writing, East Anglia was dangerously close to German-occupied France, Belgium, and Holland; it was thus easy prey for Hitler's bombers, while the nearby coast was a potential landing place for invading troops.

young woman accepts the rough living provided by his farmer's cottage. She quickly organizes their domestic life and sees to the modernization of the farm. The novel takes its title from a cherry tree the narrator had spared when he was clearing his land because it was so magnificent and because his elderly neighbors had pleaded for its survival. A severe gale finally fells it; but its life continues, in a way, during the time it supplies logs for the fire, and it soon has a successor, "a shivering sapling staked against the storm." The Norwich-born novelist R. H. Mottram called *The Cherry Tree* "one of the most beautiful farmer's calendars I've ever read."

Although the Suffolk background remains constant in Bell's works, his next novel, *Folly Field* (1933), departs from fictionalized autobiography and has a more conventional plot. It opens with scenes of idyllic life in the countryside, as children

Throughout the book the narrator is aware of this menace, and for a time his family, like so many others, is sent to stay in the northwestern part of the country. This situation leads Bell to express even more strongly his deep love of Britain and his conviction that the country will survive the current crisis as it has survived so many in the past. He also expresses his belief that even with the technological advances brought about by the war, the old country ways will never be forgotten: there will surely be a return to "natural proven living." The modern concern for ecology seems to bear out this prediction. H. J. Mas-singham, another writer of country life, described *Apple Acre* as "a work of genius," finding that the "quintessence of England is in it, the England of the wild rose, the parish church, the brown clod . . . the eternal England." Untouched by literary artifice, *Apple Acre* remains highly readable more than fifty years after it was published. Bell's non-fiction autobiography, *My Own Master,* appeared in 1961. He died on 5 September 1980.

**Reference:**
C. Henry Warren, "Bell and English Farming," *Fortnightly Review,* new series 157 (1945).

# Phyllis Bentley
*(19 November 1894 – 27 June 1977)*

Hilda Hollis
*McMaster University*

BOOKS: *The World's Bane, and Other Stories* (London: Unwin, 1918);

*Pedagomania; or, The Gentle Art of Teaching* (London: Unwin, 1918);

*Environment* (London: Sidgwick & Jackson, 1922; New York: Hillman-Curl, 1935);

*Cat-in-the-Manger* (London: Sidgwick & Jackson, 1923);

*The Spinner of the Years* (London: Benn, 1928; New York: Henkle, 1929);

*The Partnership* (London: Benn, 1928; Boston: Little, Brown, 1929);

*Carr: Being the Biography of Philip Joseph Carr, Manufacturer, of the Village of Carr Foot, in the West Riding of Yorkshire, Written by His Grand-Daughter, Mary Elizabeth Carr* (London: Benn, 1929; New York: Macmillan, 1933);

*Trio* (London: Gollancz, 1930);

*Sounding Brass: A Play in One Act* (Halifax: Stott, 1930);

*Inheritance* (London: Gollancz, 1932; New York: Macmillan, 1932);

*A Modern Tragedy* (London: Gollancz, 1934; New York: Macmillan, 1934);

*The Whole of the Story* (London: Gollancz, 1935);

*Freedom, Farewell!* (London: Gollancz, 1936; New York: Macmillan, 1936);

*Sleep in Peace* (London: Gollancz, 1938; New York: Macmillan, 1938);

*Take Courage* (London: Gollancz, 1940); republished as *The Power and the Glory* (New York: Macmillan, 1940);

*Manhold* (London: Gollancz, 1941; New York: Macmillan, 1941);

*The English Regional Novel* (London: Allen & Unwin, 1941);

*Here Is America* (London: Gollancz, 1941);

*The Rise of Henry Morcar* (London: Gollancz, 1946; New York: Macmillan, 1946);

*Some Observations on the Art of Narrative* (London: Home & Van Thal, 1946; New York: Macmillan, 1947);

*Phyllis Bentley in 1961* (Halifax Courier)

*Colne Valley Cloth from the Earliest Times to the Present Day* (Huddersfield: Huddersfield & District Woolen Export Group, 1947);

*The Brontës* (London: Home & Van Thal, 1947; Denver: Swallow, 1948);

*Life Story* (London: Gollancz, 1948; New York: Macmillan, 1948);

*Quorum* (London: Gollancz, 1950; New York: Macmillan, 1951);

*The Brontë Sisters* (London & New York: Published for the British Council and the National Book League by Longmans, Green, 1950);

*Panorama: Tales of the West Riding* (London: Gollancz, 1952; New York: Macmillan, 1952);

*The House of Moreys: A Romance* (London: Gollancz, 1953; New York: Macmillan, 1953);

*Noble in Reason* (London: Gollancz, 1955; New York: Macmillan, 1955);

*Love and Money: Seven Tales of the West Riding* (London: Gollancz, 1957; New York: Macmillan, 1957);

*Crescendo* (London: Gollancz, 1958; New York: Macmillan, 1958);

*The New Apprentice: A Play in One Act,* adapted for schools by R. S. Miles (London: French, 1959);

*The Heir of Skipton,* adapted by Miles (London: Macmillan / New York: St. Martin's Press, 1960);

*Kith and Kin: Nine Tales of Family Life* (London: Gollancz, 1960; New York: Macmillan, 1960);

*The Young Brontës* (London: Parrish, 1960; New York: Roy, 1961);

*"O Dreams, O Destinations": An Autobiography* (London: Gollancz, 1962; New York: Macmillan, 1962);

*Committees* (London & Glasgow: Collins, 1962);

*Public Speaking* (London & Glasgow: Collins, 1964);

*Enjoy Books: Reading and Collecting* (London: Gollancz, 1964);

*The Adventures of Tom Leigh* (London: Macdonald, 1964; Garden City, N.Y.: Doubleday, 1966);

*Tales of the West Riding* (London: Gollancz, 1965);

*A Man of His Time* (London: Gollancz, 1966; New York: Macmillan, 1966);

*Ned Carver in Danger* (London: Macdonald, 1967); republished as *Oath of Silence* (New York: Doubleday, 1967);

*Gold Pieces* (London: Macdonald, 1968); republished as *Forgery!* (Garden City, N.Y.: Doubleday, 1968);

*Ring in the New* (London: Gollancz, 1969);

*The Brontës and Their World* (London: Thames & Hudson, 1969; New York: Viking, 1969);

*Sheep May Safely Graze* (London: Gollancz, 1972);

*The New Venturers* (London: Gollancz, 1973);

*More Tales of the West Riding* (London: Gollancz, 1974);

*Haworth of the Brontës,* by Bentley and John Ogden (Lavenham: Dalton, 1977).

OTHER: *The Brontës,* Heather Edition, 6 volumes, edited by Bentley (London: Wingate, 1949);

*The Professor. Tales from Angria. Emma, a Fragment. By Charlotte Brontë. Together with a Selection of Poems by Charlotte, Emily, and Anne Brontë,* edited by Bentley (London & Glasgow: Collins, 1954).

Phyllis Bentley's novels and stories trace the development of the textile industry in the West Rid-ing of Yorkshire from the sixteenth to the twentieth centuries. According to Bentley in *The English Regional Novel* (1941), the regional novel is "essentially democratic" and "expresses a belief that the ordinary man and the ordinary woman are interesting and worth depicting." While her works are not much read today, the prolific Bentley was well respected in her time. Her more than forty published books include both fiction and nonfiction, but it was as a novelist that she was primarily known during her lifetime. Today she is most widely recognized for her literary criticism, especially her work on the Brontë family.

Born in Halifax in the West Riding on 19 November 1894, Phyllis Eleanor Bentley considered herself part of the "middle of the middle class." Her father, Joseph Edwin Bentley, was a textile manufacturer; the family of her mother, Eleanor Kettlewell Bentley, was also involved in the Yorkshire cloth trade. Bentley's family life and the business successes and failures of her father and brothers—she had three older brothers, the youngest of whom was six years her senior—were fertile material for Bentley's imagination, and autobiographical incidents frequently enter into her novels.

The only one of the four siblings to receive a postsecondary education, Bentley attended the Princess Mary High School for Girls in Halifax and then the Cheltenham Ladies' College, where she obtained a first-class external bachelor of arts pass degree from London University. After passing her examinations for the degree in October 1914, Bentley took a teaching position at a London high school for girls. Teaching was not her forte, but the experience, although it lasted less than a term, found its way into her short satirical work on education, *Pedagomania* (1918). Because of the shortage of teachers caused by World War I, Bentley, in a patriotic gesture, made one more attempt at teaching—this time at a Halifax boys' school—then became a clerk in the Ministry of Munitions in London. While she was working at this job, her brother Norman lent her sixty-nine pounds to have *The World's Bane, and Other Stories* (1918) published. A collection of four allegorical stories about sex, religion, class, and daydreams, it received a few favorable reviews but had little popular success: Bentley recouped only eleven pounds of her investment from sales of the book.

After the war Bentley moved back to Halifax, where she catalogued books at the local library and, in her free time, completed her autobiographical first novel, *Environment* (1922). It was accepted for publication along with its sequel, *Cat-in-the Manger* (1923). In *Environment* Bentley creates the West Riding town of Hudley, where the major events of all of

*Bentley, as an infant, with her family in 1895: brother Norman; mother, Eleanor; brothers Phil and Frank; and father, Joseph*

her regional novels will take place. Marjorie Johnson is a bookish young woman who wants to escape the limiting atmosphere of Hudley and establish an independent career. She must overcome her tendency to daydream, her adoptive aunt and uncle's desire for her to work in their store, difficulties in continuing her education, a trying teaching experience, and the temptation to marry for financial security someone she does not love. She finally marries Arthur West, a wealthy young engineer with literary interests. Bentley notes in her autobiography, *"O Dreams, O Destinations"* (1962), that this ending, which is not autobiographical–Bentley never married–was demanded by the publishers, who thought that in its original form the novel could "hardly be said to end at all." *Cat-in-the-Manger* is about Arthur West's spoiled sister, Bertha, who shows no moral or psychological development but remains selfish throughout the work. Although both books received laudatory reviews, only 500 copies of *Environment* and 360 copies of its sequel were sold.

Bentley's next novel, *The Spinner of the Years* (1928), was turned down by Sidgwick and Jackson, the publisher of her first two novels, but was accepted by Ernest Benn; her potential had been recognized by Benn's managing director, Victor Gollancz, who formed his own company in 1927; Gollancz would be Bentley's main publisher for the rest of her life. Although it sold scarcely a thousand copies on its initial publication, *The Spinner of the Years*

was praised in such London periodicals as the *Observer, The Times,* the *Morning Post,* and the *Saturday Review.* The writer J. B. Priestley commented that the book showed Bentley to be a born novelist. The consumptive, self-sacrificing Miss Hoad explains to Imogen, the young protagonist, that nature is neither benevolent nor malicious but simply "spins out the years" in an unconscious and purposeless manner. She argues that bitterness is wasted because no one intended for humanity to suffer. The only way to break through the meaninglessness is to try to do good works. Imogen attempts to forget her unwitting part in her beloved's suicide by marrying an older man whom she does not love, but her mother's financial ambitions lead to tragedy.

In Bentley's next novel, *The Partnership* (1928), Lydia, the kindly and reserved daughter of a Methodist minister, is in love with her cousin, Wilfred. She brings a poor young woman, Annice, into her parents' household as a maid; Annice's affair with Wilfred's half brother, Eric, sets off a chain of events that causes Wilfred to leave town, abandoning Lydia. Years later he returns, but Annice's relationship with a former soldier creates a misunderstanding that again drives Wilfred away. Lydia comes to accept the fact that the world is divided into hedonists, who enjoy life, and puritans, whose hard work and self-sacrifice make the hedonists' enjoyment possible.

*Carr* (1929), Bentley's personal favorite among

her novels, is a tribute to her father, who had recently died. She depicts her father's character, though not the details of his life, in Philip Joseph Carr, the type of ordinary man whom Bentley considers important to the functioning of society. The novel is written in the form of a biography, purportedly by Carr's granddaughter, Mary Elizabeth Carr; it even has an index, "quotations" from newspapers and letters, and a chronology of Carr's life. While Bentley was writing *Carr*, Priestley introduced her to many well-known literary figures and to the editors of the *Yorkshire Post*, for which she began to write regular articles.

Bentley's next novel, *Trio* (1930), is about three women growing up in the West Riding. She achieved her greatest success with her generational novel *Inheritance* (1932), which was popular both with critics and the public. It went through multiple editions, was translated into eight languages, and was serialized for radio broadcast on the BBC. The *Times Literary Supplement* (7 April 1932) praised it as a "fine historical picture," and in the *New Statesman* (16 April 1932) Gerald Bullett commented that Bentley had "the gift of holding one's attention, not only by her narrative skill, but by her own honest absorption in the lives of her *dramatis personae*."

*Inheritance* follows the conflicts and passions of three families—the mill-owning Oldroyds, the working-class Bamforths, and the intellectual Mellors—who are bound together by intermarriage and by the textile industry; it begins in 1812 and ends 119 years later. Although he is opposed to violence, Joe Bamforth jeopardizes his job at the mill by joining the loom-smashing Luddites out of sympathy with the deplorable situation of the workers. Eventually he is hanged for a murder that he did not commit because he is unwilling to abandon his friends, who include the strident Luddite George Mellor. Joe's nephew, Jonathon, or "Joth," establishes a newspaper dedicated to the welfare of the poor. A theme of thwarted love runs through *Inheritance*: hatreds arising from disputes between the manufacturers and workers spoil true love for the first generation of the families. Only Joth's marriage is happy, for he and his wife observe the conflict from the sidelines. The novel ends with David Oldroyd, whose veins contain the blood of all three families but who is "spiritually" the son of Joth, taking over the mill. Bentley would continue the story of the Oldroyds, Bamforths, and Mellors in three later novels: *The Rise of Henry Morcar* (1946), *A Man of His Time* (1966), and *Ring in the New* (1969).

Although it opened up new horizons for her, Bentley's friendship with the novelist Vera Brittain was also a source of severe distress; Bentley came to

# ENVIRONMENT

BY

PHYLLIS E. BENTLEY

LONDON
SIDGWICK & JACKSON, LTD.
3 ADAM STREET, ADELPHI, W.C. 2

*Title page for Bentley's autobiographical first novel, in which she creates the fictional Yorkshire town of Hudley*

feel that Brittain's criticisms were destroying her hard-won self-confidence. After a short period of intense friendship in 1932 Bentley and Brittain—whom Bentley affectionately called "Brighteyes"—had a major break that was triggered by Bentley's feelings of social inferiority and Brittain's frustration about her own writing, which was continually deferred because of family responsibilities. Although they would never again be as close as they were before the break, the two women were reconciled through their common friendship with the novelist Winifred Holtby.

During the 1930s Bentley grew increasingly aware of social and economic inequities and of the disturbing political solutions, such as fascism and communism, that were arising in response to them, and her novels became increasingly political. In *A Modern Tragedy* (1934) the depressed textile trade in the West Riding during the 1920s and 1930s leads a young man to engage in corrupt business practices;

*Bentley with the writers Winifred Holtby and Vera Brittain and Brittain's children, John and Shirley, in
the early 1930s*

he ruins his life and those of his family and friends. But Bentley's political views are most clearly expressed in *Freedom, Farewell!* (1936), the only novel in which she ventures completely out of her native Yorkshire. Set in ancient Rome, *Freedom, Farewell!* uses the overweening ambition of Julius Caesar as a metaphor for fascism. (Many booksellers returned their copies when they discovered that the novel lacked a Yorkshire setting.) While fascism is the main theme of *Freedom, Farewell!*, the novel also takes a feminist stance as Bentley links state tyranny with domestic patriarchal power: Caesar is as ruthless and dictatorial in his relationships with women as he is in his political ambitions. His affair with a married woman illuminates, and is illuminated by, his political career.

In an open letter titled "Creed of a Writer," published in the *Yorkshire Post* on Armistice Day 1938, Bentley took a strong stand against British prime minister Neville Chamberlain's peace negotiations with Adolf Hitler in Munich. Four days after the letter was published a translation of her novel *Sleep in Peace* (1938) was banned in Germany. Set during World War I, *Sleep in Peace* is noteworthy for its feminist viewpoint. Laura and her friend Grace are intelligent women who excelled academically as girls. While Grace is able to go to college in London, she is frustrated in her desire to study law

and become a judge: her women's college does not offer law, and women are not allowed to sit on the bench. She remains committed to education for women and becomes the principal of a women's college. At first Laura has no ambitions outside the home; but Grace's example eventually inspires her to pursue a career in art, and she becomes successful through her engravings of Yorkshire scenes. At the end of the novel Bentley looks at the next generation's tendency toward extremist political solutions: Laura's niece becomes interested in communism, while her nephew joins the British fascists.

Bentley's novel about the English Civil War, *Take Courage* (1940), published in the United States as *The Power and the Glory* (1940), demonstrates, she says in *"O Dreams, O Destinations,"* the "unnecessary cruelties which ideologies imposed by force are apt to inflict upon the human race." *Manhold* (1941), another historical novel, deals with the seventeenth-century cloth industry.

Bentley made five lecture tours to the United States during the 1930s; in 1941 she traveled throughout the United States to gain support for the British war effort. On her return she wrote the booklet *Here Is America* (1941) to introduce the geography, history, and culture of the United States to British readers. Bentley was particularly interested in the abolition of the slave trade and in what she perceived as the greater equality of women in America. The publication prompted the American Division of the Ministry of Information to give her a job writing propaganda.

In her critical study *The English Regional Novel* (1941) Bentley cites Charlotte Brontë's *Shirley* (1849) as the first great regional novel and goes on to consider the contributions to the genre of Elizabeth Cleghorn Gaskell, Anthony Trollope, George Eliot, Thomas Hardy, and Arnold Bennett. She claims the invention of the "industrial" novel as her own contribution to the development of the regional genre.

Bentley continues the story line begun in *Inheritance* in *The Rise of Henry Morcar*. The theme of true love thwarted persists, but this time love is destroyed through national, rather than class, strife. Henry Morcar, the new owner of Sykes Mill, is trapped into marrying his best friend's sister after the friend dies in World War I; their marriage is ruined because of her excessive grief for her brother. A second marriage is delayed by the outbreak of World War II; then Morcar's fiancée, Christina Harrington, dies in the London Blitz. David Oldroyd's happy life with Christina's daughter is ended by his heroic death in the war, which also ends his attempt to introduce a cooperative scheme at a small mill he had set up on old Oldroyd land. Much of the material in the book is derived from Bentley's wartime experiences in London, and her transatlantic crossings are reflected in a similar journey made by Morcar.

After the war Bentley returned to Halifax, where she spent the next five years nursing her invalid mother. During this period she wrote a promotional book, *Colne Valley Cloth* (1947), to aid local textile manufacturers who were suffering financially after the war. She also wrote *Life Story* (1948), a novel based on her mother's life and intended as a companion piece to *Carr*. Her novel *Quorum* (1950) reflects her work on various committees during this time.

Bentley was strongly influenced by the work of Charlotte, Emily, and Anne Brontë, whose home, Haworth, was only a few miles from Halifax. In addition to pamphlets for the Brontë Society, she produced five book-length studies of the sisters and their environment: *The Brontës* (1947); *The Brontë Sisters* (1950); *The Young Brontës* (1960); *The Brontës and Their World* (1969); and *Haworth of the Brontës* (1977), co-authored with John Ogden. She also brought out the six-volume Heather Edition of their writings (1949) and *The Professor. Tales from Angria. Emma, a Fragment. By Charlotte*

*Bentley as an ambulance driver in 1939*

*Brontë. Together with a Selection of Poems by Charlotte, Emily, and Anne Brontë* (1954).

After her mother's death Bentley wrote her only Gothic mystery-romance, *The House of Moreys* (1953). A resounding success, it was serialized in *Woman* magazine and made a selection of Oldhams' Companion Book Club, which sold nearly a quarter of a million copies of the work. Eleanor Moreys inherits the home in Yorkshire from which her late father was sent away in his youth for mysterious reasons. She and her Rochester-like cousin, Charles Moreys, fall in love; their impending marriage provokes an attempt on her life by the housekeeper, Adah, who is then revealed as the murderer of Charles's first wife. Adah turns out to be a Gypsy, the unacknowledged mistress of Charles's father, and the mother of his illegitimate son; she has been trying to prevent Charles from having heirs so that her grandchild will inherit the Morey fortune. Eleanor also learns that her father had been sent away from home because he displeased Adah by showing too much concern for his brother's wife. Although Bentley portrays Gypsies in a stereotypical fashion, her social conscience is evident in her criticism of the wealthy manufacturer who refuses to take responsibility for his illegitimate child.

# RING IN THE NEW

by

## PHYLLIS BENTLEY

*Ring out the old, ring in the new*
TENNYSON: IN MEMORIAM

LONDON
VICTOR GOLLANCZ LTD
1969

*Title page for Bentley's final novel written for adults, concluding the series that began in 1932 with* Inheritance

As she grew older, Bentley tended to write shorter works, including articles, book reviews, television scripts, and short stories. In the short-fiction genre Bentley was particularly known as a mystery writer; her best-known stories in this vein feature an elderly, theater-loving spinster, Miss Marian Phipps. In 1954 Bentley won third prize in the *Ellery Queen's Mystery Magazine* contest for her second Phipps story, "Chain of Witnesses." Bentley also published several collections of her stories about her Yorkshire homeland: *Panorama: Tales of the West Riding* (1952), *Love and Money: Seven Tales of the West Riding* (1957), *Kith and Kin: Nine Tales of Family Life* (1960), *Tales of the West Riding* (1965), and *More Tales of the West Riding* (1974). The stories are set in a variety of time periods, from the seventeenth century to the twentieth. Many of the tales involve characters from her novels; one of them, "The Hardaker Affair" in *Tales of the West Riding,* explores in greater detail an inci-

dent that is peripheral to the narrative of a novel in the Inheritance series, *A Man of His Time.*

The partly autobiographical novel *Noble in Reason* (1955) reflects Bentley's early career as a writer; but because the protagonist, Christopher Jarmayne, is male, it does not deal with the obstacles Bentley faced as a woman. Like Bentley, Christopher comes from a mill-owning family in the West Riding and achieves success by writing regional novels with characters that his family frequently claims are too easily recognizable. Before World War II he writes the novel *To Bury Caesar* "to investigate the contemporary European situation in terms of an earlier dictatorship." Its purpose, like that of Bentley's *Freedom, Farewell!,* is misconstrued, and it is not commercially successful. In *"O Dreams, O Destinations"* Bentley writes of a "moment of illumination" after her father's death, when she recognized the force of the Oedipus complex in her own life; Christopher has similar Freudian revelations. He also shares with his creator a tendency to excessive daydreaming.

Bentley's last adult novels were *Crescendo* (1958), about the large effects of a small act of betrayal, and two final works in the Inheritance series, *A Man of His Time* and *Ring in the New.* In these two novels David's son, Jonathon, a professor at a northern university, comments on the dealings of the materialistic Chuff, Morcar's grandson, who inherits the mill. While Jonathon protests against the nuclear arms race and the Vietnam War, Chuff is sympathetic to the racist regime of South Africa, where he spent his youngest years. A member of the Mellor family carries on the Luddite tradition as a student radical.

Toward the end of her career Bentley wrote five fairly successful juvenile historical and adventure novels: *The Adventures of Tom Leigh* (1964); *Ned Carver in Danger* (1967), published in the United States as *Oath of Silence* (1967); *Gold Pieces* (1968), published in the United States as *Forgery!* (1968); *Sheep May Safely Graze* (1972); and *The New Venturers* (1973). In the first four of these books Bentley remains on familiar territory, looking at the same events she had written about in her adult novels. *Ned Carver in Danger,* for example, deals with Luddite frame-smashing through the eyes of a fourteen-year-old boy who gets caught up with a group of rebellious croppers; George Mellor and Jonathon Bamforth appear in the book. While Bentley clearly sympathizes with the impoverished croppers, she also laments the destructive way in which they asserted their demands. At the end of the story the young protagonist wonders, "Why could not the two sides, masters and men, have sat down together and discussed the frames?"

Bentley died on 27 June 1977. Her ambition, she said in *"O Dreams, O Destinations,"* had been "to write a great novel giving a superb picture of life as it really is." At the end of her life she realized that she had not achieved that goal, but she believed that she had made a contribution, even if modest, to the "lamp of intelligence" in the West Riding. Her achievements were recognized by an honorary doctorate in literature from the University of Leeds in 1949 and by the conferral of the Order of the British Empire in 1970. The main importance of Bentley's work lies in her modernizing of the regional novel by focusing on the psychological motivations of her protagonists. Further, her feminist ideology is evident in her commitment to woman's rights in the labor force and her critique of patriarchal privilege in the home.

**References:**

Alan Bishop, ed., *Chronicle of Friendship: Vera Brittain's Diary of the Thirties 1932–1939* (London: Gollancz, 1986);

Virginia Blain, Patricia Clements, and Isobel Grundy, eds., *The Feminist Companion to Literature in English: Women Writers from the Middle Ages to the Present* (New Haven: Yale University Press, 1990), pp. 85–86;

Paul Schlueter and June Schlueter, eds., *An Encyclopedia of British Women Writers* (New York: Garland, 1988), pp. 34–35.

**Papers:**

Most of Phyllis Bentley's manuscripts are at the Halifax Central Library. A collection of her letters is at the Royal Society of Literature in London. A collection of her correspondence with Vera Brittain is in the McMaster University Archives, Hamilton, Ontario.

# George Blake
## (28 October 1893 – 29 August 1961)

### Eric Thompson
*Université du Québec à Chicoutimi*

BOOKS: *The Mother: A Play in Two Scenes* (Glasgow: Wilson, 1921);

*Clyde-Built: A Play in Three Acts* (Glasgow: Wilson, 1922);

*Vagabond Papers* (Glasgow: Wilson, 1922);

*The Weaker Vessel: A Play in One Act* (Edinburgh: Porpoise Press, 1923);

*Mince Collop Close* (London: Grant Richards, 1923; New York: McBride, 1924);

*The Wild Men* (London: Grant Richards, 1925);

*Young Malcolm* (London: Constable, 1926; New York & London: Harper, 1927);

*Paper Money* (London: Constable, 1928); republished as *Gettin' in Society* (New York & London: Harper, 1928);

*The Coasts of Normandy* (London: Faber & Faber, 1929);

*The Path of Glory* (London: Constable, 1929; New York & London: Harper, 1929);

*The Press and the Public* (London: Faber & Faber, 1930);

*The Seas Between* (London: Faber & Faber, 1930);

*Returned Empty* (London: Faber & Faber, 1931);

*Sea Tangle* (London: Faber & Faber, 1932);

*The Heart of Scotland* (London: Batsford, 1934; New York: Scribners, 1934; revised edition, London: Batsford, 1938; revised again, London & New York: Batsford, 1951);

*Rest and Be Thankful* (Edinburgh: Porpoise Press, 1934);

*The Shipbuilders* (London: Faber & Faber, 1935; Philadelphia & London: Lippincott, 1936);

*R.M.S. Queen Mary: A Record in Pictures, 1930 to 1936*, photographs by Stewart Bale and others (London: Batsford, 1936);

*David and Joanna* (London: Faber & Faber, 1936; New York: Holt, 1936);

*Down to the Sea: The Romance of the Clyde, Its Ships and Shipbuilders* (London: Collins, 1937; Boston: Houghton Mifflin, 1937);

*Late Harvest: A Novel* (London: Collins, 1938);

*The Valiant Heart: A Novel* (London: Collins, 1940; New York: Knopf, 1940);

*George Blake*

*Big Ships, Little Ships* (London: Published for the British Council by Sir I. Pitman & Sons, 1944);

*The Constant Star: A Novel* (London: Collins, 1945);

*The Westering Sun: A Novel* (London: Collins, 1946);

*British Ships and Shipbuilders* (London: Collins, 1946);

*Scottish Affairs* (London: Bureau of Current Affairs, 1947);

*Scottish Enterprise: Shipbuilding* (Edinburgh: Scottish Committee of the Council of Industrial Design, 1947);

*The Five Arches* (London: Collins, 1947);

*The Paying Guest* (London: Collins, 1949; London & New York: White Lion, 1974);

*Mountain and Flood: The History of the 52nd (Lowland) Division, 1939–1946* (Glasgow: Jackson, 1950);

*The Piper's Tune* (London: Collins, 1950);

*Barrie and the Kailyard School* (London: Barker, 1951; New York: Roy, 1951);

*The Firth of Clyde* (London: Collins, 1952);

*The Voyage Home* (London: Collins, 1952);

*The Innocence Within* (London: Collins, 1955);

*Annals of Scotland, 1895–1955: An Essay on the Twentieth-Century Scottish Novel, Related to a Series of Programmes with the Same Title to Be Broadcast by the BBC for Winter Listening, 1956–57* (London: British Broadcasting Corporation, 1956);

*B. I. Centenary, 1856–1956* (London: Collins, 1956);

*The Ben Line: The History of Wm. Thomson & Co. of Leith and Edinburgh, and of the Ships Owned and Managed by Them, 1825–1955* (London & New York: Nelson, 1956);

*Clyde Lighthouses: A Short History of the Clyde Lighthouses Trust, 1756–1956* (Glasgow: Jackson, 1956);

*The Last Fling* (London: Collins, 1957);

*The Peacock Palace* (London: Collins, 1958);

*Cruise in Company: The History of the Royal Clyde Yacht Club, 1856–1956,* by Blake and Christopher Small (Glasgow: Royal Clyde Yacht Club, 1959);

*Glasgow Electric: The Story of Scotland's New Electric Railway* (Glasgow: British Railways, 1960);

*The Loves of Mary Glen* (London: Collins, 1960);

*Lloyd's Register of Shipping, 1760–1960* (London: Lloyd's Register of Shipping, 1960);

*Scotland's Splendour as Seen by George Blake,* by Blake and others (Glasgow: Collins, 1960);

*Gellatly's, 1862–1962: A Short History of the Firm* (London: Blackie, 1962);

*The Gourock: The Gourock Ropework Co. Ltd, Port Glasgow, Scotland, Established 1736* (Port Glasgow: Gourock Ropework Co., 1963).

OTHER: *Scottish Treasure Trove,* edited by Blake (London: Newnes, 1928);

Neil Munro, *The Brave Days,* introduction by Blake (Edinburgh: Porpoise Press, 1931);

Munro, *The Looker-On,* introduction by Blake (Edinburgh: Porpoise Press, 1933);

Bill Tait, *Smiles: Cartoon Gallery,* foreword by Blake (Glasgow: Scoop Books, 1944);

*The Trials of Patrick Carraher,* edited by Blake (London: Hodge, 1951).

The Scottish novelist George Blake is remembered mainly for his Depression-era novel *The Shipbuilders* (1935). About this novel and similar ones by Blake a reviewer for the *Times* of London wrote in 1946: "To the river [Clyde] Mr. Blake brings intui-

tion and love; to the social scene knowledge and sympathy; to the individual man or woman, a somewhat commonplace insight." The last remark may seem harsh; but it is just, for Blake is not a successful portrayer of character. What is important in his work, and what has not been adequately explored by critics, is his strength as a regional author who helped shape the evolution of Scottish fiction from the period of the Kailyard romances to that of modern realism.

Born in Greenock on the Firth of Clyde, one of Scotland's principal shipbuilding centers, on 28 October 1893, Blake studied law at the University of Glasgow before enlisting for service in World War I with the Fifty-second (Lowland) Division. Wounded at Gallipoli, he became a journalist with the *Glasgow Evening News,* eventually succeeding the novelist Neil Munro as literary editor.

Blake began his authorial career as a playwright and essayist. His short plays *The Mother* (1921) and *The Weaker Vessel* (1923) were produced by the Scottish National Theatre, and some of his literary essays appeared in collected form as *Vagabond Papers* (1922). His only full-length play, *Clyde-Built,* produced in Glasgow in 1922, introduced themes that he would later develop in fictional form. It was not long before Blake was being thought of as one of the Scottish literary renaissance realists, a group that included two men who were to become the greatest twentieth-century Scottish writers: the poet Hugh MacDiarmid and the novelist Lewis Grassic Gibbon (pseudonym of James Leslie Mitchell). Although he was neither a committed socialist, like MacDiarmid, nor a realist with romantic leanings, like Gibbon, Blake shared with them a determination to present social turmoil in urban life in a realistic manner. Like them, too, he repudiated the sentimental themes of Kailyard (Scottish for "cabbage-patch"), the late-nineteenth-century style of rural poetry, drama, and fiction that had become the standard of what Scottish writing should be. Years later in his *Barrie and the Kailyard School* (1951) Blake would scorn Kailyard values, particularly the "chronic Scots disease of nostalgia."

Blake's first novels are clearly novice work. *Mince Collop Close* (1923) was influenced by John Gay's seriocomic masterpiece *The Beggar's Opera* (1728), but it lacks the sophisticated verve of the original. Bella Macfayden, crime queen of a gang of toughs and cutthroats, is the luridly drawn heroine of a badly constructed and sensationalistic story set in the industrial slums of Glasgow. Predictably, if implausibly, by the end of the novel Bella is revealing the softer side of her nature.

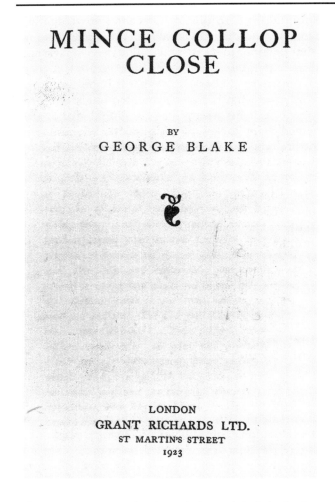

# MINCE COLLOP CLOSE

BY

G E O R G E   B L A K E

LONDON
GRANT RICHARDS LTD.
ST MARTIN'S STREET
1923

*Title page for George Blake's novel about criminals in the slums of Glasgow*

In 1923 Blake married Ellie Malcolm Lawson; they had two sons and a daughter. In 1924 Blake became an editor at *John O' London's Weekly*. His second novel, *The Wild Men* (1925), a story of industrial strife and political protest, has faults similar to those of *Mince Collop Close*. But he began to find his true voice in *Young Malcolm* (1926), in which a youth from Glasgow's mean streets rises socially and professionally to a successful medical career and marriage in London. L. P. Hartley spoke for most critics when he praised the work in the *Saturday Review* (6 November 1926) as "a touching story, preserved from sentimentality by the keenness of Mr. Blake's observation."

Blake became an editor at *The Strand Magazine* in 1928. His next book, *Paper Money* (1928), makes use of his knowledge of the river Clyde and its environs and foreshadows most of his later fiction and nonfiction. Matthew Faed, a shipworker, prospers during World War I on the strength of his ambition

and the lucrative shipbuilding contracts his company wins. At the same time his wife, Nellie, tries to climb the social ladder in a futile attempt at "gettin' in society" (the title under which the work was published in the United States the same year); instead, their neglected children get into trouble and bring disgrace upon them. The critic for the *New York Evening Post* (29 September 1928) read the book as a "sound social document, enlivened by a vein of pawky humor."

*The Path of Glory* (1929) is equally impressive, drawing on the author's experiences at Gallipoli to forge an unsentimental tale of war and lost love. John Macleod, a piper in a Highland regiment, is deceived by his wife and goes off to fight and die in the ill-fated Turkish campaign. The book was published amid the splurge of war fiction that appeared at the end of the 1920s, but it did not sell well despite favorable reviews.

In 1930 Blake became a director of the important modernist publisher Faber and Faber. His novel *The Seas Between,* published that year, is based on his adolescence in Greenock and the countryside south of the town, which lies between the Atlantic to the west and the Clyde to the east. Appearing here for the first time in Blake's works, Greenock is called Garvel; under that name it would be a major setting for many of his later works. He describes the town's "congeries of narrow eighteenth-century lanes, darkened by high irregular buildings with crow-stepped gables, built for solid burghers in the palmier days of the port," which have degenerated in modern times into slums. Blake fleshes out the reader's knowledge of the region through well-executed sketches of inland farms and villages and provides nicely detailed portraits of shipworkers and bourgeoisie. By this point Blake's style was becoming rather heavily adjectival, but usually the descriptions are functional rather than merely decorative. His major weakness continued to be an inability to create absorbing plots and characters.

In 1932 Faber and Faber acquired control of Porpoise Press, a Scottish firm, and Blake returned to Glasgow as its editor. For most of his life thereafter he divided his time between Glasgow and his home in Helensburgh, on the Firth of Clyde north of the city.

Blake never became a great plotter, but by the mid 1930s he had become a secure storyteller. *The Shipbuilders* is the central novel of his career: the story of Danny Shields and Leslie Pagan unites his previous interests in the working-class life of Glasgow with the tradition of shipbuilding in the region and the devastation wrought by the Great Depression on the industry and its workers. The economic slump has hit Clydeside hard; contracts for new hulls, refits, and maintenance have dried up with the decline in world trade. Danny, a skilled riveter, works for Leslie, the scion of a proud firm that is in serious decline. The two men have been friends since World War I, when Danny was Leslie's batman, although they seldom mix socially. Now Leslie ponders how to tell his faithful employees that he must let them go. As he stands on the deck of the last vessel his company will build, he remembers how once there were

> scores of ships ready for the launching along this reach, their sterns hanging over the tide, and how the men at work on them on high stagings would turn from the job and tug off their caps and cheer the new ship setting out to sea. And now only the gaunt, dumb poles and groups of men, workless, watching in silence the mocking passage of the vessel. It was bitter to know . . . that every feature of the *Estramadura* would come under an expert and loving scrutiny, that her passing would remind them of the joy of work and tell them how many among them would never work again.

To Leslie, the scene is a "tragedy beyond economics," the loss of an "inherited loveliness of artistry rotting along the banks of the stream." To Danny and the other men, of course, the loss of their jobs will have much more serious consequences than the inability to practice their skills with pride. For Danny and Leslie, however, the hard economic times are but the beginning of domestic miseries that eventually bring them back together: Leslie rescues Danny from scandal when his son is accused of murder, and from the humiliation of "public assistance" when he runs out of money. Blake's solution to the problems of the day, then, was for men to fall back on the solidarity they had forged in wartime. It was hardly an original message in the 1930s, but the novel conveys it through well-conceived documentary scenes. Blake came to believe that he had been unsuccessful in portraying the poverty of the industrial districts, but he is more convincing than he allowed. He captures the idiom of men in pubs, at sporting matches, and in queues; he is less successful in rendering the speech and behavior of the managerial class.

By contrast, *David and Joanna* (1936), Blake's next novel, is a whimsical potboiler about two young lovers who escape to the hills one summer for respite from Glasgow's mean streets. Their idyll has a surface charm but little to recommend it as a tale of the Depression.

Fiction was not Blake's only concern at the time. Like many others, he hoped that the construction of the mighty Cunard liner RMS *Queen Mary* in

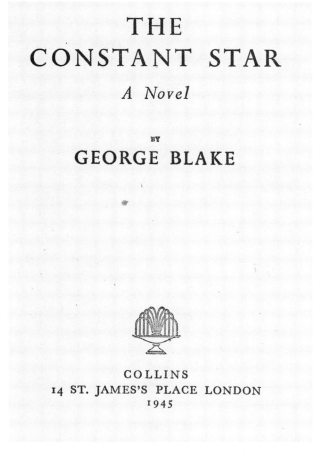

# THE CONSTANT STAR

*A Novel*

BY

# GEORGE BLAKE

COLLINS
14 ST. JAMES'S PLACE LONDON
1945

*Title page for the first of Blake's two novels about the Oliphant family*

a Clydeside yard augured a return to the great days, and when the liner was launched in 1936 he participated in the ceremonies both as a broadcaster and as the author of the text of a book of photographs of the event. This work proved to be the first of many commercial ventures: among them were histories of shipping lines, of Lloyd's Registry of Shipping (1960), of outfitters, of rope and cable makers, and of yacht clubs—accounts of firms and individuals whose accomplishments had brought fame to the region. He also became known as an anthologist of Scottish literature and a writer of travel books on the Clyde and Western Lowland regions. These projects supplemented his income during the lean years and earned him a reputation as a reliable chronicler. On a personal level, probably none of his books meant more to Blake than *Down to the Sea: The Romance of the Clyde, Its Ships and Shipbuilders* (1937), an account of the shipping heritage of Greenock and its environs.

Garvel is the setting for the humorous and acerbic *Late Harvest* (1938). The novel opens with

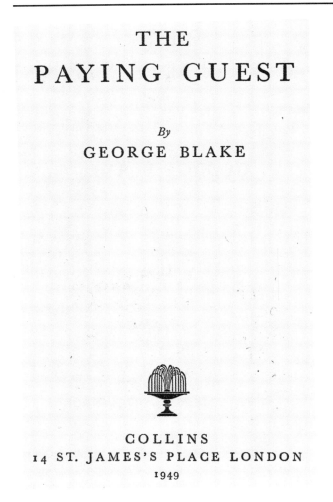

# THE
# PAYING GUEST

*By*

GEORGE BLAKE

COLLINS
14 ST. JAMES'S PLACE LONDON
1949

*Title page for Blake's novel about a woman who loses a fortune but finds love with a man she has known for twenty years*

Reverend Watson closing out his fifty-year ministry; he does not bother to say farewell to his parishioners and walks home alone, "his mind swinging . . . to the brisk allure of the Finlet Burn in spate" as he muses about the joys of fishing that await him. Meanwhile some thirty miles away Reverend Troup, a "brash and windy" evangelist, harangues his congregation. A mood of "decent inanition" grips these communities, which are stolid in the face of change; the wives and daughters, especially, are caught in webs of convention woven by their unimaginative menfolk. Blake is continuing the documentary style of *The Shipbuilders,* accompanying the narrative with the sly jabs only a native would recognize.

Blake was too old to reenlist when World War II broke out; instead he was assigned to the Ministry of Information in London to furnish propaganda for the Allied effort. It is in this light that his novel *The Valiant Heart* (1940) should be read, even if it is

World War I that provides the setting for the tale about Garvel-area people. The patriotic motif is registered early as the story focuses on an adolescent farm boy, one of those Scottish lads who have served Great Britain in "the Army, the Kirk, the Law and the Colonies" for centuries. By contrast, there is a note of bitterness as Blake criticizes Garvel for the "ultimate littleness of [its] urban life"—a littleness that has left it unfit for the strenuous fight ahead. One passage perhaps best mirrors his attitude throughout the book:

> Down the steep streets of the Clydeside town the workers streamed in thousands from the factory that topped the rise like an outsize convict prison in red brick. Behind the factory the unspoiled hills of Lennox rose green and rock-browed and detached, but the urban area below was dominated by that long range of four-storey blocks, its windows as regularly-sized, and as soulless, as a set of squares on a sheet of graph paper. The tide of humanity pouring down the slopes towards the shops and the houses confessed the dominance of the factory over the economic and social life of a sizable community.
>
> That evening crowd of released workers was made up of young, noisy girls, with a leaven of middle-aged and even elderly men. In times of peace the factory had produced a typewriting machine of world-wide repute, and the American brains behind the business had so equipped the place with machinery for the mass-production of typewriter parts that, when war came, it was not much more than an overnight job to switch the plant over to the production of time-fuses, torpedo parts and other fine contributions to the art of killing.
>
> The machine was very nearly complete master in that enormous barracks. Hot-blooded girls and sentient men minded lathes. . . . How could a girl, dreaming of her boy and of silk next her skin, think with every action of her hand that the result was possibly to be the mangling of the bodies of six Germans, the grief of a woman, the starvation of children, and then not much else but a stink and a wooden cross commemorating the unimportant?
>
> But it was Work, and it was Money. . . .

This passage shows that Blake was concerned as much about the moral and social devastation to the unique Scottish way of life wrought by war as he had been by the economic disruptions of the Great Depression. Still, it is surprising that a book published as wartime propaganda should have contained such views.

Resuming his fiction writing after the war, Blake concentrated on the social history of Greenock and Glasgow. The last fifteen years of his life turned out to be his most prolific and successful as an author: he published ten novels between 1946 and 1960, in addition to many nonfiction works.

*The Constant Star* (1945) and its sequel, *The Westering Sun* (1946), trace several generations of the Oliphant family against the backdrop of great events in European history from the early nineteenth century to the 1940s. In the first novel the cousins Julius and Mark build distinguished careers in shipbuilding and finance, respectively. Julius is an innovative engineer who makes pioneering advances in hull design and steam technology, while Mark creates a fortune by shrewdly exploiting Julius's ideas. Julius ultimately grows appalled at the sight of "sewage, rottenly suspended in windless waters, unmoved by sluggish tides"; he wants "to sweep the horror" of industrial progress away, but he realizes that it is too late. Mark, tougher and more efficient than Julius, has no such compunctions. Blake's limitations in characterization are apparent in this novel; neither man is much more than a type—the Dreamer and the Doer. He does, however, show a gift for the details of social history, as in a description of the sights and sounds of London's Great Exhibition in 1851:

> It was very wonderful, this Exhibition within the great glass-house. . . . The red-carpeted passages; the gleaming glass cases; the model engines in shining brass . . . the displays of a nation's infinitely varied manufactures in metal, from pins and fish-hooks to cotton jennies and colliery pumps; always a band playing somewhere, loud in brass or discreet on strings; palms, indiarubber plants, geraniums, fuchsias and begonias everywhere; the clatter of cups and glasses in refreshment places; and the enchanted, triumphant peoples of Britain—broad Lancashire vowels competing with Welsh sibilants, Cockney diphthongs contrasting with Scottish gutturals—streaming along the avenues, peering, explaining, exclaiming, arguing, but with never a voice or tone to suggest anything but a complete, unquestioning acceptance of this display as the perfect expression of a great nation's greatness.

Such descriptions stand out as colorful oases in a saga that is replete with plot ideas that simply fizzle out.

A main theme of the novel is the rivalry between wind and steam. While not explicitly stating a preference, Blake obviously favors the creation of beautiful sailing vessels by men like Julius over the manipulation of steam-driven ones by men like Mark. The title refers to the lovely clipper *Constant Star,* which sets speed records while plying the South Asian tea-trade routes. This achievement represents a victory of sorts for the gentle Julius, who at the end of his life reflects on the harmony that exists in nature:

> So it was with the sea—now grey and dull and flat; then green in a sort of bright anger; then blue and sparkling and young; and then, as on this night, serenely flat and pale blue shot with olive green and a ripple, as of a smile, on its face. So with the hills—so often aloof and ominous, the mist streaming over wet and cold and barren rockfaces, and again, as to-night, when they stood up in decent majesty against the northern sky, neither braggart nor humble, their summer colours of green and bronze and blue and purple enamelled with utter certainty on their great flanks.

Meanwhile Mark, despite his devious past, is rewarded with a peerage.

*The Westering Sun* continues the family history from the closing decades of the nineteenth century to the early years of World War II. While the spotlight remains on the male characters, female figures—especially Bluebell Gillanders Oliphant, who is almost the last of the line—play an increasingly prominent part. Once again Blake links the family's affairs to actual events, usually in a rather too portentous manner. At the end the Oliphants' cruising ship *Iolanthe* assists in the rescue of British soldiers at Dunkirk, and Bluebell dies beneath a collapsing wall during the London Blitz.

A second group of Garvel novels appeared in the postwar years: *The Five Arches* (1947), *The Paying Guest* (1949), and *The Piper's Tune* (1950). Although not directly connected, they have features in common besides setting: concentration on a single character; the theme of avarice; many characters who are former employees or dependents of employees of the large shipbuilding firm Tod & Bannerman; and Blake's customary overplotting, repetitive description, and awkwardness of style. In *The Five Arches* John Cram, superintendent engineer for a dockyard in China, returns home to Garvel after thirty years' absence. The arches of the title refer literally to the supports of a bridge near his grandmother's home; they symbolize the five stages of Cram's life. His relatives and friends have awaited his return expectantly, many of them hoping to share in his wealth. The reader sees Garvel society through Cram's eyes, as he notes their mannerisms and listens to their petty complaints. At length he buys a cottage beside the sea on the outskirts of the town and tries to adjust to a land of "crazy lives and haunted souls." Gradually he comes to appreciate the "cold logic of the peasantry to whom tenderness was an irrelevance when the issues of property were concerned." Blake is much more satirical in this story than usual, particularly in his depiction of "sponges" and hypocrites. Near the end of the novel Cram—implausibly, considering his age—is sent off to war, and he is captured and imprisoned by the Japanese in Hong Kong. Freed, he repeats his homeward journey, dying shortly after his arrival.

The portrait of Garvel in *The Five Arches* is sad and bitter, as though Blake had scores to settle with the land of his birth. *The Paying Guest* is an equally candid examination of the foibles of ordinary folk, but it is less judgmental. Ness Nimmo, unmarried and in her thirties, is the daughter of a foreman shipwright at Tod & Bannerman. She keeps house for the family and their tenant, Ollie Pomphrey, who has lived with them for twenty years. The monotony of her daily life is broken when she wins a lottery: she buys a yacht, lends money to her improvident brothers, and pays the nursing-home bills of a neighbor. Sailing her boat beneath "hilly bastions stretching away down to the loom of the outer islands" is a joy to Ness. But she loses her fortune through her family's bumbling, and her yacht is burned through the carelessness of her brother's fiancée. The tenant, who never tried to profit from her wealth, shyly proposes to Ness; she accepts, and then—for the first time in twenty years—they begin to call each other by their given names. Thus ends a short, sweet story that is sometimes prolix and predictable in style but always surefooted in its assessment of the effects of money on a cash-starved, conservative society.

The last of this group of novels, *The Piper's Tune,* is a similar Cinderella story but is not structured or told as well. When it begins in 1946, Jenny Rollo is running a hotel in Orlie, a village on the coast near Garvel. The story then flashes back to the 1930s to tell of the marriage of Jenny's sister to Jock Maclean. Their marriage falls apart, and the war brings further disruptions; but Jenny's secret passion for Jock endures. At the end the reader expects that the two will marry. The plot is much too crowded and melodramatic; but there are some vividly drawn scenes, and the effects of the war on Garvel are well presented.

Blake died on 29 August 1961. He had carved a small niche for himself as a regional writer, depicting the lives of working-class Glaswegians and residents of Greenock. As Maurice Lindsay puts it, he was "the only one of the older generation of Scottish Renaissance writers who faced up to the values and dilemmas of industrial society."

**References:**
Alan Bold, *Scotland: A Literary Guide* (London: Routledge, 1989), p. 170;

Beth Dickson, "Foundations of the Modern Scottish Novel," in *The Twentieth Century,* volume 4 of *The History of Scottish Literature,* edited by Cairns Craig (Aberdeen: Aberdeen University Press, 1987), pp. 50–57;

John and Julia Kray, *Collins Encyclopedia of Scotland* (London: HarperCollins, 1994), pp. 85–86;

Maurice Lindsay, *History of Scottish Literature* (London: Robert Hale, 1977), pp. 427–428;

William Power, *Literature & Oatmeal: What Literature Has Meant to Scotland* (London: Routledge, 1935), p. 189;

Edmund Stegmaier, "'Facts' and 'Vision' in Scottish Writing of the 1920s and 1930s," *Scottish Literary Journal,* 9 (May 1982): 67–78;

Roderick Watson, *The Literature of Scotland* (London: Macmillan, 1984), pp. 314, 407–408, 410;

Kurt Wittig, *The Scottish Tradition in Literature* (Edinburgh & London: Oliver & Boyd, 1958), pp. 323–324.

# Ann Bridge
## (Lady Mary Dolling Sanders O'Malley)

*(11 September 1889 – 9 March 1974)*

Teresa C. Zackodnik
*University of Alberta*

BOOKS: *Peking Picnic: A Novel* (London: Chatto & Windus, 1932; Boston: Little, Brown, 1932);

*The Ginger Griffin* (London: Chatto & Windus, 1934; Boston: Little, Brown, 1934);

*Illyrian Spring* (London: Chatto & Windus, 1935; Boston: Little, Brown, 1935);

*The Song in the House: Stories* (London: Chatto & Windus, 1936);

*Enchanter's Nightshade: A Novel* (London: Chatto & Windus, 1937; Boston: Little, Brown, 1937);

*Four-Part Setting: A Novel* (London: Chatto & Windus, 1939; Boston: Little, Brown, 1939);

*Frontier Passage: A Novel* (London: Chatto & Windus, 1942; Boston: Little, Brown, 1942);

*Singing Waters: A Novel* (London: Chatto & Windus, 1945; New York: Macmillan, 1946);

*And Then You Came: A Novel* (London: Chatto & Windus, 1948; New York: Macmillan, 1949);

*The Selective Traveller in Portugal,* by Bridge and Susan Lowndes (London: Evans, 1949; New York: Knopf, 1952; revised edition, London: Chatto & Windus, 1958; New York: McGraw-Hill, 1961);

*The House at Kilmartin* (London: Evans, 1951);

*The Dark Moment: A Novel* (London: Chatto & Windus, 1952 [i.e., 1951]; New York: Macmillan, 1952);

*A Place to Stand: A Novel* (London: Chatto & Windus, 1953; New York: Macmillan, 1953);

*Portrait of My Mother* (London: Chatto & Windus, 1955); republished as *A Family of Two Worlds: A Portrait of Her Mother* (New York: Macmillan, 1955);

*The Lighthearted Quest* (London: Chatto & Windus, 1956; New York: Macmillan, 1956);

*The Portuguese Escape: A Novel* (London: Chatto & Windus, 1958; New York: Macmillan, 1958);

*The Numbered Account: A Novel,* by Bridge and Lowndes (London: Chatto & Windus, 1960; New York: McGraw-Hill, 1960);

*Ann Bridge*

*The Tightening String: A Novel* (London: Chatto & Windus, 1962; New York: McGraw-Hill, 1962);

*The Dangerous Islands* (New York: McGraw-Hill, 1963; London: Chatto & Windus, 1964);

*Emergency in the Pyrenees* (London: Chatto & Windus, 1965; New York: McGraw-Hill, 1965);

*The Episode at Toledo,* by Bridge and Lowndes (New York: McGraw-Hill, 1966; London: Chatto & Windus, 1967);

*Facts and Fictions: Some Literary Recollections,* by Bridge and Lowndes (London: Chatto & Windus, 1968; New York: McGraw-Hill, 1968);

*The Malady in Madeira* (New York: McGraw-Hill, 1969; London: Chatto & Windus, 1970);

*Moments of Knowing: Personal Experiences in the Realm of Extra-Sensory Perception* (New York: McGraw-Hill, 1970); republished as *Moments of Knowing: Some Personal Experiences beyond Normal Knowledge* (London: Hodder & Stoughton, 1970);
*Permission to Resign: Goings-On in the Corridors of Power* (London: Sidgwick & Jackson, 1971);
*Julia in Ireland* (New York: McGraw-Hill, 1973).

Ann Bridge (Lady Mary Dolling Sanders O'Malley) was internationally successful as a novelist because of the insightful portraits of countries other than their own she offered her readers. Her novels, which have been translated into as many as sixteen languages, often resulted in an increase in tourism for the countries in which they are set. Foreign dignitaries approached her to request that she write of their homelands, for she was known for her faithful representations that resulted from rigorous research into each country's language, culture, and political history. In addition to these travelogues combined with romantic fiction that provided an insider's view of countries such as China, Yugoslavia, Italy, and Albania, Bridge wrote four novels that focus on historical events of which she had firsthand knowledge: *Frontier Passage* (1942), *The Dark Moment* (1952), *A Place to Stand* (1953), and *The Tightening String* (1962).

Mary Ann Dolling Sanders was born on 11 September 1889 in Porters, Hertfordshire, the seventh of eight children. Her mother, Marie Day Sanders, of an aristocratic Louisiana family, had met her father, James Harris Sanders, who negotiated sales between American metal and steam-engine companies and European parties, while he was in the United States on business. In *Portrait of My Mother* (1955) Bridge writes of her extremely close relationship with her mother and describes her father as "arbitrary, energetic, and very impatient; quick, competent, and thorough himself, he was remorseless in hounding down slackness or incompetence or stupidity, with wounding words and a voice frighteningly loud—to me anyhow."

James Sanders's business fortunes began to wane in 1891. To economize, the family moved from Stonington, their house in Hertfordshire, to a smaller home near Windsor Great Park in Surrey; in 1904 they moved to London. While the rest of the family thought the move to London an advantage, Mary and her mother became even closer because of their "desperate home-sickness for the country."

Educated at home, chiefly by German governesses, Mary developed a keen interest and proficiency in foreign languages. In 1906 she easily passed the examinations for admission to Oxford, but girls under eighteen could not be admitted to the university. Before her next birthday one of her brothers died; the loss devastated her mother, whose health was not sound. Realizing that it meant a great deal to her mother to have her near, Mary passed up the chance to attend Oxford and, as she says in *Portrait of My Mother,* "missed altogether the mental discipline and the serious scholarship which a University alone can give: intellectually I remained half-baked."

In 1911 James suffered financial ruin, and Mary and her siblings set about seeking employment to support themselves. Mary was an avid mountain climber who had undertaken frequent expeditions in the Alps, and it was through a fellow climber that she found a position as assistant secretary in the Chelsea branch of the Charity Organisation Society (COS). While working there she attended the London School of Economics and Political Science, receiving her diploma in 1913. In that same year a friend at the COS invited her to spend Easter in Argyll, where she met Owen St. Clair O'Malley, a Foreign Office official. They were engaged by June, and on 25 October they were married. They settled in London and had two daughters and a son.

In 1919 the O'Malleys moved to Bridge End, a home in Surrey. Owen O'Malley's first post abroad was Peking (Beijing), China, in 1925, and his family accompanied him there. In the spring of 1927 the O'Malleys' son Patrick contracted septic pneumonia; doctors advised that he would not live through another summer in China, so Mary returned to England with the children. In the autumn of that year she began writing short pieces about child rearing for *The Nursery World* and about China for *The Spectator* and *The Cornhill*. She notes in *Facts and Fictions* (1968) that "by 1929 I was making between one hundred and fifty and two hundred pounds a year by writing, which in the then state of our finances meant a great deal." When she approached a friend who was an editor at Chatto and Windus about translating Daniele Varé's short stories about China from French into English, he encouraged her to write a novel based on her experiences in China. Domestic duties restricted the time she could devote to her writing, but, working before breakfast, between six and eight o'clock, she produced *Peking Picnic* (1932). As the wife of a diplomat, she had to submit the manuscript to the Foreign Office librarian, who would censor it if necessary; moreover, the authorities insisted that she not publish the work under her real name. As she recalls in *Facts and Fictions,* "There had for a century or more been a tradition in the Service that if a diplomat's wife put pen to paper she would either ruin her husband's career, or provoke an international incident, or both." She created the pseudonym Ann Bridge from her middle name and the name of her home. *Peking Picnic* was well received by both critics and the public, and it won the third *Atlantic Monthly* Prize–$10,000 that she badly needed for her children's school fees.

*Peking Picnic* established Bridge's reputation for providing detailed inside views of foreign countries and the upper-class British diplomats stationed in them. The novel opens with reflections on the impossibility of dividing one's life between two worlds, the dilemma in which the heroine, Laura Le-Roy, finds herself. Married to an attaché to the British legation in Peking, the thirty-seven-year-old Laura has reluctantly left her son and daughter in English boarding schools while she lives a great part of the year in the Chinese capital. A weekend journey, or "picnic," to the Buddhist temple Chieh T'ai Ssu throws Laura into the company of an attractive visiting professor. The novel ranges over the Chinese countryside, providing engaging descriptions of temples and landscapes that prove to be a catalyst for romances that develop along the journey. These romances are rather contrived; only a married couple–Laura's intimidatingly beautiful niece and her husband, an American author who debates international politics with Laura–are spared Bridge's matchmaking. *Peking Picnic* should be of interest to feminist scholars for its frank treatment of Laura's sexual desires, which she pursues without seeming immoral, and Bridge's representation of the ambivalent attitude of the British upper class toward the Chinese, whom they admire as an advanced and noble civilization yet belittle as ignorant and stubborn servants, is significant in the context of postcolonial studies.

*Peking Picnic* is Bridge's only novel to receive scholarly attention. Donald Lammers argues that, with its accounts of warlords vying for control of Peking, it is a novel of the international "age of appeasement." Bridge's concern with China's unstable political landscape exemplifies, Lammers contends, the tendency of novels of the "appeasement tradition" to be concerned with world politics at a time when "the post-war international settlement was entering an especially fluxious state, with powerful new currents generated by economic collapse and political extremism carrying whole regions into choppy and ill-charted seas of change." *Peking Picnic,* in Lammers's estimation, provides a psychological background to the revisions in foreign policy the British government was forced to make in the late 1930s.

*Dust jacket for Bridge's novel about relief workers in Hungary during World War II*

While *The Ginger Griffin* (1934), Bridge's second novel, is also set in China and the social world of the British legation, it examines politics and power in that country far less than does *Peking Picnic.* After a romantic disappointment Amber Harrison, a young, pretty, thoughtful woman, leaves England to visit her aunt and uncle in Peking for a year. In Peking, Amber faces what Ellen Buell in *The New York Times Book Review* (13 May 1934) calls "her first test of spiritual strength and hardihood." She spends a great deal of time considering the nature of human relationships and pondering her own character, preconceptions, and beliefs. Her curiosity about the Chinese romanticizes China and extends only to its temples and ancient history. Amber witnesses the abduction of several terrified Chinese near the British Embassy; she is upset by the terror she sees in their faces and by the casual attitude of the British and Americans present, who take photographs and comment on how much "fun" the event is, but she never tries to learn why the Chinese were taken hostage or what their fate might be. The novel's romantic plot is as contrived as that of *Peking Picnic:* when the diplomat Rupert Benenden rejects Amber, she marries his colleague George Hawtrey despite her repeated refusals of his advances and her frank admission that she is not in love with him. Buell thought that the novel sacrifices "dramatic values to a sense of British decorum" but found its characters more realistic than those in *Peking Picnic*. *The Ginger Griffin,* for Buell, represents a "distinct advance in technique, with its added sense of smoothness and continuity." Bridge's novel *Four-Part Setting* (1939) would return to the milieu of the British diplomatic corps in China.

In Bridge's third novel, *Illyrian Spring* (1935), thirty-eight-year-old Lady Grace Kilmichael is married to a world-famous economist. Although Grace has gained a reputation as an artist, neither her husband nor her daughter take her work seriously, and they have told her so often that she is intellectually dull that she has come to believe it. She leaves her husband and daughter in Venice and travels to Yugoslavia—ostensibly to paint and sketch but really to assess the future of her marriage. There she meets Nicholas Humphries, an architecture student in his twenties who longs to be an artist. Grace recognizes his talent and begins tutoring him. Nicholas, in return, teaches Grace about young people, giving her insights into her relationship with her daughter. Through her relationship with Nicholas, Grace regains her self-confidence. Considering her husband's and daughter's treatment of her, she decides "that what provoked their attitude was . . . what she *was*. And what was more, she had become certain that freedom had something to do with it." She begins to see herself as more than the roles that have defined her: "Married women so often become more an institution than a person—to their own families a wife or mother, to other people the wife or the mother of somebody else. . . . Grace Kilmichael had been an institution for years . . . she hadn't really noticed it; but when Nicholas Humphries started treating her as a person . . . she *did* notice it. She found it something quite new and rather delightful." Grace and Nicholas gradually realize that they have fallen in love. Just at this point Nicholas's parents and Grace's husband and daughter all arrive, coincidentally, in the port city of Ragussa, where Grace and Nicholas are painting. Grace's agent, who also happens to be in Ragussa, is so impressed with Nicholas's work that he persuades Nicholas's father to support the son's pursuit of art over architecture. Grace's absence has forced her husband to realize that he had been mistreating her; he promises to do better, and the two reconcile almost effortlessly. While advising readers to "take the ending with a small grain of salt," Edith Walton

in *The New York Times Book Review* (4 August 1935) calls *Illyrian Spring* "an uncommonly agreeable and graceful story."

In 1940 Owen was briefly stationed in Turkey. During their stay there Bridge's interest in the Turkish Revolution was piqued by her friendship with Rusen and Sahlia Unaydin, supporters of Mustafa Kemal Atatürk, the leader of the revolution and Turkey's first president. Bridge returned to Turkey in the late summer of 1940 from Hungary, where her husband had been transferred, to find food and clothing for British prisoners of war. In late April 1941 the O'Malleys, fleeing advancing German troops, crossed the Soviet Union into China on the Trans-Siberian railway. After a frightening delay by Russian border guards at the Manchurian frontier, they sailed from China to San Francisco. Bridge remained in the United States for a year, discussing a possible screenplay for a film version of *Peking Picnic* that was never made. She also lectured throughout the Northeast and completed *Frontier Passage,* a novel about foreign intervention in the Spanish civil war and the first of what she called her "modern historicals." In a testament to the verisimilitude of her novels' settings, British intelligence used *Frontier Passage* to mount a second front in Spain during World War II. In June 1942 Bridge returned to Britain, where her husband had been appointed ambassador to the Polish government-in-exile. In 1943 she returned to Turkey and made her way along the historic Road of the Revolution from the Black Sea coast to its termination on the plains of Anatolia, staying with the revolutionaries who had worked with Atatürk. She became more interested in the wives of the revolutionaries, women born into lives of privilege who underwent extreme hardships to support Atatürk's modernization of Turkey. Their accounts of their lives and the lives of their mothers and grandmothers would form the basis for Bridge's modern historical *The Dark Moment.*

*Illyrian Spring* had produced a dramatic increase in tourism to Yugoslavia; when Bridge had subsequently visited Albania, government officials had asked her to write a novel set in their country. Bridge had refused, but later King Zog wrote her from exile in England, where he had fled after the Italian invasion of Albania, asking that she write about his country to "create a climate of sympathy" for it. *Singing Waters* (1945) was the result. The novel met with disapproval both from Bridge's agent and her American publisher: the agent saw the work as a sociological tract rather than a novel, and Atlantic Monthly Press refused to publish it unless Bridge cut "British anti-American cracks" from the book. Maintaining that she was merely repeating criticisms of America that were being expressed by many Europeans, Bridge refused to alter the book. *Singing Waters* was published in the United States by Macmillan in 1946; it became a Literary Guild of America selection and sold more than a million copies.

In 1945 Owen was appointed ambassador to Portugal; when he left Lisbon in the spring of 1947, Bridge remained to collect material for *The Selective Traveller in Portugal* (1949), co-authored with Susan Lowndes. In the early autumn of 1949 Bridge returned to Turkey to pursue her research into the Atatürk revolution.

In *Facts and Fictions* Bridge says of her modern historicals: "if any of my work comes to have permanent value, I feel it will be these books." *The Dark Moment,* published in 1952, seems worthy of this estimation. In *Facts and Fictions* Bridge characterizes the work as a collaboration, relating that, while sick in Greece, she worked on the novel with Sahlia Unaydin: "Together, in that hospital room . . . we arranged the whole thing, I propped up in bed making copious notes, she sitting beside me, frowning with concentration, while we planned the dramatis personae, the unfolding of the plot, and above all the names for all the characters. This was something I could never have done alone, with any real vraisemblance; the book is really as much Sahlia's as mine."

The novel spans the Ottoman Empire's decline between 1914 and 1925 and traces the friendship of a young English girl, Fanny Pierce, and Féridé Hanim, the daughter of a Turkish aristocrat. Féridé marries a young man who leaves Constantinople (today Istanbul) along with her older brother to join Atatürk at Ankara. Féridé and her sister-in-law, Nilüfer, follow their husbands. In Ankara, Féridé plays a leading role in Atatürk's efforts to bring the wives of his officers out of their traditional lives of deference and obedience into a modern Turkey in which face veils have been abolished. Bridge details female involvement in the revolution, showing how peasant women and their children transported weapons and ammunition along the Road of the Revolution to Ankara on foot. In the final chapters Fanny returns to Turkey with her uncle, joins Féridé in Ankara, and falls under the influence of Atatürk's compelling personality and romantic attentions. Nearly costing their friendship, Féridé convinces Fanny that Atatürk has become a philanderer and that for Fanny to return his advances would jeopardize the work Féridé has undertaken to bring her countrywomen into the twentieth century. Nancie Matthews in *The New York Times Book Review* (6 January 1952) hailed *The Dark Moment*

*Dust jacket for the second of Bridge's eight novels about the amateur detective Julia Probyn*

as a "fine historical novel," an "extraordinary work of reconstruction," and a "joy to read."

In addition to *Frontier Passage* and *The Dark Moment,* Bridge's historical novels include *A Place to Stand,* dealing with Hungary's Polish community and written at the request of the exiled regent, Miklós Horthy de Nagabánya, and *The Tightening String,* also set in Hungary and inspired by the frustrations Bridge had experienced with the British Red Cross in her efforts, as a member of the Prisoner's Relief Committee, to send food and clothing to British prisoners of war in Germany during World War II.

Following the publication of *A Place to Stand,* Bridge set about researching her mother's life for *Portrait of My Mother.* When that work was complete, Bridge says in *Facts and Fictions,* she "felt slightly at a loss what to do next. I had no particular plot in mind for another 'straight' novel . . . but I did not in the least want to stop writing." She became interested in writing "thrillers" about "amateur detection, preferably abroad," with a quick-witted heroine, and with the publication of *The Lighthearted Quest* (1956) the popular Julia Probyn series began. Bridge wrote eight novels featuring Probyn sleuthing near her home in Ireland and in various foreign countries: *The Lighthearted Quest, The Portuguese Escape* (1958), *The Numbered Account* (1960), *The Dangerous Islands* (1963), *Emergency in the Pyrenees* (1965), *The Episode at Toledo* (1966), *The Malady in Madeira* (1969), and *Julia in Ireland* (1973). *The Numbered Account* arose from a vacation Bridge and her husband took in Switzerland in the summer of 1958. Julia's cousin, Colin Munro, a British Secret Service agent, enlists her help in recovering his fiancée Aglaia Armitage's inheritance from her grandfather's Swiss bank account. His interest in the contents of the account is professional and is shared by the Russians. After several clever machinations, Julia succeeds in recovering Aglaia's inheritance; in the process she falls in love with John Antrobus, another Secret Service agent. Their romance is short-lived because of Antrobus's occupation, and Julia returns to England. Anthony Boucher criticized Bridge in *The New York Times Book Review* (14 August 1960) for her inability to construct a plot and for the "whopping coincidences" that advance the nov-

el's action. *The Dangerous Islands* met with equally negative reviews: Anthony Boucher in *The New York Times Book Review* (24 November 1963) called it "the season's least suspenseful suspense novel, with a minute plot." The final novel in the Probyn series, *Julia in Ireland,* was also Bridge's final work; she died on 9 March 1974.

Though Bridge's novels have generally been dismissed by critics as entertaining travelogues, her work provides fertile, though so far untouched, ground for feminist and postcolonial critics alike. Her strength, as she put it in *Facts and Fictions,* is her exploration of "serious human relationships" as those relationships are affected by geography, politics, history, and ideology.

**Reference:**

Donald Lammers, "Three 'Diplomatic Fictions' from 1932: A Literary Slant on the 'Age of Appeasement,'" *Centennial Review,* 36 (Spring 1992): 387–412.

**Papers:**

Many of Ann Bridge's manuscripts and letters are at the Harry Ransom Humanities Research Center at the University of Texas at Austin.

# Vera Brittain

*(29 December 1893 – 29 March 1970)*

## Alan Bishop
*McMaster University*

BOOKS: *Verses of a V.A.D.* (London: Erskine Macdonald, 1918);

*The Dark Tide* (London: Richards, 1923; New York: Macmillan, 1936);

*Not Without Honour* (London: Richards, 1924);

*Women's Work in Modern England* (London: Noel Douglas, 1928);

*Halcyon, or the Future of Monogamy* (London: Kegan Paul, Trench & Trübner, 1929; New York: Dutton, 1929);

*Testament of Youth: An Autobiographical Study of the Years 1900–1925* (London: Gollancz, 1933; New York: Macmillan, 1933);

*Poems of the War and After* (London: Gollancz, 1934; New York: Macmillan, 1934);

*Honourable Estate: A Novel of Transition* (London: Gollancz, 1936; New York: Macmillan, 1936);

*Thrice a Stranger: New Chapters of Autobiography* (London: Gollancz, 1938; New York: Macmillan, 1938);

*Testament of Friendship: The Story of Winifred Holtby* (London: Macmillan, 1940; New York: Macmillan, 1940);

*War-Time Letters to Peace Lovers* (London: Peace Book, 1940);

*England's Hour: An Autobiography 1939–1941* (London: Macmillan, 1941; New York: Macmillan, 1941);

*Humiliation with Honour* (London: Dakers, 1942; New York: Fellowship Publications, 1943);

*"One of These Little Ones . . . ": A Plea to Parents and Others for Europe's Children* (London: Dakers, 1943);

*Seed of Chaos: What Mass Bombing Really Means* (London: Published for the Bombing Restriction Committee by New Vision, 1944);

*Account Rendered* (New York: Macmillan, 1944; London: Macmillan, 1945);

*On Becoming a Writer* (London: Hutchinson, 1947); republished as *On Being an Author,* with an introduction and notes by George Savage (New York: Macmillan, 1948);

*Vera Brittain in 1924*

*Born 1925: A Novel of Youth* (London: Macdonald, 1948; New York: Macmillan, 1949);

*In the Steps of John Bunyan: An Excursion into Puritan England* (London: Rich & Cowan, 1950); republished as *Valiant Pilgrim: The Story of John Bunyan and Puritan England* (New York: Macmillan, 1950);

*Search After Sunrise* (London: Macmillan, 1951);

*The Story of St. Martin's: An Epic of London* (London: Reverend L. M. Charles Edwards, 1951);

*Lady into Woman: A History of Women from Victoria to Elizabeth II* (London: Dakers, 1953; New York: Macmillan, 1954);

*Testament of Experience: An Autobiographical Story of the Years 1925–1950* (London: Gollancz, 1957; New York: Macmillan, 1957);

*Long Shadows,* by Brittain and George E. W. Sizer (London & Hull: A. Brown, 1958);

*The Women at Oxford: A Fragment of History* (London: Harrap, 1960; New York: Macmillan, 1960);

*Pethick-Lawrence: A Portrait* (London: Allen & Unwin, 1963);

*The Rebel Passion: A Short History of Some Pioneer Peacemakers* (London: Allen & Unwin, 1964; Nyack, N.Y.: Fellowship Publications, 1964);

*Envoy Extraordinary: A Study of Vijaya Lakshmi Pandit and Her Contribution to Modern India* (London: Allen & Unwin, 1965);

*Radclyffe Hall: A Case of Obscenity?* (London: Femina, 1968; South Brunswick, N.J.: Barnes, 1969);

*Chronicle of Youth: The War Diary 1913–1917,* edited by Alan Bishop and Terry Smart (London: Gollancz, 1981: New York: Morrow, 1982);

*Testament of a Generation: The Journalism of Vera Brittain and Winifred Holtby,* edited by Paul Berry and Bishop (London: Virago, 1985);

*Chronicle of Friendship: Diary of the Thirties, 1932–1939,* edited by Bishop (London: Gollancz, 1986);

*Testament of a Peace Lover: Letters from Vera Brittain,* edited by Winifred and Alan Eden-Green (London: Virago, 1988);

*Wartime Chronicle: Diary 1939–1945,* edited by Bishop and Y. Aleksandra Bennett (London: Gollancz, 1989).

OTHER: Winifred Holtby, *Pavements at Anderby: Tales of "South Riding" and Other Regions,* edited by Brittain and H. S. Reid (London: Collins, 1937; New York: Macmillan, 1938);

*Above All Nations: An Anthology,* compiled by Brittain, George Catlin, and Sheila Hodges (London: Gollancz, 1945); revised and enlarged by Devere Allen and Gert Spindler (New York: Harper, 1949).

Vera Brittain's reputation centers on her achievements as an influential British feminist and pacifist and on her famous memoir of World War I, *Testament of Youth: An Autobiographical Study of the Years 1900–1925.* That work has never been out of print since first published in 1933, and its influence has been strengthened by a 1979 BBC television adaptation and new paperback editions. During her lifetime Brittain was also known internationally as a successful journalist, poet, public speaker, biographer, autobiographer, and novelist. Interest in her writings, personality, and relationships (notably her close friendship with Winifred Holtby) has grown steadily, especially among feminist critics, and the publication in 1995 of a noteworthy biography by her friend and literary executor Paul Berry with

Mark Bostridge has now provided scholarship with an authoritative account of her life and achievements.

Vera Mary Brittain was born in Newcastle-under-Lyme, a town in Staffordshire in the Midlands, on 29 December 1893. After a childhood in nearby Macclesfield she grew into what she later called "provincial young ladyhood" in Buxton, a fashionable health resort in the Peak District of Derbyshire. She was the elder child of Thomas Arthur Brittain, a prosperous businessman and partner in Brittains Limited, a paper-manufacturing company based on the paper mill established by his grandfather. He had married Edith Bervon, daughter of a Welsh-born organist and choirmaster, in 1891. The second of their two children, Edward Harold Brittain, was almost two years younger than Vera. During childhood the siblings formed a close relationship, protectively isolated as they were in their wealthy middle-class home, where they were tended by servants and a governess.

In "A Writer's Life," an article originally published in *Parents' Review* in June 1961 and later collected in *Testament of a Generation: The Journalism of Vera Brittain and Winifred Holtby* (1985), Brittain commented that "An inclination to write shows itself very early in a few fortunate individuals, who are never in doubt what their work in life is to be." She was one of those individuals: "As soon as I could hold a pen I started to write, and before that I told stories to my brother. I had written five 'novels,' illustrated with melodramatic drawings, before I was 11." Strongly influenced by her reading of such books as the sensational romances of Mrs. Henry Wood (which were among the few books in the Brittain household), her juvenile fiction has qualities that point to the five novels of her maturity: idealistic and moralistic, they are infused with references to religion and death and focus on noble, independent, self-sacrificing heroines.

By the time she came to write the five mature novels published between 1923 and 1948, Brittain's ambition was to succeed as both a critically respected and a popular writer; she consciously set out to write best-sellers. She was therefore generally content to utilize traditional forms and modes—the experimentation of Modernist contemporaries made little impression on her literary technique. She also, even more than in her juvenilia, based characters and events firmly on her own life and experience so that autobiographical elements tend to predominate over imaginative. Both tendencies were reinforced by her desire to promote, in all her writings, values associated with her social and political

activism. Her novels tend also, therefore, to be didactic.

Brittain wrote in 1925 that her "literary and
political work" were entwined: "The first . . . is simply a popular interpretation of the second; a means
of presenting my theories before people who would
not understand or be interested in them if they were
explained seriously." Toward the end of her life she
restated that position, maintaining that a writer's
highest reward comes from "the power of ideas to
change the shape of the world and even help to
eliminate its evils. . . . Contemporary writers have
the important task of interpreting for their readers
this present revolutionary and complex age which
has no parallel in history." For this purpose above
all, Brittain always championed the novel as the pre-
eminent genre. For instance, in a 1929 review
("New Fiction: Pessimists and Optimists"), she insisted that

no one can preach the gospel of optimism more successfully than the novelist who, between the sober covers of
the book, creeps unobtrusively into those households
where the politician, the ecclesiastic or the teacher
would hesitate to intrude.

So even when writing *Testament of Youth,* Brittain deliberately set out to exploit novelistic qualities: "I
wanted to make my story as truthful as history," she
wrote, "but as readable as fiction."

Her education endorsed such tendencies—and
especially the moral earnestness that marks all her
writing. As a young girl she was taught to value conventional "correct" essaylike style and novelists
such as George Eliot and Arnold Bennett, whose
books became lifelong major influences. St. Monica's, the girls' boarding school her parents sent her
to (while Edward was sent to a public school, Uppingham) was run by one of her mother's sisters,
Florence Bervon, together with Louise Heath-Jones.
The latter was an inspiring teacher who stressed
current affairs and social commitment and was sympathetic to feminism and the work of the suffra-
gettes. She introduced Brittain to *Woman and Labour*
(1911), a feminist polemic by the South African
writer Olive Schreiner—another lifelong influence
which intensified when Brittain was given a copy of
Schreiner's novel *The Story of an African Farm* (1883)
as a gift from Roland Leighton, a school friend of
Edward's with whom she fell in love.

That relationship, cemented in a brief engagement, began shortly before World War I. Brittain
admired Leighton's intellectual and poetic abilities
and his literary family: both parents were successful
popular novelists. Determined to go to university

*Brittain, in her V.A.D. uniform; her brother, Edward; and
their parents, Thomas and Edith Bervon Brittain, in 1915*

when this was still unusual for a young woman
(both Roland and Edward were expected to go as a
matter of course), Brittain persuaded her parents to
allow her to prepare for the entrance examination of
Somerville College, a women's college in Oxford,
and in the summer of 1914 she learned that she had
won a scholarship to study English literature there.

World War I began just weeks before she went
up to Oxford. Edward and Roland—and two of Edward's friends, Victor Richardson and Geoffrey
Thurlow, whom she was beginning to know well—
volunteered as officers, and within a year Brittain
decided to leave Oxford for war service as a Voluntary Aid Detachment (V.A.D.) nurse. Roland was
killed near the end of 1915; Richardson and Thurlow in 1917, when Brittain was serving in Malta;
and Edward only months before the war ended.

While at St. Monica's, Brittain had begun to
keep a diary, and from 1913 she regularly wrote
long entries until her return to England in 1917.
That diary, recording private and public events and
the anguish she suffered during the war, was pub-

lished in 1981 in edited and abridged form under her title: *Chronicle of Youth: The War Diary, 1913–1917*. A second extensive diary, kept between 1932 and 1945, has also been published, in two volumes: *Chronicle of Friendship: Diary of the Thirties, 1932–1939* (1986) and *Wartime Chronicle: Diary, 1939–1945* (1989). Brittain's literary achievement as a diarist is now firmly established, and critical attention is likely to increase. Her many fluent, trenchant letters during the first war, so far unpublished, similarly show the nature of her strongest literary talent: straightforward unmediated expression of observation and opinion.

The only other genre in which she wrote during the war was lyric poetry, and her first major publication was *Verses of a V.A.D.* (1918). Here her achievement is debatable, drawing some praise but a more frequent judgment that her poems are at best conventional and competent—a recording of intense response to events such as the death of Leighton, but in style and form so indebted to Victorian models and to Rupert Brooke's *1914 and Other Poems* (1915) that their emotional force is severely diminished.

After the war, close to a breakdown after years of strain and loss, Brittain returned to Oxford, now electing to study modern history rather than English literature. She found she was sharing her modern European history tutorials, taught by C. R. M. F. Cruttwell (dean of Hertford College), with a fellow undergraduate at Somerville: Winifred Holtby. After a sharp quarrel over Brittain's belief that Holtby had set out to humiliate her in a college debate, they went on to establish a close and fruitful friendship. They were both feminists, politically leftist (both later became members of the Labour Party), fervently committed to the cause of world peace, and ambitious to achieve success as journalists, novelists, public speakers, and social activists.

Leaving Oxford in 1921 with second-class degrees, the two young women set up a flat together in London where, until Brittain's marriage in 1925, they worked at establishing their careers. The lasting excellence of their journalism is obvious in the selection *Testament of a Generation*. Much of it is feminist in orientation; both women were members of the Six Point Group founded in 1921 by Lady Margaret Rhondda, who was also founder and editor of the influential feminist journal *Time and Tide,* in which much of their journalism was published. "I Denounce Domesticity!," first published in *Quiver* in August 1932 and collected in *Testament of a Generation,* indicates the fervor and range of Brittain's convictions:

I suppose there has never been a time when the talent of women was so greatly needed as it is at the present day. Whether great talent or small, whether political, literary, practical, academic or mechanical, its use is a social duty. . . . Even her children should not be permitted to destroy [a woman's] social effectiveness, and it is no more to their advantage than to hers that they should do so. Babies and toddlers are far happier when they can enjoy the society of their contemporaries in properly equipped day nurseries and nursery schools, than living, lonely and constantly thwarted, in houses primarily adapted—in so far as they are adapted to anything—to the needs of adults.

Brittain and Holtby also wrote on a variety of topics other than feminism, including international politics; for this reason they traveled during 1922 in war-ravaged Europe and observed League of Nations activities in Geneva. They were committed members of the League of Nations Union, valuing its promise as a peacekeeping organization, and they quickly became popular speakers at its public meetings.

In the midst of all this activity, Brittain and Holtby completed their first two novels, helping each other with advice and criticism. Brittain's *The Dark Tide* was rejected by several publishers before Grant Richards brought it out in 1923; but, as she noted in "A Writer's Life," it attracted "seventy-three reviews, including a long and favourable criticism in the *Times Literary Supplement*. This result put me 'on the map,' and led to many more freelance articles." *The Dark Tide* also attracted a threat of prosecution for libel (over an incautious statement implying that *Manchester Guardian* reporters could be bribed), a shock of anger in Oxford, and a husband. The latter was George Catlin, a young political scientist and later assistant professor at Cornell who had been Brittain's unknown contemporary at Oxford; his admiration for the novel moved him to correspond with its author, and two years later he persuaded her to marry him.

The anger in Oxford and especially in Somerville College had been earned by the unflattering depiction in the novel of life in a women's college easily identified as Somerville and of many characters whose originals were just as obvious to those who knew them. Brittain had indeed made notes for the novel while at Oxford after the war. Since the plot directly exploited events of that period, such as the incident of the Somerville debate with Holtby and was centered on the relationship of two characters who were clearly if superficially fictional representatives of Holtby and Brittain (Daphne Lethbridge and Virginia Dennison, respectively), the melodramatic characters and plot seemed all the more outra-

Page from Brittain's diary for 1915 (McMaster University Library)

geous. For instance, the outrageously villainous don Raymond Sylvester, whom Daphne agrees, disastrously, to marry just after Virginia has rejected him, could hardly escape being seen as a malicious portrait of Cruttwell, the history tutor.

Yet despite its flaws (when it was reprinted in 1935, its author acknowledged "the crude violence of its methods"), Brittain's "Oxford novel" remains interesting and enjoyable and is now something of a period piece. Its feminist main theme—women's right to independence and self-fulfillment—is, however, damaged by her failure to disentangle it from the contradictory theme of self-sacrifice in the cause of duty. As the novel ends, Virginia's long, idealistic speech eulogizing self-sacrifice exposes a confusion which Brittain herself was later to recognize and attack.

Those two themes are again prominent in Brittain's second novel, *Not Without Honour* (1924), but separated to some extent since they are now related respectively to the protagonist Christine Merivale (again a representative of Brittain herself) and the Reverend Albert Clark, whose values are submitted to severe criticism. In this novel Brittain drew even more directly on her own life, cannibalizing her diary not only for characters and incidents but also for long passages incorporated in the novel with little or no change.

The main action of *Not Without Honour* is set in 1913–1914, the period leading up to the outbreak of World War I, and its setting is Buxton—thinly disguised under the name Torborough. Recalling some years later, in *Testament of Youth,* her angry rejection of Buxton's vapidity and "social snobbery," Brittain wrote: "None of my books have had large sales and the least successful of them all was my second novel, *Not Without Honour*, but I have never enjoyed any experience more than the process of decanting my hatred into that story of the social life of a small provincial town." The plot, echoing Brittain's diary, describes the infatuation of an intelligent, ambitious girl for a charismatic Anglican curate whose unorthodox views and socialist activities bring him into conflict with the local hierarchy. Brittain's father had been witheringly hostile toward Clark's original, the Reverend Joseph Ward, who preached social change and whose church services attracted the poor. The two central characters are both highly imaginative, with "a mutual aspiration after martyrdom." Clark achieves that aspiration, killed, like Leighton, on the western front; Christine learns of his death at Oxford, where she is finding her way to independence, self-fulfillment, and the maturity that both have lacked.

This novel brings together, although still sketchily, the feminist, socialist, and pacifist themes that dominated Brittain's next novel and that she defined in her polemical writings as intrinsically connected. If *Not Without Honour* is a more coherent novel than its predecessor, it is also less vigorous. But it earned a set of largely positive reviews.

Then ensued, as far as novels are concerned, a long silence. Some of the reasons are obvious: marriage and a year of exile (as Brittain felt it to be) in the United States. She so much disliked her situation as a faculty wife at Cornell, and felt so strongly that her writing career was being destroyed by her absence from England, that she and Catlin agreed to attempt a "semi-detached marriage." She was back in London by August 1926 and almost immediately set off with Holtby for Geneva, with a commission to write articles about the League of Nations Assembly. From then until Holtby's death in 1935 they shared a home in Chelsea to which, when he was back from Cornell during vacations, Catlin was intermittently added: an arrangement that raised some eyebrows but seems to have worked extremely well for both women and for Brittain and Catlin's two children, John (born in 1927) and Shirley (born in 1930).

All through that decade Brittain was a prolific and increasingly successful freelance journalist, but she still aspired, even in her much busier daily life, to write a best-selling novel that would establish a high literary reputation. Late in the 1920s the "War Books Boom" began, and with increased fervor after seeing R. C. Sherriff's play *Journey's End* in 1929, Brittain set out to use her diary of World War I as the foundation of a novel, following the model of *Not Without Honour*. However, she found that fictionalizing this material was unsatisfactory. Avidly she had read the many recently published war memoirs, reviewing some of them for *Time and Tide;* Robert Graves's *Good-Bye to All That: An Autobiography* (1929), in particular, showed her that autobiography was a genre appropriate to her material and talent. Recognizing that no book of comparable stature had yet presented a woman's experience of the war, she threw herself into writing her "Autobiographical Study of the Years 1900–1925," *Testament of Youth.*

Its publication in 1933 and quick achievement of best-seller status changed Brittain's life: as an international celebrity she was now in constant demand for public appearances, lectures, articles, and new books. In 1934 she went on the first of three successful but grueling American lecture tours; all through it she was working, whenever she had the time and energy, on a new novel. But in 1935 disaster struck: first her father, then Winifred Holtby, died. Recovering from the double blow, she found her work as Holtby's literary executor quite demanding, especially in arranging the publication of Holtby's last novel, *South Riding* (1937); but even while correcting the proofs of Holtby's book she resumed work on her own.

*Honourable Estate: A Novel of Transition,* published in 1936, is Brittain's longest and most ambitious novel. It originated as two novels almost a decade before Holtby's death and is to some extent a companion to *South Riding:* recapturing, in different circumstances, something of the professional partnership that had supported the writing of their first novels a decade earlier. It is also a companion to *Testament of Youth,* rendering in fictional terms the same historical period and—with a different emphasis—similar central themes.

Although increasingly judged to be Brittain's best and most important novel, *Honourable Estate* has not been republished in recent years and is not easy to obtain. The main reason is that Brittain's husband, George Catlin, resented the representation of his parents as Janet and Thomas Rutherston, judging the latter characterization "grossly libellous." For, apart from fictionalizing her own experiences, as in her first two novels, Brittain had now cast her net wider to exploit the recent history of both the Brittain and Catlin families—most importantly, the marital relations of George Catlin's parents as revealed in his mother's diaries.

Edith Catlin was, Brittain wrote later in *Testament of Experience: An Autobiographical Story of the Years 1925–1950* (1957), "a turbulent, thwarted, politically-unconscious woman who died prematurely in

1917." Desperately unhappy in her marriage to a dogmatic, domineering Congregational minister, she had run away from him, abandoning her young son in 1915, and until her death two years later had worked for woman suffrage. Brittain admired Edith Catlin deeply, seeing her as a sister spirit. Soon after meeting George Catlin and learning his mother's story, she made Edith "the heroine of a projected novel called *The Springing Thorn*." Before her marriage Brittain had also made notes for a novel to be called "Kindred and Affinity," "inspired by my father's semi-apocryphal tales of his Staffordshire family. By 1925 the characters were already coming to life; the fictitious Alleyndenes bore a likeness to my forebears." Both projected novels foundered, however, until, after the publication of *Testament of Youth,* Brittain had the inspiration that eventually produced *Honourable Estate:* "Why not marry *Kindred and Affinity* to *The Springing Thorn,* make the book a story of two contrasting provincial families calamitously thrown together by chance, and then, in the next generation, join the son of one household with the daughter of the other?" Denis Rutherston, the son, is of course a depiction of George Catlin; Ruth Alleyndene, the daughter, a depiction of Brittain; and many other characters have obvious originals among Brittain's family and friends.

Apart from the Alleyndene and Rutherston family histories, with emphasis on the defective marriages of both her and Catlin's parents, Brittain drew again on her experiences in World War I. Characteristically, she also fictionalized three recent traumatic experiences: the discovery that her brother Edward had been a homosexual and had probably invited his 1918 death in battle so as to avoid disgrace; her passionate affair in the mid 1930s, while she was writing *Honourable Estate,* with her American publisher George Brett; and her quarrel in 1932 with the prolific Yorkshire novelist Phyllis Bentley (whose *Inheritance* was a best-seller that year), after a brief, intense friendship. The first two situations are worked out in the fate of Ruth Alleyndene's brother Richard and in her doomed affair with the glamorous American officer Eugene Meury (Brett is superimposed, as it were, on Leighton). But the creation of the character based on Bentley—the successful and influential playwright Gertrude Ellison Campbell, with her broken friendship with Janet Rutherston, profound spiritual connection with Ruth Alleyndene, and posthumous apotheosis at the conclusion of the novel—proved especially significant and enriching:

> Beneath the grey vaulted roof, women of every rank and profession had gathered to do honour to Ellison

# THE DARK TIDE

BY
## VERA BRITTAIN

LONDON
**GRANT RICHARDS LTD.**
ST MARTIN'S STREET
MDCCCCXXIII

*Title page for Brittain's first novel, based on her experiences at Oxford after World War I*

Campbell who had once been an arch-opponent of the women's movement. Because, by her life and work, she had indirectly conferred prestige upon them all, the women's organizations had sent their representatives.

Not only is Ellison Campbell arguably Brittain's finest characterization, but her role in the theme and the rather schematic structure of the novel complicates and strengthens both. She links the generations credibly, and as an unmarried woman and antifeminist who is powerfully creative, she deepens the central ideas. Here Brittain also successfully integrates a theme characteristic of Holtby's novels, and it seems likely that the characterization of Ellison Campbell, although primarily drawn from Bentley, gains force and complexity from Holtby associations.

In her careful foreword to the novel Brittain states that *Honourable Estate* "purports to show how the women's revolution—one of the greatest in all history—united with the struggle for other demo-

*Brittain and her husband, George Catlin, in Ithaca, New York, around 1926*

cratic ideals and the cataclysm of the war to alter the private destinies of individuals." The qualities of the three marriages that compose the main plot—extreme failure of the Rutherstons', partial failure of the Alleyndenes', and qualified success of Denis and Ruth's—filter to the reader the changing social position of women from the Victorian era to the 1930s. The title of the novel, Brittain comments in her foreword, does not refer only to the marriage service; "it also stands for that position and respect for which the world's women and the world's workers have striven" and for "that maturity of the spirit which comes through suffering and experience." Despite its burdens of wordiness, overemphasis, and earnestness, *Honourable Estate* is an impressive success in achieving Brittain's intentions; it gained wide critical approval and was a best-seller in both Britain and the United States.

After the publication of this ambitious book Brittain found herself deeply disturbed by the portents of a second world war and felt compelled to give as much time and energy as possible to writing articles and making speeches in the cause of maintaining peace. She met the Anglican priest and paci-

fist Dick Sheppard at a peace rally where they both spoke, and she decided in 1937 to abandon the foundering League of Nations Union and join his vigorous new Peace Pledge Union. Contributing that year to the pamphlet *Authors Take Sides on the Spanish War,* she proclaimed that, as "an uncompromising pacifist, I hold war to be a crime against humanity, whoever fights it and against whomever it is fought." From then to the end of her life she never wavered in her commitment, devoting extensive time and energy to committee work, speeches, and journalism in support of pacifism.

In addition, from 1939 through 1946 Brittain wrote and distributed some two hundred issues of a discussion newsletter, *Letter to Peace-Lovers;* selections were published in 1940 as *War-Time Letters to Peace Lovers* and in 1988 as *Testament of a Peace Lover: Letters from Vera Brittain.* She also published several polemical works related to the war and her pacifist beliefs, including *England's Hour: An Autobiography, 1939–1941* (1941) and *Humiliation with Honour* (1942), and forceful shorter works arguing against the blockade and saturation-bombing: *"One of These Little Ones . . . ": A Plea to Parents and Others for Europe's Children* (1943) and *Seed of Chaos: What Mass Bombing Really Means* (1944). The first draft of the latter had been published in the United States as "Massacre by Bombing" in the February 1944 edition of *Fellowship,* the magazine of the Fellowship of Reconciliation, before its British appearance; it provoked a furor, and in later years Brittain saw it as the main cause of her much-reduced popularity with American readers after the war.

Despite the demands of her pacifist activism, in the later stages of World War II and in its immediate aftermath she managed to find time and energy to write her two final novels, *Account Rendered* (1944) and *Born 1925: A Novel of Youth* (1948). Again, both were based firmly on personal experience and observation, although now primarily biographical rather than autobiographical: the personalities and lives of two men she knew well and admired deeply provided protagonists who also embody some of her own strongest values. Both novels differ strikingly from their predecessors in being dominated by Brittain's pacifist convictions, reflecting the shift in her life imposed by World War II; feminism and socialism are at most subsidiary themes. Both novels are notably shorter and less ambitious than *Honourable Estate,* and, although substantial works, they seem to show effects of Brittain's exhaustion at the end of the war.

Brittain recalled the genesis of her next novel in *Testament of Experience:*

In the autumn of 1939, I was summoned to a murder trial as a potential witness for the defense. The prisoner, a sensitive and intelligent professional man, had caused his wife's death and then attempted suicide, but afterwards claimed that he could remember nothing of the tragedy. A team of psychological specialists traced back this amnesia to a bomb explosion in 1918, and my acquaintance was found "Guilty but Insane."

Originally titled "Day of Judgment," *Account Rendered* fictionalizes this "strange and tragic story which linked the First War with the Second," allowing Brittain to demonstrate clearly the destructive effect of war on mind and spirit.

While in prison the convicted man—Leonard Lockhart, a Nottingham doctor—readily gave Brittain permission to use his story as the basis of a novel which Brittain began to write in the autumn of 1942. Unfortunately, when the text was submitted to him in April 1943, Lockhart, by then out of prison, withdrew his permission. Typically, Brittain did not give up; she set about rewriting the novel to remove any material that might make the protagonist, Francis Halkin, identifiable as Lockhart. Halkin became a musician instead of a doctor, for instance. In the process of rewriting, Brittain added several new minor characters, including—a felicitous stroke—Ruth Alleyndene, Brittain's fictional representative in *Honourable Estate,* who now, as a Labour MP, fulfills Brittain's role as observer at the trial. Perhaps the least satisfactory elements of the novel are the sentimental romance between Halkin and the self-abnegating, hero-worshiping Enid Clay and Halkin's climactic opportunity to prove himself a conventional hero through his courage after a bomb falls on the prison while he is still a prisoner. Significantly, both of these episodes are Brittain's own invention, and both are thematically damaging.

Published first in the United States, *Account Rendered* received some negative reviews (one termed Brittain an "unapologetic propagandist"); these were fueled, she was convinced, by political hostility. When the novel appeared in England some months later, it was much more successful, selling out its entire first printing of fifty thousand copies before publication and receiving better reviews.

Its successor was *Born 1925,* Brittain's "novel about Dick Sheppard." In *Testament of Experience* she revealed that the protagonist of the novel, Robert Carbury, and much of the plot were centered on the personality and life of the charismatic priest who had founded the Peace Pledge Union, converted Brittain to full pacifism, and died before World War II began. Carbury, winner of a Victoria Cross in World War I, is a priest dedicated to the preserva-

*Brittain in 1934, during her first American lecture tour*

tion of peace. Brittain alters the facts of Sheppard's life to allow Carbury to live until the war is almost over; then, like Halkin, he is given a climactic moment of moral triumph after enduring his calvary of "war-time execration." In such respects the novel repeats the pattern of *Not Without Honour.*

Through much of the novel, however, Carbury is embroiled in private domestic conflict, first with his actress wife Sylvia and then with his son. For, like *Honourable Estate, Born 1925* is a generational novel in which, through Carbury's children Adrian and Josephine—based explicitly on Brittain's children John and Shirley as she perceived them at the time she was writing the novel—Brittain seeks to demonstrate some of the changes brought about by World War II. The conflict between father and son, echoing that between John Catlin and his parents, is resolved at the end of the novel—but only after Robert is dead.

Like *Account Rendered, Born 1925* sold well in England and was respectfully received by critics. But it was not the triumph that Brittain had been hoping for, and she succumbed to depression, telling Catlin, "More and more I become just a 'popular' writer who makes money. . . . the prestige goes to hell." During the next two decades she attempted no further novels; instead, when not engaged in social action or traveling (among other countries, she visited India and South Africa), she wrote in other genres—notably autobiography, such as *Testament of Experience;* biography, including *In the Steps of John Bunyan: An Excursion into Puritan England* (1950), *Pethick-Lawrence: A Portrait* (1963), and *Envoy Extraordinary: A Study of Vijaya Lakshmi Pandit and Her Contribution to Modern India* (1965); feminist history, with *Lady into Woman: A History of Women from Victoria to Elizabeth II* (1953) and *The Women at Oxford: A Fragment of History* (1960); and pacifist history, such as *The Rebel Passion: A Short History of Some Pioneer Peacemakers* (1964). While these are worthy books, they also represent a decline from the high literary ambitions and achievements of the 1930s and through World War II.

Only once, it appears, did she seriously consider writing another novel; but her proposal, in 1960, was politely rejected by Macmillan, so her literary career did not end as she would have preferred, with success in the genre she most respected. Some years earlier she had told her daughter that she "would much rather be a writer of plays and really first-class novels, instead of the biographies and 'documentaries' to which such talent as I have seems best suited."

That depressed comment surely minimizes her literary achievement. Apart from her incontrovertible successes in other genres, notably journalism and autobiography, at least one of Brittain's novels, *Honourable Estate,* is a substantial achievement and deserves to be read widely by a new generation of readers. None of the other four lacks literary competence, interest, and thoughtful comment on central moral issues of our time. All five, revalued according to aesthetic criteria that do not automatically demote non-Modernistic writings, should be accorded a higher critical standing than they hold at present.

Brittain's novels, more than Holtby's, open themselves to easy dismissal as merely autobiographical and propagandist, but apart from their attractively straightforward narrative qualities, all of them, even the last two, present unintended complexity that should interest and challenge new readers. In *Born 1925,* for instance, Brittain's conception of a satisfactory marriage of equals, the woman maintaining her career, the husband sensitive and supportive, receives a jolt when Sylvia admits to herself that love is a random atavistic force quite beyond rational control: "Occasionally she found herself wishing that there was more unrestrained lust and less tender reverence in Robert's caresses; she longed for him just sometimes to take her inconsiderately, without asking first." Here what may be

autobiographical in origin seems to interfere with the ostensible movement of the text, stirring qualification and further consideration by the reader of the final meaning of the novel.

Brittain saw herself as representative of her generation, and as she stated in her foreword to *Testament of Youth,* she constantly endeavored in her writing "to put the life of an ordinary individual into its niche in contemporary history." Her training as a historian, and her intense concern with social issues, mark all her novels. In these, no less than in *Testament of Youth,* she avowedly fictionalized her own experiences and opinions, and those of friends and family members; but she did so with a forceful directness that infuses all five novels with moral and historical insight. Since, like all her works, they were written to reach the widest possible audience in the hope of informing and influencing as many of her contemporaries as possible, she paid minimal attention to subtlety or complexity—though, because she was an honest and intelligent analyst, these qualities nevertheless enter her texts. However much she may at times have regretted her failure to impress highbrow critics and gain a secure reputation as one of the best novelists of her day, Brittain's achievement as a novelist was nevertheless considerable, and her novels are eminently worthy of being read and revalued in our time.

**Letters:**

*Selected Letters of Winifred Holtby and Vera Brittain, 1920–1935,* edited by Brittain and Geoffrey Handley-Taylor (London & Hull: A. Brown, 1960).

**Biographies:**

Shirley Williams, "My Mother and Her Friend," *Listener,* 114 (21 November 1985): 33–34;

Hilary Bailey, *Vera Brittain* (London: Penguin, 1987);

John Catlin, *Family Quartet* (London: Hamilton, 1987);

Williams, "Testament to the Touchstone of My Life," *Independent,* 29 December 1993;

Paul Berry and Mark Bostridge, *Vera Brittain: A Life* (London: Chatto & Windus, 1995);

Deborah Gorham, *Vera Brittain: A Feminist Life* (Oxford: Blackwell, 1996).

**References:**

George Catlin, *For God's Sake, Go!* (Gerrards Cross: Colin Smythe, 1972);

Geoffrey Handley-Taylor and John Malcolm Dockeray, eds., *Vera Brittain: Occasional Papers* (London: Black Pennell, 1983);

Jean E. Kennard, *Vera Brittain and Winifred Holtby: A Working Partnership* (Hanover, N.H.: Published for the University of New Hampshire by the University Press of New England, 1989);

Lynn Layton, "Vera Brittain's Testament(s)," in *Behind the Lines: Gender and the Two World Wars,* edited by Margaret Higonnet and Jane Jenson (New Haven: Yale University Press, 1987), pp. 70–83.

**Papers:**
The Vera Brittain Archive, McMaster University, Hamilton, Ontario, Canada, has the main, extensive collection of Brittain's papers. The Winifred Holtby Archive, Hull Central Library, Albion Street, Hull, England, includes letters by Brittain. Other materials are located in the Paul Berry Collection, Stedham, Midhurst, West Sussex, England, and in the Archive of Macmillan Publishers Limited, British Library, London.

# John Brophy

*(6 December 1899 – 13 November 1965)*

Leonard R. N. Ashley
*Emeritus, Brooklyn College of the City University of New York*

BOOKS: *The Bitter End* (London & Toronto: Dent, 1928; New York: Dutton, 1928);

*Pluck the Flower: A Novel* (London & Toronto: Dent, 1929; New York: Dutton, 1929);

*Peter Lavelle: A Novel* (London & Toronto: Dent, 1929; New York: Dutton, 1929);

*Fanfare, and Other Papers,* Benington Books, no. 1 (London: Partridge, 1930);

*Flesh and Blood* (London & Toronto: Dent, 1931);

*Thunderclap* (London: Partridge, 1931);

*English Prose,* How-&-Why Series, no. 12 (London: Black, 1932);

*The Rocky Road: A Novel* (London: Cape, 1932);

*The World Went Mad: A Novel* (London: Cape, 1934; New York: Macmillan, 1934);

*Waterfront: A Novel* (London: Cape, 1934; New York: Macmillan, 1934; revised edition, London: Pan, 1950);

*The Writers' Desk Book: Articles,* by Brophy, William Freeman, L. A. G. Strong, Leonora Eyles, Eleanor Farjeon, and others (London: Black, 1934);

*I Let Him Go: A Novel* (London: Cape, 1935);

*The Five Years: A Conspectus of the Great War Designed Primarily for Study by the Successors of Those Who Took Part in It and Secondarily to Refresh the Memory of the Participants Themselves* (London: Barker, 1936);

*Ilonka Speaks of Hungary: Personal Impressions and an Interpretation of the National Character* (London: Hutchinson, 1936);

*The Ramparts of Virtue: A Novel* (London: Cape, 1936);

*Felicity Greene: The Story of a Success* (London: Cape, 1937);

*Behold the Judge: A Novel* (London: Collins, 1937);

*Man, Woman and Child* (London: Collins, 1938); republished as *City of Scandals* (London: Transworld, 1955);

*Gentleman of Stratford: A Novel* (London: Collins, 1939; New York & London: Harper, 1940);

*The Queer Fellow: Stories* (London: Collins, 1939);

*John Brophy*

*The Ridiculous Hat: A Novel* (London: Collins, 1939);

*Green Glory: A Novel* (London: Collins, 1940);

*Green Ladies: A Novel* (London: Collins, 1940); revised and republished with *Green Glory* (London: Corgi, 1957);

*Home Guard: A Handbook for the L.D.V.* (London: Hodder & Stoughton, 1940); revised as *A Home Guard Handbook* (London: Hodder & Stoughton, 1942);

*A Home Guard Drill Book and Field Service Manual* (London: Hodder & Stoughton, 1940); revised as *Home Guard Drill and Battle Drill* (London: Hodder & Stoughton, 1943);

*Advanced Training for the Home Guard: With Ten Specimen Field Exercises* (London: Hodder & Stoughton, 1941; revised, 1942);

*Solitude Island: An Entertainment* (London: Collins, 1941);

*Britain Needs Books* (London: National Book Council, 1942);

*Home Guard Proficiency* (London: Hodder & Stoughton, 1942);

*Immortal Sergeant: A Novel* (London: Collins, 1942; New York & London: Harper, 1942);

*Spear Head: A Novel* (London: Collins, 1943); republished as *Spearhead* (New York & London: Harper, 1943);

*Target Island: A Novel* (London: Collins, 1944; New York & London: Harper, 1944);

*Portrait of an Unknown Lady* (London: Collins, 1945);

*Britain's Home Guard: A Character Study* (London: Harrap, 1945);

*The Human Face* (London & Toronto: Harrap, 1945; New York: Prentice-Hall, 1946);

*City of Departures: A Novel* (London: Collins, 1946);

*The Woman from Nowhere: A Novel* (London: Collins, 1946);

*Selected Stories* (London & Dublin: Fridberg, 1946);

*Body and Soul* (London: Harrap, 1948);

*Sarah: A Novel* (London: Collins, 1948);

*Julian's Way: A Novel* (London: Collins, 1949);

*The Mind's Eye: A Twelve-Month Journal* (London: Barker, 1949);

*Turn the Key Softly: A Novel* (London: Collins, 1951);

*Windfall: A Diversion* (London: Collins, 1951);

*Somerset Maugham* (London & New York: Published for the British Council by Longmans, Green, 1952; revised edition, London, New York & Toronto: Published for the National Council & the National Book League by Longmans, Green, 1958; enlarged, 1964);

*The Prime of Life: A Novel* (London: Collins, 1954);

*The Nimble Rabbit* (London: Chatto & Windus, 1955);

*The Prince and Petronella* (London: Chatto & Windus, 1956);

*The Day They Robbed the Bank of England: A Novel* (London: Chatto & Windus, 1959);

*The Front Door Key* (London: Heinemann, 1960);

*The Human Face Reconsidered* (London: Harrap, 1962);

*The Face in Western Art* (London: Harrap, 1963);

*The Meaning of Murder* (London: Whiting & Wheaton, 1966; New York: Crowell, 1967);

*The Face of the Nude: A Study in Beauty* (New York: Tudor, 1968).

OTHER: *The Soldier's War: A Prose Anthology,* edited by Brophy (London & Toronto: Dent, 1929);

*Songs and Slang of the British Soldier: 1914–1918,* edited by Brophy and Eric Partridge (London: Partridge, 1930; revised, 1931); revised as *The Long Trail: What the British Soldier Sang and Said in the Great War of 1914–18* (London: Deutsch, 1965; New York & London: House & Maxwell, 1965);

*Hotch-Potch,* edited by Brophy (Liverpool: Council of the Royal Liverpool Children's Hospital, 1936);

*The Voice of Sarah Curran: Unpublished Letters Together with the Full Story of Her Life Told for the First Time by H. T. MacMullen,* edited by Brophy (Dublin: Privately printed, 1955);

Juris Soikans, *Under the Strange Sky,* introduction by Brophy (Kaiserslautern, Germany: Rohr, 1957);

*XX Unpublished Letters of Holbrook Jackson to Joseph Ishill,* introduction by Brophy (Berkeley Heights, N.J.: Oriole Press, 1960).

John Brophy, who said that he wrote journalism "off the surface of my mind" and kept "its depths for gestating and producing novels," was born in Liverpool on 6 December 1899 to John and Agnes Bodell Brophy. When World War I broke out in 1914, he ran away from home to join the army, serving in the infantry in France and Belgium. After the war he received a bachelor of arts degree at Liverpool University and spent a year at Durham University. In 1924 he married Charis Weare Grundy, the daughter of a Chicago clergyman, and took a teaching job in Egypt; they returned to England two years later when Charis fell ill. Brophy got a job on the advertising staff of a large store in Liverpool, then moved to London to become head copywriter for a leading British advertising firm. Later he was the chief reviewer of fiction for the *Daily Telegraph, Time and Tide,* and the BBC.

Brophy turned his military experience into his first novel, *The Bitter End* (1928). The work resembles the American classic *The Red Badge of Courage* (1895) in that it uses the battlefield–observed by Brophy, imagined by Stephen Crane–as the background for a story of a sensitive young man who experiences the horror of war. *The Bitter End* gives the reader the mud and the madness of trench warfare in a war marked by incredible incompetence of generals on both sides and by horrendous casualties. The journey of the insecure and amiable hero, Donald Foster, from adolescent innocence to sad maturity represents the crumbling of Victorian values under the weight of modern warfare. The disillusionment of the protagonist and the futility of the war are cleverly counterpointed. L. P. Hartley praised *The Bitter End* in the *Saturday Review* (5 May 1928) as

PLUCK THE FLOWER

A Novel
by
JOHN BROPHY
Author of
"THE BITTER END"

NEW YORK
E. P. DUTTON & CO., INC.

Title page for Brophy's second novel, about two brothers with contrasting characters

ers who are similar in appearance but vastly different in character. John marries a pregnant village girl, then discovers that Paul is responsible for her condition. At the same time, Paul takes the side of John's employers, the owners of a department store, whom John is battling. According to D. F. Gilman in the *Boston Transcript* (16 March 1929), "rarely have we seen a novel which dealt with life and its problems with such grave understanding." *The New York Times* (27 January 1929) called the book "a remarkably interesting study of the development of the two brothers, a skillful record of journeys starting from almost identical beginnings and ending on roads widely divergent." The *New York World* (10 February 1929), however, saying that "there is much capable writing wasted," held that "the general conception seems to be artificial, mildly old fashioned and second rate."

*Peter Lavelle* (1929), a novel of postwar disappointment and sexual dissipation, is strong when the war hero Lavelle becomes particularly embittered. The novel argues, however, that in the long run decent human values will survive all social turmoil.

*The World Went Mad* (1934) is a sprawling family history, with many partly realized characters and a variety of locales. The work centers around the Crellins, soldiers in World War I. Though some critics accused Brophy of being too impersonal with his huge cast of characters, none faulted him for the errors he made in describing places he did not personally know, such as Palestine and the United States. The novel is partially redeemed by Brophy's indignation at the waste of war, what Herschel Brickell described in the *North American Review* (March 1935) as "the author's scorn for a race that can think of no better way of settling its quarrels than of taking the youngest and finest of its members and blowing them to bits in a thousand assorted ways." By the time the novel was published, however, interest in World War I had waned. The novelist Graham Greene reviewed *The World Went Mad* for *The Spectator* (27 July 1934):

> Mr. Brophy's irony is all the better for its lack of moral indignation, its quiet acceptance of crookedness, and there is imaginative depth in such episodes as [Sir Roger] Casement's trial watched by the sick law student, and the departure of the night bombers. Any dissatisfaction one feels, is . . . with his method. . . . It is as if Mr. Brophy had been unable to accept his own episodic method and had made an unsuccessful attempt to link too many of [the episodes] into a conventional story.

excellent in its way. Nearly every writer who has tried to do what Mr. Brophy does, who complains of the coarseness of his fellows and gibes at staff-officers safe in soft jobs, defeats his own ends; shows himself a chronic grumbler and inclines our sympathy towards the sanguine animal natures whom he despises. Mr. Brophy has too much sense of humor and proportion to fall into this trap. He is not discontented but angry, and his anger rarely misses its mark. The book is as much like a work of art as a warning and an arraignment can well be.

*The New York Times* (24 June 1928) found *The Bitter End* "a good novel, because the story of Donald Foster is never subordinated to the story of the war." The *Saturday Review of Literature* (14 July 1928) said that it was "an uncommonly fine novel" from a new writer who would be one to watch.

The Brophys' daughter, Brigid Antonia, was born in 1929; she would become a novelist, short-story writer, biographer, playwright, and writer about art. Brophy's next novel, *Pluck the Flower,* was published that same year. John and Paul are broth-

Also in 1934 Brophy published *Waterfront,* the dismal story of the McCabe family: they have been deserted for fourteen years by the father, who then returns to the slums of Liverpool to commit murder and bring tragedy upon the whole brood. The Scouse waterfront is painted in a style reminiscent of the American "Ashcan School" of morbid realism: Brophy's style is stripped to its bare essentials, casting a harsh light on the miserable surroundings. *Waterfront* is a major achievement; the *Times Literary Supplement* (25 January 1934) said that the material

> is anything but sordid as told by Mr. Brophy. He extenuates nothing, but he has an ennobling touch. The defects of his characters are set down without comment of his own so as to appear the natural growth of the oppressive conditions in which they live. Often the defects of one bring out the defects of another without there being any formal antithesis.

After *Waterfront* Brophy published the minor novels *I Let Him Go* (1935) and *The Ramparts of Virtue* (1936). In 1939 came *Gentleman of Stratford,* a novel about William Shakespeare. Brophy's Bard is a clubbable, cheerful chap, not the fiercely ambitious and snobbish provincial of real life who went to the big city and, by dint of his genius, made himself an immortal. Brophy undertakes to find the man in the works, not realizing that Shakespeare, writing in the necessarily crowd-pleasing genre of drama, revealed more about his audience than about himself. Shakespeare always obeyed the rule of the theater that the good dramatist never comes on stage himself. Brophy's Shakespeare comes off as a rather wan and respectable fellow, not the lusty youth who got a much older woman pregnant and had to marry her in haste although he was already engaged to another who was closer to his own age and station. It is hard to think of Brophy's Bard poaching deer or doing any of the other things that gossip says the real Shakespeare did; worst of all, one cannot imagine the person described in this fake biography as capable of penning the sonnets or the plays. Nor does Brophy get the Elizabethan language right. The critic in the *Times Literary Supplement* (26 August 1939) calls the novel's language "Wardour Street English"; Wardour Street, in London's Soho, used to be associated with the cinema business and thereby gave its name to insensitively and inartistically elaborated speech.

During World War II Brophy edited *John O'London's Weekly* and wrote training manuals for the Home Guard. He also published patriotic war novels recounting the exploits of brave soldiers; these novels were popular in the United States as well as in Britain. His best-known such work is *Immortal Sergeant* (1942), in which three members of a British patrol in the Libyan desert in 1941 survive

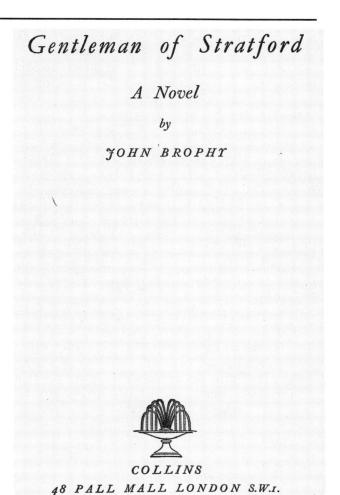

*Gentleman of Stratford*

*A Novel*

*by*

JOHN BROPHY

COLLINS
*48 PALL MALL LONDON S.W.1.*

Title page for Brophy's fictionalized biography of William Shakespeare

thanks to Corporal Spence, an inexperienced, self-effacing hero who is forced to take command when their sergeant is killed. Most critics agreed that the novel portrayed real soldiers in real war, in spite of the lack of profanity in the dialogue, although a few complained that the action was stressed at the expense of character analysis. The novel was made into a motion picture in 1943 with Henry Fonda as Spence.

*Spear Head* (1943) is an action story about British commando raids in Norway and France that leaps into high gear when the preparations are completed and the actual raids begin. The novel includes a love affair between the dashing young Irish commando O'Donovan and the captain's sister, Carol. Still another wartime action novel, *Target Island* (1944), is set in Malta. The British so admired the gallant stand of the Maltese against the Germans that King George VI gave the whole island the George Medal for bravery. In the United States this minor theater of war was almost unknown, and *The New Yorker* (20 August 1944) dismissed Brophy's tale of courageous Royal Air Force pilots and Maltese fighters as "a sentimental trifle." The story is tightly knit and exciting, but there are many clichés in the plot and the characterizations.

The postwar novels *City of Departures* (1946), *The Woman from Nowhere* (1946), *Sarah* (1948), *Julian's Way* (1949), *Turn the Key Softly* (1951), *The Prime of Life* (1954), and *The Nimble Rabbit* (1955) exhibit Brophy's easy style and energy but are forgotten today. *The Day They Robbed the Bank of England* (1959), on the other hand, was the basis for a highly successful 1960 "caper" movie, starring Aldo Ray and Peter O'Toole, that spawned many imitators. The cinema probably provided Brophy with more money for his hobby of collecting drawings by the Old Masters than did his brief appearances on best-seller lists.

Brophy's interest in art led to some specialized nonfiction books, such as *The Human Face* (1945), *The Human Face Reconsidered* (1962), *The Face in Western Art* (1963), and *The Face of the Nude: A Study in Beauty* (1968); his visual sense also added a dimension to his fictional descriptions. His many other nonfiction works include *Fanfare, and Other Papers* (1930); *English Prose* (1932); *The Writers' Desk Book* (1934), a collaborative effort with other authors; *The Five Years: A Conspectus of the Great War Designed Primarily for Study by the Successors of Those Who Took Part in It and Secondarily to Refresh the Memory of the Participants Themselves* (1936); *Ilonka Speaks of Hungary: Personal Impressions and an Interpretation of the National Character* (1936); *The Mind's Eye: A Twelve-Month Journal* (1949); *Somerset Maugham* (1952); and *The Meaning of Murder* (1966). He also edited *The Soldier's War: A Prose Anthology* (1929); *Songs and Slang of the British Soldier: 1914–1918* (1930), with Eric Partridge; the letters and biography of Sarah Curran (1955); and the correspondence of Holbrook Jackson and Joseph Ishill (1960). Although he was primarily a novelist, he produced two collections of short stories: *The Queer Fellow* (1939) and *Selected Stories* (1946).

Brophy died on 13 November 1965. A reliable and readable entertainer who wrote a wide variety of books, he is still mainly remembered as an excellent war novelist.

# Joanna Cannan

### (27 May 1896 – 22 April 1961)

## Diana Farr

BOOKS: *The Misty Valley* (London, 1922; New York: Doran, 1924);

*Wild Berry Wine* (London: Unwin, 1925; New York: Stokes, 1925);

*The Lady of the Heights* (London: Unwin, 1926);

*Sheila Both-Ways* (London: Benn, 1928; New York: Stokes, 1929);

*The Simple Pass On* (London: Benn, 1929); republished as *Orphan of Mars* (Indianapolis: Bobbs-Merrill, 1930);

*No Walls of Jasper* (London: Benn, 1930; Garden City, N.Y.: Doubleday, Doran, 1931);

*High Table* (London: Benn, 1931; Garden City, N.Y.: Doubleday, Doran, 1931);

*Ithuriel's Hour* (London: Hodder & Stoughton, 1931; Garden City, N.Y.: Doubleday, Doran, 1931); republished as *The Hour of the Angel—Ithuriel's Hour* (London: Pan, 1949);

*Snow in Harvest* (London: Hodder & Stoughton, 1932);

*North Wall* (London: Hodder & Stoughton, 1933);

*Under Proof* (London: Hodder & Stoughton, 1934);

*The Hills Sleep On* (London: Hodder & Stoughton, 1935);

*Frightened Angels* (London: Gollancz, 1936; New York & London: Harper, 1936);

*A Hand to Burn* (London: Hodder & Stoughton, 1936);

*A Pony for Jean* (London: Lane, 1936; New York: Scribners, 1937);

*Pray Do Not Venture* (London: Gollancz, 1937);

*We Met Our Cousins* (London: Collins, 1937);

*Another Pony for Jean* (London: Collins, 1938);

*Princes in the Land* (London: Gollancz, 1938);

*London Pride* (London: Collins, 1939);

*They Rang up the Police* (London: Gollancz, 1939);

*Idle Apprentice* (London: Gollancz, 1940);

*Death at the Dog* (London: Gollancz, 1940); republished as *Death at "The Dog"* (New York: Reynal & Hitchcock, 1941);

*Blind Messenger* (London: Gollancz, 1941);

*More Ponies for Jean* (London: Collins, 1943);

*Joanna Cannan*

*Hamish: The Story of a Shetland Pony* (West Drayton, Middlesex & New York: Penguin, 1944);

*They Bought Her a Pony* (London: Collins, 1944);

*Little I Understood* (London: Gollancz, 1948);

*I Wrote a Pony Book* (London: Collins, 1950);

*Murder Included* (London: Gollancz, 1950); republished as *Poisonous Relations* (New York: Morrow, 1950);

*And All I Learned* (London: Gollancz, 1951 [i.e., 1952]);

*Body in the Beck* (London: Gollancz, 1952);

*Oxfordshire* (London: Hale, 1952);

*Long Shadows* (London: Gollancz, 1955);

*People To Be Found* (London: Gollancz, 1956);

*Gaze at the Moon* (London: Collins, 1957);

*And Be a Villain* (London: Gollancz, 1958);
*All Is Discovered* (London: Gollancz, 1962).
**Editions:** *A Pony for Jean,* edited by Josephine
    Pullein-Thompson (Leicester: Brockhampton,
    1973);
*Another Pony for Jean,* edited by Pullein-Thompson
    (Leicester: Brockhampton, 1973);
*High Table,* introduction by Antony Quinton (Oxford: Oxford University Press, 1987).

OTHER: *The Tripled Crown: A Book of English, Scotch
    and Irish Verse for the Age of Six to Sixteen,* edited
    by Cannan, M. D. Cannan, and May W. Cannan (London: Frowde, 1908).

Over a period of forty years Joanna Cannan
wrote twenty-eight novels that, with one exception,
chart with remarkable accuracy aspects of the social
history of England of that time: the class system, social shibboleths, the social innuendo, and the single
word that reveals a person's background. She also
established the "pony book" genre of children's
novels, and she became one of the Gollancz publishing firm's most-celebrated crime writers. Her work
was admired by many contemporary authors, including Arnold Bennett, Ralph Partridge, Phyllis
Bentley, Doris Lessing, John Betjeman, and Julian
Symons.

Born on 27 May 1896 in Magdalen Gate
House in Oxford, Joanna Maxwell Cannan was the
third daughter of Charles Cannan and Mary Wedderburn Cannan. Charles Cannan was a classicist
and dean of Trinity College, Oxford, until 1898
when he became secretary to the delegates (chief executive officer) of Oxford University Press. His
work brought many authors to Magdalen Gate
House, including Rudyard Kipling, Henry Newbolt, A. E. W. Mason, and his onetime student Sir
Arthur Thomas Quiller-Couch. Quiller-Couch's *On
the Art of Writing* (1916) would strongly influence Joanna Cannan, bringing precision and brevity to her
style. Charles Cannan's mother, Jane Dorothea
Claude, an artist who had died young, had left behind a collection of drawings and letters she had
produced during a two-year stay in Australia; they
would be used by Joanna Cannan as the background for her novel *Pray Do Not Venture* (1937).
They are now in the Australian National Library in
Canberra. Cannan's mother was a lively and cultivated but snobbish woman whose father, the son of
a solicitor general of Scotland, had made his name
as an administrator in India. Mary Wedderburn
Cannan's aunt was the painter Jemima Blackburn, a
friend of the painter Sir Edwin Landseer and the
writers Anthony Trollope, John Ruskin, and William Makepeace Thackeray, and the first cousin of
the physicist James Clerk Maxwell.

Joanna Cannan and her sisters, Dorothea and
May, spent much of each summer on the Blackburns' estate, Roshven, on Loch Ailort in the Scottish West Highlands, which would become the setting for Joanna's children's book *We Met Our Cousins*
(1937). Other holidays were spent with their parents
rock climbing in the Lake District and mountaineering in Switzerland; Cannan would use the latter experience in *The Lady of the Heights* (1926) and *Ithuriel's Hour* (1931). Three mornings a week the sisters
attended Wychwood, Miss Anne Batty's school for
the daughters of dons, where one of Joanna's friends
was Carola Oman, the future novelist and biographer. Twice a week a French governess came to
Magdalen Gate House to instruct the girls in her language and culture. Dorothea, May, and Joanna put
out a family magazine. In addition, Joanna and
Oman edited a magazine, *Inter Multos,* to which
friends and schoolmates contributed; Cannan illustrated many of the stories. The three also edited *The
Tripled Crown* (1908), an anthology of poetry.

In 1913 Cannan attended a finishing school in
Paris. She had planned to study art at the Slade
School, but at the outbreak of World War I in 1914
she became a V.A.D. (Voluntary Aid Detachment)
nurse. She also helped out as an editor at Oxford
University Press after several members of the staff
went into the military services; one learned expert
whose manuscript she edited complained that "a
madman" had been at his work. She also prepared
the *Quarterly Journal of Medicine* for the press.

In June 1918 Cannan married Harold James
Pullein-Thompson, an infantry captain; she sometimes described how she had fallen off her bicycle
when she first saw her future husband in the Oxford
High Street. Like several of her novels' heroines,
Cannan was attracted to gentle poets who shared
her romantic ideals, but they could not, in the end,
compete with masterful and protective men like
Pullein-Thompson, a former rugby player, six feet
two inches tall, and well built, with black hair, blue
eyes, and a moustache. After a honeymoon in
Goring-on-Thames and on a houseboat at Clifton
Hampden, the Pullein-Thompsons moved into officers' quarters in Yarmouth. In 1919 they bought,
probably with help from her father, a house at 12
Crescent Road, Wimbledon.

Bored by her suburban life and determined to
be more than a housewife, Cannan began breeding
Sealyham terriers and writing. The heroine of her
first novel, *The Misty Valley* (1922), is the Oxford-
born, egotistical, and romantic Claire Wayneflete,
the daughter of a famous painter. She marries a

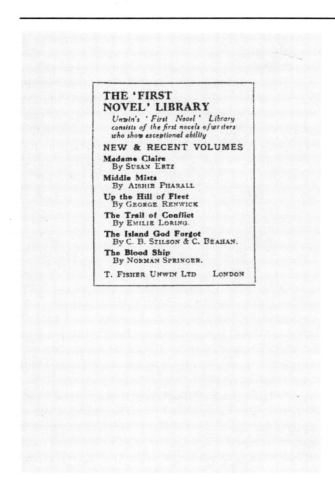

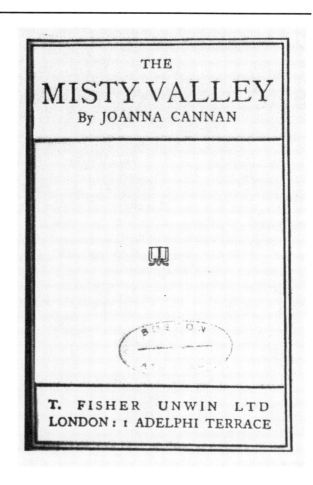

*Publisher's advertisement and title page for Cannan's first novel, about the strains in the marriage of an artist and an army captain*

dashing and handsome army captain, Roy Williams, who in civilian life cannot measure up to her impossibly poetical and idealistic marital expectations. Her hopes of studying art are, like Cannan's, thwarted by World War I, and Claire "does her bit" as a V.A.D. nurse and then as member of the Women's Royal Naval Service at Yarmouth. After the war Roy becomes a stockbroker. Claire, dissatisfied, flees to Paris and enrolls in art school. While she is in Ypres on a painting trip, however, her resentment of Roy's chauvinism and dullness—"He had never loved the far and the blue . . . Michael Angelo meant less to him than Abe Mitchell"—is countered by the guilty thought of his wartime suffering and courage: perhaps on this very spot, she thinks, "he had shivered and sweated, bivouacked." He had risked his life for people like her. She will return home, learn to cook, "address golf balls in the garden and read 'City Notes,' and dust the spars of chairs. There would be no more colour. But, looking round her, what colour had there been for Roy

in the Great War?" Meanwhile, Roy, realizing that he has withheld from Claire "all that he himself has never coveted," sells the suburban house she hated and buys one with a studio. Thus, the marriage is saved.

Cannan partly based Claire and Roy's first claustrophobic house on her home in Wimbledon, but Claire's situation was inspired by, rather than based on, Cannan's. Cannan, for example, had two servants to help her, and the birth on 14 May 1919 of her son Denis, who would become the playwright Denis Cannan, made flight difficult. And though Pullein-Thompson had once sat, like Roy Williams, "the personification of romance" astride a black mare "on a bridge above a rose river against a golden sky," he, unlike Roy, was interested in the theater and the cinema. Although Cannan later dismissed *The Misty Valley* as lightweight, it was hailed as a fine debut and especially admired for its descriptive passages. It remains notable for its freshness and vitality. Its heroine's character, shallow though it may be at times, is strongly drawn and totally convincing within the period in which it was set.

Like all of Cannan's novels, *The Misty Valley* belongs to no literary movement. Although Cannan read widely and admired some Russian and much French literature—she had special affection for the novels of Colette—she was most influenced by the English poets George Meredith, Matthew Arnold, Humbert Wolfe, Alfred Tennyson, Arthur Hugh Clough, Percy Bysshe Shelley, and Edward FitzGerald. Their work, much of which she knew by heart, inspired the rhythm in her prose.

Around 1923 the Pullein-Thompsons moved to 8 (now 4) Marryat Road, Wimbledon, where their first daughter, Josephine, was born. Cannan's mother—her father had died in 1919—built an adjacent house for herself. Cannan joined the English Centre of International P.E.N. and wrote reviews for the *Bookman* and, briefly, for the *Daily Telegraph.* Her novel *Sheila Both-Ways* (1928) depicts a mother's emotional tug-of-war between a gentle lover and her children; the children win. The publisher Allen Lane and the writers John Drinkwater, C. S. Forester, and Georgette Heyer were among Cannan's friends.

Pullein-Thompson worked for a toy manufacturer; he also invented various games but failed to market them successfully. After the Great Depression started in 1929 he was unable to hold a job, and the family's financial problems were exacerbated by the arrival of twins, Diana and Christine, only eighteen months after Josephine. (All three daughters would grow up to become writers.) Pullein-Thompson's struggles and humiliations inspired *The Simple Pass On* (1929), in which the former Etonian Laurence Danby desperately tries to sell enough vacuum cleaners to keep his spoiled wife, Wanda, in the style to which she has been accustomed. "One didn't think of money in the war," Wanda says. "I know," replies Laurence. "That's my one excuse for marrying you and bringing all this upon you." The gentle and poetic Laurence loses his wife; his friend, the former serviceman Tarrant, sums up the war heroes' postwar position: "The fact is we're nothing but junk, Danby you and I. . . . We're the generation that was born just to fight the war, and now we've fought it we've got to rot the same as those other fellows who stopped out there. . . . Why didn't we stop out there and have nice little crosses put up over us and our relations tootling out there on pilgrimages to see our graves?" Far from deserting her husband, Cannan worked all the harder to help support the family—basing many

of her characters, to his embarrassment, on his business associates.

Cannan wrote her novels in pencil in sixpenny exercise books and then typed them. She could write anywhere—sitting on a laundry basket in the kitchen, waiting in her car for her children to come out of school, on trains or park benches. Sometimes her mind was so taken up with her work that she would forget to put tea in the pot or would come downstairs with an orange peel in one hand and a letter in the other and absentmindedly put the peel on her table and the letter in the fire. She contributed polished short stories in the manner of O. Henry, whom she admired, to *John O'London's Weekly,* the *New London Magazine,* the *Daily Mail,* and the *Women's Journal.* Meanwhile, Pullein-Thompson, whose cousin was the playwright Stanley Houghton, wrote the screenplay for a silent film, *Inheritance,* and two of his plays were produced at fringe theaters. But with four children to feed he was forced to abandon his dramatic ambitions and sell refrigerators. Cannan's novel *No Walls of Jasper* was published in 1930.

In 1931 the Pullein-Thompsons moved to an old house, The Grove, on five and one-half acres at Peppard in the Chiltern Hills. In that same year Cannan's novels *High Table* and *Ithuriel's Hour* were published. These works, written at a time of stress and financial insecurity, ensured her standing as a serious novelist. *High Table,* the more acclaimed of the two, is the story of the introverted, self-conscious, myopic, and inadequate Theodore Fletcher, born in the late 1870s to a grim vicar and his even grimmer wife, who are short on love but strong on criticism. Afraid of people, he immerses himself in books. Then he meets Hester, who has come to work for her coarse father at the local pub. Theodore likes Hester's shy, mincing voice, and she likes his gentility. He lends her books and shares his favorite lines of poetry with her. Theodore sees their friendship purely as a meeting of minds until he visits her one night to read *Paradise Regained* with her. Hester comes to the door in her nightgown: "Except for his mother and Cook on the night when the boiler burst, Theodore had never seen a woman with her hair down or her figure uncorseted; but he was thinking of John Milton—was Bagehot right? Had Milton so far from justifying the ways of God to man, merely 'loaded the common theology with a new encumbrance?'" He is reading to Hester from Milton's work when their bodies touch; passion takes over. Afterward he is shocked and disgusted with himself. When Hester tells him that she is pregnant, he flees to Oxford. There he becomes a don and is eventually elected warden of St. Mary's College, not on his own merits but to keep someone else out of the position. In 1916 Theodore befriends Hester's son, the gentle officer cadet Lennie Twigg, who comes to St. Mary's for training, believing himself to be Lennie's father. Theodore attends Lennie's wedding to the brash Doreen, gives the couple money, and basks in the warmth of their astonished gratitude. After Lennie is killed on the western front, Theodore learns the truth from Hester:

> "You see, Mr. Fletcher, though it all seems such a long time ago and as if it didn't matter, I've never forgiven myself for the things I said to you. . . . And when it all turned out to be nothing, I should have let you know; but I was spiteful. I thought, well let him learn what it is like to lie awake and worry till you're half crazy, let him suffer a bit too."

> "What's that? What's that?" said Theodore.

> " . . . And I daresay you believed what I told you right up until you heard I was marrying Sam."

Theodore made no answer. He had not realized yet how it had happened, only that, on some trivial and chance error (error, that "inseparable shadow of knowledge") he had built up an illusion which had denied the failure and repaired the omissions of his life that the clear values of universal tragedy had taught him to despise. In this desolate moment, he could not estimate his loss, felt himself utterly denuded, hurried with the master instinct of such soft shelled creatures, first to hide his predicament. The woman had spoken again, was saying " . . . and considering the upset I must have caused you for what was my fault was as much as yours—don't you doubt it—I've felt that mean ever since I heard of your kindness to Lennie. . . ."

She was looking at Theodore . . . his straggly brown mustache, streaked with gray now, hid his mouth . . . not easy to read his eyes behind those thick lenses. . . . But he didn't realize that and, with an effort of will, composed his face and forced words from his aching throat.

"Of course of course," said Theodore.

After the funeral Theodore enters his lodgings, going

> into the cool and cedarn fragrance of the hall and the long dim library. And the war's over, he thought, taking off his hat . . . the war's over and it's taken its distorted outlook with it . . . he goes to his bookcase, takes down his own *History of Logic,* wondering if, after all, he *had* been rather rash in that chapter on the Peripatetics, still "ignoring clamours," we seek the good and the true.

Among the many academics Cannan had met in her youth was the provost of Oriel College, who was reputed to have silenced a lady's unwise dinner observation with "Claptrap, Madam, claptrap"; such repetition is a habit shared by Theodore, and it is likely that Theodore was inspired by the provost or some equally eccentric academic. Certainly Cannan's Oxford, with its waspish donnish rivalries, rings true. At the same time, Cannan is able to move effortlessly from the academic milieu to that of the laboring class. The result is a perceptive study of a weak and timid boy who becomes an inhibited and introverted don.

Reviews of *High Table* were favorable: "A plot of extraordinary delicacy, pathos and irony. It is rare indeed to find a tale, so ruthless in its probing of shame and grief, at the same time so sure in its grasp of significance and beauty," wrote the critic in the *Observer,* while the *Spectator* declared it a "novel of uncommon qualities. Miss Cannan has sympathy and insight, she can hit hard, she can be witty, she has a fine gift of phrase." *Ithuriel's Hour,* a story about power and domination with a mountaineering background, also received laudatory reviews. The story begins as a gentle satire of a country baronet who believes that good health, efficiency, and the will to succeed will always win through. But when tragedy strikes as he and six others pit themselves against a mountain, the strong become weak and the weak become strong.

Pullein-Thompson had lost much of Cannan's inheritance in unwise investments, and the two novels brought much-needed royalties from the United States. Cannan borrowed an additional £1,500 from the estate of her uncle, Edwin Cannan, and bought an old polo pony and chickens and ducks to add to the fowl that had come with The Grove. Thus began what she would later describe as the happiest years of her life. A Francophile with a special love for the songs of Edith Piaf, Cannan made several visits to Cap Ferrat, where her mother was living most of the year in a pension. From that ambiance she drew her inspiration for Guy's rather improbable life as a gigolo in *North Wall* (1933), one of her less successful novels.

In 1936 Cannan's first children's book, *A Pony for Jean,* was an immediate success; the reviewer for the *Times Literary Supplement* (21 November 1936) called it "a little piece of literature." Jean Leslie is based on Cannan; the collapse of her lovingly built henhouse mirrors exactly Cannan's own disastrous carpentry in Crescent Road; and Cannan, like Jean, found herself unable to bridle her first pony, who, like Cavalier in the story, was painfully thin. Other children's books followed. Cannan can "write the

ITHURIEL'S
HOUR

By
JOANNA CANNAN

HODDER AND STOUGHTON
LIMITED          LONDON
MCMXXXI

*Frontispiece and title page for Cannan's novel about a mountain-climbing expedition*

heads off almost all her rivals," wrote a reviewer of *We Met Our Cousins* (1937) in the *Times Literary Supplement* (6 November 1937): "Here is a book that neither child nor adult can set down, bubbling with humor, packed with adventure, marked by the keenest observation."

In 1939 Cannan, an admirer of Georges Simenon's work, turned her hand to crime novels with *They Rang up the Police*. For her later novels in this genre she invented the odious Inspector Price, a pompous idiot who never uses a short word when a long one is available. The characters in these fast-moving stories were largely inspired by friends and neighbors: the three ladies in *They Rang up the Police* (1939), for example, were based on three unmarried women who lived with their mother opposite The Grove; the characters in *Death at the Dog* (1940) were modeled on people Cannan and her husband met on Sundays when they visited the New Inn pub for a drink.

After the children's book *They Bought Her a Pony* (1944), inspiration failed Cannan; she wrote nothing until 1947 when she returned to the Edwardian Oxford of *High Table* for the setting of *Little I Understood* (1948). The main characters in that work and its sequel, *And All I Learned* (1952), are dreary, browbeaten Mildred and her arrogant father, Dr. Henry Oglethorpe, whose appalling self-satisfaction and selfishness, in the words of the critic for the *Sketch,* are "so cruelly yet brilliantly drawn that one finds oneself all through the book impatient for his next appearance." Poor, tactless Mildred, warped by her upbringing, never learns the intricacies of relationships or the basics of love, and she takes her anger out on the servants. Her marriage to the well-placed, sensitive Adam collapses when their daughter dies, partly through Dr. Oglethorpe's misjudgment. Brought up to believe that boys are superior to girls, Mildred dotes on her son, Michael, whom she is left to bring up alone. Finally, Michael, obstinately riding his new motorbike over ice and snow against her advice, kills her. The two novels are witty, cynical, and bitingly perceptive. "Excellent novel," wrote Elizabeth Bowen in the *Tatler* of *Little I Understood:* "There is much more to this tale than dire funniness; it suggests just how much harm one stupid woman can do—and, as an exposure of one kind of designing middle-class snobbery is without parallel." Betjeman in the *Daily Herald* said the novel was "piercingly witty about woman's weaknesses, mercilessly catty, and thoroughly entertaining. I enjoyed every page of this book with its quiet, penetrating observation." Phyllis Bentley called it "devastatingly real," and Pamela Hansford Johnson found it "absolutely fascinating."

Cannan put her experience as a regular follower of foxhounds to good use in *Murder Included* (1950), her most satiric crime novel. Battling a severe cough that she insisted was caused by her smoking, she accepted a commission to write a book on Oxfordshire for the Robert Hale County Series. She applied for an extra gasoline ration and drove through the county, revisiting villages she had not seen since her youth. The result, *Oxfordshire* (1952), is a lively, idiosyncratic, highly personal book. Always a bit of an anarchist, Cannan writes: "I dislike the University Parks: they are neat and trim, their niggling vistas marred by notice boards announcing closing times and forbidding excursions on the grass; dreamers walk better under the decaying elms and the dirty ditches of Christ Church Meadows; but the University Parks are a perfect location for the game which cricketers and followers of cricket assert have made Englishmen what they were in their most prosperous if not their finest hour." She commends the Cotswolds but loves best the Chilterns roads, which have "the architecture of the beechwoods to offer; where the trees stand back, blue distance and sometimes the shimmer of the river; and above all roads I know they have the power to bewilder, betray and benight the traveller." Cannan is historically informative about Oxford and its colleges, but she writes with more passion about nature than about buildings, telling the reader where certain birds and flowers may be found and the local names for them. The last chapter is devoted to what the poets say about the county.

In 1952 Cannan was diagnosed with tuberculosis. After a year's bed rest failed to stop the disease, she underwent an operation to splint off part of one of her lungs. She was not given a general anesthetic, and she astonished the surgeons by reciting poetry to allay her fears. The tuberculosis was halted, but her heart was irreparably damaged. Cannan's active life was at an end.

Pullein-Thompson and Cannan sold The Grove and settled with their daughter Josephine in a cottage that had once been a medieval granary in Bell Street, Henley. Cannan had by then started *Long Shadows* (1955). Her postoperation novels, although competent and eminently readable, never equaled the caliber of the best of her earlier work. But some of her verve returned for *Gaze at the Moon* (1957), her final children's book.

Pullein-Thompson died in 1957, and Cannan spent her last three and one-half years with Josephine in a thatched cottage in Stourpaine, Dorset. In the spring of 1961 Cannan was unable to fight off a bout of influenza. In the ambulance on the way to the hospital she worried about the fate of Pullein-Thompson's boxer dog, which she had inherited, and she recited Walter Savage Landor's "Finis":

> I strove with none; for none was worth my strife;
> Nature I loved, and, next to nature, art;
> I warmed both hands before the fire of life;
> It sinks, and I am ready to depart."

She died of heart failure in Blandford Cottage Hospital on the morning of 22 April, three weeks after finishing *All Is Discovered* (1962)—a murder mystery set in the countryside that is remarkable for its cynicism toward the institution of marriage.

Modern readers tend to find the class-consciousness in Cannan's novels objectionable, but she reflected life as it was between the wars; no one has bettered her descriptions of the upper-middle-class milieu of that time. She was equally at home with her male as with her female characters, and many of her psychological insights still ring true. Sometimes her prejudices leap from the page, and occasionally her plots flounder; but at her best she can hold her own against all comers in the fields of children's novels, mysteries, and Edwardian novels. Two of her children's books have been updated and republished since her death, and extracts from them are still in demand for anthologies.

**Reference:**

May Wedderburn Cannan, *Grey Ghosts and Voices* (Kineton: Roundwood Press, 1976).

**Papers:**

Joanna Cannan's papers are at Trinity College, Oxford.

# Richard Church
*(26 March 1893 – 4 March 1972)*

Margaret Crosland

BOOKS: *The Flood of Life, and Other Poems* (London: Fifield, 1917);

*Hurricane, and Other Poems* (London: Selwyn & Blount, 1919);

*Philip, and Other Poems* (Oxford: Blackwell, 1923);

*The Portrait of the Abbot* (London: Benn, 1926; New York: MacVeagh, 1927?);

*The Dream, and Other Poems* (London: Benn, 1927);

*Mood without Measure* (London: Faber & Gwyer, 1927);

*Mary Shelley* (London: Howe, 1928; New York: Viking, 1928);

*Theme with Variations* (London: Benn, 1928);

*The Glance Backward: New Poems* (London: Dent, 1930);

*Oliver's Daughter: A Tale* (London & Toronto: Dent, 1930);

*High Summer* (London & Toronto: Dent, 1931; New York: Long & Smith, 1932);

*News from the Mountain* (London: Dent, 1932);

*The Prodigal Father* (London: Dent, 1933; New York: Day, 1933);

*The Apple of Concord: A Novel* (London: Dent, 1935);

*Twelve Noon* (London: Dent, 1936);

*The Porch* (London: Dent, 1937);

*Calling for a Spade* (London: Dent, 1939);

*The Stronghold* (London: Dent, 1939);

*The Room Within* (London: Dent, 1940);

*Eight for Immortality* (London: Dent, 1941; Freeport, N.Y.: Books for Libraries Press, 1969);

*Plato's Mistake* (London: Allen & Unwin, 1941);

*The Solitary Man and Other Poems* (London: Dent, 1941);

*A Squirrel Called Rufus* (London: Dent, 1941; Philadelphia & Toronto: Winston, 1946);

*The Sampler* (London: Dent, 1942);

*British Authors: A Twentieth Century Gallery* (London: Published for the British Council by Longmans, Green, 1943; Freeport, N.Y: Books for Libraries Press, 1970; revised edition, London: Longmans, Green, 1948);

*Twentieth-Century Psalter* (London: Dent, 1943);

*Green Tide* (London: Country Life, 1945);

*Richard Church (photograph by Howard Coster)*

*The Lamp* (London: Dent, 1946);

*Collected Poems* (London: Dent, 1948; New York: AMS, 1976);

*Kent* (London: Hale, 1948);

*Richard Jefferies Centenary, 1848–1948: Memorial Lecture, Delivered at the Arts Center, Swindon, on Saturday, the 6th November, 1948* (Swindon: Council of the Borough of Swindon, 1948?);

*The Cave* (London: Dent, 1950); republished as *Five Boys in a Cave* (New York: Day, 1951);

*The Growth of the English Novel* (London: Methuen, 1951; New York: Barnes & Noble, 1961);

*Selected Lyrical Poems* (London & New York: Staples, 1951);

*A Window on a Hill* (London: Hale, 1951);

*The Nightingale* (London: Hutchinson, 1952);

*Dog Toby: A Frontier Tale* (London: Hutchinson, 1953; New York: Day, 1958);

*A Portrait of Canterbury* (London: Hutchinson, 1953; revised, 1968);

*The Prodigal: A Play in Verse* (London & New York: Staples, 1953);

*Over the Bridge: An Essay in Autobiography* (London: Heinemann, 1955; New York: Dutton, 1956);

*The Dangerous Years* (London: Heinemann, 1956; New York: Dutton, 1958);

*The Royal Parks of London* (London: Her Majesty's Stationery Office, 1956);

*Down River* (New York: Day, 1957; London: Heinemann, 1958);

*The Inheritors: Poems 1948–1955* (London: Heinemann, 1957);

*The Golden Sovereign: A Conclusion to Over the Bridge* (London: Heinemann, 1957; New York: Dutton, 1957);

*Small Moments* (London: Hutchinson, 1957; New York: Dutton, 1958);

*A Country Window: A Round of Essays* (London: Heinemann, 1958);

*The Crab-Apple Tree* (London: Heinemann, 1959);

*Richard Church* (London: Hulton, 1959);

*The Bells of Rye* (London: Heinemann, 1960; New York: Day, 1961);

*North of Rome* (London: Hutchinson, 1960);

*Calm October: Essays* (London: Heinemann, 1961);

*Prince Albert* (London: Heinemann, 1963);

*The Little Kingdom: A Kentish Collection* (London: Hutchinson, 1964);

*The Voyage Home* (London: Heinemann, 1964; New York: Day, 1966);

*A Look at Tradition* (London: Oxford University Press, 1965);

*A Stroll before Dark: Essays* (London: Heinemann, 1965);

*London, Flower of Cities All,* text by Church, drawings and paintings by Imre Hofbauer (London: Heinemann, 1966; New York: Day, 1966);

*The Burning Bush: Poems 1958–1966* (London: Heinemann, 1967);

*Twenty-five Lyrical Poems from the Hand of Richard Church* (London: Heinemann, 1967);

*Speaking Aloud* (London: Heinemann, 1968);

*The White Doe* (London: Heinemann, 1968; New York: Day, 1969);

*Little Miss Moffatt: A Confession* (London: Heinemann, 1969);

*A Harvest of Mushrooms, and Other Sporadic Essays* (London: Heinemann, 1970);

*The Wonder of Words* (London: Hutchinson, 1970);

*The French Lieutenant: A Ghost Story* (London: Heinemann, 1971; New York: Day, 1972);

*London in Colour: Illustrated by 60 Colour Photographs,* introduction and commentaries by Church (London: Batsford, 1971); republished as *London in Color: Illustrated by 60 Color Photographs* (New York: Norton, 1971);

*Kent's Contribution* (Bath: Adams & Dart, 1972);

*My England: Impression for Young Readers,* by Church and others (London: Heinemann, 1973).

OTHER: A. C. Swinburne, *Poems and Prose,* edited by Church (London: Dent / New York: Dutton, 1940);

*Poems of Our Time 1900–1942,* edited by Church and Mildred M. Bozman (London: Dent, 1945); enlarged as *Poems of Our Time 1900–1960,* edited by Church, Bozman, and Edith Sitwell (London: Dent, 1959);

*John Keats: An Introduction and a Selection,* edited by Church (London: Phoenix House, 1948);

*Poems by Percy Bysshe Shelley,* edited by Church (London: Folio Society, 1949);

*Poems for Speaking: An Anthology with an Essay on Reading Aloud,* edited by Church (London: Dent, 1950);

Phoebe Hesketh, *Out of the Dark: New Poems,* edited by Church (London: Heinemann, 1954);

*A Selection of Poems by Edmund Spenser,* introduction by Church (London, 1954);

*The Spoken Word: A Selection from Twenty-five Years of The Listener,* edited by Church (London: Collins, 1955);

*Shorter Works by Jane Austen,* introduction by Church (London: Folio Society, 1963);

*The Collected Poetry of Aldous Huxley,* edited by Donald Watt, introduction by Church (London: Chatto & Windus, 1971; New York: Harper & Row, 1971).

Between 1930 and 1969 Richard Church published thirteen novels, including the autobiographical trilogy *The Porch* (1937), *The Stronghold* (1939), and *The Room Within* (1940). Church was primarily a poet, and the controlled passion of his poetry underlies everything he wrote. His work is fluent and traditional rather than dramatic or innovative; it is typical of British writing during the 1930s and most of the following two decades—as distant as possible from the "angry young men" of

RICHARD CHURCH

# THE PORCH

'. . . for all would waste a Stoic's heart.'
*John Donne.*

LONDON: J. M. DENT & SONS LTD.

*Title page for the first novel of Church's autobiographical trilogy, which also includes* The Stronghold *and* The Room Within

the late 1950s or the outspoken productions of the "swinging sixties."

Richard Thomas Church was born on 26 March 1893 in Battersea, in southeast London, the second of the two sons of Thomas John Church, a postal worker, and Lavina Annie Orton Church. His mother was distantly related to George Eliot, but the family tended to remain quiet about this fact: they considered the great novelist to have been immoral because she had lived with the philosopher George Henry Lewes without benefit of marriage. While Church was still a boy, the family moved to the suburb of Dulwich. At Dulwich Hamlet school he won a scholarship to study art, but his father persuaded him to take up a "safe" position with the civil service at

age sixteen. He would spend twenty-four years in the service of the state, the latter part of that time in the Ministry of Labour.

He married Caroline Parfett in 1915 and published his first book, *The Flood of Life, and Other Poems,* in 1917. With his second wife, Catherina Anna Schimmer, whom he married in 1928, he had a son and three daughters.

Church had published eight volumes of poetry and a book about Mary Shelley (1928) before he began to write fiction with *Oliver's Daughter* (1930). This work is concerned with the relationship among Oliver, a provincial shopkeeper; his ailing wife; and their talented musical daughter, Jessie. The girl runs away to Paris with a composer, the son of the local doctor: but the affair ends, and she returns home alone. Her mother accuses her father of preferring Jessie to herself. Oliver dies; Jessie has a miscarriage, and, the reader must assume from the last page, she continues to reject the local boy, Tom, who had always loved her.

Church's second novel, *High Summer* (1931), is the story of Nora Holgate, who breaks away from an unsatisfactory marriage to go into business. There she finds both financial success and true love. In 1933, believing that he could earn enough to support his family through his literary work, Church retired from the Ministry of Labour.

By far the best of Church's fiction is the trilogy based on his early life. The first of these works, *The Porch,* won the French Femina Vie-Heureuse Prize in 1937 as the most distinctive novel of the year. Eighteen-year-old John Quick-shott, who has heretofore been shielded from reality by his doting mother, passes the civil service examinations and is appointed to His Majesty's Customs House in Billingsgate, in the East End of London. He has intellectual ambitions, and he discovers that some of his colleagues do also: Mouncer, for example, whose poverty-stricken background has left him embittered against society, wants to be a poet. Although Mouncer is a difficult person, when he falls ill from overwork his coworkers rally around him, but he dies. As the book ends, Quickshott is becoming closer to Dorothy, his landlord's sister, who also works for the civil service and helped him care for Mouncer. The character and fate of Mouncer are somewhat overdramatized, but the London background, from John's lodgings in Dulwich to the Custom House and the Billingsgate fish market, is evoked in a strikingly visual manner.

Readers had to wait two years for the sequel, *The Stronghold.* World War I has broken out. Mouncer has become a famous poet posthumously. Quickshott and Dorothy have become lovers but cannot marry since civil service rules at that time required that female employees must resign upon marrying. Quickshott is studying medicine at night while continuing to work at the Customs House. He is being supported financially in his studies by his colleague Matthew Brennan and also, secretly, by Dorothy. When Quickshott discovers that she has been helping him, his pride is hurt; they quarrel and separate. Dorothy goes to France to work as a nurse; there her friend Phyllis Drayton dies after giving birth to a child fathered by an uncaring, ambitious army officer. Meanwhile, Quickshott saves the lives of Dorothy's sister and the sister's baby during an air raid. When Dorothy returns home with Phyllis's baby, who is also named Phyllis, Brennan, who has been knighted and who loved the older Phyllis, raises the girl. Quickshott and Dorothy are reunited on the last page of the novel.

The younger Phyllis is the teenaged heroine of the last novel in the trilogy, *The Room Within.* Quickshott becomes a well-known doctor, and he and Dorothy marry. He dies young from overwork, and Dorothy and Brennan marry.

Church's next novel, *The Sampler* (1942), is planned, like a traditional embroidered sampler, in "four corners and a centre." The "corners" are stories about characters of widely varying backgrounds who are brought together in the "centre," set in London and titled "The Woman of Samaria." In the first corner, "The Blue Sky," two aging spinsters, Mary and Martha, are living in a cottage in Kent. Mary is a brilliant embroideress but an invalid; she is cared for by Martha, who also raises poultry and worries about money and air raids. At the end of the story Martha is summoned to London by a letter from a lawyer. In the second corner, "The Tree," Roger Haigh decides to go to London and volunteer for the Royal Air Force, breaking the "silver cord" that has tied him to his mother. The third corner, "The Grassy Foreground," presents Christopher Sims, a disillusioned veteran of World War I. In the fourth corner, "The Turbulent Water," Helen Manners decides to leave her husband and join her lover in London. In the "centre" Martha, Roger, Christopher, and Helen are staying in the same hotel in London. The hotel is bombed in an air raid; in the ordeal that follows, each character appears in his or her true colors, and they all find that their problems are solved in surprising ways—sometimes through external circumstances and the behavior of others, sometimes through their own decisions and actions. The title of the story refers to the en-

*Richard Church with his third wife, Dorothy Beale Church (Tony Stone Images)*

counter between Jesus and the woman of Samaria in chapter 4 of the Gospel of John.

The novelist Frank Swinnerton, writing in *The Observer,* called the work "a novel of character under the stress of war in which with perceptive delicacy certain lives are brought to a single point and given a thrilling elucidation." Ralph Strauss, in *The Sunday Times,* found "the pattern of the sampler" to be "beautifully complete." Norman Collins said that he read the book "with real excitement." The novelist Charles Marriott, reviewing the novel for *The Manchester Guardian,* found no sentimentality and much "crisp humour." *Modern Woman* magazine said that *The Sampler* was "Everything that a good book should be. Simple, direct and moving. . . . A rich, deep book, worth many readings." The public in wartime Britain drew comfort from the book's hopeful optimism.

The first volume of Church's autobiography, *Over the Bridge* (1955), was awarded the *Sunday Times* Prize for Literature; the novelist Howard Spring described it as "the loveliest autobiography written in our time," pointing out that the writer had "found life full of enchantment, and how not the least of its enchantments was its challenge." The second volume, *The Golden Sovereign,* appeared in 1957. That year Church was named a Commander of the British Empire by Queen Elizabeth II.

The novel Church published in 1963, *Prince Albert,* verges on the sentimental. The story is set in Kent, where Church lived for a long time and described affectionately in his novels and poetry and in several nonfiction books. Prince Albert is a pony given to young Madeleine by Tom Small, who works on her father's farm. The melodramatic plot includes a flood and Tom's involvement in near-criminal activities, but all ends happily.

The third volume of Church's autobiography, *The Voyage Home,* was published in 1964. Church's second wife died in 1965; in 1967 he married Dorothy Beale. He was a fellow of the Royal Society of Literature, and in 1970 he was elected vice president. Church died on 4 March 1972.

Richard Church wrote many other novels, but their melodramatic plots and unconvincing characters do nothing to enhance his reputation. He will be remembered mainly as a poet and critic rather than as a novelist. If some of his plots and characters seem melodramatic or artificial, the atmosphere of his novels is always convincing. He was an essentially "English" writer.

**Interview:**

Michael Hardwick, "An Interview with Richard Church," *Texas Quarterly,* 10 (1967): 188–197.

**References:**

Donald Baker, "An Eternal Patience: An Essay on Richard Church," *Texas Quarterly,* 10 (1967): 199–208;

L. A. G. Strong, "Richard Church," in his *Personal Remarks* (New York: Liveright, 1953), pp. 197–200.

# A. J. Cronin

*(19 July 1896 – 6 January 1981)*

Lisa M. Schwerdt
*California University of Pennsylvania*

BOOKS: *Hatter's Castle* (London: Gollancz, 1931; Boston: Little, Brown, 1931);

*Three Loves* (London: Gollancz, 1932; Boston: Little, Brown, 1932);

*Grand Canary* (London: Gollancz, 1933; Boston: Little, Brown, 1933);

*The Stars Look Down* (London: Gollancz, 1935; Boston: Little, Brown, 1935);

*The Citadel* (London: Gollancz, 1937; Boston: Little, Brown, 1937);

*Jupiter Laughs* (Boston: Little, Brown, 1940; London: Gollancz, 1941);

*The Keys of the Kingdom* (Boston: Little, Brown, 1941; London: Gollancz, 1942);

*Adventures of a Black Bag* (Switzerland: Phoenix, 1943; London: New English Library, 1969);

*The Green Years* (Boston: Little, Brown, 1944; London: Gollancz, 1945);

*Shannon's Way* (Boston: Little, Brown, 1948; London: Gollancz, 1948);

*The Spanish Gardener* (Boston: Little, Brown, 1950; London: Gollancz, 1950);

*Adventures in Two Worlds* (New York: McGraw-Hill, 1952; London: Gollancz, 1952);

*Beyond This Place* (Boston: Little, Brown, 1953; London: Gollancz, 1953);

*A Thing of Beauty* (Boston: Little, Brown, 1956); republished as *Crusader's Tomb* (London: Gollancz, 1956);

*The Northern Light* (Boston: Little, Brown, 1958; London: Gollancz, 1958);

*The Judas Tree* (Boston: Little, Brown, 1961; London: Gollancz, 1961);

*A Song of Sixpence* (Boston: Little, Brown, 1964; London: Heinemann, 1964);

*A Pocketful of Rye* (Boston: Little, Brown, 1969; London: Heinemann, 1969);

*Desmonde* (Boston: Little, Brown, 1975); republished as *The Minstrel Boy* (London: Gollancz, 1975);

*Lady with Carnations* (London: Gollancz, 1976);

*Gracie Lindsay* (London: Gollancz, 1978);

*Dr. Finlay of Tannochbrae* (London: New English Library, 1978).

*A. J. Cronin (photograph courtesy of Victor Gollancz, Ltd.)*

SELECTED PERIODICAL PUBLICATIONS–UNCOLLECTED: "Mascot for Uncle," *Good Housekeeping,* 106 (February 1938): 30–33;

"Prescripts for Ailing Democracy: Dictatorship," *Living Age,* 354 (July 1938): 384–387;

"Sermon from the Snows," *Reader's Digest,* 34 (April 1939): 1–4;

"Vigil in the Night," *Good Housekeeping,* 108 (May 1939): 16–19; (June 1939): 28–29; 109 (July 1939): 30–31; (August 1939): 32–33; (September 1939): 44–45; (October 1939): 48–49;

"The Most Unforgettable Character I Ever Met: Doctor of Lennox," *Reader's Digest,* 35 (September 1939): 26–30;

"Turning Point of My Career," *Reader's Digest,* 38 (May 1941): 53–57;

"Diogenes in Maine," *Reader's Digest,* 39 (August 1941): 11–13;

"Reward of Mercy," *Reader's Digest,* 39 (September 1941): 25–37;

"How I Came to Write a Novel of a Priest," *Life,* 11 (20 October 1941): 64–66;

"Drama in Everyday Life," *Reader's Digest,* 42 (March 1943): 83–86;

"Candles in Vienna," *Reader's Digest,* 48 ( June 1946): 1–3;

"Star of Hope Still Rises," *Reader's Digest,* 53 (December 1948): 1–3;

"Johnny Brown Stays Here," *Reader's Digest,* 54 ( January 1949): 9–12;

"Two Gentlemen of Verona," *Reader's Digest,* 54 (February 1949): 1–5;

"Greater Gift," *Reader's Digest,* 54 (March 1949): 88–91;

"Most Unforgettable Character I've Met," *Reader's Digest,* 55 (December 1949): 8–12;

"Irish Rose," *Reader's Digest,* 56 ( January 1950): 21–24;

"Why I Believe in God," *Woman's Home Companion,* 77 ( July 1950): 34–35, 98–99;

"Monsieur le Maire," *Reader's Digest,* 58 ( January 1951): 52–56;

"Best Investment I Ever Made," *Reader's Digest,* 58 (March 1951): 25–28;

"Doctor Remembers," *Woman's Home Companion,* 78 (October 1951): 36–37, 134, 136–137, 148–150, 152, 154, 157, 159, 182, 183, 185–187, 192; (November 1951): 26–27, 129, 136, 138–143, 165–173, 179–180;

"Quo Vadis?," *Reader's Digest,* 59 (December 1951): 41–44;

"Tombstone for Nora Malone," *Reader's Digest,* 60 ( January 1952): 99–101;

"When You Dread Failure," *Reader's Digest,* 60 (February 1952): 21–24;

"Make Marriage a Family Affair," *Woman's Home Companion,* 79 (May 1952): 36–37, 98–99;

"What I Learned at La Grande Chartreuse," *Reader's Digest,* 62 (February 1953): 73–77;

"Grace of Gratitude," *Reader's Digest,* 62 (March 1953): 67–70;

"Thousand and One Lives," *Reader's Digest,* 64 ( January 1954): 8–11;

"How to Stop Worrying," *Reader's Digest,* 64 (May 1954): 47–50;

"Don't Be Sorry for Yourself!," *Reader's Digest,* 66 (February 1955): 97–100;

"Unless You Deny Yourself," *Reader's Digest,* 68 ( January 1956): 54–56;

"Native Doctor," *Ladies' Home Journal,* 78 ( January 1961): 38–39;

"Resurrection of Joao Jacinto," *Reader's Digest,* 89 (November 1966): 153–157.

A. J. Cronin was a novelist, dramatist, and nonfiction writer whose works examine moral conflicts between the individual and society as his idealistic heroes pursue justice for the common man. His moralistic novels are known by the public for their memorable characters, powerful themes, and melodramatic plots used to set up Cronin's optimistic endings. While the early novels focus on social or moral issues of modern life, the later ones have more-spiritual themes, and the critics generally consider his ideas to be better than his skills. In Britain and the United States he is often looked upon as a hack writer, but in the former Soviet Union he is quite popular through a complete edition of his works that includes scholarly introductions and annotations. Several of his novels have been made into successful films and television adaptations.

Archibald Joseph Cronin was born on 19 July 1896 in Cardross, Dumbartonshire, Scotland, to Patrick and Jessie Montgomerie Cronin. His education at Dumbarton Academy and Glasgow University was interrupted by a stint in the Royal Naval Volunteer Reserve from 1916 to 1918, where he worked as a surgeon and achieved the rank of sublieutenant. He obtained his M.B. and Ch.B. with honors in 1919 and then worked as a physician on a ship traveling to India, followed by various appointments before continuing his education. While at Glasgow University Medical School he married Agnes Mary Gibson, also a physician, in 1921. They had three sons, Vincent Archibald Patrick, Robert Frances Patrick, and Andrew James. Cronin earned a Ph.D. in 1923, became a member of the Royal College of Physicians in 1924, and was awarded an M.D. with honors from Glasgow in 1925.

After practicing in several small Welsh mining towns, in 1924 Cronin began a four-year period working for the Ministry of Mines as medical inspector of mines, studying pulmonary disabilities in the coal fields throughout South Wales and gaining experiences he would later use in his novels. In 1925 he also began to work as a general practitioner in the fashionable West End of London, but in 1930 he went to Inveraray to recuperate from gastric ulcers. There he was able to indulge a childhood wish to be a writer, and, retiring to the attic, he began to work;

BY THE SAME AUTHOR

## HATTER'S CASTLE

"I took it about with me wherever I went from the moment I began it to the moment I finished it. . . . Those who give themselves to it . . . will feel at the end that they have been living with real people whom they will never forget, and will think the experience worth while. . . . He has made an imaginary world into which we can escape and escape again, and few living writers have done that."
—J. C. SQUIRE (*Observer*)

"I shall never forget James Brodie."—DESMOND MACCARTHY (*Sunday Times*)

"Epoch-making. . . . One wishes Arnold Bennett could have lived to see it. . . . I am too much bowled over to know whether in a month's time I shall deem it a masterpiece ; I say now that it is of that family."—JAMES AGATE (*Daily Express*)

"Its deep humanity, its creative mastery, and its epic grandeur are matters not of opinion but of self-evident fact."—*Glasgow Herald*

"The finest first novel since the war."—HUGH WALPOLE

"Almost overwhelmingly impressive."—*Everyman*

"Has a sweep and fervour that is positively awe-inspiring " (of the first part).—*News Chronicle*

"Energy and imagination enough for ten ordinary novels. James Brodie is a magnificent creation."—L. A. G. STRONG (*Spectator*)

# THREE LOVES

by

## A. J. CRONIN

*author of* Hatter's Castle

LONDON
VICTOR GOLLANCZ LTD
14 Henrietta Street Covent Garden
1932

*Publisher's advertisement and title page for Cronin's novel about a manipulative woman*

after three months he had a 250,000-word novel, *Hatter's Castle* (1931), that was accepted by the first publisher who saw it.

This novel follows James Brodie, a hatter in a small Scottish town, through his tumultuous life as he attempts to regain the position of nobility he believes may have been his birthright and his true station in life. His single-minded goal results in his harming several innocent people and leads one of his daughters to suicide. He is finally destroyed by alcohol and the death or destruction of all but one member of his entire family.

The novel has been called a horror story, but it can more properly be seen as a naturalistic examination of social problems, combined with a sentimental plot. Brodie insists that his nervous and frail younger daughter, Nessie, study night after night so that she might win a prize for the best work done by a student; she commits suicide when she fails to win the prize. The novel seems to have been influenced by George Douglas Brown's *House with the Green Shutters* (1901) in its examination of Scottish life out-

side the cities, and it established Cronin in the tradition of J. B. Priestley and other middlebrow, realist writers. Cronin's penchant for melodrama is evident when the man whom Brodie's elder daughter, Mary, loves is sent to his death along with a trainload of people. The kindly Dr. Renwick, however, finally recognizes that he really loves Mary, and he takes her away from her horrible existence. The novel appealed to popular and critical audiences and allowed Cronin to give up his successful medical practice and work full-time on his writing. The novel was filmed in 1941 by Paramount Studios and starred Robert Newton and Deborah Kerr.

In 1932 Cronin moved to Sussex. In his next work, *Three Loves* (1932), the protagonist, Lucy Moore, is a strong, vital woman who manages her life by manipulating others. She first devotes herself to her husband, but when he is killed she transfers her love to their son, Peter. She works herself to the bone so she can afford to put him through university, enabling him to become a doctor. Afraid of losing Peter when he falls in love, she tries to prevent the marriage. When he marries secretly, Lucy turns to love of God and enters a convent. She ends up alone and dies without seeing Peter again.

Cronin's ability to create believable characters deepens in this novel as readers watch Lucy's possessive love unfold. His melodramatic bent is still present, however, and is perhaps best seen in his making Lucy a passenger in the boat that accidentally runs over and kills her husband. But while her desire to be in control is reminiscent of James Brodie's in *Hatter's Castle,* here it is given gentler roots in her desire to give love rather than simply acquire it for herself. Similarly, her death after recognizing the misapplication of her affection seems closer to a tragedy rather than the comeuppance Brodie merits.

The critics saw Cronin's growth in complex characterization but thought that the novel meandered. Lucy may be more complex than James Brodie, but she neither repels the reader, as Brodie does, nor attracts the reader, as she must for the tragedy in her life to be felt rather than just seen.

Cronin tried to enlarge his canvas in his next work, using material he gathered during a trip to the Canary Islands. In *Grand Canary* (1933) Dr. Harvey Leith flees a false accusation of incompetence, traveling via ship to the Canary Islands. He interacts with various passengers and falls in love. Cronin seems here again to be primarily interested in character, but readers are presented only with surface sketches. These passengers are all stereotypes: the missionary seduced by the fallen woman; a fighter who spends his time reading the works of Plato, and the protagonist himself, whose faith in humanity and love of life are restored through the love given him by a woman. With this third novel Cronin won a rather grudging acceptance from the critics, who thought that his style and technique had become more sophisticated but that the novel lacked any real point.

When *The Stars Look Down* appeared in 1935 Cronin finally garnered both critical and popular acclaim. This story follows the difficulties of striking miners in a Welsh coal town. As starvation forces the miners back to work, readers see that both workers and managers lose when the humanity of people is forgotten.

In presenting his brief saga of the life of this community Cronin displays his strengths as well as his weaknesses. The working-class characters are drawn clearly and are not bothered by philosophical questions. The melodrama that had always been a hallmark of Cronin's art fits well with the drama inherent in the dangerous life and work of the miners.

The drowning of miners in a flood in the mine is realistic and in keeping with what readers know about this dangerous occupation. Plot becomes minimally important as Cronin presents a document of a lifestyle rather than a story per se. But the issue of the tension between labor and capital was important to Cronin's middle-class readers, as well as to his liberal-minded upper-class reviewers, and he was praised for the vivid events and sensitive human values he depicted. Carol Reed filmed the novel for M-G-M in 1941, with Michael Redgrave and Margaret Lockwood.

It is for his fifth novel, *The Citadel* (1937), an examination of the conflict between success and ethical behavior, that Cronin is best known. He clearly made use of his own experiences and feelings in his portrayal of the young Scottish doctor Andrew Manson. Manson begins as an assistant to a dying doctor in a Welsh mining town and goes on to establish a successful practice in London. A subsequent encounter with tragedy leads him to understand why he abandoned his early ideals for material success, and the story ends with his regaining his honesty and integrity. The novel pricked the conscience of the British medical community by examining the problem of fee gouging by doctors and may have helped lead to the establishment of the National Health Service.

An immediate success, *The Citadel* won the American Booksellers' Award; it was third on the U.S. best-seller list for 1937 and second for 1938. No comparable list existed in Britain, but in 1936–1937 the novel was selling up to ten thousand copies a week in hardback. A film version was produced by M-G-M in 1938 with Robert Donat and Rosalind Russell; it was remade for a ten-part television series starring Ben Cross, shown on the BBC in 1982 and on *Masterpiece Theatre* in 1983.

Critics agreed with the reading public, and *The Citadel* was proclaimed as Cronin's best effort yet. While some thought it heavy-handed and somewhat unfairly biased against the medical community, all recognized its vivid characterizations and saw more depth in the content than Cronin had previously achieved.

In the winter of 1938 Cronin, distressed about the deteriorating world situation, rented a chalet in Switzerland. As he recalls in his memoir, *Adventures in Two Worlds* (1952), he wandered into a church one day and listened to the sermon being preached in German, a language he did not understand. But when he heard the words *Christian* and *Führer,* suddenly he had a vision and understood that man had forgotten God and needed to get back to him.

Cronin's next effort, a play, seems to have been influenced by his religious experience. Produced in Glasgow and New York in 1940, *Jupiter Laughs* is the story of a young scientist who falls in love with a female missionary. After her tragic death he goes to China to carry on where she left off. The play seemed to founder without a specific point to make and had a short run. Yet the work was filmed the next year by Warner Bros. as *Shining Victory*, starring James Stephenson and Geraldine Fitzgerald. That same year Cronin's 1939 short story "Vigil in the Night" was filmed under the same name by RKO.

Success returned the next year when *The Keys of the Kingdom* (1941) appeared; it was a Book-of-the-Month Club selection and reached sales of half a million. Its reception followed the path of earlier works: popular with the public but less so with critics, who lauded its moral values but were put off by its melodrama. In the novel Cronin seems to have incorporated more directly his earlier experience in the Swiss church. Again the reader is confronted with the tension between the needs of the self and the needs of something larger than the self. Catholic priest Francis Chisholm must learn how to subdue his individuality so that he can fulfill his obligations to the church. How an individual resolves conflict between himself and an institution, and the question of where religion fits in the modern world are explored here. Although similar to Andrew Manson in his faith in his goal, Chisholm is different in having to struggle with his conscience rather than his self-interest, and readers can perhaps identify more easily with the priest's self-doubt. This novel was also adapted as a film by 20th Century-Fox, starring Gregory Peck and Rosa Stradner.

For *The Green Years* (1944) Cronin again turns to his own experiences. Robert Shannon is a young, idealistic medical student who is supervised by a department head who will let nothing and no one get in his way. Robert's faith in humanity is shaken, but he regains it when he begins to practice in a run-down area of the city and finds himself in his work. Critics viewed *The Green Years* as a falling off in the depth of Cronin's themes but generally in keeping with his style: a slight plot with somewhat stereotypical characters. The 1946 M-G-M film version starred Charles Coburn and Dean Stockwell.

Robert's story is continued in *Shannon's Way* (1948). It follows Robert as he tries to make a name for himself as a researcher. Despite being fired and having to take almost any job to survive, Robert is rewarded at the novel's close for his dedication to his cause, getting both the woman and the job he wants. The novel was viewed by critics as standard Cronin: having little to say but saying it well.

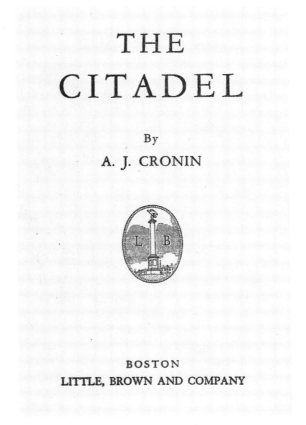

THE
CITADEL

By
A. J. CRONIN

BOSTON
LITTLE, BROWN AND COMPANY

*Title page for the American edition of Cronin's popular novel about a young Scottish doctor who loses and regains his integrity*

The book that followed, *The Spanish Gardener* (1950), did nothing to raise Cronin's star. The tale of doting Harrington Brande's affection for his semi-invalid son and his inability to get close to the boy leaves the way open for the boy to bloom under the Spanish gardener's care. There are enough events to keep the novel moving, probably because it was originally serialized, but the primary content is melodrama, and the theme of the novel—that evil will do itself in—is slighted. In 1957 Rank of America filmed the novel with Dirk Bogarde and Joan Whitely.

In 1952 Cronin wrote what is ostensibly his autobiography, *Adventures in Two Worlds*. At least one reviewer found it more entertaining than his immediately preceding two novels, and all remarked on his obvious fondness for the patients and persons he sketches. They are better presented than he, and the book may be more properly thought of as focused on his patients and friends rather than himself; readers actually get little information on what Cronin did in his life other than see patients. The work ends with a long suggestion to his readers that they cultivate a spiritual belief.

*Beyond This Place* (1953) seems to be a thesis novel, written to prove how unjust a trial by jury can be. The story of Rees Mathry, falsely imprisoned for a crime he did not commit, is about as trumped-up as Cronin tries to portray the man's trial as being. There is more plot to the novel than depth, and the characters are the stereotypes usually drawn by Cronin. The novel was filmed in 1959 as *Web of Evidence,* with Van Johnson and Vera Miles.

When *A Thing of Beauty* appeared in 1956, many felt Cronin had returned to the excellence of *The Citadel* with this tale of an English painter persecuted for his art. The rigid Englishman must leave his upper-class world and learn how to relate to people at large before he can become a true artist, but then he is shunned by his class. Cronin has the chance to draw several curious characters and present unusual slices of life, but there is no real development of character.

By this time sales of Cronin's books in the United States alone had reached seven million copies. He had lived in New England from 1939 to 1955, when he moved permanently to Switzerland, but the changes in residence did not result in any change in his work. Well known internationally, Cronin reached sales of three million copies in Russia, and his books were translated into several other languages. The products of his later years, however, were not up to the standards of his best-known works.

*The Northern Light* (1958) suffers from pale characters who seem only sketched rather than drawn. Although the novel focuses on the takeover of a virtuous small-town newspaper by a scandalous London rag, little knowledge of the newspaper business is displayed. As is usual in Cronin's work, the underdog who will not compromise his principles eventually triumphs.

*The Judas Tree* (1961) again takes up Cronin's interest in moral issues as he follows Dr. David Moray's attempt to soothe a conscience guilty over a woman he had hurt thirty years earlier. For the novel to work, readers need to understand the doctor, but the character seems to be moved by the plot requirements rather than the action coming out of the character.

Cronin said that *A Song of Sixpence* (1964), an autobiographical novel, is the work that came closest to presenting his real literary aspirations. In it Cronin tells the tale of the coming to manhood of Laurence Carroll. The Scotch Irish youngster narrates his journey to manhood, from his early childhood to receipt of his medical degree and the beginning of his practice. Critics felt the book offered nothing of note and was simply escapist fare. *A Pocketful of Rye* (1969) continues Laurence Carroll's story

and presents the conversion experience that leads him to return to his hometown. The soap-opera ending caused many to view the novel as among Cronin's more lightweight pieces.

In *Desmonde* (1975), which was published in England as *The Minstrel Boy,* Cronin shifted gears and wrote the story of his real-life friend Desmonde Fitzgerald, using a narrator called A. J. Later the narrative continues through Fitzgerald's letters that chronicle his becoming a Catholic priest, his fall from grace, and his redemption. Cronin has the opportunity to comment on music, gardening, and travel, as well as on more worldly appetites for food, wine, and sex. This large canvas leads to an odd tone in the novel as Cronin's black-and-white morality is challenged by his wonderment at Fitzgerald's activities.

Cronin's last books return to earlier material. *Lady with Carnations,* published in 1976, had previously been serialized in *Good Housekeeping* in 1936–1937. Similarly, *Gracie Lindsay* (1978) had been serialized in *Woman's Home Companion* in 1949. In both cases Cronin acquiesced to pressure from his publishers to allow these stories to appear in book form. Finally, *Dr. Finlay of Tannochbrae* (1978), a collection of stories, makes use of Cronin's early medical experiences; this and another collection, *Adventures of a Black Bag* (1943), became *Dr. Finlay's Casebook,* a popular television series shown on both the BBC and PBS. Cronin died at age eighty-four on 6 January 1981 at Valmont Clinic, Glion, Switzerland.

A. J. Cronin may be seen as a precursor to such contemporary doctor-authors as Robin Cook. Although his work evolved from plotted page-turners to somewhat deeper considerations of philosophical issues, Cronin will be remembered as a prolific writer of pleasant novels with generally credible, if sometimes stereotypical, characters; engaging, if melodramatic, plots; and, often, important moral themes.

**Bibliography:**
Dale Salwak, *A. J. Cronin: A Reference Guide* (Boston: G. K. Hall, 1982).

**References:**
Arthur Bartlett, "A. J. Cronin: The Writing Doctor," *Coronet,* 35 (March 1954): 165–169;

Vincent Cronin, "Recollection of a Writer," *Tablet,* 235 (21 February 1981): 175–176;

John T. Frederick, "A. J. Cronin," *College English,* 3 (November 1941): 121–129;

Francis Fytton, "Dr. Cronin: An Essay in Victoriana," *Catholic World,* 183 (August 1956): 356–362;

Dale Salwak, *A. J. Cronin* (Boston: Twayne, 1985).

# Rhys Davies

*(9 November 1901 – 21 August 1978)*

Jim McWilliams
*Troy State University*

See also the Davies entry in *DLB 139: British Short-Fiction Writers, 1945–1980.*

BOOKS: *The Song of Songs, and Other Stories* (London: Archer, 1927);

*Aaron* (London: Archer, 1927); revised as *Arfon* (London: Foyle, 1931);

*The Withered Root* (London: Holden, 1927; New York: Holt, 1928);

*A Bed of Feathers* (London: Mandrake, 1929; New York: Black Hawk, 1935);

*Tale* (London: Lahr, 1930);

*Rings on Her Fingers* (London: Shaylor, 1930; New York: Harcourt, Brace, 1930);

*The Stars, the World, and the Women* (London: Jackson, 1930);

*A Pig in a Poke* (London: Joiner & Steele, 1931);

*A Woman* (London: Capell at the Bronze Snail Press, 1931);

*The Woman among Women* (London: Lahr, 1931);

*Count Your Blessings* (London: Putnam, 1932; New York: Covici Friede, 1933);

*Daisy Matthews and Three Other Tales* (Waltham St. Lawrence, U.K.: Golden Cockerel, 1932);

*The Red Hills* (London: Putnam, 1932; New York: Covici Friede, 1933);

*Love Provoked* (London: Putnam, 1933);

*One of Norah's Early Days* (London: Grayson & Grayson, 1935);

*Honey and Bread* (London: Putnam, 1935);

*The Things Men Do: Short Stories* (London: Heinemann, 1936);

*The Skull* (Brockweir, U.K.: Tintern Press, 1936);

*A Time to Laugh* (London: Heinemann, 1937; New York: Stackpole, 1938);

*My Wales* (London: Jarrolds, 1937; New York: Funk & Wagnalls, 1938);

*Jubilee Blues* (London: Heinemann, 1938);

*Sea Urchin: Adventures of Jorgen Jorgensen* (London: Duckworth, 1940);

*Under the Rose* (London: Heinemann, 1940);

*Rhys Davies*

*To-Morrow to Fresh Woods* (London: Heinemann, 1941);

*A Finger in Every Pie* (London: Heinemann, 1942);

*The Story of Wales* (London: Collins, 1943; New York: Hastings House, 1943);

*The Black Venus* (London: Heinemann, 1944; New York: Howell, Soskin, 1946);

*Selected Stories* (Dublin: Fridberg, 1945);

*The Trip to London* (London: Heinemann, 1946; New York: Howell, Soskin, 1946);

*The Dark Daughters* (London: Heinemann, 1947; Garden City, N.Y.: Doubleday, 1948);

77

*Boy with a Trumpet, and Other Selected Short Stories* (London: Heinemann, 1949; Garden City, N.Y.: Doubleday, 1951);

*Marianne* (London: Heinemann, 1951; Garden City, N.Y.: Doubleday, 1952);

*The Painted King* (London: Heinemann, 1954; Garden City, N.Y.: Doubleday, 1954);

*The Collected Stories of Rhys Davies* (London: Heinemann, 1955);

*No Escape: A Play in Three Acts from His Novel "Under the Rose,"* by Davies and Archibald Batty (London: Evans, 1955);

*The Perishable Quality: A Novel* (London: Heinemann, 1957);

*The Darling of Her Heart, and Other Stories* (London: Heinemann, 1958);

*Girl Waiting in the Shade* (London: Heinemann, 1960);

*The Chosen One, and Other Stories* (London: Heinemann, 1967; New York: Dodd, Mead, 1967);

*Print of a Hare's Foot: An Autobiographical Beginning* (London: Heinemann, 1969; New York: Dodd, Mead, 1969);

*Nobody Answered the Bell* (London: Heinemann, 1971; New York: Dodd, Mead, 1971);

*Honeysuckle Girl* (London: Heinemann, 1975).

**Collections:** *The Best of Rhys Davies* (Newton Abbot, U.K. & North Pomfret, Vt.: David & Charles, 1979);

*The Selected Rhys Davies,* edited by D. A. Callard (Bristol: Redcliffe, 1993).

PLAY PRODUCTIONS: *The Ripening Wheat,* London, Royalty Theatre, 19 February 1937; revised as *The Maid of Cefn Ydlfa,* Tonypandy, Wales, 1952;

*No Escape,* by Davies and Archibald Batty, Eastbourne, 5 July 1954.

OTHER: Anna Kavan, *Julia and the Bazooka,* edited by Davies (London: Owen, 1970);

Kavan, *My Soul in China,* edited by Davies (London: Owen, 1975).

SELECTED PERIODICAL PUBLICATIONS—UNCOLLECTED: "D. H. Lawrence in Bandol," *Horizon,* 2 (October 1940): 191–208;

"From My Notebook III," *Wales,* 22 (June 1946): 13–18;

"Writing about the Welsh," *Literary Digest,* 31 (October 1949): 18–19;

"A Drop of Dew: William Price of Llantrisant," *Wales,* 31 (October 1949): 61–71.

Asked in a 1946 questionnaire for *Wales* magazine if he considered himself a Welsh writer, Rhys Davies replied, "No. I am only a writer." This simple but telling statement best sums up a man whose sole desire from his youth had been to be a professional writer. And write he did: by 1975 he had published more than forty books, nearly half of them novels; most of the other volumes were collections of short stories although he also published an autobiography, two "appreciations" of Wales, and two plays. Although he wanted to be considered "only a writer," it is for his Welsh fiction that he is most noted. Unlike some other modern Welsh writers, such as Caradoc Evans, Davies retained a love for Wales and the Welsh people. He may not have lived in Wales after he moved to London as a young man, but he frequently visited the land of his birth and always drew on it for inspiration. In spite of his success, however, he had to confront the difficulties facing a Welsh author who writes in English. As he said in a 1949 essay, "Writing about the Welsh," he found himself trapped between two worlds: on the one side were the English critics who doubted that a literary man from Wales could ever amount to much; on the other were the people of Wales, who took offense when an author tried to write honestly about Welsh customs. Further complicating matters was the political situation in Wales: members of the nationalist movement, for example, openly scorned Welshmen who lived in London and could not speak the native language. Although he was a lifelong supporter of the Labour Party and of self-government for Wales, Davies divorced himself from overt political commentary and focused on the natural beauty of his native land. He concludes "Writing about the Welsh":

> But I cannot help myself—my passion for Wales, her beauty, her individuality, her quality of perpetual youth, her struggle to keep herself uncontaminated of industrial blights, must be expressed, in the only way I know—words—and as truthfully as I am able.

Davies was born Rees Vivian Davies on 9 November 1901 (not in 1903, as he often claimed) in the colliery town of Clydach Vale in the Rhondda Valley of south Wales to Thomas Rees Davies, a grocer, and Sarah Ann Lewis Davies, a former schoolteacher. Although both parents spoke Welsh, they raised their three sons and three daughters to speak only English, fluency in which was considered essential for success in the world beyond the valley.

The district was periodically wracked by violent strikes by the miners, but the Davies family led a middle-class existence of relative calm. Davies's autobiography, *Print of a Hare's Foot* (1969), de-

Davies's parents, Thomas Rees Davies and Sarah Ann Lewis Davies

scribes his early years as idyllic; they were only occasionally upset by minor crises, such as the day his nose was broken by a rock in a fight with some other boys.

It was on his first day at Porth County School—Davies was twelve at the time—that he discovered the power and beauty of words when the teacher introduced the class to Homer's *Odyssey*. Davies read and reread the eighteen-pence schoolboy copy of the epic until he knew parts of it by heart. He then immersed himself in the works of Emile Zola, Gustave Flaubert, Leo Tolstoy, Charles Baudelaire, and Anton Chekhov. He also began to write poetry. These early verses tended to be love poems, even though Davies had yet to experience sexual passion. In his occasionally unreliable autobiography Davies invents some adolescent liaisons with girls, but even at this early age he was probably aware of his homosexuality. He devoted so much time to his literary pursuits that his grades suffered, and two years after his initial reading of the *Odyssey* Davies refused to return to Porth County School as a new term began. His obstinacy upset his parents, who believed that education would provide his only chance to escape the valley; but his father eventually accepted the boy's decision and attempted to place him in various Rhondda Valley banks or colliery offices. None of these jobs appealed to Davies, who helped out in his father's grocery store and wrote poetry whenever he had the opportunity. When he turned nineteen Davies left for London, determined to make his way in the world as a poet.

Davies found the London of the mid 1920s, with its poetry readings, art exhibits, and ballet recitals, an exciting change from the dreary life of a colliery valley. He had two poems published in a London weekly, *The New Age,* but soon afterward, having become an avid reader of the novels of D. H. Lawrence, he decided to turn to fiction. One afternoon—a rainy Sunday, as he remembered it in later years—he wrote three realistic stories that he sent to *The New Coterie,* a magazine that published works by such new writers as Liam O'Flaherty and Hugh MacDiarmid. After the first story, "A Gift of Death," appeared in the spring of 1926, Davies was introduced to Charles Lahr, proprietor of the Progressive Bookshop, where many young London intellectuals gathered to discuss aesthetics and literature. Under the imprint E. Archer, Lahr published Davies's first collection of stories, *The Song of Songs, and Other Stories* (1927), which included some of the stories from *The New Coterie,* and *Aaron* (1927), a ten-page story printed as a pamphlet in an edition of nine hundred numbered copies. (Davies would rewrite *Aaron* and publish it as *Arfon* in 1931.)

On the strength of these works the owners of the Holden Publishing firm asked Davies to write a novel. The result was *The Withered Root* (1927), which is heavily influenced by Lawrence's naturalistic fiction. Reuben Daniels, the son of a dull Rhondda Valley coal miner and his alcoholic wife, is raised in a loveless home. Reuben is introspective and odd; rather than play with the other children, he prefers to walk alone through the quiet hills around his village. At nineteen a reading of the Bible, especially the Book of Revelation, inspires him to become a fiery Baptist preacher, and he leads a religious revival in the valley. He is obsessed, however, with "fleshly" love for Eirwen Vaughan, with whom he once shared a kiss. After she rejects his plea to live with him, Reuben goes insane and dies after a long walk on a rainy night.

A naturalistic rendering of the people and landscape of the Rhondda Valley, *The Withered Root* lacks the humor for which Davies would be known later in his career. Reviewers praised the novel for its unusually frank depiction of sex and drew comparisons between Davies and Lawrence. While the work often reads like a first novel—its flat characters and trite dialogue show that Davies had much to learn about the art of fiction—the sheer intensity of *The Withered Root* places it among his best novels.

With the money from *The Withered Root,* which was also published in America, Davies went to Nice, France, in 1928. In November he received an invitation to visit Lawrence, who was then living in Bandol. The young writer and the celebrated novelist became close friends, visiting often and corresponding regularly. After six months, though, Davies's funds ran low, and he was forced to return to England. Before he left, Lawrence gave his friend the manuscript for *Pansies,* his final collection of poetry, which could not be imported into England because of its alleged indecency. Davies smuggled the manuscript past British customs officials and turned it over to Lahr, who published it in 1929. Although he never saw Lawrence again, Davies continued to correspond with his mentor until Lawrence died of tuberculosis in 1930. In London, Davies eked out a living by writing short stories for magazines; these were collected as *A Bed of Feathers* (1929) and *The Stars, the World, and the Women* (1930). He also wrote *Tale* (1930), a story published in pamphlet form in an edition of one hundred signed copies.

Davies's second novel, *Rings on Her Fingers* (1930), is again set in the Rhondda Valley. Edith Stephens—"a Welsh Emma Bovary," as Davies would describe her in his autobiography—is a woman from an unhappy, lower-middle-class background. A miner proposes to her, but she rejects him because of his poverty and vows to marry the richest man she can find, whether she loves him or not. Her subsequent marriage to a wealthy shop owner is unhappy, and she turns to a series of affairs for the excitement and passion that are lacking in her life.

The novel received mixed reviews, but nearly all of the critics agreed that *Rings on Her Fingers* was inferior to *The Withered Root.* The review in *The New York Times Book Review* (25 January 1931), for exam-

ple, suggested that Davies was too much under the influence of Lawrence. The contrived plot is obviously borrowed from Lawrence and Flaubert, and the writing is flaccid. Edith and her husband are uninteresting characters, and the reader fails to care what happens to them.

Still short of funds, Davies moved back to his family's home in Clydach Vale in late 1929. The Great Depression had begun, and many miners were unemployed. Davies used the daily scenes of misery that he witnessed as material for his next four novels. After finishing the collection *A Pig in a Poke* and the limited-edition, signed, one-story pamphlets *A Woman, Arfon,* and *The Woman among Women*—all published in 1931—Davies completed his third novel, *Count Your Blessings* (1932), and moved back to London.

*Count Your Blessings* depicts the lack of choices available to young women in the Rhondda Valley. Blodwen Jones, a miner's daughter, is determined to escape the poverty of her surroundings. After making a great deal of money as a prostitute in a fashionable bordello in Cardiff, she tires of her sordid life, returns to the valley, and marries a Baptist minister. But she is soon bored by his conventionality, and she leaves him to make a life and career independent of others. On the one hand, critics praised *Count Your Blessings* for its creation of a strong female protagonist—the first in a long line of such characters in Davies's fiction—and for its graphic, almost journalistic, descriptions of the valley and its people. Some reviewers, on the other hand, found the characters flat, and one suggested that Davies—after three novels and dozens of stories set in the Rhondda Valley—had exhausted the Welsh milieu. Just at this time Rodolphe L. Mégroz's generally laudatory *Rhys Davies: A Critical Sketch* (1932) helped to spark interest in Davies's realistic portrayals of colliery life. Davies returned to the valley as the setting for his collection *Daisy Matthews and Three Other Tales* (1932) and for his fourth novel, *The Red Hills* (1932).

The central character of *The Red Hills* is the misanthropic Iorwerth Pugh, who mines a seam of coal on a mountain near an industrial town in the Rhondda Valley. Unhappy with his situation, he considers himself an intellectual and sees the other residents of the valley as slaves to the capitalist system. He falls in love with a beautiful woman whose rebellious nature is as strong as his own; but he decides that she is not intelligent enough for him, so he breaks with her and moves even farther from civilization. By the novel's end, however, he has found a young woman he considers suitable to be his wife, and he settles with her on a small, isolated farm. In earlier works, such as *Rings on Her Fingers,* Davies had argued that passion takes precedence over intellectual kinship between a man and a woman, but here he suggests the opposite: that without an intellectual basis upon which to form a relationship, a couple is doomed to unhappiness. Reviewers saw the novel as an authentic picture of life in Wales.

After two volumes of short fiction—*Love Provoked* (1933) and *One of Norah's Early Days* (1935)—Davies published his next novel, *Honey and Bread* (1935). Set in south Wales during the first third of the nineteenth century, it would become the opening novel of a trilogy about the region. The wealthy Llewellyn family, currently headed by the spendthrift squire Tudor Llewellyn, has been established on its ancestral lands in an isolated valley for more than seven hundred years. Although his wife hates the valley, Tudor refuses to sell his birthright to the coalmining interests that are gaining a foothold in Wales. Tudor's decision pleases his sons, Owen and David, who love the valley's beauty. Financial setbacks, however, force Tudor to reconsider, and this news, coupled with an argument with his mother about his fiancée, a peasant named Bronwen, causes Owen to suffer a seizure and die. Bronwen, who is carrying his child, eventually finds happiness by marrying a young miner.

Some reviewers attacked *Honey and Bread* for its heavy-handed didacticism: Davies attempts to show that life in the Rhondda Valley was idyllic before the mines came to rape the land and corrupt the people; the reader is supposed to see the Llewellyn family and its troubles as a microcosm for all of south Wales. The novel is redeemed, however, by the passion that breathes life into the relationship of Owen and Bronwen, a young man with the soul of a poet and a young woman who nurtures and inspires that soul. They are among the most carefully drawn of Davies's early characters.

After *Honey and Bread* Davies published another collection of stories, *The Things Men Do* (1936), and another limited-edition pamphlet, *The Skull* (1936). His next novel, the second in the south Wales trilogy, was *A Time to Laugh* (1937). The work is set in the same valley as Davies's previous novel. Bronwen's grandson Tudor Morris is a young physician with socialist leanings. When he sympathizes with the striking miners of the valley, he is rejected by his family and by his snobbish fiancée. He moves his medical practice to the poorest district of the town and eventually becomes a strike leader himself. When the novel ends, there has been no economic improvement in the valley; nevertheless, it is the Christmas season of 1899 and, thus, "a time to laugh" and to be optimistic about the new century.

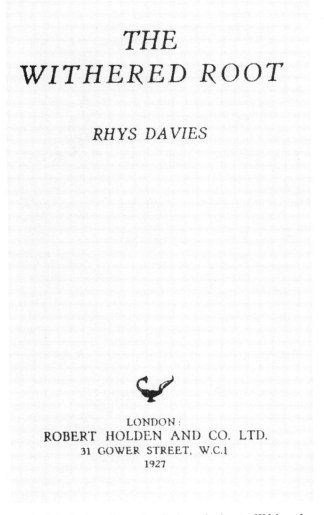

# THE
# WITHERED ROOT

## RHYS DAVIES

LONDON:
ROBERT HOLDEN AND CO. LTD.
31 GOWER STREET, W.C.1
1927

*Davies's first novel, a naturalistic work about a Welsh coal miner's son who becomes a fiery preacher*

The main characters in this didactic novel never come to life but remain types. The descriptions of the hard lives of the miners are, however, among the most moving Davies had yet produced. As a novel of social protest, *A Time to Laugh* demonstrates how the valley has declined since the Llewellyn family sold it to the mining companies: in *Honey and Bread* the hills are green, the streams clear, the air pure; in *A Time to Laugh* all of nature has been fouled by industrialization.

Before completing his south Wales trilogy Davies published a nonfiction "appreciation" of his native land, *My Wales* (1937). It is a natural companion to his fiction, offering insights into the customs of the Welsh and describing the beauty of the land. The same year Davies's first play, *The Ripening Wheat,* based on an ancient Welsh legend, was produced in London. (It would be revised and retitled

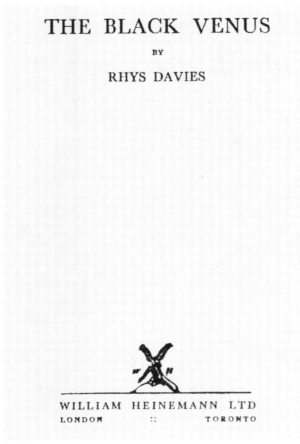

## THE BLACK VENUS

BY

## RHYS DAVIES

WILLIAM HEINEMANN LTD
LONDON      ::      TORONTO

*Title page for Davies's novel about a woman who defies the patriarchal customs of her Welsh village*

*The Maid of Cefn Ydlfa* and produced in Tonypandy, Wales, in 1952.)

*Jubilee Blues* (1938), one of Davies's best novels, completes his south Wales trilogy by bringing the story into the 1920s. Its protagonist, Cassie Jones, is filled with a vitality not often seen in the industrial valley; after most of the other characters in the novel are sapped of their strength, Cassie remains optimistic and cheerful. She is the faithful servant of an elderly justice of the peace who dies and leaves most of his money to her rather than to his greedy relatives. The judge's shiftless nephew marries Cassie, however, and they buy the Jubilee Pub. The pub's business falls off when a miners' strike breaks out, and Cassie's husband earns her contempt by being one of the first to succumb to despair. Davies suggests that the mines will lead to the downfall of Wales, that industrialization saps the strength from a people. Cassie abandons the pub and her husband and moves with her two young sons to the countryside; there she begins anew as a simple housekeeper, determined to live life to its fullest on her own terms. The reviews of *Jubilee Blues* were nearly all favorable, and the *Times Literary Supplement* made the work its "First Choice" for the week of 15 October 1938.

While working in the British War Office during World War II, Davies published *Sea Urchin: Adventures of Jorgen Jorgensen* (1940), a biography of an early-nineteenth-century Danish explorer and spy. The same year brought the publication of Davies's eighth novel and only murder mystery, *Under the Rose*. The work is divided into three sections. In the first section Rachel Lloyd, a middle-aged woman who never married after being jilted by her lover, is living a hermitlike existence; her only interest is her garden with its beautiful roses. One day the former suitor appears at her door. They reminisce, and it seems that Rachel has forgiven him; then, catching him unawares, she stabs him to death and buries him under her prized roses. The second section of the novel is an extended flashback, in which Rachel is seen as a beautiful, vivacious girl with two suitors. She chooses the one who jilts her; the change in her personality from outgoing to withdrawn is described in great detail. In the novel's final section Rachel, after burying her former lover, is again happy and adventurous. But a woman searching for Rachel's former lover arrives at the house and soon unravels the mystery of the man's disappearance, causing Rachel to commit suicide. The novel's economy of style and tripartite structure readily lent themselves to dramatic adaptation, and Davies, with the assistance of Archibald Batty, rewrote it as a three-act play titled *No Escape*. It received its first public performance at Eastbourne, England, in 1954.

Immediately after finishing *Under the Rose* Davies wrote a thinly disguised autobiography, *To-Morrow to Fresh Woods* (1941). The narrator, Penry, is a storekeeper's son who desperately wants to explore the vast world outside the Rhondda Valley. In the meantime he uses his writing as a means of imaginatively escaping from his dreary life. When he reaches adulthood, Penry leaves for London to begin his career as a writer. Although his descriptive passages are generally excellent, Davies maintains an objectivity toward his characters that turns them into stereotypes. The most interesting aspect of the novel is its depiction of Penry's love of words, but this story would be told more compellingly twenty-eight years later in Davies's autobiography. After *To-Morrow to Fresh Woods* Davies published his fourth collection of short fiction, *A Finger in Every Pie* (1942), and his second "appreciation" of his native country, *The Story of Wales* (1943).

Davies's tenth novel, *The Black Venus* (1944), is clearly his best. Having arrived at a marriageable age, Olwen Powell insists on her right to practice the ancient rural Welsh custom of *caru yn y qwely,* or "bed-courting," which allowed a suitor to climb through a bedroom window and spend several nights in the bed of his beloved. Supposedly this practice would allow the young couple to determine their compatibility. Sexual activity, however, was forbidden: the lovers were to spend the night in conversation, exchanging only occasional kisses or caresses. When *The Black Venus* opens, Olwen is on "trial" in her village in west Wales for having had too many suitors visit her bed. At the instigation of the parish priest, who was prodded into action by a nosy English gentlewoman, Caroline Drizzle, a tribunal is being held by the town's elders to determine whether bed-courting should be allowed to continue and whether Olwen and her family should be ostracized. Allowed to speak in her own defense, Olwen delivers an impassioned plea for women to have the right to determine their own destinies. This idea—that women should have the same freedoms enjoyed by men—is the central theme of the novel. Davies drives home the point by having Olwen tell one suitor that it is the duty of women to "cast off their own chains." Olwen is exonerated, and bed-courting is endorsed by the magistrate. Olwen goes on to have a few more suitors before she finally marries. Thirteen years later, having inherited her father's estate, she is an influential woman in the village. She alone has determined how she would live her life.

Along with its primary theme of female emancipation, *The Black Venus* explores the conflict of Welsh tradition, symbolized by Olwen, with the modern world, symbolized by the prudish Miss Drizzle. Davies clearly sympathizes with Olwen, showing, with his characteristic humor, how the Welsh enjoy a zest for life that the English, with their faith in progress and industry, can never understand. Ironically, the work sold well in England—it was Davies's only book to be republished in paperback—and headed the "Recommended" list in the *Times Literary Supplement* for 7 October 1944. On its publication in the United States two years later the *The New York Times Book Review* (24 February 1946) found the novel "an unusual and altogether delightful tour de force, drenched in the color of its background."

After his masterpiece Davies published two collections of short stories, *Selected Stories* (1945) and *The Trip to London* (1946). His next novel, *The Dark Daughters* (1947), is obviously indebted to William Shakespeare's *King Lear:* a cruel man ultimately re-

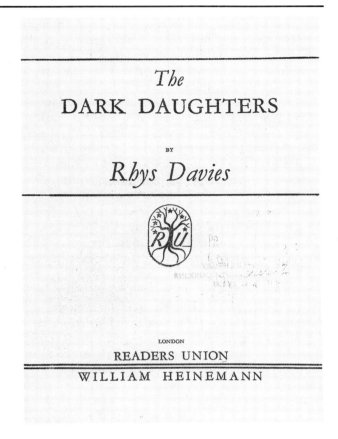

The
DARK DAUGHTERS

BY

*Rhys Davies*

LONDON
READERS UNION
WILLIAM HEINEMANN

*Title page for Davies's novel about the conflict between a cruel father and his three cruel daughters*

ceives what he deserves from his three equally cruel daughters. Although the work has moments of genuine horror, it lapses into predictable melodrama and is one of Davies's weakest novels.

Following the failure of *The Dark Daughters,* Davies published *Boy with a Trumpet, and Other Selected Short Stories* (1949). It received laudatory reviews, as had his two previous collections, and his reputation as a short-story writer began to eclipse his reputation as a novelist; his meticulously crafted stories, published in leading magazines in England and the United States, earned praise for their carefully constructed plots and subtle characterizations.

Davies did not give up writing novels, however. His twelfth, *Marianne* (1951), is about a woman's terrible retribution on a man—her twin sister's lover—who has wronged her. As in *The Dark Daughters,* Davies attempts to analyze the psychology of his characters. But he is unable to sustain suspense in the long form as well as he could in his short stories; consequently, both novels are somewhat tedious.

*The Painted King* (1954) is a satire of London's theatrical scene; at the time of the novel's publication Davies's play *No Escape* was in preparation. Judith Cottar comes to London from Dorset to find a job. Soon after taking up residence in a shabby boardinghouse she meets Guy Aspen, a composer of musical comedies; the character is based loosely on Davies's fellow Welshman Ivor Novello (real name: David Ivor Davies), the king of West End musicals in the 1940s. (One of Davies's stories, "Abraham's Glory" [1942], had been adapted into the successful London musical *Jennie Jones* in 1944.) Judith becomes Guy's secretary, then his lover; but the affection she gives him so freely is never returned, and when he achieves success he deserts her. *The Painted King* is moderately entertaining; the portrayal of Guy is quite humorous, and there are some especially funny scenes involving the hangers-on who surround him.

After publishing *The Collected Stories of Rhys Davies* (1955) Davies completed his next novel, *The Perishable Quality* (1957). Eva Pritchard returns to her hometown in south Wales after leading a mysterious life in London. Her violent former lover pursues her, but Eva outwits him. Interesting primarily because London no longer represents the escape from Wales that it did for Davies's earlier characters—here the situation is reversed—the novel is told in a series of flashbacks that do not always succeed in developing the plot.

Davies's collection *The Darling of Her Heart, and Other Stories* (1958) was followed by his fifteenth novel, *Girl Waiting in the Shade* (1960), about Lottie Curlow, who hates her mother but wants to maintain her inheritance. The novel was a failure; Davies did not publish another book for seven years, but when he did, *The Chosen One, and Other Stories* (1967) was praised as one of his best collections of short fiction. The title story, originally published in *The New Yorker*, had won the Edgar Award as the best crime story of 1966. In 1969 Davies was made an officer in the Order of the British Empire, won a prize from the Welsh Arts Council for his contributions to Welsh literature, and published *Print of a Hare's Foot*. Following this autobiography Davies published *Nobody Answered the Bell* (1971), a novel in which the tension between a lesbian couple living in a small English town is not resolved until one murders the other, and *Honeysuckle Girl* (1975), about a young

heroin addict who uses the drug to escape her miserable life. While some reviews of the two novels praised the realism with which Davies depicted the unhappiness of the characters, both sold poorly. Davies died of lung cancer in St. Pancras Hospital in London on 21 August 1978. His obituary in the 24 August 1978 *Times* of London called him "a Welsh Chekhov" and added that "he was a sweet-souled man of immense courtesy and loyalty . . . extraordinarily modest about his achievements."

Rhys Davies was ahead of his time in creating memorable female characters, independent women who win the battle of the sexes through their quick wits and enduring inner strength. Of these characters, Olwen Powell in *The Black Venus* remains the most vital.

**Bibliography:**
John Gawsworth (T. I. F. Armstrong), *Ten Contemporaries: Notes Toward Their Definitive Bibliography* (London: Benn, 1931).

**References:**
G. F. Adam, *Three Contemporary Anglo-Welsh Novelists: Jack Jones, Rhys Davies and Hilda Vaughan* (Bern: Francke, 1948), pp. 31–100;
Denys Val Baker, "Man from the Valley," *John O'London's Weekly,* 61 (20 October 1952): 1;
Glyn Jones, *The Dragon Has Two Tongues: Essays on Anglo-Welsh Writers and Writing* (London: Dent, 1968);
Rodolphe L. Mégroz, *Rhys Davies: A Critical Sketch* (London: Foyle, 1932);
David Rees, "Rhys Davies: Professional Author," *Wales,* 37 (February 1959): 70–73.

**Papers:**
The Harry Ransom Humanities Research Center at the University of Texas at Austin has an extensive collection of Rhys Davies's manuscripts, primarily from his later years, along with some of his correspondence. Another collection of manuscripts, ranging from Davies's earliest work to his final novel, is at the University of London's Sterling Library. The National Library of Wales, Aberystwyth, also has an excellent collection of his manuscripts, including some that were not published.

# Daphne du Maurier
## (12 May 1907 – 19 April 1989)

Wayne Templeton
*Kwantlen University College*

BOOKS: *The Loving Spirit* (London: Heinemann, 1931; Garden City, N.Y.: Doubleday, Doran, 1931);

*I'll Never Be Young Again* (London: Heinemann, 1932; Garden City, N.Y.: Doubleday, Doran, 1932);

*The Progress of Julius* (London: Heinemann, 1933; Garden City, N.Y.: Doubleday, Doran, 1933);

*Gerald: A Portrait* (London: Gollancz, 1934; Garden City, N.Y.: Doubleday, Doran, 1935);

*Jamaica Inn* (London: Gollancz, 1936; Garden City, N.Y.: Doubleday, Doran, 1936);

*The Du Mauriers* (London: Gollancz, 1937; New York: Literary Guild of America, 1937);

*Rebecca* (London: Gollancz, 1938; Garden City, N.Y.: Doubleday, Doran, 1938);

*Come Wind, Come Weather* (London: Heinemann, 1940; Garden City, N.Y.: Doubleday, Doran, 1941);

*Happy Christmas* (Garden City, N.Y.: Doubleday, Doran, 1940; London: Todd, 1943);

*Frenchman's Creek* (London: Gollancz, 1941; Garden City, N.Y.: Doubleday, Doran, 1942);

*Hungry Hill* (London: Gollancz, 1943; Garden City, N.Y.: Doubleday, Doran, 1943);

*The Years Between: A Play in Two Acts* (London: Gollancz, 1945; Garden City, N.Y.: Doubleday, Doran, 1946);

*The King's General* (London: Gollancz, 1946; Garden City, N.Y.: Doubleday, 1946);

*September Tide: A Play in Three Acts* (London: Gollancz, 1949; Garden City, N.Y.: Doubleday, 1950);

*The Parasites* (London: Gollancz, 1949; Garden City, N.Y.: Doubleday, 1950);

*My Cousin Rachel* (London: Gollancz, 1951; Garden City, N.Y.: Doubleday, 1952);

*The Apple Tree: A Short Novel, and Some Stories* (London: Gollancz, 1952); republished as *Kiss Me Again, Stranger: A Collection of Stories, Long and Short* (Garden City, N.Y.: Doubleday, 1953);

*Daphne du Maurier*

republished as *The Birds and Other Stories* (Harmondsworth: Penguin, 1963);

*Mary Anne: A Novel* (London: Gollancz, 1954; Garden City, N.Y.: Doubleday, 1954);

*The Scapegoat* (London: Gollancz, 1957; Garden City, N.Y.: Doubleday, 1957);

*Early Stories* (London: Todd, 1959);

*The Breaking Point: Eight Stories* (London: Gollancz, 1959; Garden City, N.Y.: Doubleday, 1959); republished as *The Blue Lenses, and Other Stories* (Harmondsworth: Penguin, 1970);

*The Infernal World of Branwell Brontë* (London: Gollancz, 1960; Garden City, N.Y.: Doubleday, 1961);

*Du Maurier's parents, Gerald and Muriel du Maurier*

*Castle Dor,* by du Maurier and Sir Arthur Thomas Quiller-Couch (London: Dent, 1962);

*The Glass-Blowers* (London: Gollancz, 1963; Garden City, N.Y.: Doubleday, 1963);

*The Flight of the Falcon* (London: Gollancz, 1965; Garden City, N.Y.: Doubleday, 1965);

*Vanishing Cornwall* (London: Gollancz, 1967; Garden City, N.Y.: Doubleday, 1967);

*The House on the Strand* (London: Gollancz, 1969; Garden City, N.Y.: Doubleday, 1969);

*Not after Midnight, and Other Stories* (London: Gollancz, 1971); republished as *Don't Look Now* (Garden City, N.Y.: Doubleday, 1971);

*Rule Britannia: A Novel* (London: Gollancz, 1972; Garden City, N.Y.: Doubleday, 1973);

*Golden Lads: Anthony Bacon, Francis and Their Friends* (London: Gollancz, 1975; Garden City, N.Y.: Doubleday, 1975);

*The Winding Stair: Francis Bacon, His Rise and Fall* (London: Gollancz, 1976; Garden City, N.Y.: Doubleday, 1977);

*Echoes from the Macabre: Selected Stories* (London: Gollancz, 1976; Garden City, N.Y.: Doubleday, 1977);

*Growing Pains: The Shaping of a Writer* (London: Gollancz, 1977); republished as *Myself When Young: The Shaping of a Writer* (Garden City, N.Y.: Doubleday, 1977);

*The Rendezvous and Other Stories* (London: Gollancz, 1980);

*The Rebecca Notebook and Other Memories* (Garden City, N.Y.: Doubleday, 1980; London: Gollancz, 1981);

*Classics from the Macabre* (London: Gollancz, 1987).

PLAY PRODUCTIONS: *The Years Between,* Manchester, The Opera House, 20 November 1944;

*September Tide,* Oxford, New Theatre, November 1948.

MOTION PICTURE: *Hungry Hill,* screenplay by du Maurier and Terence Young, Two Cities Films, 1947.

OTHER: George du Maurier, *Novels,* introductions by Daphne du Maurier and John Masefield (London: Pilot, 1947);

*The Young George du Maurier: A Selection of His Letters, 1860–1867,* edited by du Maurier (London:

Davies, 1951; Garden City, N.Y.: Doubleday, 1952);

Phyllis Bottome, *Best Stories,* edited by du Maurier (London: Faber, 1963);

George du Maurier, *Peter Ibbetson, with an Introduction by His Cousin Lady ***** (Madge Plunket),* preface by Daphne du Maurier (London: Gollancz, 1969).

SELECTED PERIODICAL PUBLICATIONS–
UNCOLLECTED: "Faces to the Sun," *Good House-keeping,* 112 (April 1941): 19;

"Menabilly: The Most Beautiful House I Have Ever Seen," *House and Garden,* 92 (August 1947): 92–97, 113, 114, 118;

"My Love Affair with Crete," *Holiday,* 49 (March 1971): 68, 78–79;

"The Place Has Taken Hold of Me," *Saturday Evening Post,* 249 (December 1977): 48–50.

*Du Maurier circa 1929*

Daphne du Maurier lived in Cornwall for forty years, twenty-five of them in Menabilly, a seventeenth-century house that she described as the most beautiful she had ever seen. Cornwall, a region of mystery and superstition, the home of legendary figures such as King Arthur and Tristan and Iseult, is a landscape easily made Gothic; it is the home, as well, of pirates both fictional and historical, with a coastline that has been responsible for innumerable shipwrecks. While never a fully assimilated Cornishwoman, du Maurier was certainly inspired by her adopted home, the setting of some of her best and best-known novels: *Jamaica Inn* (1936), *Frenchman's Creek* (1941), and *The House on the Strand* (1969). In these, and in others to a lesser degree, one finds a strong sense of place: Cornwall and Menabilly are made a dramatic part of the works, like Thomas Hardy's Dorset, D. H. Lawrence's Nottinghamshire, and, even more so, the Brontës' Yorkshire, whose moors also inspired that sense of Gothic passion, romance, and horror that characterizes du Maurier's Cornish works. It is, therefore, not surprising that du Maurier took time out from her many successful novels to write a history of Cornwall (1967) and a biography of Branwell Brontë (1960).

Du Maurier was intrigued by history–especially the history of her own family. Her paternal great-great-grandmother, Mary Anne Clarke, had been the mistress of King George III's second son, the duke of York. Clarke was the kind of woman du Maurier wished to be: strong, courageous, and capable of dealing with a man's world on her own terms. While the money inherited from Clarke enabled subsequent generations of du Mauriers to indulge in

cultural pursuits, it was Daphne's grandfather, George du Maurier, who was the first artist in the family. Initially a cartoonist for *Punch,* he later became an illustrator of novels by such authors as Hardy, Elizabeth Cleghorn Gaskell, George Meredith, and Henry James. Blinded in one eye in middle age, George du Maurier had become a novelist himself, producing *Peter Ibbetson* in 1891, *Trilby* in 1894, and *The Martian,* published posthumously in 1897. Daphne du Maurier's father, Gerald, was an actor who achieved recognition first as Raffles, the popular gentleman burglar created by the novelist E. W. Hornung, then as Bulldog Drummond, an even more popular detective created by "Sapper" (Herman Cyril McNeile). By 1914 he was actor-manager of Wyndham's Theatre in London. In 1929 he lent his name to a tobacco company, for which he was generously compensated. Daphne du Maurier's mother, the former Muriel Beaumont, was an actress.

Du Maurier was born in London on 12 May 1907, the second of three children–all daughters. Held increasingly in check, especially during her adolescence, by her puritanical and tradition-bound father, she began to experience an intense desire to be a boy. This yearning was not simply that of a girl who had become aware of gender inequality; it was the awakening of lesbian tendencies in an era when many people, including homosexuals themselves, believed that one person in a homosexual relationship must have female inclinations, the other male. As a teenager she adopted a male persona, Eric

*The Slade boatyard in Cornwall, the setting for du Maurier's first novel,* The Loving Spirit

Avon, and many of her novels' first-person narrators are male. In other areas of her life this tendency had to be repressed; for a long time she referred to it, in letters to intimates, as her "boy in a box." While du Maurier would confess to being deeply in love with several women during her life, she would never admit, even to herself, that she was bisexual.

Du Maurier's first sexual attraction was to Fernande Yvon, a teacher at a finishing school outside Paris where du Maurier studied in 1925–1926. At this time she began writing verse and short stories; the latter were influenced by Katherine Mansfield and Guy de Maupassant although in style they are more like those of Somerset Maugham. All of these early works are filled with disgust and pessimism concerning the human condition.

In 1926 the du Mauriers bought a summer home, Ferryside, in Fowey, on the south coast of Cornwall, about twenty-five miles west of Plymouth. There Daphne found the freedom from distraction she needed to write. She also found Menabilly, a secluded house owned by the Rashleigh family that was falling into disrepair, and immediately fell in love with it. She would be obsessed with

the house, visiting it frequently, until she moved into it seventeen years later.

Du Maurier's first published short story, "And Now to God the Father," appeared on 15 May 1929 in *The Bystander,* edited by her uncle, William Beaumont; she was paid ten pounds for it. On 26 June her second story, "A Difference in Temperament," was published in the same periodical. That summer du Maurier had a love affair with the future motion-picture director Carol Reed, whom she had met in France.

Du Maurier's first novel, *The Loving Spirit* (1931), was written in Fowey. It is an historical romance, one of the two kinds of novel that du Maurier would produce; the other was the Gothic or psychological thriller. Set in Cornwall, the work is based on a Cornish family named Slade whose history was filled with romance and intrigue and included a mysterious ancestor, Jane Symons. In the novel Symons becomes Janet Coombe, a woman of courage and strength who fears domesticity as a threat to her autonomy yet fervently desires love and the security of marriage. She does eventually marry, but then she becomes aloof and melancholy, never quite able to disguise her restlessness. Her only lasting satisfaction is that one of her sons, Joseph, is, like her, a "loving spirit." That spirit is inherited by subsequent generations, thereby keeping Coombe's essence alive. The novel conveys certain concerns of du Maurier's that find their way into most of her later works: her desire to be a man—here dramatized in Janet's "becoming" Joseph; her conviction that women should be strong and independent; and her belief in the inheritability of character traits.

In 1931 du Maurier met a Grenadier Guards officer, Maj. Frederick Arthur Browning, known as "Tommy" to his family and "Boy" to his colleagues. They were married on 19 July 1932 and had three children: Tessa, Flavia, and Christian. For the next twenty years the family would move frequently as Browning, who eventually attained the rank of lieutenant general, was transferred to various places within and outside the United Kingdom.

Du Maurier fought all her life to escape the influence of her powerful, jealous, and conservative father. This struggle becomes a theme in her second novel, *I'll Never Be Young Again* (1932), when the narrator, Dick, realizes that he is becoming like his despised father. Dick aspires to be a great writer, but he eventually recognizes that he does not possess the talent to distinguish himself in that field. In middle age he philosophically accepts his ordinariness, as well as his homosexuality—an orientation that, implausibly, disappears following the death of his lover, Jake, and his marriage to Hesta, who introduces him to the rewards of heterosexual passion.

The egotism displayed by Dick at the beginning of her *I'll Never Be Young Again* becomes central to du Maurier's third novel and the first of her psychological thrillers, *The Progress of Julius* (1933), in which self-preoccupation becomes diabolic. Julius Levy dedicates his life to hedonism and to the domination of everyone who is important to him, but he discovers in his daughter Gabriel both a source of pleasure beyond all others and a person he cannot control. Julius murders his daughter and avoids detection.

Du Maurier's next work was a biography of her father, *Gerald: A Portrait* (1934). Her fourth novel, *Jamaica Inn,* appeared two years later and finally persuaded the critics that she was a writer of talent. A tightly crafted Gothic horror story, much more quickly paced than her previous novels, it was her first commercial success, selling more copies in three months than her three earlier novels had in total. The work is set on the isolated, foreboding moors of Cornwall and involves characters reminiscent—as the critics noted—of those in Charlotte Brontë's *Jane Eyre* (1847) and Emily Brontë's

*Du Maurier's husband, Maj. Frederick Arthur Browning of the Grenadier Guards. They were married in 1932.*

*Wuthering Heights* (1847). Following the deaths of her parents the young, assertive Mary Yellan moves in with her aunt and uncle Patience and Joshua Merlyn, proprietors of Jamaica Inn, and Joshua's brother Jem, who becomes her lover. Mary discovers that the local vicar, a madman with a penchant for Druidic rites, is the mastermind behind a group that lures ships onto the rocks so as to plunder them. The group includes her aunt and uncle until the vicar, aware that they are about to repent and inform the police, murders them. In the end he is killed by the valiant but mysterious Jem. The novel's strength derives not so much from this plot as from the vivid characters and the dramatic landscape. This rugged and hostile environment makes considerable demands on Mary's courage as her suspicions grow; it also echoes the mysteriousness of its inhabitants as du Maurier subtly offers Mary and the reader reasons for suspecting them to be other than they at first seem to be. The depiction of the vicar, especially, is a tour de force.

It was in Alexandria, where her husband was posted in 1936, that du Maurier began her fifth novel, *Rebecca,* published in 1938. Far from home, unhappy in the company either of the British military or of the Egyptians, du Maurier often thought about Cornwall—fantasizing about, as much as recalling, its lush forests and pounding seas that stood

*The Cornish inn that became the setting for du Mauriers's fourth novel, a Gothic horror story*

in stark contrast to the stifling and arid desert. These fantasies and a sense of profound melancholy inform the mood of *Rebecca,* the story of a naive working-class woman whom the recently widowed Maxim de Winter marries and takes back to his palatial family mansion, Manderly, in the south of England. There the second Mrs. de Winter–her first name is never given–discovers that she must compete with the memory of the former mistress of the house, Rebecca, whose qualities, as the macabre housekeeper, Mrs. Danvers, constantly points out, were in dramatic contrast to those of the unsophisticated newcomer. But the bride comes to learn that she need not be jealous of her predecessor, for Max hated his first wife. Late in the novel he is charged with her murder, but during the trial evidence is introduced at the last moment that exonerates him. Returning home, the de Winters discover that the distraught Mrs. Danvers has burned Manderly down; Max and his bride are free to start their lives over again. The response to *Rebecca* was overwhelmingly positive; critics pointed out that du Maurier could no longer be compared to the Brontës or to any other novelist but had found her own voice.

The first film of a du Maurier work, *Jamaica Inn,* directed by Alfred Hitchcock and starring Maureen O'Hara as Mary and Charles Laughton as the vicar, was released in 1939. (It would be remade as a television movie in 1985, with Jane Seymour as Mary and Patrick McGoohan as the uncle.) Hitchcock, whose *Lord Camber's Ladies* (1932) had starred du Maurier's father and Gertrude Lawrence, also

made the second and possibly the most renowned film of a du Maurier novel: *Rebecca,* released in 1940, starred Joan Fontaine and Lawrence Olivier and won Academy Awards for cinematography and best picture.

Early in World War II du Maurier wrote a propaganda piece, *Come Wind, Come Weather* (1940), for the Moral Rearmament Movement; it was intended to encourage wives and mothers not to despair during the absence of their soldier husbands and sons. Her Gothic or psychological thrillers became increasingly Jungian and Poe-like as she explored the paranormal and became intrigued by the notion of the doppelgänger. Such a novel is *Frenchman's Creek;* published in 1941, it is a dark tale of Cornwall during the reign of Charles II. The protagonist, Lady St. Columb, is another woman caught between a thirst for independence and a desire for the security of domesticity. Although she returns to him in the end, Lady St. Columb leaves her husband and begins a relationship with a French aristocrat, Jean-Benoit Aubery, who has also temporarily left a claustrophobic domestic life to become a pirate. As with du Maurier's best works in this genre, *Frenchman's Creek* is enlivened by a dramatic landscape and the avoidance of stereotypes. New in this novel is the theme of the dual personality, a development of the notion of the boy in a box: Lady St. Columb is convinced that she possesses a second, deeper self–not a man but a stronger woman.

In August 1943 du Maurier leased Menabilly from Dr. John Rashleigh for a twenty-year period.

*Joan Fontaine and Dame Judith Anderson in a scene from Alfred Hitchcock's 1940 film of du Maurier's novel* Rebecca

One of the terms of the lease was that she have the house repaired at her own expense. She moved into it at the end of the year.

While *Frenchman's Creek* had been a modest success, du Maurier's next novel, *Hungry Hill* (1943), a conventional historical romance about five generations of Irish landowners, was a commercial and critical disappointment. Nevertheless, in 1947 it was made into a motion picture, starring Margaret Lockwood, Dennis Price, and Jean Simmons; du Maurier co-authored the screenplay with Terence Young. She also wrote a play, *The Years Between,* about a woman who is in the process of adjusting to the loss of her husband in the war when he suddenly reappears. It premiered in Manchester on 20 November 1944 and opened at Wyndham's Theatre in London on 10 January 1945; it was published in 1945.

In 1946 du Maurier became Lady Browning when her husband was knighted. Her next novel, *The King's General* (1946), had its inception in a local rumor that Menabilly contained a hidden chamber that had been discovered in 1824 and found to hold a human skeleton. Du Maurier set out to construct a story, set during the English Civil War, that would

account for such a discovery. Honor Harris spurns Richard Grenville's offer of marriage after she is crippled in a riding accident. Richard marries another woman, and they have a son who betrays him to Oliver Cromwell's forces. In an apparent act of remorse the son locks himself in the hidden room of their home, Menabilly, where he dies. *The King's General* was much more a commercial than a critical success: critics complained of its teenage exuberance and lack of historical accuracy.

In 1947 du Maurier traveled to New York, where she successfully defended herself in a lawsuit claiming that she had plagiarized *Rebecca* from a novel published in the 1920s. On this trip she stayed at the home of her American publisher, Nelson Doubleday, and fell in love with his wife, Ellen. In 1948 du Maurier wrote her second play, *September Tide,* about a middle-aged woman whose son-in-law, an artist, falls in love with her; she rejects him, and he returns to his wife. According to Margaret Forster's 1993 biography of du Maurier, the mother-in-law, Stella, is based on Ellen Doubleday, and the son-in-law on du Maurier herself. Stella was played by Gertrude Lawrence, to whom du Maurier also found herself sexually attracted. That same year Frederick

*Menabilly, the house near Fowey, Cornwall, where du Maurier lived from 1943 to 1969*

Browning became comptroller and treasurer to Princess Elizabeth; he moved into a London flat while du Maurier remained at Menabilly with their children and servants. The couple saw each other only during Browning's infrequent weekend visits.

Du Maurier's next novel, *The Parasites* (1949), a humorous semi-autobiographical work about a theatrical couple and their artist children, received negative reviews; John Betjeman, for example, described it in the *Daily Herald* as dull and obvious. Du Maurier reverted to her strength in *My Cousin Rachel* (1951), which was applauded by critics and outsold all of her previous works, including *Rebecca*. The narrator is the insecure orphan Philip Ashley. His guardian and cousin, Ambrose Ashley, has been vacationing at the Italian villa of their mutual cousin, Rachel, whose husband has recently died. When Philip learns that Ambrose has married Rachel, he is jealous and fearful that he has lost his lifelong friend. Then he receives another letter from Ambrose, urging him to come to Italy and suggesting that Rachel has become a threat to Ambrose's life. When he arrives in Italy, Ambrose is dead, probably of a brain tumor, and Rachel has disappeared. Believing that he has become Ambrose's alter ego, Philip swears revenge, but when he meets Rachel, he falls in love with her. Suspecting that she may have two personalities, Philip alternately revels in the exhilaration of passion and trembles in fear that he may be his cousin's next victim. But Rachel herself dies, and the novel ends with the question of her guilt unanswered. The novel was filmed in 1952, with Richard Burton as Philip and Olivia de Havilland as Rachel. That same year Princess Elizabeth

became queen, and Browning was made treasurer to her husband, Prince Philip, the Duke of Edinburgh.

Du Maurier's novel *The Scapegoat* (1957) pursues the doppelgänger theme. The narrator, John, a history teacher, is in France doing research for a series of lectures. In Le Mans he meets Jean de Gue, his exact double in appearance but his opposite in character. Over drinks de Gue proposes that the two men exchange lives; before John can respond, he passes out. He awakes the next morning in de Gue's room, the other man's chauffeur awaiting his orders. John meets de Gue's family and learns that de Gue murdered his sister Blanche's fiancé; that de Gue's wife, Françoise, and his daughter, Marie-Noel, are suicidal; and that his mother is addicted to morphine. To each family member John gives hope and a sense of purpose, encouraging de Gue's brother, Paul, to become a traveling representative of the family's glass factory and Blanche to manage the business. Just as he is beginning to succeed in saving the factory from bankruptcy he receives a message from de Gue, announcing the latter's imminent return. Wishing to retain his newfound identity, John awaits de Gue with pistol in hand, but he is discovered by a priest, who, believing him to be suicidal, persuades him that life is worth living. Abandoning his second identity but unable to return to what he believes is his worthless first life, John is driving to a monastery as the novel ends. Although sales were disappointing, critics were delighted with *The Scapegoat*. It was filmed in 1959, with Alec Guinness in the dual roles of John and de Gue and Bette Davis as de Gue's mother; the screenplay was written by Gore Vidal and the director, Robert Hamer.

In 1959 Browning retired from his service to Prince Philip and joined du Maurier at Menabilly. His health deteriorated over the next several years, partly because of excessive drinking, and he died on 13 March 1965.

*The Flight of the Falcon* (1965), a nightmarish tale of the quest for power, is one of du Maurier's most psychologically complex novels. The narrator, Armino Fabbio, is an Italian tour guide. His brother, Aldo, resembles Svengali in George du Maurier's *Trilby:* an extremely intelligent man who dominates other men and women for his own gratification, he is a combination of good and evil who believes that Christ and Satan are one being and mystically identifies himself with a fifteenth-century duke called the Falcon, who had thrown himself from a palace tower in the belief that he was the son of God and could fly. Aldo finally dons a large set of wings and jumps from a tower to his death. Armino, who has also attempted to discover a sense of his own identity in the distant past, is left to recover what is left of his life following the nightmarish passing through it of his malevolent brother.

In 1969 du Maurier lost her lease on Menabilly, which had been extended beyond its original twenty-year term; Rashleigh had died, and his heir had decided to move into the house. Du Maurier negotiated a lifetime lease on another house, Kilmarth, half a mile away from Menabilly and also owned by the Rashleigh family.

In her next novel, *The House on the Strand,* du Maurier again explores the interplay between present and past. The narrator, Dick Young (with whom du Maurier claimed that she had the strongest affinity of any of her characters, male or female), is staying at the Cornish house of his friend Magnus Lane. He takes a drug that Magnus has recently discovered and finds himself in fourteenth-century Cornwall; his name is Roger Kylmerth, and he is in love with a woman named Isolda. Each ingestion of the drug situates him a decade or so forward so that during the course of a half dozen such experiences he watches Isolda age and then die of the plague. Deteriorating rapidly from the side effects of the drug, Dick gradually loses the ability to distinguish between reality and illusion.

Du Maurier's final novel, *Rule Britannia* (1972), is a jingoistic satire set a few years in the future and dealing with the resistance of the Cornish people to the unification of Britain and America. It is generally considered the poorest of her novels.

Some of du Maurier's most accomplished works of fiction are to be found in her short-story

*Ellen Doubleday, the American publisher Nelson Doubleday's wife, with whom du Maurier fell in love in 1947*

collections: *The Apple Tree* (1952), republished as *Kiss Me Again, Stranger* (1953) and as *The Birds and Other Stories* (1963); *The Breaking Point* (1959), republished as *The Blue Lenses, and Other Stories* (1970); and *Not after Midnight, and Other Stories* (1971), republished as *Don't Look Now* (1971). Among the most notable of the stories are "The Birds," from the first collection, about a bizarre attack on a small town by thousands of birds. Hitchcock filmed the work in 1963, with Tippi Hedren, Rod Taylor, Suzanne Pleshette, and Jessica Tandy; du Maurier was highly displeased with the liberties the film took with her text. "The Alibi," in the second collection, concerns a man who, like John in *The Scapegoat*, exchanges his humdrum life for a more exciting one; by the end of the story he has been charged with murdering two people. In "Ganymede," from the same collection, a homosexual tries but fails to escape his sexual orientation; like Gustav Aschenbach in Thomas Mann's *Der Tod in Venedig* (1912; translated as *Death in Venice,* 1925), du Maurier's nameless protagonist goes to Venice and cannot resist a boy he meets there. Also set largely in Venice is "Don't Look Now," in the third collection. John and Laura, an English couple, are vacationing in Italy in an attempt to distract themselves following the death of their daughter, Christine. In Venice, John repeatedly glimpses a small figure in a red coat whom he believes to be his daughter. Meanwhile, Laura becomes friends with a pair of elderly and eccentric sisters; one of them says that she has been in communication with Christine, who has reported that John and Laura are in danger and must leave Venice immediately. Ignor-

*Du Maurier near her home, Kilmarth, in the 1970s*

ing the warning, John finally corners the figure in red; it turns out to be a dwarf, who kills John by slashing his throat with a knife. The story was made into a successful film in 1973, directed by Nicholas Roeg and starring Donald Sutherland as John and Julie Christie as Laura.

During the remainder of her life du Maurier concentrated on nonfiction; the short-story collections *Echoes from the Macabre* (1976), *The Rendezvous and Other Stories* (1980), and *Classics from the Macabre* (1987) consist of earlier works although three of those in the second volume had not been published previously. She died at Kilmarth on 19 April 1989.

Du Maurier was most proficient in creating psychological or Gothic thrillers, often having some connection to the past or set in the past, that focus on the struggle of an individual against an oppres-

sive environment. Her best novels—*Rebecca, The Scapegoat, My Cousin Rachel, The House on the Strand,* and *The Flight of the Falcon*—are strong in characterization, setting, and plot. But although she was able to live comfortably as a result of the commercial success of her works and was made a dame of the British Empire in 1969 for her literary contributions to the United Kingdom, du Maurier did not occupy a place in the literary canon during her lifetime—much to her disappointment. A reassessment of the canon has led in recent years to the "discovery" of several previously neglected figures in British literature, most of them women. This list includes Daphne du Maurier: since 1987 four full-length assessments of her life and works have appeared.

**Biographies:**

Judith Cook, *Daphne: A Portrait of Daphne du Maurier* (London: Bantam, 1991);

Martyn Shallcross, *The Private World of Daphne Du Maurier* (London: Robson, 1991);

Margaret Forster, *Daphne du Maurier* (London: Chatto & Windus, 1993).

**References:**

Avril Horner and Sue Zlosnik, *Daphne du Maurier: Writing, Identity, and the Gothic Imagination* (New York: St. Martin's Press, 1998);

Richard Kelly, *Daphne du Maurier* (Boston: Twayne, 1987).

**Papers:**

With the exception of a small collection of some correspondence with her publisher Victor Gollancz during the 1950s, which is in the Modern Records Center, University of Warwick, all of Daphne du Maurier's papers are privately held.

# C. S. Forester

## (27 August 1899 – 2 April 1966)

Neville Newman
*McMaster University*

BOOKS: *A Pawn among Kings* (London: Methuen, 1924);

*Napoleon and His Court* (London: Methuen, 1924; New York: Dodd, Mead, 1924);

*The Paid Piper* (London: Methuen, 1924);

*Josephine, Napoleon's Empress* (London: Methuen, 1925; New York: Dodd, Mead, 1925);

*Payment Deferred* (London: John Lane, 1926; Boston: Little, Brown, 1942);

*Love Lies Dreaming* (London: John Lane, 1927; Indianapolis: Bobbs-Merrill, 1927);

*Victor Emmanuel II and the Union of Italy* (London: Methuen, 1927; New York: Dodd, Mead, 1927);

*The Wonderful Week* (London: John Lane, 1927); republished as *One Wonderful Week* (Indianapolis: Bobbs-Merrill, 1927);

*Louis XIV, King of France and Navarre* (London: Methuen, 1928; New York: Dodd, Mead, 1928);

*The Shadow of the Hawk* (London: John Lane, 1928); republished as *The Daughter of the Hawk* (Indianapolis: Bobbs-Merrill, 1928);

*Brown on Resolution* (London: John Lane, 1929); republished as *Single-Handed* (New York: Putnam, 1929);

*Nelson* (London: John Lane, 1929); republished as *Lord Nelson* (Indianapolis: Bobbs-Merrill, 1929);

*The Voyage of the Annie Marble* (London: John Lane, 1929);

*Plain Murder* (London: John Lane, 1930; New York: Dell, 1954);

*The Annie Marble in Germany* (London: John Lane, 1930);

*Two-and-Twenty* (London: John Lane, 1931; New York: Appleton, 1931);

*U 97: A Play in Three Acts* (London: John Lane, 1931);

*Death to the French* (London: John Lane, 1932); republished as "Rifleman Dodd," in *Rifleman Dodd, and The Gun: Two Novels of the Peninsular Wars* (New York: Reader's Club, 1942);

*C. S. Forester*

*The Gun: A Novel* (London: John Lane, 1933; Boston: Little, Brown, 1933);

*Nurse Cavell: A Play in Three Acts,* by Forester and Carl E. Bechhofer Roberts (London: John Lane, 1933);

*The Peacemaker* (London: Heinemann, 1934; Boston: Little, Brown, 1934);

*The African Queen* (London: M. Joseph, 1935; Boston: Little, Brown, 1935);

*Marionettes at Home* (London: M. Joseph, 1936);

*The General* (London: M. Joseph, 1936; Boston: Little, Brown, 1936);

*The Happy Return* (London: M. Joseph, 1937); republished as *Beat to Quarters* (Boston: Little, Brown, 1937);

*A Ship of the Line* (London: M. Joseph, 1938); republished as *Ship of the Line* (Boston: Little, Brown, 1938);

*Flying Colours* (London: M. Joseph, 1938; Boston: Little, Brown, 1939);

*Captain Hornblower, R.N.* (London: M. Joseph, 1939)–comprises *The Happy Return, A Ship of the Line,* and *Flying Colours;* republished as *Captain Horatio Hornblower* (Boston: Little, Brown, 1939)–comprises *Beat to Quarters, Ship of the Line,* and *Flying Colours;*

*The Earthly Paradise* (London: M. Joseph, 1940); republished as *To the Indies* (Boston: Little, Brown, 1940);

*The Captain from Connecticut* (London: M. Joseph, 1941; Boston: Little, Brown, 1941);

*Poo-Poo and the Dragons* (London: M. Joseph, 1942; Boston: Little, Brown, 1942);

*The Ship* (London: M. Joseph, 1943; Boston: Little, Brown, 1943);

*The Commodore* (London: M. Joseph, 1945); republished as *Commodore Hornblower* (Boston: Little, Brown, 1945);

*Lord Hornblower* (London: M. Joseph, 1946; Boston: Little, Brown, 1946);

*The Sky and the Forest* (London: M. Joseph, 1948; Boston: Little, Brown, 1948);

*Mr. Midshipman Hornblower* (London: M. Joseph, 1950; Boston: Little, Brown, 1950);

*Randall and the River of Time* (Boston: Little, Brown, 1950; London: M. Joseph, 1951);

*Lieutenant Hornblower* (London: M. Joseph, 1952; Boston: Little, Brown, 1952);

*Hornblower and the Atropos* (London: M. Joseph, 1953; Boston: Little, Brown, 1953);

*The Barbary Pirates* (New York: Random House, 1953; London: Macdonald, 1956);

*The Nightmare* (London: M. Joseph, 1954; Boston: Little, Brown, 1954);

*The Good Shepherd* (London: M. Joseph, 1955; Boston: Little, Brown, 1955);

*The Age of Fighting Sail: The Story of the Naval War of 1812* (Garden City, N.Y.: Doubleday, 1956); republished as *The Naval War of 1812* (London: M. Joseph, 1957);

*Hornblower in the West Indies* (London: M. Joseph, 1958); republished as *Admiral Hornblower in the West Indies* (Boston: Little, Brown, 1958);

*Hunting the Bismarck* (London: M. Joseph, 1959); republished as *The Last Nine Days of the Bismarck* (Boston: Little, Brown, 1959);

*Hornblower and the Hotspur* (London: M. Joseph, 1962; Boston: Little, Brown, 1962);

*The Hornblower Companion* (London: M. Joseph, 1964; Boston: Little, Brown, 1964);

*Hornblower and the Crisis: An Unfinished Novel* (London: M. Joseph, 1967); republished as *Hornblower during the Crisis, and Two Stories: Hornblower's Temptation and The Last Encounter* (Boston: Little, Brown, 1967);

*Long before Forty* (London: M. Joseph, 1967; Boston: Little, Brown, 1968);

*The Man in the Yellow Raft* (London: M. Joseph, 1969; Boston: Little, Brown, 1969);

*Gold from Crete: Ten Stories* (Boston: Little, Brown, 1970); republished as *Gold from Crete: Short Stories* (London: M. Joseph, 1971).

PLAY PRODUCTION: *Nurse Cavell,* by Forester and Carl E. Bechhofer Roberts, London, Vaudeville Theatre, 8 March 1934.

MOTION PICTURE: *Forever and a Day,* screenplay by Forester (as C. S. Forrester) and others, RKO, 1943.

OTHER: John Porrit Wetherell, *The Adventures of John Wetherell,* edited by Forester (Garden City, N.Y.: Doubleday, 1953);

"William Joyce," in *Fatal Fascination: Was It Murder? Four Historic Cases Vividly Recreated by Four Master Storytellers,* by Forester, Nigel Balchin, Eric Linklater, and Christopher Sykes (Boston: Little, Brown, 1964), pp. 59–84; volume republished as *Fatal Fascination: A Choice of Crime* (London: Arrow, 1968);

Richard A. Hough, *Dreadnought: A History of the Modern Battleship,* introduction by Forester (London: Allen & Unwin, 1968).

C. S. Forester is best known for his series of eleven historical novels about the early-nineteenth-century British naval officer Horatio Hornblower. A prolific writer, Forester had produced twenty-four books before he conceived the nautical protagonist with whom he was to become indelibly associated. His connection to his hero has tended to obscure his other literary accomplishments, which include thrillers, novels about naval action in both world wars, travel books, and short stories. Many of his works have been adapted as motion pictures, including the classic 1951 film *The African Queen.*

The youngest of five children, Cecil Lewis Troughton Smith was born in Cairo on 27 August

1899 to George Smith, an official in the Egyptian Ministry of Education, and Sarah Troughton Smith. In his posthumously published autobiography, *Long before Forty* (1967), Forester sums up his mother's life in Egypt as "fifteen years of warmth and sunshine, of willing servants and pleasant social life." This situation ended with his father's decision that the children should be educated in England. Thus, Sarah Smith returned home with Cecil and his siblings, and at age three Cecil was enrolled in a local-authority infants' school in south London.

George Smith's choice of council schools for his children was astute: although he had a comfortable income, he had to support a family in England while maintaining himself in Egypt; the money he saved in those early years could be used later for the children's secondary education. Furthermore, the chances of winning a scholarship to one of the more-renowned English public (what Americans would call private) schools were much better for pupils who were receiving their elementary education from a local authority. As Forester recalls in *Long before Forty*: "Christ's hospital, for instance, offered scholarships to boys at L.C.C. [London County Council] schools; the lucky winner was fed and clothed and educated at quite a good public school at no cost whatever from the age of ten to that of seventeen."

Cecil Smith's upper-middle-class background set him apart from the rest of the children at the school, and he became aware of a sense of difference that, he says in his autobiography, he came "to hate more powerfully every year." In the initial period of his education he was also isolated to a considerable degree by his mother, who was concerned to ensure his scholastic success. The fascination with isolation—what he would call "the man alone"—that finds voice in his novels may have had its origin in these early years. He began to read voraciously; by the time he was seven he was, he reveals in *Long before Forty*, consuming "one book a day at least," and he developed a precocious interest in naval battles and military strategy. Some of the material that he devoured at that early age, such as Robert Leighton's *The Thirsty Sword* (1892) and H. Rider Haggard's novels, certainly influenced his later work, as can be seen in his depictions of the more-lurid details of physical combat.

In 1911 Smith received one of the coveted scholarships to Christ's Hospital. Eight years previously an older brother had been the last pupil at the school to win such a scholarship, but by this time their father's income was large enough that the school governors annulled the scholarship. In-

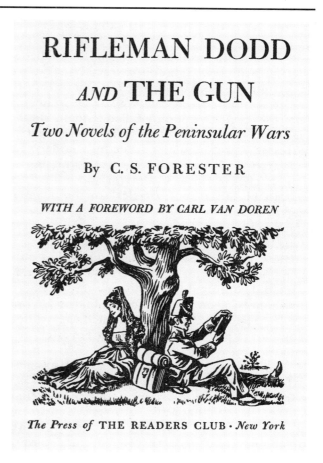

RIFLEMAN DODD
*AND* THE GUN

*Two Novels of the Peninsular Wars*

By C. S. FORESTER

*WITH A FOREWORD BY CARL VAN DOREN*

*The Press of* THE READERS CLUB · *New York*

*Title page for the American edition of two of Forester's novels about the Peninsular campaign of 1810*

stead Smith was enrolled at Alleyn's, a secondary school of excellent reputation where another older brother had been educated. In 1915, as a result of his family's change of residence, he moved to Dulwich College, a public school. At Dulwich he was a member of the Officers' Training Corps, but he was found to have a congenital heart condition that disqualified him for military service. In addition, although he was willing to serve, he was experiencing a growing distaste for the war then raging in Europe. In *Long before Forty* he writes: "there was rising inside me a terrible longing that the whole brutal, wasteful, beastly business should end." In August 1918, bereft of friends on account of the war, he went on a solitary four-week camping trip. During this time he came to terms with his rejection for military service and his changing feelings toward the war and decided, somewhat reluctantly, to enter medical school: "The profession of medicine," he writes in his autobiography, "was not entirely to my taste, but I decided that any other profession would be equally distasteful, and to that extent I was reconciled to it."

Forester found the first year of his studies at Guy's Hospital in London extremely easy: the background in science imparted to him by his earlier education served him well. The following year, however, he not only failed to maintain the pace demanded of him but also discovered that he possessed a profound ineptitude for anatomy. Increasingly unhappy with medical studies, he sought relief in riotous behavior and in the submission of "humorous articles" to the hospital magazine; he also wrote some poetry that he never intended to be published. The arrival in England of his father, whom he had not seen for six years, renewed his dedication to his studies, but only temporarily. A series of disasters in the dissecting room and continual failure in anatomy examinations impressed on him the need to find an alternative career. In 1921 he left medical school, adopted the pen name Cecil Scott Forester, and embarked on a career as an author.

His decision was not met with enthusiasm by his family, but their lack of support only acted as a goad to the neophyte writer's ambition. Reveling in the realization that he was answerable to no one but himself, he says in *Long before Forty,* he resolved "never to write a word I did not want to write; to think only of my own tastes and ideals, without a thought for those of editors or publishers." With his typical wry humor, he goes on to admit that it was "a perfectly splendid resolution to make when no single editor or publisher or member of the general public was in the least aware of my existence." He wrote his first novel in two weeks at the astonishing rate of six thousand words a day, had it typed, and sent it off to a publishing house. Within two weeks it was rejected. After three more rejections Forester began to doubt his faith in the work–which would never be published–and started another. This time he injected an element of discipline into his efforts, slashing his daily production by two-thirds; but, by his own admission, he had not yet mastered the art of fully developing his ideas prior to commencing work.

Forester would later disparage the second novel as "very bad"; nevertheless, under the title *The Paid Piper* (1924) it would become his third published book. It is a novel only in a loose sense; it is actually a series of fourteen short stories linked together by a frame. Sir William Sydenham, a government official who has recently returned to London from a term of service in Cairo, meets Mr. Cardinal, a young, educated middle-class gentleman who for some reason is posing as a Cockney street vendor. Sir William invites Cardinal home for dinner, and the latter tells the first of the stories. More stories follow on subsequent visits; most are told by Cardinal and concern his adventures in the Middle East, but Sir William and his butler, Higgins, also contribute. Toward the end of the work it is revealed that Cardinal has written a novel; his description of his writing habits and of his difficulties with publishers are clearly autobiographical.

Forester began writing his third novel as soon as the second had been dispatched to the publisher; that work, *A Pawn among Kings* (1924), about Napoleon Bonaparte's Russian campaign, was rejected twice before becoming his first published book. The pressures bearing on a man who is charged with solitary command would become a major theme in Forester's work; the novel also anticipates the psychological treatment he would give many of the central characters of his later novels. But although *A Pawn among Kings* hints at some of the strengths that would emerge in Forester's subsequent writing, there are, he says in *Long before Forty,* many "glaring weaknesses": "The motivisation [sic] had not been properly worked out at the start, with the result that I had to make use of various most unlikely changes of heart to provide a reason for various actions of the characters." The writing is frequently naive and adolescent; the plot is disjointed, and Forester has to revert to improbabilities to explain the inconsistencies. His penchant for the sensational is recognizable in his description of the suicide of Marie, a fictional mistress he creates for Napoleon: "Her white throat was burnt black with powder, and in the centre of the hideous stain was a blue spot where the bullet had entered, while her tumbled black hair was clotted together with blood and brains." On the other hand, in his stark picture of Napoleon's army retreating from Moscow, Forester captures perfectly the abject misery of defeat: "After . . . came rabble, filling up the whole road from side to side, without either order or hope, slouching along with hanging heads, not even noticing the plague-stricken skeletons which ever and anon sank down in the ditches beside them to die unremembered and uncared for."

Before *A Pawn among Kings* appeared, the work's publisher, Methuen, asked Forester to write a biography of Napoleon and paid him an advance of twenty-five pounds. It was the first money he had earned as a writer, other than a small amount he had received for some of his poetry; his first purchase with the proceeds was a pair of shoes. Forester was not particularly proud of *Napoleon and His Court* (1924), writing in his autobiography: "I do not recommend the book. The style of it was rich; one might also say gaudy."

Nevertheless, he was immediately commissioned to write another biography, *Josephine, Napoleon's Empress* (1925). He would later disparage this phase of his career as hackwork, but the advances from his publisher allowed him to live while awaiting the royalties from his first published novel. These, when they arrived, were far less than he had anticipated. To ensure a subsistence level of income, he estimated, he needed to produce at least two novels a year.

After starting and abandoning two other novels, Forester wrote the work that was to establish his reputation, the thriller *Payment Deferred* (1926), in three months. He had previously determined to write no more than a thousand words a day, but in his enthusiasm he produced the final six thousand words on the last day. It was the first work with which he felt complete satisfaction. William Marble is an alcoholic who is heavily in debt and in danger of losing his job as a bank clerk. When his recently orphaned nephew unexpectedly arrives from Australia bearing a large amount of cash, Marble sees an opportunity to solve his financial problems. He poisons the young man, buries the body in his backyard, and takes over his nephew's money. But now Marble never dares to leave his home for fear that his crime will be discovered. The disintegration of the Marble family, Marble's psychological breakdown, and an ironic twist at the end ensure retribution for the avaricious bank clerk.

The novel was not immediately accepted for publication, so Forester contracted with Methuen to write two more biographies. In *Long before Forty* he says that *Victor Emmanuel II and the Union of Italy* (1927) and *Louis XIV, King of France and Navarre* (1928) "are the poorest work I have ever done, written about subjects I know nothing about, and the sole motive for writing them was the twenty-five pounds I received on the submission of each synopsis." He supplemented his income by writing articles for trade periodicals published for such groups as goldsmiths, bus drivers, and pawnbrokers. Finally, *Payment Deferred* was accepted by John Lane. It would be adapted as a stage play in 1931 and as a motion picture (1932), with Charles Laughton as Marble in both versions. It would not be published in the United States until 1942.

In 1926 Forester married Kathleen Belcher, a sports instructor; they would have two sons, John and George. Of Forester's next novel, *Love Lies*

*French poster for the classic 1951 film based on Forester's 1935 novel*

*Dreaming* (1927), Sanford Sternlicht says: "It is a toss-up as to whether this novel or *The Shadow of the Hawk* (1928) is Forester's weakest novel." *Love Lies Dreaming* concentrates on the problems of early married life, and, as Sternlicht notes, "autobiographical elements abound": the husband, Cecil, is a novelist, and he and his wife of four years, Constance, plan to tour the French waterways, as the Foresters would do in 1928. In *Love Lies Dreaming,* however, Cecil and Constance, unlike Forester and his wife, suffer the tragedy of a stillborn son. The passage that depicts the child's funeral is full of pathos and is extremely moving. *Love Lies Dreaming* is also noteworthy for its portrayal of the class divisions in English society. Two years later, in *Brown on Resolution* (1929), Forester's description of middle-class snobbery would become savagely satiric, and in *The African Queen* (1935) he would reveal the hypocrisy that was so much a part of Britain's class system. But Forester never seems to have been able to remove himself from the conventions of that system: invariably in his novels characters from the lower social orders are inarticulate, and they often display a cringing subservience to their "betters."

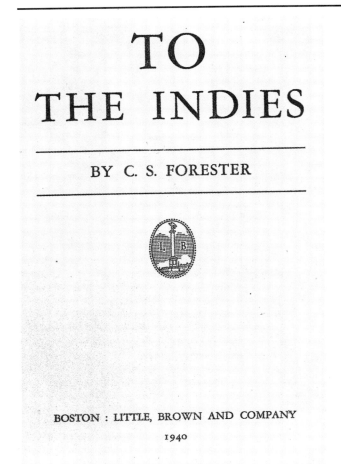

# TO
# THE INDIES

### BY C. S. FORESTER

BOSTON : LITTLE, BROWN AND COMPANY
1940

*Title page for the retitled American edition of Forester's novel*
The Earthly Paradise

Also in 1927 Forester published *The Wonderful Week*. Like *Payment Deferred,* it is a thriller, but whereas the earlier work is realistic, *The Wonderful Week* suffers from the author's apparent inability to decide whether he was writing a comic novel or a serious one. What might have been a vehicle for social satire never fulfills its promise, and the levity that characterizes the early portion is lost in an incredible plot that involves murder, discovery of a package of love letters, kidnapping, and torture. Although it is far from one of his best works, the novel again reveals Forester's ability to capture succinctly the nuances and conventions of his characters' social milieu.

*The Shadow of the Hawk* (1928; published in the United States as *The Daughter of the Hawk,* 1928) is a disjointed novel that moves from a revolution in a fictional South American country to an improbable May-December romance in England. The work was Forester's tenth published book in five years; the pace of his writing was probably

taking a toll. A vacation was called for, and Forester and his wife spent some time boating in France. The loss of a propeller through Forester's lack of navigational skills would find its way into *The African Queen;* and the intricate knowledge he acquired of the Loire River would be put to use in *Flying Colours* (1938), where familiarity with the river allows Hornblower to escape from captivity by the French.

In 1929 Forester published three books in as many genres: *Brown on Resolution* is a novel; *Nelson* is his fourth and final biography; and *The Voyage of the Annie Marble* is a travel book about the Foresters' trip across France in their dinghy named after William Marble's wife in *Payment Deferred.*

*Brown on Resolution* is Forester's first work of naval fiction. Albert Brown is the illegitimate product of a brief affair between a British naval officer and a spinster; his mother is forced to conceal the circumstances of his conception, giving Forester an opportunity to deliver a scathing commentary on English lower-middle-class hypocrisy. Brown grows up and joins the navy; during World War I his ship is sunk by the German cruiser *Ziethen,* and he is captured. When the *Ziethen* puts into Resolution Island for repairs, Brown escapes, hides in the jungle, and systematically picks off members of the crew. He is finally killed, but his actions have delayed the departure of the *Ziethen* long enough for two English vessels to arrive and sink it. Ironically, one of the English ships is commanded by Brown's father, who was never aware that his affair so many years before had resulted in the birth of a son. Forester's cynicism about war, an attitude that he never seemed to reconcile with his need to write about military heroics, emerges in the novel. His observations on civilian ingratitude to military personnel are reminiscent of Rudyard Kipling's poem "Tommy": "It had been a vain, frantic sacrifice, part of the price the Navy must pay for the glory of keeping the bellies of an unthinking population charged with their accustomed meat and bread." *Brown on Resolution* was twice adapted for the screen: as *Born for Glory* in 1935 and as *Sailor of the King* in 1953.

The success of *The Voyage of the Annie Marble* led Forester's publisher to commission him to undertake a similar trip to Germany; *The Annie Marble in Germany* was published in 1930. That same year Forester published a novel, a thriller titled *Plain Murder.* Charles Morris is in danger of losing his job as a clerk in an advertising company if his scheme to profit from a secret commission is discovered by his superior. He coerces two fellow employees to become accomplices in the superior's murder. The novel traces the psychological changes in all three, but mainly in Morris. When one of the accomplices shows signs of wanting to confess, Morris murders him by tampering with his motorcycle so that it will crash. Morris's infatuation with the daughter of the agency's owner leads him to plot the murder of his own wife. But Forester cannot permit murder to go unpunished, even if it can go undetected. Thus, as Morris attempts to murder his wife, he is killed by his other accomplice. Whereas, according to Sternlicht, "The end of *Plain Murder,* unlike that of the far superior *Payment Deferred,* lets the reader down," the *Times Literary Supplement* (17 August 1962), which mentions *Plain Murder* in the course of a review of *Hornblower and the Hotspur* (1962), describes the earlier work as "one of the most chilling analyses of a criminal psychopath in modern fiction."

Forester drew on his own experience for his next novel, *Two-and-Twenty* (1931). Its central character is a poor but poetically inclined medical student, Cecil M. Leigh, who shares with the author both his first name and an ineptitude for anatomy. Following the successful publication of two epic poems about the British navy, he gives up writing to return to medical school and the promise of a distinguished future.

In 1932, with the success of the film version of *Payment Deferred,* Forester was lured to Hollywood to write for the motion-picture industry. He moved his family to California, eventually settling in the San Francisco area, although he retained his British citizenship and spent several months of each year in England. His novel *Death to the French* (1932)—retitled "Rifleman Dodd" when it was published in the United States in 1942—deals with the adventures of a British rifleman, Matthew Dodd, who finds himself separated from his unit following a retreat by Arthur Wellesley, first Duke of Wellington, during the Peninsular campaign in 1810. Like *Brown on Resolution,* this novel includes criticism of the British class system and has an ironic conclusion.

Forester remained with the Peninsular War as the context for his next novel, *The Gun* (1933), in which a cannon, rather than a conventional human protagonist, plays the central role. The gun, abandoned by the Spanish army, is commandeered by Spanish guerrillas who use it against the French. The novel would be filmed as *The Pride and the Passion* (1957), starring Cary Grant, Frank Sinatra, and Sophia Loren. In 1934 Forester collaborated with Carl E. Bechhofer Roberts on a play, *Nurse Cavell,* which was produced in London.

*Frontispiece by N. C. Wyeth for the omnibus American edition of Forester's first three Horatio Hornblower novels*

Temporarily abandoning the historical novel in favor of a contemporary setting, Forester followed *The Gun* with *The Peacemaker* (1934). Edward Pethwick, an English schoolmaster who is also a brilliant mathematician, has invented a machine that has a contramagnetic effect. Pethwick falls in love with his headmaster's daughter, who is a pacifist; his affection is reciprocated, but the affair is thwarted by Pethwick's alcoholic wife. Pethwick employs his invention to paralyze traffic in London in an effort to influence the British government to disarm. Once more, Forester concludes the novel with a heavy irony. The *Times Literary Supplement* review of *Hornblower and the Hotspur* describes *The Peacemaker* as "one of his least successful [books] . . . an unusual concession on the author's part to the anxieties and problems of the 1930's."

The work was followed by one of Forester's greatest successes. In 1934, while he was in England, his literary agent reported that a London newspaper was intending to publish serialized novels to run in five parts each Monday through Friday. During his train ride home that evening Forester began to develop a plot; *The African Queen* was the result. In a 1952 interview with Harvey Breit, Forester said: "If you've read the original script I daresay you may be able to detect the five climaxes. Later I expanded it to the novel."

*The African Queen* takes its title from a battered river launch captained by a Cockney engineer, Charlie Allnutt, that ferries supplies to and from mining companies in Belgian-colonized Africa. The boat becomes the vehicle for an improbable attack on a German ship, the *Königin Luise*, that is stationed on Lake Wittlesbach to maintain German sovereignty in the area. The ship can only be reached by navigating the rapids and deltas of the Ulanga and Bora Rivers. Allnutt and Rose Sayer, the sister of a recently deceased missionary, make the trip, overcoming seemingly insurmountable obstacles and becoming lovers on the way. The conclusion, as was becoming a commonplace by then in Forester's work, is attended with intense irony and several surprises.

Many themes and ideas that had shown themselves in embryonic form in Forester's earlier works are more clearly developed here. Allnutt is unashamedly portrayed as an inarticulate member of Britain's lower classes, whose function is to obey his social superiors. In an episode in which Allnutt fashions a complete propeller while straightening a twisted shaft it is, significantly, the lower-middle-class Rose who is the driving force behind the repair, with the working-class Allnutt doing his mistress's bidding. But the division between the two is not so wide as to prevent a relationship between them even if Forester cannot reconcile himself to bless it with full legal and religious sanction at the novel's conclusion. Rose, as befits her background, is initially devout and totally proper; her veil of propriety is gradually removed, however, and her repression is replaced by joy as she exults in untrammeled sexual license with Allnutt. *The African Queen* is an excellent adventure story; in 1951 it was made into a highly successful film, directed by John Huston, with a screenplay by James Agee and starring Humphrey Bogart (who won an Academy Award) as Charlie and Katharine Hepburn as Rose. It was also produced as a television special on CBS on 18 March 1977, starring Warren Oates and Mariette Hartley.

In 1936 Forester published both an instructional manual on puppeteering, *Marionettes at Home,* and one of his most powerful novels, *The General.* Sternlicht asserts that "*The General* is a pacifist work," but this assessment is open to question: in the novel's criticism of the outmoded tactics that led to the slaughter of British soldiers in the trenches of France and Belgium during World War I there is an implied endorsement of more-efficient methods of waging war. The narrator comments: "Men without imagination were neces-

sary to execute a military policy devoid of imagination, devised by a man without imagination." Wry and ironic as ever, Forester shows the successful career of Lt. Gen. Sir Herbert Curzon to be the result of a combination of luck and political maneuvering. The general is to be pitied; emotionally sterile, he is unable to react to the news of the stillbirth of his son, which reaches him in the midst of the carnage at Loos. Symbolically, this event represents the end of the line for the traditional upper-class British officer corps.

It was in 1937 that Forester created the character with whom he would forever be inextricably linked, but the genesis of Horatio Hornblower had occurred some ten years earlier when Forester purchased three volumes of the *Naval Chronicle,* published between 1790 and 1820, for his library on the *Annie Marble.* Through his reading of this material he acquired an appreciation for and knowledge of naval life in the late eighteenth and early nineteenth centuries. The knowledge lay dormant until, dissatisfied with his work in Hollywood, he embarked in 1937 as a passenger on the Swedish merchant ship *Margaret Johnson,* which was bound for various Central American ports and eventually for England. During the six-week voyage Forester began to develop the character of Hornblower and some of the other personages who would eventually appear in the series.

The first Hornblower novel, published in England in 1937 as *The Happy Return* and in the United States the same year as *Beat to Quarters,* does not depict the beginning of Hornblower's career. The reason is that Forester did not write the work with the intention of writing a series of novels around his newly created character. It was only after his return from covering the Spanish civil war for *The New York Times* in 1937—his first direct experience of war—that he conceived the idea of depicting Hornblower's prior and subsequent career. In *The Happy Return* Forester maintains the elitist sympathies he had established in his earlier works. While Hornblower's origins are nonaristocratic—his father was a doctor, and references to Hornblower's poverty will become commonplace in the novels—Forester ensures that the class division between officer and common seaman is never forgotten. He writes that the crew of Hornblower's ship, the *Lydia,* "set all the store by forms and ceremonies to be expected of the uneducated." Hornblower is unapproachable and introspective, but he displays a paternal, if somewhat condescending, attitude toward his crew.

Forester has moved away from the psychological realism of his portrayal of General Curzon

*Gregory Peck, in costume as Hornblower, and the director Raoul Walsh on the set of the 1951 film* Captain Horatio Hornblower

and has created a hero. Hornblower does have human frailties: in *The Happy Return* Lady Barbara Wellesley, a fictitious sister of the duke of Wellington, takes passage in his ship, and she and Hornblower experience a mutual attraction. But Hornblower is married, and, presented with the opportunity to consummate the affair, he rejects Lady Barbara's advances. Hornblower is also an unabashed reactionary: "There was a madman called Wordsworth of whose revolutionary opinions in literature Hornblower had heard with vague horror." *The Happy Return* takes place between June and October 1808 and concerns Hornblower's encounter with El Supremo, a South American rebel with delusions of grandeur. Their relationship begins as one of cooperation, born of the necessity to thwart Spanish influence in the area, but leads to hostility when Spain becomes allied with Britain.

The second Hornblower novel, *A Ship of the Line* (1938), is set in the period May to October 1810. Lady Barbara has married the aging Rear Adm. Sir Percy Leighton, and Hornblower and his new ship, the *Sutherland,* have been assigned to Leighton's command. After a series of escapades on sea and on land, at the end of the book Horn-

blower surrenders to the French. In the next novel, *Flying Colours,* he escapes, makes his way down the Loire to the sea, is acquitted at a court-martial on his return to England, and receives a knighthood from the prince regent. His wife, Maria, dies giving birth to a son; Lady Barbara, by this time a widow, looks after the boy, and the clear inference at the tale's conclusion is that she and Hornblower will marry.

In 1938 Forester returned to Europe as a correspondent for *The New York Times,* witnessing the German annexation of Czechoslovakia between September of that year and the spring of 1939. In 1939 the three Hornblower novels were collected in Britain as *Captain Hornblower, R.N.* and in the United States as *Captain Horatio Hornblower;* they would be filmed under the latter title in 1951, with Gregory Peck as Hornblower and Virginia Mayo as Lady Barbara. In 1940 Forester went to work for the British Ministry of Information, producing propaganda material. His duties gave him the opportunity to travel on British warships.

The novel *The Earthly Paradise* (1940; published in the United States as *To the Indies,* 1940) is set against the background of Christopher Columbus's third voyage to the New World in 1498; For-

C. S. FORESTER

★

The Good
Shepherd

London
MICHAEL JOSEPH

*Title page for Forester's novel about an American naval commander in World War II*

ester weaves swashbuckling fiction into an obviously well-researched context of historical fact. Peter Monro Jack in *The New York Times Book Review* (28 July 1940) called it "an admirable tale, realistic and romantic by turns, adventurous and ingenious." A year later *The Captain from Connecticut* was published; set during the War of 1812, the novel moves from the New Jersey coast to the Caribbean. The plot, especially in the last half of the novel, is somewhat fantastic, and the book received mixed reviews. The title character, Josiah Peabody, is something of an American version of Hornblower, but Forester did not go on to write an American saga paralleling the emerging Hornblower series.

Forester's next novel, set during World War II, was considerably more accomplished. *The Ship* (1943) follows the British warship H.M.S. *Artemis* as it escorts a convoy to the besieged island of Malta. Forester intersperses descriptions of action with the personal histories of various crew members; despite Forester's propensity to overwrite, it is by far one of his best works.

In the summer of 1943 Forester was on board the U.S.S. *Tennessee,* observing the blockade of Japanese positions in the Aleutian Islands, when he began to experience severe pains in his legs. At first he put the feeling down to the chill of the Bering Sea, but the symptoms grew worse after he returned to California. He was finally diagnosed with arteriosclerosis of the legs, an incurable and crippling disease. Although friends thought that he should retire, Forester's habit of writing a thousand words a day helped him to reconcile himself to his situation. The following year his marriage of eighteen years ended in divorce.

The next novel in the Hornblower series, *The Commodore* (1945; published in the United States as *Commodore Hornblower,* 1945), is set in 1812, but Forester—cognizant of his large American readership—places Hornblower in the Baltic rather than having him engage in battle against the United States. The work appeared first as a serial in *The Saturday Evening Post,* and controversy arose over an episode in which Hornblower engages in a brief affair with a Russian countess—the first fictional depiction of adultery in the magazine's history. It should be noted that it is a combination of the countess's wiles and strong wine that ensure his seduction and that he suffers a sort of punishment for his infidelity in that he contracts typhus from being bitten by one of the fleas that infest the court of the Russian émigrés. The book concludes with Hornblower in the grips of delirium.

In *Lord Hornblower* (1946) Forester's hero is placed in charge of the city of Bordeaux, which has defected from Napoleon's cause. He again engages in an adulterous affair—this time with Marie de Graçay, whom he had met in *Flying Colours.* Forester visits retribution on Hornblower's latest paramour by having her shot when she and Hornblower are captured by the French. This was to have been the last of the series, and *The Saturday Evening Post* of 7 July 1946 so informed its readers. In that article Forester reflects on the circumstances surrounding the book's completion in 1945. He was on board H.M.S. *Swiftsure* in Tokyo Bay; the novel having been put aside for some time, Forester picked up the manuscript and began to write the final pages. Looking out over the bay, he could see the evidence of the subjugation of Adolf Hitler's final ally; since Napoleon had been, for him, a surrogate for Hitler, Forester decided that it was time to depict the emperor's final defeat at Waterloo and to bring the Hornblower saga to an end.

In 1947 Forester married Dorothy Ellen Foster; the next year he suffered a severe heart attack. As an aid to recuperation he began writing *Mr. Midshipman Hornblower* (1950). In the meantime his publisher brought out *The Sky and the Forest* (1948), a somber, pessimistic work about the slave trade in central Africa in the mid nineteenth century that is also an allegorical criticism of imperialist ideology.

With *Mr. Midshipman Hornblower,* which is less a novel than a collection of loosely connected short stories, Forester began to fill in the details of his hero's origins. At the end the eighteen-year-old Hornblower is promoted to lieutenant, despite never having passed the examination for the rank, as a reward for meritorious service.

In *Randall and the River of Time* (1950) Forester returns to World War I. A young army officer, Charles Randall, suggests improvements in a parachute flare; his promising postwar future as an inventor is destroyed, however, when he kills his wife's lover. He is acquitted of the murder charge, and the novel ends with his considering immigration to the United States. Forester's vision in this novel, as in *The Sky and the Forest,* is dark and deterministic—at opposite poles from the optimism that characterizes the Hornblower stories.

The next novel in that series, *Lieutenant Hornblower* (1952), set in 1803, continues the story of the officer's early naval career. Forester includes Hornblower's marriage to Maria, his promotion to commander, his loss of that rank as a result of the peace with France, and then, with the renewed outbreak of hostilities, his promotion again to commander. This novel was followed in 1953 by *Hornblower and the Atropos,* set in 1805. Hornblower is now an extremely junior captain—"the six hundred and first Captain out of the six hundred and two on the list," as he morosely reflects. At the beginning of the novel he is put in charge of the waterborne funeral procession that carries the body of Admiral Nelson down the Thames to St. Paul's Cathedral. Forester invests the episode with an irreverent humor that threatens to turn into burlesque: the barge carrying the body almost sinks, and Hornblower's watch temporarily becomes attached to the coffin. The conclusion of the novel, in which Hornblower's two children die of smallpox, stands in stark contrast to the comedic opening. In the year in which this novel was published Forester was offered the honor of being named a Commander of the British Empire; feeling that he did not deserve such recognition, he declined to accept.

Also in 1953 Forester published a book for older children, *The Barbary Pirates.* The following year he produced a collection of short stories, *The Nightmare,* that reflects the legacy of the Nazi death camps. The final story in the collection, "The Wandering Gentile," is a fantasy in which the narrator meets Hitler and Eva Braun in America after the war. His next novel, *The Good Shepherd* (1955), is about an American commander, George Krause, who is trying to protect a convoy from German submarines in 1943. Of all of Forester's books, this is the most intense study of the individual charged with solitary responsibility—"the man alone." In contrast to *The Ship,* in which the personal backgrounds of many of the crew members are examined, *The Good Shepherd* concentrates entirely on Krause.

Forester followed *The Good Shepherd* with a work of nonfiction, *The Age of Fighting Sail: The Story of the Naval War of 1812* (1956), published in England simply as *The Naval War of 1812* (1957). His next novel, *Hornblower in the West Indies* (1958), does not take up where *Hornblower and the Atropos* ended but instead leaps ahead to the 1820s, after the conclusion of *Lord Hornblower.* Hornblower is promoted to rear admiral and thwarts an attempt to free Napoleon from Saint Helena. Forester does not neglect domestic details in this story: Hornblower, hitherto not sure of the constancy of his wife Barbara's feelings, is finally convinced of her love.

Commissioned to write the screenplay for the motion picture *Sink the Bismarck!* (1960), about the British navy's hunt for and destruction of the German warship, Forester converted the resulting script into a serial for *The Saturday Evening Post* in 1959; the book version, titled *Hunting the Bismarck* in England and *The Last Nine Days of the Bismarck* in the United States, followed the same year. (The screenplay actually used for the motion picture was written by Edmund H. North.) It was not a critical success; the research was shallow, and the book's conversion from the screenplay was transparent. It was, however, admittedly written as an adventure story and not as a scholarly treatment of one of the major episodes of World War II, and Forester's readers were as pleased with the result as the reviewers were critical. *Hunting the Bismarck* was Forester's sole publication in 1959.

The jigsaw puzzle that was Hornblower's career was almost complete; the missing piece concerned his service in the rank of commander, which would result in his being made captain of the *Atropos*. In 1962 Forester published *Hornblower and the Hotspur* to account for the missing years. The final complete work in the series, it narrates in episodic form Hornblower's blockading duties off the French coast between 1803 and 1805. Unfettered by the political intrigues with which he had frequently been burdened previously, the commander is able to demonstrate his skill in running his ship. As Sternlicht writes, "Hornblower was at his best in single-ship, Man Alone situations. Commanding the *Hotspur* brought out the finest in Hornblower and, indeed, the best in Forester."

In 1962 Forester suffered another heart attack. Two years later he published *The Hornblower Companion,* which describes the methodology that he followed in writing the works and provides insights into Hornblower's conception and development. The book includes maps of the areas where the Hornblower saga takes place. It was the last work to be published in Forester's lifetime: he died on 2 April 1966. He had been paralyzed since suffering a stroke in September 1964 while writing *Hornblower and the Crisis* (1967). That novel, in which Hornblower participates in the Battle of Trafalgar, was published posthumously, as were

Forester's autobiography and two books of short stories: *The Man in the Yellow Raft* (1969) and *Gold from Crete* (1970).

Forester will be remembered as a writer of popular fiction. He could grasp the imagination of the public, providing it with a hero whose qualities, while stereotypically British, could flourish in the American literary market. It is surprising that so little critical or scholarly interest has been shown in the work of so prolific and socially conscious a writer. Much research still needs to be done, especially regarding his government assignments during World War II and his life during the period in which he wrote *The Commodore*.

**Interviews:**

"The Last of Hornblower," *Saturday Evening Post,* 219 (6 July 1946): 4;

Harvey Breit, "Talk with C. S. Forester," *New York Times Book Review,* 6 April 1952, p. 16.

**References:**

C. Northcote Parkinson, *The Life and Times of Horatio Hornblower* (Boston: Little, Brown, 1971);

Sanford Sternlicht, *C. S. Forester* (New York: Twayne, 1981).

# Elizabeth Goudge

*(24 April 1900 – 1 April 1984)*

P. Joan Smith
*McMaster University*

BOOKS: *The Fairies' Baby and Other Stories* (Amersham: Morland / London: Foyle, 1919);

*Island Magic* (London: Duckworth, 1934; New York: Coward-McCann, 1934);

*The Middle Window* (London: Duckworth, 1935; New York: Coward-McCann, 1939);

*A City of Bells* (London: Duckworth, 1936; New York: Coward-McCann, 1936);

*A Pedlar's Pack, and Other Stories* (London: Duckworth, 1937; New York: Coward-McCann, 1937);

*Towers in the Mist* (London: Duckworth, 1938; New York: Coward-McCann, 1938);

*Three Plays: Suomi, The Brontës of Haworth, Fanny Burney* (London: Duckworth, 1939);

*Sister of the Angels: A Christmas Story* (London: Duckworth, 1939; New York: Coward-McCann, 1939);

*The Bird in the Tree* (London: Duckworth, 1940; New York: Coward-McCann, 1940);

*Smoky-House* (London: Duckworth, 1940; New York: Coward-McCann, 1940);

*The Golden Skylark, and Other Stories* (London: Duckworth, 1941; New York: Coward-McCann, 1941);

*The Well of the Star* (New York: Coward-McCann, 1941);

*The Castle on the Hill* (London: Duckworth, 1942; New York: Coward-McCann, 1942);

*Henrietta's House* (London: University of London Press/Hodder & Stoughton, 1942); republished as *The Blue Hills* (New York: Coward-McCann, 1942);

*The Ikon on the Wall, and Other Stories* (London: Duckworth, 1943);

*Green Dolphin Country* (London: Hodder & Stoughton, 1944); republished as *Green Dolphin Street* (New York: Coward-McCann, 1944);

*The Elizabeth Goudge Reader,* edited by Rose Dobbs (New York: Coward-McCann, 1946); republished as *At the Sign of the Dolphin: An Elizabeth*

*Elizabeth Goudge*

*Goudge Anthology* (London: Hodder & Stoughton, 1947);

*The Little White Horse* (London: University of London Press, 1946; New York: Coward-McCann, 1947);

*Songs and Verses* (London: Duckworth, 1947; New York: Coward-McCann, 1948);

*The Herb of Grace* (London: Hodder & Stoughton, 1948); republished as *Pilgrim's Inn* (New York: Coward-McCann, 1948);

*Make-Believe* (London: Duckworth, 1949);

*Gentian Hill* (London: Hodder & Stoughton, 1949; New York: Coward-McCann, 1949);

*The Reward of Faith, and Other Stories* (London: Duckworth, 1950; New York: Coward-McCann, 1951);

*God So Loved the World: A Life of Christ* (London: Hodder & Stoughton, 1951; New York: Coward-McCann, 1951);

*The Valley of Song* (London: University of London Press, 1951; New York: Coward-McCann, 1952);

*White Wings: Collected Short Stories* (London: Duckworth, 1952);

*The Heart of the Family* (London: Hodder & Stoughton, 1953; New York: Coward-McCann, 1953);

*The Rosemary Tree* (London: Hodder & Stoughton, 1956; New York: Coward-McCann, 1956);

*The White Witch* (London: Hodder & Stoughton, 1958; New York: Coward-McCann, 1958);

*Saint Francis of Assisi* (London: Duckworth, 1959); republished as *My God and My All: The Life of St. Francis of Assisi* (New York: Coward-McCann, 1959);

*The Dean's Watch* (London: Hodder & Stoughton, 1960; New York: Coward-McCann, 1960);

*The Scent of Water* (London: Hodder & Stoughton, 1963; New York: Coward-McCann, 1963);

*Linnets and Valerians* (Leicester: Brockhampton Press, 1964; New York: Coward-McCann, 1964);

*The Chapel of the Blessed Virgin Mary, Buckler's Hard, Beaulieu* (Beaulieu: Privately printed, 1966);

*A Christmas Book* (London: Hodder & Stoughton, 1967; New York: Coward-McCann, 1967);

*I Saw Three Ships* (Leicester: Brockhampton Press, 1969; New York: Coward-McCann, 1969);

*The Child from the Sea* (London: Hodder & Stoughton, 1970; New York: Coward-McCann, 1970);

*The Lost Angel: Stories* (London: Hodder & Stoughton, 1971; New York: Coward, McCann & Geoghegan, 1971);

*The Joy of the Snow: An Autobiography* (London: Hodder & Stoughton, 1974; New York: Coward, McCann & Geoghegan, 1974).

**Collections:** *The Eliots of Damerosehay* (London: Hodder & Stoughton, 1957)–comprises *The Bird in the Tree, The Herb of Grace,* and *The Heart of the Family;*

*Three Cities of Bells: Wells, Oxford, Ely; Containing in One Volume Three Famous Cathedral Novels* (London: Hodder & Stoughton, 1965)–comprises *A City of Bells, Towers in the Mist,* and *The Dean's Watch;*

*The Ten Gifts: An Elizabeth Goudge Anthology,* edited by Mary Baldwin (London: Hodder & Stoughton, 1969; New York: Coward-McCann, 1969);

*Pattern of People: An Elizabeth Goudge Anthology,* edited by Muriel Grainger (London: Hodder & Stoughton, 1978; New York: Coward, McCann & Geoghegan, 1979).

PLAY PRODUCTIONS: *The Brontës of Haworth,* London, Charta Theatre, October 1932;

*Joy Will Come Back,* London, Arts Theatre, 21 March 1937;

*Suomi,* London, Cambridge Theatre, 29 May 1938;

*Fanny Burney,* Oldham, Lancashire, 1949.

OTHER: *A Book of Comfort: An Anthology,* edited by Goudge (London: M. Joseph, 1964; New York: Coward-McCann, 1964);

*A Diary of Prayer,* compiled by Goudge (London: Hodder & Stoughton, 1966; New York: Coward-McCann, 1966);

*A Book of Peace: An Anthology,* edited by Goudge (London: M. Joseph, 1967; New York: Coward-McCann, 1968);

*A Book of Faith,* edited by Goudge (London: Hodder & Stoughton, 1976; New York: Coward, McCann & Geoghegan, 1976).

The romantic novels of Elizabeth Goudge acquired an enormous readership during her lifetime, and her name appeared regularly on best-seller lists. She also wrote plays, short stories, children's fiction, biographies, and an autobiography, and she edited anthologies. Her initial popularity can be attributed in part to the timeliness of her idealism during World War II and the postwar years. However, though she herself disclaimed any scholarly aspirations, the maturity of intellect and spirit that informs her romantic imagination and the sheer artistry of her prose could account for the solidity of her enduring reputation.

Elizabeth de Beauchamp Goudge (pronounced "Goozsh") was born on 24 April 1900 in Wells, Somerset, England, the only child of Henry Leighton Goudge and Ida de Beauchamp (Collenette) Goudge. At the time of her birth her father was vice principal of the theological college at Wells Cathedral. Her mother came from a prominent French family on the island of Guernsey, and during her childhood Elizabeth visited her grandparents there annually. Her mother was chronically sick following Elizabeth's birth but retained her inherited gift for storytelling, particularly the legends of the Channel Islands. When Elizabeth was eleven years old, the family moved to Ely because her father was appointed a canon at the cathedral. The childhood influences of her father's theological intellect and her mother's pagan imagination, the Guernsey holidays, and the precincts of the ancient cathedrals in which she lived could well account for Goudge's best-known literary characteristics: her realistic understanding of human nature and experience, her fervent moral philosophy, her childlike imagination and appreciation of nature, and her mystical intuition and sense of history.

Goudge was educated at home until the outbreak of World War I when she was sent to Grassendale School, Southbourne, Hampshire. During her childhood she wrote poems, fairy stories, and other short pieces. At the age of nineteen she was sent to the Reading University School of Art for two years, and she made her first attempt to write professionally, but *The Fairies' Baby and Other Stories* (1919) failed to sell. She then spent ten years, from 1922 to 1932, writing part-time and teaching design and applied art at home, first in Ely and later in Oxford, where her father was appointed Regius Professor of Divinity. She never married. In 1932 she moved with her ailing mother away from the detrimental confines of the city to a seaside bungalow at Barton, in Hampshire, where she started writing in earnest.

After attending her first William Shakespeare play with her father during her school days, she developed a passion for the theater and the desire to be a playwright. In 1932 her first play, *The Brontës of Haworth,* was performed on a Sunday night in London. Although single performances of three more plays followed in 1937, 1938, and 1949, drama was not her forte, and she was advised to try writing novels instead. The move with her mother to Barton forced her to abandon teaching and start writing full-time, and her first novel was published two years later when she was thirty-four years old.

Set on the island of Guernsey in the nineteenth century, *Island Magic* (1934) explores the emotional upheavals of an island farming family—Andre and Rachel du Frocq and their five children—whose traditional way of life is threatened by financial loss and the presence of a mysterious stranger whom Andre has rescued from a shipwreck. The world-weary traveler lives with the family under an assumed name. Affected by the place as much as by the people, he reveals that he is Andre's lost brother, Jean de Frocq. His final actions not only save the family but also reach out to the wider community. The beauty of the island surrounds and finally transcends the human gains and losses. Drawing on the island folklore and her own childhood memories, Goudge allowed her mystical sensibility to permeate her descriptions of coastal and farm landscapes and the history and details of island family life. Her depiction of the emotional pain of personal renunciation undertaken for the long-term good of the community anticipates a literary preoccupation that would endure throughout her career.

The novel attracted attention from both sides of the Atlantic, and in her autobiography, *The Joy of the Snow* (1974), Goudge referred to it as "the first stepping stone." The second came when the literary agent Nancy Pearn commissioned her to write short stories for *Strand* magazine, and another agent, David Higham, subsequently advised her to write short stories for a living while building up a reputation with her books. For more than thirty years her stories were to appear most frequently in *The Woman's Home Companion, The Ladies' Home Journal, Good Housekeeping,* and *McCall's.* Many were to be published as collections. At least three of her later novels also were serialized in *The Ladies' Home Journal.*

Able to afford to take vacations, Goudge went hiking with a friend in the Lake District; subsequently, she was to take vacations in Scotland, north Wales, and Norway. Her second novel, *The Middle Window* (1935), is about a modern English girl, Judy Cameron, on a vacation in Scotland with her parents and fiancé. Judy feels strangely at home in the new surroundings and recognizes not only the people, the places, and the old house they are renting, but also the local young laird. One night she dreams of another, earlier Judith, who lost the husband she loved in the Jacobite rebellion of 1745. Surprising everyone, the modern Judy breaks her engagement to her conventional English fiancé in favor of remaining in Scotland with the laird.

The theme of the novel reflects Goudge's belief in the presence of the past, echoing an incident that had recurred in her home in Ely. On moonlit nights an image appeared on a bedroom wall, as if the light were shining through a stained-glass window; a suggested explanation was that a century or more previously there had been such a window instead of the plain one that then existed.

The first American edition of *The Middle Window* was published in 1939, and critical response was mixed: on 19 March 1939 Jane Spence Southron said in *The New York Times,* "It is a book that you will read a second time—and again and again," while "A.L.," the critic for *The Saturday Review of Literature* (8 April 1939), said, "It is stereotyped, sentimental romance." The latter was to become the stereotypical criticism of Goudge's work by her detractors. Goudge claimed in her autobiography that she wrote not to please critics, but herself and her readers: "We want . . . to make contact with those who

GREEN *Dolphin* STREET

ELIZABETH GOUDGE

*Binding for the American edition of Goudge's novel about two sisters in love with the same man*

ary 1937), was smitten, saying that the novel was "brimful of the same spirit that breathes in the joyfulest of Shakespeare's lyrics" and "entirely at variance with that aspect of twentieth-century realism which sees and depicts only the sordid and tragic."

With *Towers in the Mist* (1938) Goudge's sense of tradition digs deeper: this novel is set in Elizabethan Oxford, where the young Walter Raleigh and Philip Sidney are students. The daily life of Canon Gervas Leigh of Christ Church and his family of eight motherless children provides the backdrop for two stories of young love and, incidentally, for a visit to the university from Queen Elizabeth.

In *The New York Times* (22 May 1938) Southron claimed that the novel was "shot through with deeper and richer meaning" than its predecessor. The year of publication is significant: already Goudge's rising fame could be attributed in part to the salutary effect of her fiction on the prewar anxieties of her readers. In *The Saturday Review of Literature* (28 May 1938) Frances Woodward suggested that novelists wishing to escape from contemporary England should emulate Goudge: "For she does not try to make the reign of George Sixth a cozy, roselit place, but goes straight back to an earlier England, which may have been as colorful and gay as she paints it."

Goudge was by no means a scholar; it was literary skill that made her historical novels work. As "So-So," the reviewer for *The New Yorker* (21 May 1938), said: "Miss Goudge puts on an impressive show of learning about the sixteenth century, but she handles her local color with a charm and deftness that makes you refuse to care whether or not it is authentic." Well aware of her limitations, Goudge told in her autobiography how she and her father, both writers, found reading each other's books difficult: "He because he had too much intellect for mine and I because I had too little for his." After reading *Towers in the Mist* he told her, "You have a wonderful gift. . . . You can make a very little knowledge go such a long way." Goudge was fast developing this gift, for by now she had also published her first collection of short stories, *A Pedlar's Pack, and Other Stories* (1937).

In the late 1930s anxiety over the illnesses of her mother and then of her father caused Goudge to suffer a nervous breakdown. She refers to depression and melancholia as "the skeleton in the family cupboard." Her father died in the spring of 1939, and it was some time before she was able to write again.

In the interim, at the outbreak of World War II *Sister of the Angels: A Christmas Story* (1939) was published. Southron said in *The New York Times* (29 Oc-

think as we do. . . . Some of my readers have intellects that make me tremble with awe. They read me, I imagine, because of this likemindedness that has nothing to do with intellect."

Goudge's sense of history came to the fore in the two novels that followed. The first, *A City of Bells* (1936), is set in fictional Torminster (Wells) at the end of the Boer War. It tells of burnt-out Jocelyn Irvin, grandson of the saintly Canon Fordyce, opening a bookshop in an old house in the city. His fascination with the writings of Ferranti, a former occupant of the house, leads him to finish and produce a play written by Ferranti; the experience restores not only Jocelyn but also, among others, the canon's adopted grandchild, the charming Henrietta.

The theme of self-renunciation in this novel takes the form of artistic detachment. The protagonist, influenced by the spirit of the ancient cathedral city and its inhabitants, loses himself in the earlier literature; he creates a new work and is in turn recreated along with the community. Southron, reviewing the work for *The New York Times* (28 Febru-

tober 1939) that reading this "flawlessly lovely" children's book after a war bulletin was "to slip from Hades into a happy garden." While the world was in its collective Hades, Goudge was in her own. She and her mother, now considerably lacking in funds, were forced to move their permanent home from Oxford to the Barton bungalow. Unable to settle, they took a holiday in Devonshire and decided to relocate to the village of Westerland, near Paignton. Providence Cottage was nestled against a hill covered with gentians, with two nearby castles (one apparently haunted), a deep well, and a particular tree to nurture the imagination. Goudge shut herself in the bedroom and took up the novel discarded after her father's death. She strove to recapture the spirit of the mists and marshes of the Hampshire coastal region where she had been at boarding school, but she felt she "was living in another age and another time and that [the imagined places she had remembered] belonged to a lost century." At one point reaching deadlock, she prayed she might dream the rest of the book, and she did.

*The Bird in the Tree* (1940) was to be the first of three novels dealing with the contemporary Eliot family. It tells how, as a boy, David Eliot lost his parents in World War I and grew up under the wing of his grandmother, Lucilla Eliot, the family matriarch. She and her extended family live in the security and beauty of the restored old home of Damerosehay on the marshy Hampshire coast. Years later David falls in love with Nadine, the divorced wife of his uncle George, threatening the unique community he had helped to create. Lucilla, Nadine's children, and even the ancestral occupants of the old house and the land itself unite against the lovers. The couple choose to renounce their love in a positive act that restores the community.

This time Goudge provides a contemporary setting for the theme of personal renunciation. She admits, even stresses, the emotional truth of the couple's love affair yet defends the deeper integrity of traditional morality in the face of modern relative values. This defense was to remain a major concern in her fiction. One critic commented in *Books* (26 May 1940) that "It is possible for a pleasantly written novel, if it tells the truth, to lift up the spirits and make them light. So, in an hour of sinking spirits, does this story." Goudge's refusal to capitulate to the pressures of modernism no doubt contributed to her popularity during the war years and their aftermath and possibly influenced the endurance of her work. In relief at the completion of the novel, she then wrote "a light-hearted little children's book," *Smoky-House* (1940), and with these two books she earned enough to pay for Providence Cottage.

There followed a productive period induced partly by financial need and partly by the inspiration she gained from the surrounding Devonshire countryside. In her autobiography Goudge also admits that for years she worked to combat a "visiting demon" who brought darkness and was determined she should not write books. Thus, in 1941 she published another collection of short stories and a children's story, and in 1942 her sixth novel, *The Castle on the Hill*. A wartime story that reflects the unusual social situations imposed on the English people during the 1940s, *The Castle on the Hill* is set in the ancestral home of Charles Birley, who resides there with his prim housekeeper, Mrs. Brown. His sons return home; they have little in common, Richard being an airman while Stephen is a pacifist. The party grows to include Jo Isaacson, a professional musician turned street entertainer, and two young Cockney evacuees, Moppet and Poppet. The latter are two of Goudge's most unforgettable childhood portraits.

Though *The Castle on the Hill* was to be her first best-seller in the United States, the reviews were ambivalent. Southron in *The New York Times* (3 May 1942) considered the novel a victim of the wartime upheaval; the "bubbling happiness" was missing from Goudge's writing, and her personal philosophy was "tenuous, misty and unsatisfying."

However, *Henrietta's House* (1942) redressed the damage to her critical reputation. Though listed as a children's book, the story is a sequel to *A City of Bells* and tells of the exciting outcome of wishes made at a birthday picnic for Hugh Anthony, grandson of a canon of Torminster Cathedral. Here, recreating a family tradition from the island of Guernsey, Goudge bears out a comment made earlier in the *Times Literary Supplement* (19 July 1941) that "somewhere deep down, Elizabeth Goudge's imagination has a very tight hold on reality; and it is that, most easily seen in these families of children, that saves her over and over again from going sugary." In *The Saturday Review of Literature* (5 October 1942) Richard Ellis considered it "the best book about children . . . since Kenneth Grahame wrote *The Wind in the Willows*."

During this period Goudge found life in Providence Cottage with her mother a haven of peace before the wartime intrusion of the military and the later flood of postwar development. On and off, for years, she had been writing *Green Dolphin Country* (1944). By the time she completed this novel about a Guernsey great-uncle her seclusion was shattered by a nearby American-army ammunition dump. As the book grew, Goudge was warned by her literary agent that it might not be published because paper was in such short supply. After it had been sent for publication, she was amazed to hear from her American publisher that she had won an M-G-M Literary Award for $125,000.

Despite the fact that Goudge had written an author's note to explain the unlikely case of mistaken identity in the plot twist, she was nonetheless reprimanded by several reviewers "for cooking up such a fantastic story." A saga of two sisters in love with the same man, the novel traces the lives of all three characters from childhood in the Channel Islands to maturity. Due to a slip of the pen, the wrong sister, Marianne, travels to New Zealand, where the man, William, now lives, in order to marry him and raise a family. Forty years later the ill-matched couple return to their homeland to meet Marguerite, the jilted sister, a nun now become an abbess. Marianne learns that her marriage had been a mistake; she reveals the truth of William's love to Marguerite; and the three are reconciled to each other, finally accepting their circumstances.

M. L. Becker in the *Weekly Book Review* explained the appeal the novel held for Hollywood: "A right romantic tale set in strange places; not without violence, crowded with real people, it moves from scene to scene through evocations of loveliness explicit as stage directions. . . . Midsummer Day on the island provides not only an episode of vivid beauty, but a moment such as a star might covet and every young woman in the audience desire."

An M-G-M movie version titled *Green Dolphin Street* was released in October 1947 and starred Lana Turner as Marianne, Donna Reed as Marguerite, and Richard Hart as William. It was a $4 million investment, but a review by "Wit" in *Variety* (15 October 1947) predicted that it would pay off: "The double-ply premise that devotion and loyalty can finally worm a similar response from an unwilling spouse . . . [used] twice in the same opus lends a touch of corn—nonetheless, it's box-office stuff." In fact, *Green Dolphin Street* was the tenth-highest moneymaking film of the year, grossing more than $5 million at the box office and gaining an Academy Award for special effects and a nomination for cinematography. Goudge, denied success in her youthful attempts to be a playwright, unexpectedly gained it with this novel, but any wisdom the story possessed was drowned in the sea of hype. Goudge herself seemed embarrassed by the avalanche of reporters, interviews, and begging letters, but she was now an acclaimed author. Over the years the novel has sold more than one million copies.

While she was on the crest of that attention, Goudge's novel *The Little White Horse* (1946) won the 1947 Carnegie Medal for outstanding children's fic-

tion in the United Kingdom. Young Maria Merryweather first sees the little white horse on her way to the kingdom of Moonacre. Feeling a need "to find out what is wrong and put it right," she cooperates with a colorful cast of human and animal characters and courageously takes part in events that bring about a victory of good over evil. Sightings of the mystic little white horse confirm Maria's belief in the power of love to conquer hatred, and she is confident that she will continue to see it in her dreams. That same year the first anthology, *The Elizabeth Goudge Reader,* was published; it included favorite short stories with two new ones and selections from the famous novels. Her bills paid and her readership assured, Goudge was now free to develop her art in any direction she chose.

Goudge's mother died at the end of the war, compos mentis after a period of confusion. The event impressed upon Goudge the need to deal with remorse that, as she said, "rots away the very vitals of the soul," and this process was another theme that was to emerge in her later fiction. She then retired to Harewood House on the Hampshire coast—the prototype for Damerosehay, the home of the fictional Eliot family, now a shabby postwar commercial hotel—for a prolonged period during which she wrote two novels, a biography, a collection of short stories, and a book for older children.

The second of the three books about the Eliot family, *The Herb of Grace* (1948), continues the story begun in *The Bird in the Tree:* Nadine and George, now outwardly reconciled, buy a picturesque old pilgrim's inn not far from Damerosehay, where Lucilla still reigns with wisdom and understanding. Unearthing the history of the inn, each of the characters discovers the hidden heart of the house and the personal relevance of that revelation. Nadine, after considerable inner struggle, recommits herself to her marriage and family.

Goudge was thankful that she was prompted to write the Eliot family novels and that they seemed to be her readers' favorites: "As long as the three books are read, Damerosehay has not quite vanished from the world and I have not lived in vain." Once again, the timing of publication was opportune: the story of regained integrity brought hope in the postwar period. Critics hailed the escape the novel provided in depressing times and acknowledged the wisdom to be gained from the experience.

Goudge's next novel was *Gentian Hill* (1949), another historical romance; the setting was inspired, no doubt, partly by her Devonshire home and partly by the historic shipbuilding area around Keyhaven. Shipwrecked Stella is rescued and raised by a farm couple and becomes the childhood sweetheart of an orphaned boy who had deserted the navy. Their story unfolds and comes to completion after the Battle of Trafalgar. Mary Ross in the *New York Herald Tribune Book Review* (1 January 1950) described the novel's mood "of almost childlike gayety and gravity," which she attributed to the story's pre-Saxon, Roman, and medieval sources, noting Goudge's "special feeling for the continuity of living that had flowed through countless generations down to our own." Ruth Chapin in the *Christian Science Monitor* (11 January 1950), however, suggested that discriminating readers might question "how much they want to submerge themselves in [Goudge's] moral atmospherics."

During this period Goudge's work took an overtly religious turn with the publication of *The Reward of Faith, and Other Stories* (1950), a collection based on legends, the Bible, and the lives of saints; and *God So Loved the World* (1951), a life of Christ written especially for children. In the children's novel *The Valley of Song* (1951), one of her own favorites, the lyricism and mysticism increase to the extent that several reviewers claimed it would be read only by a select and sensitive few.

After the retreat in Hampshire, Goudge returned home to Providence Cottage to live alone and work on the final novel in the Eliot family series, *The Heart of the Family* (1953). She said that there was something of her mother in Lucilla Eliot and her company was comforting, but the book was a struggle; she continued to fight her personal demon, and she wondered if her writing days were over.

In this novel the four generations of Eliots gain insight into their own lives through their intuitive understanding of the tragic past of a suffering visitor who comes into their family circle. He is Sebastian Weber, secretary to David, the charismatic and achieving leading member of the Eliot family who struggles with his own tormenting past. David met Sebastian in the United States, and when the immigrant American, a refugee from Europe, arrives at Damerosehay, the spirit of the place and its occupants, both past and present, soothes and heals his pain. It appeared that Goudge's deepening spirituality was adversely affecting critical response to her work; according to Margaret Evans in the *New York Herald Tribune* (20 September 1953), the novel was about "distinctly special people, most of whom are keyed to catch nuances in their setting and relationships that would be likely to escape the attention, or at least the interest of the commonality." Nonetheless, it has had many devoted readers to this day.

*Goudge (right) with her companion, Jessie Monroe, in 1953*

It was during this period that Goudge had a sudden conviction that her demon had left for good. Later a wise friend introduced her to twenty-one-year-old Jessie Monroe, a companion for the winter in that lonely place; young enough to be Goudge's daughter, Monroe became her lifetime companion. In time the two women moved from the remoteness of Devonshire to the seventeenth-century Rose Cottage in the Oxford area, where they would be within reach of friends and relations. Goudge lived there for the rest of her life, and with Monroe she restored the neglected seventeenth-century garden.

After she had settled in Oxfordshire, Goudge finished *The Rosemary Tree* (1956). It was her goodbye to the old life in Devon, begun while she still lived there. The action takes place within the microcosm of a modern Devonshire village; the viewpoint is so permeated with Franciscan spirituality that mundane characters and events acquire magical, even heroic qualities. A quixotic vicar, John Wentworth; his abrasive wife, Daphne; his entrancing children; an eccentric aunt; and an intuitive old nanny interact with each other and the locals (including a traumatized passerby) to the ultimate edification of all of them. The book was well received though the overtly spiritual tone prompted some critical speculation about her future as a novelist.

However, *The White Witch* (1958), written after the cottage "took charge" of Goudge, once more assured her critical reputation. It was a book for Monroe, "commemorating the spells she wove in the garden." This tale of the English Civil War brings fresh insight on the conflict through the tensions, tragedies, and victories of the major characters; it is dominated by the white witch, Froniga, with her mystic gift of healing and overriding power for good. Edward Wagenknecht in the *Chicago Sunday Tribune* (5 January 1958) thought it perhaps Goudge's "very finest book," and *Time* (3 February 1958) said that though her fans thought she had already excelled, "*The White Witch* suggests that she has still not reached her peak." Indeed, there is a confidence and structural harmony in this novel that may well express the wholeness in Goudge's own life. With many personal battles won, she saw clearly the potential for good in the female nature.

To this point Goudge had been bringing her spirituality to bear upon her fiction; now she was increasingly bringing romance to her religion. She brought all her romantic sensibility to *Saint Francis of Assisi,* her 1959 retelling of the life of the saint, and won the respect of the previously skeptical M. P. Brody of *The Catholic World* (October 1959): "In a very personal way, the author has managed to communicate the compelling personality of Francis." Possibly Goudge identified with Francis in his stand against the established church, as she retained the simplicity of her own professional beliefs despite a literary establishment that in time would have her conform or withdraw from the field.

The quietness of the cottage enabled Goudge to produce two more of the novels she especially loved. *The Dean's Watch* (1960), set once again in a nineteenth-century English cathedral city, tells of the friendship of old Isaac Peabody, the humble, gifted clockmaker, and Adam Ayscough, the highly respected but intimidating dean of the cathedral. Goudge said that Adam "possessed himself" of much of her father's character. In the course of the relationship Isaac discovers his faith; Adam finds his humanity; and the lives of many in the city are enhanced.

The preoccupation in the novel with the nature of spiritual love drew critical applause, largely on account of Goudge's technical brilliance, though Shirley Barker in *The Saturday Review of Literature* (26 November 1960) said, "Few novelists have the courage nowadays to write such an unspectacular, gentle book."

As in *The Middle Window,* Goudge drew on an extrasensory experience to flavor her next novel, *The Scent of Water* (1963): there was a female presence in Rose Cottage that had been verified by several people. In this book Goudge demystifies the phenomenon: retired career woman Mary Lindsay moves to the country home bequeathed her by an eccentric cousin, seeking to resolve incomplete aspects of her life, particularly the death of her fiancé years earlier. Her intuitive nature, nurtured by the benign presence of her predecessor (sensed through the reading of her diary), leads Mary to respond to the needs of the surrounding community; in turn she finds the enlightenment for which she had hoped. In this story Goudge moves beyond romance to the metaphysical, proposing the mutation of erotic love to agape and its fulfillment within the ordinary affairs of village life.

The novel was another success for Goudge. A review by Arthur Gold in *Book Week* (15 September 1963), however, attempted to undermine Goudge:

> Miss Goudge's published work nestles comfily in the silken tradition of English Ladies fiction. . . . If one covets the feel of reality one does not read Miss Goudge, one reads literature instead. But it would be ungallant not to add that her novels are as artistically innocent as they are financially prosperous. . . . [Her] work touches those tender female places which the lesser English novelist has been mining ever since ladies first turned literate. . . . It is not so much a novel as a kind of moral institution, like tea, . . . one has no objection to one's nicer friends drinking it.

During the rest of the 1960s Goudge published two children's stories and edited three devotional anthologies. Meanwhile, she worked on a final novel, *The Child from the Sea* (1970), inspired by a stay at Monroe's vacation cottage on the Pembrokeshire coast. She was beset by many interruptions, and the book became too long, but in her autobiography she says, "I love it because its theme is forgiveness, . . . I know I can never write another novel, for I do not think there is anything else to say."

This novel is a retelling of the life of Lucy Walter, mother of the duke of Monmouth and ill-fated lover of Charles II. Lucy is a single parent, misrepresented, betrayed, imprisoned, and denied access to her children. She learns to forgive the maid who betrayed her and the husband who believed the worst and whose total allegiance she was not to regain until after her death. The book remained on the best-seller list in *Time* from 26 October 1970 to 8 February 1971 and was the Literary Guild choice for September 1970, but it was labeled "strictly for the ladies" by the reviewer in *Publishers' Weekly* (6 July 1970). After this book Goudge's last writing projects included another collection of short stories in 1971, her autobiography in 1974, and the editing of another anthology, *A Book of Faith,* in 1976.

Goudge died on 1 April 1984, at the age of eighty-three. The *Times* (London) obituary on 3 April 1984 said of her:

> Fragile in appearance but strong in spirit, she seemed at one with the peace and simplicity of her setting. Few novelists have had comparable knowledge and faith in the goodness of human nature, the beauty of childhood, and the pursuit of things lovely and of good report. As with Jane Austen, she "let other pens dwell on guilt and misery."

The comparison was apt: Goudge first read Austen during her school days, and as a literary artist she came to share, in time, the latter's wisdom, humor, love of life, and civility.

Goudge's literary career proceeded in a steady upward trajectory. The bulk of her novels, published in the years surrounding World War II, nurtured a war-sickened society and provided an environment in which problems were faced honestly, self-knowledge was gained, and the possibility of innocence and integrity was restored. Her readership was secure, though critical response to her later novels reflected the social tenor of the times. Despite the changing public mores, many of her novels remain in print and in circulation in public libraries throughout the English-speaking world. Her writings have been translated into Danish, Dutch, French, German, Italian, Spanish, and Swedish. Her work lends itself to feminist scholarship, with its emphasis on strong women handing down received wisdom to the next generation; the elements of creation-centered fantasy and myth would also appeal to modern readers. There is every reason to believe that Goudge's fiction will continue to attract new audiences.

**References:**

Thomas James Leasor, "Elizabeth Goudge," in his *Author by Profession* (London: Cleaver-Hume, 1952), pp. 142–156;

Harrison Smith, "Love and Scenery for the Millions," *Saturday Review of Literature,* 27 (26 August 1944): 7–9.

**Papers:**

Letters from Elizabeth Goudge are held in the Duckworth Papers, 1936–1941 and 1952–1953, University of London Library; in the files of the Royal Society of Literature, London (1950–1965); and in the Hodder and Stoughton correspondence files, 1965–1969, Department of Manuscripts, Guildhall Library, Aldermanbury, London.

# Robert Graves

*(24 July 1895 – 7 December 1985)*

John Ferns
*McMaster University*

See also the Graves entries in *DLB 20: British Poets, 1914-1945; DLB 100: Modern British Essayists, Second Series;* and *DLB Yearbook 1985.*

SELECTED BOOKS: *Over the Brazier* (London: Poetry Bookshop, 1916; New York: St. Martin's Press, 1975);

*Goliath and David* (London: Chiswick, 1916);

*Fairies and Fusiliers* (London: Heinemann, 1917; New York: Knopf, 1918);

*Treasure Box* (London: Chiswick, 1918);

*Country Sentiment* (London: Secker, 1920; New York: Knopf, 1920);

*The Pier-Glass* (London: Secker, 1921; New York: Knopf, 1921);

*On English Poetry: Being an Irregular Approach to the Psychology of This Art, from Evidence Mainly Subjective* (New York: Knopf, 1922; London: Heinemann, 1922);

*Whipperginny* (London: Heinemann, 1923; New York: Knopf, 1923);

*The Feather Bed* (Richmond: Hogarth Press, 1923);

*Mock Beggar Hall* (London: Hogarth Press, 1924);

*The Meaning of Dreams* (London: Palmer, 1924; New York: Greenburg, 1925);

*Poetic Unreason and Other Studies* (London: Palmer, 1925; New York: Biblo & Tannen, 1968);

*John Kemp's Wager: A Ballad Opera* (Oxford: Blackwell, 1925; New York: French, 1925);

*My Head! My Head!: Being the History of Elisha and the Shunamite Woman; with the History of Moses as Elisha Related It, and Her Questions Put to Him* (London: Secker, 1925; New York: Knopf, 1925);

*Contemporary Techniques of Poetry: A Political Analogy* (London: Hogarth Press, 1925; Folcroft, Pa.: Folcroft Library Editions, 1971);

*Welchman's Hose* (London: Fleuron, 1925; Folcroft, Pa.: Folcroft Library Editions, 1971);

*The Marmosite's Miscellany,* as John Doyle (London: Hogarth Press, 1925);

*Another Future of Poetry,* Hogarth Essays, series 2, no. 17 (London: Hogarth Press, 1926);

*Robert Graves in 1936*

*Impenetrability, or The Proper Habit of English,* Hogarth Essays, series 2, no. 3 (London: Hogarth Press, 1926);

*Lars Porsena; or, The Future of Swearing and Improper Language* (London: Kegan Paul, Trench, Trübner, 1927; New York: Dutton, 1927); revised as *The Future of Swearing and Improper Language* (London: Kegan Paul, Trench, Trübner, 1936);

*Poems (1914-1926)* (London: Heinemann, 1927; Garden City, N.Y.: Doubleday, Doran, 1929);

*Poems (1914-1927)* (London: Heinemann, 1927);

*Lawrence and the Arabs* (London: Cape, 1927); republished as *Lawrence and the Arabian Adventure*

(Garden City, N.Y.: Doubleday, Doran, 1928); republished as *Lawrence and the Arabs: Concise Edition* (London & Toronto: Cape, 1934);

*A Survey of Modernist Poetry,* by Graves and Laura Riding (London: Heinemann, 1927; Garden City, N.Y.: Doubleday, Doran, 1928);

*A Pamphlet against Anthologies,* by Graves and Riding (London: Cape, 1928; Garden City, N.Y.: Doubleday, Doran, 1928);

*Mrs. Fisher, or The Future of Humour* (London: Kegan Paul, Trench, Trübner / New York: Dutton, 1928);

*The Shout* (London: Mathews & Marrot, 1929; Folcroft, Pa.: Folcroft Library Editions, 1977);

*Good-Bye to All That: An Autobiography* (London: Cape, 1929; New York: Cape & Smith, 1930; revised edition, Garden City, N.Y.: Doubleday, 1957; London: Cassell, 1957);

*Poems, 1929* (London: Seizin, 1929);

*Ten Poems More* (Paris: Hours Press, 1930);

*But It Still Goes On: An Accumulation* (London & Toronto: Cape, 1930; New York: Cape & Smith, 1931);

*Poems, 1926–1930* (London: Heinemann, 1931);

*To Whom Else?* (Deyá, Majorca: Seizin, 1931; Folcroft, Pa.: Folcroft Library Editions, 1971);

*No Decency Left,* by Graves and Riding, as Barbara Rich (London: Cape, 1932);

*Poems, 1930–1933* (London: Barker, 1933);

*I, Claudius: From the Autobiography of Tiberius Claudius, Emperor of the Romans, Born b.c. 10, Murdered and Deified a.d. 54* (London: Barker, 1934; New York: Smith & Haas, 1934);

*Claudius the God and His Wife Messalina* (London: Barker, 1934; New York: Smith & Haas, 1935);

*"Antigua, Penny, Puce"* (Deyá, Majorca: Seizin / London: Constable, 1936); republished as *The Antigua Stamp* (New York: Random House, 1937);

*Count Belisarius* (London, Toronto, Melbourne & Sydney: Cassell, 1938; New York: Random House, 1938);

*Collected Poems* (London, Toronto, Melbourne & Sydney: Cassell, 1938; New York: Random House, 1939);

*No More Ghosts: Selected Poems* (London: Faber & Faber, 1940);

*Sergeant Lamb of the Ninth* (London: Methuen, 1940); republished as *Sergeant Lamb's America* (New York: Random House, 1940);

*The Long Week-End: A Social History of Great Britain, 1918–1939,* by Graves and Alan Hodge (Lon-

don: Faber & Faber, 1940; New York: Macmillan, 1941);

*Proceed, Sergeant Lamb* (London: Methuen, 1941; New York: Random House, 1941);

*Work in Hand,* by Graves, Hodge, and Norman Cameron (London: Hogarth Press, 1942);

*The Story of Marie Powell, Wife to Mr. Milton* (London, Toronto, Melbourne & Sydney: Cassell, 1943); republished as *Wife to Mr. Milton: The Story of Marie Powell* (New York: Creative Age, 1944);

*The Reader over Your Shoulder: A Handbook for Writers of English Prose,* by Graves and Hodge (London: Cape, 1943; New York: Macmillan, 1943; revised and abridged edition, London: Cape, 1947; New York: Vintage, 1979);

*The Golden Fleece* (London, Toronto, Melbourne & Sydney: Cassell, 1944); republished as *Hercules, My Shipmate* (New York: Creative Age, 1945);

*King Jesus* (New York: Creative Age, 1946; London, Toronto, Melbourne & Sydney: Cassell, 1946);

*Poems, 1938–1945* (London, Toronto, Melbourne & Sydney: Cassell, 1946; New York: Creative Age, 1946);

*Collected Poems (1914–1947)* (London, Toronto, Melbourne & Sydney: Cassell, 1948);

*The White Goddess: A Historical Grammar of Poetic Myth* (London: Faber & Faber, 1948; New York: Creative Age, 1948; revised and enlarged edition, London: Faber & Faber, 1952; New York: Vintage, 1958; revised and enlarged again, London: Faber & Faber, 1961);

*Watch the North Wind Rise* (New York: Creative Age, 1949); republished as *Seven Days in New Crete: A Novel* (London, Toronto, Melbourne, Sydney & Wellington: Cassell, 1949);

*The Common Asphodel: Collected Essays on Poetry, 1922–1949* (London: Hamilton, 1949; Folcroft, Pa.: Folcroft Press, 1969);

*The Islands of Unwisdom* (Garden City, N.Y.: Doubleday, 1949); republished as *The Isles of Unwisdom* (London, Toronto, Melbourne, Sydney & Wellington: Cassell, 1950);

*Occupation: Writer* (New York: Creative Age, 1950; London: Cassell, 1951);

*Poems and Satires, 1951* (London: Cassell, 1951);

*Poems, 1953* (London: Cassell, 1953);

*The Nazarene Gospel Restored,* by Graves and Joshua Podro (London: Cassell, 1953; Garden City, N.Y.: Doubleday, 1954);

*Homer's Daughter* (London: Cassell, 1955; Garden City, N.Y.: Doubleday, 1955);

*The Greek Myths,* 2 volumes (Harmondsworth: Penguin, 1955; Baltimore: Penguin, 1955);

*Collected Poems, 1955* (Garden City, N.Y.: Doubleday, 1955);

*Adam's Rib and Other Anomalous Elements in the Hebrew Creation Myth: A New View* (London: Trianon, 1955; New York: Yoseloff, 1958);

*The Crowning Privilege: The Clark Lectures 1954–1955; Also Various Essays on Poetry and Sixteen New Poems* (London: Cassell, 1955); revised as *The Crowning Privilege: Collected Essays on Poetry* (Garden City, N.Y.: Doubleday, 1956);

*¡Catacrok!: Mostly Stories, Mostly Funny* (London: Cassell, 1956);

*Jesus in Rome: A Historical Conjecture,* by Graves and Podro (London: Cassell, 1957);

*They Hanged My Saintly Billy* (London: Cassell, 1957; Garden City, N.Y.: Doubleday, 1957);

*5 Pens in Hand* (Garden City, N.Y.: Doubleday, 1958);

*The Poems of Robert Graves Chosen by Himself* (Garden City, N.Y.: Doubleday, 1958);

*Steps: Stories, Talks, Essays, Poems, Studies in History* (London: Cassell, 1958);

*Collected Poems, 1959* (London: Cassell, 1959);

*Food for Centaurs: Stories, Talks, Critical Studies, Poems* (Garden City, N.Y.: Doubleday, 1960);

*Greek Gods and Heroes* (Garden City, N.Y.: Doubleday, 1960); republished as *Myths of Ancient Greece* (London: Cassell, 1961);

*The Penny Fiddle: Poems for Children* (London: Cassell, 1960; Garden City, N.Y.: Doubleday, 1961);

*More Poems, 1961* (London: Cassell, 1961);

*Collected Poems* (Garden City, N.Y.: Doubleday, 1961);

*Oxford Addresses on Poetry* (London: Cassell, 1962; Garden City, N.Y.: Doubleday, 1962);

*The Big Green Book* (New York: Crowell-Collier, 1962; Harmondsworth: Puffin, 1978);

*New Poems, 1962* (London: Cassell, 1962; Garden City, N.Y.: Doubleday, 1963);

*The More Deserving Cases: Eighteen Old Poems for Reconsideration* (Marlborough, U.K.: Marlborough College Press, 1962; Folcroft, Pa.: Folcroft Press, 1969);

*The Siege and Fall of Troy* (London: Cassell, 1962; Garden City, N.Y.: Doubleday, 1963);

*Nine Hundred Iron Chariots* (Cambridge: Massachusetts Institute of Technology, 1963);

*Hebrew Myths: The Book of Genesis,* by Graves and Raphael Patai (Garden City, N.Y.: Doubleday, 1964; London: Cassell, 1964);

*Collected Short Stories* (Garden City, N.Y.: Doubleday, 1964; London: Cassell, 1965);

*Man Does, Woman Is* (London: Cassell, 1964; Garden City, N.Y.: Doubleday, 1964);

*Ann at Highwood Hall: Poems for Children* (London: Cassell, 1964; Garden City, N.Y.: Doubleday, 1966);

*Love Respelt* (London: Cassell, 1964; Garden City, N.Y.: Doubleday, 1966);

*Mammon: Oration Delivered at the London School of Economics and Political Science on Friday, 6 December 1963* (London: London School of Economics and Political Science, 1964);

*Mammon and the Black Goddess* (London: Cassell, 1965; Garden City, N.Y.: Doubleday, 1965);

*Majorca Observed,* by Graves and Paul Hogarth (London: Cassell, 1965; Garden City, N.Y.: Doubleday, 1965);

*Collected Poems, 1965* (London: Cassell, 1965; Garden City, N.Y.: Doubleday, 1966);

*Two Wise Children* (New York: Quist, 1966; London: Allen, 1967);

*17 Poems Missing from Love Respelt* (London: Rota, 1966);

*Colophon to Love Respelt* (London: Rota, 1966);

*Poetic Craft and Principle: Lectures and Talks* (London: Cassell, 1967);

*Poems, 1965–1968* (London: Cassell, 1968; Garden City, N.Y.: Doubleday, 1969);

*The Poor Boy Who Followed His Star* (London: Cassell, 1968; Garden City, N.Y.: Doubleday, 1969);

*The Crane Bag, and Other Disputed Subjects* (London: Cassell, 1969);

*On Poetry: Collected Talks and Essays* (Garden City, N.Y.: Doubleday, 1969);

*Beyond Giving: Poems* (London: Rota, 1969);

*Poems about Love* (London: Cassell, 1969; Garden City, N.Y.: Doubleday, 1969);

*Love Respelt Again* (Garden City, N.Y.: Doubleday, 1969);

*Poems, 1968–1970* (London: Cassell, 1970; Garden City, N.Y.: Doubleday, 1971);

*The Green-Sailed Vessel: Poems* (London: Rota, 1971);

*Poems: Abridged for Dolls and Princes* (London: Cassell, 1971; Garden City, N.Y.: Doubleday, 1971);

*Poems, 1970–1972* (London: Cassell, 1972; Garden City, N.Y.: Doubleday, 1973);

*Difficult Questions, Easy Answers* (London: Cassell, 1972; Garden City, N.Y.: Doubleday, 1973);

*Timeless Meeting: Poems* (London: Rota, 1974);

*At the Gate: Poems* (London: Rota, 1974);

*Collected Poems, 1975* (London: Cassell, 1975); republished as *New Collected Poems* (Garden City, N.Y.: Doubleday, 1977);

*An Ancient Castle,* edited by William David Thomas (London: Owen, 1980; New York: Kesend, 1981);

*Eleven Songs* (Deyá, Majorca: New Seizin, 1983).

**Collection:** *Selected Poems,* edited by Paul O'Prey (London: Penguin, 1984).

OTHER: *Oxford Poetry 1921,* edited by Graves, Alan Porter, and Richard Hughes (Oxford: Blackwell, 1921);

*The Winter Owl,* edited by Graves (London: Palmer, 1923);

*The English Ballad: A Short Critical Survey,* edited by Graves (London: Benn, 1927); revised as *English and Scottish Ballads* (Melbourne, London & Toronto: Heinemann, 1957; New York: Macmillan, 1957);

*John Skelton (Laureate),* edited by Graves (London: Benn, 1927);

*The Less Familiar Nursery Rhymes,* edited by Graves (London: Benn, 1927);

Charles Dickens, *The Real David Copperfield,* edited by Graves (London: Barker, 1933); republished as *David Copperfield, by Charles Dickens, Condensed by Robert Graves,* edited by Merrill P. Paine (New York & Chicago: Harcourt, Brace, 1934);

Frank Richards, *Old Soldiers Never Die,* rewritten by Graves (London: Faber & Faber, 1933);

Richards, *Old-Soldier Sahib,* rewritten by Graves (London: Faber & Faber, 1936; New York: Smith & Haas, 1936);

*T. E. Lawrence to His Biographer, Robert Graves: Information about Himself in the Form of Letters, Notes and Answers to Questions, Edited with a Critical Commentary,* edited by Graves (New York: Doubleday, Doran, 1938);

A. C. Swinburne, *An Old Saying: Poems,* foreword by Graves (Washington, D.C.: Mayfield, 1947);

*The Comedies of Terence,* edited by Graves (Garden City, N.Y.: Doubleday, 1962; London: Cassell, 1963).

TRANSLATIONS: Georg Schwarz, *Almost Forgotten Germany,* translated by Graves and Laura Riding (Deyá, Majorca: Seizin / London: Constable, 1936);

Lucius Apuleius, *The Transformation of Lucius, Otherwise Known as The Golden Ass* (Harmondsworth: Penguin, 1950; New York: Farrar, Straus & Young, 1951);

Manuel de Jesús Galván, *The Cross and the Sword* (Bloomington: Indiana University Press, 1955; London: Gollancz, 1956);

Pedro Antonio de Alarcón, *The Infant with the Globe* (London: Trianon, 1955; New York & London: Yoseloff, 1955);

*Graves's parents, Alfred Perceval and Amalie von Ranke Graves, in 1891*

George Sand, *Winter in Majorca,* with José Quadrado's "Refutation of George Sand" (London: Cassell, 1956);

Lucan, *Pharsalia: Dramatic Episodes of the Civil Wars* (Harmondsworth: Penguin, 1956; Baltimore: Penguin, 1957);

Suetonius, *The Twelve Caesars* (Harmondsworth: Penguin, 1956; Baltimore: Penguin, 1957);

*The Anger of Achilles: Homer's Iliad* (Garden City, N.Y.: Doubleday, 1957; London: Cassell, 1960);

*The Rubáiyát of Omar Khayyám,* translated by Graves and Omar Ali-Shah (London: Cassell, 1967);

*The Song of Songs* (New York: Potter, 1973; London: Collins, 1973).

On his death in 1985 *The Times* of London wrote of Robert Graves: "He will be remembered for his achievements as a prose stylist, historical novelist and memoirist, but above all as the great paradigm of the dedicated poet, 'the greatest love poet in English since Donne.'" This summary presents Graves's career as he would have wished; he

*Graves in his Royal Welch Fusiliers uniform during World War I*

saw himself as a poet first and a novelist second. In the latter capacity he can be fairly described as a historical novelist since only four of his seventeen novels have contemporary settings, and one is what he called "post-historical"—that is, futuristic. His historical novels range in setting from ancient Greece and Israel through imperial Rome, sixteenth-century South America and the Pacific, seventeenth-century England, and eighteenth-century North America to Victorian England.

On the surface it appears that Graves wrote novels simply to make money. He said so himself, telling an inquiring stranger in 1952:

> I make no attempt to assess myself as a novelist. I have a large family and every now and then I have to write a novel to pay for schools or dentists or holidays, and I do so: but nowadays the historical side tends to overshadow the fictional. . . . Frankly, all I really care about is poetry—that is my life, not novel-writing. My next interest is history.

On the other hand the subjects of his novels often parallel his deepest poetic and personal interests. The novel *King Jesus* (1946) and his central discussion of mythology, *The White Goddess* (1948), are closely related, as Graves explores in them what he considers male-centered mythology and the female-centered mythology that he preferred. In a 1969 interview with Peter Buckman and William Fifield, published in *Conversations with Robert Graves* (1989), edited by Frank L. Kersnowski, he said:

> My writing of prose was always thematically in line with my thought. Always myself, I never left that. That was always the background. For example, *They Hanged My Saintly Billy* [1957] was to show how Victorian England really was: how rotten, how criminal in contrast to the received version.

Of *I, Claudius* (1934), his best-known historical novel, he said in the same interview:

> The Roman historians—Tacitus, Suetonius and Dion Cassius but especially Tacitus—had obviously got Claudius wrong . . . I didn't think I was writing a novel. I was trying to find out the truth of Claudius. And there was some strange confluent feeling between Claudius and myself. . . . It's a question of reconstructing a personality. . . . There's his speech to the Aeduans, his letter to the Alexandrians, and a number of records of what he said in Suetonius and elsewhere. We know now exactly what disease he suffered from: Little's disease. The whole scene is so solid, really, that you feel you knew him personally, if you're sympathetic with him. The poor man.

Clearly, Graves's historical novels were motivated by personal sympathy and a desire for self-understanding as well as by the need to make money from works that enjoyed larger sales than his poetry. The depth of his involvement in his historical characters is confirmed by a story he told Huw Weldon in 1959 (published in *Conversations with Robert Graves*):

> When I was writing a book called *Sergeant Lamb* [*of the Ninth,* 1940], he was a Royal Welch Fusilier fighting against the Americans in the American War of Independence, my wife said: "You have laid the table for three." I had been thinking of Sergeant Lamb!

Robert von Ranke Graves was born in Wimbledon on 24 July 1895 to Alfred Perceval Graves and his second wife, Amalie (Amy) Elizabeth Sophie von Ranke Graves. His early childhood was spent between Red Branch House, Lauriston Road, Wimbledon, and the family's summer home at Harlech, North Wales. At age six he was enrolled in a dame's school in Wimbledon. He attended five more preparatory schools between 1902 and 1909; the last, Bernard Rendall's enlightened Copthorne, was the best. But Graves's years at Charterhouse, 1910 to 1914, were miserable; he says in *Good-Bye to All That: An Autobiography* (1929): "From the moment I arrived at the school I suffered an oppression of spirit that I hesitate now to recall in its fullest intensity." Bullied because of his supposed prudishness, he learned boxing in self-defense. It was at this time that he began writing poetry; in the school's poetry society he developed a platonic "pseudo-homosexual" relationship with a fellow student, "Peter" Johnstone. He won a scholarship to St. John's College, Oxford, but joined the Royal Welch Fusiliers shortly after the outbreak of World War I. On 12 May 1915 he wired his parents that he was off to France.

Graves's first attempt at novel writing occurred in September and October 1916 as he recovered from wounds received in the Battle of the Somme on 20 July. (Reported dead as a result of those wounds, Graves was one of those rare people who lived to read his own obituary.) The never-completed novel concerned his war experience. Graves went back to France when he was released from the hospital, but his superior officers thought he had returned too soon. He spent the rest of the war in England.

On 23 January 1918 Graves married the painter Nancy Nicholson, whose father and brother were the painters Sir William and Ben Nicholson. The Graveses had four children in the first six years of their marriage. During this period Graves attempted to establish himself as a poet and completed a B.Litt. in English at Oxford University. His thesis, "Poetic Unreason," was published in *Poetic Unreason and Other Studies* (1925). Graves and his wife were frequently in debt and were often supported by Graves's parents.

During the summer of 1924 Graves completed *My Head! My Head!: Being the History of Elisha and the Shunamite Woman; with the History of Moses as Elisha Related It, and Her Questions Put to Him* (1925). The novel is prefaced by the twenty-page "Argument" in which Graves gives his reasons for writing the work: "I wanted to face squarely two Biblical problems which had long puzzled me: the first, what exactly were the relations between Elisha and the Shunamite; the second, what was the sequence of events that made it necessary for Moses to die on Mount Nebo within sight of the promised land, and what was the form that his death took." The episode on which the novel is based is narrated in 2 Kings 4: 8–37. In the Bible the prophet Elisha assures a Shunamite woman that she will have a child despite her

*Nancy Nicholson in 1917. She and Graves were married the next year.*

husband's age; but "when the child was grown, it fell on a day, that he went out to his father to the reapers. And he said unto his father, My head, my head. And he said to a lad, Carry him to his mother. And when he had taken him, and brought him to his mother, he sat on her knees till noon, and then died." The Shunamite mother journeys to find Elisha, who returns to her house and restores the child to life. In Graves's version Elisha, not the woman's elderly husband, is the actual father of the child. Much of the novel is taken up with the Shunamite woman's questions to Elisha about Moses, and the prophet's answers: Moses had to die on Mount Nebo because he took the credit for striking water from the rock, rather than giving God the credit; as to the manner of his death, he drew a magic cloud about himself and could be seen conversing with a

*Robert and Nancy Graves's children—Catherine, Jenny, Sam, and David—circa 1925*

bright, glorious shape until he disappeared. In *Robert Graves: The Assault Heroic, 1895–1926* (1986) Graves's nephew and biographer Richard Perceval Graves argues that *My Head! My Head!*

is important as the precursor of a number of books clearly based upon the "associative thought" which Graves had praised in *The Meaning of Dreams* (1924). Using "associative thought" (he later called it "analeptic thought"), Graves finds solutions to historical, religious, moral and poetic problems which cannot be solved by reason alone. *My Head! My Head!* was one of Graves's first steps upon the path which later led to such major works as *I, Claudius* and *The White Goddess*.

The Graveses' fragile marriage broke down soon after Graves met the American poet Laura Riding in 1926. She accompanied the Graves family to Cairo, where Graves spent a difficult year (1926–1927) as professor of English literature at the Royal Egyptian University. After their return to London, Graves and his wife separated, and Graves and Riding began living together. On 27 April 1929 Riding tried to commit suicide by leaping from a fourth-floor window of the apartment they shared, and Graves, trying to reach her as quickly as possible, almost immediately afterward jumped from a third-floor window. Riding was much more seriously injured than Graves. After she recovered, the two moved to the Spanish island of Majorca.

Graves's second novel, *No Decency Left* (1932), was co-authored with Riding and published under the pseudonym Barbara Rich. Graves's only fictional collaboration and his least-successful novel,

*No Decency Left* takes place in Lion City, the capital of the fictional country of Lyonesse, on the twenty-first birthday of its putative author, Barbara Rich. Barbara, who is patterned after Riding, leaves her dull fiancé, Gordon; takes up with Prince Maximian; and leads a revolution. She and Maximian become king and queen.

Graves's next novelistic venture was not an original work but a condensation of Charles Dickens's *David Copperfield* (1849–1850), published in 1933. The work involved, Graves remarked in an undated 1931 letter to John Aldridge, "taking out all the monthly-part padding and general hysteria and putting what's left into some sort of intelligible order." The importance of *The Real David Copperfield* is what the exercise taught Graves about the handling of first-person narrative. Many of Graves's best novels, including those about Claudius, would employ this technique.

Graves first thought of *I, Claudius* around the time he completed his autobiography, *Good-Bye to All That*. He recorded the idea in the 5 September 1929 entry in his "Journal of Curiosities": "It is not long since a complete historical romance or interpretive biography occurred to me—'The Emperor Pumpkin.' I had been reading Suetonius and Tacitus. It was about Claudius, the emperor who came between Caligula and Nero . . . Claudius has always been a puzzle to the historians, as indeed he was to his contemporaries." In a letter to T. E. Lawrence of October 1932 he described his preparatory reading: "Tacitus, Josephus, Dio Cassius, Suetonius, Seneca, Arosius, etc. and the

Companion to Latin Studies, and Dictionary of Class. Ant." Since Claudius would be the narrator of the work, Graves studied the emperor's Aeduan speech to get a sense of Claudius's style. The ingenuous Claudius, who is regarded as an idiot by those around him, describes events that Lawrence called, in a letter to Graves of 12 November 1933, "a Chamber of Roman Horrors. . . . In every direction you [Graves] take the way of crime, so that your chronicle becomes more scandalous than the most hostile Roman story. . . . In so much human nature there would have been some good specimens, surely?" Nevertheless, Lawrence added, "It gripped me against my will . . . I have an uneasy feeling that it will be valued and collected and talked about for its vices, rather than for its force. It is not an essential book." Richard Perceval Graves contends that "Some of the strength of *I, Claudius* undoubtedly comes from the fact that Robert Graves subconsciously used it as a vehicle for expressing the dark side of his feelings for Laura Riding." Claudius's comments about his method of writing history in the novel reflect the methods Graves used in writing the work: "I like having two tasks going at the same time: when I tire of one I turn to the other. But I am perhaps too careful a writer. I am not satisfied merely with copying from ancient authorities while there is any possible means of checking their statements by consulting other sources of information on the same subject, particularly accounts by writers of rival political parties." Claudius is referring to his Etruscan and Carthaginian histories, but it is possible to see a reference to Graves's "two tasks" of writing poetry and fiction as well as to his use of various historical accounts in composing his novel. *I, Claudius* builds inexorably to Claudius's becoming emperor upon the assassination of Caligula. He has survived the poisonings perpetrated by his grandmother, Livia, and the reign of terror of Tiberius and Caligula by concealing his sensitivity and intelligence behind a mask of stammering and lameness.

Having outlived three of the worst characters in imperial Roman history, in *Claudius the God and His Wife Messalina* (1934) the new emperor finds himself married to a fourth such character. The work is an effective sequel to *I, Claudius*, though the early part lacks the tension of the first novel since Claudius is in a position of power; throughout *I, Claudius* the reader fears for Claudius's life. The first part of *Claudius the God and His Wife Messalina* is divided between Claudius's relationship with his childhood friend Herod and his military successes in Britain; the Battle of Brentwood, in which Claudius defeats Caractacus, is one of the high points of the novel. As Claudius's life is threatened by the machinations of Messalina, the tension of *I, Claudius* returns. Although Claudius defeats Messalina, he is finally defeated by Agrippinilla and Nero; the narrator of the deifications of Augustus, Tiberius, and Caligula reluctantly allows himself to be proclaimed a god.

Graves's Claudius is a prime example of a twentieth-century type: the antihero. Always Claudius presents himself in a self-deprecating manner, though such a manner can have subtle dramatic effects: "I have no dramatic gift, like my brother Germanicus," Claudius says in *Claudius the God and His Wife Messalina;* "I am merely a historian and no doubt most people would call me, in general, dull and prosy, but I have come to a point in my story where the record of bare facts unimproved by oratorical beauties should stir the wonder of my readers as greatly as they stirred me at the time." Here, as often in the two novels, the mask of dullness is used ironically to create expectation in the reader. At the conclusion of the second novel Claudius's irony is made explicit:

> Today I have made the Senate my farewell speech, and humbly recommended Nero and Britannicus to them, and given these two a long and earnest exhortation to brotherly love and concord, calling the House to witness that I have done so. But with what irony I spoke! I knew as certainly as that fire is hot and ice cold that my Britannicus was doomed, and that it was I who was giving him over to his death, and cutting off, in him, the last true Claudian of the ancient stock of Appius Claudius. Imbecilic I.

Here the self-deprecating manner strikes a tragic note. In 1935 *I, Claudius* received the Hawthornden Prize, and both novels received the James Black Tait Memorial Prize. In 1976 the two Claudius novels were combined to form the basis of the British Broadcasting Corporation television series *I, Claudius,* starring Derek Jacobi.

*"Antigua, Penny, Puce"* (1936), one of Graves's novels with a contemporary setting, is described by Robert Perceval Graves as "a story of the most venomous sibling rivalry." The rivals are the caddish Oliver Price, an unsuccessful novelist, and his sister, Jane, a successful actress and theater manager; the reader's sympathies are entirely with Jane. The title refers to a valuable stamp over which the brother and sister engage in a lifelong tug-of-war. Among the victims of the novel's satire is Graves's father, who appears as the vicar father of the protagonists. At one point Jane accuses Oliver of being

*American poet Laura Riding, for whom Graves left his wife in 1927*

Belisarius's wife, Antonia. Belisarius, a man of integrity in a decadent world, is one of the emperor Justinian's cavalry leaders. Like Germanicus in *I, Claudius,* Belisarius is a successful soldier; he defeats Carthage, the Vandals, and the Goths. But also like Germanicus, Belisarius becomes a victim of his own success: Justinian envies him and becomes his enemy. Belisarius's wife is slandered to him; he is imprisoned and blinded; and his possessions are seized. Finally, Antonia is restored to him and supports him through his last days. Graves's ambivalent attitude toward military achievement emerges in this novel: Count Belisarius is a good man, but by virtue of his occupation he is the cause of thousands of deaths, and it is his success as a soldier that leads to his downfall. The novel was awarded the Femina-Vie Heureuse Prize in 1939. In a letter to Graves, Winston Churchill said that he had read *Count Belisarius*

with the very greatest pleasure and profit. I most heartily congratulate you on this brilliant piece of work. You have "rolled back the time-curtain" in a magical way and made all this strange epoch young again. I daresay some of your readers will have felt that there was too much war, but the vivid accounts you give of those long-forgotten campaigns, in my mind, only enhance the value of the work. I delight also in the theological discussions which blend so amusingly with the easy morals.

On 4 April 1938 Graves informed his brother John that *Count Belisarius* was doing "what I required of it: namely, sell."

In late April 1939 Graves and Riding traveled to the United States. There Riding became involved with the American poet Schuyler Jackson, whom she married after his first wife divorced him. Distraught, Graves returned to England in August. He was soon joined by Beryl Hodge, who had separated from her husband, the poet Alan Hodge. They would live together until Graves's first wife agreed to a divorce; then, in May 1950, they would marry. Like his first marriage, Graves's relationship with Hodge also produced four children.

When the London publisher Methuen expressed interest in a historical novel about the American Revolution, Graves came up with the idea of using as his main character Sergeant Roger Lamb, an Irishman who had served in Graves's old regiment, the Royal Welch Fusiliers; Lamb had left behind a journal and a memoir that were published in Dublin in 1809 and 1811, respectively. In his foreword to *Sergeant Lamb of the Ninth* Graves says: "All that readers of an historical novel can fairly ask from the author is an assurance that he has nowhere

the kind of writer that, one suspects, Graves feared he might become:

A writer has to make up his mind in which of three ways he is writing: there are only three ways. The first way is to give the public what it wants, just as it wants it—the method of the popular entertainer. Then there is the way of writing without any consideration for the taste of the public; and not complaining if the public is ungrateful. That, speaking as a public entertainer, I must call the method of the eccentric. . . . But you, Oliver Price, are the third sort of writer, the sort that tries to feed the public what he thinks the public will think it ought to like because it's just a little superior.

Graves's poetry could be classed as "eccentric," done for himself to satisfy impelling needs; but in his novel writing he was in danger of becoming an Oliver Price. He was not satisfied with writing potboilers; he wanted to explore deeper levels in his novels, and he increasingly began to do so.

Graves and Riding returned to England in 1936 following the outbreak of the Spanish civil war. In his next novel, *Count Belisarius* (1938), Graves deals with a period several centuries after the age of Claudius, the sixth century A.D. The story is narrated by Eugenius, a eunuch in the service of

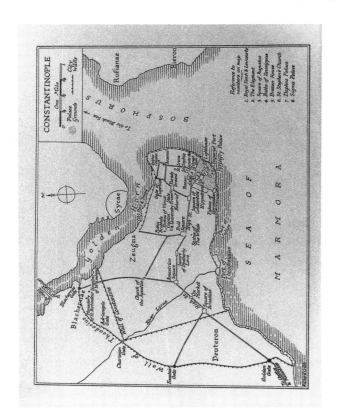 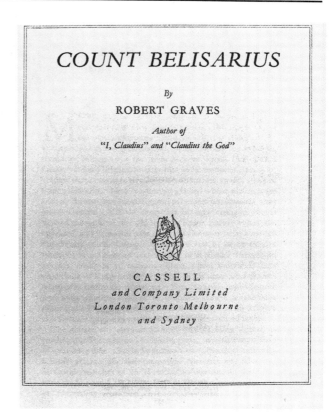

*Frontispiece and title page for Graves's novel about a Roman military leader in the sixth century A.D.*

wilfully falsified geography, chronology, or character, and that the information contained in it is accurate enough to add without discount to their general stock of history." Lamb and a fellow soldier, Richard Harlowe, are rivals for the love of Kate Weldone. Kate marries Harlowe and accompanies him to Canada when the troops are ordered to suppress the revolt by the American colonists. Lamb becomes friendly with the Mohawk chief Thayendanegea, also known as Capt. Joseph Brant, who is allied with the English, and the Mohawks teach Lamb and his friend Terry Rivers Indian woodlore. Lamb encounters Kate, who has left Harlowe and has contemplated committing suicide by throwing herself over Niagara Falls. Captain Brant marries her and Lamb in an Indian ceremony. When the time comes for him to return to the army, Lamb has to leave his pregnant wife with the Indians. At the close of the novel he is captured by the Americans.

In his foreword to the sequel, *Proceed, Sergeant Lamb* (1941), Graves says that "the chief link that I have with Lamb is that I had the honour of serving, like him, in the Royal Welch Fusiliers during a long and bloody war; and found their character as a regi-

ment, and their St. David's Day customs, happily unaltered since his day." In *Proceed, Sergeant Lamb* the sergeant escapes from imprisonment and flees through enemy territory. Kate has become the mistress of Lord Cornwallis; she is killed in the American attack on Yorktown. Later Lamb marries a war widow, Jane Cromer. After his retirement from the army he becomes a schoolmaster in Dublin; there he is visited by his and Kate's daughter, who has been brought up by an American Quaker. Thus Graves completes a story that "I first came across . . . when I was a young officer instructing my platoon in regimental history."

In his interview with Buckman and Fifield, Graves discussed the methods he used in writing historical novels and, in particular, the genesis of *The Story of Marie Powell, Wife to Mr. Milton* (1943):

Some people have gifts, like a friend of mine who can balance a glass on his finger and make it turn round by just looking at it. I have a gift of being occasionally able to put myself back in the past and see what's happening. That's how historical novels should be written. I also have a very good memory for anything I want to remember, and none at all for what I don't want to re-

*The poet Alan Hodge with Beryl Pritchard, who became Graves's second wife*

member. *Wife to Mr. Milton*—my best novel—started when my wife and I were making a bed in 1943 and I suddenly said: "You know, Milton must have been a trichomaniac"—meaning a hair-fetishist. The remark suddenly sprang out of my mouth. I realised how often his imagery had been trichomanic. So I read all I could find about him, and went into the history of his marriages. I'd always hated Milton, from earliest childhood; and I wanted to find out the reason. I found it. His jealousy. It's present in all his poems . . . Marie Powell had long hair with which he could not compete.

Graves's foray into Milton's biography contrasts sharply with the sense of responsibility to history that he displayed in his earlier novels. In *The Life of John Milton* (1983) A. N. Wilson comments:

Marriages, and what makes them a success or failure, are impenetrably difficult things to interpret. It requires the imaginative intrusiveness of Henry James to be able to fathom them; a gift singularly lacking in the malicious and crude pen of Robert Graves, whose novel *Wife to Mr. Milton* presents such a laughably improbable account of the case. He cribbed the idea of writing the book from the much better *Mary Powell* ([1849] written by Cardinal Manning's sister [Anne Manning]), but it was really George Eliot's *Middlemarch* [1871–1872] which provides the clue to Graves's fantasy. Dorothea Brooke, it will be remembered, dreamed of being married to Milton, and ended up with the unspeakable Mr. Casaubon.

*The Story of Marie Powell, Wife to Mr. Milton* is narrated by its protagonist. An Oxfordshire girl of Royalist parents, Marie is in love with a young Royalist, Sir Edmund Verney; but in 1642, at the age of sixteen, she marries the Puritan Milton because her family is in debt to Milton's father. She leaves him within a month and goes back to live with her parents but returns in 1645, bears him three children, and dies in childbirth in 1652. Graves is sympathetic to Marie and highly critical of Milton, whom he depicts as self-interested, domineering, jealous, and eager to control Marie's family's property; to Milton, Marie is nothing more than chattel. She dies while Verney is away fighting in the Civil War. While the novel drew academic ire (Professor Kelly of Princeton turned it down for Random House), it sold well.

While doing research for the novel *The Golden Fleece* (1944; published in the United States as *Hercules, My Shipmate,* 1945) Graves became fascinated with the notion that prior to the fourteenth century B.C. the worship of a moon-goddess was nearly universal in western Europe; the goddess was supposedly associated with a matriarchal social organization. Gradually, as patriarchy replaced matriarchy, the goddess was supplanted by male deities. This theory would be worked out in Graves's treatise on poetry, *The White Goddess,* but the idea underlay all of the work he did at this time. In *The Golden Fleece* the story of the Argonauts' pursuit of the golden

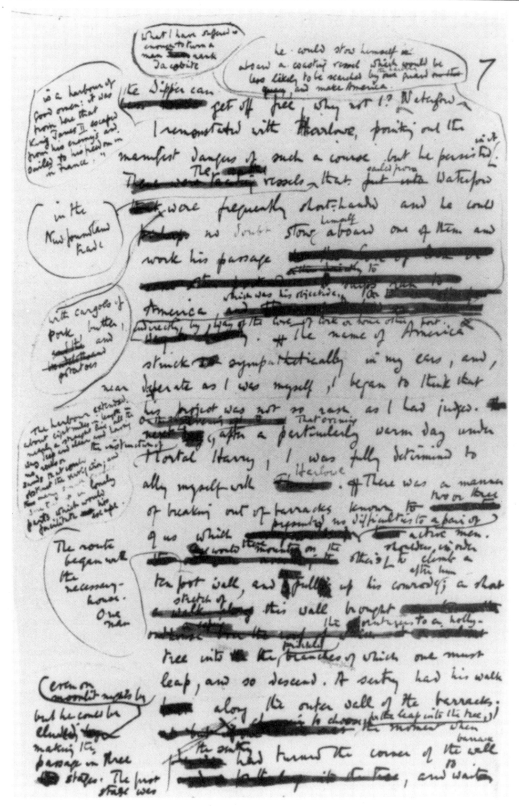

*Page from the manuscript for Graves's novel* Sergeant Lamb of the Ninth *(from Fred H. Higginson,*
A Bibliography of the Works of Robert Graves, *1966)*

The book that "usurped" *The White Goddess* was *King Jesus*. It was published in 1946, the year that Graves returned to Majorca with his family; he would live there for the rest of his life. Graves presents Jesus as the son not of God but of Herod's eldest son, Antipater. Jesus' mother is Mary, and he is later married to a second Mary—Mary of Cleophas—though their marriage remains unconsummated. The third Mary in Jesus' life is Mary the Hairdresser, the Mary Magdalene of the New Testament. The three women are representatives of the goddess. Narrated by Agabus the Deapolitan and set between the years 89 and 93, the novel shows how the triple goddess of earlier Mediterranean religion was replaced by a patriarchal god. The work provides an alternative way of interpreting the events of Christ's life.

In *Watch the North Wind Rise* (1949; published in England as *Seven Days in New Crete,* 1949), his "post-historical" novel published a year after *The White Goddess,* Graves projects his preoccupation with the goddess into the future. Edward Venn-Thomas goes to sleep in London and wakes up centuries in the future in New Crete, a pre-Christian, agricultural, matriarchal society where war is replaced by sporting contests, money is not used, and the earth's fertility is maintained through the recycling of waste. Goods are exchanged as gifts rather than bought and sold, and there is no hoarding. This ideal society cannot last, however, since "love and wisdom" require "calamity": the people have become effete, and their art has lost its originality; Venn-Thomas has been "invoked" to the future by the witch Sally to introduce such evils as lying and jealousy into the utopia. He finally returns to the present and fathers the daughter for whom he has always wished.

*The Islands of Unwisdom* (1949), which was to be titled "The She-Admiral," is based on the discovery of the Marquesas Islands in 1595 by a Spanish expedition led by Isabelle de Barretto, who took command after the death of her husband, the original commander. Graves provides a grim account of life aboard ship and of colonization, including cruelty to the Indians. In his introduction Graves assures his readers that "I have done my best to reconstruct the real story, inventing only as much as it needed for continuity."

Graves was writing fewer novels by this time; six years elapsed between *The Islands of Unwisdom* and *Homer's Daughter* (1955). This work is a fictional elaboration of Samuel Butler's idea, presented in *The Authoress of the "Odyssey"* (1897), that *The Odyssey* was written by a woman named Nausicaa, who included herself in the epic as the daughter of the king of the Phaeacians. In Graves's novel Nausicaa lives

*Graves in 1941 (Hulton Deutsch Collection)*

fleece lost by King Athamas becomes a story of the replacement of the worship of the moon-goddess by that of the patriarchal deity Zeus. In the novel the goddess's priestess at Colchis, Medea, enables the Argonauts to recover the fleece, and Jason is protected by the goddess on the island of Pelion.

On 10 February 1944 Graves wrote his biographer Martin Seymour-Smith about

> a hopelessly difficult book that has usurped the place of the one I began to write about poetry—a historical reconstruction of the whole Jesus Christ story, on which I have a rather startling new line. I have never realised how hopelessly corrupt the O.T. & N.T. texts are; hardly a single straight strand in the whole tangle—parables, lies, half-truths, miscopyings, mis-editings, mystification. Yet if one is patient a story emerges clearly: one gets it by the same means that one finds hidden arms in an African village, by grabbing an obviously dishonest text and going in exactly the other direction from the one in which it pulls you.

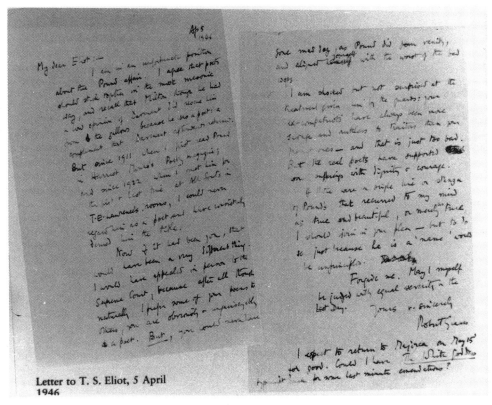

*Letter in which Graves declines T. S. Eliot's request that he sign a plea for clemency for Ezra Pound, who was charged with treason for making pro-Fascist broadcasts during World War II (from Paul O'Prey, ed.,* In Broken Images: Selected Letters of Robert Graves 1914–1946, *1982)*

**Letter to T. S. Eliot, 5 April 1946**

two hundred years after Homer, and what she writes in *The Odyssey* is derived from her own experiences. Nausicaa is pursued by suitors who plan to usurp her father's throne and who have murdered one of her brothers. Nausicaa prays for help to Athene; the goddess sends Aethon, who arrives disguised as a beggar and, assisted by Nausicaa's younger brother, slaughters the suitors.

Graves's penultimate novel, *They Hanged My Saintly Billy,* is based on the case of Dr. William Palmer, who was hanged in 1856 for murdering fourteen people in Staffordshire; in Graves's work Palmer murders no one and is wrongfully convicted and executed. Graves's dust-jacket comment declares the work a potboiler: "My novel is full of sex, drink, incest, suicides, dope, horse racing, murder, scandalous legal procedure, cross-examinations, inquests and ends with a good public hanging—attended by 30,000. . . . Nobody can now call me a specialized writer."

After *They Hanged My Saintly Billy* Graves did not publish another work of fiction for twenty-three years. *An Ancient Castle* (1980), a five-chapter children's novel, had been begun and abandoned in the 1930s. Sergeant Harington, the keeper of the ruined

Lambuck Castle on the Welsh border, lost his right arm in World War I. After an argument in a pub with Sir Anderson Wigg's chauffeur, Slark, Harington is falsely accused by Slark of insulting Sir Anderson, a profiteer who made a fortune during the war by selling poor-quality jam to the army. Anderson tries to have Harington removed from his position, but Lord Badger, lord-lieutenant of the county and the colonel of Harington's regiment during the war, prevents Harington's dismissal. Harrington's son, Giles, and Giles's friend Bronwen discover a secret room at the top of the castle that contains a six-hundred-year-old treasure. Harington, Giles, and Bronwen are given four-fifths of the treasure, and as a result of the find the castle becomes a museum that attracts two hundred thousand visitors during its first summer. Harington forgives Sir Anderson for trying to have him fired, and Sir Anderson sells Lambuck Hall to Harington and returns to London. Harington converts the hall into the Crown Hotel.

Graves died in Majorca on 7 December 1985. Because of his experiences in World War I, Graves had a lifelong preoccupation with the subject of war. His Claudius novels, *Count Belisarius,* and the

*Graves in Ireland, 1975 (photograph by Angus Forbes)*

Sergeant Lamb novels feature war prominently; in *Watch the North Wind Rise* he creates a utopian fantasy in which war is replaced by sport. Even more important for Graves is the nature of woman. His first novel depicts Elisha's relationship with the Shunamite woman; *No Decency Left* shows Barbara Rich as a proto–White Goddess figure; the Claudius novels present Livia and Messalina as powerful and destructive women; Antonia is a crucial figure in *Count Belisarius;* and Kate is important in the Sergeant Lamb novels. In *The Story of Marie Powell, Wife to Mr. Milton* the great poet is seen in an unflattering light through the eyes of his wife. The White Goddess lies behind *The Golden Fleece,* and the three Marys feature prominently in *King Jesus.* The utopia projected in *Watch the North Wind Rise* is a matriarchy, while *The Islands of Unwisdom* follows the exploits of the "she-admiral" Dona Ysabel. Finally, in *Homer's Daughter* Graves depicts a woman as the author of one of the greatest works of world literature. Although Graves regarded himself as a poet first, he will probably continue to be known primarily for his World War I autobiography, *Good-Bye to All That,* and for his novel *I, Claudius.*

**Letters:**

*In Broken Images: Selected Letters of Robert Graves 1914–1946,* edited by Paul O'Prey (London: Hutchinson, 1982);

*Between Moon and Moon: Selected Letters of Robert Graves 1946–1972,* edited by O'Prey (London: Hutchinson, 1984);

*Dear Robert, Dear Spike: The Graves-Milligan Correspondence,* edited by Pauline Scudamore (London: Sutton, 1991).

**Interviews:**

Frank L. Kersnowski, ed., *Conversations with Robert Graves* (Jackson & London: University of Mississippi Press, 1989).

**Bibliographies:**

Fred H. Higginson, *A Bibliography of the Works of Robert Graves* (London: Vane, 1966); revised by William Proctor Williams as *A Bibliography of the Writings of Robert Graves* (Winchester: St. Paul's Bibliographies, 1987);

Hallman Bell Bryant, *Robert Graves; An Annotated Bibliography* (Hamden, Conn.: Garland, 1986).

**Biographies:**

Martin Seymour-Smith, *Robert Graves: His Life and Works* (London: Hutchinson, 1982; revised edition, London: Bloomsbury, 1995);

Richard Perceval Graves, *Robert Graves: The Assault Heroic, 1895–1926* (London: Weidenfeld & Nicolson, 1986);

Graves, *Robert Graves: The Years with Laura, 1926–1940* (London: Weidenfeld & Nicolson, 1990);

Graves, *Robert Graves and the White Goddess, 1940–1985* (London: Weidenfeld & Nicolson, 1995);

Miranda Seymour, *Robert Graves: Life on the Edge* (New York: Holt, 1995).

**References:**

Harold Bloom, ed., *Robert Graves* (New York: Chelsea House, 1987);

Robert H. Canary, "The Riding-Graves Seminar at the MLA," *Focus on Robert Graves*, 5 (1976): 85–86;

Canary, *Robert Graves* (Boston: G. K. Hall, 1980);

D. N. G. Carter, *Robert Graves: The Lasting Poetic Achievement* (London: Macmillan, 1989);

J. M. Cohen, *Robert Graves* (Edinburgh: Oliver & Boyd, 1960; New York: Grove, 1961);

Douglas Day, *Swifter than Reason: The Poetry and Criticism of Robert Graves* (Chapel Hill: University of North Carolina Press, 1963);

D. J. Enright, *Robert Graves and the Decline of Modernism* (Singapore: University of Malaya, 1960); republished in *Essays in Criticism*, 2 (1961): 319–336;

Jean-Paul Forster, *Robert Graves et la dualité du reel* (Bern: Herbert Lang / Frankfurt am Main: Peter Lang, 1975);

G. S. Fraser, "The Poetry of Robert Graves," in his *Essays on Twentieth Century Poets* (Leicester: Leicester University Press, 1977), pp. 125–135;

Ronald Gaskell, "The Poetry of Robert Graves," *Critical Quarterly*, 3 (1961): 213–222;

Peter Green, "Robert Graves as Historical Novelist," *Critic*, 20 (1961–1962): 46–50;

Daniel Hoffman, *Barbarous Knowledge: Myth in the Poetry of Yeats, Graves, and Muir* (New York: Oxford University Press, 1967);

Randall Jarrell, "Graves and the White Goddess," in his *The Third Book of Criticism* (New York: Farrar, Straus & Giroux, 1966);

Patrick J. Keane, *A Wild Civility: Interactions in the Poetry and Thought of Robert Graves* (Columbia & London: University of Missouri Press, 1980);

Michael Kirkham, *The Poetry of Robert Graves* (New York: Oxford University Press, 1969);

*Malahat Review*, special Graves issue, edited by Robin Skelton and William David Thomas, 35 (1975);

T. S. Matthews, *Under the Influence* (London: Cassell, 1977);

James S. Mehoke, *Robert Graves: Peace-Weaver* (The Hague: Mouton, 1975);

Sydney Musgrove, *The Ancestry of "The White Goddess"* (Auckland, New Zealand: University of Auckland Press, 1962);

Patrick J. Quinn, *The Great War and the Missing Muse: The Early Writings of Robert Graves and Siegfried Sassoon* (Selinsgrove, Pa.: Susquehanna University Press, 1994);

Martin Seymour-Smith, *Robert Graves* (London: Longmans, Green, 1956);

Seymour-Smith, "Robert Graves," in his *Guide to Modern World Literature* (New York: Funk & Wagnalls, 1973), pp. 244–247;

*Shenandoah*, special Graves issue, 13 (1962);

Katherine Snipes, *Robert Graves* (New York: Ungar, 1979);

Monroe K. Spears, "The Latest Graves: Poet and Private Eye," *Sewanee Review*, 73 (1965): 660–678;

George Stade, *Robert Graves* (New York: Columbia University Press, 1967);

George Steiner, "The Genius of Robert Graves," *Kenyon Review*, 292 (1960): 340–365;

John B. Vickery, *Robert Graves and the White Goddess* (Lincoln: University of Nebraska Press, 1972);

A. N. Wilson, *The Life of John Milton* (Oxford: Oxford University Press, 1983), pp. 114–115.

**Papers:**

Letters and manuscripts of Robert Graves are held in the Graves Manuscript Collection at the University of Victoria, British Columbia; Lockwood Memorial Library, State University of New York at Buffalo; Berg Collection of the New York City Library; Indiana University, Bloomington; Southern Illinois University, Carbondale; the Harry Ransom Humanities Research Center of the University of Texas, Austin; the Bodleian Library, Oxford; the Imperial War Museum, London; and in the private collections of Beryl Graves and Richard Perceval Graves.

# Walter Greenwood

*(17 December 1903 – 13 September 1974)*

Paul W. Salmon
*University of Guelph*

See also the Greenwood entry in *DLB 10: Modern British Dramatists, 1900–1945.*

BOOKS: *Love on the Dole: A Tale of the Two Cities* (London: Cape, 1933; Garden City, N.Y.: Doubleday, Doran, 1934);

*His Worship the Mayor; or, "It's Only Human Nature after All"* (London: Cape, 1934); republished as *The Time is Ripe* (Garden City, N.Y.: Doubleday, Doran, 1935);

*Standing Room Only; or, "A Laugh in Every Line"* (London: Cape, 1936; Garden City, N.Y.: Doubleday, Doran, 1936);

*The Cleft Stick; or, "It's the Same the Whole World Over"* (London: Selwyn & Blount, 1937; New York: Stokes, 1938);

*Only Mugs Work: A Soho Melodrama* (London: Hutchinson, 1938);

*The Secret Kingdom* (London: Cape, 1938);

*How the Other Man Lives* (London: Labour Book Service, 1939);

*Something in My Heart* (London: Hutchinson, 1944);

*The Cure for Love: A Lancashire Comedy in Three Acts* (London: French, 1947);

*Lancashire* (London: Hale, 1951);

*So Brief the Spring* (London & New York: Hutchinson, 1952);

*Too Clever for Love: A Comedy in Three Acts* (London: French, 1952);

*What Everybody Wants* (London: Hutchinson, 1954);

*Down by the Sea* (London: Hutchinson, 1956);

*Saturday Night at the Crown* (London: Hutchinson, 1959);

*There Was a Time* (London: Cape, 1967).

PLAY PRODUCTIONS: *Love on the Dole,* by Greenwood and Ronald Gow, Manchester, Manchester Repertory Theatre, February 1934;

*My Son's My Son,* by Greenwood and D. H. Lawrence, London, The Playhouse, 26 May 1936;

*Only Mugs Work,* 1938;

*Walter Greenwood*

*Give Us This Day,* adapted from *His Worship the Mayor; or, "It's Only Human Nature after All,"* London, Torch Theatre, 1940;

*Rod of Iron,* Oldham, Oldham Repertory Theatre, 29 January 1945; produced again as *The Cure for Love: A Lancashire Comedy in Three Acts,* London, Westminster Theatre, 12 July 1945;

*So Brief the Spring,* London, 1946;

*Never a Dull Moment,* Oldham, Oldham Repertory Theatre, 1950;

*Saturday Night at the Crown: A Comedy in Three Acts,* Morecambe, June 1954; revised, Oldham, Oldham Repertory Theatre, 1956;

*Happy Days,* Oldham, Oldham Repertory Theatre, 1958;

*Fun and Games,* Salford, 1963;

*This Is Your Wife,* Bradford, September 1964;

*There Was a Time,* Dundee, Scotland, 1967; produced again as *Hanky Park,* London, Mermaid Theatre, 1 April 1971.

MOTION PICTURES: *No Limit,* screenplay by Tom Geraghty and Fred Thompson, based on a story for the screen by Greenwood, Ealing Studios, 1935;

*Love on the Dole,* screenplay by Greenwood, Barbara K. Emery, and Rollo Gamble, British National Studios, 1941;

*Eureka Stockade,* screenplay by Greenwood, Harry Watt, and Ralph Smart, from a story by Watt, Ealing Studios, 1949; released in the United States as *Massacre Hill,* 1949;

*Chance of A Lifetime,* screenplay by Greenwood and Bernard Miles, Pilgrim Pictures, 1950.

Despite being a prolific author of novels, plays, short stories, and screenplays, Walter Greenwood is remembered almost exclusively for his first novel, *Love on the Dole: A Tale of the Two Cities* (1933), and for the stage and screen adaptations of this work. *Love on the Dole,* his only novel that continues to be readily available in a paperback edition, was one of the few of his works to achieve notable commercial success. Though Greenwood's name is mentioned in many standard studies of British literature and culture in the 1930s, such mention is almost invariably in conjunction with the popular and critical success of *Love on the Dole.* While there is no simple explanation for the critical neglect of most of Greenwood's work, it seems likely that Greenwood's reputation was to an extent the victim of critical typecasting. Many of his contemporary critics heralded *Love on the Dole* as a major contribution to a strong political current in British culture whose advocates had a pronounced leftist agenda. It is not surprising, therefore, that critical disillusionment ensued when Greenwood's subsequent work failed to fit the mold anticipated for it.

In a more-balanced view of Greenwood's work, *Love on the Dole* may be regarded not as the writer's sole artistic legacy but as one of the wellsprings of a rich, though admittedly uneven, artistic vision. The transformation of *Love on the Dole* from novel to play to film reflects Greenwood's creative versatility and typifies his specific penchant for adapting his own works from one medium to another. Having emerged from the working class himself, Greenwood remained socially conscious and dismayed by the disparity between rich and poor throughout his career; he saw writing as a means of

escape from the slum. He did not disdain popular forms and often courted commercial success, though it proved elusive, nor did he repudiate the power of fiction, film, or theater to provide people with an entertaining break from the struggles of their lives.

Walter Greenwood was born on 17 December 1903 and was brought up in the Hankinson Street district of Salford, a neighborhood of working-class housing that in *Love on the Dole* and several of his other works is fictionally re-created as "Hanky Park." This area was situated just off one of the main roads into Manchester, and the so-called Two Cities of Salford and Manchester became the recurrent setting of his work in much the same way that the Five Towns feature repeatedly in Arnold Bennett's writing. Greenwood was the son of Tom Greenwood, a master hairdresser, and Elizabeth Walter Greenwood, a waitress. Walter had only one sibling, sister Betty, four years his junior. He attended the Langworthy Road Council School until he was thirteen. His father, whom Greenwood described as a man who could carry his clothes magnificently but not his liquor, died when the author was nine; this event was briefly but powerfully evoked in Greenwood's essay "The Old School: An Autobiographical Fragment," written for a collection edited by Graham Greene, *The Old School: Essays by Divers Hands* (1934), and reprinted as the final item in Greenwood's collection of prose pieces, *The Cleft Stick; or, "It's the Same the Whole World Over"* (1937). Tom Greenwood's death left Greenwood's mother to provide for the household. Greenwood held a variety of jobs when he could get work—clerking in a pawnshop, writing signs, cleaning stables, making packing cases, working in a warehouse—but none of these jobs paid more than thirty-five shillings a week. In his writing he drew on these subsistence-level experiences and on the respite he found in books or in occasional trips to the countryside.

In his autobiography, *There Was a Time* (1967), Greenwood looked back to the period of his life from childhood to the publication of his first novel. Because *There Was a Time* seldom mentions specific dates and because of its strong novelistic quality, several critics have questioned its value as autobiography. The work nevertheless provides useful insight into the formative influences on Greenwood as a writer, both in terms of specific personalities and in terms of the social context that has so obviously shaped virtually all of his writing. An important artistic and political influence on Greenwood was his maternal grandfather, a lifelong trade unionist and opera lover. From his father, whom he refers to at one point in his memoir as "the singing Irish Comedian," Greenwood absorbed a love of the music hall, which would later feed his comic dramas; from his mother, a lover of opera and serious literature, he received encouragement for his first authorial efforts.

Beyond its vision of Greenwood's inner family circle, *There Was a Time* also provides insight into the wider context of the slums of the Two Cities that were the author's artistic domain. In this world of cramped dwellings and pawnbrokers, inhabitants live in constant fear of losing their jobs, or, if already unemployed, of losing their dole and ending up in the workhouse. Greenwood chronicles the capacity of slum dwellers for both incredible generosity and acts of desperate self-interest. The specific historical context that shaped him as a writer emerges from passages depicting anti-German sentiment in his neighborhood after the sinking of the *Lusitania* during World War I, the ambivalence of slum dwellers regarding the General Strike of 1926, and the mounting frustration among the swelling ranks of the unemployed in the late 1920s.

Greenwood incorporated these materials into *Love on the Dole,* published in June 1933. This novel is a powerful work of documentary realism that chronicles the misfortunes of the Hardcastle family, who struggle for subsistence in the working-class neighborhood of Hanky Park, Salford. It particularly focuses on the fortunes of Harry and Sally Hardcastle, who are brother and sister, but in the manner of Charles Dickens the story includes a gallery of memorable characters. As the novel begins, Harry has just finished school and is starting full-time work at the pawnshop where he had already been working long hours while others assumed that he was in school. Harry chafes at the intolerable boredom of work at the pawnshop and covets a job at Marlowe's, the great engineering works. He finally secures a job there as an apprenticing engineer. While working as an apprentice Harry wins twenty-two pounds on a three-pence horse-race bet and goes on an idyllic holiday by the sea with Helen, a local girl who is the object of his romantic affections. At the beginning of *Love on the Dole* Sally's fortunes seem similarly promising. She is employed and begins a relationship with Larry Meath, a self-educated socialist who introduces Sally to his friends and associates at the Labour Club.

As the novel progresses, however, the fortunes of both Harry and Sally sharply decline. As soon as his apprenticeship is over, Harry is let go by the engineering works since keeping him on would necessitate paying him higher wages. Harry's love affair with Helen ends in a shotgun marriage and, dis-

owned by his family, Harry is tempted to turn to crime in order to support his wife and child. Larry Meath, already seriously ill with a wracking cough, is savagely beaten during a workers' protest march and dies soon after. In desperation Sally gives in to the entreaties of the mercenary Sam Grundy, a local bookie whose sole interest in her is sexual. In a highly equivocal ending that offers a glimmer of hope dashed with bitter irony, Sally secures jobs at the bus offices for her brother and her father through Grundy's influence. Although the narrative is at times overly melodramatic, the novel deserves praise for honestly capturing the impoverished world and the colorful dialogue of its North Country characters.

Almost universally hailed by critics and readers alike, the novel went through a succession of printings upon its initial release and was quickly translated into many languages. The immediate respect for *Love on the Dole* among intellectuals, along with the grim material circumstances of its author at the time of its publication, can be illustrated by Greenwood's contact at the time with the novelist Graham Greene. According to Greene's biographer, Norman Sherry, Greene was deeply moved by *Love on the Dole* and, prior to the publication of his own review of the book in the *Spectator,* wrote a congratulatory letter to the author. Greenwood promptly replied to Greene, and Sherry quotes the following entry from Greene's journal: "Heard from Walter Greenwood . . . a pathetic letter referring to the hard life he had had, his broken engagement, etc. Living now on 30/- a week wages at Salford. Glad I had written." According to Sherry, Greene was so moved by the vision of squalor evoked in Greenwood's letter that the following day he wrote to fellow author Naomi Mitchison asking whether something might not be done for Greenwood through the Authors' Society.

Perhaps it was with the prospect of helping him partly in mind that Greene soon solicited an essay from Greenwood for *The Old School,* which gathered reminiscences of school experiences from such prominent writers of the time as W. H. Auden, Harold Nicolson, Elizabeth Bowen, Anthony Powell, and Greene himself. In "The Old School: An Autobiographical Fragment," Greenwood's bleak recollections of his education are vividly revealed. He opens the essay by indicating that his ability to quit school in 1916 at the age of thirteen was an exquisite pleasure, the enjoyment of which was only dampened by the necessity of being expected to work at the pawnbroker's shop. Elsewhere in the essay he describes school as a "punishment for being young" and claims that the "teachers' disgust of us was only equaled by our disgust of them and of the School."

Greenwood followed *Love on the Dole* with the novel *His Worship the Mayor; or, "It's Only Human Nature after All,"* first published in September 1934 and eventually adapted by Greenwood for the stage as *Give Us This Day* in 1940. Although an ambitious work that develops the social concerns of Greenwood's first novel, *His Worship the Mayor* is ultimately disappointing. Like *Love on the Dole,* it is set in the Two Cities. The novel chronicles the simultaneous rise to social position of Edgar Hargraves and the inexorable fall of the impoverished Shuttleworth family. In this work Greenwood is at pains to show that Hargraves's social ascent is not achieved through any deserving character qualities but is made possible mainly through the convenient—and, by Hargraves, eagerly awaited—death of his eccentric aunt, Phoebe, who leaves him a substantial fortune. The Shuttleworths are similarly, but negatively, the pawns of fate. Joe Shuttleworth loses his job at a coal mine, and this blow to his dignity depresses him deeply and leads ultimately to his death. His young son, Jimmy, seizes the chance to help the family by getting a job at the local rubber works but soon acquires the debilitating lung illness experienced by many of his coworkers.

The basic structuring principle of the novel is a crude dialectic whereby a scene concerning Hargraves's rise is juxtaposed with a scene dealing with the Shuttleworths' decline. From time to time the two plotlines directly connect, most strikingly at the beginning of the novel, which includes one of its strongest scenes. One of Mrs. Shuttleworth's jobs is cleaning the Hargraves shop, and while engaged in her duties there she steals a shawl, an act that results in her serving a term in prison. The incident is a richly ambivalent one in which the reader's temptation to judge the act in moral terms is complicated by knowledge of the Shuttleworths' desperate poverty and of the pomposity, hypocrisy, and greed of Hargraves.

While the crosscutting effect of *His Worship the Mayor* is simplistic and too often seems contrived, it does yield some benefits. For example, the technique enables Greenwood to develop an ironic parallel between how slum neighbors pull together to help each other, especially during the crisis of Mrs. Shuttleworth's incarceration, and the way in which the social climbers of Hargraves's circle grease each other's palms. Yet a fundamental problem remains, arising from the conflicting modes of the two plotlines. While the plotline concerning the Shuttleworths resonates with the kind of documentary realism that was a source of artistic strength in *Love on*

'Love on the Dole.   A Tale of the Two Cities.   By Walter Greenwood

'The Time is ripe, and rotten ripe, for change;
Then let it come . . .'
                                    JAMES RUSSELL LOWELL

Doubleday, Doran & Company Inc.
Garden City     1934     New York

*Title page for the American edition of Greenwood's first novel*

*the Dole,* the Hargraves plotline is dominated by caricature and comic hyperbole. Although Hargraves is intended to be emblematic of the exploitative system that imprisons the Shuttleworths, it is all too easy to dismiss Hargraves and his plotline as the products of literary exaggeration.

There is a close parallel between *Love on the Dole* and *His Worship the Mayor* in terms of closure. At the end of each work there is a direct echo both of the language and the situation with which the novel opens. The plight of the Hardcastles and Shuttleworths (emblematic of their class) seems inescapable because of this emphasis on what one critic, Valentine Cunningham, calls "a closed economic circle." Not surprisingly, such apparent pessimism on Greenwood's part was attacked by Marxist critics of the time, who would have preferred to see the depiction of a more assertive and activist proletariat capable of taking its collective destiny into its own hands. As Richard Johnstone notes:

When . . . *His Worship the Mayor* appeared in 1934, the *Left Review* praised its faithfulness to life only to conclude that 'it lacks ultimate direction, and its most serious fault is the complete absence of any suggestion of a solution to the state of vulgar bigotry and exploitation on the one hand and unrelieved misery and want on the other.' The proletarian novel, while it described conditions as they were, failed to point to the necessity of political action, and for this it was condemned.

In *Standing Room Only; or, "A Laugh in Every Line"* (1936) Greenwood turns his analytical gaze to the London theatrical world. In this novel Henry Ormerod, a store clerk from the Two Cities, is the author of a play, *A Laugh in Every Line.* Unexpectedly Henry's play arouses the interest of rival London theatrical agents; he is propelled into the heady world of the West End of London; and his play becomes a hit. The basic structuring principle of the novel involves the contrast between the naiveté and inexperience of the insecure store clerk and the slick, cynical opportunism of such characters as Harry Ellis, a theatrical agent; Henry's own father, an aging vaudevillian with delusions of grandeur; and Sir Walter Brierly, whose patronage of the play stems mainly from his sexual attraction to its leading lady.

The action of *Only Mugs Work: A Soho Melodrama* (1938) centers on the conflict between two rival groups of criminals. The Gorelli gang, run by Tony Gorelli, conducts a variety of nefarious enterprises including the smuggling into England of illegal aliens fleeing the rise of Nazism in Europe. The other gang is led by a mysterious personage referred to only as the "Con Man," whose actual identity is not revealed until late in the novel. Both gangs use a variety of quasi legitimate activities as fronts for their more-illicit ventures. As the novel opens, tension between the two groups has escalated because of the Con Man's involvement in the slot-machine racket, which had hitherto been monopolized by Gorelli. At the center of the heightening of narrative conflict is Mario Gorelli, Tony's younger brother. Mario is jealous of his older brother and resents Tony's position of supremacy within the group. Tired of being expected to consult with Tony before conducting gang business, Mario rashly decides to frame the Con Man by using one of the Con Man's own cars to pull a heist at a fur warehouse. Predictably, the scheme backfires, and Mario's fatal shooting of a policeman during the robbery forces him to flee. In the end Mario's action precipitates the demise of the Gorelli gang.

There are several connections between *Standing Room Only* and *Only Mugs Work* that actually point up the weaknesses of both. The two works share the laudable ambition of revealing to the reader the darker side of certain social strata (the world of the theater in the former and the London underworld in the latter). But in both books this documentary impulse clashes with stereotypical conventions and especially with the kind of simplistic genre tropes one would expect a social commentator studiously to avoid. The authenticity of the portrait of gangsters in *Only Mugs Work* is undermined by the pervasiveness of gangster film iconography and of Greenwood's incongruous weaving of a romantic plotline into the work. Similarly, *Standing Room Only* abounds with stock characters such as Henry's self-willed and shrewish mother and Edna, the young woman in love with Henry who patiently waits for him to come to his senses after the glamour of West End has cast its spell. Exemplifying the awkward tensions in *Standing Room Only* is the character of Roger Morden, the director of the stage production of Henry's play. Morden espouses socialist views that echo Greenwood's own and that point up the grasping selfishness rampant in the world of the theater. Yet, although Morden almost emerges as worthy of the reader's attention, this more complex character finds himself in a world of stock characters, rather like a good actor trapped in a bad play.

A more insidious dimension of both novels involves ethnic stereotyping. In *Only Mugs Work* the emphasis on the Italian heritage of several of the Gorelli gang fails to transcend the limits of a simplistic stock mafioso characterization. In *Standing Room Only* there is a strand of anti-Semitism that is no less painful for being subtle. Jake Macpherson (who has changed his name from Jacob Loblensky) is a stereotypical Jewish entertainment mogul whose obsession with money is one of his defining characteristics and to whom one character says: "Once a Jew, always a Jew. Can't you *ever* do a deal without haggling?" Quite apart from being painfully racist, such stereotypes point up the social scapegoating from which they often originate. In *Only Mugs Work* any critique of the corruption of the London underworld is mitigated by the inference that such corruption can be blamed, at least in part, on the influence of "foreigners," specifically Italian immigrants. Similarly, in *Standing Room Only* the figure of the Jewish business mogul becomes a scapegoat for the rapacious greed and self-interest that typify the London theatrical world.

In 1937 Greenwood married Pearl Alice Osgood, an American actress. That year also saw the publication of *The Cleft Stick,* a volume of fifteen short stories that retains considerable interest on several levels. In his "Author's Preface" to the volume Greenwood indicates that most of the stories in the collection were actually composed between 1928 and 1931, prior to the publication of *Love on the Dole*. *The Cleft Stick* therefore provides insight into the genesis of *Love on the Dole*, particularly since several characters and situations from the stories resurface in the novel. As in *Love on the Dole*, Greenwood is at his best in the stories documenting the social realities of the slum dwellers of the Two Cities. For example, in the title story of the collection, "The Cleft Stick," Greenwood manages to avoid bathos in the haunting portrait of a woman in the slums whose misery tempts her to contemplate suicide but who finds that she lacks the coppers necessary to start the gas oven that she intends to use for this purpose. In "Joe Goes Home" a blind old man whose lifelong career had been to rap on people's windows in the morning to wake them up realizes that a trip he is about to take to the hospital will be his last trip anywhere. In "Any Bread, Cake or Pie?" a growing young boy's desperate battle with hunger leads him to commit theft.

*The Cleft Stick* garnered many positive reviews, both in Britain upon its initial release and a year later upon its release in the United States. Writing in *New Statesman and Nation* (11 December 1937), Brian Howard ended a strongly favorable review of the work as follows: "Imaginative, unideological, stimulating, yet truthful, this volume would make a splendid Christmas present for persons who need an effective, first push to the Left." The reviewer for *The New York Times Book Review* (2 October 1938), Jane Spence Southron rightly saw that *The Cleft Stick* is most fully appreciated as a story sequence: "This volume must not be regarded as a collection of isolated stories, but as fifteen chapters in the contemporary life of two English cities, Manchester and Salford, described by the author in his preface as 'of indescribable ugliness,' the nearest approach to which in America, he is assured by his wife, an American, is Pittsburgh."

Along with *Only Mugs Work* and the American edition of *The Cleft Stick*, Greenwood's next novel, *The Secret Kingdom*, was published in 1938. This novel, like almost all of Greenwood's fiction, is set in the Two Cities. It is a saga of the fictitious Byron family with a particular focus on Paula, Viola, and Anne, the three daughters of William Byron, a master craftsman. In the novel Paula struggles against the effects of poverty to improve the circumstances of herself and her family and to attain some degree of artistic culture, eventually focusing her energies on the musical talents of her son, William. Several episodes are drawn with particular power, including the struggle of Paula's husband, Robert Treville, with alcohol; an accident at the local mine that kills both Viola's husband, Chris Winter, and Anne's husband, Sam Hardie; and the declining fortunes of William Byron, whose way of life is destroyed by the onset of mass production.

In *The Secret Kingdom* several interrelated themes are explored, including the grinding adversity of poverty, the negative effect of mass production on the quality of workmanship, and the manipulative power of advertising. One particularly intriguing example of this latter theme involves the way in which advertisements for ale and liquor consumption are drawn into the account of Treville's urge to drink. On one level the omnipresent ads become a medium of seduction, tempting Treville away from the path of sobriety. On another level an ironic contrast is suggested between the glamorous world invoked by the ads and the actual degraded depths to which Treville has sunk.

*The Secret Kingdom* is arguably Greenwood's most overtly autobiographical novel. Like Robert Treville, Greenwood's father struggled with alcohol, was a barber, was locally known for his singing voice, and died when his son was still a child. Paula, with her love of music and opera and her desire to instill these into her son, is surely based on Greenwood's mother, while William Byron, with his love of music and his deep socialist convictions, is probably based on Greenwood's grandfather. Paula's son, William, with his artistic creativity, love of music, and guilt over not doing his share for his mother and sister, is no doubt an alter ego for the author himself.

Concurrently with his role as a novelist, Greenwood was a man of the theater. *Love on the Dole* was itself redrafted for the stage in 1934 by its author and Ronald Gow, a dramatist who had long wanted to work on a project dealing with unemployment. The play was first performed in February 1934 in Gow's hometown of Manchester at the Manchester Repertory Theatre. In 1936, following a run of 391 performances in London, the play opened in New York. It helped launch the rise to stardom of actress Wendy Hiller, who played the role of Sally in both the Manchester and London productions.

The reviewers of the stage production of *Love on the Dole* were impressed, and a useful overview of the almost unanimous praise of the production is provided by Stephen Constantine in his 1982 article "'Love on the Dole' and its Reception in the 1930's": "*The Stage* claimed that 'It is a long time since London has seen a play so sincere and so powerful,' while *John O'London* thought it an 'admirable and extremely moving play.' Even *The Illustrated Sporting and Dramatic News* described it as 'an epic written with the realism of Tchechov,' and *The*

*Deborah Kerr in a scene from the 1941 film version of Greenwood's* Love on the Dole

*Times,* after some guarded criticisms, conceded that 'being conceived in suffering and written in blood, it profoundly moves its audience.'" Constantine notes, furthermore, that there were "a score of curtain calls on the first night. It was claimed that fully one million people had seen the play in England before the end of 1935, and it then ran successfully on Broadway in 1936 and in Paris in 1937."

Greenwood's dramatic career spanned five decades, from plays in the 1930s such as *Love on the Dole* and *My Son's My Son* (1936), which he completed from a work begun by D. H. Lawrence, to *Hanky Park,* a stage adaptation of his autobiography that had a limited run at the Mermaid Theatre in London in 1971. One intriguing strand of his theatrical career involves his dramatizations of his own fiction. There was a stage adaptation of *Only Mugs Work* in 1938, and *Give Us This Day,* first produced in 1940, is an adaptation of *His Worship the Mayor.* One of Greenwood's one-act plays, *The Practised Hand,* is an adaptation of a chilling story in *The Cleft Stick* about a woman who makes money through her talent for discreetly terminating the lives of dying people whose next of kin are eagerly awaiting the opportunity to redeem insurance policies. Yet Greenwood was never to have another play that enjoyed the commercial success of *Love on the Dole.*

After *Love on the Dole* Greenwood's two most successful theatrical ventures, and certainly the most representative of his turn toward broad Lancashire comedy, were *The Cure for Love: A Lancashire Comedy in Three Acts,* first produced by Douglas Emery (under the title *Rod of Iron*) at the Oldham Repertory Theatre on 29 January 1945, and *Saturday Night at the Crown: A Comedy in Three Acts* (1954). After a preliminary provincial tour *The Cure for Love* was presented by the company at Westminster Theatre, London, beginning on 12 July 1945, under the direction of the well-known British actor Robert Donat, who himself played central character Jack Hardacre. The comic plot takes place in Salford toward the last stages of World War II and turns on the complications arising from a basic love triangle involving Jack Hardacre, a soldier home on leave; Janey Jenkens, whose dubious claim that she and Jack are engaged is based on the fact that she used a monetary gift from Jack to buy an engagement ring; and Milly, a young woman from London who is billeted with Jack's mother, Sarah, and is working at a factory for the duration of the war. Though Jack initially feels obligated to honor his engagement with Janey, his love for Milly confuses and frustrates him and raises the hackles of both Janey and her mother, who work together to ensnare Jack. The romance plot is further complicated by the courting of Milly by Joe Truman; in a subordinate plot strand the proprietor of the Flying Shuttle pub, Harry Lancaster, attempts to woo Sarah, whose gruff, unsentimental exterior makes her seem impervious to romance. The play ends predictably with Jack and Milly coming together, Sarah capitulating to Harry, and Joe and Janey consoling each other for their respective romantic losses.

The main interest of *The Cure for Love* resides not in its pedestrian plot but in its glimpses of working-class British society during the war that jut through the rather flimsy comic surface: the wartime work in factories undertaken by women; the damage done to cities during the Blitz; rationing; and the potential for jealous tension between soldiers on leave, tired of being asked when they will be returning to action, and men in "civvies," who are unable to compete with the sexual allure of a man in uniform. A screen adaptation by Donat, Albert Fennell, and Alexander Shaw was released in 1950 under the direction of Donat, who reprised the role of Jack Hardacre.

*Saturday Night at the Crown* was first produced in June 1954, but it was not seen in London until a revised version (produced in Oldham in 1956) opened at the Garrick Theatre on 9 September 1957. The "Crown" of the title is the neighborhood pub, and the loosely structured plot of this work provides a pretext for much conversation among the regular pub patrons. As the play opens, several characters are enjoying a pint, including Ada Thorpe and her husband, Herbert, and two brothers-in-law, Sam and Charlie. Their talk is mainly centered on three subjects: the recent death of old Mrs. Hardy and the family feud over money that this death has precipitated; the extreme nervousness of Tom Fielden, whose wife is having a baby; and the possible trajectory of several love affairs involving various patrons and employees of the pub. Wilbur, an American soldier, is in love with Sally, the barmaid, and his overtures to her provoke the jealousy of Harry Boothroyd, the owner of the pub, who has long adored Sally without articulating the truth about how he feels. The pretentious widow Eunice Sidebottom shows her love for Harry by giving him a fishing rod for his birthday—a gift that elicits plenty of banter among the patrons about catching a mate. The resolution of these romantic intrigues is as predictable as in *The Cure for Love*. Sally and Harry come to realize their mutual affection, leaving Wilbur and Eunice to console each other for their disappointments. Again, as in *The Cure for Love,* the strength of the play resides not in its plot but in the accuracy with which Greenwood captures the tart drolleries of Lancashire pub patrons. In an interesting reversal of Greenwood's frequent adaptations of his fiction into plays, *Saturday Night at the Crown* was

adapted by the author into a novel by the same title that was published in 1959.

A facet of Greenwood's work that deserves further research is his role as a screenwriter, which, like his roles as novelist and dramatist, began at the outset of his literary career. Greenwood's first screenplay was *No Limit* (1935), a comedy that he wrote for George Formby, the popular working-class comedian who, like Greenwood, was a North Country man. In the film Formby plays a motor mechanic determined to win an important dirt-bike race on the Isle of Man. Success was immediate, and the film had many revivals.

In his 1992 history of British cinema, *The Age of the Dream Palace: Cinema and Society in Britain, 1930–1939,* Jeffrey Richards documents the complex history of Greenwood's next film, an adaptation of *Love on the Dole*. According to Richards the press reported in 1936 that negotiations for making a film of *Love on the Dole* were in progress. But, interestingly, this proposal by the British division of the French studio Gaumont was blocked by the British board of film censors. As another commentator, Valentine Cunningham, notes: "It was a curious back-handed compliment to the power of Greenwood's story that the censors found it too disturbing to present before a popular audience in the 1930's." Late in 1940, in a political climate made more favorable by the onset of the war, the filming of *Love on the Dole* finally began on location in the English North Country, with a script by Greenwood, Barbara K. Emery, and Rollo Gamble. *Love on the Dole* was directed by John Baxter for British National Studios and starred the as-yet-unknown Deborah Kerr, whose acting career the film helped to launch. The film was greeted with glowing reviews of a kind reminiscent of the original critical reaction to the novel and the stage adaptation. As Peter Stead notes, "The climax of the film was probably one of the most shocking moments that British audiences of that period had ever seen, for the young girl goes off to become a bookie's tart so as to improve her family's fortunes." The durability and adaptability of *Love on the Dole* is suggested by the fact that it was resurrected as a stage musical in 1970.

After World War II Greenwood worked on the scripts for several films, including *Eureka Stockade* (1949), released in the United States as *Massacre Hill* (1949). Greenwood cowrote the film with Ralph Smart and the well-known documentarian Harry Watt, who also directed the picture. The film is set during the Australian gold rush of the 1850s and concerns the adventures of a group of Australian gold miners who revolt against a harsh governor. The well-armed government forces easily subdue the rebels, but public opinion shifts in favor of the miners, and the government is forced to make concessions to the miners' demands. Featured in the cast was Chips Rafferty, a popular Australian screen personality of the period, who played Peter Lalor, the leader of the rebellious miners.

Greenwood next collaborated with Bernard Miles on the script for *Chance of a Lifetime* (1950), which Miles also directed and acted in. In this film the workers in a small engineering plant conduct a strike against what they perceive to be inefficient management, accepting a challenge from their bosses to run the factory themselves. The workers' discovery that they have taken on more than they can handle leads to a reconciliation between the union and management sides. While the film would probably be regarded now as politically naive, it was welcomed by some critics at the time of its release for its willingness to address labor issues and for its emphasis on the need for cooperation between labor and management.

Three years before his death from heart failure in 1974, Greenwood was made an honorary D.Litt. by Salford University. While the author was undoubtedly deserving of such recognition, today he is rarely paid the tribute of being read. Undoubtedly part of the blame for such neglect must be attributed to Greenwood himself. The intensity of his dedication to the social realities around him often left him careless about the formal and stylistic aspects of his work. On the other hand, this same preoccupation with the experiences of the working class infuses the best of his works with a rich sociohistorical value that makes them deserving of further evaluation.

**References:**

Stephen Constantine, "'Love on the Dole' and its Reception in the 1930's," *Literature and History*, 8 (Autumn 1982): 233–247;

Valentine Cunningham, *British Writers of the Thirties* (Oxford: Oxford University Press, 1988), pp. 83–84, 131–132, 137, 284, 306, 315–316, 322;

Andrew Davies, *Leisure, Gender and Poverty: Working-Class Culture in Salford and Manchester 1900–1939* (Philadelphia: Open University Press, 1992), pp. 9, 40, 46–48, 57–58, 76, 81, 83, 85, 94, 149, 153–154;

Richard Johnstone, *The Will to Believe: Novelists of the Nineteen-Thirties* (Oxford: Oxford University Press, 1982), pp. 32–34;

Jeffrey Richards, *The Age of the Dream Palace: Cinema and Society in Britain, 1930–1939* (London: Routledge, 1984), pp. 119–120, 198–199, 254, 302;

Norman Sherry, *The Life of Graham Greene,* volume 1 (London: Cape, 1989), p. 478;

Peter Stead, *Film and the Working Class: The Feature Film in British and American Society* (London: Routledge, 1989), p. 127.

# Charlotte Haldane
### (27 April 1894 – 16 March 1969)

### Judith Adamson
*Dawson College, Montreal*

BOOKS: *Man's World* (London: Chatto & Windus, 1926; New York: Doran, 1927);

*Motherhood and Its Enemies* (London: Chatto & Windus, 1927; Garden City, N.Y.: Doubleday, Doran, 1928);

*Brother to Bert* (London: Chatto & Windus, 1930);

*I Bring Not Peace* (London: Chatto & Windus, 1932);

*Youth Is a Crime* (London: Faber & Faber, 1934);

*Melusine; or, Devil Take Her!* (London: Barker, 1936; New York: Arno, 1978);

*Music, My Love!: One Listener's Autobiography* (London: Barker, 1936);

*Russian Newsreel: An Eye-Witness Account of the Soviet Union at War* (London: Secker & Warburg, 1942; Harmondsworth & New York: Penguin, 1943);

*Truth Will Out* (London: Weidenfeld & Nicolson, 1949; New York: Vanguard, 1951);

*Marcel Proust* (London: Barker, 1951; New York: Roy, 1951);

*The Shadow of a Dream* (London: Weidenfeld & Nicolson, 1952; New York: Roy, 1953);

*Fifi and Antoine: A Romance* (London: Harvill, 1956);

*The Galley Slaves of Love: The Story of Marie d'Agoult and Franz Liszt* (London: Harvill, 1957);

*Mozart* (London & New York: Oxford University Press, 1960);

*Alfred: The Passionate Life of Alfred de Musset* (London: Blond, 1960; New York: Roy, 1961);

*Daughter of Paris: The Life Story of Céleste Mogador, Comtesse Lionel de Moreton de Chabrillan, Told by Herself* (London: Hutchinson, 1961);

*Tempest over Tahiti* (London: Constable, 1963);

*The Last Great Empress of China* (London: Constable, 1965; Indianapolis: Bobbs-Merrill, 1966);

*Queen of Hearts: Marguerite of Valois ("La Reine Margot") 1553–1615* (London: Constable, 1968; Indianapolis: Bobbs-Merrill, 1968);

*Charlotte Haldane with her second husband, the geneticist J. B. S. Haldane*

*Madame de Maintenon: Uncrowned Queen of France* (London: Constable, 1970; Indianapolis: Bobbs-Merrill, 1970).

PLAY PRODUCTIONS: *The Crooked Sapling,* Cambridge Arts Theatre, May 1944;

*The Age of Consent,* London, Princes Theatre, August 1953.

RADIO SCRIPTS: "The World Goes By," British Broadcasting Corporation, 1943;

*The World Today,* British Broadcasting Corporation World Service, 1948–1951;

*Justice Is Deaf,* British Broadcasting Corporation, 1951;

"Woman's Hour" and "Children's Hour," British Broadcasting Corporation, 1952;

*Books and People,* British Broadcasting Corporation, 1954.

OTHER: Charlotte Yonge, *The Heir of Redclyffe,* preface by Haldane (London: Duckworth, 1964).

TRANSLATIONS: Johannes Lange, *Crime and Destiny* (New York: Boni, 1930); republished as *Crime as Destiny: A Study of Criminal Twins* (London: Allen & Unwin, 1931);

Michelle Lorraine, *Castle in the Sea* (London: Harvill, 1956; Boston: Beacon, 1957);

Heinz Woltereck, *A New Life in Old Age* (London: Reinhardt, 1958); republished as *A New Life in Your Later Years* (New York: Dial, 1959);

Michel Join-Lambert, *Jerusalem: Ancient Cities and Temples* (London: Elek, 1958; New York: Putnam, 1958);

Alphonse Daudet, *Sidonie* (London: Blond, 1958; New York: Roy, 1958);

Anne Rives, *Over the Tunnel* (London: Harvill, 1962; New York: Dutton, 1962);

Jean Héritier, *Catherine de Médici* (London: Allen & Unwin, 1963; New York: St. Martin's, 1963);

Catherine Devilliers, *Lieutenant Katia* (London: Constable, 1964);

Jean Décarreaux, *Monks and Civilization: From the Barbarian Invasions to the Reign of Charlemagne* (London: Allen & Unwin, 1964).

Charlotte Haldane was one of the first newswomen on Fleet Street, a novelist, biographer, political essayist, playwright, music critic, and radio broadcaster—in short, a versatile woman of letters. She was an ardent, albeit quirky, feminist and, in the 1930s, an indefatigable activist for the British Communist Party. Her novels and newspaper articles are a valuable register of British life from the 1920s to the 1950s, especially as it concerned women; her autobiography includes an account of her loss of belief in communism that is as compelling as Stephen Spender's account of his own disillusionment. In spite of these accomplishments, she has received attention from scholars chiefly as the wife of the geneticist J. B. S. Haldane.

Charlotte Franken was born on 27 April 1894 in Sydenham, in south London, to the Jewish immigrants Joseph and Mathilde Saarbach Franken. Her father was a wealthy German fur merchant; her mother, born in New York City, had adopted German manners in her teens after moving to Frankfurt am Main to live with an aunt.

Charlotte Franken was educated at South Hampstead High School in London until her father's business took the family to the Continent in 1906; she then attended the Allgemeine Deutsche Schule in Antwerp. She was discouraged from writing poems and stories by her German governess, who tore them up, and by her parents, who were indifferent to her talent. Nonetheless, by the time the family returned to London in 1910 she was determined to be a writer. She was planning to study languages at Bedford College for Women, but a decline in her father's business resulted in her being sent to secretarial school. She went to work for a concert agent, where her duties included translating Anna Pavlova's ballet synopses from the French, and then for a music publisher, where she ghostwrote articles under the names of music-hall stars for women's twopenny weeklies.

During World War I her father, who had never become a British subject, was declared an enemy alien. To avoid being interned he went to the United States with his younger daughter, Elizabeth, and his American-born wife. Charlotte chose to remain in London even though she was excluded by her father's situation from the war work for which her language and secretarial skills suited her. Using the pseudonym Charlotte Franklyn to disguise her German surname, she published her first short story in *The Bystander* in 1916.

In 1918 Franken married Jack Burghes, who had been shell-shocked in the war. Their son, Ronald John McLeod Burghes, was born in January 1919. Charlotte supported the family by free-lancing for the *Daily Express* and other London newspapers. In 1921 the *Daily Express* hired her, first as social editor and then as a reporter; she also free-lanced for the separately run *Sunday Express.* Her articles took up the feminist cause; she championed married women—especially those who, like her, were supporting families—and often used court reports to argue for changes in the divorce laws. She believed that women should emancipate themselves from traditional roles but that they should not try to copy men; her idealization of marriage and motherhood led some feminists to condemn her.

In 1924, amid widespread interest in the possibility of ectogenesis (gestation outside the womb), Charlotte Burghes interviewed the country's leading geneticist, John Burdon Sanderson Haldane. They were married in 1926, after Jack Burghes divorced her; J. B. S. Haldane was named as corespondent in the highly publicized case, which nearly cost him his readership in biochemistry at Cambridge.

Muriel C. Bradbrook, who was then a student at Girton College, called Roebuck House, the Haldanes' home, "the most advanced political household in Cambridge." The young scientists, musicians, actors, and writers who gathered there included William Empson, Michael Redgrave, Hugh Sykes Davies, John Davenport, Martin Case, and Malcolm Lowry.

In 1926 Haldane left the staff of the *Daily Express* and published her first novel, *Man's World,* to critical acclaim. The work is a dystopia set in the future. It depicts a society ruled by and for men in which women are categorized according to their biological capabilities; those who do not want children are free to be artists or administrators and to have sexual relations with whomever they choose, but they must be sterilized to safeguard the future of the race. Their contributions to society are considered inferior to those of "vocational mothers," who predetermine the sex of their children by performing "Perrier exercises" during pregnancy and who make up motherhood councils that control the genetic stock and regulate the proportions of male and female babies. *Man's World* remains Haldane's best-known novel. In some ways it foreshadows Aldous Huxley's *Brave New World* (1932), which she would review favorably in *Nature* (23 April 1932). Huxley, too, describes ectogenesis as the final result of industrial rationality, but in Huxley's novel men and women are affected equally by the system. The world Haldane envisions is closer to the one Margaret Atwood would create six decades later in *The Handmaid's Tale* (1985).

In 1924, in *Daedalus; or, Science and the Future,* Haldane's new husband had optimistically predicted a future in which the division between pure and applied science would no longer exist; babies would be bred in test tubes; and the world would be rationally and humanely controlled by biochemists. As her novel shows, Charlotte Haldane was highly skeptical about the advantages of such a situation, especially for women. She was, nonetheless, fascinated by science, and she was so quick to understand the principles of the experiments that J. B. S. Haldane and his colleagues were conducting in the Cambridge laboratories that she set up the Science News Service to simplify and sell scientific articles to the popular press. She continued to run the agency, writing most of the articles herself, for the next ten years.

Haldane's second book, *Motherhood and Its Enemies* (1927), is a nonfiction work that the feminist historian Sheila Jeffreys calls an "antifeminist classic." Haldane's notion that the "normal" woman, "on attaining maturity, mates and bears children"

*Haldane with some of the young people who gathered at her home in Cambridge: William Empson, J. L. Cowan, Malcolm Lowry, Ronald Burghes (Haldane's son by her first marriage), an unidentified man, and Robert Lazarus*

seems outdated today; at the same time, she is remarkably perceptive about the changes in relationships between men and women that were occurring with the increased use of birth control and about the effect of smaller families on children. Her call for access to contraceptives for married women, the use of anesthetics in childbirth, and research into the education of children was forward-looking. Her suggestion that the unemployment and old-age benefits provided for working women be extended to mothers who were not employed outside the home was revolutionary.

In 1927 and 1928 the Haldanes traveled extensively, selling copies of *Motherhood and Its Enemies* at the World Population Conference in Geneva and the Genetical Congress in Berlin. After a trip to the Soviet Union in 1928 they became increasingly involved in left-wing politics.

In her second novel, *Brother to Bert* (1930), Haldane draws on knowledge she had gained from translating Johannes Lange's *Verbrechen als Schicksal* (1929) as *Crime and Destiny* (1930). Lange had argued for the genetic determination of behavior by showing that if one identical twin had criminal propensities the other was likely to have them also. Haldane's novel shows, on the contrary, that environment plays a larger role in behavior than heredity. Her protagonists are identical Cockney twins who dance in music halls and chase girls. One brother, damaged in childhood by a blow to the head, is so evil as to be unusual even among criminals. By the end of the novel he has murdered the mistress he shared with his gentler twin, who is reformed by a working-class girl. The book is an interesting character study and shows Haldane's skill at fictionalizing biological and sociological concepts.

Haldane's third novel, *I Bring Not Peace* (1932), is set mainly in Paris in the 1930s. Its protagonist, the musically gifted and ingenuous young American James Dowd, is based on Lowry, whom she called "the most romantic undergraduate of that period in Cambridge" and who shared her love of music, especially jazz. Dowd falls in love with Michal, an independent, sexually free journalist. Because she intends to marry a French biochemist, Dowd leaves for London with a bisexual friend who commits suicide in circumstances similar to those of an early acquaintance of Lowry, Paul Fitte. The characters have a hardness befitting their wayward, often drunken lives. The novel gave rise to a rumor that Haldane and Lowry had had an affair; they had not.

In the autumn of 1932 the Haldanes moved to London, where J. B. S. became professor of genetics at University College the next year. In the spring of 1933 they visited Spain to participate in a scientific and literary conference sponsored by the League of Nations. Haldane's fourth novel, *Youth Is a Crime* (1934), is in large part autobiographical. Like the author, its Jewish protagonist, Elizabeth Hermann, is uprooted from a London girl's school and taken to Antwerp, where she is placed in an anti-Semitic German gymnasium. Haldane had always spoken up for young people in her newspaper articles; here she fictionalizes the injustices unknowingly done to girls. Although brilliant, Elizabeth is discouraged from academic achievement and groomed for marriage. A friend, seduced by a man who deserts her, has an abortion and is sent away by her family because of the disgrace she has brought upon them. The novel was highly successful commercially and was well received by the critics.

In 1936 Haldane published a romance, *Melusine; or, Devil Take Her!,* a feminist rendition of a medieval legend of the sorceress Melusine of Lusignan. Haldane had been interested in card tricks and fortune-telling since childhood, and the work allowed her, she says in her 1949 autobiography, *Truth Will Out,* to explore in fiction "what it felt like to be a sorceress, to practise magic arts." She and her family experimented with tarot cards; they were joined in this activity by their friend John Morris, who had participated in the first Mount Everest expedition. When Morris returned to India in 1936 to prepare for the third Everest climb, he and Haldane tried to communicate telepathically. Although Haldane did not take such experiments particularly seriously, she used them as material for a later novel.

When the Spanish civil war began in the summer of 1936 Haldane helped the British Communist Party recruit volunteers for the International Brigade. She was honorary secretary of the party's Dependents and Wounded Aid Committee for most of the war, and from March to May 1937 she clandestinely guided the British volunteers through Paris. Initially her sixteen-year-old son, Ronnie, signed up with the International Brigade behind her back, but she gave her worried consent for him to go and fight. She returned to Spain at the beginning of 1938 as guide and interpreter for the American singer, actor, and black activist Paul Robeson, and in May 1938 she spoke about the Spanish situation at the Second World Congress against Fascism in Marseilles. Later that year she went to China.

Throughout the 1930s Haldane continued to write articles for the *Express* papers, for *The News Chronicle,* and, during her trip to China, for *The Daily Herald.* From February 1939 until December 1940 she was the editor of the magazine *Woman Today,* contributing essays and editorials. During that time she also gave popular lectures in Britain and France on the situations in Spain and China. In May 1940 she joined the St. Pancras Borough Council Air Raid Precautions Emergency Committee (A.R.P.) in London.

According to her autobiography, Haldane suffered "mental discomfort, but not rebellion" over the German-Soviet Nonaggression Pact of 23 August 1939, and when Germany attacked Russia in June 1941 she, like most British Communists, still looked to Moscow for political direction. She had a deep concern for the Russian people and signed on as a war correspondent for the *Daily Sketch*—the first British woman to hold such a position—so she could join a convoy that was headed there. She found that conditions in the Soviet Union had been misrepresented by the British Communist Party. She had expected to find well-organized urban populations and healthy, productive collective farmers; instead, the cities were full of panic, disease, and poverty, and the farms were crippled by the "final hopelessness" of people who had been forced off their own land into collective ventures. The sight of a young mother carrying her starved baby to a graveyard became a metaphor for Haldane's sense of betrayal. The child, she says in *Truth Will Out,* represented "the revolt of my sense of morality, the re-awakening of my mind . . . from a deep, drugged sleep"; for her, the Soviet Union had ceased to be "the hope of the toilers of the world."

On the return voyage she began *Russian Newsreel: An Eye-Witness Account of the Soviet Union at War* (1942), in which she avoids political controversy and expresses her admiration for the Russian people. The reviewer for the *Times Literary Supplement* (16 May 1942) found her an "unfailingly sympathetic eye-witness" to "the heroic immensity of the Russian effort, the prodigious labors and sacrifices of the people of Russia in the common cause of destroying the Nazi enemy."

Haldane remained a socialist, but she broke with the Communist Party as soon as she arrived home. She immediately became what she called "a political leper," shunned by her former friends; the party faction in Fleet Street kept her from getting another job as a war correspondent. But she was also considered suspect by British Intelligence, which kept dossiers on all party members in wartime England. Since 1939 she and her husband had wanted to divorce, but the party had discouraged them doing so for fear that the publicity would reflect poorly on the morals of communists at a politically delicate time. In 1941, however, it encouraged them to divorce and urged J. B. S. Haldane, who at the time was chairman of the editorial board of the party newspaper, *The Daily Worker,* as well as a government consultant, openly to join the party so as to counter the adverse effect it expected from his wife's defection.

In *Truth Will Out* Haldane tells why many of her generation had become communists and gives an impassioned account of her loss of belief in the party. The year before the book was published, three chapters were separately printed in *The Tribune.* They provoked a storm of letters to the editor, including an angry one (3 September 1948) from her former sister-in-law, the writer Naomi Mitchison, accusing her of "superficial analysis." Many readers appreciated what one called Haldane's "heroic honesty" (10 September 1948), but their support was trifling beside the problems her defection had created for her.

To earn a living she wrote articles on world and domestic affairs for *Everywoman,* which ca-

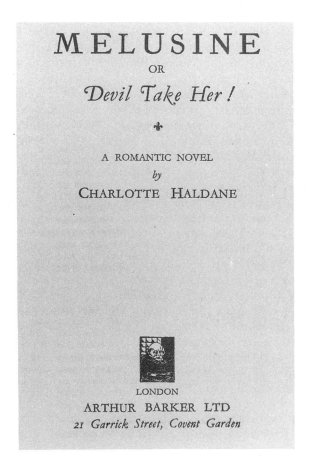

MELUSINE
OR
*Devil Take Her!*

❧

A ROMANTIC NOVEL
*by*
CHARLOTTE HALDANE

LONDON
ARTHUR BARKER LTD
*21 Garrick Street, Covent Garden*

*Title page for Haldane's 1936 novel about a medieval sorceress*

tered to lower-middle-class housewives and which appreciated her feminism. In August 1943 her friend John Morris, who had become an assistant in the Eastern Service of the British Broadcasting Corporation, got her a job in the same section. When George Orwell vacated the position she became "talks producer" in the Indian Section of the British Broadcasting Corporation's Eastern Service. She continued to write and broadcast for the BBC into the 1950s. In 1951 she published a biography of Marcel Proust; she would continue to write biographies for the rest of her life.

In 1952 Haldane published her sixth novel, her first in more than a decade. *The Shadow of a Dream* takes up her earlier fascination with extrasensory perception. In the work ESP is used by strong and independent women to heal. In her final novel, *Fifi and Antoine* (1956), a charming love story about two dogs and their master and mistress, the playfulness present in several of her earlier books finds a natural outlet. These two novels suggest the stature Haldane might have reached as a novelist had she not depleted her energies in political work just as she was reaching her maturity as a writer.

After 1956 Haldane occupied herself with biographies, mostly of creative, unorthodox, sexually liberated, powerful women. Nearly blind, she died of pneumonia on 16 March 1969. Her final work, *Madame de Maintenon: Uncrowned Queen of France* (1970), was published posthumously to laudatory reviews.

Charlotte Haldane's career as a novelist was cut short by her antifascist activities and the isolation to which she was subjected after she left the British Communist Party. Her early characters tended to be stylized, her psychological analysis not well developed. Nonetheless, *Youth Is a Crime* is an admirable novel, and *I Bring Not Peace* is highly evocative of its period; written when she was fifty-eight, *The Shadow of a Dream* shows her novelistic powers still strong. Haldane was a talented and versatile writer who was staggeringly productive and always passionately engaged in the social and cultural issues of her day. Her novels and her journalism form a unique record of the most important movements of the twentieth century. Her biographies continue to provide role models for women.

**Biography:**
Judith Adamson, *Charlotte Haldane: Woman Writer in a Man's World* (London: Macmillan, 1997).

**References:**
Gordon Bowker, *Pursued by Furies* (London: HarperCollins, 1993), pp. 101–111;

Muriel C. Bradbrook, *Malcolm Lowry: His Art and Early Life* (Cambridge: Cambridge University Press, 1974), p. 174;

Ronald W. Clark, *J. B. S.: The Life and Work of J. B. S. Haldane* (London: Oxford University Press, 1968), pp. 77–85;

Sheila Jeffreys, *The Spinster and Her Enemies* (London: Pandora, 1985), p. 174;

Conrad Knickerbocker, "Singing the Paradise Street Blues," *Paris Review,* 38 (Summer 1966): 88;

Elizabeth Russell, "The Loss of the Feminist Principle in Charlotte Haldane's *Man's World* and Katherine Burdekin's *Swastika Night,*" in *Where No Man Has Gone Before,* edited by Lucie Armitt (London: Routledge, 1991), pp. 15–28;

Susan M. Squier, "Sexual Biopolitics in *Man's World,*" in *Rediscovering Forgotten Radicals: British Women 1889–1939,* edited by Angela Ingram and Daphne Patai (Chapel Hill: University of North Carolina Press, 1993), pp. 137–155.

# Radclyffe Hall

*(12 August 1880 – 7 October 1943)*

Kathy March

BOOKS: *'Twixt Earth and Stars: Poems,* as Marguerite Radclyffe-Hall (London: Bumpus, 1906);

*A Sheaf of Verses: Poems,* as Radclyffe-Hall (London: Bumpus, 1908);

*Poems of the Past and Present,* as Radclyffe-Hall (London: Chapman & Hall, 1910);

*Songs of Three Counties and Other Poems,* as Radclyffe-Hall (London: Chapman & Hall, 1913);

*The Forgotten Island,* as Radclyffe-Hall (London: Chapman & Hall, 1915);

*The Forge* (London: Arrowsmith, 1924);

*The Unlit Lamp* (London & New York: Cassell, 1924);

*A Saturday Life* (London: Arrowsmith, 1925; New York: Cape & Smith, 1930);

*Adam's Breed* (London: Cassell, 1926; Garden City, N.Y.: Doubleday, Page, 1926);

*The Well of Loneliness* (London: Cape, 1928; New York: Covici-Friede, 1928);

*The Master of the House* (London: Cape, 1932; New York: Cape & Ballou, 1932);

*Miss Ogilvy Finds Herself* (London: Heinemann, 1934; New York: Harcourt, Brace, 1934);

*The Sixth Beatitude* (London: Heinemann, 1936; New York: Harcourt, Brace, 1936).

**Editions:** *The Well of Loneliness,* introduction by Alison Hennegan (London: Virago, 1981);

*The Unlit Lamp,* introduction by Zoe Fairbairns (Toronto: Dennys, 1981);

*Adam's Breed,* introduction by Hennegan (London: Virago, 1985).

SELECTED PERIODICAL PUBLICATIONS–
UNCOLLECTED: "The Attack on Psychical Research," *The World: A Journal for Men and Women* (20 February 1917): 175–176;

"On a Series with Mrs. Leonard Osborne," by Hall and Una Troubridge, *Proceedings of the Society for Psychical Research,* 30 (1920): 399–554;

*Radclyffe Hall in 1928*

"A Veridical Apparition," *Journal of the Society for Psychical Research,* 20 (April 1921): 78–88.

The literary contribution of Radclyffe Hall is often overshadowed by the notoriety of the obscenity trial of her *The Well of Loneliness* (1928), the first openly lesbian novel in English. In fact, however, before the appearance of that work she was the author of five volumes of poetry and four other novels, ranging from social comedies to spiritual quests, which sold well and won prestigious awards. The negative reaction to *The Well of Loneliness* led her to turn to religious novels. Her short stories, collected in *Miss Ogilvy Finds Herself* (1934), reflect her interests in religion, spiritualism, and the psychological development of the individual.

Marguerite Antonia Radclyffe-Hall was born on 12 August 1880 at Sunny Lawn, West Cliffe, Bournemouth, Hampshire, to Radclyffe Radclyffe-Hall and Mary Jane Diehl Sager Radclyffe-Hall, who was originally from Philadelphia. Her paternal grandfather, a tuberculosis specialist who ran a sanatorium in Torquay, had established the family fortune that relieved her father of the necessity of pursuing a career. Radclyffe-Hall's parents separated a few weeks after her birth; her mother filed for divorce in 1882 and in 1889 married Alberto Visetti, who taught singing at the Royal College of Music in London. The family moved to the Kensington section of London in 1889. During her childhood and adolescence Radclyffe-Hall experienced loneliness and alienation; she was neglected by her mother, her father, and her stepfather. Although her maternal grandmother provided some emotional support, her relationship with her family would remain strained throughout Radclyffe-Hall's life. She was educated by governesses and at day schools. Her father, whom she saw on only two or three occasions, died when she was eighteen.

At twenty-one Radclyffe-Hall inherited the family fortune. She traveled throughout Europe and twice to America and continued her academic pursuits for two terms at King's College in London and for a year in Dresden, Germany. She loved dogs, horses, and the countryside, and in 1906 she purchased a house in Malvern Wells, Worcestershire.

Radclyffe-Hall's first book of poetry was published in 1906. Of the eighty poems in *'Twixt Earth and Stars,* twenty-one were later set to music. The poems' sentimentality, love of the countryside, and affirmation of the goodness of nature made the volume popular with the reading public.

In 1907 Radclyffe-Hall's initial poetic success brought her into contact with Mabel Veronica Batten, known as "Ladye" to her family and friends, an amateur singer and society figure; they became lovers in 1908. Under Batten's influence Radclyffe-Hall converted to Catholicism. As Radclyffe-Hall became aware of her lesbianism she adopted a masculine appearance and the nickname John. Her next volume, *A Sheaf of Verses* (1908), includes poems, such as "Ode to Sappho" (which includes the phrase "Immortal Lesbian!") and "The Scar," that reflect a growing self-confidence about her homosexuality. *Poems of the Past and Present* was published in 1910 and *Songs of Three Counties and Other Poems* in 1913. The latter volume includes her most popular poem, "The Blind Ploughman":

Set my hands upon the plough
My feet upon the sod;
Turn my face towards the East,
And praise be to God!
. . . . . . . . . . . . . . . . .
God has made the sun to shine
On both you and me;
God who took away my eyes
That my *soul* might see.

The influence of A. E. Housman's rural and nostalgic poetry is apparent. The motifs of spiritual awareness, understanding, and revelation would be further developed in her novels.

During World War I Radclyffe-Hall became active with the Red Cross. Her next collection of poems, *The Forgotten Island,* was published in 1915. The speaker of the poems remembers a past life on the island of Lesbos and celebrates a love that has run its course. While writing the poems Radclyffe-Hall was caring for Batten, who was gravely ill with high blood pressure and circulatory problems; at the same time she became involved with Una Vincent Troubridge, Batten's cousin and the wife of Adm. Ernest Troubridge. Una became her lifelong companion. After accusing Radclyffe-Hall of infidelity, Batten died of a stroke in 1916. Guilt over Batten's death and a desire to believe in an afterlife led Radclyffe-Hall to join the Society for Psychical Research. She and Troubridge also resolved to make their lives and work a living memorial to Batten; they referred to this concept as "Our Three Selves."

In 1924 *The Forge,* a social comedy, became Radclyffe-Hall's first published novel, although it had been written after *The Unlit Lamp,* which was published later the same year. With *The Forge* she dropped her first name and the hyphen between her surnames and began writing under the pseudonym Radclyffe Hall. The two novels are related in theme but contrast in style and mood. Originally titled "Chains," *The Forge* deals with the ties that bind a couple together. Hilary Brent, a poet and aspiring novelist, and his wife, Susan, a painter, feel trapped in their marriage; their country home does not provide satisfaction; and moving back to London changes little. They separate, but after some time they reconcile; they realize that they cannot be successful artists without the stability and security provided by marriage. The novel sold well and was described by reviewers as both serious and delightful.

The inspiration for *The Unlit Lamp,* originally titled "Octopi," came from watching a spinster care for her elderly mother at a seaside resort in Devon in 1922. Hall exclaimed, "Isn't it ghastly to see these unmarried daughters who are just unpaid servants and the old people sucking the very life out of them like octopi!" In the novel Joan Ogden wants to become a doctor; Elizabeth Rodney, her governess, tries to help her achieve this goal. But loyalty to Joan's overbearing mother, especially after the deaths of Joan's tyrannical colonel father and her younger sister, keeps Joan in the small seaside town. She makes several attempts to escape, but she cannot; her mother manipulates and exploits her and stymies her emotional development. Joan and Elizabeth plan to move to London so that Joan can pursue her medical studies, but when Joan is drawn one last time into her mother's grasp, Elizabeth finally leaves and marries. After her demanding mother dies, Joan, having no other options, becomes the spinster caretaker to an old man. As in *The Forge*, people are bound together, but whereas Hilary and Susan Brent were able to break their ties and choose to return to them, Joan is not strong enough to escape. Frustration, loneliness, and sadness pervade the novel. The work received favorable reviews and established Hall as a serious writer.

Hall's next work, *A Saturday Life* (1925), is a social comedy in the vein of *The Forge*. The title is derived from Eastern philosophy and refers to one's seventh incarnation. Sidonia Shore, a creative and energetic young woman, attempts to discover an appropriate outlet for her artistic impulses. From childhood onward she progresses through dance, drawing, poetry, piano, sculpting, and singing. At nineteen she wins a scholarship to study art in Italy, but when she gets there, she decides to study music instead. Her teachers, Einar Jensen and Liza Ferrari, are kind, compassionate mentors for Sidonia. She returns to England to begin her musical career but meets and marries David, settling for a conventional marriage and motherhood. Sidonia has matured and has discovered the natural order of the world.

The inspiration for Hall's next novel came from observing an obsequious waiter. She said, "I am going to write the life of a waiter who becomes so utterly sick of handling food that he practically lets himself die of starvation." Originally titled "Food," *Adam's Breed* (1926) became her most successful novel, going through several printings and winning prestigious prizes including the Prix Fémina Vie Heureuse, the James Tait Black Award, and the American Eichelbergher Award. Troubridge had found the title in the Rudyard Kipling poem "Tomlinson," in which the devil wishes to be reunified with God, like all of "Adam's breed." Gian-Luca is born out of wedlock to an Italian immigrant family in London's Soho district; his mother dies in childbirth without revealing the identity of his father. Gian-Luca is raised by his mother's mother, Teresa, with the help of her extended fam-

*Mabel Veronica Batten ("Ladye"), Hall's first lover, circa 1907*

ily. Nevertheless, he grows up isolated and lonely; his grandmother is bitter over the death of her daughter, for which she blames Gian-Luca, and even rejects God. Gian-Luca becomes the head-waiter at the Doric Restaurant and marries Maddalena, a simple Italian girl. Drafted in World War I, he hopes to serve on the front but is assigned to the catering corps. He returns from the war a changed man; he has lost his ambition. His job at the restaurant cannot provide for his spiritual needs; all he sees about him is gluttony and greed. Even the writings of the Italian poet Ugo Doria no longer bring him joy, especially after he has the bitter experience of serving the man—who turns out to be his natural father—a meal. A trip to Italy causes him to question further the cruelty and sorrow in the world. The sight of a beggar and her blind son causes childhood emotions to reemerge: he remembers crying at the sight of slaughtered lambs in his family's food shop and of beautiful flowers in the

*Hall and her lifelong companion, Una Troubridge, in 1931*

park. He leaves his wife and sets off into the New Forest to live as a hermit and find God. He discovers that God created both the material and the spiritual worlds, and that the split between the two can be overcome through God's love. He realizes that he has to participate in the world in order to be part of God's love and compassion. He decides to return to Maddalena, but he has grown so weak during his months in the forest that he dies. As they view his body, Maddalena whispers to the priest that he looks strange, as if he were not there. The priest says, "Why should Gian-Luca be here? . . . Did our Lord remain in His Tomb?"

*Adam's Breed* has been compared to Hermann Hesse's *Siddhartha* (1922) for its moving and poetic qualities. It also presents rare psychological insights. The artistic weaknesses of the work include overlong yet superficial descriptions of the characters. Nevertheless, its vivid depiction of the struggle of the protagonist makes *Adam's Breed* perhaps her best novel.

*The Well of Loneliness,* published in 1928, brought the issue of female homosexuality into the public sphere; it remained "*the* book about lesbianism" for many years. Hall believed that it was her mission to explain the condition of the "invert," or "born lesbian," as she held herself to be. Supported by the research of Havelock Ellis and Richard von Krafft-Ebing, which claimed that homosexuality was congenital and not a freely chosen orientation, Hall called for understanding of and compassion for those, like her, who were born this way.

In *The Well of Loneliness* Stephen Gordon, born into an aristocratic family and given a masculine name because her parents had longed for a son, discovers that she is an invert. As a man she would have led a model life, but as a woman she is "unnatural." She resembles her father, with whom she is extremely close as a child; on his death, her relationship with her mother becomes all the more strained. Rejecting a marriage proposal, she falls in love with Angela Crossby, the wife of a businessman. The relationship goes awry, and her mother exiles her from the family home. She writes a novel and becomes part of the artistic homosexual community even though she is still confused about her own nature. During World War I she joins the women's ambulance brigade and meets Mary Llewellyn, a Welsh girl; after the war they set up house together in Paris, where Stephen rejoins the artistic set. Mary becomes unhappy with their isolation from conventional society, and Stephen sacrifices herself by "giving" Mary to Martin Hallam, the man whose proposal she rejected in her youth. The novel ends with Stephen's prayer: "Acknowledge us, oh God, before the whole world. Give us also the right to our existence!"

There are no explicit sex scenes in the novel; nevertheless, because of its subject matter, and despite the success of *Adam's Breed,* Hall had difficulty finding a publisher for the work. Finally, Jonathan Cape took a chance on it, paying Hall an advance of £500 and adding a commentary by Ellis in which the eminent psychologist said: "So far as I know, it is the first English novel which presents, in a completely faithful and uncompromising form, one particular aspect of sexual life as it exists among us today." Initial sales were good; critics admired the work's honesty but questioned its stereotypical psychology and propagandistic tendencies. But on 19 August 1928, less than a month after the novel's publication, James Douglas, editor of the *Sunday Express,* condemned the work as "moral poison" and called on the home secretary to ban it. Cape announced that the book was being withdrawn from publication, but he immediately subleased the rights and sent molds for the casting of new printing plates to the Pegasus Press in Paris. When copies of the novel were smuggled in to Leonard Hill, a London bookseller, charges were brought against Cape and Hill under the 1857 Obscene Publications Act. Writers who offered to testify for the defense included Bernard Shaw, H. G. Wells, Leonard and Virginia Woolf, E. M. Forster, A. P. Herbert, and Vita Sackville-West, but their testimony was rejected by the court as irrelevant. *The Well of Loneliness* was found obscene; it would not be republished in Britain until 1949, although copies continued to be printed in Paris and smuggled into the country. The work's American publisher, Covici-Friede, was taken to court by John S. Sumner, superintendent of the New York Society for the Suppression of Vice; the action caused sales of the book to double. Sumner seized 865 copies of the work from the publisher's offices, but Covici-Friede had moved the printing plates to a New Jersey plant. Covici-Friede was convicted in 1929 under the then-prevailing standard known as the Hicklin Rule, which held that obscene passages rendered an entire work obscene. The judge acknowledged that the work was "a well written, carefully constructed piece of fiction" and included "no unclean words" but found that it "pleads for tolerance on the part of society" for homosexuals. The conviction was reversed on appeal, and the Hicklin Rule was overturned by the United States Supreme Court in 1934 in *United States* v. *One Book Entitled "Ulysses."*

Some critics regretted that a better novel could not have been found to challenge the censorship laws. Rebecca West thought that the work's attempt to persuade readers to be sympathetic to the characters overshadowed its literary merits. Leonard Woolf, in *The Nation and Athenaeum* (4 August 1928), criticized the book's lack of emotional realism. Since the 1970s, however, writers have tended to attack the novel for being too weak in its defense of lesbianism. According to Jane Rule, Hall's inability to reconcile her lesbianism with her Catholicism, even though she believed that her sexual orientation was a fact of nature, resulted in the sense of guilt that pervades the novel. Esther Newton criticizes the depiction of Stephen Gordon as a stereotypical mannish lesbian. Rebecca O'Rourke faults the novel for failing to address the choices lesbians make in their struggle against oppression; instead, the work deterministically views lesbianism as an "affliction."

Personal attacks took their toll on Hall. The one that most traumatized her was a book of satiric drawings by Beresford Egan titled *The Sink of Solitude* (1928); a caricature of her on a crucifix with a naked young woman at her hip was especially offensive to her. She withdrew from society and tried to make "amends for that insult to her Lord and to her

*Caricature of Hall by Beresford Egan (from his* The Sink of Solitude, *1928)*

Faith" with her next novel, which began as "The Carpenter's Son" and was published as *The Master of the House* (1932). The novel was inspired by a carpenter's shop she saw in Frejus, France, on her way to Saint-Tropez. Christophe Benedit is the son of a poor carpenter, Jouse, and his wife, Marie, and has a cousin named Jan (the similarities to Jesus' family—Joseph, Mary, and John the Baptist—are obvious). Throughout his childhood and adolescence Christophe is subject to trances in which he has experiences similar to episodes in the life of Jesus, and in his waking hours he bears stigmata and is able to heal sick and injured animals. As he grows up in his seaside village, he develops a compassion for all living creatures. During World War I he is drafted and sent to Palestine; wandering across a battlefield in a dreamlike state, he attempts to convince the soldiers on both sides that they all belong to a unified humanity. Captured by the enemy, he is nailed to a plank and executed. The novel ends with a crucifixion tableau, with Christophe looking toward the rising sun as he dies.

The novel briefly made the best-seller lists, but the reviews were highly negative. There is a lack of character development, especially of the protagonist; since Christophe is spiritually perfect from the

*Hall's study at her home in Rye*

beginning, the quest or struggle motif that made *Adam's Breed* so appealing is absent. The work is long and often plodding, and the descriptions of the town and its colorful characters are superficial. Some critics called the novel a travelogue.

*Miss Ogilvy Finds Herself,* a volume of short stories Hall had written between 1924 and 1933, was published in 1934. The book was not well received, but several of the stories include the sort of psychological insights that made her early works so successful. Protagonists react to impulses and influences that are beyond their control and reveal the darker side of their natures. In the title story Miss Ogilvy, who had been an ambulance driver in World War I, is suffocating in her conventional life in Surrey. Vacationing on an island off the coast of Devon where a Bronze Age culture had existed, she goes into a trance and finds herself transformed into a caveman who is loved by a maiden. They consummate their love; the next morning Miss Ogilvy is found dead. "The Lover of Things" is a novella-length story about a young man, Henry Dobbs, who

grows up in poverty but loves beautiful objects. He steals a statuette, is jailed, and loses his family, but he believes that it was worth it; only objects, not people, can provide him with what he needs. Hall clearly shows how his early psychological development has led to this attitude. The title character of "Fraulein Schwartz" is a middle-aged German spinster living in a boardinghouse in London. During World War I the other boarders turn on her as she tries to explain her belief in a unified humanity. After her beloved cat is poisoned, she drowns herself. Unlike other Hall characters, she wishes for a conventional life, but it is denied her. In "The Rest Cure" Mr. Duffell is a businessman who suffers a nervous breakdown. He decides that he can be anything he chooses to be—a horse, a tree, even a stone, and he descends into madness as he attempts to become an object that does not feel pain. An attendant at the mental hospital attempts to explain that even stones can have personality traits, and the story ends with Mr. Duffell trying to strangle him. In "Upon the Mountains" the brothers Mateo and

Tino and Tino's wife, Fiora, become involved in a strange triangle. Mateo and Fiora force Tino to promise that if he dies first, he will send back a sign as to which of them loved him better. Tino dies in a plane crash; two years later Mateo has chosen not to continue to participate in their competition to serve Tino's memory. He dies, and a message is found in his hand that implies that his love for Tino was stronger than Fiora's. The triangular relationship of the "Three Selves" is reflected in the story.

Hall's final novel sold only six thousand copies in Britain and two thousand in America, and the reviews were generally negative, but she and Troubridge considered it her finest work. The protagonist of *The Sixth Beatitude* (1936), thirty-year-old Hannah Bullen, supports her two illegitimate children, her parents, and her siblings. The sixth beatitude rewards those who are pure in heart; this description fits Hannah, who, "seeing life clearly[,] neither feared nor despised it." She has physical relationships with various men, thereby fulfilling her role as the eternal feminine, part of a natural, life-affirming process.

While she was writing *The Sixth Beatitude* Hall had become involved with Eugenia Souline, a Russian nurse who had been brought in to help care for Troubridge during an illness. Troubridge remained loyal to Hall despite the unhappiness Hall's pursuit of Souline caused her.

Hall's health declined during the early 1940s. She quit smoking but was diagnosed with tuberculosis. She underwent surgeries on her eyes and had to give up writing; she contracted double pneumonia and finally developed colon cancer. With Troubridge at her bedside, she died in London on 7 October 1943. She was buried at Highgate Cemetery next to Batten; the inscription on her tombstone is from Elizabeth Barrett Browning's "Sonnets from the Portuguese" (1850): "And if God Choose I Shall But Love Thee Better After Death." Until her own death in 1963 Troubridge protected the copyrights of Hall's works, especially *The Well of Loneliness*. Current scholarship is primarily concerned with Radclyffe Hall's role in the history of lesbianism and censorship.

**Letters:**

*Your John: The Love Letters of Radclyffe Hall,* edited by Joanne Glasgow (New York & London: New York University Press, 1997).

**Biographies:**

Una Troubridge, *The Life of Radclyffe Hall* (New York: Citadel, 1961);

Michael Baker, *Our Three Selves: The Life of Radclyffe Hall* (London: Hamish Hamilton, 1985);

Sally Cline, *Radclyffe Hall: A Woman Called John* (Bergenfield, N.J.: Overlook, 1998).

**References:**

Margot Gayle Backus, "Sexual Orientation in the (Post) Imperial Nation: Celticism and Inversion Theory in Radclyffe Hall's *The Well of Loneliness," Tulsa Studies in Women's Literature,* 15 (Fall 1996): 253–266;

Michèle Aina Barale, "Below the Belt: (Un)covering *The Well of Loneliness,"* in *Inside/Out: Lesbian Theories, Gay Theories,* edited by Diana Fuss (New York & London: Routledge, 1991), pp. 235–257;

Vera Brittain, *Radclyffe Hall: A Case of Obscenity?* (New York: Barnes, 1969);

Terry Castle, *The Apparitional Lesbian: Female Homosexuality and Modern Culture* (New York: Columbia University Press, 1996);

Castle, *Noël Coward and Radclyffe Hall: Kindred Spirits* (New York: Columbia University Press, 1993);

Lovat Dickson, *Radclyffe Hall at the Well of Loneliness: A Sapphic Chronicle* (London: Collins, 1975; New York: Scribners, 1975);

Claudia Stillman Franks, *Beyond the Well of Loneliness: The Fiction of Radclyffe Hall* (Amersham: Avebury, 1982);

Leigh Gilmore, "Obscenity, Modernity, Identity: Legalizing *The Well of Loneliness* and *Nightwood," Journal of the History of Sexuality,* 4 (April 1994): 603–624;

Angela Ingram, "Unutterable Putrefaction and Foul Stuff: Two Obscene Novels of the 1920s," *Women's International Forum,* 9 (1986): 341–356;

Adrienne Kertzer, "Voices in the Well: Elizabeth Jolley and Radclyffe Hall," *World Literature Written in English,* 32, no. 1 (1992): 122–132;

Jane Marcus, "Sophistry: The Woolf and the Well," in *Lesbian Texts and Contexts,* edited by Karla Jay and Joanne Glasgow (New York & London: New York University Press, 1990), pp. 164–181;

Esther Newton, "The Mythic Mannish Lesbian: Radclyffe Hall and the New Woman," in *Hidden from History: Reclaiming the Gay and Lesbian Past,* edited by Martin Duberman, Martha Vicinus, and George Chauncey Jr. (New York: Meridian, 1989), pp. 281–293;

Richard Ormrod, *Una Troubridge: The Friend of Radclyffe Hall* (London: Cape, 1984);

Rebecca O'Rourke, *Reflecting on "The Well of Loneliness"* (London & New York: Routledge, 1989);

Adam Parkes, "Lesbianism, History, and Censorship: *The Well of Loneliness* and the Suppressed Randiness of Virginia Woolf's *Orlando*," *Twentieth Century Literature*, 40 (Winter 1994): 434–460;

Jean Radford, "An Inverted Romance: *The Well of Loneliness* and Sexual Ideology," in *The Progress of Romance*, edited by Radford (London & New York: Routledge & Kegan Paul, 1986);

Katrina Rolley, "Cutting a Dash: The Dress of Radclyffe Hall and Una Troubridge," *Feminist Review*, 35 (Summer 1990): 54–66;

Sonja Ruehl, "Inverts and Experts: Radclyffe Hall and the Lesbian Identity," in *Feminism, Culture, and Politics*, edited by Rosalind Brent and Caroline Rowan (London: Lawrence & Wishart, 1982), pp. 15–36;

Jane Rule, *Lesbian Images* (Garden City, N.Y.: Doubleday, 1975);

Joan Scanlon, "Bad Language vs. Bad Prose: *Lady Chatterley* and *The Well*," *Critical Inquiry*, 38 (Autumn 1996): 3–13;

Catharine Stimpson, "Zero Degree Deviancy: The Lesbian Novel in English," *Critical Inquiry*, 8 (1981): 363–380;

Rebecca West, "Concerning Censorship," in her *Ending in Earnest: A Literary Log* (Garden City, N.Y.: Doubleday, Doran, 1931), pp. 6–12;

Gillian Whittock, "Everything Is Out of Place": Radclyffe Hall and the Lesbian Literary Tradition," *Feminist Studies*, 13 (Fall 1987): 555–582.

# Patrick Hamilton
### (17 March 1904 – 23 September 1962)

### Rosemary Erickson Johnsen
*Michigan State University*

See also the Hamilton entry in *DLB 10: Modern British Dramatists, 1900–1945.*

BOOKS: *Monday Morning* (London: Constable, 1925; Boston: Houghton Mifflin, 1925);

*Craven House* (London: Constable, 1926; Boston: Houghton Mifflin, 1927; revised edition, London: Constable, 1943);

*Twopence Coloured* (London: Constable, 1928; Boston: Little, Brown, 1928);

*The Midnight Bell: A Love Story* (London: Constable, 1929; Boston: Little, Brown, 1930);

*Rope: A Play, with a Preface on Thrillers* (London: Constable, 1929); republished as *Rope's End: A Play, with a Preface on Thrillers* (New York: R. R. Smith, 1930);

*The Siege of Pleasure* (London: Constable, 1932; Boston: Little, Brown, 1932);

*The Plains of Cement* (London: Constable, 1934; Boston: Little, Brown, 1935);

*Twenty Thousand Streets Under the Sky: A London Trilogy* (London: Constable, 1935)—includes *The Midnight Bell, The Siege of Pleasure,* and *The Plains of Cement;*

*Gas Light: A Victorian Thriller in Three Acts* (London: Constable, 1939); republished as *Angel Street: A Victorian Thriller in Three Acts* (New York: French, 1942);

*Impromptu in Moribundia* (London: Constable, 1939);

*Money With Menaces & To the Public Danger: Two Radio Plays* (London: Constable, 1939);

*Hangover Square; or, The Man with Two Minds: A Story of Darkest Earl's Court in the Year 1939* (London: Constable, 1941; New York: Random House, 1942);

*This is Impossible: A Play in One Act* (London: French, 1942);

*The Duke in Darkness: A Play in Three Acts* (London: Constable, 1943);

*The Slaves of Solitude* (London: Constable, 1947); republished as *Riverside* (New York: Random House, 1947);

*Patrick Hamilton*

*The West Pier* (London: Constable, 1951; Garden City, N.Y.: Doubleday, 1952);

*Mr. Stimpson and Mr. Gorse* (London: Constable, 1953);

*The Man Upstairs* (London: Constable, 1954);

*Unknown Assailant* (London: Constable, 1955).

PLAY PRODUCTIONS: *Rope,* London, Ambassadors Theatre, 25 April 1929;

*The Procurator of Judea,* London, Arts Theatre, 2 July 1930;

*John Brown's Body,* London, Phoenix Theatre, 11 January 1931;

*Gaslight,* Richmond, Surrey, Richmond Theatre, 5 December 1938; as *Angel Street,* New York, John Golden Theatre, 5 December 1941;

*The Duke in Darkness,* Edinburgh, Lyceum Theatre, 7 September 1942;

*The Governess,* Glasgow, February 1945;

*The Man Upstairs,* Blackpool, Grand Theatre, 19 January 1953.

RADIO SCRIPTS: *Rope,* BBC, 18 January 1932; *Money With Menaces,* BBC, 4 January 1937; *To the Public Danger,* BBC, 25 February 1939; *This is Impossible,* BBC, 27 December 1941; *Caller Anonymous,* BBC Home Service, 7 March 1952.

SELECTED PERIODICAL PUBLICATION—UNCOLLECTED: "The Quiet Room," *Printer's Devil,* 1 (May 1990).

Patrick Hamilton is best remembered for his plays *Rope* (1929) and *Gas Light* (1939), which were made into well-known films and have been performed in countless amateur and professional stage productions. But Hamilton referred to his plays deprecatingly as "thrillers" and wanted to be remembered primarily for the novels he had published. Beginning in the 1930s he had a popular reputation based both on his novels and his plays; in 1956 John Betjeman described him in an article in the *Spectator* as "one of the best English novelists." His work suffered a period of near invisibility after his death, although, as Doris Lessing noted in September 1987 in the *Listener,* "his books were on the shelves of people who make sure their special authors don't get thrown out." The resurgence of interest in his work that began in the late 1980s focused on the original appeal of Hamilton's novels: they are, according to Lessing, "minor classics," representations of a fictional milieu largely overlooked by other novelists. In September 1951 the *Times Literary Supplement* described Hamilton's characters as "the faithless, the uprooted, the lonely souls"; the settings for Hamilton's stories are accurately portrayed boardinghouses, pubs, and cafés.

Anthony Walter Patrick Hamilton was born on 17 March 1904 at Hassocks, Sussex, the last of three children. His mother, Ellen Adèle Hockley, was forty-three; his father, Bernard Hamilton, was forty. The marriage was the second for both. Hamilton's mother was the middle-class daughter of a dentist. Hamilton's father was upper middle class, with a public-school education and a master of arts from Cambridge. He had inherited a considerable sum of money at age twenty-one but ran through it, so that by the time his son was born the family fortunes were dwindling. Most of Patrick's childhood was spent in ever-changing leased houses or respectable boardinghouses catering to middle-class people who were experiencing hard times; such establishments are a principal focus of Hamilton's early fiction.

Hamilton's secondary education consisted of two terms at Westminster Public School in autumn 1918 and winter 1919. During this period his first publication—a poem, "Heaven"—appeared in the respected journal *Poetry Review.* He left school when he was barely fifteen, and the only further education he received was a short course in typing and shorthand, taken under pressure from his father, who was urging him to find a profession. Hamilton wanted to be a writer, but his father objected that Hamilton needed a career more likely to provide financial support.

Hamilton's chance to work in the arts was provided by his older sister, Lalla, whose involvement with a married man, Sutton Vane, whom she eventually married, had great consequences for her youngest brother as well as herself. Vane was a playwright and actor, and Lalla acted in his plays. In 1921 she got Hamilton a job as a bit-part actor and assistant stage manager. While no actor, Hamilton learned a great deal about dramatic technique and the elements of a successful production, knowledge on which he drew when writing his own plays. His experiences also provided material to be used in his first three novels, *Monday Morning* (1925), *Craven House* (1926), and *Twopence Coloured* (1928). Theatrical life plays a minor role in the first two and is the focus of the third. More important than this service, however, was the financial assistance his sister and Vane provided following the huge financial success of Vane's play *Outward Bound* in 1923.

Hamilton spent 1924 in a rented room in West Kensington. Supported financially by his mother, who paid his rent, and his sister, who gave him cash and other gifts, he worked full time on his first novel. By the end of the year it was finished. His sister's connections provided him with a literary agent, and after a few rejections *Monday Morning* was accepted by Constable. Just days after his twenty-first birthday Hamilton signed his contract and began a career-long relationship with Michael Sadleir, the noted Victorianist, who had accepted the novel for Constable.

The title of *Monday Morning* refers to the young protagonist's often-repeated resolutions to begin life, or at least the novel he would like to write, on the next Monday morning. Hamilton used his experiences in an Earl's Court residential hotel as the basis for the book. The plot follows Anthony Forster as he arrives in London from Sussex to cram with an examination tutor. A fellow resident of the hotel gets him a job as assistant stage manager and bit-part actor with a touring show, and at the end of the novel Anthony is engaged to the love interest, Diane. The novel is light and humorous, taking as its main subject the postures and inconsistencies of youth as the author gently mocks his own experiences and aspirations, and it can be seen as a preliminary venture into what later became Hamilton's principal territory: life in the haunts of people on the margin. *Monday Morning* came out that autumn to reasonably good press; the *Times Literary Supplement* reviewer captures the tone of its reception when he advises that "as a holiday book this is to be strongly recommended."

Hamilton soon began work on his second novel, using his experiences in a Kew boardinghouse as its basis. By the end of summer 1926 *Craven House* was done. Constable was so pleased by the book, the firm offered him a five-novel contract. *Craven House* is set in a genteel boardinghouse in Chiswick and takes boardinghouse life as its principal subject. Hamilton exposes the agonizing absurdities of such a life, from "the Long Evening Problem" to the laundry-airing battles. The residents are middle class but in reduced circumstances, and while the novel exposes their faults, it also offers some sympathy for them. The world of *Craven House* is presented compellingly and in meticulous detail while the main plot once again involves the coming of age of a young man. The hero, Master Wildman, first appears as a schoolboy. Later, he must find a profession to support himself; he works in a city office, writes a hit play that ensures his future as a writer, and becomes engaged to fellow resident Elsie Nixon. *Craven House* is more assured than its predecessor, and the improvement is reflected in the reviews.

After the success of *Craven House* Hamilton decided to write a longer and more serious novel. He spent 1927 working on *Twopence Coloured,* an exposé of the theatrical world. Jackie Mortimer, a young woman from Hove, decides on a stage career. She meets an established actor, Richard Gissing, who gets her started in the business; the novel traces her undistinguished theatrical career and her relationship with the married Gissing. After his sudden death she renounces the stage and accepts a proposal of marriage from Gissing's brother. Contemporary reception was favorable, but the book has not held much interest for subsequent critics. Hamilton's usual verisimilitude, so compelling when applied to other subjects, is less interesting when his

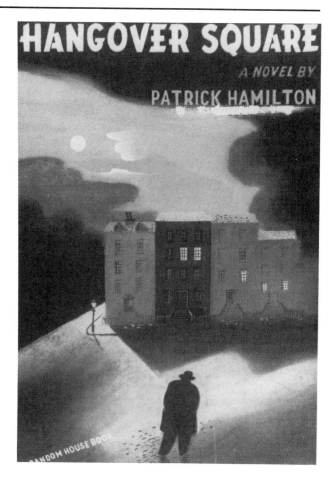

*Dust jacket for Hamilton's novel about an alcoholic, schizophrenic loner who commits murder and suicide*

subject is the lower reaches of the theatrical world.

The year 1927 also saw the beginning of a relationship that had an enormous impact on Hamilton's life and work. It is not known exactly when he met Lily Connolly, who was a prostitute, but he first mentions her in a letter to his brother in the summer of 1927. He partly rationalized this relationship as research, saying that he planned to write a novel "about both servants *and* harlots (possibly the slow transformation of the one into the other)." There is no doubt, however, that his infatuation was profound, even unbalanced, and that it cost him a great deal of time, nervous energy, and money. Later, he drew on his experiences with Lily Connolly and her world—a memorable night in a cheap boardinghouse in Drury Lane, tea at her flat with her fellow-prostitute flatmates, the frustrations of romantically pursuing someone who must play by different rules—to create the verisimilitude of his pub trilogy, *Twenty Thousand Streets Under the Sky* (1935). On the publication of *Twopence Coloured* in 1928 Hamilton began work on *The Midnight Bell: A Love*

*Story,* the first novel of the trilogy.

*The Midnight Bell,* published in June 1929, marks the shift to Hamilton's more-mature style. Bob, a waiter at a pub named the Midnight Bell, aspires to be a writer. He becomes obsessed with a young prostitute, Jenny Maple, whom he hopes to reclaim from the streets. Bob loses everything because of this destructive relationship: his savings, his job at the pub, even his hope of writing a novel. He returns to being a sailor. This book marks the beginning of Hamilton's novelistic advocacy of London's marginal people. Bob is, in many respects, an unlikely hero, and his behavior is hardly heroic; but Hamilton's sympathy for him and anger at his circumstances create a powerful condemnation of society. The restrictions and rootlessness of Bob's life are shown in harrowing detail, and Hamilton shares with readers his own knowledge of this largely overlooked class of people.

Another major event in 1929 was the advent of *Rope.* It had a tryout production on 3 March at the Strand Theatre in London, and the first full production opened on 25 April at the Ambassadors Theatre. Running for six months, the play was highly profitable because of its single set and small cast. It made a great deal of money for Hamilton and continued to be a major source of income for the rest of his life. Between the great success of *Rope* and the glowing reviews of *The Midnight Bell,* Hamilton became quite a literary celebrity. He enjoyed his new status, although it distracted him from his writing.

On 31 July 1930 Hamilton's domineering father died. On 6 August, Hamilton married Lois Martin. The marriage came as a surprise to Hamilton's family; his mother learned the news by letter after the fact. Three years older than Hamilton, Lois was, like him, recovering from an unhappy romance. Each offered the other security and stability. Prior to the marriage the only writing that Hamilton was doing was *John Brown's Body,* a play about a scientist murdering a man who tries to destroy his research; it had only a single tryout on 11 January 1931 at the Phoenix Theatre. It was never published, and, according to biographer Nigel Jones, only one line survives. Lois took over her husband's business affairs, and after their honeymoon he started work on *The Siege of Pleasure* (1932), which is Jenny Maple's story. When he continued to have trouble working, Lois proposed living in the country. They leased a cottage in Norfolk and spent most of 1931 there. Lois banned alcohol and only lifted her ban late in the year after *The Siege of Pleasure* was finished. While the narrative frame of that novel is tied to the aftermath of Bob's story, most of its action takes place before the events in *The Midnight Bell* to show how Jenny went from being a servant to becoming an alcoholic and a prostitute.

The following year was a disastrous one for Hamilton. It began well enough, with his new novel finished and a highly publicized attempted ban of a BBC radio broadcast of *Rope.* Val Gielgud, head of drama at the BBC, had created the attention by broadcasting and publishing a warning statement about the strong content of the play. The broadcast, on 18 January 1932, was an enormous success; but less than a week later, on 24 January, Hamilton was run down by a speeding car. Hamilton was walking, accompanied by his wife and sister, on a street with no sidewalks off Earl's Court Road when he was struck by the car and dragged before being thrown off. His injuries were life-threatening. Hamilton suffered compound fractures of his thigh and wrist and serious lacerations, notably to his face. He spent three months in the hospital, was transferred to a nursing home, and then required a period of private convalescence. The accident left him with physical scars: his face required plastic surgery, but visible scars remained, and one arm and one leg never fully healed. The accident also left him with psychological scars: he was sensitive about his appearance, became more introverted, and for a period of two years produced no substantial work. The driver of the car was not charged with drunken driving but was given a small fine for careless driving. Hamilton sued the driver in 1933 and was awarded £6,000. This experience found its way into his work several times; the first was the addition of a drunk driving accident to the final draft of *The Siege of Pleasure* before its late 1932 publication.

In 1933 Hamilton became seriously interested in Marxism. That September, his brother made a trip to the Soviet Union; Hamilton did not accompany him but was reading Karl Marx and Lenin and devouring his brother's letters, lamenting that they were insufficiently detailed and laudatory. Critics have debated the importance to Hamilton's life and work of his "conversion" to Marxism, with no conclusive results. Leftist critics generally believe Hamilton's Marxism was an important force in his work, while others tend to find his Marxism simplistic and to see his sympathy for marginalized people as a result of a more general humanitarianism.

Early in 1934 Hamilton's mother committed suicide in the face of a serious illness. Hamilton returned to Norfolk and devoted himself to finishing *The Plains of Cement* (1934) by spring. This final novel in the pub trilogy is the story of Ella, the barmaid at the Midnight Bell. Plain, kindhearted, and uninterested in consuming the alcohol she dispenses to others, she nourishes an unrequited love for Bob.

In *The Midnight Bell* she is a partial witness to his self-destruction, and she is the antithesis of Jenny. In *The Plains of Cement* Hamilton reveals the circumstances of her life that are contemporaneous with Bob's story: she is caught in a dead-end job, aware of the hopelessness of her love for Bob, but trying to hope for something better. The novel follows the development of Ella's possible escapes from her confined life. The smallness of these hopes and their ultimate defeat underscore Hamilton's championing of London's invisibles.

Ella is pursued by Mr. Eccles, a ridiculous and annoying middle-aged suitor who, nonetheless, offers the possibility of financial support and thus is tolerated by Ella as long as she can manage it. The luxuries he offers her—a night at the theater, a meal at the Lyons' Corner House—show how limited are her means. Furthermore, her disliked stepfather is seriously ill, and for a time it looks as if he will die, leaving her mother in peace and both women with a small legacy. Finally, she gets a lead on a job as nanny to the children of a wealthy family about to go to India. Ultimately, however, Mr. Eccles becomes unbearable; her stepfather recovers; and she does not get the job with the wealthy family. Bob leaves the pub to return to the sea, and Ella is left even more alone than she was when the novel started. *The Plains of Cement,* a strong novel on its own, gains greater power as it ties together the two earlier novels in the trilogy. It was published in 1934, and the following year Constable published a one-volume edition of the trilogy under the title *Twenty Thousand Streets Under the Sky: A London Trilogy.* Noted author J. B. Priestley wrote a preface for the book, which was another sign of Hamilton's growing literary reputation.

Late in 1937 Hamilton made a trip to the United States and then visited his brother in Barbados. On his return he decided to leave Norfolk; he rented rooms in Oxford, and during a search for more-permanent lodgings he began work on his Marxist dystopia, *Impromptu in Moribundia* (1939). He and Lois moved into a flat in Henley-on-Thames in the spring of 1938. Henley would be his main home until after World War II. *Gas Light: A Victorian Thriller in Three Acts,* Hamilton's second big theatrical success, opened in December of that year; this famous story of a villainous husband's attempt to drive his wife insane remains one of his best-known achievements.

The following year *Impromptu in Moribundia* appeared in print. Its central device is the narrator's trip to the planet of Moribundia, a satirical and exaggerated version of England. The book chiefly attacks advertising and class stereotypes (the belief in

*Hamilton in his apartment in the Albany, 1947 (photograph by Bill Brandt)*

Cockney humor, for example), and several celebrated writers and scientists are singled out for derision. The mock science-fiction approach is not a success, however, and the device of backwards spelling—*gnikrow ssalc* and *Raglafart Erauqs*—is simply cumbersome. This book was not a commercial success and is the only one of Hamilton's books never to be reprinted. Some leftist critics admire it, but for most critics it lacks the power of Hamilton's best work, which re-creates a milieu of lonely and forgotten people. In 1939 Constable also published a pair of Hamilton's radio plays, *Money with Menaces* and *To the Public Danger,* which had been broadcast earlier. The latter play had been commissioned and dealt with the subject of drunk driving and auto safety. During this period Hamilton was busy and successful, working on a variety of projects and serving briefly as drama critic for *Time and Tide.*

At the end of the year Hamilton turned to his next novel, *Hangover Square,* which he completed early in 1941 and which was published later that year. This novel, inspired in part by Hamilton's obsession with the rising actress Geraldine Fitzgerald, is perhaps his best; it returns to Earl's Court to trace events in the life of George Harvey Bone during the period leading up to World War II. Bone, like most of Hamilton's characters, is a loner, but he is also an alcoholic and a schizophrenic. His obsession with the cruel and disdainful Netta Longdon leads eventually, after many painful turns, to his murdering her and her lover, Peter, while in one of his "dead" moods. The novel concludes with Bone's suicide as the radio announces the declaration of war with Germany. Many of Hamilton's usual concerns are here—the monotonous lives of marginal people, the hotels in which they live, and the pubs, cinemas, and cafés in which they try to escape their loneliness—but he has added alcoholism, mental illness, and murder, both individual (Bone's) and societal (the Nazis and the war).

*Hangover Square* was a great success, and Hamilton turned to writing *The Duke in Darkness* (1943), an historical play that is the most political of his dramas. A revised edition of *Craven House* was also published in 1943. Declared unfit for military service, Hamilton did some broadcast writing for the Entertainment National Service Association, but this work turned out to be nothing of substance, as he complained to others. During the war he took a flat in the Albany apartment block to use as a London base, while maintaining the Henley flat.

The experience of World War II in Henley formed one basis for Hamilton's picture of life on the home front in *The Slaves of Solitude* (1947). His progress on that novel was intermittent; he began work late in 1943 but set it aside the following spring. Late that autumn he reported to his brother that he was writing again, but he was still working on the project after the war was over. He finally finished the novel in 1946, and it came out the following year. Miss Roach, a spinster nearing middle age, has been bombed out of her home in London and has taken up residence in a boarding-house in Thames Lockdon, a fictionalized Henley, from which she commutes to her job in a London publisher's office. As Hamilton records the war years, there is little of the heroic about life on the home front. For people like Miss Roach, the war is a series of petty irritations and confusing conflicts between enforced inactivity and unavoidable encounters with other people. Miss Roach is miserable in her boardinghouse, tormented by Mr. Thwaites, an elderly, malicious, and mentally unstable fellow resident. Her life is complicated beyond her comprehension and ability to cope when an American lieutenant begins a relationship with her. The final blow comes when a German woman she knows moves into the boardinghouse. The combination of repressive boardinghouse life, wartime restrictions and dislocations, and this odd assortment of characters

drives Miss Roach to distraction. At the end of the novel she receives the break Ella never got in *The Plains of Cement:* she receives an inheritance from her aunt and returns to London to face the war there. Hamilton charts a version of the homefront unlike anyone else's, and *The Slaves of Solitude* is considered by many critics to be his best novel.

By this time, however, his drinking had become a visible problem, and he had received medical advice to cut back, or preferably eliminate, his alcohol consumption. His older brother estimated Hamilton's intake after the war at about three bottles of scotch a day; as Sean French, one of Hamilton's biographers, notes, the contemporary parallel in terms of cost, given the effects of war and rationing on the availability of hard liquor, would be a cocaine habit. Hamilton wrote during periods of abstinence or relative abstinence, however, not while drunk. He finished *The Slaves of Solitude* shut up in his bedroom, with his wife, Lois, bringing meals on trays. One explanation for his slowing output is that those periods in which he was willing and able to work became less frequent and of shorter duration.

Hamilton spent part of 1947 working with Alfred Hitchcock on the movie version of *Rope,* but their collaboration was not a success. Hamilton felt he had little real input into the film—aside from having written the play text upon which it was based—and he did not like the movie. After this frustrating experience he went on a drinking binge which put him in a nursing home for recovery.

In 1948 Hamilton began to plan his next novel. Work on it was slow, ceasing altogether at times. In 1949 he bought a house on the Isle of Wight, hoping the change of scene would help him write, but he resold the house at a loss a few months later. Hamilton's life was complicated by a whole series of disruptions and dissatisfactions, including an affair. It is not certain when he met Ursula Stewart, born Lady Ursula Chetwynd-Talbot, but in September 1949 he was writing to his brother about their relationship, which had been going on for some time. She was also a writer and had published five novels under the name Laura Talbot. After the Isle of Wight house was sold, Hamilton rented a house in Hove. He lived there with "La," as her friends called her, and spent weekends with his wife, Lois, in his Albany flat. Hamilton floundered in this triangle, apparently unable to make a change, and would remain in it, with some variation, for the rest of his life.

When La returned to her Chelsea flat, Hamilton sold his Albany flat, bought a converted stable at Whitchurch, near Pangbourne, and installed Lois there. In spite of the uproar in his private life, he was working on the first Gorse novel, finishing it in an intense burst in the autumn of 1950. The Gorse novels, which were intended from the beginning to be a series, examined a sociopathic criminal, Ralph Ernest Gorse. The novels, unlike Hamilton's other fiction, are set retrospectively in the interwar period. The allusions throughout the novels to Gorse's murderous career and eventual end on the gallows are characteristic of true-crime writing. The first novel, *The West Pier* (1951), portrayed Gorse's early career. His criminal tendencies are evident even during his school days, and the central crime in this novel is his defrauding of Esther Downes, a young working-class girl. Gorse takes her savings, painstakingly built up through the efforts of her mother, and leaves her stranded at a country inn, unable even to pay the bill for their tea. An important feature of this novel is that Hamilton focuses his attention on Brighton. Hamilton knew Brighton well, having spent much of his childhood in Hove, and frequently returned there. It figures in his other novels as a destination but is the principal setting only in *The West Pier*. No less an authority than Graham Greene describes it as "the best novel written about Brighton."

Hamilton began work on the second novel, *Mr. Stimpson and Mr. Gorse* (1953), almost immediately after *The West Pier* was finished, but he was working around the complications of his personal life. Divorce proceedings were started, then put on hold; meanwhile, Hamilton continued to divide his time between his mistress in Chelsea and his wife in Whitchurch. La herself was getting a divorce from her second husband, Michael Stewart. In June 1953 Lois and Hamilton were divorced; in 1954 Hamilton and La were married in London. These years were marked, among other troubles, by conflict with Inland Revenue.

In the second Gorse novel, Gorse switches his territory to Reading and his criminal attentions to Mrs. Plumleigh-Bruce, a colonel's widow. Once again, in spite of much doom-laden foreshadowing, Gorse's crimes consist only of swindling Mrs. Plumleigh-Bruce of £500 and humiliating her socially, although Mr. Stimpson tries to foil Gorse's efforts. Hamilton's longtime publisher, Michael Sadleir, did not care for the novel, complaining that all of its characters are unpleasant; but it was favorably reviewed upon publication.

His final play, *The Man Upstairs*, was to be produced in 1954 but suffered from a crippling series of delays. The next year, with some misgivings and stung by the criticisms of Sadleir and his brother on the first two Gorse novels, Hamilton began work on *Unknown Assailant*. The book, his least substantial in every respect, came out that same year and depicted

Gorse swindling a naive barmaid, Ivy Barton, of her savings, assisted greatly—if unintentionally—by Ivy's snobbish father, who loses £200 of his own money in the bargain. It was the last published work of his career and makes clear the huge gap between Gorse's actions and the dramatic commentary of the three novels. These novels retain a certain interest through Hamilton's depiction of local atmosphere, snobbery, and the sociopathic personality, but they are not his best work and certainly do not live up to the plan he had conceived for them. When they were made into a miniseries for British television, a great deal of material was added to make the action more consonant with the rhetoric. The television adaptation of the Gorse books, however, introduced many new American readers to Hamilton's work in the early 1990s.

As he worked on the Gorse novels, Hamilton's increasingly dysfunctional personal life began to take up all of his time and energy, and his drinking only compounded the problems. The divorce from Lois had not meant the end of their relationship, and he continued to visit her much as he had earlier. In 1955, at the urging of his second wife, Hamilton agreed to try a cure for his alcoholism. La's former husband recommended a program developed by Dr. John Dent that involved taking apomorphine. Hamilton underwent treatment in the autumn, but the "cure" did not work, probably because Hamilton was not a willing participant; after being released from the nursing home, he refused to follow the rules regarding alcohol consumption and the required medication. He and La moved to Norfolk, thinking that a change of scene and fresh air would be good for Hamilton. These factors had no lasting effect, however, and the relationship between Hamilton and his wife deteriorated while he continued to spend periods of time with Lois.

Hamilton's drinking problem worsened, and he became clinically depressed. Late in 1956 Dent proposed that Hamilton undergo electroconvulsive therapy. He agreed to a series of six treatments and underwent seven for good measure. He returned to Norfolk, believing himself to be cured. Facing the same complicated personal life, his drinking continued, and he had further alcohol-induced stays in the hospital. His writing life was effectively over, though during one of his stays in the hospital he began working on an autobiography. He later revised that first attempt, "Memoirs of a Heavy Drinking Man," into a second version, but neither was ever completed. In 1961 he wrote a few chapters of a new novel, "The Happy Hunting Grounds," but never got any farther than that.

By the summer of 1962 Hamilton was failing

fast; he was seriously ill and nearly bedridden, but still drinking. He died 23 September 1962 from complications of his alcoholism. Lois visited him for a few days near the end, and both wives took part in the funeral. His will left two-thirds of his estate to his second wife and one third to his first wife, continuing the triangle to the bitter end. This disposition of property greatly upset his brother, Bruce, who had expected to inherit at least part of the estate. The relationship between the brothers was always complex, and this final insult is not unimportant. Bruce Hamilton wrote the first biography of Hamilton, establishing a record that must be perpetuated or actively refuted. Virtually all the papers Hamilton left behind upon his death eventually became the property of his brother.

Hamilton's fiction is in many ways accomplished, but perhaps his greatest achievement is his creation of a record of people on the margins, what he called the "semi-proletariat." Many writers of the interwar period took an interest in leftist politics, but Hamilton's work captures a way of life usually ignored by other writers. His characteristic subjects and distinctive writing style have won him many readers, although until recently his work has received little attention from academic critics. The reviews of reprinted editions of his novels reveal a series of rediscoveries by admiring readers.

### Biographies:

Bruce Hamilton, *The Light Went Out: A Biography of Patrick Hamilton* (London: Constable, 1972);

Nigel Jones, *Through a Glass Darkly: The Life of Patrick Hamilton* (London: Scribners, 1991);

Sean French, *Patrick Hamilton: A Life* (London: Faber & Faber, 1993).

### References:

Angus Hall, "After the Hangover," *Books and Bookmen,* 13 (July 1968): 11–12;

Michael Holroyd, "Out of Print" and "Patrick Hamilton," in his *Unreceived Opinions* (New York: Holt, Rinehart & Winston, 1974), pp. 102–118, 149–152;

Brian McKenna, "Confessions of a Heavy-Drinking Marxist," in *Beyond the Pleasure Dome: Writing and Addiction from the Romantics,* edited by Sue Vice, Matthew Campbell, and Tim Armstrong (Sheffield: Sheffield Academic Press, 1994), pp. 231–244;

Arnold Rattenbury, "Literature, Lying and Sober Truth: Attitudes to the Work of Patrick Hamilton and Sylvia Townsend Warner," in *Writing and Radicalism,* edited by John Lucas (London & New York: Longman, 1996), pp. 201–244;

John Russell Taylor, "Patrick Hamilton," *London Magazine,* 6, no. 2 (1966): 53–60;

Donald Thomas, "The Dangerous Edge of Things," *Encounter,* 69, no. 2 (1987): 32–40;

Peter J. Widdowson, "The Saloon Bar Society: Patrick Hamilton's Fiction in the 1930s," in *The 1930s: Challenge to Orthodoxy,* edited by Lucas (London & New York: Harvester/Barnes & Noble, 1978), pp. 117–137.

### Papers:

Boston University has several important play manuscripts in their special collections: *Gaslight, To the Public Danger,* and *Money with Menaces.* The Lilly Library, Indiana University, has some movie scripts along with Michael Sadleir's copies of many of Hamilton's novels, inscribed by the author. The Manuscripts Department of the Library of the University of North Carolina, Chapel Hill, has some of Hamilton's correspondence with Sadleir in the Michael Sadleir Papers. A collection of letters and other manuscript material that belonged to Bruce Hamilton was auctioned off in the early 1990s; its present whereabouts are unknown.

# John Hampson
## *(1901 – 26 December 1955)*

### Chris Hopkins
*Sheffield Hallam University*

BOOKS: *Saturday Night at the Greyhound* (London: Hogarth, 1931);

*The Sight of Blood* (London: Ulysses Bookshop, 1931);

*Two Stories: The Mare's Nest; The Long Shadow* (London: Lahr, 1931);

*O Providence* (London: Hogarth, 1932);

*Strip Jack Naked* (London: Heinemann, 1934);

*Man about the House* (London: Grayson, 1935);

*Family Curse* (London: Chapman & Hall, 1936);

*The Larches,* by Hampson and L. A. Pavey (London: M. Joseph, 1938);

*Care of "The Grand"* (London: Chapman & Hall, 1939);

*The English at Table* (London: Collins, 1944);

*A Bag of Stones* (London: Verschoyle, 1952).

When he died in 1955, John Hampson's obituary in the *Times* of London said that he was "the author of the well-known novel *Saturday Night at the Greyhound*" and

> the grandson of Mr. Mercer Hampson Simpson, sometime manager of the Theatre Royal, Birmingham, and he spent most of his life in the Midlands, in his early years as an employee in the catering trade. This experience he put to good use not only in *Saturday Night at the Greyhound* . . . but also in *Care of "the Grand"* and *The English at Table.* . . . the only novel he wrote after the last war was *A Bag of Stones.*

As the obituary indicates, Hampson was, and is, remembered principally for his first novel, *Saturday Night at the Greyhound* (1931). The details of his life are obscure: there is no entry on him in the *Dictionary of National Biography* or in any post–World War II literary reference book, nor is he listed in standard works of his time, such as Stanley Kunitz and Howard Haycraft's *Twentieth Century Authors: A Biographical Dictionary of Modern Literature* (1942). This obscurity is particularly striking when Hampson is compared with his contemporary James Hanley: the two have sometimes been mentioned to-gether, but where Hampson has slipped out of literary memory, Hanley is fully established. (Ironically, Hampson, in a letter of 7 March 1931 to the publisher E. Lahr, said that one of Hanley's novels "is terrible: it made me shud[d]er.") There is a lack, then, both of public record of periods of Hampson's life and of substantial critical discussion of his work; the only exceptions in regard to the latter are an unpublished master of arts dissertation by Mercer Simpson (1975) and an account of Hampson's role in the "Birmingham group" of writers in Andy Crofts's *Red Letter Days* (1990). Yet he certainly was famous for one work in the 1930s; and his other six novels of the period were, at least, respectfully reviewed at the time and can give insights into aspects of the interwar novel. The best of Hampson's novels, *Saturday Night at the Greyhound* is certainly a major achievement; but even it has been neglected.

John Frederick Norman Hampson Simpson was born in Handsworth, near Birmingham, in 1901; the exact date is unknown. His father, Mercer Hampson Simpson, came from a family that had been connected with theater management since the 1860s and had made a good deal of money from its ownership of theatrical leases. Mercer Hampson, however, was the manager and part-owner of a brewery, which suffered a financial collapse in 1907. The family found itself in relative poverty until 1912, when Mercer Simpson obtained another post as a manager. John Hampson left home in 1917 and took a series of jobs. E. M. Forster had heard an account of how Hampson made his living before his success as an author; P. N. Furbank's 1979 biography of Forster recounts the story, as well as giving some details of Hampson's appearance and eccentricities:

> At much the same period [September 1932], Forster also made the acquaintance of "John Hampson." . . . Simpson, who was now in his late thirties, lived with a family named Wilson, near Birmingham. He was tiny, and in appearance rather grotesque, with a cow-lick and a Hapsburg chin and dressing from head to foot in brown (he had a mania for the colour brown, writing in brown ink on nearly-brown paper). The Wilsons employed Simpson as a nurse to the Wilsons' idiot son, Ronald. Before taking this post he had worked in hotel kitchens and had supported himself for a time as a book thief–though, as he said, "only taking the best books." Forster . . . took to him greatly, considering him a most admirable and saint-like character. He [Forster] soon became a frequent visitor to him and the Wilsons.

Hampson related to friends a few further details about this period: the book thefts led to a short spell in prison; he had also been a munitions worker, a waiter in Nottingham and in London, a barman in a Derbyshire pub, and a chef in the city of Derby. He had taken the job as caretaker for Ronald Wilson in 1925.

*Saturday Night at the Greyhound* was published by Virginia and Leonard Woolf's Hogarth Press. John Lehmann–who, later in the decade, was to become a centrally important figure in publishing new work–had started work at the press shortly before the novel appeared. He recalls in a letter quoted in his memoir *Thrown to the Woolfs* (1978) that the work was "a distinct success": "Hampson seems to me a great hope . . . the book is already going very fast, embarrassingly fast when the first edition is quite small. We've already ordered a second."

The novel has a concentrated and unusual atmosphere that partly results from its formal austerity and economy. It has a small cast of characters, all of whom are viewed only in their connection with the Greyhound pub. The novel preserves the Aristotelian dramatic unities most strictly: the narrative takes place within the course of a single day–or, in this case, a single night; the action has a single setting, the country pub; and there is a single plot, the fall of the landlord's family. The novel is divided into three parts: "Nightfall at the Greyhound," "The Open House," and "The House Closes." Each part is divided into sections, each of which is devoted to the internal monologue of one of the characters. The reader first meets Mrs. Tapin, the Greyhound's hardened and shrewd housekeeper and cook. She has seen fourteen previous landlords of the pub fail to make a living out of it, and she knows that the present tenant, Fred Flack, will follow their example. Opposing her own country cunning–"things nearly always happened as she expected them to"–to the town-bred folly of Flack, she filches food, drink, and money from her employer at every opportunity. Her past includes an affair with the squire of the village of Grovedon, of which her daughter, Clara, is the illegitimate product.

The next section belongs to Tom Oakley, the brother of Fred Flack's wife, Ivy. Tom and Ivy's parents kept a highly successful pub in Birmingham, and Tom is as aware as Mrs. Tapin that the Greyhound is doomed to fail: "Business would be poor that night. . . . It had been a mistake ever to come." The failure is particularly galling for Tom, who has a talent for the business and who came to the Greyhound only because of his sister. He previously held an excellent position as a waiter in a London hotel, where he took intense pleasure in his skill: "he found the severe, unchangeable mode of serving a meal correctly had a quality of satisfaction about it." He dislikes his brother-in-law, partly because Fred is a drunkard–a fatal flaw in a publican–and partly because Tom has an unusually strong affection for his sister. This love takes the place of any desire for other relationships, either sexual or social, though there is some suggestion that he is a homosexual: "Women had no attraction for him. Men respected rather than liked him."

Subsequent sections in part 1 introduce the viewpoints of Ivy, Fred, and Clara, who is having an affair with Fred. In the following two parts the only variation is in the order in which the characters' sections appear. Ivy knows that Fred is a failure, but she refuses to acknowledge the depth of the problem: "the truth about him was too unpleasant to believe; she only accepted the obvious faults which could not be disregarded." She is so entranced by Fred's erotic appeal that she wills herself to forget the only too apparent flaws in his character, thinking only of "the beauty of his straight limbs . . . the whiteness of his body, the tender secret things of which she alone knew." Such an emphasis on sexuality is unusual for a novel of this period.

Tom has considerable insight into Ivy's passion for Fred, and, though explicitly critical of Fred's exploitation of his appeal, is careful to avoid any direct conflict with his sister's commitment to this source of destructive pleasure. In fact, Tom's feelings for Ivy constitute a similar foolish passion. When he left his job at the London hotel to join her in a venture that he already knew would be doomed by Fred's character flaws, he thought:

> In all the wide world there was no other as Ivy was, no one. . . . From all that was ugly, from all bitterness he wished to shield her. The feelings he had for her were too ecstatic to set in a frame of words.

Tom's highest values are businesslike conduct, hard work, and realism; it is only in regard to Ivy that he lapses from these virtues. Similarly, Ivy is realistic about everything except the possibility that Fred will change: "Hope was so vivid in her thoughts that she found it incredible that Freddy remained the same easy-going man."

Just as Ivy hopes that every day will bring her a reformed Fred, Fred vaguely supposes in regard to his business that one day "things might improve." But where Ivy and Tom's suspension of common sense in certain cases is damaging to themselves, Fred's more-general lack of prudence does not seem to affect him negatively; on the contrary, it gives him license to do whatever he wishes, while others have to suffer the consequences.

The events that take place during the single night depicted in the novel result from these situations and character flaws. Fred is the chief instigator of the pub's decline: he has spent Ivy's savings without reducing their debts, but he continues to give away free drinks and to drink heavily himself. He plays cards with his customers, who cheat him at every opportunity. Clara tells him that she is pregnant by him, but he refuses to take any re-

*Dust jacket for Hampson's first novel*

sponsibility in the matter. Mrs. Tapin maliciously strangles the greyhound, Naxi, that Ivy loves. Fred had bought Naxi as a mascot for the pub–he was cheated even here, for the villagers who sold him the dog charged him more than it was worth. Tom discovers the body but conceals the knowledge from Ivy, realizing that "after her first grief, she would see in Naxi's terrible end foredoomed failure for all her plans for success." At the end of the novel Fred loses everything in a rigged card game, and the village policeman catches him illegally serving customers after closing time; Clara has informed on him in revenge for his indifference to her condition. He will never be able to keep a pub again. The novel concludes with the simple sentence "They had reached the day's end," suggesting both the ordinariness of the events and their symbolic and tragic value for the characters. Ivy's hopes are ruined; Tom's fears are fulfilled; and even Fred must face the fact of his own failure. The only hopes left are those of Clara and Mrs. Tapin, who enjoy a sense of superiority at, and take a brutal pleasure in, the downfall of another incumbent of the Greyhound.

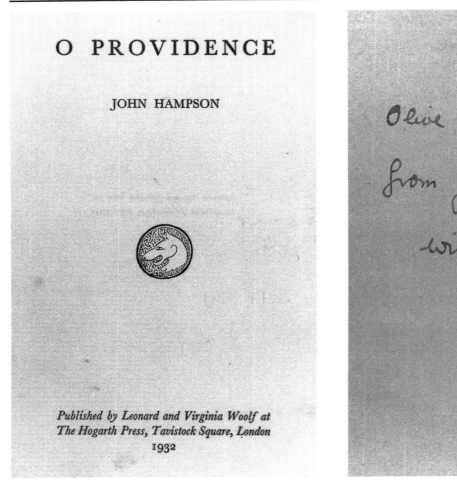
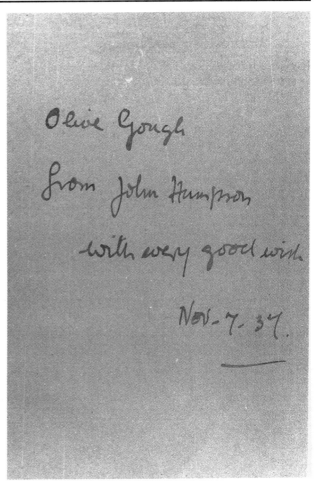

*Inscribed endpaper and title page for Hampson's chronicle of the Stonetun family (Arizona State University Library)*

The uniqueness of the novel lies in its ability to combine a starkly contemporary realism with an aura of classical tragedy. The blend of an innovative modernist form with a realist or even naturalist content and social milieu is also striking. Categorizing the novel's tone as tragicomic, the *Times Literary Supplement* (12 March 1931) said that the "use of the professional aspect of publichouse life as a background for the unfolding drama deserves special praise." It said that the plot was given added impact by limiting the action to the course of one night, while also revealing the principal characters' past and future lives. The novel was widely read: the Hogarth Press brought out five impressions between 1931 and 1935; in 1937 the novel appeared as Penguin paperback number 94, a sure sign of continuing success, and a second Penguin impression appeared later in the year. The novel has rarely been critically discussed at any length, but where it has been mentioned it has

been regarded as possessing a distinction all its own. The novelist and critic Walter Allen—who, like Hampson, was part of the "Birmingham group"—said that it seemed to "owe nothing to anything that has gone before."

The reception of the novel brought Hampson into contact with literary figures such as Forster, with whom he began a lifelong friendship. He generously used these contacts to help other writers, especially those—among them Allen and Walter Brierley—from working-class backgrounds in Birmingham.

Hampson's next publications, both in 1931, were small volumes of short stories that were noticed by reviewers as much for their aesthetic value as products of the bookmaker's art as for their literary merit. *The Sight of Blood* was only eight pages long and comprised only the title story. Aimed at bibliophiles, it was published in a limited edition of 145 copies, each signed by the author. The *Times Literary Supplement* (28 January 1932) commented that the pieces in *Two Stories: The Mare's Nest; The Long Shadow* were "slight in content as in quantity"; nevertheless, the review praised Hampson's "integrity and craftsmanship." The publication of these collectors' editions, as well as the comments made about them, suggest the impact made by *Saturday Night at the Greyhound:* though Hampson was the author of only one novel, he had already established a reputation.

Hampson's next novel, *O Providence,* published by the Hogarth Press in 1932, is less innovative than *Saturday Night at the Greyhound;* based on the history of an upper-middle-class family, it is reminiscent of such traditional English novels as John Galsworthy's trilogy, *The Forsyte Saga,* published between 1906 and 1921. Novelists considered modern writers, including Forster and even Christopher Isherwood, however, also produced works of this type: Isherwood's family narrative, *The Memorial: Portrait of a Family,* was published by the Hogarth Press in the same year as *O Providence.* As is shown by his use of the stream-of-consciousness technique, Hampson has by no means turned his back on modernism; but in most respects his novel works in quite traditional ways, retaining, for example, a strong sense of the third-person authorial narrator. Gone is the austerity of narration and setting that makes *Saturday Night at the Greyhound* so distinctive; missing, too, is the narrative drive given by the strict unities of the earlier novel. The work is an account of the fairly wealthy Stonetun family; the narrator reinforces the viewpoint of the youngest son, Justin, as normative. Showing signs of the influence of James Joyce's *A Portrait of the Artist as a Young Man* (1916), the novel begins with Justin's earliest memories; it ends with the departure of his father, Victor, to serve in the army in 1914.

The main emphasis is on Justin's childhood and on his perception of the social conditioning his family tries to inflict on him. Justin is a sensitive boy who refuses to abide by the norms laid down for his class. He is attracted to games and toys that his family regards as feminine or simply as odd: he plays with dolls; has an imaginary companion, the Fairy Godmother; and engages in various kinds of storytelling. His values are artistic ones, and, like Tom Oakley in *Saturday Night at the Greyhound,* but more explicitly, he has homosexual tendencies. His oddity, his sexuality, and his status as an artist in embryo derive from a conception of the "artistic" that was established by the nineteenth-century aesthetes and continued to

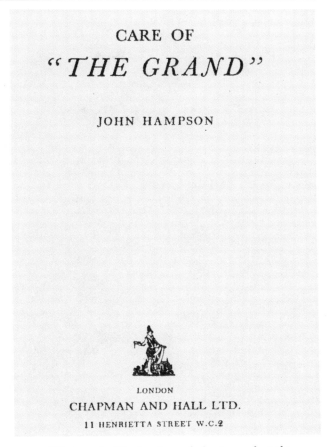

CARE OF

## "*THE GRAND*"

JOHN HAMPSON

LONDON
CHAPMAN AND HALL LTD.
11 HENRIETTA STREET W.C.2

*Title page for Hampson's novel about a week at the Grand Hotel*

have considerable currency into the 1930s. At the end of the novel Justin asserts his independence from his family:

> He was no longer a child. That was all behind him....
> Justin was glad to be alone....
> He thought of tomorrow.
> He considered the future, dreaming, and saw a straight path mounting steadily towards a pinnacle. He knew that he would reach the top. The vista of things to come was rosy and gleaming.

There is, however, little concrete evidence of a change in Justin or in his relationship with his family. Although the early part of the novel gives the impression that it will be a bildungsroman about Justin's development into an artist, Justin never achieves that status. This feature may be partly a result of the influence of *A Portrait of the Artist as a Young Man,* which concludes with its protagonist a potential rather than an actual artistic success. But it may also be that Hampson could not envisage Justin as an adult: Justin is trapped in his role of sensitive child, somewhat as Isher-

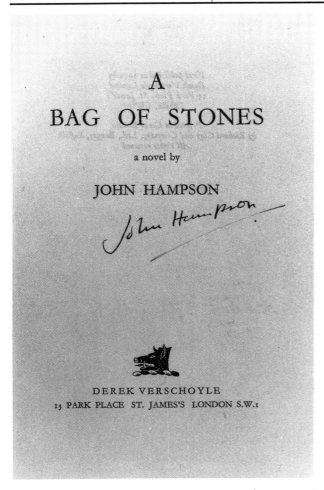

*Autographed title page for Hampson's final novel (University of Wisconsin at Milwaukee)*

wood's sensitive and quasi-artistic protagonists in *The Memorial* and in his earlier *All the Conspirators* (1928) remain locked in dependent relationships with their families.

*O Providence* was less successful than Hampson's first novel had been. The *Times Literary Supplement* (14 April 1932) observed that this work was less experimental than *Saturday Night at the Greyhound;* while considering this difference an advance in technique, the reviewer also noted that it produced an excessively low-key effect. And, though commending the novel's interest in the mundane, the review criticizes its "monotony of drabs and greys." The work suffers from a lack of narrative pace and from a lack of closure; in these respects it is representative of Hampson's remaining novels. Reviewers during the rest of his career would repeatedly praise Hampson's style but would have reservations about his ability to develop his plots.

The Woolfs had similar doubts. In her diary entry for 15 January 1933 Virginia Woolf comments, "Hampson's new novel is so bad we are going to advise against publishing it." The novel in question was, presumably, his third, *Strip Jack Naked,* which was published in 1934 by the William Heinemann firm. Hampson's relations with the Woolfs seem to have continued, but not wholly amicably. In her diary for 11 March 1936 Virginia Woolf records how busy Leonard is and remarks, "and here's Hampson cooly applying . . . for help about his miserable contracts." The Hogarth Press published no more of Hampson's works, but Leonard Woolf may have assisted him in negotiating contracts with other publishers—*Family Curse* (1936) has a dedication thanking Woolf for his help. After 1932 Hampson's novels appeared under the imprints of several major publishers, suggesting possible difficulties as well as continuing faith in him as a novelist.

*Strip Jack Naked* was reviewed slightly more favorably than *O Providence,* though, again, the *Times Literary Supplement* (14 June 1934) found fault with its being set in a "minor key." The same review, however, praised the novel's construction as "harmonious," and there is, indeed, a more certain handling of plot development and closure than in *O Providence.* The story concerns two brothers: Alf (who may have been based on Hampson's brother, a motorcycle-racing champion who rode under the name Jimmy Hampson) is an extroverted truck driver who likes, in the *Times Literary Supplement* reviewer's words, "noise and movement" and is "run after by the girls," while Ted, who works at home in their father's shoe shop, is a familiar Hampson character type: he is solitary, sensitive, and fond of reading and introspection. Alf and Ted clearly represent heterosexual and homosexual modes of masculinity, respectively. The *Times Literary Supplement* reviewer noted that Hampson "characteristically . . . sets [Ted] in the centre of the picture." Ted is devoted to Alf and loves to perform domestic work to make him happy and comfortable. When Alf is killed in a road accident on the eve of his wedding to Laura, who is pregnant by him, Ted is griefstricken. His father comments, "You can't go down to the grave, but you would if you could." Instead, Ted marries Laura, taking his brother's place as a husband and father. The *Times Literary Supplement* suggests that "this final sacrifice on the altar of his idolatrous affection" is the beginning of his own "liberation . . . to come to know the actuality of love and marriage and the completion of manhood." The real interest of the novel, however, seems to be in Ted's homoerotic feelings for Alf; making the two men brothers and having Alf die gave Hampson room to explore homosexual love within the conventions of a publishable novel. This subtext was by no means deeply hidden from contemporary readers who cared to look for it.

In 1935 Hampson published *Man about the House,* another short story in a limited edition. In 1936 he married the German actress Therese Giehse; the marriage was W. H. Auden's idea and was designed to provide Giehse with British citizenship so that she could escape the Nazi regime. Earlier in the year Auden himself had married Erika Mann, Thomas Mann's daughter, for the same reason. Although the marriage was a legal union, Hampson and Giehse did not live together as man and wife.

Hampson's main publication in 1936 was *Family Curse.* Like *O Providence,* it is a family history; but this time the narration is presented from multiple points of view, clearly demarcated by chapter and section—a return to the narrative technique of *Saturday Night at the Greyhound* but without that novel's starkness and economy. As in *O Providence,* there is a critique of the conformism of a wealthy bourgeois family—the Sumerles—and a characteristic interest in various kinds of sexual nonconformity. There is the typical Hampson homosexual artist in the younger son, Johnny, who, like Justin Stonetun, rejects the family at the end of the story. What is new is a greater interest in female characters, who make much more substantial appearances here than in previous novels. The book was received moderately well.

Hampson's next novel, *The Larches* (1938), was a new departure in that it was co-authored with L. A. Pavey. It nevertheless includes much that is to be expected in a Hampson novel. It concerns the Blake family, particularly the contrasted values of the father, Stephen, and the mother, Margaret. In ways that are reminiscent of family politics in Forster's novels, the father and mother represent, respectively, complacent acceptance of convention and a more imaginative emotional response to life. Their son, Francis, is torn between these values, though he sympathizes more fully with his mother. The narration is presented retrospectively from the day on which Stephen remarries, some years after Margaret's death. In the end, father and son are reconciled. The usual "minor key" criticism was leveled at the work; one reviewer said that it belonged to "the simmering or watched-pot school of novel, whose characters have boiled yesterday and may possibly boil tomorrow, but . . . will never boil today."

Hampson's final novel of the interwar period returned to a setting similar to that of *Saturday Night at the Greyhound* and also to some of that novel's narrative method. *Care of "The Grand"* (1939) is set in a hotel and narrated through a series of internal monologues. Instead of taking place in a single night, however, this novel covers a week at "The Grand." It is divided into seven sections, one for each day of the week, and each day is divided into subsections titled "Morning," "Noon," and "Night." Variety is provided by altering the sequence in which characters "speak" within this strict structure. As in Hampson's first novel, the structure helps to give unity and pace to the narrative and avoids some of the lack of control that is found in his earlier novels that have large casts of characters. The work also shows Hampson taking an interest in the sort of documentary concerns that engaged other writers in the 1930s: in a prefatory note Hampson says that he is indebted to the journal *FACT* "for much of the practical information on which this novel is based . . . especially to a study . . . written by an assistant hotel manager," and the *Times Literary Supplement* (22 July 1939) noted that the novel was particularly interested in the "workings of the staff" and in "everyday . . . routine." *Care of "The Grand"* was positively reviewed, with few of the reservations that had been expressed by critics of Hampson's other works.

From 1941 until the early 1950s Hampson did some writing for BBC radio. During World War II Hampson published only one book, *The English at Table* (1944), a nonfiction work about culinary traditions in England that was inspired, perhaps, like Evelyn Waugh's treatment of food in his novel *Brideshead Revisited* (1944), by the hardships caused by wartime rationing. He was one of the close friends who were invited to Forster's seventieth birthday party on 1 January. His next, and final, work was the novel *A Bag of Stones* (1952). The protagonist is a typical Hampson figure—a sensitive boy who, like Francis Blake in *The Larches,* identifies with his passive mother and fears his oppressive father.

Little is known of Hampson's later life. His correspondence with a New York antiquarian bookseller, H. A. Rappaport, shows that in 1954 Hampson was in the curious position of not owning copies of his own novels. Rappaport was able to find a copy of the first edition of *Saturday Night at the Greyhound,* and Hampson asked him to look out for copies of *The Larches* and *Man about the House.* The novelist's difficulties in buying copies of his books suggest how swiftly neglect had overtaken his earlier reputation. In a letter dated 7 September 1954 Hampson tells Rappaport that he has been busy writing a Christmas feature for radio and revising a "new novel." The novel's title is not mentioned, and it was never published. It is clear from the letters that Hampson was still active, optimistic, and proud of his earlier work. He died on 26 December 1955.

Contemporaries' judgments of John Hampson's work seem largely correct: his first novel, *Saturday Night at the Greyhound,* was an extraordinary achievement with, as Allen puts it, "an original distinction and idiosyncrasy." His subsequent novels had less impact, but all of them manifest originality and quality. Study of Hampson's work can reveal much about the literary, historical, and cultural contexts of the novel in Britain between the wars. It is unfortunate that a writer whose novels have suggestive parallels with those of E. M. Forster and Christopher Isherwood should have been so neglected.

**References:**

Walter Allen, *Tradition and Dream—The English and American Novel from the Twenties to Our Time* (London: Dent, 1964), pp. 226–227;

Andy Crofts, *Red Letter Days—British Fiction in the 1930s* (London: Lawrence & Wishart, 1990), pp. 159–183;

Valentine Cunningham, *British Writers of the Thirties* (Oxford: Oxford University Press, 1989; New York: Oxford University Press, 1989), p. 149, 152, 171, 303, 306, 314;

P. N. Furbank, *E. M. Forster—A Life* (Oxford: Oxford University Press, 1979), pp. 179–180;

John Lehmann, *Thrown to the Woolfs* (London: Weidenfeld & Nicolson, 1978), p. 15;

Mercer Simpson, "The Novels of John Hampson," M.A. thesis, University of Wales, 1975.

# James Hanley
*(3 September 1901 – 11 November 1985)*

Sheri P. Midkiff
*Williams Baptist College*

BOOKS: *Drift: A Novel* (London: Partridge, 1930);
*The German Prisoner* (London: Privately printed, 1930);
*A Passion before Death* (London: Privately printed, 1930; New York: Privately printed, 1935);
*Boy* (London: Boriswood, 1931; New York: Knopf, 1932);
*The Last Voyage,* Furnival Books, no. 5 (London: Joiner & Steele, 1931);
*Men in Darkness: Five Stories* (London: John Lane, 1931; New York: Knopf, 1932);
*Ebb and Flood: A Novel* (London: John Lane, 1932);
*Stoker Haslett: A Tale* (London: Joiner & Steele, 1932);
*Aria and Finale* (London: Boriswood, 1932);
*Captain Bottell* (London: Boriswood, 1933);
*Resurrexit Dominus* (London: Privately printed, 1934);
*Quartermaster Clausen* (London: Arlan at the White Owl Press, 1934);
*The Furys: A Novel* (London: Chatto & Windus, 1935; New York: Macmillan, 1935);
*At Bay* (London: Grayson & Grayson, 1935); enlarged as *At Bay and Other Stories* (London: Faber & Faber, 1944);
*Stoker Bush* (London: Chatto & Windus, 1935; New York: Macmillan, 1936);
*The Secret Journey* (London: Chatto & Windus, 1936; New York: Macmillan, 1936);
*Half an Eye: Sea Stories* (London: John Lane, 1937);
*Broken Water: An Autobiographical Excursion* (London: Chatto & Windus, 1937);
*Grey Children: A Study in Humbug and Misery* (London: Methuen, 1937);
*Hollow Sea: A Novel* (London: John Lane, 1938);
*People Are Curious* (London: John Lane, 1938);
*Between the Tides* (London: Methuen, 1939); republished as *Towards Horizons,* as James Bentley (London: Mellifont, 1949);
*Our Time Is Gone* (London: John Lane, 1940; revised edition, London: Phoenix House, 1949);
*The Ocean* (London: Faber & Faber, 1941; New York: Morrow, 1941);

*James Hanley*

*No Directions* (London: Faber & Faber, 1943);
*Sailor's Song* (London: Nicholson & Watson, 1943);
*Crilley, and Other Stories* (London: Nicholson & Watson, 1945);
*What Farrar Saw* (London: Nicholson & Watson, 1946);
*Selected Stories* (Dublin: Fridberg, 1947);
*Emily* (London: Nicholson & Watson, 1948);
*A Walk in the Darkness* (London: Phoenix House, 1950);
*Winter Song* (London: Phoenix House, 1950);
*The House in the Valley,* as Patric Shone (London: Cape, 1951); republished as *Against the Stream,* as Hanley (New York: Horizon, 1981);
*The Closed Harbor* (London: Macdonald, 1952; New York: Horizon, 1953);

*Don Quixote Drowned* (London: Macdonald, 1953);

*Collected Stories* (London: Macdonald, 1953);

*The Welsh Sonata: Variations on a Theme* (London: Verschoyle, 1954; New York: Horizon, 1978);

*Levine* (London: Macdonald, 1956; New York: Horizon, 1956);

*Dock Leaves: A John Cowper Powys Number,* by Hanley and others (Pembroke Dock, Wales: Dock Leaves Press, 1956);

*An End and a Beginning* (London: Macdonald, 1958; New York: Horizon, 1958);

*Say Nothing* (London: Macdonald, 1962; New York: Horizon, 1962);

*The Inner Journey: A Play in Three Acts* (London: Black Raven, 1965; New York: Horizon, 1965);

*Plays One* (London: Kaye & Ward, 1968)—comprises *The Inner Journey* and *A Stone Flower;*

*The Face of Winter* (Loughton, Essex: Ward, 1969);

*John Cowper Powys: A Man in the Corner* (Loughton, Essex: Ward, 1969);

*Herman Melville: A Man in the Customs House* (Loughton, Essex: Dud Norman, 1971);

*Another World* (London: Deutsch, 1972; New York: Horizon, 1972);

*A Woman in the Sky* (London: Deutsch, 1973; New York: Horizon, 1973);

*The Darkness* (London: Covent Garden, 1973);

*A Dream Journey* (London: Deutsch, 1976; New York: Horizon, 1976);

*A Kingdom* (London: Deutsch, 1978; New York: Horizon, 1978).

**Editions and Collections:** *Boy,* foreword by Liam Hanley (London: Penguin, 1992);

*The Last Voyage and Other Stories,* introduction by Alan Ross (London: Harvill, 1997).

PLAY PRODUCTIONS: *Say Nothing,* London, Theatre Royal, Stratford East, 14 August 1962;

*Forever and Ever,* Hamburg, 1966;

*The Inner Journey,* Hamburg, 1966;

*Leave Us Alone,* London, 1972.

TELEVISION SCRIPTS: "The Inner World of Miss Vaughan," British Broadcasting Corporation, 1 April 1964;

"Another Port, Another Town," Granada Television, 4 May 1964;

"Mr. Ponge," British Broadcasting Corporation, 9 December 1965;

"Day out for Lucy," British Broadcasting Corporation, 1 July 1965;

"A Walk in the Sea," British Broadcasting Corporation, 9 March 1966;

"That Woman," British Broadcasting Corporation, 31 May 1967;

"Nothing Will Be the Same Again," British Broadcasting Corporation, 6 October 1968;

"It Wasn't Me," British Broadcasting Corporation, 17 December 1969.

RADIO SCRIPTS: "S.S. *Elizabethan,*" British Broadcasting Corporation, 1941;

*Freedom's Ferry* (series), British Broadcasting Corporation, 1941;

*Open Boat* (series), British Broadcasting Corporation, 1941;

"Return to Danger," British Broadcasting Corporation, 1942;

"A Winter Journey," British Broadcasting Corporation, 1 April 1957;

"The Ocean," British Broadcasting Corporation, 19 May 1958;

"A Letter in the Desert," British Broadcasting Corporation, 12 October 1958;

"Gobbet," British Broadcasting Corporation, 6 October 1959;

"The Queen of Ireland," British Broadcasting Corporation, 19 April 1960;

"Miss Williams," British Broadcasting Corporation, 13 November 1960;

"Say Nothing," British Broadcasting Corporation, 25 April 1961;

"A Pillar of Fire," British Broadcasting Corporation, 24 June 1962;

"A Walk in the World," British Broadcasting Corporation, 1 January 1962;

"A Dream," British Broadcasting Corporation, 13 November 1963;

"The Silence," British Broadcasting Corporation, 13 January 1968;

"Sailor's Song," British Broadcasting Corporation, 1970;

"One Way Only," British Broadcasting Corporation, 1970;

"A Terrible Day," British Broadcasting Corporation, 7 November 1973;

"A Dream Journey," British Broadcasting Corporation, 23 September 1974;

"Another World," British Broadcasting Corporation, 1980.

OTHER: Fedor Ivanovich Shaliapin, *Chaliapin: An Autobiography as Told to Maxim Gorky; with Supplementary Correspondence and Notes, Translated from the Russian,* edited by Hanley and Nina Froud (London: Macdonald, 1968 [i.e., 1967]; New York: Stein & Day, 1967).

In work that spans a half-century, James Hanley depicts situations and characters that reflect the complexity of modern life. His characters, many of whom are from the lower classes, face isolation and loneliness and seek love, acceptance, and self-understanding. While their lives seem to be characterized more by defeat than by triumph, they maintain their dignity and sense of worth in the midst of misfortune. While his early novels are primarily concerned with those whose livelihoods depend on the sea, his later works are set in locales ranging from remote Welsh villages to London.

Born in Dublin on 3 September 1901, Hanley was raised in Liverpool. He became a merchant seaman—his father's occupation—at fourteen; in 1917 he jumped ship at Saint John, New Brunswick, to join the Canadian Expeditionary Force and fight in World War I. Following his military service in France he returned to England for a time, lived in the Welsh village of Llangyllwych from 1932 until 1963, and spent the remainder of his life in London. He married a woman named Timothy; they had a son, Liam. His two years as a seaman and his work as a journalist, railway porter, and racetrack cashier after World War I provided him with experiences he would use to portray, accurately and sympathetically, the lives of the poor and the working class.

Hanley's first novel, *Drift,* was published in 1930 after being rejected by nineteen publishers. Joe Rourke lives in Liverpool with his parents, Mick, who works in a slaughterhouse, and Martha. Devout Roman Catholics, Mick and Martha are concerned about their son's rejection of the church; they are particularly upset because Joe is seeing a young prostitute, Jane. After many conflicts with his parents Joe leaves home to live with Jane. Martha dies soon afterward, and Joe's grief and guilt over his treatment of his mother show Jane that they can never be happy together. While Joe is attempting to reconcile with his father, Jane leaves with another man. Joe is rejected by his father, and he is unable to find peace even after going to a church to confess.

One of the earliest works for which Hanley received critical acclaim was *Boy* (1931). Arthur Fearon is a thirteen-year-old from the lower class who dreams of becoming a schoolmaster or a pharmacist, but his parents need him to help provide income for the family and remove him from school. Arthur runs away from home and stows away on a ship; when he is discovered, he is made a member of the crew. In port one of the other sailors introduces him to the delights of sex by taking him to a prostitute; for the first time Arthur experiences a form of pleasure over which he has some measure of control. But the encounter results in his being infected with syphilis. Realizing that Arthur is doomed to die an agonizing death, the captain smothers him. Even

*Title page for Hanley's first novel*

though Arthur's life ends tragically, he has tried to take control of his destiny rather than submit to the wishes of others.

In 1934 the publisher of *Boy,* Boriswood, brought out an edition of the novel with a cover depicting a nearly nude belly dancer. Reactions to both cover and content led to a court case in which the publishers were fined £500, and the novel was removed from circulation. Nevertheless, the work was praised by such notables as William Faulkner and E. M. Forster for its honesty and integrity and was republished in 1992 with a foreword by Hanley's son, Liam. According to Liam the notoriety surrounding the novel was distasteful to Hanley and increased his desire for privacy.

The title character of Hanley's novel *Captain Bottell* (1933) is the well-respected, fifty-year-old master of the *Oroya.* One of the passengers on a voyage to the Persian Gulf is Mrs. Willoughby, who is traveling to join her husband, a government official serving in Basra. Bottell is strongly attracted to Mrs.

*James Hanley*

# A WOMAN IN THE SKY

ANDRE DEUTSCH

*Title page for Hanley's tragic novel about two elderly women
who cannot bear to be separated*

Willoughby; finally, he is overcome by his desire for her, and his officers have to confine him to his cabin. Bottell's loss of self-control is paralleled by a storm that causes the ship to sink. Mrs. Willoughby escapes, along with many of the crew, but Bottell goes down with the ship. The loneliness of life at sea is portrayed through comments to Mrs. Willoughby by a crew member named Mulcare; the insights provided by Mulcare make Bottell's gradual disintegration easier to comprehend.

Some of Hanley's most effective writing can be found in his series of novels about the Furys, a working-class Irish family living in England. He began the saga with *The Furys* (1935); the rest of the five-volume chronicle comprises *The Secret Journey* (1936), *Our Time Is Gone* (1940), *Winter Song* (1950), and *An End and a Beginning* (1958). Most of the novels are set in the slums of the fictional city of Gelton, which is based on Liverpool. Life is hard for Denny and Fanny Fury and their children, Desmond, Anthony, Maureen, and Peter. Fanny is the driving force of the family; she is determined that her chil-

dren—especially her youngest son, Peter—will rise above their origins. She wants Peter to be a priest and insists that the rest of the children contribute part of their earnings to support his education; as a result the others resent Peter greatly. The family's situation and the relationships among its members are reminiscent of those of the Morels in D. H. Lawrence's *Sons and Lovers* (1913): Fanny is as domineering as Gertrude Morel, but her children and husband have the strength to rebel against her demands. While Fanny can be a tyrant, she can be considered heroic in her efforts to insure happiness and security for her loved ones. The series begins with Peter's return home from the university in disgrace and ends, after the deaths of Fanny and Denny, with the children reflecting on the meaning of their struggles and those of their parents. The first novel, *The Furys*, has been particularly praised for its character portrayals and its treatment of the themes of loneliness, isolation, the need for love, and the search for identity.

Another highly regarded novel is *The Ocean* (1941). Five men are adrift in a lifeboat after their ship is torpedoed by a German submarine. The sailor Joseph Curtain takes charge: he organizes the rowing rotations, rations the food and water, tends to the elderly priest Father Michaels, sees to the burial at sea of another sailor who dies, and puts down an attempted rebellion by three of the men. Curtain is described as "the plan working," "the cause and the effect, the order and the hope, the plan and its achievement." As each man takes refuge in his own thoughts and memories, the reader gains insight into the characters. The novel ends with Father Michaels sighting a rescue boat.

Some of Hanley's best fiction was published after World War II. In *The Closed Harbor* (1952) Eugene Marius, one of two survivors of a shipwreck during the war, has lost his captain's license because the ship sank under mysterious circumstances and because he accidentally killed his nephew, who was a member of the crew, in a fight prior to the sinking. Marius's efforts throughout the novel are directed at regaining a ship and, thereby, his honor and sense of identity. Finally, he retreats into the world of insanity, where he is still a captain.

Several of Hanley's postwar novels are set in Wales, where he found the solitude he needed for his writing. In *Don Quixote Drowned* (1953) he describes the Welsh as "courteous and cunning, eccentric, provincial artistic, insular, poetic, dramatic, fierce, and sometimes mad."

*The Welsh Sonata: Variations on a Theme* (1954) is the story of the disappearance of a tramp named Rhys from a Welsh village. The novel is narrated through the journal of the investigating policeman, Goronwy Jones. As Jones searches for the tramp, his journal provides insights not only into Rhys's life but also into those of the villagers.

In *Levine* (1956) Felix Levine, a native of Poland, is the sole survivor of a shipwreck off the coast of England. As he seeks passage on another ship, he endures the hostility of the authorities and the country folk because he is a foreigner. He becomes involved with Grace Helling, who was freed from her parents' domination when they were killed in the London blitz. When Levine attempts to leave her, Grace clings to him; finally he kills her to regain his freedom.

*Say Nothing* (1962) originated as a radio play in 1961; as he composed the novel, Hanley used the same material for his stage play. A few months after the publication of the novel, the play premiered at the Theatre Royal Stratford East in London. Hanley focuses in *Say Nothing* on three people who live together in a boardinghouse in the northern industrial town of Garlston. The inability of the Baineses and Mrs. Baines's sister, Winifred, to communicate with each other or to change their situation makes their existence a living hell, like that of the characters in Jean-Paul Sartre's *Huis clos* (produced, 1944; published, 1945; translated as *In Camera,* 1946, and as *No Exit,* 1947) and Samuel Beckett's *Waiting for Godot* (1953). (Hanley considered "A Conversation with the Damned" and "A Sojourn with the Damned" as alternative titles for the work before settling on *Say Nothing*.) They are indifferent to one another except when there is an occasion for ridicule or criticism. A young boarder, Charles Elston, moves in, and from the first evening he is deluged with confidences from the three: each describes his or her misery to him and asks him to "say nothing" to the others. When he tries to talk to any of them about changing their lives, each indicates that change is not possible; their very identities seem to be maintained by their conflict with one another. Elston realizes that the inhabitants of the house are prisoners of their own fears and obsessions and that they have damned each other, and he leaves after less than a month so that he will not suffer the same fate.

After the publication of *Say Nothing* Hanley spent the next ten years writing poetry, nonfiction, and plays for radio, television, and the stage. He returned to novel writing in the early 1970s. *Another World* (1972) is set in the Welsh village of Garthmeilo. Mrs. Gandell, the Englishman who owns the Decent Hotel, and her Welsh manservant, Islwyn Jones, struggle to keep the hotel from going bankrupt. Depending on one another for companionship and support, they are viewed with suspicion and disgust by the villagers. Meanwhile, the village minister, Mervyn Thomas, is in love with the mysterious Miss Rhiannon Vaughan, a typist who dwells simultaneously in the worlds of reality and unreality. While Mrs. Gandell and Jones eventually find contentment, Miss Vaughan escapes from involvement with Thomas by drowning herself in the ocean; Thomas subsequently kills himself, as well.

In the *Sewanee Review* (Summer 1974) Jonathan Yardley says that in *A Woman in the Sky* (1973) "Hanley is writing about people who 'don't matter,' and with great tenderness he shows us how very much indeed they do matter." Brigid Kavanaugh and Lena Biddulph are elderly friends who live in London and try to maintain their independence. But when Biddulph is arrested for shoplifting, Kavanaugh, who is mentally ill and depends on her friend to maintain her connection to reality, cannot endure her loneliness and isolation, and she kills herself. Lil Winten, a neighbor of Kavanaugh's, and Luke Tench, Kavanaugh's former employer, are forced by the suicide to reassess their sensitivity to people such as Kavanaugh and Biddulph. They are also made more aware of the joylessness and sterility of their own lives as they learn about the women's courage and endurance.

*A Dream Journey* (1976) chronicles the deterioration of the relationship of Clem Stevens, an artist, and his common-law wife, Lena, from their first meeting at a tea shop in Euston in the mid 1930s through the stillbirth of their child, Lena's breast cancer, Clem's infidelities, and his decline as an artist. Finally, Clem refuses to venture out of the apartment. One day, while Lena is gone, he dies from burns suffered in a gas explosion. Lena has spent her life providing love and acceptance for one who came to depend solely upon her; but she, in turn, derived her sense of identity from her role as Clem's supporter and encourager.

*A Kingdom* (1978) is set on a country estate in Wales. Cadi and Lucy are sisters who are reunited after twenty years when they must arrange for the burial of their father. Cadi had set aside her own needs to care for their father after Lucy eloped and moved away, and the sisters have communicated little since then. Although Lucy has escaped the isolation of life with her father, she has sacrificed her identity to her husband's demands. Cadi may be alone, but she is her own mistress; the estate, Pen y Parc, is her kingdom, where her wishes reign supreme.

Hanley's vision of modern life is bleak but not hopeless. His characters are never moderate in their response to the challenges they face. Those who transcend the boundaries of loneliness and isolation are persistent in their quest for love, acceptance, and a sense of identity. Thus, Hanley acknowledges the indomitable nature of the human spirit.

Hanley's wife died in 1980; Hanley died on 11 November 1985. He was buried in Llanfechain Churchyard in Wales.

**Interview:**

Ion Trewin, "James Hanley," *Publishers Weekly,* 27 (December 1976): 14,16.

**Bibliography:**

Linnea Gibbs, *James Hanley: A Bibliography* (Vancouver: Hoffer, 1980).

**References:**

Walter Allen, *The Modern Novel in Britain and the United States* (New York: Dutton, 1964), pp. 227–228, 232, 262;

Fred D. Crawford, *Mixing Memory and Desire:* The Waste Land *and British Novels* (University Park & London: Pennsylvania State University Press, 1982), pp. 71–75;

Frank G. Harrington, "Considering and Collecting James Hanley," *American Book Collector,* 8 (May 1987): 3–10; revised and enlarged as *James Hanley: A Bold and Unique Solitary* (Francestown, N.H.: Typographeum, 1989);

"A Novelist in Neglect: The Case for James Hanley," *Times Literary Supplement,* 11 (June 1971): 675–676;

Edward Stokes, *The Novels of James Hanley* (Sydney: Halstead, 1964);

Patrick Williams, "'No Struggle but the Home': James Hanley's *The Furies,*" in *Recharting the Thirties,* edited by Patrick J. Quinn (Selinsgrove, Pa.: Susquehanna University Press / London: Associated University Presses, 1996), pp. 134–145.

**Papers:**

Collections of James Hanley's papers are at the Paley Library at Temple University, the Northern Illinois University Library, the Canaday Library of Bryn Mawr College, and the Lockwood Memorial Library at the State University of New York at Buffalo.

# A. P. Herbert
*(24 September 1890 – 11 November 1971)*

## Margaret Crosland

See also the Herbert entry in *DLB 10: Modern British Dramatists, 1900–1945.*

BOOKS: *Poor Poems and Rotten Rhymes* (Winchester: P. & G. Wells, 1910);

*Play Hours With Pegasus* (Oxford: Blackwell, 1912);

*Half-Hours At Helles* (Oxford: Blackwell, 1916);

*The Bomber Gipsy, and Other Poems* (London: Methuen, 1918; revised and enlarged, 1919);

*The Secret Battle* (London: Methuen, 1919; New York: Knopf, 1920);

*The House by the River* (London: Methuen, 1920; New York: Knopf, 1921);

*Light Articles Only* (London: Methuen, 1921); republished as *Little Rays of Moonshine* (New York: Knopf, 1921);

*The Wherefore and The Why: Some New Rhymes for Old Children* (London: Methuen, 1921);

*"Tinker, Tailor . . . ": A Child's Guide to the Professions* (London: Methuen, 1922; Garden City, N.Y.: Doubleday, Page, 1923);

*Four One-Act Plays: Double Demon, by A. P. Herbert; St. Simon Stylites, by F. Sladen Smith; Thirty Minutes in a Street, by Beatrice Mayor; Pan in Pimlico, by Helen Simpson* (Oxford: Blackwell, 1923); republished as *Double Demon, and Other One-Act Plays* (New York: Appleton, 1924);

*The Man About Town* (London: Heinemann, 1923; Garden City, N.Y.: Doubleday, Page, 1923);

*Laughing Ann, and Other Poems* (London: Unwin, 1925; Garden City, N.Y.: Doubleday, Page, 1926);

*The Old Flame* (London: Methuen, 1925; Garden City, N.Y.: Doubleday, Page, 1925);

*Riverside Nights: An Entertainment,* by Herbert and Nigel Playfair (London: Unwin, 1926);

*She-Shanties* (London: Unwin, 1926; Garden City, N.Y.: Doubleday, Page, 1927);

*Fat King Melon and Princess Caraway: A Drama in Five Scenes* (London: Humphrey Milford, 1927);

*Plain Jane* (London: Unwin, 1927; Garden City, N.Y.: Doubleday, Page, 1927);

*A. P. Herbert as a petty officer in the Royal Navy during World War II*

*The Red Pen* (London: British Broadcasting Corporation, 1927);

*Two Gentlemen of Soho* (London: French / New York: French, 1927);

*Misleading Cases in the Common Law* (London: Methuen, 1927; New York: Putnam, 1930);

*Honeybubble & Co.* (London: Methuen, 1928);

*The Trials of Topsy* (London: Unwin, 1928);

*Topsy, M.P.* (London: Benn, 1929); republished as *Topsy* (Garden City, N.Y.: Doubleday, Doran, 1930);

*La Vie Parisienne: A Comic Opera in Three Acts,* by Herbert and Alfred Davies-Adams (London: Benn, 1929);

*Ballads For Broadbrows* (London: Benn, 1930; Garden City, N.Y.: Doubleday, Doran, 1931);

*More Misleading Cases* (London: Methuen, 1930);

*The Water Gipsies* (London: Methuen, 1930; Garden City, N.Y.: Doubleday, Doran, 1930);

*Tantivy Towers: A Light Opera in Three Acts* (London: Methuen, 1931; Garden City, N.Y.: Doubleday, Doran, 1931);

*Derby Day: A Comic Opera in Three Acts* (London: Methuen, 1931);

*Helen: A Comic Opera in Three Acts Based Upon "La Belle Hélène" by Henri Meilhac and Ludovic Halévy* (London & New York: Chappell / London: Methuen, 1932);

*"No Boats on the River" . . . With a Technical Essay by J. H. O. Bunge* (London: Methuen, 1932);

*A. P. Herbert* (London: Methuen, 1933);

*Still More Misleading Cases* (London: Methuen, 1933);

*Holy Deadlock* (London: Methuen, 1934; Garden City, N.Y.: Doubleday, Doran, 1934);

*Mr. Pewter* (London: Methuen, 1934);

*Uncommon Law: Being Sixty-six Misleading Cases Revised and Collected in One Volume, Including Ten Cases Not Published Before* (London: Methuen, 1935; Garden City, N.Y.: Doubleday, Doran, 1936);

*What a Word! Being an Account of the Principles and Progress of "The Word War" conducted in "Punch," to the Great Improvement and Delight of the People, and the Lasting Benefit of the King's English, with Many Ingenious Exercises and Horrible Examples* (London: Methuen, 1935; Garden City, N.Y.: Doubleday, Doran, 1936);

*Mild and Bitter* (London: Methuen, 1936; Garden City, N.Y.: Doubleday, Doran, 1937);

*The Ayes Have It: The Story of the Marriage Bill* (London: Methuen, 1937; New York: Doubleday, Doran, 1938);

*Sip! Swallow!* (London: Methuen, 1937; Garden City, N.Y.: Doubleday, Doran, 1938);

*General Cargo* (London: Methuen, 1939; New York: Doubleday, Doran, 1940);

*Let There Be Liberty* (London: Macmillan, 1940);

*Siren Song* (London: Methuen, 1940; New York: Doubleday, Doran, 1941);

*Let Us Be Gay* (London: Methuen, 1941);

*Let Us Be Glum* (London: Methuen, 1941);

*"Well, Anyhow . . . "; or, Little Talks* (London: Methuen, 1942);

*Bring Back the Bells* (London: Methuen, 1943);

*A. T. I. "There is No Need for Alarm"* (London: Ornum Press, 1944);

*A Better Sky; or, Name This Star* (London: Methuen, 1944);

*"Less Nonsense!"* (London: Methuen, 1944);

*Light the Lights* (London: Methuen, 1945);

*Big Ben: A Light Opera in Two Acts* (London: Methuen, 1946);

*The Point of Parliament* (London: Methuen, 1946);

*Topsy Turvy* (London: Benn, 1947);

*Bless the Bride: A Light Opera in Two Acts* (London: French, 1948);

*Leave My Old Morale Alone* (Garden City, N.Y.: Doubleday, 1948)—comprises *Siren Song; Let Us Be Glum; Bring Back the Bells; "Well, Anyhow . . . "; or, Little Talks; "Less Nonsense!"; Light the Lights;*

*Mr. Gay's London, With Extracts from the Proceedings at the Sessions of the Peace, and Oyer and Terminer for the City of London and County of Middlesex in the Years 1732 and 1733* (London: Benn, 1948);

*The English Laugh* (London: Oxford University Press, 1950);

*Independent Member* (London: Methuen, 1950; Garden City, N.Y.: Doubleday, 1951);

*Come to the Ball; or, Harlequin: A New Libretto by A. P. Herbert and Reginald Arkell for the Music of Die Fledermaus* (London: Benn, 1951);

*Number Nine; or, The Mind-Sweepers* (London: Methuen, 1951; Garden City, N.Y.: Doubleday, 1952);

*Codd's Last Case and Other Misleading Cases* (London: Methuen, 1952);

*"Full Enjoyment" and Other Verses* (London: Methuen, 1952);

*Why Waterloo?* (London: Methuen, 1952; Garden City, N.Y.: Doubleday, 1953);

*Pools Pilot; or, Why Not You?* (London: Methuen, 1953);

*The Right to Marry* (London: Methuen, 1954);

*"No Fine on Fun": The Comical History of the Entertainments Duty* (London: Methuen, 1957);

*Made for Man* (London: Methuen, 1958; Garden City, N.Y.: Doubleday, 1958);

*Anything But Action? A Study of the Uses and Abuses of Committees of Inquiry* (London: Published for the Institute of Economic Affairs by Barrie & Rockliff, 1960);

*Look Back and Laugh* (London: Methuen, 1960);

*"Public Lending Right": Authors, Publishers & Libraries; A Preliminary Memorandum Humbly Submitted to the Society of Authors* (Shrewsbury: Published by Wilding & Son for the Society of Authors, 1960);

*Silver Stream: A Beautiful Tale of Hare & Hound for Young and Old* (London: Methuen, 1962);

*Bardot M. P.? And Other Modern Misleading Cases* (London: Methuen, 1964; Garden City, N.Y.: Doubleday, 1965);

*The Thames* (London: Weidenfeld & Nicholson, 1966);

*Wigs at Work* (Harmondsworth: Penguin, 1966);

*Sundials Old and New; or, Fun with the Sun* (London: Methuen, 1967);

*The Singing Swan: A Yachtsman's Yarn* (London: Methuen, 1968);

*In the Dark: The Summer Time Story and the Painless Plan* (London: Bodley Head, 1970);

*A. P. H.: His Life and Times* (London: Heinemann, 1970).

**Collections:** *Wisdom for the Wise: Being "Tinker, Tailor . . . " and The Wherefore and the Why* (London: Methuen, 1930);

*A Book of Ballads: Being the Collected Light Verse of A. P. Herbert* (London: Benn, 1931)—comprises *Laughing Ann, and Other Poems; She-Shanties; Plain Jane; Ballads for Broadbrows;* republished as *Ballads for Broadbrows, and Others* (Garden City, N.Y.: Doubleday, Doran, 1931);

*The Topsy Omnibus, Comprising The Trials of Topsy, Topsy, M.P., and Topsy Turvy* (London: Benn, 1949).

PLAY PRODUCTIONS: *The Blue Peter,* music by Armstrong Gibbs, London, Royal College of Music, 12 February 1924;

*The King of the Castle,* by Herbert and William Armstrong, music by Dennis Arundell, Liverpool, Playhouse, 20 December 1924;

*At the Same Time,* London, Aldwych Theatre, 2 July 1925;

*Riverside Nights,* by Herbert and Nigel Playfair, music by F. Austin and Alfred Reynolds, Hammersmith, Lyric Theatre, 10 April 1926;

*The White Witch,* London, Haymarket Theatre, 29 September 1926;

*Two Gentlemen of Soho,* Liverpool, Playhouse, 3 September 1927; Hammersmith, Lyric Theatre, 24 October 1928;

*Plain Jane; or, The Wedding Breakfast,* music by R. Austin, Croydon, Greyhound Theatre, 26 December 1927;

*Double Demon: An Absurdity in One Act,* Liverpool, Playhouse, 26 March 1929;

*La Vie Parisienne,* adaptation by Herbert and Alfred Davies-Adams from the libretto by Henri Meilhac and Ludovic Halévy for the opera by Jacques Offenbach, Hammersmith, Lyric Theatre, 18 April 1929;

*Tantivy Towers: A Light Opera in Three Acts,* music by Thomas F. Dunhill, Hammersmith, Lyric Theatre, 16 January 1931;

*Helen: A Comic Opera in Three Acts,* adaptation by Herbert from the libretto by Meilhac and Halévy for *La Belle Hélène* by Offenbach, London, Adelphi Theatre, 30 January 1932;

*Derby Day: A Comic Opera in Three Acts,* music by Alfred Reynolds, Hammersmith, Lyric Theatre, 24 February 1932;

*Mother of Pearl,* songs by Oscar Straus, Manchester, Gaiety Theatre, 27 January 1933;

*Streamline,* by Herbert and Ronald Jeans, music by Vivian Ellis, London, Palace Theatre, September 1934;

*Home and Beauty,* London, Adelphi Theatre, 2 February 1937;

*Paganini,* adaptation by Herbert from the operetta by Franz Lehár, London, Lyceum Theatre, 20 May 1937;

*Big Ben: A Light Opera in Two Acts,* music by Ellis, London, Adelphi Theatre, 17 July 1946;

*Bless the Bride: A Light Opera in Two Acts,* music by Ellis, London, Adelphi Theatre, 26 April 1947;

*Tough at the Top,* music by Ellis, London, Adelphi Theatre, 15 July 1949;

*The Water Gipsies,* adaptation by Herbert from his novel, music by Ellis, London, Winter Garden Theatre, 31 August 1955;

*Better Dead,* adaptation by Herbert from his *Made for Man,* London, Richmond Theatre, 1962.

OTHER: "The Rate for the Reading: An Appeal to Parliament from Authors and Publishers," in *Libraries: Free-for-All? Some Issues in Political Economy,* by Ralph Harris (London: Institute of Economic Affairs, 1962), pp. 19–58;

*Watch This Space—Six Years of It: An Anthology of Space-Fact, 4 October 1957–4 October 1963,* compiled and edited by Herbert (London: Methuen, 1964).

Few authors of the twentieth century can claim that through their published fiction they have directly or indirectly helped to bring about significant changes in the laws of Britain. A. P. Herbert, who was knighted in 1945 and made a Companion of Honour in 1970, was one of those few. The vitality and exceptionally wide range of his work are remarkable: he is perhaps best known as a humorist and contributor to *Punch* magazine, with which he was associated for sixty years; but he also wrote successful musical comedies, poetry, nonfiction, and novels. Much of his writing reveals his unrivaled talent for comedy and drama, and even his serious

*Herbert aboard his boat,* Water Gipsy, *at Westminster Pier in 1939*

treatment of what he saw as injustice and unnecessary confusion was always applied with penetrating thought, mockery, and satire that prove in the end to be more effective than mere condemnation.

The eldest of three brothers, Alan Patrick Herbert was born on 24 September 1890 at Ashstead Common, between Epsom and Leatherhead in Surrey. His father, Patrick Herbert, who had been born in County Kerry, Ireland, came from an Irish Catholic background and had attended Trinity College, Dublin, during the same period as Oscar Wilde. Herbert's mother, Beatrice Selwyn Herbert, whose family had included several Anglican bishops, died when her eldest son was only seven. The family moved to London, where Herbert's father worked in the India Office. The future writer was sent to The Grange, a preparatory school at Folkestone, and in 1904 he went on to Winchester, one of the oldest English public schools. He remained there for six years, and during that time he began writing poetry. His compositions earned him the King's Gold Medal for English verse in addition to the Silver Medal for English speech and a prize for Latin verse. Next came four years, 1910–1914, at New College, Oxford, where he read classics and obtained a degree in law.

The year he graduated from the university saw the outbreak of World War I, which led Herbert to join the Royal Naval Volunteer Reserve. He married Gwendolen Harriet Quilter, a cousin of the composer Roger Quilter, on 31 December 1914; they would have a son and three daughters. By May 1915 he was in Gallipoli with the British forces; he was wounded in action and later decorated. Somehow he still found time and energy to write, and before the end of the war he published two collections of war poetry in Britain.

The war provided the inspiration for Herbert's first and most serious novel, *The Secret Battle* (1919). "I did not descend to prose," he wrote characteristically in his 1970 autobiography, *A. P. H.: His Life and Times,* "till 1918." Having written the novel, he was summoned to the office of the London publisher Methuen, where he received the classic treatment meted out to young unknown writers who might feel dangerously optimistic. *The Secret Battle* had been read by the experienced essayist E. V. Lucas, who pointed out its considerable literary merit but could promise no commercial success. The author later borrowed a phrase from Noel Coward: the book, he said, was *un flop d'estime.* The novelist Arnold Bennett praised it, however, and Prime Minister David Lloyd George recommended it to his minister of war, Winston Churchill.

The novel describes the life of the hero, Harry Penrose, in the British army at Gallipoli and in

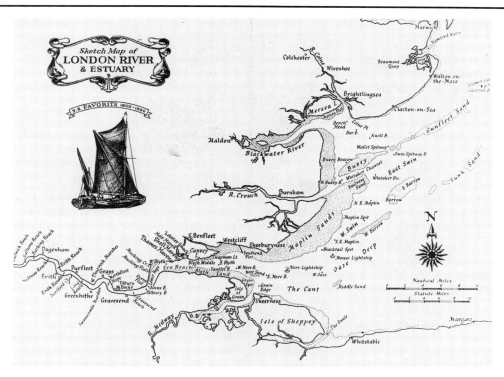

*Endpapers for Herbert's final novel,* The Singing Swan

France. In describing the unimaginable hardships of these campaigns Herbert wrote from firsthand experience. Harry is a man who always had been aware of his desperate lack of confidence, dedicating his life to overcoming it. Harry is also a hero, but owing to the jealousy of various officers and the overwhelming military bureaucracy, he is falsely accused of being a coward and a deserter; he is court-martialed and finally shot by his own men. Churchill agreed with the lesson taught by the author: the conduct of courts-martial must be improved and made truly fair. The novel came into its own in 1928 when Churchill wrote a foreword to the third edition; later Field Marshal Bernard Montgomery wrote of his great admiration for it. Significantly, as late as 1993 a posthumous pardon was granted to former members of the British army who had suffered the same fate as Harry Penrose in World War I.

Herbert's sense of fairness and his imaginatively radical approach to the solving of social abuses made him wish to reform many traditional practices which he knew to be wrong, and he participated actively in public affairs throughout his life. He was called to the bar in 1918, and although he did not practice as a barrister, he gained valuable experience during two years spent as private secretary to a member of Parliament who was himself a barrister. From 1935 to 1950 Herbert represented Oxford University as an Independent member of the House of Commons and no doubt would have continued to do so had university seats not been abolished. He also continued to use his writing to expose and mock injustices as well as to entertain.

Despite Herbert's publishing activity in so many fields, it is the novel published in 1930, *The Water Gipsies,* that has remained his best-known book. No other tale expresses in such detail, with so much understanding, humor, and gentle criticism, the lives of the many contrasting people who lived and worked by the river Thames. The author describes the middle-class Raven household and in particular the life and aspirations of their maid, Jane Bell, whose father and sister live on the barge *Blackbird.* Jane reluctantly marries Ernest, a militant left-winger; after he drowns, she finds a happier marriage with Fred. Herbert was a keen observer of the ways in which the various social classes lived and worked, and the reader inevitably sympathizes with characters such as Jane, who work hard in service, rather than with those such as George Gordon Bryan, the painter who, like the other aristocrats, appears almost as a caricature. Bryan is attracted to Jane, whom he paints, but because of class issues he lacks the courage to commit himself to her and feels guilty. Bryan escapes from her and more particularly from his upper-class fiancée by buying a boat, *The Water Gipsy,* and sailing away. This moving and humorous book includes memorable portraits of Jane's incorrigible father and her sister Lily, so different from Jane and drawn into what could be described briefly as "low life." Fellow authors Hilaire Belloc and John Galsworthy praised the novel, and H. G. Wells found it "human and true."

In 1934 Herbert published his next novel, *Holy Deadlock,* presented as farcical entertainment with the intent of making a serious point. It reveals the background against which the author worked so hard to obtain reform of the divorce laws. Mrs. Mary Adam decides she wants to marry Martin Seal, and therefore she must divorce her husband John, despite the romantic start of their marriage. The story traces, with much comedy, what the three people have to do to obtain a divorce without scandal, what the various members of the legal profession think and do, and what goes wrong. The absurdities of the contemporary divorce laws in Britain are ruthlessly exposed through a constantly entertaining narrative. Eventually those laws were changed—Herbert was an active proponent of the Marriage Bill that passed Parliament in 1936—and no book has been as important as *Holy Deadlock* in persuading the law officers and the appropriate government departments to pay attention to this social problem. In his autobiography Herbert quotes a 1934 letter from Rudyard Kipling saying that the novel "will be the reference work, as well as arsenal and magazine to draw on, for future work by men and women who have been driven more than half crazy by the existing state of things."

In his literary and political activities Herbert also paid attention to such varied issues as the tax on entertainment, the hope that authors could profit from library borrowings, the need to improve general English word usage and writing style, and the uses of a classical education. All aspects of entertainment were especially important to him since he had devoted many years of his life to the theater and to musical comedies. Herbert was also devoted to the water; he and his boat, *Water Gipsy,* served during World War II, first as part of the River Emergency Service, a fleet of private vessels on the Thames, and later as part of the Royal Navy.

*Why Waterloo?* (1952) is an historical novel about Napoleon's life on, and escape from, the island of Elba after his defeat and abdication in April 1814. Marie Walewska, Napoleon's Polish mistress, visits him, bringing their young son, Alexandre. His mother and his sister, Pauline, also arrive, and the social life of Elba becomes entertaining and colorful. Herbert quotes from many historical documents, from letters to ships' logs; the historical notes are more absorbing than the novel itself.

In 1968 Herbert published his last novel, the culmination of his lifelong passion for sailing and for the river Thames. This book was *The Singing Swan: A Yachtsman's Yarn,* named for one of the last sailing barges on the river; the boat plays a gallant part in the dramatic story involving an ambitious industrialist and many theatrical personalities. The real *Singing Swan* was also involved in complex activities on the river and around the coast, including the 1940 evacuation of Allied troops from the French port of Dunkirk on the North Sea. In his autobiography Herbert called this novel "a labour of love" and "a last salute to a noble breed," but the book received little attention from the critics.

Herbert, who died on 11 November 1971, was an outstanding member of his generation. On 19 April 1928 John Galsworthy wrote Herbert a letter full of praise, including a pronouncement with which readers today can still agree: Herbert was by "far the best humourist we have had for ages." If his theatrical work now belongs to the past, his few pieces of sustained fiction, plus the "near novels," to use his phrase, remain surprisingly relevant to later generations of readers, especially those interested in social history and those who want their novels full of action and laced with humor.

**Bibliography:**
Gilbert H. Fabes, *The First Editions of A. E. Coppard, A. P. Herbert and Charles Morgan: With Values and Bibliographical Points* (London: Myers, 1933), pp. 55–125.

**Biography:**
Reginald Pound, *A. P. Herbert: A Biography* (London: M. Joseph, 1976).

**Reference:**
Susan Glasspool, comp., *Sir Alan Herbert, 1890–1971: A Brief Guide to His Literary Work* (Hammersmith: Hammersmith Public Libraries, 1973).

# Georgette Heyer

*(16 August 1902 – 5 July 1974)*

Kenneth Womack
*Penn State Altoona*

See also the Heyer entry in *DLB 77: British Mystery Writers, 1920–1939.*

BOOKS: *The Black Moth* (London: Constable, 1921; Boston & New York: Houghton Mifflin, 1921);

*The Great Roxhythe* (London: Hutchinson, 1922; Boston: Small, Maynard, 1923);

*The Transformation of Philip Jettan,* as Stella Martin (London: Mills & Boon, 1923); republished as *Powder and Patch,* as Heyer (London: Heinemann, 1930; New York: Dutton, 1968);

*Instead of the Thorn* (London: Hutchinson, 1923; Boston: Small, Maynard, 1924);

*Simon the Coldheart* (London: Heinemann, 1925; Boston: Small, Maynard, 1925);

*These Old Shades* (London: Heinemann, 1926; Boston: Small, Maynard, 1926);

*Helen* (London & New York: Longmans, Green, 1928);

*The Masqueraders* (London: Heinemann, 1928; New York: Longmans, Green, 1929);

*Beauvallet* (London: Heinemann, 1929; New York & Toronto: Longmans, Green, 1930);

*Pastel* (London & New York: Longmans, Green, 1929);

*Barren Corn* (London & New York: Longmans, Green, 1930);

*The Conqueror* (London: Heinemann, 1931; New York: Dutton, 1966);

*Devil's Cub* (London: Heinemann, 1932; New York: Dutton, 1966);

*Footsteps in the Dark* (London & New York: Longmans, Green, 1932; New York: Buccaneer, 1976);

*Why Shoot a Butler?* (London & New York: Longmans, Green, 1933; Garden City, N.Y.: Doubleday, Doran, 1936);

*The Unfinished Clue* (London & New York: Longmans, Green, 1934; Garden City, N.Y.: Doubleday, Doran, 1937);

*The Convenient Marriage* (London: Heinemann, 1934; New York: Dutton, 1966);

*Georgette Heyer in 1946*

*Death in the Stocks* (London & New York: Longmans, Green, 1935); republished as *Merely Murder* (Garden City, N.Y.: Doubleday, Doran, 1935);

*Regency Buck* (London & Toronto: Heinemann, 1935; New York: Dutton, 1966);

*The Talisman Ring* (London & Toronto: Heinemann, 1936; Garden City, N.Y.: Doubleday, Doran, 1937);

*Behold, Here's Poison!* (London: Hodder & Stoughton, 1936; Garden City, N.Y.: Doubleday, Doran, 1936);

*They Found Him Dead* (London: Hodder & Stoughton, 1937; Garden City, N.Y.: Doubleday, Doran, 1937);

*An Infamous Army* (London & Toronto: Heinemann, 1937; Garden City, N.Y.: Doubleday, Doran, 1938);

*A Blunt Instrument* (London: Hodder & Stoughton, 1938; Garden City, N.Y.: Doubleday, Doran, 1938);

*Royal Escape* (London: Heinemann, 1938; Garden City, N.Y.: Doubleday, Doran, 1939);

*No Wind of Blame* (London: Hodder & Stoughton, 1939; Garden City, N.Y.: Doubleday, Doran, 1939);

*The Spanish Bride* (London: Heinemann, 1940; Garden City, N.Y.: Doubleday, Doran, 1940);

*The Corinthian* (London & Toronto: Heinemann, 1940; New York: Dutton, 1966);

*Beau Wyndham* (Garden City, N.Y.: Doubleday, Doran, 1941);

*Faro's Daughter* (London: Heinemann, 1941; Garden City, N.Y.: Doubleday, Doran, 1942);

*Envious Casca* (London: Hodder & Stoughton, 1941; Garden City, N.Y.: Doubleday, Doran, 1941);

*Penhallow* (London: Heinemann, 1942; Garden City, N.Y.: Doubleday, Doran, 1943);

*Friday's Child* (London & Toronto: Heinemann, 1944; New York: Ace, 1944);

*The Reluctant Widow* (London & Toronto: Heinemann, 1946; New York: Putnam, 1946);

*The Foundling* (London: Heinemann, 1948; New York: Putnam, 1948);

*Arabella* (London: Heinemann, 1949; New York: Putnam, 1949);

*The Grand Sophy* (London: Heinemann, 1950; New York: Putnam, 1950);

*The Quiet Gentleman* (London: Heinemann, 1951; New York: Putnam, 1952);

*Duplicate Death* (London: Heinemann, 1951; New York: Dutton, 1969);

*Detection Unlimited* (London: Heinemann, 1953; New York: Dutton, 1969);

*Cotillion* (London: Heinemann, 1953; New York: Putnam, 1953);

*The Toll-Gate* (London: Heinemann, 1954; New York: Putnam, 1954);

*Bath Tangle* (London: Heinemann, 1955; New York: Putnam, 1955);

*Sprig Muslin* (London: Heinemann, 1956; New York: Putnam, 1956);

*April Lady* (London: Heinemann, 1957; New York: Putnam, 1957);

*Sylvester; or, The Wicked Uncle* (London: Heinemann, 1957; New York: Putnam, 1957);

*Venetia* (London: Heinemann, 1958; New York: Putnam, 1959);

*The Unknown Ajax* (London: Heinemann, 1959; New York: Putnam, 1960);

*Pistols for Two and Other Stories* (London: Heinemann, 1960; New York: Dutton, 1964);

*A Civil Contract* (London: Heinemann, 1961; New York: Putnam, 1962);

*The Nonesuch* (London: Heinemann, 1962; New York: Dutton, 1963);

*False Colours* (London: Bodley Head, 1963; New York: Dutton, 1964);

*Frederica* (London: Bodley Head, 1965; New York: Dutton, 1965);

*Black Sheep* (London: Bodley Head, 1966; New York: Dutton, 1967);

*Cousin Kate* (London: Bodley Head, 1968; New York: Dutton, 1969);

*Charity Girl* (London: Bodley Head, 1970; New York: Dutton, 1970);

*Lady of Quality* (London: Bodley Head, 1972; New York: Dutton, 1972);

*The Georgette Heyer Omnibus* (New York: Dutton, 1973);

*My Lord John* (London: Bodley Head, 1975; New York: Dutton, 1975).

The author of nearly sixty volumes, Georgette Heyer is primarily known today as the originator and most prolific practitioner of the "Regency" historical romance. Ellen Pall, who writes Regency novels under the pseudonym Fiona Hill, defines the genre as consisting of novels that "take place in the better drawing rooms of England and are written in a dense, slang-ridden version of the diction of their period, the years from 1811 to 1820 when the Prince Regent, the future George IV, reigned in place of his mad father—the eponymous Regency." Heyer's Regency novels are notable for her extraordinary attention to historical detail, including the style of her characters' dress and their use of language—elements of her fiction that reveal her affinity for the works of Jane Austen. Heyer's concern for such issues of characterization and period is underscored by the voluminous notebooks she left behind at her death in 1974, which include detailed drawings and notes for projected novels. Although her novels rarely received critical acclaim, they always sold well. By the time of her death Heyer's fiction had been translated into more than ten languages, and at least fifty of her novels were still in print.

Heyer was born on 16 August 1902 in the posh London suburb of Wimbledon to George Heyer, a fur merchant, and Sylvia Watkins Heyer. Her father was elected to the exclusive Wimbledon Literary and Scientific Society in 1909 and published well-received translations of the poems of François Villon in 1924.

Heyer inaugurated her writing career with a romantic adventure tale, *The Black Moth* (1921). Originally composed to entertain her hemophiliac younger brother, Boris, the novel about Devil Andover's search for love includes some of the themes that would be common in Heyer's later work: young love, the melancholy hero, and the extravagant wife.

Following the commercial success of *The Black Moth,* Heyer published several experiments in the historical mode: *The Great Roxhythe* (1922), *The Transformation of Philip Jettan* (1923), *Instead of the Thorn* (1923), and *Simon the Coldheart* (1925). Her father died of a heart attack in the spring of 1925 after playing tennis with Heyer's fiancé, George Ronald Rougier, leaving Heyer's fiction the main means of support for her family. She married Rougier on 18 August 1925; his career as a mining engineer required them to live in eastern Africa until 1928 and in Yugoslavia in 1929.

Meanwhile, Heyer continued to publish novels: *These Old Shades* in 1926, *Helen* and *The Masqueraders* in 1928, *Beauvallet* and *Pastel* in 1929, and *Barren Corn,* her most ambitious and darkest novel, in 1930. A beautiful young milliner, Laura, and an English aristocrat, Hugh Salinger, fall in love after meeting in the south of France. All during their courtship and marriage he attempts to teach her the social graces so that she will receive the approval of his peers; she, on the other hand, is troubled by his snobbery and his obsequiousness to his rich relatives. He fails in his endeavor to alter his wife's demeanor, and she, with no other way to escape her painful situation, commits suicide. In *Barren Corn* Heyer treats the theme of class differences that would pervade much of her later work. *Barren Corn* was followed by the historical novel *The Conqueror* (1931). Her son, Richard, was born in 1932.

During the 1930s and early 1940s Heyer departed from the Regency genre to produce a series of commercially successful mystery novels with a contemporary setting: *Footsteps in the Dark* (1932), *Why Shoot a Butler?* (1933), *The Unfinished Clue* (1934), *Death in the Stocks* (1935; republished in the United States as *Merely Murder,* 1935), *Behold, Here's Poison!* (1936), *They Found Him Dead* (1937), *A Blunt Instrument* (1938), *Envious Casca* (1941), and *Penhallow* (1942). She temporarily abandoned the mystery genre in the early 1940s but would return to it in the early 1950s with *Duplicate Death* (1951) and *Detection Unlimited* (1953). Critics consider her mysteries uneven, although they, like her Regency novels, remain in print because of her substantial popular audience. Earl F. Bargainnier attributes Heyer's success as a mystery writer to her knack for combining

*Dust jacket for the American edition of Heyer's novel about the first Norman king of England. The jacket design is a reproduction of the Bayeux Tapestry.*

the romantic attributes of the Regency novel with the darker elements of the thriller: "Her achievement as a writer of detective fiction lies in her occasional ability to combine the comic and her special type of romance with the conventions of the Golden Age mystery to create a kind of detective comedy of manners."

In the early 1940s, as Heyer's husband began to find success as a barrister, the family settled in Brighton, a resort town on the English Channel. During this period Heyer produced four of her most substantial and fully realized historical novels: *The Spanish Bride* (1940), *The Corinthian* (1940), *Faro's Daughter* (1941), and *Friday's Child* (1944).

While researching an earlier novel, *An Infamous Army* (1937), Heyer had consulted *The Autobiography of Lieutenant-General Sir Harry Smith* (1901); Smith's Spanish wife, Juana, is the heroine of *The Spanish Bride*. Smith encounters the fourteen-year-old Juana the day after the British capture Badajoz, the Spanish town where she lives, during the Peninsular War of 1808 to 1814. Their wedding follows quickly thereafter: "No honeymoon for this bride; no driving away in a chaise-and-four, with the wedding-guests waving farewell, and corded trunks full of wedding clothes piled high on the roof. One small portmanteau contained the few necessities

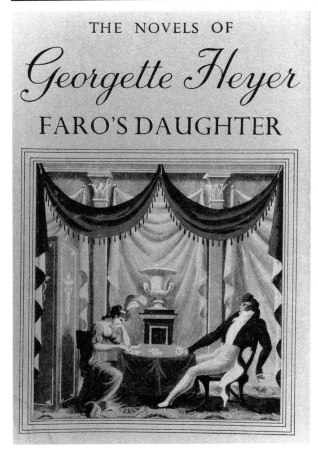

THE NOVELS OF

*Georgette Heyer*

FARO'S DAUGHTER

*Dust jacket for Heyer's novel featuring a couple who spar verbally before succumbing to mutual attraction*

which had been procured for Juana at Elvas, and one small tent was her first home." Heyer's descriptions of her characters are vivid, as in her introductory account of Smith: "The Brigade-Major was a wiry young man, rising twenty-five, with a dark, mobile countenance, a body hardened by seven years' service in the $95^{th}$ rifles, a store of inexhaustible energy, and a degree of luck in escaping death that was almost uncanny." The novel largely traces the couple's initial, uneasy union through their happy marriage. It shows how Heyer often extended the Regency mode beyond the "better drawing rooms of England."

The hero of *The Corinthian,* Beau Wyndham, exemplifies the characteristics of several of Heyer's male protagonists. The quintessence of the elegant, wealthy gentleman, Wyndham first appears in the novel as "a very notable Corinthian. From his windswept hair (most difficult of all styles to achieve) to the toes of his gleaming Hessians, he might have posed as an advertisement for the Man of Fashion. . . . His air proclaimed his unutterable boredom, but no tailoring, no amount of studied nonchalance, could

conceal the muscle in his thighs, or the strength of his shoulders." The enigmatic Wyndham falls in love at first sight with a young woman, Penelope Creed, who is preoccupied with her ineffectual childhood sweetheart; later she is, predictably, overcome by Wyndham's remarkable charm. Two noteworthy minor characters are Cedric Brandon, a drunkard and rake who provides many of the novel's comic moments, and Lady Luttrell, the heroine's strong-willed, intelligent older friend. Heyer supplements her study of the couple's budding relationship with subplots that threaten to derail the lovers' path to romantic bliss.

*Faro's Daughter* reveals a debt to William Shakespeare's comedy *Much Ado about Nothing* (circa 1588–1589): the novel's main characters, Max Ravenscar and Deb Grantham, spar verbally in the fashion of the play's Beatrice and Benedick. At their first appearance Heyer describes Max as "very tall, with a good pair of legs, encased in buckskins and topboots, fine broad shoulders under a coat of superfine cloth, and a lean, harsh-featured countenance with an uncompromising mouth and extremely hard grey eyes," while Deb is "built on queenly lines, carried her head well, and possessed a pretty wrist, and a neatly turned ankle. She looked to have a good deal of humour, and her voice, when she spoke, was low-pitched and pleasing." Deb inaugurates their tempestuous relationship with a playful barb: "Who is our new friend, my lord? A Puritan come amongst us?" Although Max and Deb's initial mutual dislike eventually gives way to romance, in *Faro's Daughter* Heyer relaxes somewhat the rigid formula that is found in so many of her novels.

Heyer's next Regency novel, *Friday's Child* (1944), was her personal favorite; in a 1943 letter to her publisher, William Heinemann, she defended it against possible future critics with ironic self-deprecation: "I think myself I ought to be shot for writing such nonsense, but it's unquestionably good escapist literature, and I think I should rather like it if I were sitting in an air-raid shelter, or recovering from the flu. Its period detail is good; my husband says it's witty—and without going to these lengths, I will say that it is very good fun." Far from being mere "nonsense," *Friday's Child* is a triumph of plot and characterization. Hero Wantage, a poor orphan, discovers that her cousin, the wealthy and attractive Lord Sheringham, has married her mainly to secure his inheritance. Resolving to win Sheringham's love, Hero tries to fit into fashionable London society; there she encounters the memorable variety of minor characters that marks Heyer's fiction, including Lord Wrotham and the Honourable

*Dust jackets for four of Heyer's Regency novels of the 1960s and early 1970s*

*Heyer in 1970*

Ferdy Fakenham. Failing to meet Lord Shering-ham's social standards, Hero runs away. The couple reunites at the novel's end, and Hero realizes her dream of a passionate marriage to Lord Shering-ham.

After *Friday's Child* Heyer published a series of successful Regency novels: *The Reluctant Widow* (1946), *The Foundling* (1948), *Arabella* (1949), *The Grand Sophy* (1950), *The Quiet Gentleman* (1951), and *Cotillion* (1953). The last of these has two heroes—the ineffectual Freddy Standen and the handsome Jack Westruther—who are vying for the affections of the beautiful Catherine Charing. Standen first appears in the novel as a "slender young gentleman, of aver-age height and graceful carriage. His countenance was unarresting, but amiable; and a certain vague-ness characterized his demeanor," while Heyer's ini-tial description of Westruther recalls Beau Wynd-ham in *The Corinthian:* he is a "tall man whose air and bearing proclaimed the Corinthian. Coat, neck-cloth, fobs, seals, and quizzing-glass, all belonged to

the Dandy; but the shoulders setting off the coat so admirably, and the powerful thighs, hidden by satin knee-breeches, betrayed the Blood, the out-and-outer not to be beaten on any sporting suit." The near duplication of a description from an earlier novel underscores the rigidity of the formula of the Regency novel. After the usual comic machinations by secondary characters—particularly the elderly spinster Miss Fishguard—the novel concludes with Catherine's engagement to Standen, *Cotillion* offers one of Heyer's most entertaining and well-designed plots.

Heyer continued to turn out Regency novels through the 1950s, 1960s, and early 1970s: *The Toll-Gate* (1954), *Bath Tangle* (1955), *Sprig Muslin* (1956), *April Lady* (1957), *Sylvester; or, The Wicked Un-cle* (1957), *Venetia* (1958), *The Unknown Ajax* (1959), *A Civil Contract* (1961), *The Nonesuch* (1962), *False Col-ours* (1963), *Frederica* (1965), *Black Sheep* (1966), and *Cousin Kate* (1968). In *Charity Girl* (1970) Viscount Desford confides to his friend Hetta Silverdale his infatuation with the beautiful runaway Cherry Steane, the "charity girl," only to realize belatedly that he is in love with Silverdale. Although the novel was, like most of Heyer's works, financially successful, its plot is less substantial than such works as *Faro's Daughter* and *Friday's Child*. Her biographer, Jane Aiken Hodge, calls it "a happy book, full of mellow laughter, even if it does have the occasional repetition, a little too much slang, and, for once, some slightly jolting changes of subject."

*Lady of Quality* (1972), the last novel Heyer would publish in her lifetime, is set in Bath. Annis Wychwood is rich and beautiful but unmarried at the age of twenty-nine. In Oliver Carleton, who is well known for his rudeness, she discovers the one man who strikes her fancy. At their first meeting Annis sees the "challenge" in Carleton's eyes and the "satirical curl of his lips," and soon the two are engaging in a series of verbal spars in the tradition of Max Ravenscar and Deb Grantham in *Faro's Daughter*. Unlike most of her earlier novels, *Lady of Quality* goes beyond the rites of courtship and engagement to depict the couple's married life.

Diagnosed with lung cancer in May 1974, Heyer died on 5 July. Her obituary in the *Manchester Guardian* called her "one of the great queens of historical fiction"; the *Sunday Telegraph* noted that she was "sometimes known as the twentieth-century Jane Austen." In 1975 *My Lord John,* a novel about the House of Lancaster that she had researched and planned for many years, was published posthumously.

Although she has been criticized for the repetitiveness of the narrative elements in her Regency romances, Georgette Heyer's attention to historical research and concern for matters of style, characterization, and description, as well as her phenomenal sales records, separate her from other authors who have worked in the genre she pioneered. Hodge concludes her 1984 biography of Heyer by saying, "It would be a suitable irony, and no surprise, if a reappraisal in the next few years were to give her work the critical acclaim it never achieved in her lifetime. The need for escape is not likely to grow less." That reappraisal has not yet occurred.

**Biography:**

Jane Aiken Hodge, *The Private World of Georgette Heyer* (London: Bodley Head, 1984).

**References:**

Earl F. Bargainnier, "The Dozen Mysteries of Georgette Heyer, *Clues,* 3 (1982): 30–39;

James P. Devlin, "A Janeite's Life of Crime: The Mysteries of Georgette Heyer," *Armchair Detective,* 17 (1984): 300–315;

E. R. Glass and A. Mineo, "Georgette Heyer and the Uses of Regency," in *La Performance del Testo,* edited by Franco Marucci and Adriano Bruttini (Siena: Ticci, 1986), pp. 283–292;

Helen Muriel Hughes, "Changes in Historical Romance, 1890s to the 1980s: The Development of the Genre from Stanley Weyman to Georgette Heyer and Her Successors," dissertation, University of Bradford, 1988;

Ellen Pall, "In the Grasp of Romance: My Life as Fiona Hill," *New York Times Book Review,* 30 April 1989, pp. 1, 37.

**Papers:**

Collections of Georgette Heyer's manuscripts and correspondence are in the Duke University Library in Durham, North Carolina.

# Winifred Holtby

*(23 June 1898 – 29 September 1935)*

Alan Bishop
*McMaster University*

BOOKS: *My Garden and Other Poems* (London & Hull: Brown, 1911);

*Anderby Wold* (London: John Lane, 1923);

*The Crowded Street* (London: John Lane, 1924);

*The Land of Green Ginger: A Romance* (London: Cape, 1927; New York: McBride, 1928);

*Eutychus; or, The Future of the Pulpit* (London: Kegan Paul, Trench, Trübner / New York: Dutton, 1928);

*A New Voter's Guide to Party Programmes: Political Dialogues* (London: Kegan Paul, Trench, Trübner, 1929);

*Poor Caroline* (London: Cape, 1931; New York: McBride, 1931);

*Virginia Woolf* (London: Wishart, 1932);

*Mandoa, Mandoa! A Comedy of Irrelevance* (London: Collins, 1933; New York: Macmillan, 1933);

*The Astonishing Island: Being a Veracious Record of the Experiences Undergone by Robinson Lippingtree Mackintosh from Tristan da Cunha during an Accidental Visit to Unknown Territory in the Year of Grace MCMXXX–?* (London: Lovat Dickson, 1933; New York: Macmillan, 1933);

*Truth Is Not Sober* (London: Collins, 1934; New York: Macmillan, 1934);

*Women and a Changing Civilisation* (London: John Lane, 1934; New York: Longmans, Green, 1935); republished as *Women* (London: John Lane, 1939);

*The Frozen Earth, and Other Poems* (London: Collins, 1935);

*South Riding: An English Landscape* (London: Collins, 1936); republished as *South Riding: A Novel* (New York: Macmillan, 1936);

*Pavements at Anderby: Tales of "South Riding" and Other Regions,* edited by H. S. Reid and Vera Brittain (London: Collins, 1937; New York: Macmillan, 1938);

*Take Back Your Freedom* by Holtby and Norman Ginsbury (London: Cape, 1939);

*Testament of a Generation: The Journalism of Vera Brittain and Winifred Holtby,* edited by Paul Berry and Alan Bishop (London: Virago, 1985).

*Winifred Holtby in the early 1930s*

As a writer Winifred Holtby is best remembered for *South Riding: An English Landscape* (1936), the last of her six novels, and for her impressive journalism. Holtby died at the age of thirty-seven, but in that comparatively short life her achievements were many. With her close friend Vera Brittain she became, in her twenties, a prominent social activist for the causes of feminism and world peace, and after a visit to South Africa in 1926 she worked also to eradicate racism there. A forthcoming biography by Marion Shaw is likely to contribute strongly to a growing interest in Holtby's life and achievements.

Winifred Holtby was born on 23 June 1898 in Rudston, Yorkshire, the younger of two daughters of a prosperous farmer, David Holtby, and his forceful, philanthropic wife, Alice, who was elected a member of the East Riding County Council and became the first woman alderman of the area. An independent and precocious child, Holtby showed narrative ability at an early age; as she recalled in the 1934 article "Mother Knows Best," republished in *Testament of a Generation: The Journalism of Vera Brittain and Winifred Holtby* (1985): "At the ages of three and four I was as implacable a narrator of impossibilities as the Ancient Mariner." Her literary interests were encouraged at Queen Margaret's School, Scarborough, and when she was thirteen her first book, *My Garden and Other Poems* (1911), appeared—a collection of poems whose publication had been secretly arranged by her mother.

Although she continued to write poetry intermittently throughout her life, Holtby was soon drawn to journalism and fiction. World War I had begun while she was still at school—her first exploit in journalism was an eyewitness account, written when she was sixteen and published not only by the local newspaper but as far away as Australia, of the German bombardment of Scarborough at the end of 1916. After a short period as an assistant in a London nursing home, Holtby went up to Somerville College, Oxford, in 1917, following her mother's wishes; but a year later she left to act as a Women's Army Auxiliary Corps hostel forewoman in France until the war ended.

Returning to Somerville, she encountered in her modern history tutorials the woman who was to become her closest friend and colleague: Brittain. Initial hostility gave way to a deep understanding in which their literary ambitions, some similarities of experience, and their leftist social and political views allowed them to help and encourage each other creatively. Physically and temperamentally they were quite different, however: Holtby tall, fair, sociable, enthusiastic, and equable; Brittain small, dark, pretty, shy, and volatile. These differences complicated and strengthened their relationship.

After completing second-class degrees, the two young women took a flat together in London and within a few years had established themselves as successful journalists and public speakers promoting feminism and world peace. They joined the Six Point Group established in 1921 by Lady Margaret Rhondda, who had also founded the feminist journal *Time and Tide,* of which Holtby was to be appointed a director in 1926 at the age of twenty-eight. They also joined the League of Nations Union (then the apparent best hope for maintaining peace),

speaking and writing on its behalf, reporting on League of Nations meetings in Geneva, and touring Europe observing the effects of World War I.

By temperament Holtby was generous, dutiful, and inclusive, qualities that strongly mark her writing. A statement defining her feminist position (in a 1926 article, "Feminism Divided," republished in *Testament of a Generation*) is significant:

> Personally, I am a feminist . . . because I dislike everything that feminism implies. I desire an end of the whole business, the demands for equality, the suggestions of sex warfare, the very name of feminist. I want to be about the work in which my real interests lie, the study of inter-race relationships, the writing of novels and so forth. But while the inequality exists, while injustice is done and opportunity denied to the great majority of women, I shall have to be a feminist, . . . with the motto Equality First. And I shan't be happy till I get it.

Although they were extremely prolific journalists, Holtby and Brittain also published two novels each during the four-year period up to Brittain's marriage in 1925. Holtby's were *Anderby Wold* (1923) and *The Crowded Street* (1924). In them she established a recurrent theme: the quest for fulfillment and independence, and its cost. Several of her major characters (such as David Rossitur, the young outsider who has promoted rural socialist change and fallen in love with the conservative Mary Robson in the first novel) are thwarted in personal relations, suffer in isolation, and die young. For the protagonists—notably Muriel Hammond in *The Crowded Street*—life brings deprivation and suffering, but these are recognized finally as the price of the freedom to find oneself through dedication to socially valuable work.

*Anderby Wold* and *The Crowded Street* are regional novels; the first clearly draws on Holtby's love of the family farm, her knowledge of farming life, and her close observation of people who shared her early years—the characters of Mary Robson and Sarah Bannister, Mary's acerbic sister-in-law, appear to have some qualities of Alice Holtby. The author later commented in "Mother Knows Best" that this novel was rooted in her father's decision, during the war, to sell the family farm and retire. Disturbed deeply by that loss, she set out to write a novel "to instruct myself in the reason for that change which had previously seemed to me an unmitigated tragedy," inventing "a story of a young woman . . . married to a much older farmer, and confronted by circumstances similar to those which proved too much for my frail and gentle father."

Those circumstances center on an intensifying conflict between traditional conservatism and the

*Page from a 19 January 1926 letter from Holtby to Vera Brittain (from Paul Berry, ed.,* Testament of a Generation: The Journalism of Vera Brittain and Winifred Holtby, *1985)*

new socialist values that aim to improve the lives of the poor and powerless: another recurrent theme in Holtby's novels. After David's melodramatic death Mary recognizes her loss, but she also knows that "If the changes which David desired in Anderby were to come, then she and [her husband] must go. For, if they stayed, they would prevent the completion of his work. They could not help it. They were made like that."

What helps to give these two early novels distinctiveness is a friction between the bracing wit and vigor of the dialogue and authorial comment, on the one hand, and the often depressing and melodramatic events of the plots on the other. And although both are essentially realistic regional novels in the tradition of George Eliot and Arnold Bennett, from

the beginning a sharp satiric element is evident—for instance, in the portrait of Sarah Bannister. In fact, tension between realism and satire runs through Holtby's novels, with realism dominating her first two and her last one, *South Riding,* while the three central novels tilt toward satire.

Complicating, and to some extent resolving, the tension between realism and satire are two other authorial tendencies, both mitigating the harsh and negative, both increasingly forceful in the later novels. The first Holtby terms "romance"—escape into an alternative imagined world of fantasy. As she wrote in a letter to Brittain, "My brain thinks realistically and satirically, but my pen will run away into romance." Her characteristic desire to balance, to include, is evident. Second, there is her tendency to treat generously characters (most strikingly Robert Carne of *South Riding*) whose traditionalist opinions and behavior Holtby cannot endorse intellectually and to render as less than attractive those characters who represent values close to her own. In this way a further balance is struck, with no character allowed the status of hero or villain, no character available for the reader's thoughtless adulation or rejection. Easy conclusions are characteristically frustrated in Holtby's novels; complications and reversals are common. In *Anderby Wold,* for instance, the charming Mary's "lady bountiful" behavior is often morally disreputable, while her critic, the inelegant and unpleasant schoolteacher Coast, is morally in the right.

Muriel Hammond, the protagonist of Holtby's second novel, *The Crowded Street,* undergoes a long internal struggle before, with the help of political activist Delia Vaughan (a character based on Vera Brittain), she is able to find independence and fulfillment. To reach this point she must throw off the stultifying, negative values of her provincial society, especially its prescription of marriage as the only acceptable female destiny. Unable to save her sister Connie from being destroyed by a desperate, inappropriate marriage, Muriel at last decides her own future and joins Delia in London. Having taken this brave step, she eventually refuses marriage to Godfrey Neale, the handsome, unimaginative, ultraconservative country gentleman whom she has loved silently since her girlhood. The central, feminist theme of the novel—that a woman can and should seek fulfillment in a career—is forcefully expressed in the final pages.

Despite its positive and effective statement of the "single woman" theme generally crucial in the decade following World War I and personally crucial for Holtby, *The Crowded Street* is a weaker novel than its predecessor: episodic and awkwardly structured, with distracting shifts of focus and tone. Its five sections are titled for the main feminine influences on Muriel's life as it unfolds until, in the aftermath of World War I, Muriel herself seizes control; but this structure has an irritatingly factitious quality since it only partially accords with the plot and chronology.

Holtby's third novel, *The Land of Green Ginger* (1927), is much more effective formally and abandons the crammed diversity of *The Crowded Street* for concentration on the life of its protagonist, Joanna Leigh. Holtby began writing this novel while in South Africa. She had decided, after Brittain's marriage and departure for the United States in 1925, to visit her close friend Jean McWilliam, whom she had met during her war service in France, and to travel to South Africa lecturing on behalf of the League of Nations Union. Observation and experience convinced her of the iniquity of racist South African government policies and brought her into close contact with the nascent black trade-union movement there, thus giving her a third cause to work for when she returned to England. She also garnered material for use in her next three novels.

The first chapter of *The Land of Green Ginger* establishes the central theme of conflict between reality and romance as Edith, "tall, brown-haired and dreamy," leaves Kingsport (Hull) for South Africa as the wife of a missionary. There Joanna is born; but because her mother has died bearing her, she is sent to Kingsport to be brought up by relatives. She grows up just as drawn to romance as her mother had been: her romantic response to the name of a street in Hull, "The Land of Green Ginger," predicts the problems she will have adjusting to a life whose inimical reality will thwart her steadily. She thinks, "When I leave school I shall see all the world, and travel for ever and ever": but, just nineteen, she makes an unwise marriage during World War I. Teddy Leigh seems to her a brilliant, vigorous young man who will fulfill her romantic yearnings; but he has concealed from her that he has contracted tuberculosis, and as he sinks further and further into selfish invalidism on a remote Yorkshire farm, Joanna, now mother of two children, must struggle against harsh odds. When Paul Szermai, a Hungarian aristocrat supervising Finnish laborers, comes advantageously into her life and falls in love with her, she is caught between her romantic aspirations and the challenge to her marriage vows. After Szermai's departure, Teddy's death, and a daughter's severe illness, she recognizes the destructive effects of romanticism: "Fool, fool, to feed upon fantasy till the life of the flesh betrayed you. Fool, to think in your vanity that you could conquer disease and poverty by a dream." As the novel ends, Joanna leaves for South Africa to join a school friend, Rachel (as Muriel Hammond had joined Delia Vaughan in London).

Thematically, *The Land of Green Ginger* is complex. Its satiric attack on romantic escapism, emphasized by the ironic subtitle of the novel, is not permitted to stand unchallenged; for Joanna's survival, despite the long deprivation and suffering in her life, has been sustained by her generosity of spirit and the fertile imagination that enables her to find romance in hostile circumstances. Although she arrives ultimately at the bleak realization that "Everyone has to find his own security. The awful thing about life is that we are really alone in it," her journey to South Africa opens into a "pilgrimage" cater-

*First page of the manuscript for Holtby's novel* South Riding *(reproduced by permission of Kingston upon Hull Public Libraries Committee, the estate of Winifred Holtby, and W. Collins Sons & Co. Ltd.)*

ing to "her delight in the comical and strange and splendid things." Holtby's repetition of the first chapter title for the final chapter may suggest fulfillment or negative closure. But clearly conflict between reality and romance is not absolute: although romanticism is delusive and destructive, especially for a woman unwise enough to expect mere marriage to provide fulfillment, there is nevertheless in reality the potential for joy and wonder. *The Land of Green Ginger* is a more unified as well as a more complex novel than its predecessor.

Holtby's fourth novel, *Poor Caroline* (1931), appears at first to be thoroughly satiric; yet it too submits its adverse criticism to complication and authorial generosity, steadily undermining the complacent negative judgment of the protagonist implied by the title. Shifting her setting from Yorkshire to London, Holtby again uses, with greater success, the device of structuring her novel by character; each chapter focuses on one of the six varied individuals whose lives become entangled with Caroline Denton-Smyth and her Christian Cinema Company. Caroline is broadly similar to Joanna Leigh of *The Land of Green Ginger*: both are women of imaginative and physical vitality obsessed by a romantic vision, and both are saved ultimately from moral disaster. At first presented as tiresomely simpleminded, with her considerable vitality fastened on exploiting acquaintances for her own ends, Caroline gains moral stature as her story evolves until, dying in a hospital, she commands sympathetic admiration. Even what readers have judged to be sheer self-deception—her ambition that the Christian Cinema Company should benefit mankind—is partially achieved when it provides various lesser benefits to its directors and others.

A similar shift in evaluation occurs in the reader's response to the six directors as, apart from Eleanor de la Roux, each is shown to have selfish reasons for becoming involved with Caroline's project. Eleanor, a young South African feminist socialist, emerges as the moral conscience of the novel. The centrality of her relationship with the older woman, Caroline, is another of Holtby's repeated narrative patterns, begun in *Anderby Wold* and most strikingly developed in Sarah Burton's relationship with Mrs. Beddows in *South Riding*. As in the latter novel, a major theme of *Poor Caroline* is the moral importance of avoiding narrow judgments and of fully acknowledging human complexity and individuality.

This novel also ends on what seems to be an unironic and more conventionally happy note than any other by Holtby: Eleanor will surely marry the man she loves, Roger Mortimer. "'The present generation of feminists must marry,' thought Eleanor,

listening to Roger's voice. . . . After all, marriage was not the only cause of failure." And she sends him a note: "You might at least pay me the compliment of asking me to marry you. I do love you, you know."

*Poor Caroline*—the first of Holtby's novels to match commercial with critical success—was written in a period of happiness and achievement after Brittain's return from the United States in 1926 had reestablished the close relationship of the two women. Brittain's husband, George Catlin, was away teaching at Cornell University most of the year, and Holtby enjoyed being an "aunt" to Brittain's two small children in the Chelsea house they shared. Since the satire of the novel surely includes the author, whose consuming social activism and generosity in responding to the needs and demands of others was lamented by her literary friends, the positive trend of judgment in the novel is another indication of happiness.

Holtby's next novel, the ambitious *Mandoa, Mandoa! A Comedy of Irrelevance* (1933), was written in less fortunate circumstances, for she had just suffered the first serious episode of Bright's disease, the kidney ailment that would kill her a few years later. Before she completed the novel, she had been warned that her time was short; three months before its publication she suffered the further blow of finding her novel preempted by Evelyn Waugh's *Black Mischief* (1932), which had been similarly inspired by the coronation in 1930 of the Emperor Haile Selassie of Ethiopia.

Again—and to much greater effect—Holtby drew on memories of South Africa for characters and events. The bored, autocratic Lord High Chamberlain of Mandoa, Safi Talal, hellbent on westernizing his country according to defective Hollywood-based concepts, is based on Clements Kadalie, leader of the black trade union that Holtby supported and promoted. The opening section of *Mandoa, Mandoa!* exemplifies Holtby's vivid, humorous, and effective satire of the cultural confusion created by colonialism. Talal watches "as a religious procession passed along the street, the nodding statues of saints and virgins followed by acolytes who beat drums and sang an old Mandoan hymn to a tune from the great all-singing, all-talking film, 'College Girls Must Love.'" Surrounded by leprous hawkers, he notices "a refractory slave being driven to execution" and meditates on the need for change: "He would have streets and baths and gramophones and cocktails. By the Holy Saints, by the Gods of old Mandoa, by the Sisters Gish and Mary Pickford, so he would!" As Brittain commented, *Man-*

*Dust jacket for Holtby's final novel*

doa, Mandoa! includes some "savage humour." And the satire is double-edged, for it embraces contemporary England, itself increasingly influenced by American popular culture and no less confused than Mandoa in its values, as Holtby set out to demonstrate in the pure satire she published later in 1933, *The Astonishing Island: Being a Veracious Record of the Experiences Undergone by Robinson Lippingtree Mackintosh from Tristan da Cunha during an Accidental Visit to Unknown Territory in the Year of Grace MCMXXX–?*.

The plot of *Mandoa, Mandoa!* swings between Mandoa and England, where a battle for the soul of Mandoa has begun. On one side is Prince's Tours Ltd, a travel agency (no doubt modeled on Cook's) whose owner, Sir Joseph Prince, sees lucrative opportunity in opening Mandoa to tourism. Maurice Durrant, one of the major characters, has just been elected a Conservative member of Parliament but retains his directorship with the agency; he arranges for his brother Bill, of whom he is deeply jealous, to be sent to Mandoa to prepare the way for Prince's. Bill Durrant, attractive but unreliable, unprejudiced but easily influenced, is a version of Harry Pearson, the man Holtby had fallen in love with when she was a girl, before the war apparently damaged him psycho-

logically; in later years he wandered back into her life at unpredictable intervals. The protagonist, Jean Stanbury—who finds herself in Mandoa as representative of the International Humanitarian Association, on a commission investigating alleged abuses by Prince's—to some extent represents Holtby. The commission itself yields further opportunity for Holtby's satire as its ill-assorted members flounder toward disaster.

*Mandoa, Mandoa!* is a long novel with a complicated plot and a large gallery of characters, qualities that make it a forerunner of *South Riding*. But its vigorous satire is counterpointed by realistic passages in which satire dwindles and disappears, so that tone and theme become uncertain and even problematic. Arthur Rollett is a key character in defining the serious political attack of the novel on the iniquities of British imperialism, which is accused of tolerating and indeed promoting various forms of slavery. As a doomed reformer, he is a descendant of David Rossitur; and as the conscience of the novel, he is deliberately given some unattractive qualities. Arthur's death, however, appears to change little, and the eventual resolution—which will depend primarily on Mandoan politics—is left uncertain, although weighted toward defeat. Bill remains: "A series of chances had led him to Mandoa. He represented a firm that pursued its own profit, and a nation that considered its own prestige. Yet, while he stayed in the country, the runway would be kept clean and the office occupied." Talal still yearns for "'Elevators and factories and electric cars. We will make a great city.' But the clouds swam together again, drowning both light and darkness."

For Jean, however, there is apparent resolution. She marries Bill's brother Maurice and settles into domesticity—a second conventionally "happy ending," perhaps contradicting the feminist decision of Muriel Hammond. Here uncertainty is surely related to the oscillation in the novel between satire and realism. Our final view of Jean is ambiguous: she loves Maurice because, unlike Bill, he needs her; she has come to agree with her husband's colonial exploitation and conservatism; yet she is thinking of Bill, "her lost lover, her lost friend, the man who had tried to make Mandoa," as she asks "Shall we have coffee in the other room?"

As Holtby's novels became more technically assured, they increasingly—and perhaps paradoxically—expressed skepticism, complexity, and a preference for individuality over doctrinal generalities. Balance and inclusion continued their active role in her imagination. Her final novel, *South Riding*, gives prominence to death and suffering, balancing them against life and happiness. In her critical study *Virginia Woolf* (1932) Holtby had written: "Death balances the picture. It completes the pattern. It makes even cruelty fall into place. It is completion." Several of the central characters in *South Riding* suffer severe illness and die—Annie Holly, Robert Carne, and Lily Sawdon most prominently and movingly. Joe Astell, the dedicated socialist councillor who, in succession to David Rossitur and Arthur Rollett, is the conscience of the novel, has tuberculosis. All of the main characters are shadowed by their mortality.

Holtby wrote *South Riding* in little more than two years, under sentence of death, knowing that her illness might end her life even before she could complete the most ambitious of her novels. That she wrote in frequent pain, and in spite of severe interruptions as she continued to serve her family and friends whenever they needed her, is itself a testimony to her determination, generosity, and literary ambition. After Holtby's death in September 1935 Brittain, as literary executor, arranged for publication of the novel.

The marvel is that this rich book, by common agreement Holtby's masterpiece, is also, as Brittain wrote in *Testament of Friendship: The Story of Winifred*

*Brittain at Holtby's grave in 1954*

*Holtby* (1940), "a hopeful and lovely book, never morbid, and often vital with gay satiric humour." The conclusion radiates a hard-earned optimism, as Emma Beddows and Sarah Burton (who has just escaped death herself) smile at each other: Sarah "knew at last that she had found what she had been seeking. She saw that gaiety, that kindliness, that valour of the spirit, beckoning her on from a serene old age."

The book is reminiscent of George Eliot's *Middlemarch* (published in parts, 1871–1872) as a regional novel portraying the effects of social change on a representative set of characters through interweaving plots. As its epigraph ("'Take what you want,' said God. 'Take it—and pay for it.'") indicates, *South Riding* also focuses on the preeminence of human individuality. Holtby's long-established theme of the quest for independence and fulfillment, and its cost, is now given its fullest expression. Of the large cast of characters—more than 150 in the somewhat facetious list prefacing the text—at least twenty are significant. But steadily the novel centers on three: Sarah Burton, a forceful, middle-aged reformist head of a girls' school; elderly Mrs. Beddows, an influential and popular local politician; and the man they both love, the conservative squire

Robert Carne. Again, characteristically, love is thwarted in any full expression: Sarah decides to become Carne's mistress, since he is imprisoned by his love for an institutionalized wife, but he suffers a disabling angina attack before consummation; and Mrs. Beddows, as an older, married woman, cannot even state her love. Yet the effects of even thwarted love are seen as ultimately beneficent.

In anatomizing the intersection of public and private through political machinations and their consequences, *South Riding* complements *Mandoa, Mandoa!,* demonstrating how even the smallest decisions of local government may change individual lives no less than the headlined incursions of international imperialism do. Lydia Holly, intelligent daughter of poor parents, is finally freed from the burden of caring for her younger siblings, hoping to find fulfillment through education, when the county council's decision to build a housing estate promotes her father's remarriage. Moreover, because of that decision "slums would be pulled down, a certain number of families would move out into the red-roofed, neatly-ordered council houses. Fewer mothers would die in childbirth, fewer babies would sicken in airless basement bedrooms, fewer housewives would collapse into lethargy, defeated by the unending battle against dirt and inconvenience."

The intense desire held by several of the major characters to serve their community, to improve their small world even while rumors of "Hitler's Nazi movement in Germany" cast shadows over it, is strongly endorsed. "'I believe,' said Sarah gravely, 'in being used to the fullest limit of one's capacity.' 'And you expect people to choose their own ways of fulfilment?' 'Yes. To a large extent.'" Sarah's fulfillment, and the positive effect she has on her society, spring from those convictions, allied with the vigor, determination, and administrative ability that link her strongly with Emma Beddows.

One of the most moving characters in this novel is Agnes Sigglesthwaite, an incompetent science teacher held to a daily round of pain and frustration by the need to support her mother. Sarah is sympathetic, but as school head she must ultimately give precedence to the needs of the children and force Miss Sigglesthwaite to resign. Miss Sigglesthwaite is saved from despair as Holtby had been herself: by the sight of lambs in early spring, an emblem of the hope and glory of life. And she too earns a second chance; Sarah, opening a letter from her with foreboding, reads, "I can now report that my own health has already shown great improvement, and that I have found another

post. I am now installed as daily companion to an elderly lady living here who is almost blind." Reading to this employer from popular romantic novels has "opened up a new world for me," and Miss Sigglesthwaite ends her letter with the noble grace of a newfound self-respect. She has paid the cost and achieved a degree of independence and fulfillment.

Optimism, compassion, reconciliation, emphasis on the significance of generous effort on behalf of the public good—these are dominant themes of *South Riding*. Moral failure is not, of course, absent, but even that can have positive results—the self-deceiving Councillor Huggins may earn a measure of personal discomfiture, but the slimy maneuvers of the wealthy manipulator Alderman Snaith ultimately result in general social good.

As the novel moves toward its conclusion, the main theme is explicitly recalled and reconsidered as Sarah meditates on her earlier certainties:

> Take what you want, said God: take it and pay for it. She remembered Mrs. Beddows' caveat: Yes, but who pays? And suddenly she felt that she had found the answer. We all pay, she thought; we all take; we are members one of another. We cannot escape this partnership. This is what it means—to belong to a community; this is what it means, to be a people.

Brittain perceived in *South Riding* "both an end and a beginning. It is an end in the sense that, when compared with her first novel, *Anderby Wold*, it gives an uncanny appearance of completion to her literary cycle." And indeed, in returning to Holtby's beloved Yorkshire after three novels set away from it, in echoing characters and situations, in restoring and enriching such early themes as the conflict between tradition and socialism, *South Riding* does seem a conscious revisiting of *Anderby Wold*. But, Brittain continues, *South Riding* is also "a beginning because it clearly indicates what she could and would have done had she survived even for another decade. From its pages we can estimate the real measure of her quality."

Holtby's six novels recommend themselves to later generations for their imaginative vigor, for their convincing characterization and other technical strengths, and for their always interesting and still-relevant themes. They are also a fitting testament to a noble life that creatively reconciled social activism and literary achievement.

**Letters:**
*Letters to a Friend,* edited by Alice Holtby and Jean McWilliam (London: Collins, 1937; New York: Macmillan, 1938);

*Selected Letters of Winifred Holtby and Vera Brittain, 1920–1935,* edited by Vera Brittain and Geoffrey Handley-Taylor (London & Hull: Brown, 1960).

**Bibliography:**

Geoffrey Handley-Taylor, comp. and ed., *Winifred Holtby: A Concise and Selected Bibliography, Together with Some Letters* (London & Hull: Brown, 1955).

**Biographies:**

Evelyne White, *Winifred Holtby As I Knew Her: A Study of the Author and Her Works* (London: Collins, 1938);

Vera Brittain, *Testament of Friendship: The Story of Winifred Holtby* (London: Macmillan, 1940; New York: Macmillan, 1940);

Jean E. Kennard, *Vera Brittain and Winifred Holtby: A Working Partnership* (Hanover, N.H.: University Press of New England, 1989).

**Papers:**

The main collection of Holtby's papers is the Winifred Holtby Archive, Hull Central Library, Hull, England. Other materials are located in the Winifred Holtby Collection, Bridlington Public Library, East Yorkshire, England; the Vera Brittain Archive, McMaster University Library, Hamilton, Ontario, Canada (mainly letters and published writings); and the Winifred Holtby Memorial Collection, Fisk University Library, Nashville, Tennessee.

# R. C. Hutchinson
*(23 January 1907 – 3 July 1975)*

### Mark A. Graves
*Bowling Green State University*

BOOKS: *Thou Hast a Devil: A Fable* (London: Benn, 1930);

*The Answering Glory* (London: Cassell, 1932; New York: Farrar & Rinehart, 1932);

*The Unforgotten Prisoner* (London: Cassell, 1933; New York: Farrar & Rinehart, 1934);

*One Light Burning: A Story* (London: Cassell, 1935); republished as *One Light Burning: A Romantic Story* (New York: Farrar & Rinehart, 1935);

*Shining Scabbard: A Story* (London: Cassell, 1936; New York: Farrar & Rinehart, 1936);

*Testament: A Novel* (London: Cassell, 1938; New York: Farrar & Rinehart, 1938);

*The Fire and the Wood: A Love Story* (London: Cassell, 1940; New York: Farrar & Rinehart, 1940);

*Interim* (London: Cassell, 1945; New York: Farrar & Rinehart, 1945);

*Elephant and Castle: A Reconstruction* (New York: Rinehart, 1949; London: Cassell, 1949);

*Paiforce: The Official Story of the Persia and Iraq Command, 1941-1946,* anonymous (London: His Majesty's Stationery Office, 1949);

*Journey with Strangers* (New York: Rinehart, 1952); republished as *Recollection of a Journey: A Novel* (London: Cassell, 1952);

*The Stepmother: A Novel* (New York: Rinehart, 1955; London: Cassell, 1955);

*March the Ninth* (New York: Rinehart, 1957; London: Bles, 1957);

*Image of My Father: A Novel* (London: Bles, 1961); republished as *The Inheritor* (New York: Harper, 1962);

*A Child Possessed: A Novel* (London: Bles, 1964; New York: Harper, 1965);

*Johanna at Daybreak* (London: M. Joseph, 1969; New York: Harper, 1969);

*Origins of Cathleen: A Diversion* (London: M. Joseph, 1971);

*Rising* (London: M. Joseph, 1976);

*"The Quixotes" and Other Stories: The Selected Short Stories of R. C. Hutchinson,* edited by Robert Green (Manchester: Carcanet, 1984).

*R. C. Hutchinson*

PLAY PRODUCTION: *Last Train South,* St. Martin's Theatre, London, 11 August 1938.

SELECTED PERIODICAL PUBLICATIONS–UNCOLLECTED: "To Commerce via the University," *Nineteenth Century,* 106 (November 1929): 661-671;

"The Six Bobber," *English Review,* 50 (January 1930): 102-107;

"Cars of Yesterday: The Rocket Reviewed," *Punch* (20 May 1936): 562-564;

"Apostasy," *Punch* (15 June 1938): 648-649;

"How Long Should a Novel Be?," *Swinton and Pendlebury Public Libraries Bulletin,* 12 (May 1939): 5-7;

"Open Letter from a Shaving Man to the Manager of His Seaside Hotel," *Punch* (23 August 1939): 216;

"Aliens at Bow Street," *Spectator* (23 September 1939): 404–405;

"Bag and Bowler Hat," *St. Martin's Review*, 584 (October 1939): 454–457; republished as "Salesman, Diplomat, Clerk-on-Wheels," *Synopsis*, 4 (November 1939): 69–72;

"Marriage under Repair," by Hutchinson and Margaret R. Hutchinson, *St. Martin's Review*, 590 (April 1940): 182–185;

"My Apologia," *John O'London's Weekly* (15 April 1949): 23; republished as "If One Must Write Fiction," *Saturday Review of Literature*, 22 (3 September 1949): 6–7, 37;

"My First Novel," *Listener* (2 April 1953): 567–568;

"The Pace for Living," *Listener* (17 September 1953): 457–458;

"Birth of *A Child Possessed*," *Mental Health*, 26 (Spring 1967): 26–27.

R. C. Hutchinson chronicled in his novels the impact on individuals of world war and revolution in the twentieth century. Often uneven in his narrative structure and pacing, Hutchinson admitted that his "inventiveness" at times resulted in long novels. His works reflect belief in Christian stoicism, of which he said, in answer to a request for information from *Twentieth Century Authors* (1942), that "no other attitude towards the mystery of pain, which is the great mystery, has any value."

Hutchinson's reputation steadily declined after 1964 although he would publish three major novels before succumbing to a heart attack eleven years later. His sterling achievement in the early part of his career was *Testament* (1938), a novel of the Russian Revolution that won the *Sunday Times* gold medal for fiction. His other noteworthy accomplishments include being named a fellow of the Royal Society of Literature in 1962 and winning the W. H. Smith and Son Prize for *A Child Possessed* (1964).

Ray Coryton Hutchinson was born in the north-London suburb of Finchley, Middlesex, on 23 January 1907 to Mr. and Mrs. Harry Hutchinson. He lived there until the age of thirteen, when he entered the Monkton Combe Boarding School in Bath. At the school Hutchinson suffered three miserable years of homesickness and wrote his first novel, a twenty-thousand-word "thriller" titled "The Hand of the Purple Idol" that was never published.

After Monkton, Hutchinson matriculated at Oriel College, Oxford, where he rowed in the boat crew and, as he put it, spent part of his time falling off horses as a member of the cavalry's Reserve Of-ficers Training Corps. He transferred to the air squadron and, he said, succeeded in landing a plane or two without wrecking. "I wasted my time at Oxford," Hutchinson told *Twentieth Century Authors*. "The only sensible thing I did was to pay court to Margaret [Owen] Jones," the daughter of Capt. Owen Jones. In 1927 he received his master of arts and joined the advertising department at J. and J. Colman, a mustard manufacturing firm in Norwich. He published his first short story, "Every Twenty Years," in *Empire Review* (January 1928); he had written it while still an undergraduate at Oxford. Hutchinson and Jones were married in September 1929 and had four children: Ann, born in 1930; Jeremy, born in 1932; Elspeth, born in 1934; and Piers, born in 1937.

Hutchinson later came to consider his first published novel, *Thou Hast a Devil: A Fable* (1930), "balderdash." Set in some undetermined time in the future, the novel chronicles a native uprising in a British colony governed according to the values and prejudices of the upper classes, attitudes the author clearly despises. The novel's hero is a charismatic black revolutionary whose career is cut short by the conflict between political and religious factions that arise after Western influence wanes in the emerging nation.

Although Hutchinson's next several novels are set in the present or the recent past, their locales are almost as foreign to his own experience as was the futuristic colony of his first novel. *The Answering Glory* (1932) details a young woman's training as a missionary and her experiences on an island off the coast of Africa. The novel was made a Book-of-the-Month Club recommendation in the United States. In *The Unforgotten Prisoner* (1933) the young half-English, half-German orphan Klaus Gotthold struggles to survive in the demoralization and economic turmoil of Germany after World War I. Even though Hutchinson had been only eleven years old when the war ended and had experienced none of the situations he depicts firsthand, he was able to imagine them so vividly that some reviewers were convinced that he had been an eyewitness to them. The novel was a Book Society choice in England and sold fifteen thousand copies in its first month. In *One Light Burning* (1935) Alan Wild, an Oxford philosopher, searches for a lost Russian missionary in sub-Arctic Siberia but finds love instead. The novel was a Book-of-the-Month Club recommendation in the United States; its success led Hutchinson to resign as chief assistant to the manager of advertising at Colman's to devote himself full-time to writing. His fifth novel, *Shining Scabbard* (1936), is about a provincial French family, the Séverins, who

# SHINING SCABBARD

BY

R. C. Hutchinson

FARRAR & RINEHART, Incorporated

New York                                                    Toronto

*Title page for the American edition of Hutchinson's novel about a French family trying to regain its lost honor*

strive on the eve of World War I to regain the honor that was lost when the patriarch was charged with cowardice and stripped of his commission during the Franco-Prussian War. It was a Book-of-the-Month Club selection in America and sold seventy-eight thousand copies there within two weeks.

The 732-page *Testament,* which won the 1938 *Sunday Times* gold medal for fiction and was translated into Swedish, German, Norwegian, French, and Spanish, tells of the bond between Count Anton Scheffler, badly wounded and imprisoned by the Austrians early in World War I, and Capt. Alexei Otraveskov, Scheffler's onetime fellow prisoner, who gains Scheffler's release while struggling to be united with his wife and crippled son amid the turmoil of the Russian Revolution. The breakdown of Ostraveskov's family structure serves as a microcosm of the dismantling of autocratic tradition. The novel is at its best in profiling the adjustments of the principal characters to conditions in postrevolutionary Russia; it suffers, though, from the introduction of seemingly irrelevant secondary characters and

unnecessary plot complications that obscure the main narrative. Despite these distractions, critics praised the work; in *The Saturday Review of Literature,* for example, Phyllis Bentley called it the most outstanding British novel of 1938. Again, many readers—including a nurse who had worked in Russia and wrote to Hutchinson—were convinced that he was writing from firsthand experience even though he had never set foot in Russia.

The critical success of *Testament* coincided with the failure of Hutchinson's only produced play, *Last Train South* (1938), after less than a month's run in London's West End. The play, set in a railway station in Russia in 1919–1920, closed two days before the novel was published. Although several unproduced play manuscripts remain among his papers, fiction was Hutchinson's main interest; in addition to the novels, he wrote short stories throughout his career. Twenty-six of them were published posthumously as *"The Quixotes" and Other Stories* (1984).

By 1940 Hutchinson and his family were living in a sixteenth-century farmhouse in the Cotswolds. There he completed *The Fire and the Wood: A Love Story* (1940), which became a Book Society choice in England and a Literary Guild selection in the United States. Forbidden by the Nazi authorities to continue his research on tuberculosis at the hospital, the young Jewish doctor Josef Zeppichmann converts a room in the boardinghouse where he lives into a makeshift laboratory. There he conducts medical experiments on rats in a desperate attempt to cure the housemaid, Minna, a Gentile with whom he is in love, of the disease. Finally, he loses his job and is interned in a labor camp. Minna, by now a patient at a sanitarium, arranges his escape, and they flee in a canal boat across the German border to safety.

The end of the novel seems to have been rushed, probably because Hutchinson expected that he would soon be inducted into the army; in March 1940, three months before the work was published, he was commissioned a captain. "This is a day for journalists," he commented in *Twentieth Century Authors* in 1942. "The novelists can't keep up with the stream; the breadth and depth and fullness and lovely proportions of the art . . . cannot show themselves in this uproar." Hutchinson was assigned to the Eighth Battalion of the East Kent Regiment ("the Buffs"), stationed in Buckinghamshire and Devon. In 1943 he was transferred to the Staff College in Camberley, and in 1944 he served in the War Office in London. Living during the week in an apartment in Kensington, he bicycled the seventeen miles to his home to spend Saturdays with his family. In December 1944 he composed King George VI's speech for the Stand-Down Parade of the Home Guard. While serving in the army he wrote *Interim* (1945), a departure from his usually lengthy narrative style: the novel is only 143 pages long in its British edition (186 in the American edition). The work shows the impact of a British squad's brief billeting in a Cumberland village during the war by exposing, layer by layer, the lives of the members of one household. A journey through Egypt, Iraq, and Palestine in 1945 resulted in the anonymously published *Paiforce* (1949), an official history of the British command in Iraq and Persia in World War II.

Discharged with the rank of major in October 1945, Hutchinson attended some sessions of the Nuremberg War Crimes trials; the impressions he acquired there would reverberate through his fiction in the 1950s. In January 1946 he returned to a novel he had begun in 1940: *Elephant and Castle: A Reconstruction* (1949), a lengthy and panoramic work similar to his best prewar sagas, was an immediate best-seller. Set in a London suburb between the wars—the title refers to an Underground station on the south side of the Thames—the novel covers a twenty-year period in the life of the upper-middle-class Armorel Cepinnier, who is twenty-two at the beginning of the work. After an unsuccessful first love affair she sets her sights on the working-class Gian Ardee, a young man wrongfully accused, in Armorel's opinion, of striking a constable. The novel follows the unlikely marriage of the two as Armorel unleashes her relentless energy to transform Gian into the man of her expectations. In the process it is revealed that the lower-class "criminal" is morally superior to his social-climbing wife. The narrative, like that of *Testament,* is cluttered with a plethora of characters who seem to have been included merely to create local color.

Like *Elephant and Castle,* Hutchinson's next three novels were published in the United States a few months before they appeared in England. In *Journey with Strangers* (1952; republished the same year in England as *Recollection of a Journey*) Hutchinson draws on his experiences in the Middle East to depict an aristocratic Polish family that emigrates from its homeland after the German and Soviet invasions at the beginning of World War II to find freedom in the British-ruled Persian Gulf area. The narrator is Stefanie Kolbeck, the daughter-in-law of the head of the family, Gen. Stanislas Kolbeck. Hutchinson's characters have to recall nightmarish moments from their pasts so as to gain insight and peace in the present. Although the number of tragedies befalling one family, even in wartime, begins to strain credulity,

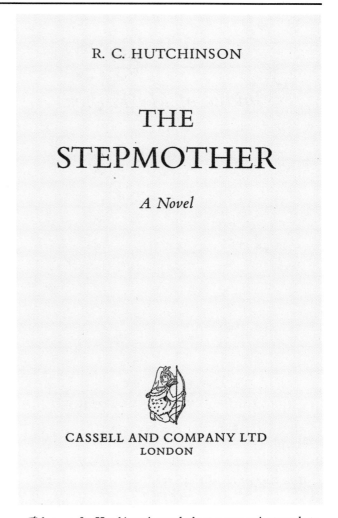

R. C. HUTCHINSON

# THE STEPMOTHER

*A Novel*

CASSELL AND COMPANY LTD
LONDON

*Title page for Hutchinson's novel about a woman's struggle to fit into an established family*

Hutchinson's rather maudlin diction aptly reflects the lethargy and world-weariness of the characters. The Kolbecks' fierce loyalty to Poland and to one another is steadfast throughout their misfortunes. Above all else Hutchinson emphasizes in the novel the importance of resiliency.

Discarding a draft of a manuscript about a woman who perpetrates atrocities in a concentration camp, Hutchinson continued his examination of family life in *The Stepmother* (1955). Forty-six-year-old Catherine de Lauzun, from Quebec, marries Lawrence Ashland, a fifty-seven-year-old British civil servant with two grown children. Catherine gradually realizes that she cannot take the place of Lawrence's long-suffering, deceased, and virtually deified first wife, Josephine. As she contends with Lawrence's increased workaholism, one stepson's besmirched military career, and the meddling of the

R. C. HUTCHINSON

*Image of My Father*

A NOVEL

GEOFFREY BLES · LONDON

*Title page for Hutchinson's novel about a man's search for his identity*

A Book Society selection, *March the Ninth* was the last of Hutchinson's books to attract a substantial readership. His income from novel writing decreased dramatically in the 1960s even though he would publish four more substantial works and would win a major literary prize.

The resonances of war are felt in *Image of My Father* (1961), a novel that, as Robert Green puts it, reveals "the contrast between the mores of the English bourgeois, ignorant of invasion and occupation, and those of Belgians who suffered war more directly." Like Klaus Gotthold in *The Unforgotten Prisoner,* Vincent Selborne is searching for the identity of his British father and, thereby, for his own identity; the quest provides his hope for healing and rebirth after his imprisonment in a German labor camp. The novel was a Book Society recommendation in England; published in the United States as *The Inheritor* (1962), it was a Book-of-the-Month Club recommendation there.

Published in 1964, *A Child Possessed* won the W. H. Smith and Son Prize and was a Book-of-the-Month Club recommendation in the United States. The work opens at a sanitarium in Switzerland where Hélène, a celebrated actress, must decide whether to subject her daughter, Eugénie, to a brain operation that has only a minimal chance of improving the child's Down's syndrome. But she discovers that the decision is not hers alone: since she is not legally divorced from the child's father, he must grant permission for the surgery, as well. Stephan, a truck driver who has been unaware of his daughter's existence, much less her condition, refuses and takes the girl from the institution that has been her only home almost since birth. The dilemma humanizes and reunites the parents. Hutchinson skillfully avoids allowing the story to lapse into maudlin sentimentality.

In *Johanna at Daybreak* (1969), another Book-of-the-Month Club recommendation, Hutchinson resurrects a theme that preoccupied him early in his postwar career: the role of memory. The reader discovers that the fictions that the amnesiac Johanna Schecter has spun around herself mask her betrayal of her Jewish husband to the Nazis, which led to his death in Dachau, and her abandonment of her children. Like the characters in *Journey with Strangers,* Johanna cannot achieve healing until she admits the reality of the past. Hutchinson reveals his protagonist's repressed memories bit by bit so that by the time she realizes the true magnitude of her transgressions, readers feel only sympathy, not disgust, for her.

Hutchinson's only comic novel, *Origins of Cathleen: A Diversion* (1971), was recognized by many

first wife's young sister, Catherine serves as the conduit through whom conflicting and fragmentary perceptions of Ashland family life emerge. Hutchinson's skillful treatment of the rearranging of established family ties was called "sensitive and civilized" by one reviewer. A Book-of-the-Month Club recommendation in the United States, the novel was adapted as a play by Warren Chetham-Strode and produced in London in November 1958.

The title of Hutchinson's next novel, *March the Ninth* (1957), refers to the date in 1943 when a group of Nazis quashed resistance in a Yugoslavian town by executing four innocent citizens. Four years later Eugen Reichenbach, a surgeon performing relief work in Trieste, discovers that a wounded man he is treating is Ludwig Kern, one of the Nazis who was involved in the crime. Reichenbach is torn between the demands of justice, which would mean revealing the hiding place of the fugitive, and his duty as a doctor to heal his patient. Reichenbach's quandary is heightened by the fact that he has fallen in love with Kern's wife.

critics as a profound work of fiction. Cathleen results from the union of an Irish nationalist and a German governess, both unschooled in the ways of love. Young Ryan Hutchinson—the author uses his own surname for his narrator—chronicles their courtship in an eclectic household that includes Ryan's anglicized Irish father, his Russian mother, and a host of international houseguests lingering for stays of undetermined lengths. The intertwining courses of the two families are brought full circle in the marriage of Ryan and Cathleen years later.

Hutchinson's final novel, *Rising* (1976), about class struggle in a fictional South American country at the turn of the twentieth century, reflects his reading of Marcel Proust's *A la recherche du temps perdu* (1913–1922; translated as *Remembrance of Things Past,* 1927–1931) and a trip to South America with his wife in 1971. On 3 July 1975 Hutchinson's work on the conclusion of *Rising* was interrupted by a visit from two old friends; he died of a heart attack later that day, and the novel was published with the final chapter incomplete.

In his article "My Apologia" (1949) Hutchinson had remarked, "The desire to write novels sometimes seems to me a kind of disease. It afflicts many people, either early or late in life, but the majority make a good recovery. I have been less fortunate." His obituary in the *Times* of London said that he "combined narrative skill with a sympathetic insight into human character" and "had a high reputation among a discerning public." R. C. Hutchinson should be remembered as a novelist whose imagination transformed events and places of which he had little or no personal experience into rich narrative territories and who was able to plumb the psychological depths of his characters.

**Letters:**

*Two Men of Letters: Correspondence between R. C. Hutchinson, Novelist, and Martyn Skinner, Poet, 1957–1974,* edited by Rupert Hart-Davis (London: M. Joseph, 1979).

**Bibliography:**

Robert Green, *R. C. Hutchinson: The Man and His Books* (Metuchen, N.J. & London: Scarecrow Press, 1985).

**References:**

Phyllis Bentley, "Is the British Novel Dead?," *Saturday Review of Literature,* 19 (28 January 1939): 3–4;

"Hutchinson, Ray Coryton," in *Twentieth Century Authors,* edited by Stanley J. Kunitz and Howard Haycraft (New York: Wilson, 1942), pp. 696–697.

**Papers:**

Many of R. C. Hutchinson's manuscripts and letters are at the Harry Ransom Humanities Research Center at the University of Texas at Austin.

# Naomi Jacob

*(1 July 1884? – 27 August 1964)*

Michael Jasper
*Bilkent University, Turkey*

BOOKS: *Jacob Ussher* (London: Butterworth, 1925);
*Rock and Sand* (London: Butterworth, 1926);
*Power* (London: Butterworth, 1927);
*The Plough* (London: Butterworth, 1928);
*Saffroned Bridesails,* as Ellington Gray (London: Butterworth, 1928);
*"That Wild Lie—"* (London & Melbourne: Hutchinson, 1930);
*Roots* (London: Hutchinson, 1931);
*"Seen Unknown . . ."* (London: Hutchinson, 1931);
*Props* (London: Hutchinson, 1932);
*Young Emmanuel* (London: Hutchinson, 1932);
*A Novel, Groping* (London: Hutchinson, 1933);
*Poor Straws!* (London: Hutchinson, 1933);
*Me—a Chronicle about Other People* (London: Hutchinson, 1933);
*Four Generations* (London: Hutchinson, 1934; New York: Macmillan, 1934);
*The Loaded Stick* (London: Hutchinson, 1934; New York: Macmillan, 1935);
*"Honour Come Back—"* (London: Hutchinson, 1935; New York: Macmillan, 1935);
*Me—in the Kitchen* (London: Hutchinson, 1935);
*"Our Marie" (Marie Lloyd): A Biography* (London: Hutchinson, 1936);
*Barren Metal* (London: Hutchinson, 1936; New York: Macmillan, 1936);
*The Founder of the House* (New York: Macmillan, 1936; London: Arrow, 1965);
*Time Piece* (London: Hutchinson, 1936; New York: Macmillan, 1937);
*Me—Again* (London: Hutchinson, 1937);
*Fade Out* (London: Hutchinson, 1937; New York: Macmillan, 1937);
*The Lenient God* (London: Hutchinson, 1937; New York: Macmillan, 1938);
*No Easy Way* (London: Hutchinson, 1938);
*Straws in Amber* (London: Hutchinson, 1938; New York: Macmillan, 1939);
*More about Me* (London: Hutchinson, 1939);
*Full Meridian* (London: Hutchinson, 1939; New York: Macmillan, 1940);

*Naomi Jacob*

*This Porcelain Clay* (London: Hutchinson, 1939; New York: Macmillan, 1939);
*Me—in War-time* (London & Melbourne: Hutchinson, 1940);
*Sally Scarth* (London & Melbourne: Hutchinson, 1940);
*They Left the Land* (London & Melbourne: Hutchinson, 1940; New York: Macmillan, 1940);
*The Cap of Youth* (London & Melbourne: Hutchinson, 1941; New York: Macmillan, 1941);
*Under New Management* (London & Melbourne: Hutchinson, 1941);

*Leopards and Spots* (London & New York: Hutchinson, 1942);

*Private Gollantz* (London & New York: Hutchinson, 1943);

*White Wool* (London & New York: Hutchinson, 1943);

*Me and the Mediterranean* (London & New York: Hutchinson, 1945);

*Susan Crowther* (London: Hutchinson, 1945);

*Me—over There* (London & New York: Hutchinson, 1947);

*Honour's a Mistress* (London: Hutchinson, 1947);

*A Passage Perilous* (London: Hutchinson, 1947);

*Opera in Italy,* by Jacob and James C. Robertson (London & New York: Hutchinson, 1948);

*Gollantz: London, Paris, Milan* (London & New York: Hutchinson, 1948);

*Mary of Delight* (London: Hutchinson, 1949);

*Me and Mine (You and Yours),* preface by W. H. Elliott (London & New York: Hutchinson, 1949);

*Me—Looking Back,* foreword by Bransby Williams (London & New York: Hutchinson, 1950);

*The Heart of the House* (London & New York: Hutchinson, 1951);

*Robert, Nana and Me: A Family Chronicle* (London: Hutchinson, 1952);

*The Gollantz Saga,* 2 volumes (London: Hutchinson, 1952, 1953)—comprises *The Founder of the House, "That Wild Lie—," Young Emmanuel;*

*Just about Us* (London: Hutchinson, 1953);

*The Morning Will Come* (London: Hutchinson, 1953);

*Me—Likes and Dislikes* (London: Hutchinson, 1954);

*Antonia* (London: Hutchinson, 1954);

*Second Harvest* (London: Hutchinson, 1954);

*The Irish Boy: A Romantic Biography* (London: Hutchinson, 1955);

*Prince China, by Himself but Dictated to Naomi Jacob* (London: Hutchinson, 1955);

*Tales of the Broad Acres: Comprising Sally Scarth, The Loaded Stick, Roots* (London: Hutchinson, 1955);

*Wind on the Heath* (London: Hutchinson, 1956);

*Me—Yesterday and To-day* (London: Hutchinson, 1957);

*Late Lark Singing* (London: Hutchinson, 1957);

*Gollantz and Partners* (London: Hutchinson, 1958);

*What's to Come* (London: Hutchinson, 1958);

*Search for a Background* (London: Hutchinson, 1960);

*Three Men and Jennie* (London: Hutchinson, 1960);

*Strange Beginning* (London: Hale, 1961);

*Great Black Oxen* (London: Hale, 1962);

*Yolanda* (London: Hale, 1963);

*Me—and the Swans* (London: Kimber, 1963);

*Me—and the Stags* (London: Kimber, 1964);

*Me—Thinking Things Over* (London: Kimber, 1964);

*Long Shadows* (London: Hale, 1964);

*Flavia* (London: Hale, 1965).

**Collection:** *The Gollantz Saga,* 7 volumes (New York: New American Library, 1973–1974)—comprises *The Founder of the House; "That Wild Lie—"; Young Emmanuel; Four Generations; Private Gollantz; Gollantz: London, Paris, Milan; Gollantz and Partners.*

In Naomi Jacob's novel *Late Lark Singing* (1957) Ann Power reflects on her husband, Silas, on the morning after their wedding night:

> His passion of the night which had passed had been that, she felt, of a child. A child crying, "I want, I want—give me, give me what I want." There had been little or no delicacy in his love-making, and even for that she made the excuse that it proved that he knew nothing of love. . . . she had indulged in dreams, and they had been very different from reality. Perhaps she had been wrong, and allowed the ideas of romance to colour her thoughts; perhaps this mysterious love-making was something put into the world to make men happy, and not to give any real joy to women—except the joy of giving.

The passage is illustrative of Jacob's portrayals of women and their first husbands in her popular Yorkshire romance novels. The women are refined romantics: at one point Ann Power gushes to a bookseller over Emily Brontë's *Wuthering Heights* (1847), "It's like feelin' the wind off the moors in your face—a coldish wind, a wind that's strong and fierce but—oh, sir." Like Ann Power, Ann Harrington in *Full Meridian* (1939) has received from her father a love of books and some claim to refinement, and her love for her father has given her an idealistic, nearly Rousseauian view of men. Jacob's heroines are attracted to men who are, at first glance, like the wind off the moors: "coldish," strong, and fierce, with the concomitant positive associations of virility and sexual romance. The reality of life with these strong, silent men quickly sets in, however. Jacob's fictional first husbands—Silas Power, William Harrington, and Abel Moss in *White Wool* (1943), for example—soon prove themselves to be atavistic brutes who have either never reached full humanity or have reverted to a level below it. They stink and refuse to bathe; they shovel great forkfuls of food into their maws and chew noisily with their mouths open; they rut like animals in the marriage bed; they swear; they physically abuse their wives and children; they stifle their wives' desire to realize their full potentials; and they are unfaithful. Silas Power dashes a child—the product of his own infidelity—to its death against the hearthstones and beats Ann into unconsciousness for having tried to adopt it.

Jacob's women come to recognize their husbands' true natures, but out of a sense of personal honor they will neither leave the brutes nor take lovers. Instead, they engage in a series of minor revolts—refusing to clean muddy boots, surreptitiously borrowing books—that escalate into full-scale rebellions in which they withhold sex and refuse to be anything more than mistresses of their homes and mothers to their children. Eventually these women meet men of refinement and sensitivity and, through a series of Dickensian plot twists and timely coincidences, reach states of financial independence: Ann Harrington, for example, becomes the manager of Harrington's Department Store in London. Often they wind up supporting their second husbands, as Ann Power does George Bramforth. They attain emotional and spiritual well-being—Ann Power exclaims when Silas dies in prison: "I'm free! Now I'll begin to make summat out of my own life, not just let myself be a reflection of the life of someone else!"—and the novels have classic matrimonial happy endings. Most of Jacob's romantic plots focus on this process of personal emancipation of her Yorkshire heroines.

Naomi Ellington Jacob was born in Ripon, Yorkshire, on 1 July, but the year is a matter of some dispute. A few generally reliable sources give the year as 1889, but her obituary in the *Times* of London says that she was eighty when she died on 27 August 1964, which would make 1884 the year of her birth. Jacob's autobiographical writings—the first is fittingly titled *Me—a Chronicle about Other People* (1933)—are of little use in settling this question. Although she often ridicules men and women who try to hide their years by dressing in "modern" fashions or using excessive makeup, she is reticent about her own age and rarely states it unequivocally. In *Me and the Mediterranean* (1945) she revels in relating one of her common stage routines: "Would you believe I'm eighty-five years old?" she heartily asks a crowd of soldiers in an Entertainments National Service Association (ENSA) theater. "No!" they reply in unison. "Well, I'm not," she says with a Cheshire-cat grin. As between 1884 and 1889, the former year is given by the majority of sources and can be more easily reconciled to her age at other key moments in her life.

Jacob maintained a lifelong identification with the area of Yorkshire in which she grew up. In *Me—Yesterday and To-day* (1957) she writes lovingly of her simple childhood:

Those canny cottages in Bongate—perhaps they were not fitted with the latest gadgets, but people always seemed to manage very well, to live there very comfortably, and keep in good health. I look back on my nurse's kitchen as one of the nicest rooms I have ever known. The kitchen range shone like satin, there were two kettles—one, the black "sookey" also polished until it shone and looked as if it had been made of the best Whitby jet.

This kitchen was to be replicated in *Late Lark Singing*. Jacob's mother was Nina Ellington Collinson, a novelist who wrote under the pen name Nina Abbott. "Any writing ability I may have, I inherit from my mother," Jacob says in *Me—Yesterday and To-day*. Her mother's family were yeomen who owned the same piece of land in Yorkshire for more than three hundred years. Much less is known about her father, and Jacob's silence about him may indicate that he was the model for the brutish Yorkshire men in her novels. From her father's side of the family she obtained the pride in the Jewish people and hatred for anti-Semitism and fascism that would form the second major theme of her fiction and would also thread throughout her many *Me* volumes. Although Jacob was a member of the Church of England in her youth, her father's family had come from Spain and had worked their way, over the course of several hundred years, through Holland and finally into Poland. Her great-grandfather and great-grandmother were killed in pogroms in Poland, and her grandfather had escaped from Poland to Germany as a boy. Her Jewish heritage led Jacob to write a series of seven sprawling epic novels of the Jewish experience in England. These are the Gollantz novels, which trace the history of a Jewish family in London, and they include her first major success, *Four Generations* (1934). She says in *Me—Yesterday and To-day* that "the whole trouble with Jews is not that they are so different from other races, but that they are so like them." In her Gollantz novels, says Jane Spence Southron in *The New York Times Book Review* (3 January 1937) of Jacob's *Barren Metal* (1936), "she has set out to show . . . the best features of Jewish character."

"How I hated it," Jacob writes in *Me—Yesterday and To-day* of her schooling. She was educated at a series of private Yorkshire schools, including Skelfield, near Ripon, run by the Dixon sisters, and a school run by a Miss Meade and a Miss Browne. "They liked my sister—," Jacob writes of the latter school in *Me—Yesterday and To-day,* "everyone did—but Miss Meade loathed me. Nothing I could do was right. Well, I admit that I didn't do much right, but there were some subjects at which I was pretty good. Then I was accused of 'showing off.'" Jacob was a

*Frontispiece and title page for Jacob's 1955 book about her Pekingese*

large, gawky, and masculine child, and her teachers and classmates seem to have been put off by her appearance and her assertive, sometimes acerbic, "mannish" personality. Jacob completed her formal education at Middlesbrough High School and, as she often put it, "in the world in general."

Because of what she refers to only as "family reverses"—one of them may have been the death of her father—Jacob was forced to go to work at fifteen as a teacher in Middlesbrough. "I loved teaching, I loved children, but I hated the petty restrictions, the limitations and the bullying," she says in *Me—Yesterday and To-day*. She attempted to enliven her teaching by replacing the deadly-dull practices of the time with methods that anticipate late-twentieth-century pedagogical innovations. She used real money to improve the children's grasp of abstract mathematics, and she read to them the life and poetry of George Gordon, Lord Byron. If she sensed that they were becoming bored she would halt the lesson and engage them in conversation about their homes, their pets, and their families. She did not, however, neglect genuine learning but tried to impart to her pu-

pils both taste and factual knowledge. In *Me—Yesterday and To-day* she says:

> The young mind must be led gently from "Hearts and Flowers" or some dreadful blaring piece of boogy-woogy to the delicacies of Mozart, Purcell, and to Beethoven and Bach. Let them gaze their fill at the goitre-necked lovelies of Rossetti, and the slick portraits; they'll slowly come to realize—if they have any perception at all—what is worth looking at, learning about and analyzing.

At eighteen Jacob left her teaching position and became the secretary (later the manager) of the variety performer Marguerite Broadfoote. At about the same time she converted to Roman Catholicism. She also immersed herself in the woman suffrage movement. In *Me and the Mediterranean* she notes that she wore her hair "tied in a horse's tail with a big bow" and was called "the Baby Delegate" at suffragist meetings. "I was very frightened and equally imbued with the fierce determination that women ought to have the same rights as are, or may be accorded, to men." She called herself a socialist and joined the Labour Party.

When World War I broke out Jacob was a member of the Actresses Franchise League. The organization's wartime efforts included the Women's Emergency Corps, which received offers of help from women volunteers and assigned them to various tasks. One of the corps's projects was a toy factory that was started in a deliberate attempt to replace German prewar dominance in the industry. Jacob was the secretary; she recalls in *Me–in War-time* (1940): "we had a factory, small but quite good, and a staff of about eighty girls." In addition to making toys, the factory housed "a knitting department, making Balaclava helmets and things for the troops." Soon Jacob formed her own offshoot of the Women's Emergency Corps, the Three Arts Employment Fund, which channeled unemployed theatrical personnel into war work: "We had workrooms, and admitted people who could prove they had been connected with Art, Music, and Drama." In 1916 Jacob was working for Three Arts as a welfare supervisor at a munitions factory in Willesden; she left that year for a captain's commission in the Women's Legion, which recruited those who were unable to join the regular services. Jacob's disqualification for regular service may have had to do with her health: she spent more than a year in a sanitarium after the war, recuperating from tuberculosis. In 1920, following her convalescence, she made the first of her many stage and screen appearances, in which she usually played a drab or a harridan. Her career as a novelist began in 1925 with *Jacob Ussher.*

In 1928 Radclyffe Hall published the novel *The Well of Loneliness,* about a lesbian's search for identity and happiness in a homophobic society. To Jacob, who bought the work at the Times Bookshop on the day of its publication, it must have seemed like the story of her own life. "Reading it in 1928," she writes in *Me–and the Swans* (1963), "it would never have occurred to me that there was a single sentence or phrase which could be criticised on the ground of being immoral or offensive." Jacob initiated a correspondence with Hall and Hall's longtime companion, Una Troubridge, in 1929. The correspondence quickly developed into a close friendship.

Jacob left England in 1930: "I was flung down steps and into horse ponds as a result of my [suffrage] efforts; my health decided that I must live out of England," she says in *Me–Yesterday and To-day.* She immigrated to Sirmione, Italy, which would be her home for the rest of her life. Jacob writes about her friendship with Hall and Troubridge, who were her frequent guests in Italy, in *Me and the Mediterra-*

nean and at greater length in *Me–and the Swans,* the title of which is taken from one of Hall's novels. Freed from the restrictive social atmosphere of England, Jacob openly displayed her sexual identity. She adopted the nickname Mike or Mickie (Hall was known as John), began to wear men's suits, and cut her hair in a short, masculine style.

In 1934 *Four Generations,* the fourth of the Gollantz novels, became Jacob's first major success. She made her name in popular letters both in Great Britain and in the United States during the rest of the decade. She also had some success as an actress: in 1936 she appeared with Sir John Gielgud in the Edgar Wallace play *The Ringer.* "A very good actress she was," Gielgud recalls in *Early Stages* (1939).

At the beginning of World War II Jacob returned to England. The war years, chronicled in *Me and the Mediterranean,* were the most notable period of Jacob's life; in fact it is fair to say that it is because of her wartime activities in the Entertainments National Service Association (ENSA) rather than for her novels that her name is recognized today. Founded by Basil Dean in 1938 to provide entertainment for British and Allied forces and war workers, ENSA reached the camps, factories, and hostels on the home front and on war fronts from the Mediterranean to India and Africa. It was in ENSA that Jacob brokered a moderate literary and theatrical standing into full membership in the British cult of personality. Cropping her hair into a near crewcut and adopting what would become her signatory affectation, a monocle, she became famous both at home and abroad for her flamboyantly masculine appearance and aggressive behavior. Vera Brittain says that "few men had a greater addiction to the whiskey bottle" than did Jacob. She also insisted on wearing her World War I Women's Legion uniform, complete with captain's bars. Dean relates in *The Theatre at War* (1956) an incident in which Jacob, in uniform and monocle, was approached by a young Cockney soldier who saluted and asked, "Sir or madam, is this the way to the ENSA theatre?"

Jacob initially joined the Hospital Concert Section of ENSA, headed by Dame Sybil Thorndike and Dame Lillian Braithwaite and headquartered on Drury Lane in London, but she soon grew bored with home service and left for the Mediterranean and Africa as ENSA welfare supervisor; later she became public-relations officer. According to Dean,

Shortly after her arrival in Algiers a succession of signals in cipher arrived at the War Office, angrily demanding who was the woman parading about Algiers in unauthorized uniform and purporting to belong to ENSA? Finally, there came one from our senior officer:

the military authorities were threatening her immediate arrest if she were not recalled.

Jacob imperiously refused to change the uniform, to be recalled, or to curtail her ENSA activities. The War Office relented, and Jacob wore her defunct uniform for the duration of the war.

Jacob's virulent hatred of Nazism emerges sporadically in *Me and the Mediterranean.* Among her mildly amusing anecdotes about famous entertainers are passages that are striking in their anger. Germans, Jacob sneers,

> will sing their hearts out over songs which extol the glories of Germany or the appearance of the first snowdrop, but that is superficial only. Under those moist eyes is something hard as steel. Drunk with the teachings of Naziism, they could watch—dry-eyed and mocking—old women being forced to scrub pavements, old men kicked and beaten, young girls raped and driven mad, babies snatched from their mother's arms to suffer death in its most terrible forms.

Perhaps Jacob's greatest literary failing is her inability consistently to maintain this spirit either in her fiction or, inexplicably, in her autobiographical nonfiction. Her Gollantz saga is weak as a work of social commentary because of its feeble and emaciated spirit of outrage. *Me and the Mediterranean* is mainly a collection of pleasant stories in which she seems concerned mostly with trying to be witty through understatement. Only occasionally does the reader feel Jacob's emotional reaction to what is happening around her: "An old Italian said to me, 'This'—pointing to the shabby buildings—'typifies Fascism. Never stone, always plaster made to appear like stone.'" This emotional distance about the war is found only in her writing, however; in her personal life Jacob's warm humanity endeared her to the troops. In addition to entertaining them, she counseled them on religious issues and on matters of love and loneliness. She wrote letters for them and held gatherings at her home in Sirmione at which she was able to satisfy her passion for cooking.

After the war Jacob retired to Sirmione to write novels and raise her Pekingese—her whimsical *Prince China* (1955) is purportedly "by" her Pekingese of that name, as "Dictated to Naomi Jacob." In 1947 she left the British Labour Party and, labeling herself a "conservative Socialist," joined the Conservative Party. "Nobody who loves England can do otherwise," she was quoted in *The New York Times* (14 June 1947). "The [Clement] Atlee government is approaching fascism in its . . . refusal to give equal pay to women and its insults to housewives." She went on to say that "what Britain is seeing now is a

travesty of socialism. As an old member of the party I have lived through the great days of socialists. Today our leaders are not merely inefficient and shortsighted. They are not even ashamed of their failures." This defection—and the rather extreme language in which it was announced—alienated Jacob from her former public life. The traditionally liberal artistic community, except for some old friends, ostracized her, and she never acted again. Furthermore, this pioneer of suffrage was not welcome among the younger generation of feminists. The ostracism continues to this day: modern feminist literature, which reveres Hall, rarely mentions Jacob—nor do histories of the Atlee government or specialized works on women in the Labour Party in the early twentieth century.

Jacob ceased writing the Gollantz novels with *Gollantz and Partners* (1958); from then on, more an exile than an émigré, she nostalgically reached back to her childhood to concentrate on her Yorkshire romances and memoirs. She died of a heart attack on 27 August 1964. Her friend Bransby Williams described Jacob as "one of the best fiction-writers of today. She is unlike some of her novels, a jolly, boisterous laughing companion."

While Jacob admired Hall's courage in publishing *The Well of Loneliness,* which nearly ruined Hall's literary career, Jacob never wrote openly about lesbianism either in her novels or in her memoirs. She did, however, write almost exclusively about alienated individuals who struggle to find their way out of "wells of loneliness." Her fiction is mainly valuable for this delineation of character. Her standard plot—the heroine's youthful and ill-advised plunge into a loveless marriage, struggle for identity in such a relationship, and happiness with a true soul mate after the death of the first husband—is dated and commonplace. Her style, in spite of her adoption of the interior monologue in such novels as *Late Lark Singing* and *Long Shadows* (1964), is notable mainly for its hyperromanticism. For instance, in *Long Shadows* the protagonist, Sidone Heriot, reflects in a Paris cafe:

> Even now there were parts of the city which were peopled for Sidone by men and women who had lived hundreds of years ago. Madame de Maintenon, Diane de Poitiers, the Empress Josephine, Ninon, all passed by in their coaches. She often thought she saw D'Artagnan swaggering down some of the narrow old streets, or fancied that she saw the young Corsican Lieutenant leaving the tall, old house where he lodged for twenty francs a month, and even that rent was often terribly in arrears. Dumas Pere rolled along with Ada Isaacs Menken on his arm, and sometimes when she re-visited the Left Bank, in some cafe she would see a man who had

once been handsome . . . sitting alone; staring into space perhaps dreaming of the poems which he would never write.

If such passages underscore the modesty of Jacob's talents, however, they also illustrate her strengths as a writer. While she may never explore great depths in her novels, nor attempt to find an answer to the great mysteries of the human condition, her characters do come to life on the page. The reader cannot help but be moved by the yearnings of her characters as they wait and pray for a way out of their suffering. Jacob's most valuable gift was her ability to portray the quiet pain of unfulfilled hope.

Referring to her fan mail, Jacob wonders in *Me and the Mediterranean* "if these kind, generous folk know what a joy it is when they do things of that kind, how it makes everything so very well worth while, makes you feel that even if you will never be a 'stylist,' never write really good literature, that you have not completely wasted your time and your publisher's paper?" She was, as Theodore Purdy Jr. called her in his review of *Fade Out* (1937) in the *Saturday Review of Literature* (1 January 1938), "a good light romantic novelist . . . full of sure-fire tricks, but presenting them always in a new guise." Her novels, Purdy says, are "acceptably written and with much genuine humor." This humor, and her ability to draw characters "who seem to detach themselves from their background and move about in a special atmosphere," as Currie Cabot put it in a review of *The Cap of Youth* (1941) in the *Saturday Review of Literature* (30 August 1941), are the qualities for which her novels are remembered—when they are remembered. In spite of her adoption of the interior monologue technique from Hall, she is a weak stylist. She is prone to unnecessary and often jarring pauses indicated by dashes, as in two passages from *Me and the Mediterranean*: "Do you remember how as children you loved—picture books"; "Nothing mattered except—doing the job." Her memoirs tend, as she admits, to flit from flower to flower in a sort of free association; for example, in *Me and the Mediterranean* she goes immediately from discussing the use of a hot plate "to make ducks—who may be 'comical birds' anyway—do the 'goose step'" to "I heard a rather pleasant story the other day about an oyster." While Naomi Jacob's works are, perhaps, not worth remembering, her life, as documented in her *Me* series of memoirs, definitely is.

**References:**

Vera Brittain, *Radclyffe Hall: A Case of Obscenity?* (London: Femina Books, 1968), pp. 99, 103–105, 216;

Basil Dean, *The Theatre at War* (London: Harrap, 1956), p. 81;

John Gielgud, *Early Stages* (London: Macmillan, 1939), p. 125;

Richard Ormrod, *Una Troubridge: The Friend of Radclyffe Hall* (New York: Carroll & Graf, 1985), pp. 88–89, 226–227;

"Pioneer Quits Laborites to Fight Atlee Regime," *New York Times,* 14 January 1947, p. 24;

Bransby Williams, *Bransby Williams, by Himself* (London: Hutchinson, 1954), pp. 95–97, 145.

**Papers:**
Fearing that they might contain anti-Hitler or anti-Fascist material, her maid destroyed all of Naomi Jacob's papers when the Germans moved into Italy during World War II.

# Doris Leslie
*(before 1902 – 31 May 1982)*

Leonard R. N. Ashley
*Emeritus, Brooklyn College of the City University of New York*

BOOKS: *The Starling* (New York & London: Century, 1927);

*Fools in Mortar* (New York & London: Century, 1928);

*The Echoing Green* (London: Hurst & Blackett, 1929);

*Terminus* (London: Hurst & Blackett, 1931);

*Puppets Parade* (London: John Lane, 1931);

*Full Flavour* (London: Macmillan, 1934; New York: Macmillan, 1934);

*Fair Company* (London: John Lane, 1936; New York: Macmillan, 1936);

*Concord in Jeopardy* (London: Hutchinson, 1938; New York: Macmillan, 1938);

*Another Cynthia: The Adventures of Cynthia, Lady Ffulkes (1780–1850) Reconstructed from Her Hitherto Unpublished Memoirs* (London: Hutchinson, 1939; New York: Macmillan, 1939);

*Royal William: The Story of a Democrat* (London & Melbourne: Hutchinson, 1940; New York: Macmillan, 1941);

*House in the Dust* (London: Hutchinson, 1942; New York: Macmillan, 1942);

*Polonaise* (London & New York: Hutchinson, 1943);

*Folly's End* (London: Hutchinson, 1944);

*The Peverills* (London: Hutchinson, 1946);

*Wreath for Arabella* (London & New York: Hutchinson, 1948);

*That Enchantress* (London & New York: Hutchinson, 1950);

*The Great Corinthian: A Portrait of the Prince Regent* (London: Eyre & Spottiswoode, 1952; New York: Oxford University Press, 1953);

*A Toast to Lady Mary* (London: Hutchinson, 1954);

*Peridot Flight: A Novel Reconstructed from the Memoirs of Peridot, Lady Mulvarnie, 1872–1955* (London: Hutchinson, 1956);

*Tales of Grace and Favour* (London: Hutchinson, 1956)—comprises *Folly's End, The Peverills, Another Cynthia*;

*The Perfect Wife* (London: Hodder & Stoughton, 1960); republished as *The Prime Minister's Wife* (Garden City, N.Y.: Doubleday, 1961);

*Doris Leslie*

*As the Tree Falls* (London: Hodder & Stoughton, 1958);

*I Return: The Story of François Villon* (London: Hodder & Stoughton, 1962); republished as *Vagabond's Way: The Story of François Villon* (Garden City, N.Y.: Doubleday, 1962);

*This for Caroline* (London: Heinemann, 1964);

*Paragon Street* (London: Heinemann, 1965);

*The Sceptre and the Rose* (London: Heinemann, 1967);

*The Marriage of Martha Todd* (London: Heinemann, 1968);

*The Rebel Princess* (London: Heinemann, 1970);

*A Young Wives' Tale* (London: Heinemann, 1971);

*The Desert Queen* (London: Heinemann, 1972);

*The Dragon's Head* (London: Heinemann, 1973);

*The Incredible Duchess: The Life and Times of Elizabeth Chudleigh* (London: Heinemann, 1974);

*Call Back Yesterday* (London: Heinemann, 1975);

*Notorious Lady: The Life and Times of the Countess of Blessington* (London: Heinemann, 1976);

*The Warrior King: The Reign of Richard the Lion Heart* (London: Heinemann, 1977);

*Crown of Thorns: The Life of Richard II* (London: Heinemann, 1979).

The author of more than sixteen novels and seventeen biographies, Doris Leslie was the darling of book-club readers—six of her books were popular choices of Britain's National Book Club—and she had a considerable following among those who liked to get a little historical knowledge while being entertained by diverting stories. She was once cited in a journalism poll as the second-most-famous historical novelist, and her *As the Tree Falls* was ranked by *Books and Bookmen* as the best historical novel of 1958.

Doris Oppenheim was born in London around the turn of the twentieth century—she was always reticent about her age and her early life. Educated privately in London and Brussels, she at first thought that she might become a painter and studied art in London. At fifteen she decided she wanted to become an actress; her father was opposed to the idea, but without his knowledge she obtained a scholarship to the dramatic section of the Guildhall School of Music. She made her stage debut at the Old Vic as Viola in William Shakespeare's *Twelfth Night* and also acted with the Birmingham Repertory. While still in her teens she married another actor, John Leslie, whose surname she would use as her pen name. John Leslie died soon after the marriage, and Doris Leslie married R. Vincent Cookes. She later said that she did not acknowledge this marriage for "religious reasons."

After her first husband's death Leslie lost interest in acting and returned to her earlier interest in art. She went to Florence to study, but the success of her first novel, *The Starling* (1927), which is set in Florence, convinced her to abandon painting and become a writer.

*The Starling* was followed swiftly by *Fools in Mortar* (1928), *The Echoing Green* (1929), *Terminus* (1931), and *Puppets Parade* (1931). Leslie later characterized these novels as "trivial"; she dated her arrival on the literary scene with *Full Flavour* (1934), a tremendous success that was adapted for the stage and translated into five languages. It was one of the dynasty chronicles that were so popular at the time, especially with women readers. The novel's picaresque episodes are held together by the striking central figure of Catherine Ducroix. Brought up as a demure Victorian lady, she inherits her father's tobacco business and makes a success of it. Catherine's business and personal career, including two marriages with dramatic ups and downs, are treated in considerable detail. The narrative concludes as she is sending her grandson off to fight in World War I, which was to destroy the world of the Victorians and Edwardians. Herschel Brickell in the *New York Post* (1 September 1934) called the work a "pleasant, leisurely written chronicle, with many characters and much detail" and predicted: "it will be popular." "Varied events and scenes," wrote Virginia Barney in the *North American Review* (September 1934), "crowd the pages of this vivid story of the seventy-year life of one woman." E. H. Walton noted in *Forum* (October 1934) that "Miss Leslie never permits the background to steal the story"; actually, however, the background is the novel's saving grace: its somewhat anachronistic picture of the times is essential to the appeal of the narrative.

The women in this woman's story are better realized than the men although J. S. Southron in *The New York Times* (2 September 1934) objected strongly to "the American girl like none has ever met" as "one character too many." In one of the few haughty dismissals of the novel, the anonymous critic for *The Nation* (5 September 1934) contended that "Miss Leslie has a gift for creating atmosphere, but she seems to have little talent for portraying intricate characters and even less, if this book is any indication, for contriving original plots." Iris Barry in *Books* (2 September 1934), on the other hand, called the novel

> a readable and human book; the old familiar story of growth and courtship, heartbreak, solace and growing old should never seem wearisome if it is as well told as here. A peculiar charm of this book is its delightful attitude toward childhood. There are many passages, and those the best, devoted to characters under fifteen years of age and all of them are successful, extremely lively and full of flavor.

Fanny Butcher said in the *Chicago Tribune* (1 September 1934) that the novel had "insidious charm":

> It comforts the reader, not actively, but by implication. It amuses him. It is, in a word, everything that a novel can be without being a masterpiece. And just as ordinary human beings are much more comfortable to live with than geniuses, so "Full Flavour," which has every virtue of the simple, charming chronicle, will probably find a home in every home.

Having hit the market bull's-eye with *Full Flavour,* Leslie was to try again and again to repeat her success with "leisurely written" but dramatic stories of characters—mainly women—against sketchy historical backgrounds. Not as popular as *Full Flavour,* but rather more ambitious, was *Fair Company,* which followed in 1936. The novel traces four generations of an English family from the Regency period to the mid 1930s. Several women carry the story; the most important, Sabrina, is as rakish as her twin brother, who lost an eye in the battles over the Reform Bill of 1832. The huge cast of characters is somewhat confusing for the reader—Dorothea Kingsland complained in *The New York Times* (6 September 1936) that "we cannot find great sympathy for these shadows; there are too many of them and their lives are too remote"—and there are anachronisms of language and other details; but the *Times Literary Supplement* (26 September 1936) allowed that "the author's freshness of outlook and inventive energy make her story pleasant and lively," and that was all that Leslie's readers wanted.

Some of the minor figures from *Full Flavour* and *Fair Company* reappear in *Concord in Jeopardy* (1938), where the list of characters fills three pages. The novel centers, however, on the title character, a painter born in the late Victorian era who dies in World War I. In his strengths and his inhibitions he embodies the spirit of the period that perished in that conflagration. The writing is "so long-winded that occasionally its interest sags," according to *The New Republic* (20 July 1938), but Margaret Wallace in *The New York Times* (26 June 1938) thought that Concord's story was "important enough individually to command the reader's undivided interest." Some reviewers were tired of reading novels about World War I as the Nazi threat began to be noticed: Frances Woodward wrote in *The Saturday Review of Literature* (2 July 1938):

> The book is thoughtful, but on questions long since solved.... It is all eminently readable, but there is about it the faint sentimental flavor evoked by watching a revival of some play we saw in 1916.... This is not an effect deliberately created by Doris Leslie. She is not writing in the manner of another day, but seems herself to be a part of it, and one of the dozens of competent English novelists who appear to have been permanently deafened by the Ypres guns, and unaware that there are now new thunders over England.

The reviewer for the *Times Literary Supplement* (25 June 1938) was immune to the neurotic charm of Leslie's hero: "Concord is a strange, unhappy, not very convincing figure; others in the book, his friends and intimates, are much more alive; perhaps it is the author's insistence on the magnitude of Concord's achievements that rather irritates the

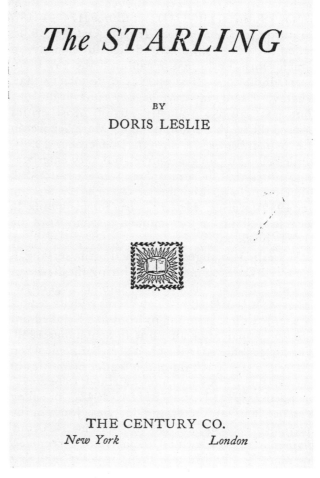

*The STARLING*

BY
DORIS LESLIE

THE CENTURY CO.
New York          London

*Title page for Leslie's first book*

reader by arousing his resistance." Leslie's desire to be more "literary" than the genre permits, by trying to make Concord into a kind of symbol, is the major flaw in this work: historical romance can seldom carry much mythical freight.

More successful was *Another Cynthia: The Adventures of Cynthia, Lady Ffulkes (1780–1850) Reconstructed from Her Hitherto Unpublished Memoirs* (1939). It is a work to which the word *lively,* common in critical reactions to Leslie's works, can appropriately be applied. Cynthia is a modern Moll Flanders who rises in the world to become the mistress of a lord and settles down in the end to live happily ever after with another titled lover. Along the way she has a series of adventures of the kind that were common in eighteenth-century fiction and are debased in modern "bodice-ripper" paperbacks. These events are reported in entries from Cynthia's diaries; this narrative technique recalls, in a more sprightly fashion, the long epistolary novels of the period in which the work is set, such as Samuel Richardson's *Pamela* (1740-1741) and *Clarissa* (1747-1748). Southron in *The New York Times* (1 October 1939) called the book "an utterly delightful comedy, in which Doris Leslie has recaptured the gay lightheartedness and effervescence of a society that, whatever else it may have been, was never dull . . . [but was] always robustly alive." Most critics praised the work's historical color; Mark Schorer in the *Boston Evening Transcript* (14 October 1939), while calling it "no great novel, but very entertaining," noted that the atmosphere was accurate. Wilfrid Gibson in the Manchester *Guardian* (22 September 1939) praised *Another Cynthia* for providing "a pleasant relief from the ominous possibilities of the nightly black-out."

Leslie was slightly wounded while serving in the Civil Defence in London during the Battle of Britain. The war enters directly into her next novel, *House in the Dust* (1942), which begins with its central figure, Jennifer, standing in front of a bombed-out London house after air raids in September 1940. The house reduced to dust had been her home when she was a girl. Back flood the tender memories of her childhood—"a very clumsy method, to be sure," snapped *The New Yorker* (15 March 1942), "of telling a rather familiar Victorian tale." Bess Jones in the *Saturday Review of Literature* (21 March 1942) complained to the reader that "the narrator is reminiscing more for her own sake than for yours" and that Jennifer, though a compelling woman, is too remote from the remembered action she describes. Most critics, however, liked Jennifer's independent ways, although they are a bit incredible in a woman of her upbringing and time: Jennifer rejects the weakling to whom she is engaged in favor of a dashing Irishman, who turns out to be a drunkard. The self-assured Jennifer is what Leslie's female readers would want to be, not what Victorians actually were. In fact, all of the Victorians in Leslie's novels ring a trifle false. The problem is not so much that characters in *House in the Dust* refer in the 1880s to George Du Maurier's novel *Trilby*, which was not published until 1894 (as the critic for the *Times Literary Supplement* [14 March 1942] pointed out), or use twentieth-century expressions as that their ideas and attitudes are those of Leslie and her readers, not those of the Victorian period. What is most Victorian about *House in the Dust* is Leslie's imitation of the narrative techniques of the sloppier Victorian novelists.

In 1946 Leslie married a London physician, Walter Fergusson Hannay; he was knighted in 1951. In 1956 the Hutchinson firm republished three Leslie novels—*Another Cynthia*, *Folly's End* (1944), and *The Peverills* (1946)—with success as *Tales of Grace and Favour* (1956). As the 1960s began, Leslie's *Peridot Flight: A Novel Reconstructed from the Memoirs of Peridot, Lady Mulvarnie, 1872–1955* (1956) was being enjoyed by a whole new audience, as well as by her longtime fans, in a dramatic adaptation presented on BBC television.

Leslie's husband died in 1961; that same year she converted to Roman Catholicism. Moving to Devon, where she bred and showed English bulldogs, she went on to write the novels *A Young Wives' Tale* (1971), *The Dragon's Head* (1973), and *Call Back Yesterday* (1975).

Leslie's novels were less successful, both commercially and aesthetically, than her biographies. *Royal William: The Story of a Democrat* (1940), *Polonaise* (1943), *Wreath for Arabella* (1948), *I Return: The Story of François Villon* (1962; republished as *Vagabond's Way*, 1962), and *The Sceptre and the Rose* (1967) are among the best of these works, all of which appeal both to the reader's high-minded desire to learn something about the past and to his or her interest in scandal and gossip. When she ventured farther back in time than the Victorian period, as in *The Warrior King: The Reign of Richard the Lion Heart* (1977) or *Crown of Thorns: The Life of Richard II* (1979), she was less successful but still enjoyable. She died in Sussex on 31 May 1982.

Doris Leslie entertained the public during an era in which other women, such as Elizabeth Bowen, Jean Rhys, Ivy Compton-Burnett, and Muriel Spark, were writing more-important novels in Britain. Readers today are not apt to share the enthusiasm for Leslie's historical novels that led Gertrude Bayley in the *Boston Evening Transcript* (24 October 1936) to say of *Fair Company*: "Miss Leslie's fine artistry has given the story color and perfection of detail, and has shown in the life of her characters the spirit which has made England what it is today." Leslie's novels were the sort of innocuous reading of which the critic Leslie A. Fiedler was speaking when he looked forward to a day when one would see "bonfires made of the last historical romance hailed as the novel of the year in the last book review section of the last *New York Times*."

**Reference:**
Leslie A. Fiedler, *Waiting for the End: The Crisis in American Culture and A Portrait of 20th Century American Literature* (New York: Stein & Day, 1964).

# Ethel Mannin

*(11 October 1900 – 5 December 1984)*

## Margaret Crosland

BOOKS: *Martha* (London: Parsons, 1923; New York: Duffield, 1923; revised edition, London: Jarrolds, 1929);

*Hunger of the Sea* (London: Jarrolds, 1924; New York: Duffield, 1924);

*Sounding Brass* (London: Jarrolds, 1925; New York: Duffield, 1926);

*Pilgrims* (London: Jarrolds, 1927; New York: Doran, 1927);

*Green Willow* (London: Jarrolds, 1928; Garden City, N.Y.: Doubleday, Doran, 1928);

*Crescendo, Being the Dark Odyssey of Gilbert Stroud* (London: Jarrolds, 1929; Garden City, N.Y.: Doubleday, Doran, 1929);

*Children of the Earth* (London: Jarrolds, 1930; Garden City, N.Y.: Doubleday, 1930);

*Confessions and Impressions* (London: Jarrolds, 1930; revised edition, London: Hutchinson, 1936);

*Bruised Wings, and Other Stories* (London: Wright & Brown, 1931);

*Common-Sense and the Child: A Plea for Freedom* (London: Jarrolds, 1931; Philadelphia: Lippincott, 1932);

*Green Figs* (London: Jarrolds, 1931);

*Ragged Banners: A Novel with an Index* (London: Jarrolds, 1931; New York: Knopf, 1931);

*The Tinsel Eden, and Other Stories* (London: Wright & Brown, 1931);

*All Experience* (London: Jarrolds, 1932);

*Linda Shawn* (London: Jarrolds, 1932; New York: Knopf, 1932);

*Love's Winnowing* (London: Wright & Brown, 1932);

*Dryad* (London: Jarrolds, 1933);

*Venetian Blinds* (London: Jarrolds, 1933; New York: Knopf, 1933);

*Forever Wandering* (London: Jarrolds, 1934; New York: Dutton, 1935);

*Men Are Unwise* (London: Jarrolds, 1934; New York: Knopf, 1934);

*Cactus* (London: Jarrolds, 1935; revised, 1944);

*The Falconer's Voice* (London: Jarrolds, 1935);

*The Pure Flame* (London: Jarrolds, 1936);

*South to Samarkand* (London: Jarrolds, 1936; New York: Dutton, 1937);

*Common-Sense and the Adolescent* (London: Jarrolds, 1937; revised, 1945);

*Women Also Dream* (London: Jarrolds, 1937; New York: Putnam, 1937);

*Darkness My Bride* (London: Jarrolds, 1938);

*Rose and Sylvie* (London: Jarrolds, 1938);

*Women and the Revolution* (London: Secker & Warburg, 1938; New York: Dutton, 1939);

*Privileged Spectator: A Sequel to "Confessions and Impressions"* (London: Jarrolds, 1939; revised, 1948);

*Christianity—or Chaos?: A Re-statement of Religion* (London: Jarrolds, 1940);

*Julie: The Story of a Dance-Hostess* (London: Jarrolds, 1940);

*Rolling in the Dew* (London: Jarrolds, 1940);

*Red Rose: A Novel Based on the Life of Emma Goldman—"Red Emma"* (London: Jarrolds, 1941);

*The Blossoming Bough* (London & New York: Jarrolds, 1942);

*Captain Moonlight* (London & New York: Jarrolds, 1942);

*Castles in the Street* (London: Dent, 1942);

*Commonsense and Morality* (London & New York: Jarrolds, 1942);

*No More Mimosa* (London: Jarrolds, 1943);

*Proud Heaven* (London: Jarrolds, 1943);

*Bread and Roses: An Utopian Survey and Blue-print* (London: Macdonald, 1944);

*Lucifer and the Child* (London & New York: Jarrolds, 1945);

*The Dark Forest* (London: Jarrolds, 1946):

*Selected Stories* (Dublin: Fridberg, 1946);

*Comrade O Comrade; or, Low-down on the Left* (London & New York: Jarrolds, 1947);

*Connemara Journal* (London: Westhouse, 1947);

*German Journey* (London & New York: Jarrolds, 1948);

*Late Have I Loved Thee* (London: Jarrolds, 1948; New York: Putnam, 1948);

*Every Man a Stranger* (London: Jarrolds, 1949);

*Bavarian Story* (London: Jarrolds, 1949; New York: Appleton-Century-Crofts, 1950);

*Jungle Journey* (London & New York: Jarrolds, 1950);

*At Sundown, the Tiger* (London & New York: Jarrolds, 1951);

*The Fields at Evening* (London & New York: Jarrolds, 1952);

*This Was a Man: Some Memories of Robert Mannin by His Daughter* (London & New York: Jarrolds, 1952);

*The Wild Swans, and Other Tales Based on the Ancient Irish* (London: Jarrolds, 1952);

*Moroccan Mosaic* (London & New York: Jarrolds, 1953);

*Lover under Another Name* (London & New York: Jarrolds, 1953; New York: Putnam, 1954);

*Two Studies in Integrity: Gerald Griffin and the Rev. Francis Mahony ("Father Prout")* (London: Jarrolds, 1954; New York: Putnam, 1954);

*So Tiberius* (London: Jarrolds, 1954; New York: Putnam, 1955);

*Land of the Crested Lion: A Journey through Modern Burma* (London: Jarrolds, 1955);

*The Living Lotus* (London: Jarrolds, 1956; New York: Putnam, 1956);

*The Country of the Sea: Some Wanderings in Brittany* (London: Jarrolds, 1957);

*Pity the Innocent* (London: Jarrolds, 1957; New York: Putnam, 1957);

*Fragrance of Hyacinths* (London: Jarrolds, 1958);

*The Blue-Eyed Boy* (London: Jarrolds, 1959);

*Brief Voices: A Writer's Story* (London: Hutchinson, 1959);

*Ann and Peter in Sweden* (London: Muller, 1959);

*Ann and Peter in Japan* (London: Muller, 1960);

*The Flowery Sword: Travels in Japan* (London: Hutchinson, 1960);

*Sabishisa* (London: Hutchinson, 1961);

*Ann and Peter in Austria* (London: Muller, 1962);

*Curfew at Dawn* (London: Hutchinson, 1962);

*With Will Adams through Japan* (London: Muller, 1962);

*A Lance for the Arabs: A Middle East Journey* (London: Hutchinson, 1963);

*The Road to Beersheba* (London: Hutchinson, 1963; Chicago: Regnery, 1964);

*Aspects of Egypt: Some Travels in the United Arab Republic* (London: Hutchinson, 1964);

*Bavarian Story* (London: Arrow, 1964);

*Rebel's Ride: A Consideration of the Revolt of the Individual* (London: Hutchinson, 1964);

*The Burning Bush* (London: Hutchinson, 1965);

*The Lovely Land: The Hashemite Kingdom of Jordan* (London: Hutchinson, 1965);

*Loneliness: A Study of the Human Condition* (London: Hutchinson, 1966);

*The Night and Its Homing* (London: Hutchinson, 1966);

*An American Journey* (London: Hutchinson, 1967);

*The Lady and the Mystic* (London: Hutchinson, 1967);

*Bitter Babylon* (London: Hutchinson, 1968);

*England for a Change* (London: Hutchinson, 1968):

*The Midnight Street* (London: Hutchinson, 1969);

*The Saga of Sammy-cat* (Oxford & New York: Pergamon, 1969);

*Practitioners of Love: Some Aspects of the Human Phenomenon* (London: Hutchinson, 1969; New York: Horizon, 1970);

*England at Large* (London: Hutchinson, 1970);

*Free Pass to Nowhere* (London: Hutchinson, 1970);

*My Cat Sammy* (London: M. Joseph, 1971);

*Young in the Twenties: A Chapter of Autobiography* (London: Hutchinson, 1971);

*The Curious Adventure of Major Fosdick* (London: Hutchinson, 1972);

*England My Adventure* (London: Hutchinson, 1972);

*Mannin and her daughter, Jean, preparing to fly from Croydon to Paris in 1925*

*Mission to Beirut* (London: Hutchinson, 1973);
*Stories from My Life* (London: Hutchinson, 1973);
*An Italian Journey* (London: Hutchinson, 1974);
*Kildoon* (London: Hutchinson, 1974);
*The Late Miss Guthrie* (London: Hutchinson, 1976);
*Sunset over Dartmoor: A Final Chapter of Autobiography* (London: Hutchinson, 1977).

Ethel Mannin was nothing if not prolific: she published 102 books, including novels, collections of short stories, travel books, polemical essays on social and political issues, biographies, children's stories, and books on education. She was an independent, exceptionally honest woman whose life and work reflect the changing intellectual and social fashions of the 1930s and the following decades. Several of her many novels remain readable for their forward-looking discussions of topics such as the problems of marriage, sexual relationships in general, and feminism.

Ethel Edith Mannin was born on 11 October 1900 in the London suburb of Clapham to Robert Mannin, a postal worker, and Edith Gray Mannin. She wrote in her first autobiography, *Confessions and Impressions* (1930), that she had inherited her Irish father's imagination and the practicality of her country-born mother. At six she was enrolled in a small, local private school; two years later she transferred to a boarding school, then took a commercial course. From childhood she wanted to be an "authoress," and as she passed through the adolescent stages of platonic love affairs, she began to write poetry. She also became a socialist. When she was fifteen, she went to work as a stenographer for the Charles F. Higham advertising agency in London. Two years later she became associate editor of a small theatrical magazine, *The Pelican.*

Shortly before her nineteenth birthday Mannin married a copywriter at the agency, John Alexander Porteous, who was thirteen years older than she; within a year they had a daughter, Jean. At first Mannin resented the child's arrival because it interfered with her writing; she came to love her daughter, however, and in spite of her maternal responsibilities succeeded in writing what she called "novelettish" stories, countless articles, and, soon, novels. Several years later she stated her belief that women writers should have a "masculine mind"; unlike the novelist Naomi Mitchison, Mannin believed that pregnancy and creative work did not go together.

The now-forgotten novelist Douglas Goldring, helping to judge the First Novel Competition in 1923, was impressed by Mannin's *Martha;* Mannin's novel was a runner-up in the competition and was published the same year. She and Goldring became friends; in his autobiography, *Odd Man Out* (1935), he describes her in the early 1920s as a "slim blonde, Madonna-like girl who concealed her flaming vitality under a cloak of the utmost demureness." She already looked like a "personality," Goldring says: "She was crude, and raw, not very well dressed and as pretty as they make 'em. But what lent her distinction was her complete lack of affectation, her di-

*Mannin in her garden (photograph by Paul Tanqueray)*

rectness and essential simplicity." He adds that her later success did not impair these qualities.

Mannin's first commercial success in the field of fiction was *Sounding Brass* (1925), based on her experiences in advertising, and it earned enough money that she was able to fulfill her desire to travel; she would remain an energetic traveler for the rest of her life, and her experiences would find their way into her novels, short stories, and travel books. Her novel *Pilgrims* (1927) was inspired by her admiration for the painter Vincent Van Gogh; she had been introduced to Van Gogh's work by a Dutch friend in Paris, where she lived for a time. In 1929 she bought Oak Cottage in Wimbledon; it would remain her home base for the next forty years. Her *Ragged Banners: A Novel with an Index* (1931) is the story of an unusual man, "half-genius, half-faun"; the dedication says that it was written "For the great legion of the valiant undefeatable defeated." It is a melodramatic novel that embodies the author's knowledge of Europe and her plea for understanding for unconventional people. The index includes the names of many real people and also abstract ideas, such as "Intellectuality, Curse of"

and "Philistines, Philosophy of." *Linda Shawn* (1932), a novel about a child, allows Mannin to express her views on education.

The novel *Men Are Unwise* (1934), dedicated "To all who love mountains," is about more than mountain climbing; it includes discussions of love, marriage, fidelity, and the acceptance of reality. Mannin tried to adapt it as a play but failed. In another of her autobiographies, *Privileged Spectator: A Sequel to "Confessions and Impressions"* (1939), she is honest, as usual, about what she saw as a failed novel: "the mountain-loving hero emerges as tiresome and apparently it is difficult to care whether he climbs a mountain or not. . . . I wanted the conflict between his passion for mountains and his love for his wife to be a big thing, something really profound; but I failed to bring it off, which is more disappointing to me than it could possibly be to any reader."

On the other hand, she regarded *Cactus* (1935) as one of her better novels; it was the first one in which she introduced her political views. She dedicated it to Ernst Toller, a German revolutionary; writing about the novel later, she pointed out that it had foreshadowed the civil war in Spain. *South to Samarkand* in 1936 records her travels in the Soviet Union and expresses her disappointment with the bureaucracy that, as she saw it, was destroying socialism. She soon decided that she was an anarchist rather than a socialist. Her first marriage ended in 1938; that same year she married Reginald Reynolds, like herself a writer and a pacifist.

In 1938 Mannin opened her nonfiction work *Women and the Revolution* with a dedicatory letter to the anarchist Emma Goldman because "your whole life has been dedicated to the revolutionary cause, and because you are the greatest living woman revolutionary." The Lithuanian-born Goldman had emigrated from Russia to the United States in 1885, had been deported to the Soviet Union in 1919, and after 1921 had worked in Europe for the same causes that Mannin supported, including the struggle of the Spanish Republicans against the fascist dictator Francisco Franco from 1936 to 1939. The two women had met and corresponded before Goldman's death in Toronto in 1940. Mannin's novel *Red Rose* (1941) is based on Goldman's life.

In Mannin's novel *Proud Heaven* (1943) a rich music lover involved in an empty marriage has an affair with a violinist; the narrator, his friend Robert Charles, falls in love with the violinist after the music lover's death. Charles meditates on "heroic love" and maintains that it cannot happen twice in one lifetime; in fact, for most people it does not happen once. "Then let there be plurality of marriages," he says; "one more or less it makes no difference, since all are equally counterfeit." He comes to a pragmatic conclusion: "We have to do the best for ourselves in the wilderness of living." Writing at the height of World War II, Mannin has Charles engage in political speculation: "The common people of the world, not the politicians and the intellectuals and the professional revolutionaries, but the toiling masses— these are the people who can save the peace, salvage civilisation." In a "rational society," he maintains, there would be a place for the artist and the intellectual; "but ours is not even a rational society in the making, and we have to do the best for ourselves."

Mannin wrote several books about her travels in the Middle East; she also used the area as a setting for her fiction. In 1956 she published *The Living Lotus,* the story of an Anglo-Burmese girl who is separated from her parents during the Japanese invasion of the country. Eight years later her British father finds her and takes her home with him to Britain. The novel poses the question whether the father had the moral right to uproot his daughter from the culture in which she had grown up; at the end of the work the girl returns to Burma (today Myanmar). A reviewer in the magazine *Time and Tide* regarded the book as "one of the best novels Ethel Mannin has given us for a long time . . . [her] Burma is a country and a people we can believe in."

At the end of the 1960s Mannin moved from Wimbledon to Overhill, a house in Shaldon, Devonshire, that her daughter had found for her. She wrote about the area in her final autobiography, *Sunset over Dartmoor* (1977). In July 1984 she was injured in a fall at her home; she died at Teignmouth Hospital on 5 December.

Since the 1930s, when she was at her best, some of the issues Mannin confronted in her fiction and nonfiction have been at least partially resolved in directions that she advocated: the role of women has been clarified and their social position improved; contraception is freely available; divorce laws have been rationalized; and the importance of the individual has been more widely recognized. Serious novelists have gone beyond her by avoiding melodrama and sentimentality and integrating social commentary more tightly into their plots. But Ethel Mannin, who was a pioneer in many ways, remains a representative of her time.

**References:**

Andy Croft, "The Red Rose of Love and the Red Flower of Liberty," in *Rediscovering Forgotten Radicals: British Women Writers, 1889–1939,* edited by Angela Ingram and Daphne Patai (Chapel Hill: University of North Carolina Press, 1993), pp. 205–225;

Douglas Goldring, *Odd Man Out: The Autobiography of a "Propaganda Novelist"* (London: Chapman & Hall, 1935), p. 294;

Rebecca O'Rourke, "Were There No Women? British Working Class Writing in the Inter-War Period," *Literature and History,* 14 (Spring 1988): 48–63;

Reginald Reynolds, *My Life and Crimes* (London: Jarrolds, 1956).

# Naomi Mitchison

*(1 November 1897 –   )*

## Margaret Crosland

See also the Mitchison entry in *DLB 160: British Children's Writers, 1914–1960*.

BOOKS: *The Conquered* (London: Cape, 1923; New York: Harcourt, Brace, 1923);

*When the Bough Breaks, and Other Stories* (London: Cape, 1924; New York: Harcourt, Brace, 1924);

*Cloud Cuckoo Land* (London: Cape, 1925; New York: Harcourt, Brace, 1926);

*The Laburnum Branch: Poems* (London: Cape, 1926; New York: Harcourt, Brace, 1926);

*Black Sparta: Greek Stories* (London: Cape, 1928; New York: Harcourt, Brace, 1928);

*Anna Comnena* (London: Gerald Howe, 1928);

*Nix-Nought-Nothing: Four Plays for Children* (London: Cape, 1928; New York: Harcourt, Brace, 1929);

*Barbarian Stories* (London: Cape, 1929; New York: Harcourt, Brace, 1929);

*Comments on Birth Control* (London: Faber & Faber, 1930);

*The Hostages, and Other Stories for Boys and Girls* (London & Toronto: Cape, 1930; New York: Harcourt, Brace, 1931);

*Kate Crackernuts: A Fairy Play for Children* (Oxford: Alden, 1931);

*Boys and Girls and Gods* (London: Watts, 1931);

*The Corn King and the Spring Queen* (London: Cape, 1931; New York: Harcourt, Brace, 1931);

*The Price of Freedom: A Play in Three Acts,* by Mitchison and Lewis E. Gielgud (London: Cape, 1931);

*The Powers of Light* (London: Pharos, 1932);

*The Delicate Fire: Short Stories and Poems* (London & Toronto: Cape, 1933; New York: Harcourt, Brace, 1933);

*The Home and a Changing Civilisation* (London: John Lane, 1934);

*Naomi Mitchison's Vienna Diary* (London: Gollancz, 1934; New York: Smith & Haas, 1934);

*Beyond This Limit,* pictures by Wyndham Lewis (London: Cape, 1935);

*Naomi Mitchison in the 1920s*

*We Have Been Warned: A Novel* (London: Constable, 1935; New York: Vanguard, 1936);

*The Fourth Pig: Stories and Verses* (London: Constable, 1936);

*An End and a Beginning, and Other Plays* (London: Constable, 1937);

*Socrates,* by Mitchison and Richard H. S. Crossman (London: Hogarth Press, 1937; Harrisburg, Pa.: Stackpole, 1938);

*The Moral Basis of Politics* (London: Constable, 1938; Port Washington, N.Y.: Kennikat Press, 1971);

*The Alban Goes Out* (Harrow, Middlesex: Raven, 1939);

*As It Was in the Beginning: A Play in Three Acts,* by Mitchison and Gielgud (London: Cape, 1939);

*The Kingdom of Heaven* (London & Toronto: Heinemann, 1939);

*Historical Plays for Schools* (London: Constable, 1939);

*The Blood of the Martyrs* (London: Constable, 1939; New York: McGraw-Hill, 1948);

*The Bull Calves* (London: Cape, 1947);

*Men and Herring: A Documentary,* by Mitchison and Denis Macintosh (Edinburgh: Serif, 1949 [i.e., 1950]);

*The Big House* (London: Faber & Faber, 1950);

*Spindrift: A Play in Three Acts,* by Mitchison and Macintosh (London: French, 1951);

*Lobsters on the Agenda* (London: Gollancz, 1952);

*Travel Light* (London: Faber & Faber, 1952; New York: Penguin Books-Virago Press, 1987);

*Graeme and the Dragon* (London: Faber & Faber, 1954);

*The Swan's Road* (London: Naldrett, 1954);

*The Land the Ravens Found* (London: Collins, 1955);

*To the Chapel Perilous* (London: Allen & Unwin, 1955);

*Little Boxes* (London: Faber & Faber, 1956);

*Behold Your King: A Novel* (London: Muller, 1957);

*The Far Harbour: A Novel for Boys and Girls* (London: Collins, 1957);

*Five Men and a Swan* (London: Allen & Unwin, 1957);

*Other People's Worlds* (London: Secker & Warburg, 1958);

*Judy and Lakshmi* (London: Collins, 1959);

*A Fishing Village on the Clyde,* by Mitchison and George William Lennox Paterson (London: Oxford University Press, 1960);

*The Rib of the Green Umbrella* (London: Collins, 1960);

*The Young Alexander the Great* (London: Parrish, 1960; New York: Roy, 1961);

*Karensgaard: The Story of a Danish Farm* (London: Collins, 1961);

*Presenting Other People's Children* (London: Hamlyn, 1961);

*The Young Alfred the Great* (London: Parrish, 1962; New York: Roy, 1963);

*Memoirs of a Spacewoman* (London: Gollancz, 1962; New York: Berkley, 1973);

*The Fairy Who Couldn't Tell a Lie* (London: Collins, 1963);

*Alexander the Great* (London: Longmans, 1964);

*Henny and Crispies* (Wellington: New Zealand School Department of Education, School Publications Branch, 1964);

*Ketse and the Chief* (London: Nelson, 1965; Camden, N.J.: Nelson, 1967);

*When We Become Men* (London: Collins, 1965);

*A Mochudi Family* (Wellington: New Zealand Department of Education, School Publications Branch, 1965);

*Friends and Enemies* (London: Collins, 1966; New York: Day, 1968);

*Return to the Fairy Hill* (London: Heinemann, 1966; New York: Day, 1966);

*The Big Surprise* (London: Kaye & Ward, 1967);

*Highland Holiday* (Wellington: New Zealand Department of Education, School Publications Branch, 1967);

*African Heroes* (London & Sydney: Bodley Head, 1968; New York: Farrar, Straus & Giroux, 1969);

*Don't Look Back* (London: Kaye & Ward, 1969);

*The Family at Ditlabeng* (London: Collins, 1969; New York: Farrar, Straus & Giroux, 1970);

*The Africans* (London: Blond, 1970);

*Sun and Moon* (London: Bodley Head, 1970; Nashville: Nelson, 1973);

*Cleopatra's People* (London: Heinemann, 1972);

*Small Talk . . . : Memories of an Edwardian Childhood* (London: Bodley Head, 1973);

*A Life for Africa: The Story of Bram Fischer* (London: Merlin, 1973; Boston: Carrier Pigeon, 1973);

*Sunrise Tomorrow: A Story of Botswana* (London: Collins, 1973; New York: Farrar, Straus & Giroux, 1973);

*The Danish Teapot* (London: Kaye & Ward, 1973);

*Oil for the Highlands?* (London: Fabian Society, 1974);

*All Change Here: Girlhood and Marriage* (London: Bodley Head, 1975);

*Sittlichkeit* (London: Birkbeck College Press, 1975);

*Solution Three* (London: Dobson, 1975; New York: Feminist Press at the City University of New York, 1995);

*Snake!* (London: Collins, 1976);

*The Brave Nurse and Other Stories* (Cape Town & New York: Oxford University Press, 1977);

*The Two Magicians,* by Mitchison and Dick Mitchison (London: Dobson, 1978);

*The Cleansing of the Knife and Other Poems* (Edinburgh: Canongate, 1979);

*You May Well Ask: A Memoir, 1920–1940* (London: Gollancz, 1979);

*The Vegetable War* (London: Hamish Hamilton, 1980);

*Images of Africa* (Edinburgh: Canongate, 1980);

*Mucking Around: Five Continents over Fifty Years* (London: Gollancz, 1981);

*Margaret Cole, 1893–1980* (London: Fabian Society, 1982);

*What Do You Think Yourself? Scottish Short Stories* (Edinburgh: Harris, 1982);

*Not by Bread Alone* (London & New York: Boyars, 1983);

*Among You, Taking Notes: The Wartime Diary of Naomi Mitchison 1939–1945,* edited by Dorothy Sheridan (London: Gollancz, 1985);

*Beyond This Limit: Selected Shorter Fiction of Naomi Mitchison,* edited by Isobel Murray, The Scottish Classics, no. 5 (Edinburgh: Scottish Academic Press in conjunction with the Association of Scottish Literary Studies, 1986);

*Naomi Mitchison* (Edinburgh: Saltire Society, 1986);

*Early in Orcadia* (Glasgow: Drew, 1987);

*A Girl Must Live: Stories and Poems* (Glasgow: Drew, 1987);

*The Oath-Takers* (Nairn, Scotland: Balnain, 1991);

*Sea-green Ribbons* (Nairn, Scotland: Balnain, 1991).

PLAY PRODUCTIONS: *Full Fathom Five,* by Mitchison and L. E. Gielgud, London, Embassy Theatre, 25 January 1932;

*The Price of Freedom,* Cheltenham, 1949;

*The Corn King,* music by Brian Easdale, London, 1950;

*Spindrift,* Glasgow, 1951.

OTHER: *An Outline for Boys and Girls and Their Parents,* edited by Mitchison (London: Gollancz, 1932);

*Re-Educating Scotland: Being a Statement of What Is Wrong with Scottish Education and What It Might Yet Become, with a Number of Practical Proposals for Its Betterment, Put Forward by the Education Committee of Scottish Convention,* edited by Mitchison, Robert Britton, and George Kilgour (Glasgow: Published by Scoop Books for Scottish Convention, 1944);

Frederic Bartlett and others, *What the Human Race Is Up To,* edited by Mitchison (London: Gollancz, 1962);

"The Little Sister," in *Pulenyane's Secret,* by Ian Kirby (Cape Town: Oxford University Press, 1976);

"The Wild Dogs," in *The Animal That Hides in the Trees,* by Megan Biesele (Cape Town: Oxford University Press, 1977).

SELECTED PERIODICAL PUBLICATION—UNCOLLECTED: "Writing Historical Novels," *Saturday Review of Literature,* 11 (27 April 1935): 645–646.

During her long and creative life Naomi Mitchison has achieved a remarkable reconciliation between the practical everyday world and the realms of myth, remote cultures, and history. At the age of sixty she began to write about the future while continuing to produce, as she had during her entire writing life, poems, plays, books for children, reviews, essays, and articles on a variety of social, moral, and political themes. She has also published three volumes of memoirs.

Naomi Margaret Haldane was born on 1 November 1897 in Edinburgh to the physiologist John Scott Haldane and Louisa Kathleen Trotter Haldane. The Haldanes were an ancient Scottish family that had owned land near Gleneagles, Perthshire, for many generations. Naomi's mother assumed that her daughter would grow up to participate in conventional Edinburgh social life, as she herself had done during late Victorian times. John Scott Haldane held progressive social and political views, but the responsibility for bringing up the children was left to their mother. Naomi's elder brother, John (Jack) Burdon Sanderson, born in 1892, who would become the famous geneticist J. B. S. Haldane, was her early role model; as children the two kept guinea pigs in the hope of conducting genetic experiments with them.

Despite the security of her family life the future novelist experienced secret terrors and unidentifiable fears that seem to have caused her a high degree of anguish. She confided them to the historian, poet, and novelist Andrew Lang, one of the many well-known and erudite people who frequented the Haldane circle. Best remembered now for his collections of fairy tales, Lang has been described as a "renegade academic." Although Naomi was only nine when they met, and he was in his sixties, a rapport developed between them, and Naomi never lost interest in the subjects—folklore, magic, and the relationship between humans and animals—that preoccupied him.

When Haldane reached school age, her father held an important academic post at the University of Oxford that enabled her to attend the progressive Dragon School for boys there; a few other girls had recently been admitted. Her life as a writer began in a small way in 1913 when she wrote a play that was performed at the school. When she reached adolescence, her "proper" mother removed her from the school; Naomi could see no reason for the change, and it probably contributed to the feminist beliefs she would come to hold. Nevertheless, she received a sound education at home from a governess. Holidays were spent mainly at the family estate, Cloan, near Auchterarder, Scotland; there were also visits to Cornwall.

After World War I broke out in August 1914, Haldane obtained permission to work as a volunteer nurse at Saint Thomas's Hospital in London, where she was able to see for the first time how people from the less-privileged classes lived out their far-from-easy lives. She was forced to return to Oxford when she caught scarlet fever. She did some volunteer work there and also studied part-time with the Saint Anne's Society at the university, concentrating on physics and botany.

In February 1916 Haldane married Gordon Richard Mitchison, known as Dick; all her writings would be published under her married name. They had become friends two years earlier, and the marriage was more or less arranged by the two families. Later, Naomi Mitchison would describe in her memoirs the astonishing degree of sexual ignorance from which both partners suffered. It seems, however, that she was ready to accept early marriage—usual at the time and even more so because of the war—because she wanted to gain independence from her parents. She was already capable of overruling her parents-in-law by insisting on a quiet wedding and refusing to wear a conventional bridal gown. A week after the wedding her husband was back at the front, where he was badly wounded, but he made a total recovery and became a successful barrister and, later, a Labour member of Parliament for Kettering in Northamptonshire. Their first son, Geoffrey, was born in 1918; he would die of meningitis at the age of nine. There were to be six other children. Fortunately for Naomi, who wanted to concentrate on writing, her mother in Oxford was willing to look after the children at least part of the time while they were young.

In 1919 the family moved to Cheyne Walk in London's Chelsea. There Mitchison began to write her fiction on a piece of board attached to the perambulator in which she wheeled her children through the streets. Her first novel, *The Conquered* (1923), was published by the enterprising Jonathan Cape after many others had rejected it. The book was a risky venture: the author was young and unknown, and the novel, about Julius Caesar's subjection of Gaul between 58 and 46 B.C., followed no fashionable trend. But Mitchison seems to have known from the start of her career how to bring history to life by creating credible characters in believable and vividly described surroundings. The central characters, the young Celt Meromic and his sister Fiommar, are handsome, idealized creatures. Fiommar kills herself on the "last day of freedom"; Meromic's transmutation into a wolf is described in mysterious poetry on the last page. The book was dedicated to Mitchison's brother, who contributed a

*Mitchison with her husband, Richard, and her brother, J. B. S. Haldane, in 1916*

sixteen-line poem that appears at the conclusion of the novel. The story is highly imaginative but has a sound historical basis; Mitchison supplies a brief bibliography that includes Caesar's *De Bello Gallico* (*The Gallic Wars*). The political scientist Ernest Barker, an authority on Irish history, wrote a preface to the novel.

In 1923 the Mitchisons moved into a large house, River Court, in Hammersmith Mall by the Thames, a West London district favored by writers and other intellectuals. Among the friends they acquired there were the writers A. P. Herbert and E. M. Forster. In 1924 she was made an officer of the French Academy. Mitchison's next novel, *Cloud Cuckoo Land* (1925), as well as her story collections *When the Bough Breaks, and Other Stories* (1924) and *Black Sparta: Greek Stories* (1928), deal with the same period of history as her first. In a note to *When the Bough Breaks* she wrote: "Not unnaturally one always used to take sides with the barbarians against Rome—But it's the Northerner, one's possible ancestor, who is really thrilling." These works confront violence in humanity and challenge traditional sexual and social norms.

Mitchison's early sexual ignorance had been overcome by her discovery of the pioneer work by

*Mitchison in 1928 in Greece, where she went to do research for her novel* The Corn King and the Spring Queen *(courtesy of Naomi Mitchison)*

Dr. Marie Stopes, who wrote about birth control and opened a clinic in London. Recognizing the contribution scientific birth control could make to the independence of women, Mitchison became involved in the administration of a similar clinic in North Kensington. She wrote widely on the controversial subject, and she and her husband agreed that they could experience extramarital relationships.

Mitchison's masterwork, the seven-hundred-page novel *The Corn King and the Spring Queen* (1931), takes place between 228 and 187 B.C. and concerns a three-cornered culture clash among Sparta, the other Greek city-states, and a mythical country of Marob on the shores of the Black Sea. The young Erif Der, the Spring Queen, is vital to the culture and survival of Marob; she can work magic and possesses power and independence. The Spartan women, on the other hand, even those from the upper classes, lead lives of repression and subjugation. Themes treated in this exceptionally rich work include the Stoic philosophy and the Spartan attitude to unwanted children. The reader unfamiliar with ancient history will be grateful for the summaries that the author adds after each of the five parts of her book. The novelist Winifred Holtby pronounced *The Corn King and the Spring Queen* the best novel of 1931—a year that also saw the publication of Virginia Woolf's *The Waves*, Pearl S. Buck's *The Good Earth*, William Faulkner's *Sanctuary*, and Victo-

ria Sackville-West's *All Passion Spent*. The book has remained in print since its first appearance, and Mitchison has been ranked with such other outstanding women writers of historical fiction as Mary Renault in Britain and Zoe Oldenbourg and Marguerite Yourcenar in France.

Mitchison joined the Labour Party in 1931. She visited the Soviet Union in 1932 and Austria in 1934 and wrote nonfiction works about her experiences; she also wrote poetry and stories for children. In the distinctly adult novel *We Have Been Warned* (1935) she turns to contemporary issues, using material from her travels to write freely about birth control and sex outside of marriage. Neither Cape nor Victor Gollancz would publish the book; finally, the Constable firm did so after Mitchison reluctantly agreed to some modifications of the more-outspoken passages.

Four years later Constable published *The Blood of the Martyrs,* a novel in which Mitchison compares the early Christians persecuted by Nero to modern-day socialists. The mistake made by both groups, as Mitchison saw it, was to remain too isolated from the rest of society. While she was writing this book, the artist Wyndham Lewis painted a striking portrait of her; her face wears an expression of near-angry concentration.

During the World War II years Mitchison lived mainly in Carradale, a house in Scotland.

There she wrote *The Bull Calves* (1947), her first Scottish historical novel, which deals with the aftermath of the Jacobite rising of 1745. She used the story to express her belief that women could supply vital help in the postwar renaissance of the country. Mitchison herself became involved in the regeneration of the Highlands after the war, a topic she treats in *Lobsters on the Agenda* (1952), about a small westcoast fishing community divided over whether to construct a village hall. In the short-story collection *Five Men and a Swan* (1957) she deals with the prehistory of the human race.

Mitchison saw science fiction as an opportunity to introduce her radical ideas about the role of women in sexual relationships and in society in general. Her first and best-known novel in this genre is *Memoirs of a Spacewoman* (1962), which develops the theme of the interconnectedness of all life forms. It includes a mother-child relationship that is memorable for its intensity and sensuality. Her other science-fiction novels are *Solution Three* (1975); *The Vegetable War* (1980); and *Not by Bread Alone* (1983), which features a lesbian protagonist.

In 1963 Mitchison agreed to become a "mother" to Linchwe, a newly appointed tribal chief in Botswana (formerly the British protectorate of Bechuanaland) whom she had met when he visited Carradale as a student. She made regular trips to Botswana until the late 1960s and wrote often about her experiences, notably in *Return to the Fairy Hill* (1966). Her husband was created a life peer as Baron Mitchison in 1964, but she continued to prefer to be known simply as Naomi Mitchison. Her husband died in 1970.

Mitchison continued to publish novels and short stories into her nineties. In *Early in Orcadia* (1987) she imaginatively reconstructs a journey by neolithic people from Caithness across the Pentland Firth to Orkney. In *A Girl Must Live* (1987), she gathered previously published, as well as unpublished, poems and short stories. She apparently concluded her prolific novel output in 1991 with two short historical quest novels, *The Oath-Takers,* dealing with ninth-century European turmoil, and *Sea-green Ribbons,* about a young woman's attraction to the Levellers in Cromwellian England.

Through her life and work Naomi Mitchison has made a unique contribution to the twentieth century. She received honorary doctorates from Sterling University in 1979 and from Strathclyde University in 1983. An exhibition in celebration of her one-hundredth birthday was mounted by the National University of Scotland in 1997. It is her fiction more than any other aspect of her writing that endows her with classic status.

*Mitchison at ninety-one, in the garden of her home, Carradale, in Scotland (courtesy of Jill Benton)*

**Biographies:**

Jill Benton, *Naomi Mitchison: A Biography. A Century of Experiment in Life and Letters* (London: Pandora, 1990);

Jenni Calder, *The Nine Lives of Naomi Mitchison* (London: Virago, 1997).

**References:**

Beth Dickson, "From Personal to Global: The Fiction of Naomi Mitchison," *Chapman,* 10 (Summer 1987): 34–40;

Sarah Lefann, "Difference and Sexual Politics in Naomi Mitchison's *Solution Three,*" in *Utopian and Science Fiction by Women: Worlds of Difference,* edited by Jane L. Donawerth and Carol A. Kolmerten (Syracuse: Syracuse University Press, 1994), pp. 153–165;

Marilyn K. Nellis, "Anachronistic Humor in Two Arthurian Romances of Education: *To the Chapel Perilous* and *The Sword and the Stone,*" *Studies in Medievalism,* 2 (Fall 1983): 57–77;

Alison Smith, "The Woman from the Big House: The Autobiographical Writings of Naomi Mitchison," *Chapman,* 10 (Summer 1987): 10–17.

# Nancy Mitford

*(28 November 1904 – 30 June 1973)*

Allan Hepburn
*University of Toronto*

BOOKS: *Highland Fling* (London: Butterworth, 1931; revised edition, London: Hamilton, 1951);

*Christmas Pudding* (London: Butterworth, 1932; revised edition, London: Hamilton, 1951);

*Wigs on the Green* (London: Butterworth, 1935);

*Pigeon Pie: A Wartime Receipt* (London: Hamilton, 1940; New York: British Book Center, 1959);

*The Pursuit of Love: A Novel* (London: Hamilton, 1945; New York: Random House, 1946);

*Love in a Cold Climate* (London: Hamilton, 1949; New York: Random House, 1949);

*The Blessing* (London: Hamilton, 1951; New York: Random House, 1951);

*Madame de Pompadour* (London: Hamilton, 1954; New York: Random House, 1954; revised edition, London: Hamilton, 1968; New York: Harper & Row, 1968);

*The Nancy Mitford Omnibus* (London: Hamilton, 1956)–comprises *The Pursuit of Love, Love in a Cold Climate, The Blessing*;

*Voltaire in Love* (London: Hamilton, 1957; New York: Harper, 1957);

*Don't Tell Alfred* (London: Hamilton, 1960; New York: Harper, 1961);

*The Water Beetle* (London: Hamilton, 1962; New York: Harper & Row, 1962);

*The Sun King* (London: Hamilton, 1966; New York: Harper & Row, 1966);

*Frederick the Great* (London: Hamilton, 1970; New York: Harper, 1970);

*A Talent to Annoy: Essays, Articles and Reviews 1929–1968,* edited by Charlotte Mosley (London: Hamilton, 1986).

**Collection:** *The Best Novels of Nancy Mitford* (London: Hamilton, 1974)–comprises *The Pursuit of Love, Love in a Cold Climate, The Blessing, Don't Tell Alfred.*

PLAY PRODUCTION: André Roussin, *The Little Hut,* translated by Mitford, Edinburgh, Lyceum Theatre, August 1950.

*Nancy Mitford around 1948*

OTHER: *The Ladies of Alderley: Being the Letters between Maria Josephs, Lady Stanley of Alderley, and Her Daughter-in-Law, Henrietta Maria Stanley, during the Years 1841–1850,* edited by Mitford (London: Chapman & Hall, 1938);

*The Stanleys of Alderley: Their Letters between the Years 1851–1865,* edited by Mitford (London: Chapman & Hall, 1939);

Marie Madaleine Pioche de la Veigne, Comtesse de La Fayette, *The Princesse de Clèves,* translated, with a preface, by Mitford (London: Euphorion, 1950);

André Roussin, *The Little Hut,* translated by Mitford (London: Hamilton, 1951);

Alan S. C. Ross and others, *Noblesse Oblige: An Enquiry into the Identifiable Characteristics of the English Aristocracy*, edited, with contributions, by Mitford (London: Hamilton, 1956; New York: Harper, 1956).

Although Nancy Mitford claimed in *The Water Beetle* (1962) to remember "almost nothing" about her childhood—"It is shrouded in a thick mist which seldom lifts except on the occasion of some public event"—she plundered material from her life for her eight comic novels. To tease her friends and family she often cast them as characters in her fictional plots; for instance, her irascible father appears as the wrathful General Murgatroyd in *Highland Fling* (1931) and the volatile Uncle Matthew in *The Pursuit of Love* (1945). Not just transformed autobiographies, Mitford's novels define a style that combines physical humor, verbal sharpness, and the high-society glamor of the decades immediately before and after World War II. Like her friend Evelyn Waugh, Mitford satirizes the pretensions and shortcomings of the aristocracy; the heroines of her novels are both upper class and hopelessly gullible.

The daughter of David Bertram Ogilvy Freeman Mitford and Sydney Bowles Mitford, Nancy Freeman Mitford was born on 28 November 1904 at 1 Graham Street, Chelsea, London. Her grandfather, Algernon Bertram Freeman Mitford, an ambassador to Russia and Japan, had been created Baron Redesdale in 1902 for his service to the British Empire; David Mitford succeeded to the title when his father died in 1916. The family owned extensive property and a Georgian house in Gloucestershire, where Nancy grew up.

The eldest of the Mitford children, and the only one with dark hair in a family of blonds, Nancy tyrannized her five sisters and one brother. Her sister Jessica remembered: "She might suddenly turn her penetrating emerald eyes in one's direction and say, 'Run along up to the schoolroom: we've all had quite enough of you.'" Mitford received little formal education; she proudly claimed later in life that all she acquired in the way of instruction as a child was a knowledge of French and an ability to ride. She attended a finishing school, Hatherop Castle, which emphasized "feminine" gentility rather than intellectual inquiry. The highlight of her school experience was a trip to the Continent in 1922 that inaugurated a lifelong love affair with France.

In 1925 Mitford made her London debut. Living on an allowance of £125 a year from her father, she entered the smart set of London that established standards of taste and hedonism for the 1920s. In the company of aesthetes, lords, homosexuals, Oxo-

nians, and debutantes Mitford dashed from nightclubs to house parties and from house parties to country houses. From 1928 until 1933 she was engaged to James Alexander (Hamish) St. Clair Erskine, the second son of the earl of Rosslyn and a member of the set known as the "Bright Young Things." They shared a fondness for party-going and high jinks but quarreled over Erskine's drinking, debts, and irresponsibility; she insisted in a letter of 17 April 1930 that he was "pure gold" under his "ghastly exterior." The relationship ended when Erskine unexpectedly announced his engagement to another woman.

Erskine appears as the suave artist Albert Gates in *Highland Fling,* Mitford's first novel. The work dramatizes the battles of the avant-garde against the old guard, represented by younger and older generations, respectively. After two years of painting in Paris, Albert returns to London and is whisked into the club-hopping society of his friends Walter and Sally Monteath, who spend far more money than they have. These "Bright Young People" traipse off to Dalloch Castle in Scotland when the Monteaths' relatives ask them to preside at a hunting season in the Highlands. Jane Dacre accompanies them and falls madly in love with the epicene Albert. While the older generation loathes the clutter of nineteenth-century decor, the Bright Young People admire its lavishness. Albert discovers boundless Victorian treasures in the castle and spends his time photographing them, to the great consternation of General Murgatroyd, Lord and Lady Prague, and other elderly philistines. Albert goes out of his way to irritate them by wearing orange clothes and rhapsodizing about Victorian paintings. Dalloch Castle burns to the ground, provoking despair in Albert and delight in the philistines, who hate the "rubbish" of the last century.

The plot turns on the upper hand taken by women in the marriage game. "I'd no idea women—nice ones, you know—ever proposed to men, unless for some very good reason," Walter says to Sally when she proposes to him in a taxicab. Jane, too, has to woo the indifferent Albert, who lives for pleasures other than matrimonial ones. Jane sees marriage mainly as an opportunity to upset her family: "Marriage had always seemed to her rather a dull and pompous business, but to run away to Paris as the mistress of a handsome young artist would be the height of romance, and would properly scandalize her parents and relatives." The novel ends with the arrival of prenuptial gifts and a postponement of the wedding by Jane.

The marriage of Mitford's sister Diana to Bryan Guinness, scion of the beer fortune, had been

*Mitford at her wedding to Peter Rodd on 4 December 1933*

the society wedding of 1929. Nancy, a bridesmaid, wrote up the event for *Vogue* magazine (6 March 1929) and recycled the material in *Highland Fling*. In her essay, "The Secret History of a London Wedding," she decries the horror of wedding presents such as "a silver soup tureen that might have come out of an ogre's castle, a beaten brass tray, and cut glass and bubble glass so dreadful that it has to be seen to be believed." A similar mound of hideous presents fills the home of Jane's parents in *Highland Fling*.

Mitford's second book, *Christmas Pudding* (1932), is another "country house" novel. The spiteful, elegant, gossipy Sir Roderick (Bobby) Bobbin, a student at Eton, manipulates his mother into hiring the novelist Paul Fotheringay to tutor him over the Christmas holidays. Fotheringay arrives at the family's Gloucestershire estate, Compton Bobbin, under false pretenses. He has no interest in Bobby's education but wants to peruse the diary and papers of the illustrious Victorian poet Lady Maria Bobbin; Bobby's mother, the granddaughter of Lady Maria, had refused to give him access to the materials. The ruse works because it has the participation of Amabelle, a courtesan who has risen to become a refined salon hostess. Amabelle, who has more than a pass-

ing knowledge of the arts of seduction, says that she has never believed in true love although she fears that it may exist. Nobody, she says, falls in love only once in a lifetime; marriage is a practicality, not a romantic torrent of passion. This is true of most marriages in Mitford's comedic novels: the laughter depends on the recognition that love is an illusion and that marriage merely consolidates strategic alliances or wins a good livelihood. In *Christmas Pudding* the frumpy Philadelphia Bobbin, Bobby's sister, learns that the bright young novelist Fotheringay cannot be trusted and that she may as well rely on the boring Lord Lewes, who will bring her millions but no passion. "'When one's friends marry for money they are wretched, when they marry for love it is worse,'" Paul says. "'What is the proper thing to marry for, I should like to know?'"

On 4 December 1933 Mitford married Peter Murray Rennell Rodd. Nicknamed "Prod," Rodd was the son of the distinguished diplomat, linguist, and classical scholar Sir Rennell Rodd but had inherited none of his father's talents. Peter Rodd lived a dissolute and transient life, drifting from job to job. His philandering and prodigality cast Mitford on her own resources throughout their marriage.

Given the political frenzy of the 1930s, it is not surprising that Mitford followed the fashion of her generation and wrote a political satire, *Wigs on the Green* (1935). Noel Foster and Jasper Aspect leave London in search of wives. Noel is pursuing the richest heiress in England, Eugenia Malmains, who has become a propagandist for the fascist Union Jack Movement. Jasper meets another heiress, Poppy St. Julien, who has run away from home and assumed a false identity. Noel ultimately returns, unmarried, to London; Jasper marries Poppy. The novel ends with a free-for-all between the Union Jack contingent and an artistic, pacifist group led by Anne-Marie Lace. Eugenia is based on Mitford's sister Unity, who belonged to Adolf Hitler's circle of acquaintances. When Baron and Lady Redesdale visited Munich in 1938, Unity took them to tea with Hitler; afterward, Baron Redesdale defended Hitler in the House of Lords. Unity attempted suicide on the day war between Germany and England was declared in 1939. Hitler had her transported to Switzerland, and her mother and her sister Deborah brought her back to England. In 1936 Diana Mitford, after divorcing Bryan Guinness, had married Sir Oswald Mosley, leader of the British Union of Fascists; the fascist rallies in *Wigs on the Green* are based on Mosley's demonstrations. While Mitford's parents and her sisters Unity and Diana had fascist tendencies, Jessica Mitford moved to the United States and became a communist. As Selina Hastings

*Mitford (second from left) with her family in 1934: mother, Sydney Bowles Mitford, Lady Redesdale;
sisters Diana and Unity; brother, Tom; sisters Pamela and Jessica; father, David Bertram Ogilvy
Freeman Mitford, Lord Redesdale; sister Deborah*

writes in her 1985 biography of Mitford, "Nancy remained all her life politically immature, her opinions too frivolous and too subjective to be taken seriously—a limitation which restrained her not at all in the airing of these opinions." At times a socialist, at other times a republican, Mitford eschewed the extremist beliefs of her fascist and communist sisters. Later she would want to distance herself from *Wigs on the Green,* writing Waugh on 8 November 1951: "Too much has happened for jokes about Nazis to be regarded as funny or as anything but the worst of taste."

Sophia Garfield, the blithe heroine of Mitford's fourth novel, *Pigeon Pie: A Wartime Receipt* (1940), is forced by her well-to-do businessman husband to entertain members of The Brotherhood, a religious cult to which he belongs. Sophia falls in love with Rudolph Jocelyn, who, for amusement, attends the lavish weekend parties the Garfields give for The Brotherhood. To help in the war effort she volunteers at a hospital, where "emergencies" are just drills. Her dear friend and godfather, Sir Ivor King, a beloved singer and wearer of tatty wigs, disappears; soon he begins broadcasting Nazi propaganda to England, apparently having defected to Germany. Sophia's German maid also disappears

under mysterious circumstances. On the evening that the maid's body is found in the drain beneath the hospital, Sophia discovers that Sir Ivor is not in Germany at all but has been abducted by German infiltrators and forced to make the nightly broadcasts from her own house. After Sophia's bulldog is taken hostage by the Germans, Sophia commits some clever counterespionage, such as sneaking a message to Rudolph and following a trail of curls that have fallen from Sir Ivor's wig. The novel satirizes underground brotherhoods, communist sympathizers, spy novels, and sentimental attachment to pets. Published only four days before the German invasion of Holland and Belgium, the novel disappeared without a trace. The comic treatment of air raids and German infiltration of England caused Mitford to add a prefatory remark to a 1952 reprint of the novel in which she pointed out that it had been written during the Phony War, when such possibilities were not taken seriously.

During the war Mitford worked in Heywood Hill's bookstore and volunteered at a first-aid post at St. Mary's Hospital in Paddington. In September 1942 she met Gaston Palewski, a diplomat who was representing Charles De Gaulle's Free French forces in London, and began an affair with him. After the

*Dust jackets for two of Mitford's novels and
a biography*

war "the Colonel," as Mitford called Palewski, was named *chef de cabinet* in De Gaulle's provisional government. In 1945 Mitford invested £5,000 she had received from her father in Hill's bookshop, negotiating a partnership in which she would serve as a buyer of French literature for his store. She spent three months in Paris at the end of the year, ostensibly purchasing books but really waiting for Palewski to make some time for her in his hectic schedule.

Palewski served as the model for all of Mitford's glamorous French heroes, including Fabrice de Sauveterre in *The Pursuit of Love*. Published in December 1945, the novel marks a newfound maturity in Mitford's writing. Linda Radlett first marries a dull banker and then a dedicated communist. Having failed in both marriages, she is weeping atop her luggage outside the Gare du Nord in Paris when "a short, stocky, very dark Frenchman in a black Homburg hat" laughs at her. The stranger, de Sauveterre, sweeps Linda into a tempestuous affair, installing her in an apartment as his mistress. He then proceeds to pop into and out of her life with maddening irregularity. With the outbreak of World War II Fabrice becomes involved in the Resistance, and Linda has to return to London. *The Pursuit of Love* is narrated by Fanny Logan, Linda's cousin. Fanny's mother, "the Bolter," cannot settle down with one man and leaves Fanny housed with her cousins, a batch of high-spirited girls closely resembling the Mitford sisters, and her Uncle Matthew, who, like Mitford's father, bellows and storms at the slightest provocation.

Mitford moved permanently to Paris in 1946, taking up residence at 7, rue Monsieur. Palewski refused to marry her on the grounds that her status as a divorcée would ruin him politically; he probably also feared that Mitford's name would conjure up memories of Unity Mitford's friendship with Hitler. Mitford complained to her sister Diana in a letter dated 29 June 1948 that she was forced to behave like a character in a farce: "When I go round to the Colonel's flat it is like some dreadful spy film & I end by being shut up in a cupboard or hiding on the escalier de service & being found by the concierge—so undignified I nearly die of it—apart from the fact that the whole of the time is taken up by these antics & I get about 5 restless minutes of his company!"

After moving to Paris, Mitford corresponded regularly with Waugh, who counseled her on plot details for *The Pursuit of Love* and suggested the novel's title. In a letter of 24 October 1948 he recommended that she rewrite her next novel, *Love in a Cold Climate* (1949). "Most of the minor characters are flops," he said, advising her to "start again." Mitford was right not to follow his suggestion: the sequel to *The Pursuit of Love* was a million-copy bestseller as well as a critical success. Narrated again by Fanny, *Love in a Cold Climate* follows the fortunes of Polly, one of the richest heiresses in England. Polly's mother, Lady Montdore, wants to marry her off to a worthy gentleman. To spite her mother, Polly marries Boy Dougdale, who is several decades older than she and had previously been Lady Montdore's lover. Polly and Boy travel on the Continent to avoid the wrath of Lady Montdore. Disinherited and out of love with her husband, Polly finally returns to England. Through the offices of Cedric Hampton, a distant Canadian cousin and brilliant gossip, harmony is restored among Boy, Polly, and Lady Montdore. Polly takes a lover while Cedric, Boy, and Lady Montdore motor off to France.

Cedric is the great comic creation of *Love in a Cold Climate*. He enters Hampton Court like a giant insect and tosses himself abjectly at the feet of the Montdores, from whom he expects to inherit a monumental fortune:

> A glitter of blue and gold crossed the parquet, and a human dragon-fly was kneeling on the fur rug in front of the Montdores, one long white hand extended towards each. He was a tall, thin young man, supple as a girl, dressed in rather a bright blue suit. . . . "Don't speak," he said, "just for a moment. Just let me go on looking at you—wonderful, wonderful people!"

A connoisseur of face creams and diets, jewels and wainscoting, Cedric throws Lady Montdore into paroxysms of pleasure. He makes her lose weight and beautify herself until she looks like a young girl. He also recommends that she fix an expression of delight on her face by uttering the word *brush* before entering a room. A busybody with a tender spot for animals, Cedric combines the qualities of Mitford's many homosexual friends, including her companion Mark Ogilvie-Grant and her former fiancé, Erskine. In his letter of 24 October 1948 Waugh had particularly sneered at the "Parisian pansy." Writing to Waugh on 11 January 1949, Mitford admitted that American readers objected to her unabashed portrayal of Cedric's homosexuality: "*The Woman's Home Journal* says he is revolting & that neither they nor any other American mag will touch him." On 20 January she wrote Waugh: "It seems in America you can have pederasts in books so long as they are fearfully gloomy & end by committing suiãide. A cheerful one who goes from strength to strength like Cedric horrifies them." Mitford's inclusion of openly homosexual characters in her novels was a daring move in the 1940s.

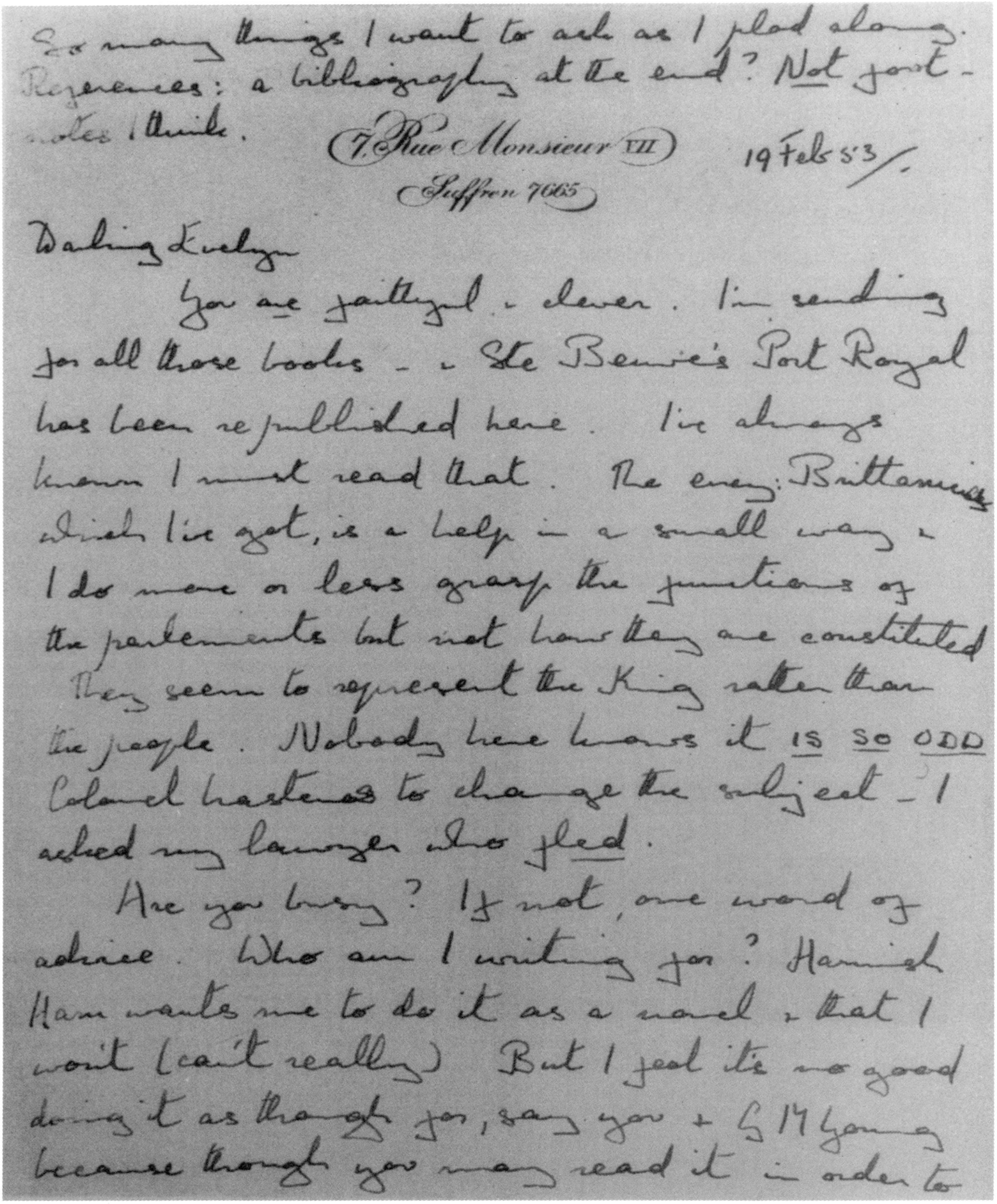

So many things I want to ask as I plod along.
References: a bibliography at the end? <u>Not</u> foot-
notes I think.

*7 Rue Monsieur VII)*
*Suffren 7665*                          19 Feb 53/.

Darling Evelyn

You are faithful & clever. I'm sending
for all those books — & Ste Beuve's Port Royal
has been re published here. I've always
known I must read that. The ency: Brittanica
which I've got, is a help in a small way &
I do more or less grasp the functions of
the parlements but not how they are constituted
They seem to represent the King rather than
the people. Nobody here knows it <u>IS SO ODD</u>
Colonel hastens to change the subject — I
asked my lawyer who <u>fled</u>.

Are you busy? If not, one word of
advice. Who am I writing for? Hamish
Ham wants me to do it as a novel & that I
won't (can't really) But I feel it's no good
doing it as though for, say you & G M Young
because though you may read it in order to

*Page of a letter from Mitford to Evelyn Waugh, asking for advice on her* Madame de Pompadour *(British Library)*

234

Mitford's passion for France is evident in her novel *The Blessing* (1951). In 1940 Grace Allingham, an Englishwoman, marries an energetic Frenchman, Charles-Edouard de Valhubert. Valhubert disappears for the next seven years, leaving Grace to bring up their son, Sigi. Reunited in 1947, the family moves to Valhubert's country home in Provence. Grace is subjected to the merciless scrutiny of relatives and the local clergyman but seems not to notice, so entranced is she with French literature, landscapes, and life. Unwilling to accept Valhubert's infidelities, Grace leaves him. Sigi, who imagines that he will receive double the affection and gifts if his parents remain separated, contrives to keep them apart; but his schemes are exposed, and Grace and her husband are reunited. Grace has to relinquish the English notion of romantic exclusivity and accept French promiscuity.

The place of the unmarried woman is a persistent motif in Mitford's biographies, which, except for her final one, *Frederick the Great* (1970), have French subjects. Her first biography, *Madame de Pompadour* (1954), documents the sway of Louis XV's mistress over the court at Versailles; the political battles and intrigues of the court ultimately reflect Madame de Pompadour's romantic hold on Louis's affections. Mitford says that Madame de Pompadour's "politics will not give much satisfaction to the feminist. . . . To her, as to most women, politics were a question of personalities."

Mitford provoked a public outcry in September 1955 with her article "The English Aristocracy" in *Encounter* magazine. The piece shows how verbal signs betray class: for instance, a speaker of "U" (upper-class) English eats "vegetables," while a "non-U" speaker eats "greens"; the U speaker rides a "bike," the non-U speaker a "cycle"; someone with a great deal of money is "rich" to the U speaker, "wealthy" to one who speaks non-U English. The article had many people checking their vocabularies with alarm to see whether they were aristocratic in speech, if not in title; many others were miffed by what they took to be Mitford's elitist attitude. The essay, which was actually intended as a "tease," was included the following year in a volume edited by Mitford under the title *Noblesse Oblige;* the book sold fourteen thousand copies in a few months in Britain and ten thousand copies in a week in the United States.

In her second biography, *Voltaire in Love* (1957), Mitford shows that the writer's mistress, Emilie, the Marquise du Châtelet, compelled him to defy kings to prove his love for her. The work opens: "The love of Voltaire and the Marquise du

*Mitford's lover, the French diplomat Count Gaston Palewski*

Châtelet was not an ordinary love. They were not ordinary people."

Palewski was appointed ambassador to Italy in 1957, serving until 1962; the Romans dubbed him "l'Embrassadeur" for his libertine behavior. Mitford and Rodd had been separated for many years; in December 1957 he finally asked for a divorce, and she agreed.

Palewski's ambassadorship was part of the inspiration for Mitford's final novel, *Don't Tell Alfred* (1960). Fanny, the narrator of *The Pursuit of Love* and *Love in a Cold Climate,* finds herself relocated to the British embassy in Paris when her husband, Alfred Wincham, an Oxford don, is appointed ambassador. Fanny has to face a series of crises: the former ambassador's wife (modeled on Mitford's friend Diana Cooper, the wife of the former ambassador to France, Duff Cooper) refuses to leave the premises; Fanny's errant son arrives with his pregnant girlfriend; her assistant, Northey, is beset by French suitors and is constantly breaking into tears. Mitford's anti-Americanism is reflected in the portrait of the yawning bore, Hector Dexter, a double agent who returns to the West because he cannot bear life in the Soviet bloc. The running joke in *Don't Tell Al-*

*Mitford in the garden of her home at 4, rue d'Artois, Versailles, in 1971 (photograph by Roger Gain,* Sunday Times, *London)*

*fred* is that the embassy is really run not by the ambassador but by Fanny, who resolves the crises without letting Alfred know that anything is wrong.

Mitford remained devoted to Palewski through his many infidelities, and the theme of abiding love is central to her biography *The Sun King* (1966):

"Louis XIV fell in love with Versailles and Louise de La Vallière at the same time; Versailles was the love of his life." Mitford herself fell in love with the former home of the French court; in January 1967 she moved from the rue Monsieur to a house at 4, rue d'Artois in Versailles. In 1969, without informing Mitford beforehand, Palewski married Violette de Talleyrand-Perigord, the Duchesse de Sagan. Nevertheless, Mitford and Palewski remained on friendly terms until her death.

For the last four years of her life Mitford suffered intense pain from a rare form of Hodgkin's disease. In 1972 she was awarded the Legion of Honor by the French government and appointed a Commander of the British Empire. She died at her home in Versailles on 30 June 1973 and was buried in the Cotswolds.

Nancy Mitford is notable for her insistence on maintaining a comic vision in her novels throughout such trying times as the Great Depression, World War II, and the Cold War. In her novels she poked fun at eccentricity, protocol, and self-deception.

### Letters:

*The Letters of Evelyn Waugh,* edited by Mark Amory (New Haven & New York: Ticknor & Fields, 1980);

*Love from Nancy: The Letters of Nancy Mitford,* edited by Charlotte Mosley (London: Hodder & Stoughton, 1993; New York: Houghton Mifflin, 1993).

### Biographies:

Harold Acton, *Nancy Mitford: A Memoir* (London: Hamilton, 1975);

Jonathan Guinness and Catherine Guinness, *The House of Mitford* (London: Hutchinson, 1984);

Selina Hastings, *Nancy Mitford* (London: Hamilton, 1985).

### Papers:

The bulk of Nancy Mitford's papers are held by her literary executor, the duchess of Devonshire, at Chatsworth.

# Edwin Muir
## (15 May 1887 – 3 January 1959)

Raymond N. MacKenzie
*University of St. Thomas*

See also the Muir entries in *DLB 20: British Poets, 1914–1945* and *DLB 100: Modern British Essayists, Second Series.*

BOOKS: *We Moderns: Enigmas and Guesses,* as Edward Moore (London: Allen & Unwin, 1918); as Muir (New York: Knopf, 1920);

*Latitudes* (London: Melrose, 1924; New York: Huebsch, 1924);

*First Poems* (London: Hogarth Press, 1925; New York: Huebsch, 1925);

*Chorus of the Newly Dead* (London: Hogarth Press, 1926);

*Transition: Essays on Contemporary Literature* (London: Hogarth Press, 1926; New York: Viking, 1926);

*The Marionette* (London: Hogarth Press, 1927; New York: Viking, 1927);

*The Structure of the Novel* (London: Hogarth Press, 1928; New York: Harcourt, Brace, 1929);

*John Knox: Portrait of a Calvinist* (London: Cape, 1929; New York: Viking, 1929);

*The Three Brothers* (London: Heinemann, 1931; New York: Doubleday, Doran, 1931);

*Poor Tom* (London: Dent, 1932);

*Six Poems* (Warlingham, Surrey: Samson, 1932);

*Variations on a Time Theme* (London: Dent, 1934);

*Scottish Journey* (London: Heinemann/Gollancz, 1935);

*Social Credit and the Labour Party: An Appeal* (London: Nott, 1935);

*Scott and Scotland: The Predicament of the Scottish Writer* (London: Routledge, 1936; New York: Speller, 1938);

*Journeys and Places* (London: Dent, 1937);

*The Present Age from 1914,* volume 5 of *Introductions to English Literature,* edited by Bonomy Dubrée (London: Cresset, 1939; New York: McBride, 1940);

*The Story and the Fable: An Autobiography* (London: Harrap, 1940); revised and enlarged as *An Autobiography* (London: Hogarth Press, 1954; New York: Sloane, 1954);

*Edwin Muir (photograph by Mark Gerson)*

*The Narrow Place* (London: Faber & Faber, 1943);

*The Voyage and Other Poems* (London: Faber & Faber, 1946);

*The Scots and Their Country* (London: Longmans, Green, 1946);

*The Politics of King Lear* (Glasgow: Jackson, 1947; New York: Haskell House, 1970);

*Essays on Literature and Society* (London: Hogarth Press, 1949; revised and enlarged, 1965; Cambridge, Mass.: Harvard University Press, 1965);

*The Labyrinth* (London: Faber & Faber, 1949; Folcroft, Pa.: Folcroft, 1977);

*Collected Poems, 1921–1951,* edited by J. C. Hall (London: Faber & Faber, 1952; New York: Grove, 1953);

*Prometheus* (London: Faber & Faber, 1954);

*One Foot in Eden* (London: Faber & Faber, 1956; New York: Grove, 1956);

*Collected Poems, 1921–1958,* edited by Hall and Willa Muir (London: Faber & Faber, 1960; revised and enlarged, 1963; New York: Oxford University Press, 1965);

*The Estate of Poetry* (London: Hogarth Press, 1962; Cambridge, Mass.: Harvard University Press, 1962);

*Selected Poems,* edited by T. S. Eliot (London: Faber & Faber, 1965);

*Uncollected Scottish Criticism,* edited by Andrew Noble (London: Vision, 1982; Totowa, N.J.: Barnes & Noble, 1982);

*Selected Prose,* edited by George Mackay Brown (London: John Murray, 1987);

*The Truth of Imagination: Some Uncollected Reviews and Essays,* edited by Peter H. Butter (Aberdeen: Aberdeen University Press, 1988);

*The Complete Poems of Edwin Muir,* edited by Butter (Aberdeen: Association for Scottish Literary Studies, 1991).

**Editions:** *Poor Tom,* introduction by Peter H. Butter (Edinburgh: Harris, 1982);

*The Marionette,* afterword by Paul Binding (London: Hogarth Press, 1987).

TRANSLATIONS: Lion Feuchtwanger, *Jew Süss,* translated by Muir and Willa Muir (London: Secker, 1926); translation republished as *Power* (New York: Viking, 1926);

Franz Kafka, *The Castle,* translated by Muir and Willa Muir (London: Secker, 1930; New York: Knopf, 1930);

Kafka, *The Great Wall of China and Other Pieces,* translated by Muir and Willa Muir (London: Secker, 1933);

Kafka, *The Trial,* translated by Muir and Willa Muir (London: Gollancz, 1937; New York: Knopf, 1937);

Kafka, *America,* translated by Muir and Willa Muir (London: Routledge, 1938; New York: New Directions, 1946).

Edwin Muir's reputation today rests primarily on his poetry and secondarily on his criticism, autobiography, and translations. Between 1927 and 1932, however, he wrote three novels that served his personal purposes by developing his writing ability and by allowing him to confront, understand, and exorcize some inner conflicts that had gnawed at him since his youth. None of these novels received much critical acclaim, and none sold particularly well, but all have qualities that will amply repay the modern reader who seeks them out. They are highly unusual and fundamentally experimental works that communicate some of the intellectual excitement that Muir felt in writing them.

The youngest of six children, Muir was born on Pomona, the largest of the Orkney Islands, on 15 May 1887 to James Muir, a tenant farmer, and Elizabeth Cormack Muir. When Edwin was two the family moved to Wyre, one of the smallest of the islands, on which there were only seven farms. Muir grew up in an environment that, he says in *An Autobiography* (1954), was essentially no different from the way it had been hundreds of years before, with scarcely any visible traces of the modern world. The isolation, the windswept and barren landscape, and the surrounding sea combined to work on the boy's imagination and to make his childhood a mythlike experience. He says in *An Autobiography* that "the Orkney I was born into was a place where there was no great distinction between the ordinary and the fabulous; the lives of living men turned into legend." The family's beliefs were strongly tinged with Calvinism, and the Muirs participated in the waves of religious revival that swept the islands during the first ten years or so of Edwin's life; but for the young Muir the landscape, the open sky, and the farm animals—some gentle and some, such as the horses, frightening but beautiful and mysterious—seemed to offer a more benign view of God's creation than the one that was presented at the revival meetings.

Throughout his life Muir would return frequently to the Orkneys, both in person and in his novels and poetry. The archetypal story that recurs throughout his work, especially his poetry, is that of the expulsion from Eden; clearly, tiny Wyre played the role of his personal Eden. George Marshall has demonstrated that during Muir's childhood the Orkneys were, in fact, much less idyllic than he paints them; they were undergoing many painful transitions as they moved toward the twentieth century. But for Muir, apparently, the dislocations and upheavals were much less memorable than the Edenic peace he recalled. His family, though poor, was close-knit; his parents seemed to him to be "fixed allegorical figures in a timeless landscape."

James Muir's farming on Wyre did not satisfy his landlord, and when Edwin was eleven the family moved back to Pomona to work a farm near the village of Kirkwall. Two years later his father gave up farming, and the family moved into the town. Their financial condition continued to worsen, and in 1901 they moved to Glasgow; Muir's two older brothers already had gone there to work.

The move to Glasgow was an uprooting from which Muir never fully recovered. Although the family moved into a relatively comfortable flat, the surrounding poverty, the harshness and noise, and the street violence were deeply disturbing to him. His formal schooling had ended by the age of fourteen, and he took a succession of clerking jobs. He spoke later of Glasgow as an abyss into which his family sank, one by one, along with the happiness and rightness of his youth. During their first year there his father died; less than a year later Muir's elder brother Willie was diagnosed with tuberculosis, and he, too, died. Soon afterward his brother Johnnie began complaining of headaches, which turned out to be symptoms of a brain tumor. Almost immediately after Johnnie's death, their mother fell ill; she died a few months later. Muir himself was sick much of the time—which kept him from passing the physical examination for military service during World War I—and suffered from depression. One of his worst experiences came when, to get out of Glasgow, he took a job at a bone-rendering factory in the town of Fairport; his memories of the place would include rotting meat, the smell of burned bones, and maggots. The contrast with his Edenic Orkney could not have been more complete. He began to experience panic attacks that included a sense that inanimate objects could come forward somehow and do him harm.

Looking for a way to strengthen himself mentally, he wrote to A. R. Orage, editor of the magazine *New Age,* asking for advice on reading matter; Orage suggested works by several authors, including the German philosopher Friedrich Nietzsche. Nietzsche soon became Muir's intellectual hero, helping him to slough off what remained of the religious beliefs in which he had never found much comfort and to develop a stoic outlook. He began to write aphorisms and brief essays in imitation of Nietzsche, and Orage published them. Muir soon collected enough such writings to publish a book, *We Moderns: Enigmas and Guesses* (1918), for which he used the pseudonym Edward Moore.

In the winter of 1918, shortly after *We Moderns* came out, Muir met Wilhelmina (Willa) Anderson. She had a sense of certainty and an inner strength that were gradually communicated to Muir, putting an end to the spiral of misery on which he had entered when he came to Glasgow. They married on 7 June 1919 and moved to London.

Over the next few years Muir produced a stream of essays and reviews that made his name known in both England and America. In 1921 he and Willa went to the Continent, living in Prague and Dresden and traveling in Austria and Italy. He

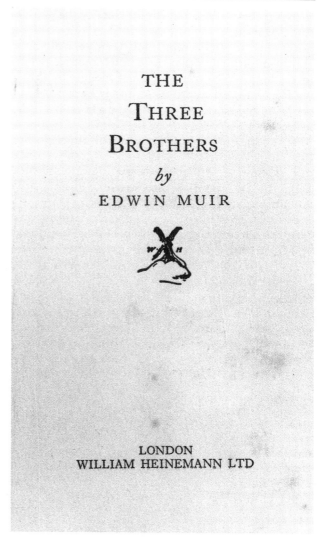

THE
THREE
BROTHERS
*by*
EDWIN MUIR

LONDON
WILLIAM HEINEMANN LTD

*Title page for Muir's novel about the conflicts within the
Blackadder family in Scotland*

learned German, and with Willa, who had already mastered the language, began translating German novels—an activity that would help pay many of their bills over the ensuing years. They moved back to England in 1924; Muir's first book of criticism, *Latitudes,* appeared that year, and his *First Poems* was published in 1925. The Muirs moved to Saint-Tropez in 1926; in 1927 they returned to England, where their son, Gavin, was born in October. In 1927 Muir also published his first novel, *The Marionette,* a work he had begun planning in Austria in 1924.

*The Marionette* is an odd and disturbing book; it was heavily influenced by Muir's reading of the writings of Johann Wolfgang von Goethe, as well as by the general atmosphere of modernist German fiction. The story takes place in modern Salzburg, but there are few details that would identify the place or time. Martin, a well-to-do widower, virtually ignores his feeble-minded fourteen-year-old son, Hans, until the day that their housekeeper, Emma, forces him to take some notice of the boy by thrusting Hans into his study. After this awkward encounter Martin decides to try to bring Hans out of his fantasy world. He takes the boy on walks, which at first are frightening experiences for Hans: to him the natural world is "a terrifying heraldry," a chaotic assemblage of threatening and ominous signs and animals. Muir's narrative style, while objective and unsentimental, is highly effective in conveying the boy's consciousness, which is at various times tortured and uncomprehending, childishly pleased, and filled with incoherent rage. Martin takes Hans to the marionette theater, where he has arranged for a private showing. He hopes that the show will help to bring Hans out of his shell; but the reader, who is privy to Hans's mental processes, realizes that the boy's fascination is rooted in incomprehension: Hans half believes that the marionettes are living creatures. The show put on for the boy is a miniature version of Goethe's *Faust* (1808, 1832), and the father arranges with the owner for Hans to take home the marionette of Gretchen. Hans's perception of reality becomes more confused than ever—just the opposite of what his father had intended. He imagines that he is Faust and begins wearing clothes like those of the Faust marionette, and he falls pathetically in love with the Gretchen figure. But the marionette never comes to life as it had in the show, and Hans's frustration is accompanied by feelings of anger and guilt. Seeing his reflection in a mirror, he begins to believe that there is a second Hans, the one in the mirror, who lives happily with a real Gretchen. He vividly imagines the world where the other Hans lives; it is a duplication of his own world but happier and more peaceful.

Some neighborhood boys find him wearing his Faust suit in the garden and taunt him; overcome with shame, he tries to undo his fantasy by avoiding the clothes and the Gretchen marionette. But he returns to the puppet one day and, in one of the most disturbing sequences in the novel, undresses it. Seeing that it is built just like his other dolls, he puts it back in its box. But soon afterward he returns and tries desperately to recapture his vision of a real Gretchen. He dons the Faust suit once more, recites some lines from the play, and undresses the marionette again. In an effort to get Gretchen to speak to him, he beats the marionette and tears off one of its limbs; then, feeling an "evil resolve" grow in him, he hammers a nail into its head. He believes that he has

destroyed Gretchen and the "other" Hans as well. But then he finds dead Gretchens everywhere, as numberless as the leaves in the garden, all of them killed by him. He breaks down completely, and his father finds him naked, beating his head against the garden wall.

Soon Hans has a healing dream in which Gretchen comes to life. His father repairs the marionette, but Hans declares that he is no longer interested in it. The story ends ambiguously; the final paragraph suggests both gain and loss:

> Hans is at present between twenty and thirty. He is less afraid of people than he used to be, and may be seen, with his father, tramping the less frequented roads near Salzburg. Through long association father and son have come to resemble each other in their gestures and ways of speech. Emma alone has remained unaltered.

Hans's fantasy world has been shattered, and he has become more "normal," but the agony he has had to endure makes the reader wonder if the change has been worth it. And the hinted alteration in the father suggests that the endeavor has been costly for both of them.

*The Marionette* includes some autobiographical elements: Hans's fears and anxieties are informed by those Muir had experienced in Glasgow, and his dreams and visionary experiences sometimes echo dreams Muir wrote about later in his autobiography. Clearly, Muir was projecting himself into the character of the idiot boy Hans. But the many literary and religious parallels and allusions in the book suggest larger meanings. Muir wanted the work to be read allegorically, as he said in a letter of 10 November 1926 to the American publisher Benjamin W. Huebsch:

> I hope you will like the book. It is less a novel than a sort of metaphysical or symbolical tragedy, and at the same time a perfectly straightforward tale. My hope is that the human significance of the book will transpire through this. Some parts of it you may find rather horrible, but the theme dictated this, and there was no getting out of it.

The work's epigraph is a quotation from Goethe that accuses God: "You lead us into life, and in accord with your will we poor wretches fall into sin, and then we are made to suffer; for on this earth there is retribution for every sin." Hans can similarly accuse his Maker, for his sufferings are none of his doing; his earthly father, in trying to improve him, only leads him into more and more grief and agony. Hans can be seen as a kind of Everyman, and Martin as God trying to make something of his decayed offspring. The novel suggests that God is a kind of puppeteer who puts his creatures through pain for reasons they cannot begin to understand. But the work cannot be summed up in this simple allegory. The role of Gretchen is complex: she is Eve-like in her "tempting" of Hans to violence, but she is also muselike in helping him to create his beautiful fantasy world. Thus, the novel can be interpreted as a parable not about Everyman but about the artist or writer who cannot help but move into and out of fantasy, who must create alternate realities while understanding only imperfectly what is happening. Moreover, the effect of the artist on the reader is suggested when Hans's fantasy beguiles his father, who senses that Hans's imaginary world "existed, a reduplication of the actual world, and as he felt its completeness, it seemed to Martin that existing thus, in rivalry, it made the existence of the actual world more arbitrary." Hans's helplessness, along with the book's strange intermixture of the real and the fantastic, are reminiscent of Franz Kafka's fiction, but Muir had not yet encountered Kafka's work when he wrote *The Marionette*. When he read Kafka's *Das Schloß* (1926)—which he and Willa translated into English as *The Castle* (1930)—he called it "a purely metaphysical and mystical dramatic novel" in a letter of 8 July 1929 to American novelist and translator Sydney Schiff, adding that "it appeals particularly to the part of me which wrote *The Marionette*." Muir came to see Kafka as an allegorist, but as Ritchie Robertson has pointed out, for Muir allegory was not a matter of simple one-to-one correspondences but was much looser and more fluid, maintaining something deeply mysterious within it that allowed the continual teasing out of additional meanings.

Most reviewers of *The Marionette* expressed puzzlement over the allegorical intent of the novel but praised the compelling style in which it is told. Muir's biographer, Peter H. Butter, calls it his best novel; as the most modernist of all Muir's fiction it is certainly the one most directly related to the spirit of its age, evoking comparisons with writers such as Kafka and William Faulkner. Muir wrote a great deal about that spirit in his reviews and essays; in "Contemporary Fiction," published in his *Transition: Essays on Contemporary Literature* (1926), he contends that the modern writer must be always groping, always uncertain of both the materials and the ends, and can hope, at most, for only partial achievements.

Muir developed his ideas about the novel in *The Structure of the Novel* (1928); the book is less well known than Percy Lubbock's *The Craft of Fiction* (1921) or E. M. Forster's *Aspects of the Novel*

(1927)—works to which it refers frequently and which it resembles in general tone—but it is at least as valuable to the student of the genre as those studies. Muir's speculations on the distinctive roles of time and space in various types of novels lead to many insights about authors as diverse as Jane Austen and Leo Tolstoy, and they also reveal much about Muir's intentions in his own novels. What Muir calls the "dramatic novel," for example, has its world primarily in time rather than in space and lends itself to the legendary, the archetypal, and the universal. His best example of this type of novel is Emily Brontë's *Wuthering Heights* (1847), but one can infer that *The Marionette* belongs in this category. The most capacious form of novel, according to Muir, is the "chronicle novel," in which the organizing element is not character or action but life or even time itself, which is almost an arithmetical constant that has power over the characters and events. The chronicle novel, he says, must be based on some sort of religious belief or some sense of an externalized Fate.

Muir's next novel, *The Three Brothers* (1931), is an attempt to work within this arena. *The Three Brothers* is set in sixteenth-century Scotland, a period Muir had recently researched for his 1929 biography of the religious reformer John Knox, and is the story of the Blackadder family. The father is a humanist, having traveled on the Continent and brought back some of the new sensitivities and tolerances. His sons lead troubled lives: Sandy, the eldest, becomes a fanatical Calvinist, while the twins Archie and David seem fated to be set against each other. David, the principal protagonist, is somewhat like Hans in that he is timid and inept socially. His father, like Hans's, takes charge of his education and gradually builds his self-confidence. The religious conflicts of the time are brought home to the boys as they watch from their farm a battle between French troops and Protestant rebels. Muir makes this historical situation real, showing how it tears apart a family and a whole country. The growing antipathy toward Catholics is memorably depicted in the scene in which the boys' mother dies: she is a Catholic and wants the last rites, but the only available priest is a drunkard who is suspicious of everyone and frightened of those who were once his parishioners; David must literally beat him to the family's house during a thunderous downpour.

Muir's attitude toward the Calvinism in which he had been raised had become highly negative; he saw it as repressive and destructive both to the individual and to Scotland itself. He had concluded his biography of Knox by declaring that the reformer had robbed Scotland of the benefits of the Renais-

POOR TOM

by

EDWIN MUIR

LONDON
J. M. DENT & SONS LTD.

*Title page for Muir's final novel, an autobiographical
bildungsroman*

sance and had relegated the country for centuries afterward to a "savage provincialism." This view of Calvinism is clearly reflected in *The Three Brothers*.

The boys grow up and leave home, taking up residence together in rooms above Sandy's Edinburgh shop. Sandy becomes increasingly hardened in his Calvinism; his rigid division of humanity into the damned and the elect causes him pain, but he clings to it in desperation. Conflicts erupt between Archie and David, the climactic one coming when Archie steals Ellen, the woman David loves. After Ellen becomes pregnant by Archie, a jealous lover from her past finds and kills her and nearly kills Archie. Soon afterward Sandy falls ill and dies a slow and painful death. Buffeted by one tragedy after another, David tries to understand how such a world could have been created and overseen by a loving God. *The Three Brothers*, then, is an attempt to confront the classic philosophical and theological prob-

lem of evil, a theme that Muir also explores in many of his poems. Some of Muir's best and most impassioned prose is to be found in the final pages of the novel, in which David has a breakdown and undergoes a seemingly total loss of faith. After many days of suffering, he has an extended vision of the Day of Judgment that includes an image of time becoming spatial; the whole history of the world is visible, like a vast ocean whose tossing waves have suddenly frozen in place. The image shows David that God sees human suffering in a fundamentally different way from that in which people experience it. This vision modulates into an even more powerful one in which all humanity stands on a vast beach, facing God on the Last Day. Despite the terror of the scene, the visions bring David comfort. In his diary he writes: "I cannot comprehend Thee, O God, I throw myself in humility before Thee, and no longer question thy inscrutable ways." He accepts the mystery and no longer insists on a humanly acceptable explanation. His father helps him with a simple parable about a blind man who, though he cannot see the road, knows that there is one. The novel concludes with David leaving Scotland for the Continent, like an Adam leaving a corrupted Eden for a new and strange world.

*The Three Brothers* received some praise in contemporary reviews, but the negative tone of most of them led Muir to say in an 11 April 1931 letter to Schiff that the novel was "a pretty complete failure publicly." The novel has not found much of an audience since then: Margery McCulloch emphasizes its inadequacy as historical fiction; Elgin W. Mellown treats it as essentially a preliminary draft for Muir's autobiography, in which events in David's life would later be described—almost verbatim, in some instances—as Muir's own experiences; and Robertson says that Muir is dealing with the problem of evil rather than telling a well-shaped tale and that he does not fully develop his characters, especially Sandy. Yet to some readers these flaws will be forgivable in a novel that is so passionately meant as this one. Muir was earnestly working toward a faith that would make sense of the suffering in his past and would help him to go on. In *The Structure of the Novel* he had said that such a faith is essential to the greatest novels: the chronicle novels, such as Tolstoy's *War and Peace* (1865–1869), that place individual experience within the largest and most inclusive canvas. He also said that modern writers—including the greatest, such as James Joyce and D. H. Lawrence—lacked such a faith and that without it they were condemned to pursue mere originality, having no set of values that they could affirm. *The Three Brothers* is Muir's attempt to move his work onto a larger canvas. If it ultimately fails, it remains a rich and rewarding attempt.

Muir's final novel, *Poor Tom* (1932), is another intriguing blend of the autobiographical with the fictional. Like the other novels, it is a bildungsroman that ultimately centers on the main character's struggle for a faith or philosophy that will allow him to make sense of life's sufferings. *Poor Tom* is set in early-twentieth-century Glasgow, the time and place of Muir's own greatest trials. It is divided into three parts, the latter two of which mostly consist of increasingly oppressive descriptions of the horrible death of Tom Manson from a brain tumor. The main character is Tom's elder brother "Mansie," who develops a deepening sense of guilt over his brother's illness. The Manson family resembles Muir's own family during their Glasgow years, although it has only four members: Mansie; Tom; their younger sister, Jean; and their mother. Muir does not identify himself directly with Mansie, whom he describes as a young man "without any great intelligence or sincerity of mind," but many of Mansie's experiences are exactly the same as ones that were eventually reported in Muir's autobiography.

When the story opens, Tom discovers that Mansie has secretly begun dating Helen, who had recently broken off with Tom. Her name is suggestive: like Helen of Troy in Homer's *Iliad,* she is unwittingly responsible for causing profound pain to two brothers—brothers whose lives, like those of the sons of Atreus in the *Iliad,* seem to be cursed. Tom is unable to accept Mansie and Helen's relationship, and he spirals downward into depression, anger, and alcoholism. One night he drunkenly falls from a tramcar, striking his head on the curb. He develops blinding headaches, and eventually a brain tumor is diagnosed. Mansie blames his relationship with Helen for Tom's drinking, the resulting accident, and the tumor caused by the accident. As Tom's condition worsens, Mansie turns cold toward Helen; when the doctor tells Mansie that there is no hope for Tom's recovery, Mansie writes a letter breaking off with her. He commits himself totally to the care of his brother and to his own agonizing guilt.

Helen is depicted sympathetically; she shares some of Mansie's guilt over Tom's condition but does not torture herself as he does. Her love for Mansie is genuine; the reader glimpses her pain as Mansie slowly cuts her out of his life. The motif of a woman causing emotional havoc in the male character's life is common to all three of Muir's novels—if the marionette Gretchen can be considered a female character—and one may be led to suspect an element

of misogyny in Muir's psychological makeup. Mellown, in fact, sees the novels as a kind of therapy in which Muir tried to purge painful emotions, including unconscious feelings of hostility to his mother. But Muir may simply have been building his story on the traditional version of the Fall, which puts the blame on Eve. Many of his later poems—culminating in the 1956 volume *One Foot in Eden*—make use of the Eden story; but in those works the woman is no longer at fault. "Adam's Dream," for instance, treats the Fall as almost inevitable, and in the closing lines the grief-stricken Adam finds a measure of peace in "Eve's encircling arms." Women in the poems are often healers, such as Helen in "The Charm," and they are often heroic, such as Penelope in "Telemachos Remembers," who at her loom "wove into her fears / Pride and fidelity and love." But in the three novels, the primary female characters—Gretchen, Ellen, and Helen—all play disruptive roles.

One scene in *Poor Tom* seems to be based on an incident in Willa Muir's life. Before she met Muir, Willa had been in love with a medical student who was unfaithful to her. On a pier at St. Andrews she took off the ring he had given her—"a pretty ring of diamonds and sapphires," she says in her autobiography, *Belonging* (1968)—and threw it into the sea before the young man's eyes. In *Poor Tom* Mansie, idly toying with a locket around Helen's neck, discovers a lock of Tom's hair inside it. Helen, distraught, throws the locket into the sea as a gesture of commitment to Mansie, but the act accomplishes the opposite of what she had intended: instead of reassuring Mansie it contributes to his uneasiness with the relationship and to his sense of guilt:

> And while he was still wondering that she should carry about Tom's hair clasped in a locket, and still thinking of Tom's hair drowned in the sea—that gave one an uncanny feeling, as if part of Tom had been drowned without his knowing it—the spell stole over him again, the trance held them suspended, and when at last they rose and walked back the flashing arc made by the locket as it fell into the sea had been lost in the web of their dream.

Most of the external action of the novel occurs in the first part; the next two parts are devoted to a minute psychological study of Tom's illness and Mansie's reactions to it. In these two parts Muir begins building up the larger themes of the story: *Poor Tom* is not only an attempt to exorcise some of the pain Muir felt over the deaths of his family members but also an effort to choose between the two systems of belief that were competing for his allegiance—socialism and religion. Muir abandoned his youthful enthusiasm for socialism in favor of a religious worldview, and Mansie goes through the same intellectual process. At first, socialism seems to Mansie to offer the promise of an egalitarian society in which the poverty and misery he sees in places such as the Eglinton Street slums of Glasgow will be eradicated. His enthusiasm reaches its climax at a May Day demonstration: as Mansie marches with the crowds, he feels a profound sense of acceptance and oneness with those around him, "for all outward semblance was inessential, all distinction had fallen away like a heavy burden borne in some other place." Mansie walks home in a state of bliss, convinced that he has found the answer—until he opens the door and sees Tom, and his sense of isolation and guilt returns. As Mansie continues to ruminate about socialism, he decides that the May Day revelation was a delusion.

In the remarkable nineteenth chapter of the novel Muir interrupts the narrative to speak directly to the reader in an eloquent essay (a tactic Tolstoy frequently employs in *War and Peace*). In the essay Muir holds that our modern predicament results from our having abandoned the "Why" question in favor of the much less significant "How." The answer to the How can never transfigure our lives. In a world without the Divine, we are left easy prey to "the shadows of fear and mortality." Socialism is involved only with the How, and while it can deceive us for a time, it can never be the all-encompassing philosophy it pretends to be; its emptiness must ultimately be revealed, as it is to Mansie. (Muir continued to develop these ideas after the publication of *Poor Tom;* on 26 January 1940 he wrote to the critic Herbert Read about a projected book-length study that would compare Calvinism and communism, both of which he saw as being built on an unhealthy wrath.) Muir adds another essay in chapter 22, this one a powerful description of the psychology of one brought to death by an illness. Muir develops this essay from a meditation on Giovanni Bellini's painting of Christ in Gethsemane, suggesting that Christianity will provide the Why that socialism ignores.

Mansie continues to be tormented by guilt and fear, but he slowly and timidly begins to speculate about the possibility of an afterlife—not a better future in this life but a wholly different reality. Socialism cannot account for death, Muir points out; it can only reduce the enormous fact of the individual's death to a mere step on the road to Utopia. The theme of time that Muir had explored in *The Three Brothers* is revived as Mansie realizes that what he needs is a philosophy that is above and outside of time, and he ponders the reality of the heaven he had believed in as a child. Riding home on a tramcar

one night, he experiences another epiphany, but this one is more solid and permanent than the May Day revelation. Mansie realizes that his predicament is that of all humanity: "they have all gone through it," he thinks, and at that moment "a great weight rolled from his heart."

Tom dies soon afterward, and the novel concludes with Mansie experiencing an even greater revelation while standing alone before his brother's coffin in the darkened room. He now sees the greatness of death, of the "everlasting and perfect order, the eternal destiny of all men, the immortality of his own soul." Tom's suffering and death have been the means of leading Mansie toward an expiation of his guilt; Tom functions, therefore, as a Christ figure (Muir had suggested a parallel between Tom and Christ in the meditation on the Gethsemane scene in chapter 22). With Tom's death Mansie's suffering leads to a felt and understood acceptance and resolution; he now feels "embedded in life, fold on fold." He leaves the room and closes the door; like David in *The Three Brothers* he has reached a new state of maturity and is ready to confront life on a higher plane.

William Heinemann, the publisher of *The Three Brothers,* rejected *Poor Tom,* and Muir found a new publisher in Richard Dent. Reviews of the novel were lukewarm at best, and most of them lumped it in with other new novels rather than treating it individually. William Johnstone, who did the illustrations for the dust jacket, told Peter H. Butter, editor of *Selected Letters of Edwin Muir* (1974), that only about eighty copies of *Poor Tom* were sold.

Muir at one time planned to continue the story, as he indicated in a 29 September 1932 letter accompanying a copy of the novel that he sent to his and Willa's friends George and Lizzie Thorburn:

> I hope Lizzie won't look for any living model (or dead one either) for any of the characters: that would be completely wrong, for they are all synthetic, made up of scraps taken from all sorts of nooks and corners, and mostly pure imagination, like the main situation. The book is unfortunately a very lugubrious one; but I had to get it out of my system; and I look upon it only as the first third of a whole, the second of which I look upon as noisily comic—if I can bring it off. Meantime, I hope that this instalment won't give the whole of you the blues—George, being the man of the house, should try it first.

This passage reveals Muir's almost apologetic attitude toward his novel; also, his insistence that it is completely fictional suggests that he was confused about the role his own experiences played in his novels. He never sorted out this confusion, and although he went on to write much poetry and criticism, he never published any more fiction.

Muir did try his hand at fiction one more time, though he never completed or tried to publish the result. In 1940 he wrote some forty pages of a detective novel, titled "The Highland Mystery." The typescript survives in the National Library of Scotland. He wrote to Read on 26 January 1940 about his financial concerns, and said:

> Willa and I have actually been thinking of starting on a detective story, which we have been making up in our minds for several months now for our own entertainment; but I don't know, either, whether detective stories are profitable. I wonder whether you could give some idea about that: our story would be quite an amusing one.

Clearly, Muir saw the book as a potboiler, but gave it up when he came to feel it would not be salable; however, the draft—though utterly unlike anything else he had ever written—is highly enjoyable genre fiction and might have been much more successful than he believed. The light tone and the fast pace, so different from the textures of Muir's other novels, probably owe much to the influence of Willa. The story involves the mysterious murder of a widely disliked English gentleman who had recently settled near the Highland village of Inverallochan. Muir sets up the plot deftly, with one key obvious suspect but also a host of others who might have done the killing.

The characters in this fragment are not at all like the tortured protagonists of his finished novels. The main characters evidently would have been Long John Campbell, a mathematically inclined laird in his fifties, and his grumbling, "egalitarian" manservant, Logan. There is an English inspector, Ambler, who condescends to the rural Scots and as a result is himself manipulated and outsmarted; Logan explains that Ambler got involved in the case only because the murdered man was also English, and "the English are terrible clannish." The novel would have continued no doubt in this satiric vein, providing humor at the expense of the smug Sassenachs such as Ambler. The interplay between Campbell and Logan could well have developed into a clever Scottish version of Lord Peter Wimsey and Bunter. A romance element between Campbell and the daughter of the murdered man is hinted at and Muir evidently intended to work in a subtheme regarding socialism and people's varying attitudes toward it. So "the Highland Mystery" is rich in potential. It seems unlikely, however, that there would have been room in the story for Muir's recurring

*Muir's wife, Willa, in 1945*

themes of the Fall and the problem of evil, and part of Muir's dissatisfaction with the draft may have come from a sense that the story lacked importance to him. He abandoned it, and continued work on his poetry and criticism.

In *Belonging* Willa Muir suggests that Muir's novels did not find a public because they were too downbeat for the early years of the Depression. While there is no doubt some truth in that observation, Muir's ambiguous feelings about his fiction led him to create tales that few readers were ready to appreciate. Modern readers, however, who can read the novels in the context of Muir's autobiography will be able to see more of interest in them than their contemporary readers could.

In the nearly three decades of his life after *Poor Tom,* Muir and his wife were highly productive writers, translators, and teachers. They moved to St.

Andrews, Scotland, in 1934; in 1941 Edwin went to work for the British Council in Edinburgh. He was transferred to Prague in 1945, Cambridge in 1948, and Rome in 1949. He was made warden of Newbattle Abbey College near Edinburgh in 1950; in 1955-1956 he was a visiting professor of poetry at Harvard University. Returning to England, the Muirs settled in Swaffham, Surrey, where Muir died on 3 January 1959.

Muir might have written more fiction had there been a more appreciative reading public for his novels, but it appears that his real genius was for poetry and criticism. In "The Poetic Imagination," published in his *Essays on Literature and Society* (1949), Muir minimizes the differences between the poet and the prose storyteller; he claims that writers as disparate as William Wordsworth and Fyodor Dostoyevsky provide readers with "a more profound and various understanding of life than personal experience or practical sense ever can." This thesis points to the most important aspect of Muir's novels, whether one regards them as failures or as successes: they are evidence of an artist working to understand and explain human existence through the medium of prose fiction. Muir's three novels, each utterly unlike the others yet all combining similar autobiographical and mythical strands, offer a remarkable experience to the modern reader adventurous enough to seek them out.

**Letters:**
*Selected Letters of Edwin Muir,* edited by Peter H. Butter (London: Hogarth Press, 1974).

**Bibliographies:**
Elgin W. Mellown, *Bibliography of the Writings of Edwin Muir* (University: University of Alabama Press, 1964; revised edition, London: Vane, 1966);

Mellown and Peter C. Hoy, *Supplement to the Bibliography of the Writings of Edwin Muir* (University: University of Alabama Press, 1971);

Hoy and Mellown, *A Checklist of Writings about Edwin Muir* (Troy, N.Y.: Whitston, 1971).

**Biography:**
Peter H. Butter, *Edwin Muir: Man and Poet* (Edinburgh: Oliver & Boyd, 1966; New York: Barnes & Noble, 1967).

**References:**
Glen Cavaliero, "Autobiography and Fiction," *Prose Studies,* 8 (1985): 156-171;

W. S. Di Piero, "On Edwin Muir," *Chicago Review,* 37 (1990): 80-88;

Amos Handel, "The Sense of Estrangement from One's Previous Self in the Autobiographies of Arthur Koestler and Edwin Muir," *Biography,* 9 (1986): 306-323;

Roger Knight, *Edwin Muir: An Introduction to His Work* (London: Longman, 1980);

C. J. M. MacLachlan and D. S. Robb, eds., *Edwin Muir: Centenary Assessments* (Aberdeen: Association for Scottish Literary Studies, 1990);

George Marshall, *In a Distant Isle: The Orkney Background of Edwin Muir* (Edinburgh: Scottish Academic Press, 1987);

Margery McCulloch, *Edwin Muir: Poet, Critic and Novelist* (Edinburgh: Edinburgh University Press, 1993);

Elgin W. Mellown, "Autobiographical Themes in the Novels of Edwin Muir," *Contemporary Literature,* 6 (1965): 228-242;

Mellown, *Edwin Muir* (Boston: Twayne, 1979);

Thomas Merton, "The True Legendary Sound: The Poetry and Criticism of Edwin Muir," *Sewanee Review,* 75 (April-June 1967): 317-325;

Kenneth Muir, "Edwin Muir's Chorus of the Newly Dead and Its Analogues," *Connotations: A Journal for Critical Debate,* 6 (1996-1997): 203-206;

Willa Muir, *Belonging: A Memoir* (London: Hogarth, 1968);

Murray G. H. Pittock, "Armorial Weed: The Landscape of Edwin Muir," in *Northern Visions: The Literary Identity of Northern Scotland in the Twentieth Century,* edited by David Hewitt (East Lothian: Tuckwell, 1995), pp. 70-81;

Robert Richman, "Edwin Muir's Journey," *New Criterion,* 15 (April 1997): 26-33;

Ritchie Robertson, "Edwin Muir as Critic of Kafka," *Modern Language Review,* 79, no. 3 (1984): 638-652;

Robertson, "Goethe, Broch, and the Novels of Edwin Muir," *Forum for Modern Language Studies,* 19, no. 2 (1983): 142-157;

J. R. Watson, "Edwin Muir and the Problem of Evil," *Critical Quarterly,* 6 (1964): 231-249.

**Papers:**
The majority of Edwin Muir's letters, papers, and manuscripts—including the typescript for "The Highland Mystery"—are in the National Library of Scotland, Edinburgh. A large collection of Willa Muir's papers, including some of Edwin Muir's, is housed at St. Andrews University Library, Scotland. The BBC Script Collection in the Scottish Theatre Archive, Glasgow University Library, includes some of Muir's radio scripts; the BBC Archives in London also include scripts by Muir and about him.

# Beverley Nichols

## (9 September 1898 – 15 September 1983)

### Margaret Crosland

BOOKS: *Prelude: A Novel* (London: Chatto & Windus, 1920);

*Patchwork* (London: Chatto & Windus, 1921; New York: Holt, 1922);

*Self* (London: Chatto & Windus, 1922);

*25: Being a Young Man's Candid Recollections of His Elders and Betters* (London: Cape, 1926; New York: Doran, 1926);

*Are They the Same at Home? Being a Series of Bouquets Diffidently Distributed* (London: Cape, 1927; New York: Doran, 1927);

*Crazy Pavements* (London: Cape, 1927; New York: Doran, 1927);

*The Star-Spangled Manner* (London: Cape, 1928; Garden City, N.Y.: Doubleday, 1928);

*Oxford, London, Hollywood: An Omnibus by Beverley Nichols; Containing "Twenty-five," "Are They the Same at Home?," and "The Star-Spangled Manner"* (London: Cape, 1931);

*Women and Children Last* (London: Cape, 1931; Garden City, N.Y.: Doubleday, 1931);

*Down the Garden Path* (London: Cape, 1932; Garden City, N.Y.: Doubleday, Doran, 1932);

*Evensong: A Novel* (London: Cape, 1932; Garden City, N.Y.: Doubleday, Doran, 1932);

*Evensong: A Play in Three Acts,* adapted by Nichols and Edward Knoblock (London: French, 1932; New York: French, 1932);

*In the Next War I Shall Be a Conscientious Objector* (London: Friends' Peace Committee, 1932?);

*For Adults Only* (London: Cape, 1932; Garden City, N.Y.: Doubleday, Doran, 1933?);

*Cry Havoc!* (London: Cape, 1933; Garden City, N.Y.: Doubleday, Doran, 1933);

*Failures: Three Plays* (London: Cape, 1933)—comprises *The Stag, Avalanche, When the Crash Comes;*

*A Thatched Roof* (London: Cape, 1933; Garden City, N.Y.: Doubleday, Doran, 1933);

*Official Handbook of the Corporation of Brighton,* by Nichols and others (Brighton, Sussex: Corporation of Brighton, 1933);

*The Valet as Historian* (London: Forsyth, circa 1934);

*A Village in a Valley* (London: Cape, 1934; Garden City, N.Y.: Doubleday, Doran, 1934);

*How Does Your Garden Grow?,* by Nichols, Compton Mackenzie, Marion Cran, and Vita Sackville-West (Garden City, N.Y.: Doubleday, Doran, 1935);

*The Fool Hath Said . . .* (London: Cape, 1936; Garden City, N.Y.: Doubleday, Doran, 1936);

*No Place Like Home* (London: Cape, 1936; Garden City, N.Y.: Doubleday, Doran, 1936);

*Mesmer: A Play in Three Acts* (London: Cape, 1937);

*News of England; or, A Country without a Hero* (London: Cape, 1938; New York: Doubleday, Doran, 1938);

*Green Grows the City: The Story of a London Garden* (London: Cape, 1939: New York: Harcourt, Brace, 1939);

*Revue* (London: Cape, 1939; Garden City, N.Y.: Doubleday, Doran, 1939);

*Men Do Not Weep* (London: Cape, 1941; New York: Harcourt, Brace, 1942);

*Verdict on India* (London: Cape, 1944; New York: Harcourt, Brace, 1944);

*The Tree That Sat Down* (London: Cape, 1945);

*The Stream That Stood Still* (London: Cape, 1948);

*Shadow of the Vine: A Play in Three Acts* (London: Cape, 1949);

*All I Could Never Be: Some Recollections* (London: Cape, 1949; New York: Dutton, 1952);

*Yours Sincerely,* by Nichols and Monica Dickens (London: Newnes, 1949);

*Uncle Samson* (London: Evans, 1950);

*The Mountain of Magic: A Romance for Children* (London: Cape, 1950);

*A Pilgrim's Progress* (London: Cape, 1952);

*Merry Hall* (London: Cape, 1951; New York: Dutton, 1953);

*The Queen's Coronation Day: The Pictorial Record of the Great Occasion* (London: Pitkin Pictorials, 1953);

*Laughter on the Stairs* (London: Cape, 1953: New York: Dutton, 1954);

*No Man's Street* (London: Hutchinson, 1954; New York: Dutton, 1954);

*Beverley Nichols' Cat Book* (London: Nelson, 1955);

*The Moonflower* (London: Hutchinson, 1955); republished as *The Moonflower Murder* (New York: Dutton, 1955);

*Sunlight on the Lawn* (London: Cape, 1956; New York: Dutton, 1956);

*Death to Slow Music* (London: Hutchinson, 1956; New York: Dutton, 1956);

*The Rich Die Hard* (London: Hutchinson, 1957; New York: Dutton, 1958);

*The Sweet and Twenties* (London: Weidenfeld & Nicolson, 1958; New York: British Book Centre, 1958);

*Murder by Request* (London: Hutchinson, 1960; New York: Dutton, 1960);

*Cats' A. B. C.* (London: Cape, 1960; New York: Dutton, 1960);

*Cats' X. Y. Z.* (London: Cape, 1961; New York: Dutton, 1961);

*Garden Open Today* (London: Cape, 1963; New York: Dutton, 1963);

*Forty Favourite Flowers* (London: Studio Vista, 1964; New York: St. Martin's Press, 1965);

*A Case of Human Bondage* (London: Secker & Warburg, 1966; New York: Award, 1966);

*Powers That Be* (London: Cape, 1966; New York: St. Martin's Press, 1966);

*The Tree That Sat Down, and The Stream That Stood Still* (New York: St. Martin's Press, 1966);

*The Art of Flower Arrangement* (London & Glasgow: Collins, 1967; New York: Viking, 1967);

*Garden Open Tomorrow* (London: Heinemann, 1968; New York: Dodd, Mead, 1969);

*The Sun in My Eyes; or, How Not to Go around the World* (London: Heinemann, 1969);

*The Wickedest Witch in the World* (London: W. H. Allen, 1971);

*The Gift of a Garden; or, Some Flowers Remembered,* edited by John E. Cross (London: W. H. Allen, 1971; New York: Dodd, Mead, 1972);

*The Gift of a Home* (London: W. H. Allen, 1972; New York: Dodd, Mead, 1973);

*Father Figure* (London: Heinemann, 1972; New York: Simon & Schuster, 1972);

*Down the Kitchen Sink* (London: W. H. Allen, 1974);

*The Unforgiving Minute: Some Confessions from Childhood to the Outbreak of the Second World War* (London: W. H. Allen, 1978);

*Twilight: First and Probably Last Poems* (Maidstone, Kent: Bachman & Turner, 1982).

PLAY PRODUCTIONS: *The Stag,* London, Globe Theatre, 2 April 1929;

*Avalanche,* Edinburgh, 1931;

*Evensong,* by Nichols and Edward Knoblock, London, Queen's Theatre, 30 June 1932;

*When the Crash Comes,* Birmingham, 1933;

*Mesmer,* London, Tavistock Little Theatre, March 1938;

*Shadow of the Vine,* London, Wyndham's Theatre, 14 February 1954.

OTHER: Nellie Melba, *Melodies and Memories,* ghostwritten by Nichols (London: Butterworth, 1925; New York: Doran, 1926);

Charles Sedley, *The Faro Table; or, The Gambling Mothers,* introduction by Nichols (London: Nash & Grayson, 1931);

*A Book of Old Ballads,* compiled by Nichols (London: Hutchinson, 1934; New York: Loring & Mussey, 1934?);

*The Making of a Man: Letters from an Old Parson to His Sons,* foreword by Nichols (London: Nicholson & Watson, 1934);

*Receipt Book,* preface by Nichols (London: Woolf, 1968);

Jan Styczyński, *Cats in Camera,* preface by Nichols (London: Deutsch, 1962).

Few popular writers of the twentieth century have had such a long, varied, and successful career as Beverley Nichols. Of his nearly seventy books, twelve are novels; the rest include a collection of short stories; plays; an autobiography; travel books; polemical essays; books about gardening, flowers, flower arranging, and cats; and children's stories. Although most of his work went out of print long before his death at eighty-five, several titles have become classics of their kind and are collected by bibliophiles, at least in Britain. While fiction forms a relatively small proportion of a large output, his success in his other work resulted in large part from his use of narrative techniques in nonfictional genres.

John Beverley Nichols was born on 9 September 1898 at Long Ashton, near Bristol in Somerset, the youngest of the three sons of John Nichols, a successful solicitor, and Pauline Zoe Lilian Shalders Nichols. He attended preparatory school in Torquay and then Marlborough College and enrolled at Balliol College, Oxford, in 1917. After one term at the university Nichols was commissioned a second lieutenant in the Labour Corps. After working briefly with the War Office he served as aide to the vice chancellor of the University of Cambridge, Sir A. E. Shipley, during Shipley's University Mission to the United States in late 1918. Nichols then returned to Balliol, where he studied modern history

Beverly Nichols (right) with Edward Knobloch, his collaborator on the 1932 play version of
Evensong (Tony Stone Images)

from 1919 to 1921. At the university he became well known for his indiscreet sexual behavior and his controversial views. He was president of the Oxford Union debating society for one term in 1920, edited the student magazine *Isis,* and founded and edited the left-wing literary magazine *Oxford Outlook.*

Nichols's first novel, *Prelude,* written during his long train journeys in the United States during 1918, was published in 1920. It was based on incidents remembered from his school days. The reviews were good; according to the author's obituary in the *Times* of London, the book was "still readable" in 1983. Its success launched him on a busy career in journalism and the theater. *Patchwork* (1921) is about an Oxford student who becomes a successful New York playwright; Nichols broke with tradition by stating that the characters were not fictitious but, good and bad alike, were based on real people. His third novel, *Self* (1922), was a best-seller although Nichols himself described it later as "about the worst novel ever written." The "self" is Becky Sharp, a modern-day version of the unscrupulous, clever, and ambitious heroine of William Makepeace Thackeray's *Vanity Fair* (1847–1848). In 1926 he published his first volume of memoirs, *25: Being a Young Man's Candid Recollections of His Elders and Betters.* His 1927 novel *Crazy Pavements* included outspoken passages about drug taking and homosexuality that were considered shocking at the time, and the book narrowly escaped legal action for libel. In 1928–1929 he edited the magazine *American Sketch.*

Nichols composed music as well as lyrics for various stage shows, notably *C. B. Cochran's 1930 Re-*

*vue.* Two years later he published a book that has remained popular ever since: *Down the Garden Path,* embellished with delightful drawings by the popular illustrator Rex Whistler. It employs techniques drawn from fiction writing in portraying incidents and characters such as the Lady Gardener. Its usefulness as a practical gardening book is minimal, but it appeals to gardeners and nongardeners alike because it is consistently amusing, especially in its dialogue. Since it evokes a near-ideal village life, it has always been enjoyed more by city dwellers than by country people. It was followed during the next thirty years by several other titles on the themes of gardening, country life, flowers, and flower arrangement, but the first title has retained its status as a classic.

Also in 1932 Nichols published the novel *Evensong,* based on the later years of the Australian singer Dame Nellie Melba. Her autobiography, *Melodies and Memories* (1925), had largely been ghostwritten by Nichols; he had hoped that her manuscript would repeat some of the lurid stories she had told him, but it had not done so. He therefore put the stories into his own book, which was extremely successful. It came out the year after Melba died, and she was widely recognized as the model for the heroine, Irela. The novelist J. B. Priestley, reviewing the work in the London *Evening Standard,* called the novel "brilliant" and its heroine "colossal"; according to Priestley, the author had "exhibited his fascinating monster with the most admirable skill." Working with Edward Knoblock, Nichols adapted *Evensong* for the theater; Edith

EVENSONG

*A Novel*

BY

BEVERLEY NICHOLS

JONATHAN CAPE
THIRTY BEDFORD SQUARE
LONDON

*Title page for Nichols's fictionalized biography of the Australian
singer Dame Nellie Melba*

Evans's performance as Irela was the first popular
success of her career.

In September 1932 Nichols, who was an intimate of many celebrities of the time, began a gossip
column in the form of a diary for the *Sunday Chronicle;*
he continued to write it for the next fourteen years. He
never missed an opportunity to call attention to himself by supporting or attacking controversial ideas. By
the early 1930s he believed that only the fascist British
National Party, led by Sir Oswald Mosley, could prevent a second war between Britain and Germany; he
would later repudiate that position. In *Cry Havoc!*
(1933) he advocated pacifism and disarmament, and
in *Verdict on India* (1944) he supported the Indian Mus-
lims and criticized Mohandas (Mahatma) Gandhi. A
second volume of autobiography, *All I Could Never Be:
Some Recollections,* appeared in 1949.

In 1954 Nichols's work as a novelist took a new
turn when he began writing detective stories. In *No
Man's Street* he introduces a detective, Horatio Green,
whose success in solving crimes is based on a knowledge of plants, both ordinary and rare, and a keen
sense of smell. Green is a convincing character,
without the eccentricities of such series sleuths as
Agatha Christie's Hercule Poirot. He appears in all
five of Nichols's detective novels; the final work in
the series, *Murder by Request,* was published in 1960.

In his memoirs published in the London *Sunday
Express* in 1962 as *Looking Back,* the writer W. Somerset
Maugham had written cruelly about his former wife,
Syrie. Nichols had known Maugham and his wife, and
after Maugham's death in December 1965 Nichols set
out to put the record straight. Adapting the title of
Maugham's 1915 novel, he published *A Case of Human
Bondage* (1966), which became a best-seller. According
to biographer Bryan Connon, the impression left by
the book is that Nichols's own role in this situation
had not been entirely honorable.

In 1968 Nichols published *Garden Open Tomorrow,* about the garden he had designed at Sudbrook
Cottage, Ham Common, Surrey, his home for the last
twenty-five years of his life. His third volume of memoirs, *Father Figure* (1972), is a particularly revealing
book if it is true, and even if it is not. Alleging that his
father was a sadistic alcoholic who treated the family
with great cruelty, Nichols claims that he tried to kill
his father on three occasions: when he was fifteen, he
dissolved a bottle of aspirin in his father's soup; a few
months later he tried to run over his passed-out father
with a lawn roller; and when he was thirty-one, returning to his own home and discovering that his father had let himself in, wrecked the house, and passed
out, Nichols dragged the man outside and left him in a
snowdrift to freeze to death. (His father survived and
eventually died of natural causes.) Nichols's final volume of autobiography, *The Unforgiving Minute: Some
Confessions from Childhood to the Outbreak of the Second
World War,* appeared in 1978.

Nichols died on 15 September 1983 after a fall.
Some of his poetry volumes, several of his books for
children, and the classic *Down the Garden Path* are still
in print in Britain.

**Biography:**

Bryan Connon, *Beverley Nichols: A Life* (London: Constable, 1991).

**References:**

Victoria Glendinning, "Excursions from Paradise,"
*Times Literary Supplement,* 8 September 1978, p.
984;

Ethel Mannin, *Confessions and Impressions* (London:
Hutchinson, 1930);

Francis Yeats-Brown, *Dogs of War!* (London: Davies,
1934).

# Adelaide Eden Phillpotts
# (Adelaide Ross)

### (23 April 1896 – 4 June 1993)

## James Y. Dayananda
*Lock Haven University*

BOOKS: *Illyrion, and Other Poems* (London: Palmer & Hayward, 1916);

*Arachne* (London: Palmer, 1920);

*Man: A Fable* (London: Constable, 1922);

*Savitri, the Faithful: A Play in One Act* (London: Gowans & Gray, 1923);

*The Friend* (London: Heinemann, 1923);

*Camillus and the Schoolmaster: A Play in One Act* (London: Gowans & Gray, 1923);

*Yellow Sands: A Comedy in Three Acts,* by Phillpotts and Eden Phillpotts (London: Duckworth, 1926; New York: French, 1927);

*Lodgers in London* (London: Butterworth, 1926; Boston: Little, Brown, 1926);

*Akhnaton: A Play* (London: Butterworth, 1926);

*Tomek the Sculptor* (London: Butterworth, 1927; Boston: Little, Brown, 1927);

*Devonshire Plays: The Farmer's Wife and Devonshire Cream* (London: Duckworth, 1927);

*A Marriage* (London: Butterworth, 1928);

*The Atoning Years* (London: Butterworth, 1929);

*Yellow Sands: The Story of the Play* (London: Chapman & Hall, 1930);

*The Youth of Jacob Ackner* (London, Benn, 1931);

*The Good Old Days: A Comedy in Three Acts,* by Phillpotts and Eden Phillpotts (London: Duckworth, 1932);

*The Founder of Shandon* (London: Benn, 1932);

*The Growing World* (London: Hutchinson, 1934);

*Onward Journey* (London: Hutchinson, 1936);

*Broken Allegiance* (London: Hutchinson, 1937);

*The Gallant Heart* (London: Rich & Cowan, 1938);

*What's Happened to Rankin?* (London: Rich & Cowan, 1938);

*The Round of Life* (London: Rich & Cowan, 1939);

*Laugh with Me* (London: Rich & Cowan, 1941);

*Our Little Town* (London: Rich & Cowan, 1942);

*From Jane to John* (London: Rich & Cowan, 1943);

*The Adventurers* (London: Rich & Cowan, 1944);

*The Lodestar* (London & New York: Rich & Cowan, 1946);

*The Fosterling* (London & New York: Rich & Cowan, 1949);

*Stubborn Earth* (London: Rich & Cowan, 1951);

*A Song of Man,* as Adelaide Ross (London: Linden, 1959);

*Panorama of the World,* as Ross (London: Hale, 1969);

*A Wild Flower Wreath,* as Ross (Bude, Cornwall: Published by the author, 1975);

*Reverie: An Autobiography,* as Ross (London: Hale, 1981);

*Village Love: A Country Romance,* as Ross (Crawley, West Sussex: Rigby & Lewis, 1988);

*The Beacon of Memory,* as Ross (Crawley, West Sussex: Rigby & Lewis, 1991).

PLAY PRODUCTIONS: *Yellow Sands,* by Phillpotts and Eden Phillpotts, London, Haymarket Theatre, 3 November 1926;

*My Lady's Mill,* by Phillpotts and Eden Phillpotts, London, Lyric Theatre, 2 July 1928;

*The Good Old Days,* by Phillpotts and Eden Phillpotts, Birmingham, Repertory Theatre, December 1931.

OTHER: John Cowper Powys, *Letters to Nicholas Ross,* selected by Phillpotts, as Adelaide Ross, and Nicholas Ross, edited by Arthur Uphill (London: Rota, 1971).

Although Adelaide Eden Phillpotts Ross and her works have virtually disappeared from sight, her publishing career spanned some seventy-five years. Compared to her father, Eden Phillpotts, who published more than 225 books, her output is small: between 1916 and 1991 she published 37 books in a variety of genres. Although largely neglected by critics even in her own day, she produced novels, plays, and poems of great charm that show considerable talent. Many of her works are realistic portrayals of women who share a capacity for suf-

*Adelaide Eden Phillpotts in 1976 (photograph by James Y. Dayananda)*

fering, a suspicion of middle-class values, and a distrust in the ability of men to make women happy.

Mary Adelaide Eden Phillpotts was born on 23 April 1896 at Ealing, the second of two children of Eden and Emily Topham Phillpotts. She grew up in a home in Devon that was dominated by writing. In *Reverie: An Autobiography* (1981) she relates, "We had to be silent when our father was working—all morning and after ten until supper. I recall being told to walk on tiptoe because he had a 'splitting headache.'" Among the well-known writers who visited the Phillpotts home were Thomas Hardy, Agatha Christie, and Arnold Bennett. Adelaide Phillpotts frequently vacationed on Dartmoor with her father and older brother, Henry; during these trips Eden Phillpotts made notes for his well-known Dartmoor Cycle novels.

After a period of education under a governess, Adelaide Phillpotts was sent to a local boarding school, Girton House, and later to Gressendale—a school "for the daughters of gentlemen"—at Southbourne. When she was fourteen she traveled to Paris with her mother and experienced the thrill of a fresh perspective: "I was filled with joy. 'All men are brothers!' I sang to myself. . . . Henceforth there would be no more barriers, no frontiers between races. Every journey would be from home to home." In 1915–1916 she worked for the *Cambridge Magazine*. While she was in Cambridge she attended lectures on the art of writing by Sir Arthur Quiller-Couch at the university. She concluded her education with a social science course at Bedford College in London in 1921–1922. Among the friends she made in London were the philosopher L. Susan Stebbing and the actress Sybil Thorndike.

Phillpotts and her father coauthored *Yellow Sands* (1926), a comedy that ran for 619 performances at the Haymarket Theatre in London; later they turned the play into a novel (1930). The play and the novel deal with the disposition of an old woman's estate. Adelaide's *Akhnaton* (1926), a play in verse and prose that was never performed, presents the pharaoh's revolutionary attempt to introduce monotheism to Egypt in the fourteenth century B.C. Father and daughter collaborated again on the plays *My Lady's Mill* (produced in 1928) and *The Good Old Days: A Comedy in Three Acts* (produced in 1931; published in 1932).

In addition to their joint writing projects, Phillpotts and her father dedicated books to each other, and Eden Phillpotts wrote sonnets to his daughter. According to Adelaide, the relationship extended beyond literary collaboration and fatherly affection to incest and extreme jealousy and cruelty on his part. She tells the story in *Reverie*:

> He had begun deeply to love me. I think he looked on me as an extension of himself, for he would take me into his bed and fondle me, compare my limbs with his

and say "Look! Your hands and feet are just like smaller editions of mine. You are so like me. And you are going to be a writer too." He kissed me all over and said: "You must never marry!" At six or seven that meant nothing to me. Yet I did not forget those words, which all through my youth and afterwards were repeated. I loved him too but only as a father, and for fear of hurting him I let him do whatever he liked.

Adelaide Phillpotts seems to have compensated for her father's domination by creating independent female protagonists. Her heroines are not modern career women but warm and sensitive mothers and not-so-submissive wives. The protagonist and narrator of *A Marriage* (1928), Janet Finlay, is the daughter of a poor clerk in an accounting firm. A woman of average looks, she gives up hope of marriage and goes to work as a stenographer-typist for Matthew Hammond, an author and reader in English literature at a London college. Hammond falls in love with her and proposes marriage. When Matthew's family invites Janet and her parents to dinner, Janet is exposed to upper-class prejudice; Matthew's mother, especially, looks down on Janet's family. Matthew, however, is too large minded and generous of spirit to notice such things as her father's "eating his soup with the point of his spoon." The novel lingers over Janet's courtship, wedding, and honeymoon, "since it forms really but a short time compared to the years which followed, but it was the foundation on which those years were built, and I think every woman whose marriage is not a failure likes to dwell on the early days of it." She has a miscarriage; goes on to bear two children, Jane and James; and supports Matthew through his recurrent bouts of depression. Some of his plays become successful productions in London, and Janet experiences jealousy when he becomes attracted to some of the young and beautiful actresses who appear in them—especially the stunning Asia: "She was to him everything that is beautiful to a man on the verge of age: romance, youth, beauty, and besides these a truly noble character without alloy." The couple remains together in a reasonably happy marriage until Matthew's death.

After the historical novel *Broken Allegiance* (1937), about Benedict Arnold, Phillpotts returned to her stories of independent heroines with *The Gallant Heart* (1938). Leah Vinnicombe is born in a workhouse, orphaned, raised in an institution for destitute children, and released at the age of thirteen to become a scullery maid in a boardinghouse. After running away from one hopeless situation after another, she finds work at Izet Northmoor's Friar's Farm. Izet's son, Nathaniel, falls in love with Leah and wants to marry her; his mother opposes the marriage and drives both of them from the farm. Nathaniel and Leah marry and go to work at Bencombe Farm. There Leah is a successful manager:

> She did this so well—often better than a man would have done it—that the next time they needed an extra laborer, they came to her again. One stipulation she made: her wages must be equal to a man's, not only because they would otherwise be underselling their labour, but because she believed in equal pay for equal work. . . . The village women . . . professed to be shocked by Leah and her goings-on—her unwomanly pursuits, her rough garments, her indifference to criticism and gossip, her unlikeness to themselves.

Leah is clearly a woman ahead of her time. When another woman says, "Love and childbearing be the bestest life for woman—no gain-saying it," Leah responds: "Depends on the woman. Don't suit all and some it makes mighty narrow-natured. . . . As if there ba'nt nothing to life but love and child-rearing." She and Nathaniel have two daughters, Ruth and Grace. Grace's lover, Nicholas Grendon, falls in love with Leah, who, in her forties, is "slim, tall, graceful and tough, with shining brown eyes . . . brimming with vitality." Leah discourages him and remains faithful to Nathaniel. Hers is the "gallant heart": morally strong and unyielding to temptation.

*The Round of Life* (1939) follows another strong woman, Lily Lark, from childhood to old age. Strong, assertive, and energetic, Lily makes her way up in the world. Born in a poorhouse, a "gutter child," she grows up to marry Basil Bingham and moves into his suburban house. Bingham, however, tries to turn her into a lady: "Your upbringing has been so unconventional that I think it would be a good play if you tried to get rid of that Cockney accent, Lillian. Perhaps if you copy the way I speak. . . ." Bingham's attempt to play Henry Higgins to Leah's Eliza Doolittle fails miserably, and she leaves him. She then marries Sir Havergall Clyde and moves into his country house after a honeymoon in Scotland. Lily goes through many husbands and lovers and becomes an actress for a time; finally her life goes full circle, and she dies as she was born—in a poorhouse.

*Our Little Town* (1942) is the story of Lisa Broad, a village doctor's daughter. "A small town like ours of three thousand souls," says Dr. Barnaby Broad, "is like my round Convex mirror there. In miniature it reflects the whole world . . . know Littleton and you know mankind." Lisa wants to escape from the little town, "to travel over the whole world, marry the man she most wanted, and have children who would be the sort she desired; to complete a full personal life, and help reform the world."

*Phillpotts's father, the author Eden Phillpotts*
*(Hulton-Deutsch Collection)*

But it is not to be. She becomes involved with two men, Lawrence Standing and Christopher Walton. Lawrence is killed, and Christopher is blinded, in World War II. At the end of the novel Lisa decides to remain with Christopher: "She was glad to do what she could for her old friend. Why should the fact that long since, as it seemed, she had refused his offer of marriage, and Lawrence had been killed, prevent her from helping him. . . . Grief had enkindled, not blown out, her loving kindness and generosity."

*From Jane to John* (1943) is an epistolary novel; it is told in a series of letters from Jane Moor, a young woman living in the West Country village of Netherfold, to John Mann, a soldier, from October 1939 to February 1942. During the course of their correspondence John comes home on leave, and he and Jane marry; later they have a child, Jonathan Forward. All of the letters are from Jane; none of John's is included. The war remains in the background as the reader sees the little world of Netherfold through Jane's eyes: she experiences loneliness, love, and motherhood; she describes her mother, her cat, her garden, her dreams, her neighbors, her walks on the moor, and her trips to Cornwall. "The old laburnum is out in Reddaway garden, John, and the lilies of the valley, lupius, irises, tulips, and white clematis. . . . That's what I love about England."

*The Fosterling* (1949) is told by Alison Westaway, a midwife at Marronmouth General Hospital in Devon. Anthony Gilbert, the town librarian, proposes to her, but she refuses his offer of marriage because she is preoccupied with adopting the fosterling, Giles. A gallery of interesting characters is presented: Alison's father, Thomas, who runs the Gallean Inn; her animal-loving grandfather, "the Captain"; her domineering grandmother, "the Commodore"; her great-aunt Carrie, "eternally young in spirit and eternally cheerful"; and her stepmother, Rosalie, who keeps "the house spic and span, and always looked comely and fresh." After Giles grows up and disappears from the village, Anthony proposes to Alison a second time and is accepted. At the end of the novel Giles is discovered in Rio de Janeiro with a circus.

In *Stubborn Earth* (1951) Hannah Northway and her son Oliver work the intractable soil of Hillhead Farm, which had been wrested from the West Country moorland by their ancestors three centuries before. Hannah wants to unite Hillhead with Chase Farm, a larger and richer establishment, by having Oliver marry Isabella, the daughter of Chase Farm's owners, Jemima and Joseph Northway. Oliver, however, loves Selina Coombe, a poor orphan. Hannah protests Oliver's choice, and after he and Selina are married she makes their lives miserable with her ceaseless nagging of her daughter-in-law. The clashes only increase after the birth of Oliver and Selina's son, Alfred, a year after their marriage: "Selina likened her mother-in-law to the tough bracken shoots which pushed up through the hardest ground in spring, even cracking asphalt and cement." Pushed beyond endurance, Selina runs away from home but returns after a day; the shock of her disappearance produces a change of heart in Hannah. "Don't cry any more. Kiss me. Henceforth my heart will beat for both of you," Hannah tells Selina, finally accepting her as one of the family.

Phillpotts herself remained single until she was fifty-five. On 25 August 1951, at the Newton Abbot Registry Office, she married Nicholas Ross, an American from Boston who had settled in Britain. Her experience was similar to that of Oliver in *Stubborn Earth:* her father was vehemently opposed to the marriage. When she told him of her plans, "He belittled my information, did not take it seriously, laughed at me, bade me put the whole daft notion out of my head. What on earth was I dreaming of?" After the marriage, until his death in 1960, Eden

Phillpotts refused to speak to his daughter. The marriage was a happy one, lasting until Nicholas died on 28 July 1967. After her marriage Phillpotts published her writings under the name Adelaide Ross.

In 1963 Ross and her husband had traveled around the world; she told the story of the thirty-thousand-mile voyage in *Panorama of the World* (1969). Her autobiography, *Reverie,* also describes her extensive travels, as well as her vivid memories of her friendships with such literary figures as Thomas and Florence Hardy Bennett.

Ross spent most of the last years of her life in the village of Kilkhampton, Cornwall, six miles north of Bude. When she became blind and too weak to live independently, she moved into Trelana Nursing Home, Poughill, Bude, where she died on 4 June 1993. She had produced a body of work that is impressive in its range and richness. Her most notable achievement is the fiction in which she explored the struggles of oppressed and abandoned women with sensitivity and sympathy.

## Letters:

*Eden Phillpotts (1862–1960): Selected Letters,* edited by James Y. Dayananda (Lanham, Md.: University Press of America, 1984).

## Papers:

The major collections of Adelaide Eden Phillpotts's correspondence and manuscripts are at the Humanities Research Center of the University of Texas at Austin and at Stevenson Library of Lock Haven University at Lock Haven, Pennsylvania.

# William Plomer

(10 December 1903 – 21 September 1973)

D. A. Boxwell
*U.S. Air Force Academy*

See also the Plomer entries in *DLB 20: British Poets, 1914–1945* and *DLB 162: British Short-Fiction Writers, 1915–1945.*

BOOKS: *Turbott Wolfe* (London: Leonard & Virginia Woolf, 1925; New York: Harcourt, Brace, 1926);

*I Speak of Africa* (London: Hogarth Press, 1927);

*Notes for Poems* (London: Hogarth Press, 1927);

*The Family Tree* (London: Leonard & Virginia Woolf, 1929);

*Paper Houses* (London: Leonard & Virginia Woolf, 1929; New York: Coward-McCann, 1929);

*Sado* (London: Leonard & Virginia Woolf, 1931); republished as *They Never Come Back* (New York: Coward-McCann, 1932);

*The Case Is Altered* (London: Leonard & Virginia Woolf, 1932; New York: Farrar & Rinehart, 1932; revised edition, London: Chatto & Windus, 1970);

*The Fivefold Screen* (London: Hogarth Press, 1932; New York: Coward-McCann, 1932);

*Cecil Rhodes* (London: Davies, 1933; New York: Appleton, 1933);

*The Child of Queen Victoria, and Other Stories* (London: Cape, 1933);

*The Invaders* (London: Cape, 1934);

*Ali the Lion: Ali of Tebeleni, Pasha of Jannina, 1741–1822* (London: Cape, 1936); republished as *The Diamond of Jannina: Ali Pasha, 1741–1822* (New York: Taplinger, 1970);

*Visiting the Caves* (London: Cape, 1936);

*Selected Poems* (London: Hogarth Press, 1940);

*Double Lives: An Autobiography* (London: Cape, 1943; New York: Noonday, 1956);

*The Dorking Thigh and Other Satires* (London: Cape, 1945);

*Four Countries* (London: Cape, 1949);

*Museum Pieces* (London: Cape, 1952; New York: Noonday, 1954);

*A Shot in the Park* (London: Cape, 1955); republished as *Borderline Ballads* (New York: Noonday, 1955);

*Janet Stone, University of Durham Library*

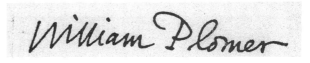

*At Home: Memoirs* (London: Cape, 1958; New York: Noonday, 1958);

*A Choice of Ballads* (London: Cape, 1960);

*Collected Poems* (London: Cape, 1960; enlarged, 1973);

*Conversation with My Younger Self* (Ewelme, U.K.: Stellar, 1963);

*Address Given at the Memorial Service for Ian Fleming: St. Bartholomew the Great, September 15th, 1964* (London: Privately printed, 1964);

*Taste and Remember* (London: Cape, 1966);

*The Planes of Bedford Square* (London: Printed at the Bookbang, 1971);

*Remarks When Opening the George Gissing Exhibition at the National Book League, London, 23 July* [i.e., June] *1971* (London: Enitharmon, 1971; Folcroft, Pa.: Folcroft Library Editions, 1977);

*Celebrations* (London: Cape, 1972);

*The Butterfly Ball and the Grasshopper's Feast,* by Plomer, Alan Aldridge, and Richard Fitter (London: Cape/Times Newspapers in association with Aurelia Enterprises, 1973); revised by Edward G. Atkins (New York: Grossman, 1975);

*The Autobiography of William Plomer* (London: Cape, 1975; New York: Taplinger, 1976);

*Electric Delights,* edited by Rupert Hart-Davis (London: Cape, 1978; Boston: Godine, 1978).

**Edition:** *Turbott Wolfe,* introduction by Laurens van der Post (London: Hogarth Press, 1965; New York: Morrow, 1965).

OTHER: Haruko Ichikawa, *Japanese Lady in Europe,* edited by Plomer (London: Cape, 1937; New York: Dutton, 1937);

Robert Francis Kilvert, *Kilvert's Diary, Selections from the Diary of the Rev. Francis Kilvert,* edited by Plomer (3 volumes, London: Cape, 1938–1940; 1 volume, New York: Macmillan, 1947; revised edition, 3 volumes, London: Cape, 1960);

Herman Melville, *Selected Poems,* edited by Plomer (London: Hogarth Press, 1943);

William D'Arfey (Anthony Butts), *Curious Relations,* edited by Plomer (London: Cape, 1945; New York: Sloane, 1947);

George Gissing, *A Life's Morning,* introduction by Plomer (London: Home & Van Thal, 1947);

Benjamin Britten, *Gloriana: Opera in Three Acts,* libretto by Plomer (London: Boosey & Hawkes, 1953);

*New Poems 1961: A P.E.N. Anthology of Contemporary Poetry,* edited by Plomer, Anthony Thwaite, and Hilary Corke (London: Hutchinson, 1961);

Herman C. Bosman, *Unto Dust,* foreword by Plomer (London: Blond, 1963);

Richard Rumbold, *A Message in Code: The Diary of Richard Rumbold, 1932–60,,* edited by Plomer (London: Weidenfeld & Nicolson, 1964);

Britten, *Curlew River: A Parable for Church Performance,* libretto by Plomer (London: Faber & Faber, 1964);

Britten, *The Burning Fiery Furnace: Second Parable for Church Performance,* libretto by Plomer (London: Faber Music, 1966);

Britten, *The Prodigal Son: Third Parable for Church Performance,* libretto by Plomer (London: Faber Music, 1968);

Ingrid Jonker, *Selected Poems,* translated by Plomer and Jack Cope (London: Cape, 1968).

In his final decade the novelist, biographer, and poet William Plomer attained the kind of recognition generally conferred on establishment literary figures: he was made a fellow of the Royal Society, a Commander of the British Empire, and president of the Poetry Society, and was awarded the Queen's Gold Medal for Poetry and an honorary doctorate of letters from Durham University. But in *At Home,* his 1958 autobiography, Plomer had disclaimed any desire for a high-profile career: "My temperament and talent did not impel me to try and make a living by writing books; they impelled me to write books only when I wished and only whatever kind I wished. . . . Literature has its battery hens; I was a wilder fowl."

Plomer gained notoriety at the outset of his career as a novelist by deliberately offending the establishment. Hurling a bomb titled *Turbott Wolfe* (1925) at his fellow South Africans, Plomer was a provocateur who prompted the outrage of the critic in *The Natal Advertiser,* whose review was headed "A Nasty Book on a Nasty Subject," and the condemnation of the reviewer for *The South African Nation,* who called the novel "pornographic." Plomer described the reception of the work in his earlier autobiography, *Double Lives* (1943): "Leading South African newspapers devoted long lead articles to vituperation, which served very well as advertisement." Virginia Woolf—who, with her husband, Leonard, published the novel—commented on Plomer's complexity in her diary entry of 19 August 1929: "a compressed inarticulate young man, thickly coated with a universal manner fit for all weather and people: tells a nice dry prim story, but has the wild eyes which I . . . take to be the true index of what goes on within." Plomer's five widely ranging novels belie the author's diffident public persona: they are urgent and strongly articulated explorations of the complex connections among desire, class, and race.

A product of the heyday of British imperialism, William Charles Franklyn Plomer (pronounced "Plumer") was born in Pietersburg, Transvaal, on 10 December 1903 to Charles Plomer, a civil servant in the Department of Native Affairs, and Edythe Waite-Browne Plomer. In *At Home* William Plomer describes his English parents as sensible mid-Victorians, "faithful but not fanatical Anglicans" who "believed that it was an obligation to help those less fortunate than themselves, as a matter of

*Plomer's parents, Charles and Edythe Waite-Browne Plomer*

ordinary humanity and Christian charity." His parents' relatively enlightened views served as a guiding principle in Plomer's fiction. In *At Home* he writes that "it is the business of the novelist not so much to see life as it is to see from the point of view of others." This self-effacing desire to represent empathetically the perceptions of other classes and races was also fostered by a peripatetic childhood spent migrating between South Africa and England; Plomer's fiction is marked by his sense of being simultaneously an involved but detached observer. He was educated in England at Beechmont and Rugby, and at St. John's College in Johannesburg. Completing his formal schooling at seventeen, he embarked on brief careers as a farmer and as a merchant. At Marsh Moor, an isolated farm in the Eastern Province of the Cape Colony, and later at his trading post at Entumeni in Zululand, Plomer experienced the provincial racism that would be the subject of his sensational first novel.

Begun when Plomer was only nineteen, *Turbott Wolfe* is the work of an idealistic young man lashing out against the injustices and brutalities of racially divided South African society. "My impulse was to present in fictional form, partly satirical, partly lyri-

cal, partly fantastic," an evocation of contemporary South Africa, Plomer wrote later in *At Home*. The writing was an exercise in catharsis, an attempt, he says, "to externalize the turmoil of feelings" the subject aroused in him. "To speak of it as a novel is perhaps a misnomer: it was a violent ejaculation, a protest, a nightmare, a phantasmagoria." Yet the novel is far more subtle and complex than this self-critique would suggest. Hailed by liberals as a pioneering work, *Turbott Wolfe* has been a touchstone in South African literary history; of all Plomer's novels it has attracted the most critical attention. In his introduction to the 1965 republication of the novel—which was banned in South Africa because of its advocacy of miscegenation as a solution to racial conflict—Laurens van der Post says that Plomer's first work "was a book of revelation" to South Africans, the most significant literary exploration of the country since Olive Schreiner's *The Story of an African Farm* (1883). This opinion was shared by the South African writers Nadine Gordimer and Alan Paton.

The novel is structured as a series of disillusioned and highly ambivalent reminiscences of the title character's life in South Africa, told on his deathbed to his former schoolmate "William Plo-

*Plomer with his students in Tokyo in 1928 (University of Durham Library)*

mer"; ostracized by his South African neighbors, Wolfe has returned to England broken and embittered. The distancing established by the indirect narration, typical of Plomer's often-criticized reticence as a writer, mitigates the emotional "turmoil" that incited the production of the novel. "William Plomer" gradually recedes from the work, failing to make a final reappearance to bring closure to the story. *Turbott Wolfe* ends, instead, with several "appendices," consisting of unfinished notes for a caricature and three poems. The inconclusiveness of the novel attests to the defeatism felt by all those who challenged the white-supremacist culture of South Africa.

Wolfe, the keeper of a trading post in rural South Africa, comes into conflict with the philistine and racist white farmers Bloodfield, Flesher, and Schwerdt, whose "vulgarity only emphasized the colossal disastrous significance of their background," because of his enlightened racial attitudes and his interest in the arts. Wolfe criticizes "the combined ruthlessness of the poor white and the missionary and the official," who join together to oppress the natives; he calls one Protestant mission "nothing more or less than a house of ill-fame on the lines of a garden-village." Wolfe is, however, hardly Plomer's mouthpiece; the rich modernist texture of the novel is a consequence of Wolfe's unreliability as a narrator. His description of the two interracial romances at the center of the novel—his own unconsummated infatuation with Nhliziyombi and his outrage at the freethinking Mabel van der Horst's marriage to Zachary Msomi—reveals how lacking in self-

awareness he is. He idealizes Nhliziyombi in an unconsciously racist way: "She was an ambassadress of all that beauty (it might be called holiness), the intensity of the old wonderful unknown primitive African life—outside history, outside time, outside science." Immobilized by his idealization of Nhliziyombi and fearful of the consequences of pursuing the native woman, Wolfe "dare[s] not touch her." His unacknowledged racism is also apparent in his reaction to Mabel's marriage to Zachary: "Then this idea of miscegenation. How can I believe in it? It is a nightmare. This girl could not really mean to give herself to an African. She would be cutting herself clean off from her own world."

In the wake of the publication of the book Plomer found himself part of a South African literary community that included such like-minded figures as van der Post and Roy Campbell; the three established the literary magazine *Voorslag* (Whiplash) in 1926. Soon afterward Plomer and van der Post made a spontaneous decision to sail for Japan. Plomer's three years of traveling and teaching there resulted in a collection of short stories, *Paper Houses* (1929), and the novel *Sado* (1931).

Like *Turbott Wolfe,* Plomer's delicately observed second novel is about the impossibility of establishing lasting cross-cultural and interracial relationships. The homosexual love affair of Victor Lucas, a painter sojourning in Tokyo to expand his artistic horizons, and his model, the student Sado Masaji, founders on the shoals of cultural differences. After the consummation of their relationship on a picnic—obliquely, yet daringly, portrayed by

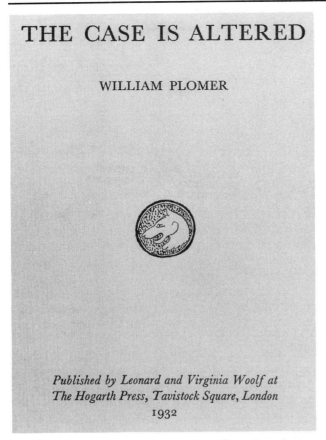

# THE CASE IS ALTERED

### WILLIAM PLOMER

*Published by Leonard and Virginia Woolf at
The Hogarth Press, Tavistock Square, London*
1932

*Title page for Plomer's novel about class conflict and murder in a
London boardinghouse*

Plomer—the two men are left "with little but the knowledge of failure." Victor distances himself from Sado and commits himself to his European friends and artistic heritage, leaving Sado devastated. Victor reflects that

> since the picnic he had tried to make himself believe that the new turn in his relationship with Sado had supplied that very stimulus of which for some time he had unconsciously felt in need. But now he saw that he was wrong, that he had led himself into a blind alley, and probably Sado as well. For what, after all, he now asked himself, had he expected of Sado? Had he not acted almost as if he had assumed that Sado might be a permanent part of his life? If so, would that not have involved either Sado leaving Japan or Lucas's staying there? He now shuddered at the idea, which he had never before entertained, of the possibility of being obliged to establish himself in Japan—and who could imagine Sado separated from his country?

The interracial marriage of Komatsu, Victor's patron and host, and his British-born wife, Iris, also founders. The Komatsus' marriage had been entered into out of a mutual effort at cross-cultural contact; Iris's alienation from England "and the limitations of a family life dominated by dead and dying ideas" had led her to "take the very independent step of trying to find a new life in a new country." But the effort is revealed to be misguided when the unhappily married and homesick Iris unsuccessfully pursues Victor, who has moved into the Komatsus' guest house with Sado. Learning from the Komatsus' example, Victor renounces exile and the possibility of life with Sado in Japan.

Reviewers compared the novel favorably to Plomer's friend E. M. Forster's *Where Angels Fear to Tread* (1905), which had explored the same theme. *Everyman* praised Plomer for a "power of detachment rare in youth, and a quality of unprejudiced observation found in few writers of full maturity." The muted depiction of the homosexual relationship at the heart of the novel, however, made Harold Nicolson impatient in his *Action* review: "If I started out to write a book on inversion I think I should be more plucky about it from the start." But in the wake of the trials of both the British and American publishers of Radclyffe Hall's lesbian novel, *The Well of Loneliness* (1928), Plomer had chosen to avoid bringing down the wrath of official British censorship.

In the spring of 1929 Plomer left Japan for England by way of Manchuria, Siberia, Russia, and Poland. In England he underwent what he called an incomplete "re-occidentation," and his final three novels were written from an expatriate's perspective. "Displacement," he says in *At Home,* "had enabled me to understand, as I could not otherwise have understood, something of the strangeness a foreigner approaching England for the first time might feel." His return to England was eased by his entrée into the London literary scene provided by the Woolfs, and by his attachment to the painter Anthony Butts, who encouraged Plomer in his view—borne out by the events of the 1930s—that Western cultures were doomed to catastrophic devastation unless they renounced violence. Plomer and Butts traveled in France, Germany, and Italy and lived in Greece for a time, returning to England in 1932.

The first of Plomer's novels with a British setting, *The Case Is Altered* (1932), was inspired by a sensational real-life event: the murder of his landlady by her obsessively jealous common-law husband in November 1929. In her diary entry for 30 November Virginia Woolf recorded how Plomer's "eyes—the representative part of him—flashed and goggled" as he related the story to her. The same lively narration energizes *The Case Is Altered,* which begins as a comedy of manners and ends in what Phyllis Bentley, reviewing the novel in *The New*

*Plomer in 1934 with his mentor and publisher, Virginia Woolf (University of Durham Library)*

*Statesman and Nation* (16 July 1932), called a "superb murder scene . . . completely real and convincing." Bentley praised Plomer for his "grim humor and essentially modern view of life," which she found "as refreshingly acid as a lemon." The novel shows that violence is a fact of life even in the most placid and mundane of London's domestic milieus, the lower-middle-class boardinghouse; it also shows that social class, like racial difference in *Turbott Wolfe* and *Sado,* impedes human connection. Beryl Fernandez's London boardinghouse, a microcosm of British society in which people from differing class backgrounds come into conflict, reflects Plomer's attempt to come to grips with the baroque complexities of the British class system.

Cambodia Crescent is a street in symbolic transition, a decaying Victorian neighborhood undergoing its final death throes before being demolished and replaced by modern high-rise buildings. The narrator speaks of the "dreary respectability" of the street, its vulgarly large houses carved into apartments filled with "thwarted hopes, and all the horrors of life at its worst in the bourgeois backwaters." The lodgers at Beryl's house are victims of a destructive and exploitative class system. Those who struggle unsuccessfully to rise above their origins include the attractive greengrocer's assistant Eric Alston and the grasping Mrs. Gambitt, who wishes to be "taken for a decayed gentlewoman." There are also actual "decayed gentlewomen" who are trying to keep themselves from falling further

down the social hierarchy, such as Mrs. Petherham-Porter, who dabbles in escapist occultism, and Constantia Brixworth, one of "these lonely, nomadic women" who subsist on failing investments.

It is Beryl's effort to position herself more securely by buying the house that finally costs her her life: her successful entrepreneurial spirit is resented by her husband, Paul, a failed businessman who feels emasculated by being supplanted as the breadwinner. He lives in the "anti-social dream-world of the madman," groundlessly suspecting his wife of infidelity with every man with whom she comes into contact, and his paranoid rages culminate in his murdering Beryl on the staircase in front of her young daughter. Her masochistic acceptance of Paul's destructive passion is significant for the political theme of the novel: the narrator asserts that Beryl is symbolic of "modern life, which is Jewish, feminine, and paradoxical. The little movements of her life were like the large movements of the world we live in—a world . . . which seeks negation instead of the godlike, desires death, perhaps, rather than life." The pessimism of *The Case Is Altered,* as well as its unconscious anti-Semitism and sexism, is typical of liberal British writing of the 1930s.

With one exception, class conflict structures every character's relationship with virtually every other character in the novel. For example, Eric's girlfriend, Amy Pascall, laments that "he's ambitious. . . . Socially ambitious, I mean. . . . Anyway I sometimes thinks I'm not good enough for him!"

*The painter Anthony Butts, Plomer's longtime companion and the model for the protagonist of Plomer's novel* Museum Pieces *(University of Durham Library)*

The only successful relationship in *The Case Is Altered* is a homosexual one between the petty-bourgeois Eric Alston and Amy's adventurous working-class brother, Willy Pascall. In the final scene of the novel Eric nurses Willy's wounds after a violent political rally at which working-class men have protested the appearance of a right-wing upper-class candidate and his supporters:

> Pascall got a nasty cut on the hand from a piece of glass falling from a broken window. Alston managed to fight a way through the crowd and get him outside, where he produced a handkerchief and tied up the place as carefully as he could. In his eyes shone something like the bright, fanatical devotion of the beardless Achilles kneeling to bind up the wounded arm of Patroclus, who, seated on the ground and in pain, clenches his white teeth between his bearded lips (eager that no complaint shall escape from them) and turns away his graceful head, the two men forming, for an instant of time and for ever, an image of courage, beauty, and love.

Like *The Case Is Altered, The Invaders* (1934) is marked by a profound pessimism about the ability of the British people to surmount class conflict. Two decades after its publication he commented in *At Home,* "The book was also thought well of by those of my friends who had experience of social work and a better idea of the gulf that separated South Kensington from the purlieus of the Edgware Road than had certain literary intellectuals of the know-all type." The settings of the novel range from affluent Holland Park, the home of the Presteigns, to the sweatshops of Soho and the military barracks near Marble Arch, the habitats, respectively, of Mavis Steel and her brother, Chick. *The Invaders* interweaves its characters through encounters between working-class migrants to London from the provinces—the "invaders" of the title—and members of the financially secure urban middle class. Chief among the latter is the disillusioned World War I veteran Nigel Edge, who moves among the various locales restlessly searching for a meaningful homosexual relationship and for independence from his stereotypically Edwardian uncle, Col. Maurice Presteign. Clearly the character with whom Plomer most identifies, Nigel is ambivalent about everything; he is representative of what the narrator calls "the damaged generation—they needed another war, but they were all pacifists; they needed a cause and had none; they needed something to look forward to and found nothing." While *The Case Is Altered* is optimistic about the possibility of fulfilling homosexual relationships, *The Invaders* is a depiction of the effects of homophobia. Nigel is attracted to two working-class men, Tony Hart and Chick Steel, both of whom are recent migrants to the metropolis. Uncle Maurice condemns his nephew's "unnatural" relationships with men; Chick, who does not requite or fully understand Nigel's desire, fears "that his association with Nigel might be open to misconstruction"; and Nigel is blackmailed by Tony's vicious brother, Len. Ultimately, Chick and Tony pull away from Nigel's financial support and emotional neediness. The working-class characters realize that London will not provide the economic salvation and class mobility for which they had hoped. Encountering more-overt hostility from the middle classes in the pressured confines of urban life, and subject to economic and sexual predation in ways for which their rural origins have ill prepared them, the "invaders" are defeated. Broken by their encounters with contemporary urban society, Tony, Chick, and Mavis leave the city. Working-class life in the Midlands and North of England is difficult, but it is less anomic and rootless than modern urban existence. At the end of the novel Nigel is alone but "calm and resigned, and hopeful about the future. He did not know why he was hopeful, but he felt that a phase of his life was ended. He felt as if he knew where he was."

*The Invaders* was published by Jonathan Cape, for whom Plomer became a reader and editorial adviser in the mid 1930s. Abandoning novel writing, he turned to biography, autobiography, criticism, and, especially, poetry. During World War II he worked for the Naval Intelligence Division of the Admiralty. It was not until the early 1950s that he wrote another novel; *Museum Pieces* (1952) was his last work in the genre and, in his opinion, the finest. "I have a special affection for it, and would not alter a word or comma," he said in *At Home*. Critics agreed: John Raymond in *The New Statesman and Nation* (20 September 1952) called *Museum Pieces* a "triumph. It is witty, stylish, supremely entertaining, and it has a wonderfully elegiac centre."

The novel is a roman à clef about, and a tribute to, Plomer's friend Butts, who had committed suicide in 1941 in despair at the carnage of World War II. It was inspired by Plomer's editing of *Curious Relations* (1945), Butts's memoir of his family. In telling the story of Toby D'Arfey and his domineering mother, Susannah Mountfaucon, the novel scrupulously adheres to the facts of the lives of Butts and his mother, Mary Colville-Hyde; but the strategies of fiction enable Plomer to elevate Butts as the representative figure of a tragic anachronism: the sensitive artist whose aristocratic and premodern ethos leaves him unable to survive the horrors of the twentieth century. Butts believed, as Plomer says in *At Home,* "that Europe had lost its way and that the benefits it had brought to Asia and Africa had been fatally outweighed by arrogance, exploitation, want of imagination, want of foresight and puritanical materialism."

The narrator of *Museum Pieces* is the archivist Jane Valance, a longtime friend of Toby and his mother. Jane is an observer; she relates almost nothing about herself. As the novel opens, Jane questions the extent to which anyone's life can be narrated:

> Am I setting out to write a memoir in the form of a novel, or a novel in the form of a memoir? I owe a little debt, I feel, to the truth, and I intend to pay: it is my debt and I am the only person who can pay it. That is more important to me than contriving a plot, keeping potential readers in a state of tension, flattering their prejudices, and so on. . . . Even the lives of some of the people one knows best are "seen, lost, and seen," like dragonflies on a summer morning—especially the lives of people like Toby, who was so greatly concerned to keep his friends segregated from one another or even completely ignorant of one another's existence.

Here Plomer is signaling his reasons for using fiction, rather than biography, to memorialize the man who had been his most intimate friend for more than a decade. Jane eulogizes Toby as "a civilized man. He was always on the side of creators against destroyers, he was an enemy of the banal, and if he had strayed in search of easy amusement, he knew and always returned to what was enduring and vigorous and best." Plomer's pessimism about the ability of the creators to withstand the onslaught of the destroyers reaches its apex in *Museum Pieces*. Perhaps the most telling scenes in the novel are those that detail Toby's gradual physical extinction via drug abuse in a nursing home surrounded by the bombed sites of former London neighborhoods. The Luftwaffe bombs destroy the stored possessions of the D'Arfey and Mountfaucon families, which symbolize the cultural and artistic heritage of Britain. Like *Between the Acts* (1941), his mentor Virginia Woolf's final novel, *Museum Pieces* is an affectionate but rue-laden elegy for a Britain attempting to cope with the descent of the West into barbarity.

Plomer's literary career continued for another twenty years after his last novel. He died of a heart attack on 21 September 1973 in Hassocks, Sussex. Critics have often regretted that Plomer's novels lack the direct intensity of his poetry; Paton calls him "the soul of reticence" for his muted persona and self-effacing fiction. *Turbott Wolfe* is still prominent in discussions of South African literary history, but Plomer's subsequent novels are generally ignored. Nevertheless, they would reward renewed critical attention.

**Biography:**

Peter F. Alexander, *William Plomer: A Biography* (New York: Oxford University Press, 1989).

**References:**

"About William Plomer," *London Magazine,* new series 13 (December 1973/January 1974): 5–29;

Peter F. Alexander, "An Archetypal Anti-Apartheid Novel: The Writing of Turbott Wolfe," *Durham University Journal,* 81 (June 1989): 281–287;

Geoffrey V. Davis, "'Look Elsewhere for Your Bedtime Story': William Plomer and the Politics of Love," *Matatu: Journal of African Culture and Society,* 2 (Autumn 1988): 255–275;

John Robert Doyle, *William Plomer* (New York: Twayne, 1969);

Nadine Gordimer, "A Wilder Fowl," in *Turbott Wolfe,* by Plomer, edited by Stephen Gray (Johannesburg: Donker, 1980), pp. 165–168;

Stephen Gray, "'Doubly Involved and Doubly Detached': William Plomer's Creative Use of the Colonial-Motherland Bond," *Commonwealth Essays and Studies,* 11 (Autumn 1988): 46–54;

Gray, "Edward Wolfe and Turbott Wolfe: A Note Concerning William Plomer," *Contrast: South African Literary Journal,* 4 (December 1987): 31–41;

Cecily Lockett, "*Turbott Wolfe:* A Failed Novel or a Failure of Criticism?," *Unisa: English Studies,* 25 (May 1987): 29–34;

Alan Paton, "William Plomer: Soul of Reticence," *Theoria: A Journal of Studies in the Arts, Humanities and Social Sciences,* 46 (1976): 1–15;

David Rabkin, "Race and Fiction: God's Stepchil-dren and *Turbott Wolfe,*" in *The South African Novel in English: Essays in Criticism and Society,* edited by Kenneth Parker (New York: Africana, 1978), pp. 77–94;

Michael Wade, "William Plomer, English Liberalism, and the South African Novel," *Journal of Commonwealth Literature,* 8, no. 1 (1973): 20–32.

**Papers:**
William Plomer's papers are at the University of Durham in England.

# Ernest Raymond

*(31 December 1888 – 14 May 1974)*

George J. Johnson

BOOKS: *Tell England: A Study in a Generation* (London: Cassell, 1922; New York: Doran, 1922);
*Rossenal* (London & New York: Cassell, 1922);
*Damascus Gate* (London & New York: Cassell, 1923; New York: Doran, 1923);
*The Shout of the King* (London: Hodder & Stoughton, 1924; New York: Doran, 1924);
*Wanderlight* (London & New York: Cassell, 1924);
*Daphne Bruno* (London & New York: Cassell, 1925; New York: Doran, 1926);
*The Business of Living* (Dover: Dover & County Chronicle, 1926);
*The Fulfillment of Daphne Bruno* (London & New York: Cassell, 1926; New York: Doran, 1926);
*Morris in the Dance: A Novel* (London: Cassell, 1927);
*The Old Tree Blossomed: A Realistic Romance* (London: Cassell, 1928);
*Through Literature to Life: An Enthusiasm and an Anthology* (London: Cassell, 1928; Folcroft, Pa.: Folcroft Library Editions, 1976);
*The Berg: A Play in Three Acts* (London: Benn, 1929);
*A Family That Was* (London: Cassell, 1929; New York: Appleton, 1930);
*The Jesting Army* (London: Cassell, 1930; New York: Appleton, 1931);
*Mary Leith* (London: Cassell, 1931; New York: Appleton, 1932);
*Once in England: A Novel* (London: Cassell, 1932)—comprises *A Family That Was, The Jesting Army, Mary Leith*;
*The Multabello Road: A Play in Three Acts* (London: Cassell, 1933);
*Newtimber Lane: Being a Writing of Sir Edmund Earlwin of Cowbourne in Sussex* (London: Cassell, 1933);
*Child of Norman's End* (London: Cassell, 1934);
*We, the Accused* (London: Cassell, 1935; New York: Stokes, 1935);
*Don John's Mountain Home* (London: Cassell, 1936);
*The Marsh* (London: Cassell, 1937; New York: Stokes, 1937);
*In the Steps of St. Francis* (London: Rich & Cowan, 1938; New York: Kinsey, 1939);
*The Miracle of Brean* (London: Cassell, 1939);

*Ernest Raymond*

*A Song of the Tide* (London: Cassell, 1940);
*The Last to Rest* (London: Cassell, 1941; New York: Kinsey, 1942);
*Was There Love Once?: A Novel* (London: Cassell, 1942);
*The Corporal of the Guard: A Novel* (London: Cassell, 1943);
*For Them That Trespass: A Novel* (London: Cassell, 1944; New York: Dutton, 1976);
*Back to Humanity,* by Raymond and Patrick Raymond (London: Cassell, 1945);
*The Five Sons of Le Faber* (London: Gifford, 1946);
*The Kilburn Tale* (London: Cassell, 1947);
*In the Steps of the Brontës* (London & New York: Rich & Cowan, 1948);

*Gentle Greaves* (London: Cassell, 1949; New York: Saturday Review Press, 1972);

*The Witness of Canon Welcome* (London: Cassell, 1950);

*A Chorus Ending* (London: Cassell, 1951);

*The Chalice and the Sword* (London: Cassell, 1952);

*Two Gentlemen of Rome: The Story of Keats and Shelley* (London: Cassell, 1952);

*The Nameless Places* (London: Cassell, 1954);

*To the Wood No More: A Novel* (London: Cassell, 1954);

*The Lord of Wensley* (London: Cassell, 1956);

*The Old June Weather* (London: Cassell, 1957; New York: Saturday Review Press, 1974);

*The City and the Dream* (London: Cassell, 1958; New York: Saturday Review Press, 1975);

*The Quiet Shore* (London: Cassell, 1958);

*The Visit of Brother Ives* (London: Cassell, 1960);

*Mr. Olim* (London: Cassell, 1961);

*Paris, City of Enchantment* (London: Newnes, 1961; New York: Macmillan, 1961);

*The Chatelaine* (London: Cassell, 1962);

*One of Our Brethren* (London: Cassell, 1963);

*Late in the Day: A Novel* (London: Cassell, 1964);

*The Tree of Heaven* (London: Cassell, 1965);

*The Mountain Farm* (London: Cassell, 1966; New York: Saturday Review Press, 1973);

*The Bethany Road* (London: Cassell, 1967);

*The Story of My Days: An Autobiography, 1888–1922* (London: Cassell, 1968);

*Please You, Draw Near: Autobiography 1922–1968* (London: Cassell, 1969);

*Good Morning, Good People: An Autobiography—Past and Present* (London: Cassell, 1970);

*A Georgian Love Story* (London: Cassell, 1971; New York: McCall, 1971);

*Our Late Member: A Novel* (London: Cassell, 1972);

*Miryam's Guest House: A Novel* (London: Cassell, 1973);

*Under Wedgery Down: A Novel* (London: Cassell, 1974).

**Editions:** *We, the Accused* (New York: St. Martin's Press, 1981);

*We, the Accused* (Harmondsworth & New York: Penguin, 1983).

PLAY PRODUCTIONS: *The Berg*, London, Q Theatre, 5 March 1929;

*The Multabello Road*, London, St. Martin's Theatre, 24 April 1932.

OTHER: *The Autobiography of David ———*, edited by Raymond (London: Gollancz, 1946).

SELECTED PERIODICAL PUBLICATION— UNCOLLECTED: "The Brontë Legend, Its Cause and Treatment," *Essays by Divers Hands, Being the Transactions of the Royal Society of Literature of the United Kingdom,* third series 26 (1953): 127–141.

Labeled a "popular" novelist, Ernest Raymond published fifty-nine books in fifty-two years. His first, *Tell England: A Study in a Generation* (1922), sold three hundred thousand copies by 1939, reached its fortieth edition by 1965, and was made into a motion picture. His second-most-celebrated novel, *We, the Accused* (1935), was, as he said in *Please You, Draw Near: Autobiography 1922–1968* (1969), "a steady seller for thirty years"; received the 1935 Book Guild Medal; and was selected by readers of the *Sunday Times* as one of the Hundred Best Crime Stories. Three years before his death the eighty-three-year-old Raymond reentered the American fiction market after a thirty-year absence with *A Georgian Love Story* (1971); it was followed in each of the succeeding five years by a novel that had been previously published in England and in the early 1980s by several editions of *We, the Accused,* one of them a companion to the 1983 television version. In the *New York Times Book Review* (25 July 1926) Percy A. Hutchison claimed that "the public has more to do with determining art-direction than have the artists" and that Raymond provided that public with "a turning away from the novel of sophistication." This approach allowed Raymond to display his skill as a storyteller, his broad-minded views, his concern for his realistic characters—evident in the intimate asides he provides—and the humor and social satire that enliven his narration.

Born on 31 December 1888 in Argentieres, France, purportedly to William and Florence Bell Raymond, Ernest Raymond was brought to England in 1891. He was raised in London, along with another child—whom he identifies in *The Story of My Days: An Autobiography, 1888–1922* (1968) only as Dots—by his "Auntie," Miss Emily Calder. Frequently beaten by Calder, Raymond became an isolated and shy dreamer. Calder's sister, whom Raymond knew as Aunt Ida, lived nearby with her husband, Dr. Franz Broenner, and a son, Percy Wilkinson, who was five years older than Raymond and was supposedly the product of a previous marriage. Raymond's frequent visits to Ida led to displays of affection on her part that, as a child, he did not understand. He gradually discovered that he and Dots were the children of Maj. Gen. George Frederick Blake and had been conceived in the same year by the Calder sisters—Dots by Emily and Ernest by Ida; he deduced that Percy was also the general's son. While Blake, of whom Ernest was fond, never admitted the relationship, Ida did so shortly before her death; she explained that "General Blake always said I was not to be troubled" and that he had paid Emily to care for Raymond.

Blake provided for Raymond's education at Colet Court and, when he was twelve, at St. Paul's, a highly regarded London public school (what Americans would call a private school). There, in 1901, the lonely and sensitive Raymond discovered Charles Dickens's *Pickwick Papers* (1836–1837) and immediately felt the desire to emulate Dickens by earning everlasting acclaim as a writer.

The general's death in 1904 and Aunt Emily's decision, as trustee, to apply Raymond's bequest to herself meant that Raymond had to enroll in a cheaper school. A year later he ended his education and went to work in a store in London. In 1908 he became a teacher at Glengorse School, a preparatory school in Eastbourne, Sussex. In 1911 he moved to St. Christopher's School in Bath, where he taught until the following year.

Attracted to Anglo-Catholicism during his time in Bath, in 1912 Raymond entered Chichester Theological College, where, aided by a photographic memory and driven by a desire to prove himself to his disdainful Aunt Emily, he graduated first in his class. He went on to receive an L.Th. from Durham University and was ordained a priest in the Church of England in 1914. He was a chaplain with the Tenth Manchester Regiment from 1915 to 1917 and with the Ninth Worcestershire Regiment from 1917 to 1919; he saw action at Gallipoli in August 1915 and also served in Egypt, France, Mesopotamia, Persia (today Iran), and Russia. Returning to England, he became curate at Brighton Parish Church. In 1921 he married Zoe Irene Maude Doucett; they had two children, Patrick and Lella.

After being rejected by twelve publishers, *Tell England: A Study in a Generation* was published by Cassell on 16 February 1922; the firm would be Raymond's main British publisher for the rest of his career. The first half of the novel follows the escapades of the narrator, Rupert Ray, and his friends Edgar Doe and Archie Pennybet during their five years at Keningstowe, a boys' school. Begun when Raymond was eighteen, this half lacks form and is quite mawkish in comparison to the still-emotional but more-controlled second half, set during World War I. Pennybet is killed at Neuve Chappele in 1914; Ray and Doe join the ill-fated Dardanelles expedition in late 1915, and Doe dies heroically while creating a diversion for the evacuation of Suvla. Ray survives that action but perishes in Belgium near the war's end; the "editor" of the work, Padre Monte,

*Maj. Gen. George Frederick Blake, the family friend whom Raymond discovered to be his father*

includes Ray's final letter and describes the circumstances of his death. The novel's title comes from a paraphrase of Simonides' tribute to the Spartan heroes of Thermopylae: "Tell England, ye who pass this monument / We died for her and here we rest content."

Critical opinion of the novel was sharply divided. L. Moore said in the *Literary Review* (2 September 1922) that the work presented "a clearer account of heroism and the making and make-up of heroes than any other novel of the war"; the *Nation and Atheneum* (29 April 1922) called it "a sentimental, coarse and pretentious book—a vulgar book" but praised Raymond's descriptive powers. Mary Cardogan and Patricia Craig say that it "became a best seller because it pandered openly to certain romantic ideas of youth and its attitude to war." Raymond later admitted embarrassment at its failings, but the reading public had no such doubts: the novel was reprinted five times by April 1922 and was still being published more than thirty years later.

In *Please You, Draw Near* Raymond confesses that "the four or five novels that succeeded *Tell England* . . . were not, as wholes, good enough, and, were it possible, I would cheerfully see them pulped." The first of these, *Rossenal,* was published in August 1922. The title is the surname bestowed on the illegitimate protagonist, David. David is raised by a guardian, Katie Macassa; his "aunt," Dora Chartreuse, finally confirms his suspicion that she is his mother, but Sir Gordon Hay never confesses to being David's father. David is left in poverty by the embezzling of Katie and her lawyer brother; but the discerning schoolmaster Mr. Aitch helps him to find a teaching position in Eastbourne, which leads to David's involvement with the wealthy Angus family and to the beginning of his writing career. Despite Raymond's feelings about the work, the reviewer for *Punch* (20 September 1922) found *Rossenal* "very good company to the end."

In 1922 Raymond became one of the earliest members of the International P.E.N. Club. The following year he filed a Deed of Relinquishment, resigning from the priesthood, and also published *Damascus Gate.* The novel details the relationship of two soul-mate cousins, Oscar Pool Shattery and Lella Shattery Pool. A brilliant and dynamic inventor, Oscar relies on the patient Lella to see him through the failure of his marriage and the loss of his business empire, while she must cope with her marriage to the ambitious and hypocritical clergyman Henry Guard. Finally realizing that their obsessions can only damage their relationships, the characters experience conversions in their views of themselves that parallel Saint Paul's transformation outside the gates of Damascus. In general, the reviews were positive, with the *Times Literary Supplement* (14 June 1923) claiming that the work's "strength and firmness of characterization" were superior to those of the two previous novels. In *Wanderlight* (1924) the war veteran Hilary Down has a love affair and undergoes a crisis of conscience just before his consecration as an Anglican priest. The *Times Literary Supplement* (12 June 1924) said that Raymond's love of his youthful characters "enables him to win our sympathy for them."

*Daphne Bruno* (1925) was followed in 1926 by its sequel, *The Fulfillment of Daphne Bruno.* The first novel follows the late-Victorian, upper-middle-class heroine from her birth through her failed romance with the American Henry Detmould; through a literary career that creates problems with her already-distant author-father, Tenter Bruno; to her loveless marriage to her uninteresting childhood playmate, Roger Muirhead, and the birth of their daughter,

Evie. In the sequel Daphne and Roger establish a successful preparatory school, and Daphne writes a well-received novel, inherits her father's wealth, and attains a balance between reason and emotion that enables her to counsel her headstrong and talented daughter in the turbulent postwar period. The first novel was criticized for a lack of substance; Percy A. Hutchison noted in *The New York Times Book Review* (25 July 1926) that Raymond was able to sum up its content "in less than two pages at the outset of its sequel." Hutchinson found *The Fulfillment of Daphne Bruno* "less a novel to enthrall than a work to which he felt compelled to yield respect."

Late in 1926 Raymond, who had never skied, accepted an invitation to join a skiing party in the Austrian Tyrol. On New Year's Day 1927, while Raymond was skiing on the beginner's slope, six members of the party were buried by an avalanche; only one survived. Raymond conducted the funeral service for the victims.

Although Raymond was dissatisfied with his next novel, *Morris in the Dance* (1927), he was upset by a friend's comment: "I really can't think why publishers trouble to publish such books"; in *Please You, Draw Near* he likened the remark to a disparaging comment about one's child. Reviewers were kinder, however, to the story of Morris's early years in Temple Gowring, a town based on the resort city of Brighton. Employed as a shop clerk, Morris secretly desires to start a repertory theater; the fulfillment of that dream brings a Russian girl, Pandora, into his life. The novel follows the vicissitudes of their relationship after the failure of the theater. The *Times Literary Supplement* (17 June 1927) commended the novel for its "freedom [from] cheap emotionalism."

In 1928 Raymond published *The Old Tree Blossomed: A Realistic Romance.* The "old tree" is the family tree of Robert Gallimore and his son, Stephen, who are descended from troubadours and crusaders but are reduced to working as head clerk and junior clerk, respectively, in a London department store. Stephen pursues and marries Florrie; he later discovers, to his horror, that she had formerly been a barmaid. World War I brings the snobbish Stephen a commission and entrée to a world of country houses, a relationship with the aristocratic Dorothea, and, eventually, a senseless but heroic death in the Middle East.

In August 1928 Cassell published a collection of Raymond's essays, *Through Literature to Life;* the book was reprinted four times before Christmas and would still be in print in the 1960s. On the basis of the volume Raymond was invited to participate in a conference on "Literature and Leisure" in Vancouver, British Columbia, in April 1929; afterward he gave talks in several Canadian cities. In Toronto he met Hazel Reid Marsh, with whom he fell in love.

Raymond's first play, *The Berg,* a dramatization of the last two and a half hours of the *Titanic,* was published in 1929. It enjoyed a brief run in London's West End and became a favorite of repertory theaters and amateur dramatic societies. Adapted for the screen under the title *Atlantic,* it appeared worldwide in English, French, and German versions.

Also in 1929 Raymond published *A Family That Was;* when the novel appeared in the United States the following year, the *Saturday Review of Literature* (26 July 1930) called it "honest and often interesting for all its lack of direction and discipline." The novel chronicles the lives of the family of Dr. Ernest O'Grogan, vicar of St. Austin's, Kensington, from 1893 to 1914. Their idyllic existence is shattered in 1906 by the vicar's sudden departure with a pregnant married member of the congregation, forcing the family into near poverty and the five children into a search for careers. The youngest, Tony, becomes a teacher in a prep school in Sussex; his sister Peggy is converted to Anglo-Catholicism and marries her priest, who is twenty years her senior. At the end of the novel all of their lives are changed by the advent of World War I.

In 1930 Maj. F. J. Ney, the organizer of the conference in Vancouver, brought some young people to tour England and Europe; Marsh came with them and resumed her affair with Raymond. In October, Raymond left on a six-week lecture tour of Canada arranged by Ney; Marsh remained in England to seek employment.

*The Jesting Army* (1930) follows Tony O'Grogan, who is now a soldier, through accurately described campaigns at Gallipoli, in Palestine, and in France. While the novel's sentimentality was criticized, Raymond was also praised for avoiding the grim realism of many contemporary authors and portraying the cheerfulness with which the troops disguised their fear and loneliness.

During Raymond's absence Marsh decided that she could not continue their illicit relationship. When he returned from Canada, she broke off with him, despite his entreaties.

In *Mary Leith* (1931) Tony O'Grogan returns from the war to his wife, Honor, and becomes a curate in a church. His satirical article on his colleagues, "Sanders Sent the Wrong Wine," brings him literary fame but, together with his affair with Mary Leith, a Canadian girl he meets in New York, leads to his withdrawal from the church. These events occur against the background of labor un-

*Emily and Ida Calder, whom Raymond believed to be his aunts; in fact, Ida was his mother*

rest, allowing Raymond to present the working-class view through Tony's former batman, Joe Wylie, who has become a Socialist agitator. The three O'Grogan novels were republished together the following year under the title *Once in England.*

The narrator of *Newtimber Lane* (1933), Sir Edmund Earlwin, is patterned after Raymond's father, Major General Blake. In his Sussex home, Newtimber Lane, Earlwin recalls his abusive father; his expulsion from Oxford for an affair with a local woman; his elopement with and abandonment of Edith Reeding; his affair in Boulogne with Paula Shard-Wells, whom he also abandoned; and his brief romance at fifty with a young American, Grace O'Connan. The novel's prolixity is somewhat relieved by its vivid descriptions of rural Sussex and its comic minor characters.

The year 1933 also saw the publication of Raymond's second play, *The Multabello Road,* which had premiered the previous year at St. Martin's Theatre, and his assumption of the presidency of the Young

P.E.N. Club, following such notables as E. M. Forster and Bertrand Russell. He spent much of 1933 and 1934 in intensive research on criminal law, prisons, and police methodology, and in interviewing a young man who had been sentenced to death and received a last-minute reprieve, all in preparation for the writing of *We, the Accused.* In 1934 he published *Child of Norman's End,* the story of young Cynthia Coventry of the West London suburb of Norman's End: her conflicts with her scandal-mongering grandmother; her affair with the philandering sculptor O'Kelvie; and her rescue by her former playmate, Leo Damien. Raymond's authentic picture of this quarter-mile-square neighborhood in the twilight of the Edwardian period is enlivened by the theatrics of the genuinely caring vicar, Mr. Guilder.

In May 1935 Raymond took what he called "a flight from publication" to Spain to avoid being in England when *We, the Accused* appeared; in *Please You, Draw Near* he says that "not one of the seventeen books which preceded it had meant so much or cost so much." In Barcelona, Raymond read Compton Mackenzie's headline review in the *Continental Daily Mail*—the first of many positive comments. Paul Presset, a middle-aged teacher, is unhappily married to the bullying Elinor. Attracted to another teacher, Myra Bawne, he poisons Elinor. Raymond draws vivid portraits of the police inspector, Boltro, who pursues Presset through Sussex, Surrey, and Cumberland; the ambitious prosecutor, Sir Hayman Drewer; and the prison officials involved in Presset's eventual hanging. Raymond learned that all the members of the commission charged with reforming the prison system had read his book and that a prominent prosecuting counsel, Norman, Lord Birkett, could find no legal or technical errors in it. The review in the *Manchester Guardian* (30 May 1935) ended: "Given another half-dozen novels as powerful as this, and in fairly quick succession, and the death penalty should be a thing of the past." At a P.E.N. meeting Raymond was quizzed about the book by nineteen-year-old Diana Young, who herself had already published a novel; five years later she would become his second wife.

In 1936 Raymond published *Don John's Mountain Home,* a tragicomedy centering on the governess Margaret Elms; her employer, the curate Mr. Several; Cyril Woodward, the schoolmaster she loves; and Don John, a large, deformed communist who is utterly out of place in conservative Avonsmead. Mr. Several and various local institutions—the school, the British Legion, and the Servitor's Club—are butts of Raymond's good-natured humor. Calling it "an author's holiday from *We, the Accused*," the *Times*

*Literary Supplement* (2 May 1936) found *Don John's Mountain Home* pleasant reading.

The title of Raymond's 1937 novel, *The Marsh,* refers to the low-lying slum area along the Thames in which Danny Counsel is raised. The novel follows Danny's training in crime by Meyer Sleeman and Ben the Russky; his romances with Jenny Lemaitre and San Morris; his encounters with the police, judges, and "gaolers"; and his murder with his own gun by Detective Sergeant "Rump" Huckstead, who pleads self-defense. This harsh examination of the making of a criminal is lightened by a sympathetic portrayal of the confused but dedicated church worker, Miss Rachel.

In 1937 Raymond toured Italy, Egypt, and the Holy Land, gathering material for his biography-travel book *In the Steps of St. Francis* (1938). At the P.E.N. Congress in Prague in June 1938 he received a manifesto for peace signed by forty-one Czech writers. Raymond became an air raid warden that year, and in 1939 he assisted in the evacuation of two thousand children from London to his Sussex hometown, Haywards Heath. His first marriage ended in divorce that year, and in the fall he learned that Hazel Marsh had died two years earlier, while he was in Egypt. In 1939 Raymond published *The Miracle of Brean.* The "miracle" is the discovery by plain, forty-plus Lettie Meadows that her blind lover, a married war veteran, is unworthy of her and that permanent love requires unselfishness and understanding. This revelation allows her to leave the Sussex community of the title and start life anew in Italy, where her child will be born.

London south of the Thames forms the backdrop for *A Song of the Tide* (1940), the tragic love story of Roddy Stewart, a grocer's delivery boy who is promoted to shop assistant, and Fay Warren, a silly but optimistic theater usherette. While the setting and characters are lifelike, the plot seems contrived.

Having been rejected for service with the Ministry of Information in 1939, Raymond joined the Home Guard in 1940. That same year he moved to the London suburb of Hampstead; from there he had a panoramic view of the blitz. In the fall he married Diana Young. Their son, Peter, born the following June, nearly died of jaundice as an infant.

Raymond's next novel, *The Last to Rest* (1941), concerns the middle-aged accountant Stanley Shepherd; his romance-writer wife, Clara; and their children, eighteen-year-old Peter and sixteen-year-old Enid. While Enid remains at home to prepare for examinations, the rest of the family attends the Prague Writers Conference in the summer of 1938. There, father and son are inspired by the Czech love of freedom. After the war begins, the family moves to Hampstead, where Stanley becomes an air raid warden, Peter an anti-aircraft gunner, and Enid an ambulance driver; Clara moves to the relative safety and comfort of the country. Reviews were generally complimentary; the *Times Literary Supplement* (6 September 1941) said, "it is a book worthy to stand beside the best that has been written about the Nazi *Blitzkrieg*."

The protagonist of *Was There Love Once?* (1942) is Judith Fear, an attractive typist in a government office. The novel examines the influence on her of three men: her father, the Reverend Basil Fear, a selfish bully; her fellow employee, Lee, whose mistress she becomes in a meaningless affair; and Father Porteous, an Anglo-Catholic priest whom she joins in caring for poverty-stricken East-Enders during the blitz.

The title character of *The Corporal of the Guard* (1943) is fifty-year-old Miles Amery, a druggist in the London suburb of Hodden who has a younger wife, Bell, and a year-old son, Eric. The novel traces the triumphs and tragedies of a group of men, unfit for service overseas mainly because of their age, who were the backbone of England's home defense during World War II. Amery's dedicated service earns him a promotion to corporal but also leads to the decline of his business. Meanwhile, Bell becomes fascinated with the glamorous stories of Iraq recounted by the mysterious Alastair McKennedy. The novel is similar to many written at the time depicting the life of "the little man" during the war.

*For Them That Trespass* (1944) begins with the celebration of the twenty-fifth anniversary of the successful playwright and poet Christopher Byron Drew and his wife, Mary, then flashes back thirty years to the "trespasses": Christopher was involved with a prostitute named Frankie, who was murdered by Jim Heal, the man with whom she lived; unaware of Christopher's relationship with Frankie, Jim had framed her lover Herb Logan for the murder. Christopher had suspected the truth all along but had said nothing. He recognizes his moral obligations only after Jim's deathbed confession releases Herb from prison. In a review of the American edition, which was not published until two years after Raymond's death, *Booklist* (1 December 1976) noted that "there is little suspense in the book's outcome; its major enticement is the realistic creation of [London] settings and characters, particularly through dialogue replete with cockney accents or stiff Victorian prose."

The years 1945 and 1946 were devoted mainly to nonfiction pursuits. With his son, Patrick, a wing commander in the Royal Air Force, Raymond wrote

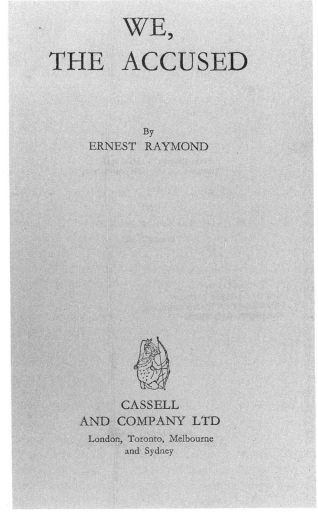

WE,
THE ACCUSED

By
ERNEST RAYMOND

CASSELL
AND COMPANY LTD
London, Toronto, Melbourne
and Sydney

*Title page for Raymond's novelistic examination of the British criminal-justice system*

*Back to Humanity* (1945), a plea for a return to human values after the dehumanization of the war; one section of the book recounts Patrick's wartime experiences. In 1946 Raymond edited *The Autobiography of David ———*, a detailed record of a mental patient's attempts to lead a normal life; Raymond is quoted in the *Times Literary Supplement* (8 June 1946) as saying that his "contribution is limited to the arrangement of the writings . . . and to the elimination of 'comment and moralizing.'"

*The Five Sons of Le Faber* (1946) follows the career of Justin, the eldest son, who is the frustrated headmaster of a second-rate Hammersmith preparatory school. Burdened with an unappealing wife and a senile father-in-law, Justin is also subjected to the hectoring of his brothers—especially the fourth, Robin, who flaunts his material success. Finally, Justin loses his mind.

Raymond's contribution to British literature was recognized in 1947 by his appointment as a fellow of the Royal Society of Literature. That same year he published *The Kilburn Tale*. In the following year another travelogue-biography, *In the Steps of the Brontës,* appeared.

In *Please You, Draw Near* Raymond calls *Gentle Greaves* (1949) his favorite novel because it "embraces the two deepest loves in the first half of my life." Gen. Allen Mourne, the dignified, simplehearted father of the central character, Theodore Mourne, is based on Raymond's father, George Frederick Blake, while Theodore's cousin, Gentle Mary Greaves, his love since childhood, is modeled on Hazel Reid Marsh. Ostensibly written by Theodore in 1946 as a memoir for his daughter, the novel describes his Edwardian childhood, which was dominated by his sadistic mother but made bearable by his affectionate father and the love of Gentle Mary; his ignominious expulsion from school; his rise to success as a publisher, during which he saved his former headmaster from ruin; his tragic reinvolvement with Gentle Mary during the war, when both were married to others; and their conception of a child—the daughter for whom Mourne is writing the journal. While the novel is overly sentimental, its characterization and its re-creation of the stifling Edwardian atmosphere are masterful.

*The Witness of Canon Welcome* (1950) chronicles the affairs of an ambitious and hypocritical North London curate, Canon Humbert Welcome, whose parish is 10 percent middle class and 90 percent lower class. The assignment of a former shoe salesman, Peter Baynes, as his assistant forces Welcome to become more deeply involved with the poor members of his congregation. Welcome's testimony frees Ricky Carman, who has been arrested for attempting to burglarize the canon's home; and with the aid of a would-be lover, Lilian Eadie, Welcome perjures himself to save Phil Janey, Carman's daughter, who has killed her brutal seducer, Ned Horby. The canon's "witness" is rewarded at the end with a bishopric.

*A Chorus Ending* (1951) is a story within a story: the frame story concerns the amateur investigation being conducted in Chalk Farm, an area in north London, by the retired civil servant Bryan Filmer; the embedded story, which constitutes the main plot of the novel, takes place thirty-five years earlier and is told to Filmer by his fellow hotel guest, Cicely Piers. Piers, whose real name is Elfreda Du Cray, recalls her stifled life with her domineering, hypocritical mother; her lover, the ambitious but insecure librarian Everett Armidy, who murdered Mrs. Du Cray to assert his Nietzschean mastery and suppress

her vilification of him; the investigation of the crime; the trial; and Armidy's execution. The use of the framing device makes the novel excessively long.

In 1952 Raymond returned to the theme of religion in the London slums in *The Chalice and the Sword.* A former army officer, the Anglo-Catholic Father Dawbeny has ministered for twenty years to a motley collection of parishioners while dealing with the aftereffects of the war, a murder, and a contrived charge of sexual assault against him. The *Times Literary Supplement* (12 December 1952) found the priest "a still figure" in contrast to the vibrant minor characters. In the same year Raymond published a double biography, *Two Gentlemen of Rome: The Story of Keats and Shelley* (1952). Nothing was published in 1953, possibly because Raymond was preoccupied with his campaign to win election as a Liberal to the Tory-controlled Hampstead Town Council. He lost the election, but he did persuade the St. Pancras Town Council to mount a plaque on the wall of Samuel Taylor Coleridge's last home in Highgate Village.

Two novels appeared in 1954: *The Nameless Places* and *To the Wood No More.* In the latter work, which is set during the Edwardian period, the rural rector Albany Grahame becomes a baronet, with a large income and a Regency house in fashionable St. John's Wood, as a result of his brother's suicide. Already doubtful about his religious vocation, Sir Albany eagerly anticipates the new life that awaits him. The novel traces the vicissitudes of that new life and his relative success in dealing with them. The *Times Literary Supplement* (5 March 1954) likened the structure of *To the Wood No More* to that of a William Makepeace Thackeray novel, praising Raymond's depiction of Sir Albany for giving the novel "vitality . . . when it wavers and straggles."

Raymond ran for town council again in 1956 and in 1959; he was not elected, although he did receive more votes each time. During that period he published *The Lord of Wensley* (1956) and *The Old June Weather* (1957). In the latter novel several illegitimate nursery-school children from Kensington, aided by their aunts, search for and find their parents. The *Times Literary Supplement* for 28 March 1958 carried a letter to the editor from Raymond decrying "the pitiable condition of Coleridge's tomb" in Highgate Churchyard and pleading for something to be done about it.

With *The City and the Dream* (1958) Raymond concluded his "London Gallery" of sixteen novels depicting fifty years of London life, the series he had started in 1934 with *Child of Norman's End.* Set in the Clerkenwell district of London, the novel follows the attempts of the minor clerk Kerry Betterkin to write a story about the Knights of St. John, who had dwelt in the area during the Middle Ages. Beset by difficulties but determined to succeed for his own sake and for that of his sister, Pearl, Kerry ultimately triumphs. The novel, which includes a rich diversity of characters, is in part a satire of the British publishing industry.

Raymond used his Gallipoli experience as the basis for *The Quiet Shore* (1958), a recollection of that failed campaign by a former Light Infantry officer. Although the battle was lost, the narrator's memory of the bravery, resolution, and dignity of his fellow officers fills him with pride. In a letter to the *Times Literary Supplement* (27 May 1960) Raymond protested that the previous issue's review of his murder mystery *The Visit of Brother Ives* had missed the point of his ridicule of the dialogue of Headmaster D'Acres and D'Acres's two assistants.

For the 1961 Hampstead Borough Council elections Raymond facetiously suggested that his wife's cousin, the novelist Pamela Frankau, also run as a Liberal. As a result both Raymond and Frankau, as well as a third Liberal candidate, were elected in the Town Ward, historically a Tory stronghold. That year also marked the fruition of Raymond's efforts to have the Coleridge family remains moved to a new vault in St. Michael's Church, Highgate. The campaign had been supported by many prominent British literary figures and by large contributions from the United States.

Raymond's status with critics during the 1960s is indicated by the fact that his books received only one-paragraph reviews in the *Times Literary Supplement* under the heading "Other New Novels." The eccentric title character of *Mr. Olim* (1961) is based on the Reverend Horace Elam, the headmaster of St. Paul's school during Raymond's time as a student there. The story concerns Davey, a student at Olim's school; the cruel aunt with whom Davey lives; and the aunt's lover, Mr. Bray. In *Please You, Draw Near* Raymond claims that *The Chatelaine* (1962) failed with readers because the title character, an Englishwoman living in France, refuses to shelter her own son when he is shot down by the Germans during World War II because she does not want to endanger her cherished chateau. While the son and other members of the family, who work with the Resistance, forgive the woman, readers disliked her. The experience led Raymond to list as his first criterion for a successful novel that the central character cannot "play against the house."

In *Please You, Draw Near* Raymond cites his next novel, *One of Our Brethren* (1963), as a violation of his second criterion: "the end crowns the work."

# TO THE WOOD NO MORE

A NOVEL

by

ERNEST RAYMOND

CASSELL AND COMPANY LIMITED
LONDON

*Title page for Raymond's novel about a country vicar who inherits a title and a house in a fashionable London neighborhood*

Set in the cathedral town of Casterton in the 1920s and narrated by a candidate for the priesthood, the novel deals with an ambitious archdeacon who is charged with improper behavior in a London hotel. According to Raymond, readers objected to the withholding of the archdeacon's deathbed penance, which the narrator could not reveal because of the seal of the confessional.

In 1964 Raymond was named a Knight Officer, Order of Merit of the Italian Republic, because of his two nonfiction works—on Saint Francis and on John Keats and Percy Bysshe Shelley—set in Italy. That year he published the novel *Late in the Day*, drawn from his experience of returning to Ypres alone in October 1962—he had been at the third battle of Ypres in the fall of 1917—and again in May

*Raymond in 1968*

1963 with Diana so that she could see the grave of her father, who had been killed when she was one year old. In the novel the sixty-four-year-old veteran Stephen Blaize returns to the Ypres battlefield; later he joins the pacifist Quakers. The novel was criticized by the *Times Literary Supplement* (28 May 1964) for lacking a point and for being "sentimental, arch, and facetious." Diana's novel based on the 1963 trip, *The Noonday Sword* (1965), was much more successful.

In *The Tree of Heaven* (1965) the widowed fifty-eight-year-old surgeon Mark Dolman, the Labor Party mayor of the fictitious London borough of Keys, brings a prostitute to his home—only to have her die of a heart attack. The novel traces the deceits through which Dolman attempts to protect his reputation with his sister, son, niece, and constituents.

Set in the fictitious Sledden Valley in Cumberland, *The Mountain Farm* (1966) focuses on the romance of the farm girl Greta Whinlake and the dashing mountain climber Norry Kingharben; after his death she recovers from her grief through the ministrations of the adoring hunchback, Johnny Blenco. When the book was republished in the United States seven years later, Martin Levin said in *The New York Times* (16 December 1973) that "its heart . . . belongs to 1931 and the age of lost innocence."

In the spring of 1966 Raymond visited the Holy Land to try to recover his lost faith. Out of this trip came *The Bethany Road* (1967), in which the central character deals with the same problem—first on the road from Bethany to Jerusalem and then as an observer at a communion service in a London church.

In early June 1967 Diana Raymond's beloved cousin, Pamela Frankau, died after a painful illness. A few months earlier she had been attempting to cheer Raymond up during his five-week stay in the hospital following an operation. Possibly because the events of 1967 turned his thoughts to the prospect of his own mortality, Raymond devoted his energies for the next three years to writing his autobiography. The first part, *The Story of My Days: An Autobiography, 1888–1922*, begins with his bizarre family situation and ends with the success of *Tell England*. Raymond's son Patrick provided the title for the second volume, *Please You, Draw Near*, and suggested that it consist of a collection of ideas about writing, loosely connected with events from Raymond's career. Patrick also suggested that the third book be a statement of Raymond's renewed faith; published in 1970, it took its title, *Good Morning, Good People*, from Saint Francis's words to the people of Poggio Bustone, Italy.

In 1971 Raymond became president of the Dickens Fellowship of London. That same year he published the best-selling *A Georgian Love Story,* which also appeared in the United States—his first novel to do so in thirty years. Its narrator looks back almost seventy years to the Edwardian and Georgian eras to tell of the romance of the upper-middle-class but impoverished Stewart O'Murry of Hollen Hill—the narrator himself—and Raney Darby, a tobacconist's daughter from the disreputable Hollen Dene. Ending with the outbreak of World War I and Raney's death, the novel evokes an authentic bygone world peopled with flesh-and-blood characters: Stewart's self-important and pompous father, Augustus; his sympathetic Uncle Douglas; his rebellious sisters Aldith and Augusta; and Raney's parents, who are members of the Plymouth Brethren. In a seven-hundred-word review in *The New York Times* (19 September 1971) Auberon Waugh, while confessing that a generation gap clouded his assessment of the novel, noted its "ability to bring a lump to the throat and a tear to the eye."

Raymond received the Order of the British Empire in 1972. In April, James Farrant noted in *Books and Bookmen* the fiftieth anniversary of Raymond's association with Cassell by saying of *Our Late Member* (1972): "he can still write as unflaggingly and provocatively as ever." The title character, Rodney Merriwell, has been the Liberal member of Parliament for the fictitious Ridgeway constituency in North London since 1918; the novel depicts only the four years leading to his defeat in 1946. His party is already losing ground when his son Everard, a bomber pilot, persuades his father to take the unpopular position of speaking out against the bombing of German cities. His other son, Stanley, an anti-aircraft gunner in Kent, disappears from his base shortly before a former lover is found stabbed to death in an orchard.

Raymond's last two novels received scant attention in England; *Miryam's Guest House* (1973) was ignored by reviewers, and *Under Wedgery Down* (1974), the story of an Edwardian's spiritual journey from faith to doubt and back again, was, once more, lumped under "Other New Novels" in the *Times Literary Supplement* (10 November 1974). Raymond died on 14 May 1974 and was buried in Hampstead Cemetery.

*Tell England* established Raymond's reputation as a writer. As he matured, his novels became less sentimental, and he learned to draw characters who did not share his upper-middle-class background and to depict life in the less-affluent parts of London and in rural England. These qualities, along with his strong plots, vivid descriptions, feeling for atmosphere, and concern with religious issues, made his works popular with readers for more than half a century.

## References:

Gillian Avery, *Childhood's Pattern* (London: Hodder & Stoughton, 1975), p. 185;

Mary Cardogan and Patricia Craig, *Women and Children First: The Fiction of Two World Wars* (London: Gollancz, 1978), pp. 89–94, 287.

# Naomi Royde-Smith

*(1875 – 28 July 1964)*

Karen M. Carney
*University of Illinois at Urbana-Champaign*

*Una and the Red Cross Knight, and Other Tales from Spenser's Faery Queene* (London: Dent / New York: Dutton, 1905);

*The Tortoiseshell Cat: A Novel* (London: Constable, 1925; New York: Boni & Liveright, 1925);

*The Housemaid: A Novel in Three Parts* (London: Constable, 1926; New York: Knopf, 1926);

*A Balcony: A Play in Three Acts* (London: Benn, 1927; Garden City, N.Y.: Doubleday, Doran, 1928);

*John Fanning's Legacy* (London: Constable, 1927);

*Skin-Deep; or, Portrait of Lucinda, with a Prologue and an Epilogue from the London Adventure of Arabell Holdenbrook* (London: Constable, 1927; New York: Knopf, 1927);

*Children in the Wood: A Novel* (London: Constable, 1928); republished as *In the Wood: A Novel in Three Parts* (New York & London: Harper, 1928);

*The Lover* (London: Constable, 1928; New York & London: Harper, 1929);

*Summer Holiday; or, Gibraltar: A Novel* (London: Constable, 1929); republished as *Give Me My Sin Again* (New York & London: Harper, 1929);

*The Island: A Love Story* (London: Constable, 1930; New York & London: Harper, 1930);

*Pictures and People: A Transatlantic Criss-Cross between Roger Hinks in London and Naomi Royde-Smith (Mrs. Ernest Milton) in New York, Boston, Philadelphia during the Months of January, February, March in the Year 1930* (New York & London: Harper, 1931);

*The Double Heart: A Study of Julie de Lespinasse* (London: Hamilton, 1931; New York: Harper, 1931);

*Mrs. Siddons: A Play in Four Acts* (London: Gollancz, 1931);

*The Delicate Situation* (London: Gollancz, 1931; New York & London: Harper, 1931);

*The Mother* (London: Gollancz, 1931; Garden City, N.Y.: Doubleday, Doran, 1932);

*The Bridge* (London: Gollancz, 1932; Garden City, N.Y.: Doubleday, Doran, 1933);

*Naomi Royde-Smith*

*Incredible Tale* (London: Benn, 1932);

*Madam Julia's Tale, and Other Queer Stories* (London: Gollancz, 1932);

*David: A Tale in Three Parts* (London: Benn, 1933; New York: Viking, 1934);

*The Private Life of Mrs. Siddons: A Psychological Investigation* (London: Gollancz, 1933); republished as *Portrait of Mrs. Siddons: A Study in Four Parts* (New York: Viking, 1933);

*Pilgrim from Paddington: The Record of an Experiment in Travel Made by Naomi Royde-Smith between August 22, 1932, and July 30, 1933* (London: Barker, 1933);

*The Queen's Wigs: A Romantic Novel* (London: Gollancz, 1934; New York: Macmillan, 1934);

*Van Lords; or, The Sport of Removing: Being a Postscript to "Pilgrim from Paddington"* (London: Barker, 1934);

*Jake: A Novel* (London: Macmillan, 1935; New York: Macmillan, 1935);

*All Star Cast: A Novel* (London: Macmillan, 1936; New York: Macmillan, 1936);

*For Us in the Dark: A Novel* (London: Macmillan, 1937; New York: Macmillan, 1937);

*Miss Bendix* (London: Macmillan, 1938);

*The Younger Venus: A Tale* (London: Macmillan, 1938; New York: Macmillan, 1939);

*The Altar-Piece: An Edwardian Mystery* (London & New York: Macmillan, 1939; New York: Macmillan, 1939);

*Urchin Moor: A Tale* (London: Macmillan, 1939);

*Jane Fairfax: A New Novel* (London: Macmillan, 1940);

*Outside Information: Being a Diary of Rumours Collected by Naomi Royde Smith; Together with Letters from Others and Some Account of Events in the Life of an Unofficial Person in London and Winchester during the Months of September and October 1940* (London: Macmillan, 1941);

*The Unfaithful Wife; or, Scenario for Gary: A Tale* (London: Macmillan, 1941);

*Mildensee: A Romance* (London: Macmillan, 1943);

*Fire-Weed: A Novel* (London: Macmillan, 1944);

*The State of Mind of Mrs. Sherwood: A Study* (London: Macmillan, 1946);

*Love in Mildensee: A Novel* (London: Low, Marston, 1948);

*The Iniquity of Us All: A Prelude* (London: Low, 1949);

*Rosy Trodd* (London: Low, 1950);

*The New Rich* (London: Low, 1951);

*She Always Caught the Post* (London: Hale, 1953);

*Melilot: A Tale* (London: Hale, 1955);

*Love at First Sight: A Story of Three Generations* (London: Hale, 1956);

*The Whistling Chambermaid: A Tale* (London: Hale, 1957);

*How White is My Sepulchre: A Tale* (London: Hale, 1958);

*A Blue Rose: A Tale* (London: Hale, 1959);

*Love and a Birdcage* (London: Hale, 1960).

PLAY PRODUCTION: *A Balcony,* London, Everyman Theatre, 25 August 1926.

OTHER: *The Pillow Book: A Garner of Many Moods,* collected by Royde-Smith (London: Methuen, 1906);

*Poets of Our Day,* edited, with an introductory essay, by Royde-Smith (London: Methuen, 1908);

*The Westminster Problems Book: Prose and Verse,* compiled by Royde-Smith (London: Methuen, 1908);

*The Second Problems Book: Prizes and Proximes from the Westminster Gazette, 1908–1909,* compiled by Royde-Smith (London: Sidgwick & Jackson, 1909);

*A Private Anthology,* collected by Royde-Smith (London: Constable, 1924);

Jules Supervielle, *The Ox and the Ass at the Manger,* translated by Royde-Smith (London: Hollis & Carter, 1945);

Eugénie de Guérin, *The Idol and the Shrine: Being the Story of Maurice de Guérin, Together with Translated Extracts from the Journal of Eugénie de Guérin,* translated by Royde-Smith (London: Hollis & Carter, 1949).

A true woman of letters, Naomi Royde-Smith enjoyed a fifty-five-year career as a novelist, journalist, editor, translator, playwright, and biographer. Although her books are little read today, she was an important popular novelist and literary influence in England in the period between the world wars.

Naomi Gwladys Smith was born in Llanwrst, Wales, in 1875, the eldest daughter of Ann Daisy Williams Smith and Michael Holroyd Smith; the surname Royde-Smith, a variation on her father's middle and last names, seems to have been her own invention. Her childhood was spent in Halifax, Yorkshire; she would draw on the people and events of those years for several of her novels, including the heavily autobiographical *Children in the Wood* (1928). After her family moved to London, Royde-Smith was educated at Clapham High School and at a private school in Geneva.

Royde-Smith's career as a writer began in 1905 with a children's version of Edmund Spenser's *The Faerie Queene* (1590–1613). Shortly afterward she began a sixteen-year association with the *Westminster Gazette.* As editor of the popular Saturday "Problems and Prizes" page she compiled two collections of contributors' prose and verse, *The Westminster Problems Book* (1908) and *The Second Problems Book* (1909). In 1912 she became the paper's literary editor, a position that led to connections with such notable writers as Walter de la Mare, Katherine Mansfield, Wyndham Lewis, Rupert Brooke, and Rose Macaulay. Royde-Smith and Macaulay became particularly close: Macaulay frequently stayed at Royde-Smith's large house in Kensington, and after World War I the two held a salon there every Thursday evening. The writer Mary Agnes Hamilton remembered these literary evenings fondly:

THE LOVER

BY

NAOMI ROYDE-SMITH

LONDON
CONSTABLE AND CO LTD
1928

*Title page for Royde-Smith's short novel about a chance meeting
of an artist and a former lover*

There was excellent coffee; there were chocolates and cigarettes—hard liquor had not yet come into vogue with the intelligentsia; there was conversation.... Over a long series of years, everybody in the literary world, the not yet arrived as well as the established, was to be met with, there, at one time or another.

Virginia Woolf, who attended one of the evenings in 1921, was less enthusiastic in her diary: "It was a queer mixture of the intelligent and the respectable. I detest the mixture of ideas and South Kensington."

A combination of "ideas and South Kensington" forms the core of Royde-Smith's first novel, *The Tortoiseshell Cat* (1925), about Gillian Armstrong, a young woman struggling to make an independent life in London as a schoolteacher and later as personal secretary to an aristocrat. Reviewers praised the novel's original and often comic rendering of contemporary British culture; *The New York Times* (15 November 1925) noted that "readers 'fed up' with much of the output of the Mayfair and pseudo-Mayfair school will turn to this novel with a

chuckle of delight." Both *The Tortoiseshell Cat* and its successor, *The Housemaid* (1926), were considered "modern" not only in subject matter—the books treated such previously taboo subjects as homosexuality and suicide—but also in the author's deft, understated handling of her material.

After the demise of the *Westminster Gazette* in 1923 Royde-Smith worked for several years as a freelance book reviewer and drama critic. The latter occupation led to an acquaintance with Ernest Milton, a popular English actor fifteen years younger than she; they were married shortly after he starred in the London production of her first play, *A Balcony* (1926; published, 1927). Royde-Smith would write four more plays and a novel, *All Star Cast* (1936), that attempts to merge the genres of drama and fiction and was described by *The New York Times* (23 August 1936) as "a most instructive lesson in how to see plays."

Royde-Smith once estimated that it took her about four months to write a novel. Between 1927 and 1929 she published five of them; most enjoyed a modest success with the reading public but received mixed critical reviews. Critics pointed out several weaknesses in her writing, particularly a tendency to dwell on character at the expense of plot. Reviewing *Children in the Wood,* the *Times Literary Supplement* said: "We fear that character and episode so beguile this author that she sees no necessity to provide strong [plot] connexions." *The Lover,* also published in 1928, is a noteworthy exception to this criticism. The story of a chance meeting of a successful but jaded artist and the woman he loved years before, the novel skillfully weaves past and present in a plot containing only a few lines of dialogue. A mere eighty-nine pages in length, *The Lover* is a tiny masterpiece of modernist prose.

In December 1929 Royde-Smith accompanied her husband to the United States, where he was appearing in Patrick Hamilton's play *Rope's End* (the basis for Alfred Hitchcock's 1948 film *Rope*). Disappointed to be leaving London just before an exhibition of Italian painting was to arrive there, Royde-Smith arranged for her friend the art critic Roger Hinks to write to her about the exhibition; in return she promised to see "as many Italian and other pictures in New York as I can compass and let you know how they look in America." Their correspondence, published as *Pictures and People* (1931), demonstrates Royde-Smith's appreciation of the arts and of people in all walks of life. Her letters chronicle the famous (Will Rogers, Vachel Lindsay, Mrs. Jack Gardner), the infamous (bootleggers and gamblers), and the unsung (diners at the Automat, elevator operators, taxicab drivers). Her observations on

American culture are often slyly humorous, as when she describes the Manhattan skyline:

> When you get up to the open spaces where Fifth Avenue is cut by 59th Street and look back, the first impression is funny and rather frightening, as though you saw the work of a set of high-spirited and rather malignant children who had spent a week playing with all the toy bricks in the world. At any minute one of them might give one of the towers a push and it might fall and knock another across the middle, and then what a slashing and crashing and scattering there'd be! If a really intelligent Bolshevik started working out the relative positions of the tallest of them he would only have to select a suitable tower and prepare a strong enough bomb to play ninepins with the lot.

On her return to England in 1930 Royde-Smith embarked on *The Double Heart* (1931), a biography of the eighteenth-century French writer Julie de Lespinasse. Royde-Smith notes that as a girl she had always admired "the great French ladies who held salons" and that she had taken Lespinasse and Marie DeVichy-Chamrond, Marquise du Deffand, as role models when she and Macaulay held their salons after the war. That same year she published a play about the life of the nineteenth-century English actress Sarah Kemble Siddons; the work formed the basis of her biography *The Private Life of Mrs. Siddons: A Psychological Investigation* (1933).

Royde-Smith's interest in mid-Victorian culture is also apparent in her most critically acclaimed work, *The Delicate Situation* (1931): in a small English town in 1861 Mary Paradise, a young woman, falls in love with an aristocrat who deserts her for a wealthy heiress. Critics praised the work for its sensitive portrayal of Victorian people and attitudes: in *The Spectator* L. A. G. Strong called it "a book steady, sane, and humorous, which reaches back confidently to its Victorian ancestors."

One of Royde-Smith's greatest talents was her ability to ferret out the unexpected and remarkable in the most pedestrian situations. Certainly this is true of her whimsical account of traveling England by rail, *Pilgrim from Paddington* (1933). When Royde-Smith and her husband moved from Hatfield to Chelsea, she chronicled the experience in *Van Lords; or, The Sport of Removing: Being a Postscript to "Pilgrim from Paddington"* (1934).

Royde-Smith's 1935 novel, *Jake,* a tale of a musical genius, was published by the giant Macmillan firm, which would continue to publish her novels until 1946. The Macmillan works run the

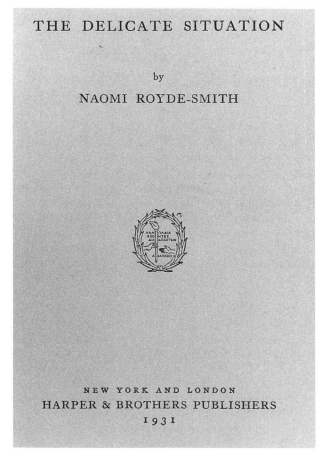

THE DELICATE SITUATION

by

NAOMI ROYDE-SMITH

NEW YORK AND LONDON
HARPER & BROTHERS PUBLISHERS
1931

*Title page for the American edition of Royde-Smith's novel about a Victorian girl who is deserted by her aristocratic lover*

gamut of genre and subject: most notable among them are *For Us in the Dark* (1937), a modern retelling of Robert Browning's *The Ring and the Book* (1868–1869); *The Younger Venus* (1938), a contemporary love story that merges two of Royde-Smith's favorite subjects, Italian painting and English fiction; and *The Altar-Piece: An Edwardian Mystery* (1939).

In 1941 Royde-Smith published *Outside Information,* an account of events "in the life of an unofficial person" during the blitz. The following year she and her husband converted to Roman Catholicism. Several of her postwar novels, including *The Iniquity of Us All: A Prelude* (1949), have Catholicism as a theme.

If there is a unifying thread in all of Royde-Smith's work, it is her keen interest in and appreciation for the lives of women—her fictional heroines, the subjects of her biographies, and those who appear in her travel books. Her novels are populated by strong, intelligent female characters who take the lead in a variety of roles—schoolmistresses, clergymen's wives, shop owners, nurses, artists. Throughout her literary career Royde-Smith took pains to acknowledge her debt to women writers of past generations. In the author's note to her 1940 novel, *Jane Fairfax,* a retelling of and tribute to Jane Austen's *Emma* (1815), Royde-Smith thanks "the shades of Miss Austen, Miss [Fanny] Burney, Miss [Maria] Edgeworth, Mrs. [Mary Martha] Sherwood." In 1946 she published a critical study of Sherwood, an early-nineteenth-century children's novelist whose *The History of the Fairchild Family* (1818–1847) Royde-Smith had read as a girl. In the introduction Royde-Smith says that Sherwood is "an Englishwoman who deserves to be remembered quite as much for her indomitable character as for the vigour and vivacity of her now forgotten writings"–a comment that today applies as well to its author as to her subject.

Royde-Smith continued to write until 1960. She died in a London hospital on 28 July 1964; her husband survived her by ten years. Lovat Dickson noted in his memorial piece on Royde-Smith for the *Times* of London that those less than forty years of age would hardly remember Naomi Royde-Smith, but anyone older than sixty, particularly those of a literary bent, could hardly forget her.

## References:

Mary Agnes Hamilton, *Remembering My Good Friends* (London: Cape, 1944);

Virginia Woolf, *The Diary of Virginia Woolf: 1920–1924,* edited by Anne Olivier Bell (New York: Harcourt Brace Jovanovich, 1978).

# Edward Sackville-West
### (13 November 1901 – 4 July 1965)

## Margaret Crosland

BOOKS: *Piano Quintet* (London: Heinemann, 1925; New York: Knopf, 1925);

*The Ruin: A Gothic Novel* (London: Heinemann, 1926; New York: Knopf, 1927);

*The Apology of Arthur Rimbaud: A Dialogue* (London: Woolf, 1927);

*Mandrake over the Water-Carrier: A Recital* (London: Heinemann, 1928);

*Simpson: A Life* (London: Heinemann, 1931; New York: Knopf, 1931; revised edition, London: Weidenfeld & Nicolson, 1951);

*The Sun in Capricorn: A Recital* (London: Heinemann, 1934);

*A Flame in Sunlight: The Life and Work of Thomas de Quincey* (London: Cassell, 1936); republished as *Thomas de Quincey: His Life and Work* (New Haven: Yale University Press, 1936);

*Graham Sutherland* (Harmondsworth: Penguin, 1943; revised, 1955);

*The Rescue: A Melodrama for Broadcasting Based on Homer's* Odyssey, music by Benjamin Britten (London: Secker & Warburg, 1945);

*And So to Bed: An Album Compiled from His B.B.C. Feature* (London: Phoenix House, 1947);

*Inclinations* (London: Secker & Warburg, 1949; New York: Scribners, 1950);

*The Record Guide,* by Sackville-West and Desmond Shawe-Taylor (London: Collins, 1951; revised, with contributions by Andrew Porter and William Mann, 1955; Westport, Conn.: Greenwood Press, 1978);

*The Record Year: A Guide to the Year's Gramophone Records Including a Complete Guide to Long Playing Records,* 2 volumes, by Sackville-West and Shawe-Taylor (London: Collins, 1952, 1953).

OTHER: Rainer Maria Rilke, *Duineser Elegien: Elegies from the Castle of Duino,* translated by Sackville-West and Vita Sackville-West (London: Hogarth Press, 1931);

*Edward Sackville-West (Tony Stone Images)*

"Fear in Fancy Dress," in *Little Innocents: Childhood Reminiscences* (London: Cobden-Sanderson, 1932), pp. 50–54;

*Goya: Drawings from the Prado,* translated by Sackville-West (London: Horizon, 1947);

Thomas De Quincey, *Recollections of the Lake Poets,* edited by Sackville-West (London: Lehmann, 1948);

De Quincey, *Confessions of an English Opium-Eater, Together with Selections from the Autobiography,* edited by Sackville-West (London: Cresset, 1950; New York: Chanticleer, 1950);

*The Correspondence between Richard Strauss and Hugo von Hofmannsthal,* translated by Hans Hammelmann and Ewald Osers, introduction by Sackville-West (London: Collins, 1961).

Although Edward Sackville-West is probably best remembered as a music critic, he wrote five unusual novels that earned him a place in the history of literature during the 1920s and 1930s. They did not remain in print for long and, with one exception, have not been republished. They are, however, likely to appeal to readers who enjoy subtle plotting, complex interplay of characters, and close attention to detail.

Edward Charles Sackville-West was born in London on 13 November 1901 to Maj. Charles John Sackville-West of the King's Royal Rifle Corps, a professional soldier who had served in India and South Africa, and Maud Cecilia Bell Sackville-West. From his mother Edward Sackville-West inherited an incurable disease, telangiectasia, that caused debilitating nosebleeds. He also inherited from her a love of and remarkable talent for music: he could play the organ and piano, including works by Richard Wagner, before he learned to read, but only in the key of C major; he would memorize pieces by ear and transpose them into this key. He later said of his mother that "the perpetual struggle between Romance and Reality was the mainspring of her strange and vivid personality." A similar struggle can be discerned in her son's life and work.

As a child Sackville-West frequently stayed at Knole, the house in Sevenoaks, Kent, that had been in his family's possession for centuries. It was then occupied by his great-uncle Lionel, third Baron Sackville, and was often filled with distinguished guests. The house and its atmosphere have been immortalized in *Knole and the Sackvilles* (1922) by Edward's cousin Vita Sackville-West.

When he was ten Edward Sackville-West was sent to a newly opened preparatory school, South Lodge, at Enfield, Middlesex. Two years later he went to Eton College, where he took music lessons from the concert pianist Irene Scharrer and won the Eton music prize in 1918. He visited Paris with his father and at seventeen began to read the works of the "decadent" French writer Joris-Karl Huysmans, whose best-known novels were *A rebours* (1884; translated as *Against the Grain,* 1922) and *Là-bas* (1891; translated as *Down There,* 1924). He left Eton in 1919, considered composing musical settings for works by Edgar Allan Poe and Gabriele d'Annunzio, visited Germany, and returned to France, where he became interested in Stendhal.

Sackville-West entered Christ Church, Oxford, in 1920. During the next few years he met there, at Knole, and at other great houses many people who were already famous or were to become so, including Raymond Mortimer, David Cecil, Maurice Bowra, L. P. Hartley, Virginia Woolf, and Lady Ottoline Morrell. He probably experienced homosexual liaisons with some of the men in this group. There is no doubt, however, about his fascination with a fellow student, Jack McDougal, because it supplied material for *The Ruin* (1926), a novel he wrote while he was at Oxford; it was his first piece of sustained writing although it was published after the second novel he wrote, *Piano Quintet* (1925).

After leaving the university and visiting France again, Sackville-West was the music critic for the weekly review *The Spectator* in 1924 and 1925. His first published novel, *Piano Quintet,* concerns the complex and obscure relationships among the three men and one woman who make up the Poller String Quartet and the pianist who joins them when they play the César Franck piano quintet. The novel, which follows their tour across Europe, is divided not into chapters but into "movements," each of which opens with a quotation from an author such as Lamartine or Fyodor Dostoyevsky. The book has two epigraphs, one from Rainer Maria Rilke (whose *Duineser Elegien* [1923] were translated in 1931 by Sackville-West and Vita Sackville-West) and one from the sixteenth-century French poet Maurice Scève, linking music and love.

Critics today would accuse *Piano Quintet* of preciosity, but on its publication it received favorable reviews. *The Evening News* in London praised the "finesse and finish usually associated with a mature writer"; the *Sunday Times* called it a "remarkable piece of work, worthy to be judged by high standards." *The Daily Chronicle* admired "the exquisite character-drawing of this well-written book"; Mortimer praised it in *Vogue,* while Edwin Muir in the *Nation and Athenaeum* (9 October 1926) found it to be "one of the most promising [novels] which had appeared for several years."

The title of *The Ruin* refers to the decline of the family that lives in Vair, a magnificent old house filled with splendid furniture and works of art and patterned after Knole; it also refers to a purposely constructed ruin in the parkland surrounding the house. Vair is inhabited by the ailing Lady Torrens, who dies before the end of the novel; her eccentric husband, who spends most of his time playing the scores of obscure nineteenth-century operas on a piano in a remote room; and their four grown children. Their daughter Ariadne is so possessive of her brother Nigel that she destroys his love affair with

Antonia; she and Nigel seem to be having an incestuous relationship. A visitor, Marcus Fleming, modeled on Jack McDougal, fascinates Denzil, the younger brother. Nigel's sister Helen might have loved Marcus, but the latter makes only a half-hearted attempt to "intrude" into her life. Nigel drowns himself, and Ariadne enters a convent; the "ruin" of the family is complete.

Sackville-West's third novel, *Mandrake over the Water-Carrier: A Recital* (1928), is set in the Channel Islands and involves astrology, magic, and witchcraft. Julian Maclaren-Ross said of it in the *Times Literary Supplement:* (11 May 1951):

> The plot is excessively complicated, involving several family skeletons, the uneasy relationship between a young man and his father, and even more uneasy love-affair between a dumb girl (who later recovers the power of speech) and a peripatetic boxer named Tamerlane, a painter, his predatory wife, and a mandrake, the authenticity of which is often in doubt, but which nevertheless has a symbolical effect on the lives which revolve around its sinister presence in the gloom-ridden conservatory. Mr Sackville-West maintains a firm hold upon the threads of his story, occasionally using them skilfully to gag and bind the reader into a state of attention; one closes the book with the impression of awaking from an hypnotic trance. The total effect is that aimed at by surrealist poetry (though no book could be less "automatically written") and remains long in the recollection of anybody who has once surrendered to its spell; though symbols such as Bertram Glove's wig or the figure of Tilton Crowner (which, compounded initially of a false beard and a falsetto voice, as a practical joke, emerges later, as a living entity, outside the British Museum) may not be immediately understood, they are none the less haunting, while the reader comes to dread the periodical appearances of Godfrey Leboucher's malignant mirror-twin ("His Very Image") as much as does its unfortunate victim.

The title character of Sackville-West's next novel, *Simpson: A Life* (1931), seems to have been based on Ada Annie Hutton, the nanny who had raised him. The story begins at the end of the nineteenth century with the young Simpson's decision to leave home to take up a career as a nanny. Her first post is at Vair, the house from *The Ruin,* with Lady Torrens and three of her children. She goes on to serve at homes in Wimbledon, Aldershot, Folkestone, and, during World War I, in East Prussia. Simpson is totally devoted to each of her charges. In one of her posts a child named Salathiel clutches her apron: "They were shown to each other in a perfect ecstasy of direct knowledge; so that Simpson felt his heart descend into her own, falling like a stone into a well, and finding itself enveloped." After World

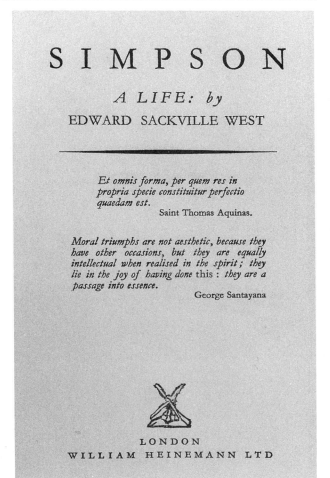

# SIMPSON

## A LIFE: by
### EDWARD SACKVILLE WEST

*Et omnis forma, per quem res in propria specie constituitur perfectio quaedam est.*
Saint Thomas Aquinas.

*Moral triumphs are not aesthetic, because they have other occasions, but they are equally intellectual when realised in the spirit; they lie in the joy of having done* this : *they are a passage into essence.*
George Santayana

LONDON
WILLIAM HEINEMANN LTD

*Title page for Sackville-West's novel about a nanny*

War I Simpson returns to Germany because a child there needs her, but she is killed in a Nazi street riot.

Sackville-West's final novel, *The Sun in Capricorn: A Recital* (1934), has a complex plot involving the transformation of a schoolboy argument into "terms of political and philosophical ideology" and a crown that is said to have belonged to the medieval alchemist and physician Paracelsus; Denzil Torrens, the youngest of the children in *The Ruin* and *Simpson,* reappears in the story.

In addition to fiction, Sackville-West wrote two biographies; neither is a conventional presentation of a life story. *The Apology of Arthur Rimbaud: A Dialogue* (1927) is presented as an imagined dialogue between the poet and Sackville-West, who was particularly interested in the French writer's decision to give up literature early in life. In the *Sunday Times* (19 April 1936) Desmond MacCarthy found Sackville-West's *A Flame in Sunlight: The Life and Work of Thomas de Quincey* (1936) subtle and sensitive, but he also

*Portrait of Sackville-West painted in 1954 by Graham Sutherland.
It is displayed at Sackville-West's ancestral home, Knole
(National Trust).*

noted "lapses from clarity" and pronounced the book "carelessly written" and lacking in polish. Nevertheless, the book won the James Tait Black Memorial Prize.

During the 1940s Sackville-West's main activity was reviewing gramophone records in collaboration with Desmond Shawe-Taylor. In 1943 the composer Benjamin Britten dedicated to Sackville-West his *Serenade for Tenor, Horn and Strings, Opus 31.* Soon afterward the two collaborated on *The Rescue: A*

*Melodrama for Broadcasting Based on Homer's* Odyssey, which was broadcast in two parts in 1943 and published in 1945.

In August 1945 Sackville-West, along with Shawe-Taylor and another friend, bought Long Crichel House in Dorset. Sackville-West wrote a few radio scripts and some literary criticism; the latter was collected in 1949 as *Inclinations*. Because of poor health he was unable to complete a novel that was provisionally titled "The Eyes of the Statue." He was disappointed in 1951 when none of his books was included in the National Book League exhibition of the one hundred best works by British authors published during the previous thirty years. Visits with the novelist Elizabeth Bowen at her home in Ireland inspired Sackville-West, who had converted to Roman Catholicism in 1949, to buy Cooleville House, near Clogheen in County Tipperary, in 1955. After his father's death in 1962 at the age of ninety-two, Sackville-West became the fifth Baron Sackville, but he did not spend much time at Knole, which had become a tourist attraction. (His father had transferred it to the National Trust in 1946, retaining a lease on part of the house for the family.) He died at Clogheen on 4 July 1965 and was buried in the local churchyard. Apart from his unusual novels and his contribution to music criticism, Sackville-West has acquired another form of immortality: in Nancy Mitford's novel *Don't Tell Alfred* (1960) he appears as the eccentric, hypochondriacal but lovable Uncle Davey; friends have attested that the portrait is accurate. A full-length 1954 portrait by Graham Sutherland, about whose art Sackville-West had written a book in 1943, is displayed at Knole; it depicts a serious and somewhat melancholy man.

To date, *Simpson,* which Sackville-West revised in 1951, is his only novel to be republished. The subtlety, complexity, and eccentricity of his work have prevented Sackville-West from occupying a major place in twentieth-century fiction, but his few novels reflect an unusual and fascinating mind. Their oblique reflections of life in Britain during the 1920s and 1930s present an image that is different from that found in virtually all other contemporary British writing.

**Biography:**
Michael De-la-Noy, *Eddy: The Life of Edward Sackville-West* (London: Bodley Head, 1988).

**Reference:**
Jocelyn Brooke, "The Novels of Edward Sackville-West: An Appreciation," *Month,* 6 (1951): 99–107.

# Siegfried Sassoon

### (8 September 1886 – 1 September 1967)

Sanford Sternlicht
*Syracuse University*

See also the Sassoon entry in *DLB 20: British Poets, 1914–1945.*

BOOKS: *Poems,* anonymous (London: Privately printed, 1906);
*Orpheus in Diloeryum,* anonymous (London: Printed by J. E. Francis, 1908);
*Sonnets and Verses,* anonymous (London: Privately printed, 1909);
*Sonnets,* anonymous (London: Privately printed, 1909);
*Poems,* anonymous (London: Chiswick, circa 1910);
*Twelve Sonnets,* anonymous (London: Chiswick, 1911);
*Hyacinth: An Idyll,* anonymous (London: Chiswick, 1912);
*Melodies,* anonymous (London: Chiswick, 1912);
*An Ode for Music* (London: Chiswick, 1912);
*The Daffodil Murderer: Being the Chantrey Prize Poem,* as Saul Kain (London: Richmond, 1913);
*Discoveries* (London: Chiswick, 1915);
*Morning-Glory* (London: Chiswick, 1916);
*The Old Huntsman, and Other Poems* (London: Heinemann, 1917; New York: Dutton, 1918);
*Counter-Attack, and Other Poems* (London: Heinemann, 1918; New York: Dutton, 1918);
*Picture Show* (Cambridge: Privately printed, 1919); republished as *Picture-Show* (New York: Dutton, 1920);
*The War Poems of Siegfried Sassoon* (London: Heinemann, 1919);
*To My Mother* (London: Faber & Gwyer, 1920);
*Recreations* (London: Chiswick, 1923);
*Lingual Exercises for Advanced Vocabularians,* anonymous (Cambridge: Cambridge University Press, 1925);
*Selected Poems* (London: Heinemann, 1925);
*Siegfried Sassoon* (London: Benn, 1926);
*Satirical Poems* (London: Heinemann, 1926; New York: Viking, 1926; enlarged edition, London: Heinemann, 1933);
*Nativity* (London: Faber & Gwyer, 1927; New York: Rudge, 1927);

*Siegfried Sassoon*

*The Heart's Journey* (New York: Gaige / London: Heinemann, 1927; enlarged edition, London: Heinemann, 1928; New York: Harper, 1929);
*Memoirs of a Fox-Hunting Man,* anonymous (London: Faber & Gwyer, 1928); as Sassoon (New York: Coward-McCann, 1929);
*In Sicily* (London: Faber & Faber, 1930);
*Memoirs of an Infantry Officer,* anonymous (London: Faber & Faber, 1930); as Sassoon (New York: Coward-McCann, 1930);
*On Chatterton: A Sonnet* (Winchester: Privately printed, 1930);

*Poems,* as Pinchbeck Lyre (London: Duckworth, 1931);

*To the Red Rose* (London: Faber & Faber, 1931);

*Prehistoric Burials* (New York: Knopf, 1932);

*The Road to Ruin* (London: Faber & Faber, 1933);

*Vigils* (Bristol: Privately printed, 1934; enlarged edition, London: Heinemann, 1935; New York: Viking, 1936);

*Sherston's Progress* (London: Faber & Faber, 1936; Garden City, N.Y.: Doubleday, Doran, 1936);

*The Complete Memoirs of George Sherston* (London: Faber & Faber, 1937; republished as *The Memoirs of George Sherston* (Garden City, N.Y.: Doubleday, Doran, 1937);

*My Mother* (London: Faber & Gwyer, 1938);

*The Old Century and Seven More Years* (London: Faber & Faber, 1938; New York: Viking, 1939);

*On Poetry* (Bristol: Printed for the University of Bristol by J. W. Arrowsmith, 1939);

*Rhymed Ruminations* (London: Chiswick, 1939; enlarged edition, London: Faber & Faber, 1940; New York: Viking, 1941);

*Poems Newly Selected, 1916–1935* (London: Faber & Faber, 1940);

*The Flower Show and Other Pieces* (London: Faber & Faber, 1941);

*The Weald of Youth* (London: Faber & Faber, 1942; New York: Viking, 1942);

*Siegfried's Journey, 1916–1920* (London: Faber & Faber, 1945; New York: Viking, 1946);

*Collected Poems* (London: Faber & Faber, 1947; New York: Viking, 1949);

*Meredith* (London: Constable, 1948; New York: Viking, 1948);

*Common Chords* (Stanford Dingley: Mill House, 1950);

*Emblems of Experience* (Cambridge: Rampant Lion, 1951);

*Renewals* (Worcester: Stanbrook Abbey Press, 1954);

*The Tasking* (Cambridge: Cambridge University Press, 1954);

*An Adjustment* (Royston, Hertfordshire: Golden Head, 1955);

*Sequences* (London: Faber & Faber, 1956; New York: Viking, 1957);

*Lenten Illuminations; Sight Sufficient* (Cambridge: Cambridge University Press, 1958);

*The Path to Peace* (Worcester: Stanbrook Abbey Press, 1960);

*Collected Poems, 1908–1956* (London: Faber & Faber, 1961);

*An Octave: 8 September 1966* (London: Arts Council of Great Britain, 1966);

*Something about Myself, by Siegfried Sassoon, Aged Eleven* (Callow End, Worcester: Stanbrook Abbey Press, 1966);

*Selected Poems* (London: Faber & Faber, 1968);

*Siegfried Sassoon Diaries 1920–1922,* edited by Rupert Hart-Davis (London: Faber & Faber, 1981);

*Siegfried Sassoon Diaries 1915–1918,* edited by Hart-Davis (London: Faber & Faber, 1983);

*The War Poems of Siegfried Sassoon,* edited by Hart-Davis (London: Faber & Faber, 1983);

*Siegfried Sassoon Diaries 1923–1925,* edited by Hart-Davis (London: Faber & Faber, 1985).

OTHER: Wilfred Owen, *Poems,* introduction by Sassoon (London: Chatto & Windus, 1920; New York: Huebsch, 1921).

Although Siegfried Sassoon lived almost to the age of eighty-one and published poetry, fiction, and criticism over a period of sixty years, it was his experience in the years 1916 to 1918 that stoked his genius and informed almost all of his subsequent writing–a corpus that places Sassoon in the first rank of twentieth-century British writers. He won his muse the hard way: as a combat infantry officer at the Somme and in a half-dozen subsequent battles.

Sassoon's unique literary achievements are threefold. First, through the authentic voice of a fighting soldier and a genuine poet he created a new language of war, breaking with the romanticized, distanced pictorialization of soldiering and battle exemplified by Alfred Tennyson's "The Charge of the Light Brigade" (1854) and the poetry and fiction of Rudyard Kipling and Kipling's imitators. By portraying the soldier's pain, misery, disgust, and horror, he shocked much of the British public out of its lust for victory at all costs, led the way for the acceptance of such other combat poets as Wilfred Owen and Robert Graves, and made war a subject of modernism.

Second, Sassoon spent much of the last forty years of his life twice reliving and rewriting the first thirty-five by producing three autobiographical novels–*Memoirs of a Fox-Hunting Man* (1928), *Memoirs of an Infantry Officer* (1930), and *Sherston's Progress* (1936)–and then returning to the same memories in three autobiographies: *The Old Century and Seven More Years* (1938), *The Weald of Youth* (1942), and *Siegfried's Journey, 1916–1920* (1945). In doing so he not only established himself as a master crafter of prose and a prizewinning novelist but also created an evocation of a long-past bucolic Victorian and Edwardian England: a place of country houses and large agricultural estates, a time of slowly passing

*Sassoon (left) with his father, Alfred Ezra Sassoon, and his brothers, Michael and Hamo (Hulton Getty Picture Collection)*

seasons filled with hunts and harvests, cricket and croquet, and comity between the social classes. A monstrous war destroyed that world and left in its ruins a modern industrial society in which Sassoon and many others could never be comfortable.

Third, with the anonymous publication of the award-winning *Memoirs of a Fox-Hunting Man* Sassoon started the flood of World War I remembrance literature that included Edmund Blunden's *Undertones of War* (1928), R. C. Sherriff's drama *Journey's End* (1928), Graves's *Good-bye to All That* (1929), Richard Aldington's *Death of a Hero* (1929), and Ernest Hemingway's *A Farewell to Arms* (1929).

Siegfried Loraine Sassoon, the second of three children—all sons—was born to luxury and privilege on 8 September 1886 at his parents' country house, Weirleigh, near Warminster, Kent. The Sassoons were descendants of eighteenth-century Mesopotamian Jewish merchants who had extended the family business enterprises from Baghdad to Persia and then to India, where they had come under the Union Jack, and finally to England itself. Stanley Jackson has called the family the "Rothschilds of the East." Near the end of his life Sassoon explained that "the daemon in me is Jewish. . . . I have always wanted to be a kind of minor prophet."

Sassoon's father, Alfred Ezra Sassoon, avoided business and trained as a concert violinist but never became a professional. The first Sassoon to marry out of his religion, he was disowned by his family. Theresa Georgiana Thornycroft Sassoon, Siegfried's mother, was an Anglican who came from Cheshire gentry. Her family included gifted sculptors, painters, and engineers; she herself was a competent artist and had studied with Ford Madox Brown. Oblivious to the fact that Richard Wagner was a notorious anti-Semite, she named her half-Jewish second son out of admiration for the composer of the music drama *Siegfried* (1863). In 1891 Alfred Sassoon left Theresa and set up housekeeping in London with a woman who had been her best friend; he died of tuberculosis in 1895.

Initially educated at home, Sassoon attended the New Beacon School from 1900 to 1902 and then enrolled at Marlborough College. There he began to write poetry, joined the Rifle Corps, and became

*Sassoon's mother, Theresa Georgiana Thornycroft Sassoon, in the garden of their country house, Werleigh*

the school's student organist. He entered Clare College, Cambridge, in 1906; that same year he published, at his own expense, *Poems,* the first of ten poetry collections he would bring out privately before he joined the army in 1914. Cambridge was a disaster academically: Sassoon took no interest in his studies but spent his time reading and writing poetry and golfing. At the end of his second year he left without a degree and moved back in with his mother at Weirleigh. The literary lion Edmund Gosse, a family friend, encouraged Sassoon; Gosse was especially impressed by *The Daffodil Murderer: Being the Chantrey Prize Poem* (1913), a clever parody of John Masefield's narrative poetry. A friend of Gosse's, the anthologist Edward Marsh, persuaded Sassoon to move to London and introduced him to the poet Rupert Brooke, who became a role model for Sassoon.

On 31 July 1914 Sassoon, bored with his indolent life in Kent, bicycled thirty miles to Rye, where he enlisted in the Sussex Yeomanry Regiment the next day. Three days later Great Britain declared war on Germany. The uniforms were colorful, and

war seemed to Sassoon, Brooke, and others of their class a great adventure. Sassoon envisioned glorious mounted chases not too different from foxhunting: "My heart was in my boots," he would say in *The Weald of Youth.* He did not try to obtain a commission because he was not sure that he had leadership qualities.

Fifteen months passed before Sassoon reached the trenches. While recovering from a broken arm suffered in a fall from his horse, he realized that cavalry would be of little use in trench warfare; consequently, he sought and was granted a commission as a lieutenant in the Royal Welch Fusiliers, a distinguished infantry regiment. After officer training he was sent to France in November 1915 as transportation officer for the regiment's First Battalion. At battalion headquarters he met and became friends with Graves, a captain and combat veteran.

Sassoon's poetry still treated war as a grand adventure and test of manhood even though his younger brother had already been killed at Gallipoli. But his first taste of modern battle burned the romance of war out of Sassoon; he would never again write limpid pre-Raphaelite verse. In January 1916 the First Battalion took up its position in a line of trenches on the River Somme as the British army prepared for its greatest offensive of the war. In April, Sassoon rescued wounded comrades from no-man's-land under fire and was awarded the Military Cross for valor; his fellow soldiers nicknamed him Mad Jack. The First Battle of the Somme began on 1 July; on 6 July Sassoon single-handedly captured a German trench. Late in the month he came down with acute gastroenteritis—perhaps typhoid fever—and had to be evacuated to England. The illness probably saved Sassoon from death or mutilation in the battle, which lasted for four and one-half months, cost 420,000 British and Commonwealth dead and wounded and almost as many German, resulted in only a few miles of captured enemy territory, and was followed by two more years of a war of attrition. Sassoon was recommended for the Victoria Cross, Britain's highest award for valor, for capturing the German trench, but the award was disallowed because the overall action was a failure. Recuperating in an Oxford military hospital, Sassoon was visited by the art critic Robert Ross, who had once been Oscar Wilde's lover. Ross introduced Sassoon to the London hostess and patron of the arts Lady Ottoline Morrell, whose husband, Philip Edward Morrell, was a leader in the small but influential British peace movement. While being lionized as a poet-hero, Sassoon underwent a crash course in radical politics and turned against the war.

Back in the front line in early 1917, Sassoon was shot in the shoulder during the Battle of Arras while leading an attack on a German position. Once more he was evacuated to England, this time to a London hospital. After meeting the leading British pacifist, the philosopher Bertrand Russell, he began what Edmund Blunden later called his "splendid war on the war." On 15 June 1917 he wrote "A Soldier's Declaration," in which he claimed that the war was being deliberately prolonged by British politicians and that the original aims of the war had been subverted so that the soldiers no longer knew what they were fighting for. Copies of the protest were sent to influential authors; it was printed in *The Times* and read aloud in Parliament. Sassoon refused further military duty, hoping to be court-martialed and become a martyr to the antiwar cause. But Graves intervened to save Sassoon from what Graves saw was a futile gesture and a useless sacrifice: without Sassoon's knowledge he convinced Sassoon's superior officers that Sassoon was "shell-shocked" (in today's terminology, that he was suffering from posttraumatic stress disorder) and should be examined by a medical board. The appeal

*Sassoon as a lieutenant in the Royal Welch Fusiliers in 1915*
*(Hulton Getty Picture Collection)*

was passed up the chain of command, and the War Office decided to hush up the embarrassing incident. Ordered before a medical board, Sassoon—who in the meantime had torn his Military Cross ribbon from his tunic and thrown it in the Mersey in Liverpool—was, thanks to Graves's testimony, sent to a military convalescent home at Craiglockhart, near Edinburgh. There he was "treated" by Dr. William H. R. Rivers, a compassionate neurologist; wrote some of his finest war poems; and became a friend and mentor to Owen, a younger poet and fellow officer who was also a patient there.

When Sassoon could no longer bear to remain in the hospital undergoing a sham convalescence while his comrades were suffering and dying in France, Rivers reluctantly helped him to pass another medical board. In February 1918 he was sent to the campaign in Palestine with the Twenty-fifth Battalion, Royal Welch Fusiliers; in May the battalion was rushed to France to help contain the German breakthrough. On 13 July, Sassoon, who had been promoted to captain and made a company commander, was returning from a patrol in no-

*Sassoon with his wife, Hester Gatty Sassoon*

man's-land when he was shot in the head by one of his own men who mistook him for a German. Believing that his life was over, Sassoon actually felt a wave of relief, but he survived and was again evacuated to a London hospital. While he was there his collection *Counter-Attack, and Other Poems* (1918) was published, establishing him as the outstanding British war poet. When he was released from the hospital he went home to Weirleigh to convalesce. Sassoon's friends struggled to prevent him from returning to the front for the fourth time; the armistice, signed on 11 November 1918, removed the threat.

*Picture Show* and *The War Poems of Siegfried Sassoon* appeared in 1919 to almost universal acclaim, and Sassoon's position as a major British poet was confirmed. Recovered from his wounds, Sassoon, who at this point considered himself a socialist, enrolled at Oxford to study economics so that he could help the Labour Party in the 1919 election. He soon grew bored with his studies, and he felt less and less comfortable working with people who were not of his social class, but he did not abandon socialism until after he had unsuccessfully campaigned for the Pacifist Socialist candidate Philip Snowden and had accepted the only salaried civilian job he would ever hold: literary editor of the socialist *Daily Herald*. In 1920 he traveled to America for a lecture tour.

Sassoon tried to apply the satiric skills he had so successfully employed in his war poetry to civilian topics, but he achieved only limited success in

such volumes as *Satirical Poems* (1926) and *The Road to Ruin* (1933). Lyric collections, including *The Heart's Journey* (1927) and *Vigils* (1934), were also coolly received, and Sassoon's reputation as a poet began what would be a lifelong decline. His poetic interests would eventually turn to meditative and religious themes.

After the war Sassoon entered into a series of less-than-satisfactory homosexual relationships with artistic or aristocratic men who were twenty years his junior; the most significant such involvement was with the notorious social butterfly Stephen Tennant. When Tennant jilted him, Sassoon rebounded into a marriage with Hester Gatty, daughter of the late chief justice of Gibraltar, on 18 December 1933. They had known each other for only three months; he was forty-seven, and she was twenty-eight. After a Continental honeymoon they established a residence, Heytesbury House, in Wiltshire; Sassoon would live there for the rest of his life. They had one child, George, who was born in 1936; the marriage ended in separation.

Sassoon was not happy with the century in which he had been forced to live; his mind and his heart continually returned to late-Victorian and Edwardian times. Throughout the 1920s he had nightmares about the war, and he sorely missed lovers and comrades who had been killed: they remained young and beautiful in his mind as he grew older, and the world seemed to grow stranger and more vicious. The solution for Sassoon was to record his earlier life, up to and including his military service. He chose the novel form for his first attempt, with the character George Sherston as his alter ego in an epic bildungsroman that comprises *Memoirs of a Fox-Hunting Man, Memoirs of an Infantry Officer,* and *Sherston's Progress;* the three novels were republished in a single volume as *The Complete Memoirs of George Sherston* (1937). In the trilogy, which covers the period 1895 to 1918, Sassoon evokes a nostalgic picture of upper-class English life and shows the impact of war on that privileged and much-envied existence. Writing the novels was a therapeutic exercise in remembering and forgetting, both of which Sassoon had great need to do. *The Complete Memoirs of George Sherston* served Sassoon as *Á la recherche du temps perdu* (Remembrance of Things Past, 1913–1927) served Marcel Proust.

Sassoon's most successful novel, *Memoirs of a Fox-Hunting Man,* was published anonymously, but the public quickly guessed the author's identity: although George Sherston is not a writer and, unlike Sassoon, is mildly vacuous, snobbish, hero-worshiping, and interested mainly in horses and hunting, the events in the novel largely parallel those in the early life of the internationally known poet. The work celebrates pastoral life in Victorian-Edwardian country houses and the beautiful English countryside, as well as the pleasant activities of the young and wealthy: cricket, riding, horse racing, and, of course, foxhunting. The novel is like a portfolio of snapshots, freezing time and place and ironically underscoring the seeming timelessness of a well-ordered, closed, class-ridden, inward-looking– and doomed–society.

George Sherston, an orphan, lives at Butley with his Aunt Evelyn. The groom, Tom Dixon, who serves as a role model of manly behavior for the lonely boy, teaches George to ride and takes him to watch a foxhunt. George is immediately smitten with the sport. He sees a boy of his own age doing well in the chase; later, at a dance, he meets the boy, whose name is Dennis Milden. At twelve George goes off to school at "Ballboro'"; after Ballboro' he enrolls at Cambridge but leaves without a degree and returns to his aunt's home, where Dixon revives his interest in foxhunting. Visiting a friend from Ballboro', Stephen Colwood, in Sussex, George finds his dream horse, Cockbird (the name is that of Sassoon's favorite mount, which he left behind when he went off to war). Aunt Evelyn sells one of her rings to help her nephew buy the horse, on which he wins the Colonel's Cup Race. He renews his friendship with Dennis Milden, who is now master of the Ringwell Hounds. When Dennis moves north to the Midlands to become master of the Packlestone Hunt, George goes with him.

With the advent of the war, George enlists in the cavalry but breaks his arm in a fall from a horse and is sent home to recuperate. At his request a neighbor, Captain Huxtable, recommends him for a commission in the infantry, which he receives. In camp he becomes friends with Dick Tiltwood, a young man fresh from school (based on Sassoon's closest comrade in the war, David Thomas). When the battalion is sent into battle George is assigned to headquarters, and Dick is killed in the trenches. George also learns that Dixon, who was also in the army and was trying to be transferred to George's unit, has died of pneumonia. The grief-stricken George, furious that the war has consumed his best friends, requests immediate combat duty. As the novel ends, George is a primitive savage with a club in his hand, waiting to kill an enemy soldier he has never seen before. *Memoirs of a Fox-hunting Man* was enormously successful in Britain and America, winning the Hawthornden Prize and the James Tait Black Memorial Prize and establishing Sassoon as a major writer of prose.

*Memoirs of an Infantry Officer* shows the soldier's lot as one of fear, misery, pain, and death and satirizes the officer class's insistence on well-bred behav-

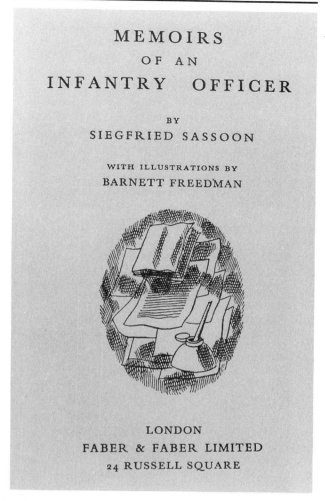

MEMOIRS
OF AN
INFANTRY OFFICER

BY
SIEGFRIED SASSOON

WITH ILLUSTRATIONS BY
BARNETT FREEDMAN

LONDON
FABER & FABER LIMITED
24 RUSSELL SQUARE

*Title page for the second volume of Sassoon's autobiographical bildungsroman*

ior, good form, emotional detachment, and stoic indifference to suffering. When the novel opens in 1916 Sherston is exhausted from combat. His colonel sends him to the rear for extra training; ironically, the instruction is provided by officers who have never been in combat, and the curriculum is devoted to open warfare in the mistaken belief that the "breakthrough" is imminent. Back in the trenches, he goes into no-man's-land to retrieve some of the British casualties after a disastrous raid and is awarded the Military Cross for his heroism. He is sent home on leave; before returning to his unit he stops in London to buy better equipment than that issued by the army. When his companion, Kendle, is cut down by a sniper, George single-handedly attacks and captures a German trench; not knowing what to do with it, he returns to the British lines, only to be reprimanded by his colonel for his failure to hold the trench or get help. He comes down with enteritis before the Battle of the Somme

# PRELUDE.

Far off in earliest remembered childhood I can overhear myself repeating the words 'Water-cress Well'. I am kneeling by an old stone well-head; my mother is standing beside me and we are looking into the water. My mother tells me that it is 'a very deep-rising spring'; but I do not want to be told anything about it, even by her. I want nothing at all except to be gazing at the water which bubbles so wonderfully up out of the earth, and to dip my fingers in it and scatter the glittering drops.

From its well-head the spring overflows into cressy shallows; hence it wanders away as a gurgling and purposeful runnel which may, some day, for all I can tell, arrive at being a real Kentish river. The well reflects the empty sky; I can see myself in it, rather obscurely, when I am not watching the bubbles climbing up in the middle of the crystal-clear water.

Many a half-hour's pilgrimage we made from our house to Water-cress Well, which, after having been one of my favourite places to go to, now becomes a symbol of life itself in an opaque and yet transparent beginning. From that so intensely remembered source, all my journeyings now seem to have started. If I were to go back and look for it I might find that it has vanished; but in my thoughts it is for ever the same. Around and above it whisper the woodland branches; times wavering shadows fall across the glade; but there will be no sunset for that pictured afternoon. Light as a leaf, a robin drops down and decides to have a drink. I look again; the robin is not there. The well-head is alone with its secret energy of life. My mother and I are voices out of sight, for we are half way across the breezy meadow, leaving behind us Water-cress Well and the rivulet that goes running through the wood, talking to itself in the wordless language of water and roots and stones.

＊                          ＊                          ＊

Again, from those lost years of childhood, I hear my voice. This time it asks a question. "What will the seeds be like when they come up?" I am standing beside my mother, who is making a water-colour sketch of a man sowing. It is a dry bright morning in early spring and we are sheltered from the cold east wind by the catkined hazels of a little copse where I have been picking primroses. The ploughed land slopes upwards. Marching across it, the sower in his sackcloth apron scoops and scatters

*Page from the manuscript for* The Old Century and Seven More Years, *the first volume of Sassoon's autobiography (from* Geoffrey Keynes, A Bibliography of Siegfried Sassoon, *1962)*

and is sent to a hospital in Oxford. After recovering he returns home on leave for a month of foxhunting. In February 1917 he is back in the front lines, commanding one hundred grenadiers in the Battle of Arras; they clear the enemy trenches, but George is wounded when the mission is nearly completed. In England once more, he comes under the influence of pacifists, including the philosopher Thornton Tyrell (based on Bertrand Russell), who helps him write a letter refusing to return to combat because the war is being unnecessarily prolonged by vested interests. George expects to be court-martialed and, perhaps, executed, but his superiors order him to go before a medical board to test his sanity. On the advice of his friend Capt. David Cromlech (based on Graves) he allows the board to declare him shell-shocked and order him placed in a hospital for mental casualties.

*Sherston's Progress* is artistically the least satisfactory novel of the trilogy. Sassoon seems to have grown tired of the project; six years passed between the publication of *Memoirs of an Infantry Officer* and *Sherston's Progress*. Also, Sassoon inserts seventy-three diary-like pages into the narrative—an authorial intrusion that decreases the work's verisimilitude. The title of the novel is meant to create an association in the reader's mind between George's journey into and out of no-man's-land and Christian's journey in John Bunyan's *The Pilgrim's Progress* (1678, 1684) from the City of Destruction to the City of Zion. Sassoon also connects T. S. Eliot's poem *The Wasteland* (1922) with his own recasting of the war on the western front.

When *Sherston's Progress* opens in the summer of 1917, Sherston is in Slateford War Hospital for shell-shock victims. He is attended by a wise and compassionate physician, Capt. W. H. R. Rivers— the real name of Sassoon's neurologist and friend. Although he is not actually suffering from shell shock, Sherston is nervous and apprehensive. Understanding, rest, good food, and golf bring him around, and by autumn he feels guilty that his convictions have separated him from his comrades and sheltered him from their dangers. He dreams of the dead, of blasted landscapes, and of skeletons. He finally decides "that going back to the War as soon as possible was my only chance of peace," and a new medical board restores him to duty at his own request. He serves in Ireland and then in Palestine, and with the German breakthrough of March 1918 he is rushed back to France. In May he is back at the Fourth Army School, hearing the same lectures he heard almost two years before. The battle lines have changed little; the only difference from his last time at the school is that hundreds of thousands of men have been killed in the interim.

*Sassoon near the end of his life*

A captain and a company commander at thirty-one, George looks out for the welfare of his men as best he can and takes inordinate personal risks on their behalf. Going out on an unnecessary night patrol, he is shot in the head by his own sergeant, who mistakes him for a German in the darkness. George is sure that he is mortally wounded and is almost relieved that his despair and suffering are soon to be over, but the wound is not fatal. He is evacuated to England, where Dr. Rivers almost magically waves away his depression and restores his mental health. The trilogy ends with George Sherston reborn; his last words spoken aloud sound like a schoolboy's: "Oh Rivers, I've had such a funny time since I saw you last!" His last thoughts, however, are more profound: "It is only from the innermost silence of the heart that we know the world for what it is, and ourselves for what the world had made us." The goal of Sassoon's epic first-person narrative—self-comprehension—has finally been achieved. *The Complete Memoirs of George Sherston* is an allegorical everyman's journey from innocence to experience, from the shallow sporting triumphs of youth through the valley of the shadow of death to the knowledge that the world is a hospital and a graveyard.

Sassoon continued to examine his life in his biographies, *The Old Century and Seven More Years, The Weald of Youth,* and *Siegfried's Journey, 1916–1920.* In the fictional trilogy the central figure is a sportsman, a soldier, and a man of action; in the biographical trilogy he is a literary artist and a philosopher.

Sassoon spent the rest of his life writing poetry at Heytesbury House. During World War II he invited war refugees and British and American troops into his home. He was not a pacifist in that conflict, believing that fascism had to be stopped by force. Faber and Faber published his *Collected Poems* (1947) and his *Collected Poems, 1908–1956* (1961), but most of Sassoon's introspective, personal, and religious later verse was privately printed. In 1951 he was made a Commander, Order of the British Empire; in 1953 he was named an honorary fellow of Clare, his old college at Cambridge; in 1957 Queen Elizabeth II awarded him the Queen's Gold Medal for poetry; and in 1965 Oxford University honored him with a doctor of letters degree. He converted to Roman Catholicism at age seventy and died in his sleep at Heytesbury House on 1 September 1967.

Sassoon's fiction was therapy for him: it helped him to compensate for an unhappy personal life and assuaged his grief over the losses of his youth and the loss of youth itself. In his Sherston trilogy he created, in some of the best English prose written between the world wars, a joyous recollection of late-Victorian and Edwardian country life. He also created a tortured account of a terrible experience that thousands of his readers had shared and could relive and better understand through the pain, grief, anger, and pity of George Sherston.

**Letters:**

*Letters to a Critic,* edited by Michael Thorpe (Nettlestead: Kent Editions, 1976).

**Bibliography:**

Geoffrey Keynes, *A Bibliography of Siegfried Sassoon* (London: Hart-Davis, 1962).

**Biography:**

Felicitas Corrigan, *Siegfried Sassoon: Poet's Pilgrimage* (London: Gollancz, 1973).

**References:**

Bernard Bergonzi, *Heroes' Twilight* (London: Constable, 1965), pp. 92–102;

Edmund Blunden, *Undertones of War* (London: Collins, 1964), p. 169;

Adrian Caesar, *Taking It Like a Man: Suffering, Sexuality and the War Poets: Brooke, Sassoon, Owen, Graves* (New York: Manchester University Press, 1993);

F. J. Harvey Darton, *From Surtees to Sassoon: Some English Contrasts (1838–1928)* (London: Morley & Kennerley, 1931);

Avrom Fleischman, "The Memoirs of George Sherston," in his *Figures of Autobiography: The Language of Self-Writing in Victorian and Modern England* (Berkeley: University of California Press, 1983), pp. 337–353;

Paul Fussell, *The Great War and Modern Memory* (London & New York: Oxford University Press, 1975);

Robert Graves, *Goodbye to All That* (London: Cape, 1929; New York: Cape & Smith, 1930);

John Hildebidle, "Neither Worthy nor Capable: The War Memoirs of Graves, Blunden, and Sassoon," in *Modernism Reconsidered,* edited by Robert Kiely, Harvard English Studies, no. 11 (Cambridge, Mass.: Harvard University Press, 1983), pp. 1010–1021;

Philip Hoare, *Serious Pleasures: The Life of Stephen Tennant* (London & New York: Penguin, 1990);

Samuel Hynes, *A War Imagined: The First World War and English Culture* (New York: Atheneum, 1991), p. 156;

Stanley Jackson, *The Sassoons* (London: Heinemann, 1968);

Thomas Mallon, "The Great War and Sassoon's Memory," in *Modernism Reconsidered,* pp. 81–99;

Paul Moeyes, *Siegfried Sassoon: Scorched Glory. A Critical Study* (New York: St. Martin's Press, 1997);

John Onions, *English Fiction and Drama of the Great War 1918–1939* (New York: St. Martin's Press, 1990), pp. 35–43;

Patrick J. Quinn, *The Great War and the Missing Muse: The Early Writings of Robert Graves and Siegfried Sassoon* (Cranbury, N.J.: Susquehanna University Press, 1994);

Elaine Showalter, "Rivers and Sassoon: The Inscription of Male Gender Anxieties," in *Behind the Lines: Gender and the Two World Wars,* edited by Margaret Randolph Higonnet (New Haven: Yale University Press, 1987), pp. 61–69;

Sanford Sternlicht, *Siegfried Sassoon* (New York: Twayne, 1993).

**Papers:**

Collections of Siegfried Sassoon's papers are at the Columbia University Library, the Harry Ransom Humanities Research Center at the University of Texas at Austin, the Lilly Library at Indiana University, the McFarlin Library at the University of Tulsa, and in the Edmund Blunden Collection at the University of Iowa.

# R. C. Sherriff

## (6 June 1896 – 13 November 1975)

### Kenneth Womack
*Penn State Altoona*

See also the Sherriff entry in *DLB 10: Modern British Dramatists, 1900–1945.*

BOOKS: *Journey's End: A Play in Three Acts* (London: Gollancz, 1929; New York: Brentano's, 1929);

*Journey's End: A Novel,* by Sherriff and Vernon Bartlett (London: Gollancz, 1930; New York: Stokes, 1930);

*Badger's Green: A Play in Three Acts* (London: Gollancz, 1930); republished as *Badger's Green: A Comedy in Three Acts* (London & New York: French, 1934); revised as *Badger's Green: A Comedy in Two Acts* (London: French, 1962);

*The Fortnight in September: A Novel* (London: Gollancz, 1931; New York: Stokes, 1932);

*Two Hearts Doubled: A Playlet* (London & New York: French, 1934);

*St. Helena: A Play in Twelve Scenes,* by Sherriff and Jeanne De Casalis (London: Gollancz, 1934; New York: Stokes, 1935);

*Greengates* (London: Gollancz, 1936; New York: Stokes, 1936);

*The Hopkins Manuscript* (London: Gollancz, 1939; New York: Macmillan, 1939); revised as *The Cataclysm* (London: Pan, 1958);

*Chedworth: A Novel* (New York: Macmillan, 1944);

*Another Year: A Novel* (London: Heinemann, 1948; New York: Macmillan, 1948);

*Quartet: Stories by W. Somerset Maugham, Screenplays by R. C. Sherriff* (London: Heinemann, 1948; Garden City, N.Y.: Doubleday, 1949);

*Miss Mabel: A Play in Three Acts* (London: Gollancz, 1949);

*Trio: Stories by W. Somerset Maugham, Screen Adaptations by W. Somerset Maugham, R. C. Sherriff, and Noel Langley* (Garden City, N.Y.: Doubleday, 1950);

*Home at Seven: A Play in Three Acts* (London: Gollancz, 1951);

*The White Carnation* (London: Heinemann, 1953);

*King John's Treasure: An Adventure Story* (London: Heinemann, 1954; New York: Macmillan, 1954);

*The Long Sunset* (London: Elek, 1955);

*The Telescope: A Play in Three Acts* (London: French, 1957);

*A Shred of Evidence: A Play in Three Acts* (London: French, 1961);

*The Wells of St. Mary's* (London: Heinemann, 1962);

*No Leading Lady: An Autobiography* (London: Gollancz, 1968);

*The Siege of Swayne Castle* (London: Gollancz, 1973).

PLAY PRODUCTIONS: *Profit and Loss,* Surbiton, Gables Theatre, 10 January 1923;

*Cornlow-in-the-Downs,* Surbiton, Gables Theatre, 10 December 1923;

*Journey's End,* London, Apollo Theatre, 9 December 1928;

*Badger's Green,* London, Prince of Wales' Theatre, 12 June 1930;

*St. Helena,* by Sherriff and Jeanne De Casalis, London, Old Vic, 6 October 1936;

*Miss Mabel,* London, Duchess Theatre, 23 November 1948;

*Home at Seven,* London, Wyndham's Theatre, 7 March 1950;

*The Long Sunset,* Birmingham, Birmingham Repertory Theatre, 30 August 1955;

*A Shred of Evidence,* London, Duchess Theatre, 27 April 1960.

MOTION PICTURES: *The Old Dark House,* screenplay by Sherriff, Benn W. Levy, and J. B. Priestley, adapted from Priestley's novel *Benighted,* Universal, 1932;

*The Invisible Man,* screenplay by Sherriff and Philip Wylie, adapted from H. G. Wells's novel, Universal, 1933;

*One More River,* screenplay by Sherriff, adapted from John Galsworthy's novel, Universal, 1934;

*Dracula's Daughter,* screenplay by Sherriff, Garrett Fort, and others, Universal, 1936;

*The Road Back,* screenplay by Sherriff and Charles Kenyon, adapted from Erich Maria Remarque's novel, Universal, 1937;

*R. C. Sherriff*

*The Four Feathers,* screenplay by Sherriff and Lajos Biró, adapted from A. E. W. Mason's novel, United Artists, 1939;

*Goodbye, Mr. Chips,* screenplay by Sherriff, Claudine West, and Eric Maschwitz, adapted from James Hilton's novel, M-G-M, 1939;

*That Hamilton Woman,* screenplay by Sherriff and Walter Reisch, Korda, 1941;

*This above All,* screenplay by Sherriff, adapted from Eric Knight's novel, Twentieth Century-Fox, 1942;

*Forever and a Day,* screenplay by Sherriff and others, RKO, 1943;

*Odd Man Out,* screenplay by Sherriff and F. L. Green, adapted from Green's novel, Universal, 1947;

*Quartet,* screenplay by Sherriff, adapted from stories by W. Somerset Maugham, Eagle Lion, 1949;

*Trio,* screenplay by Sherriff, Maugham, and Noel Langley, adapted from stories by Maugham, Gainesborough/Rank, 1950;

*No Highway in the Sky,* screenplay by Sherriff, Alec Coppel, Oscar Millard, and Nevil Shute, Twentieth Century-Fox, 1951;

*The Dam Busters,* screenplay by Sherriff, Associated British Corporation, 1954;

*The Night My Number Came Up,* screenplay by Sherriff, Ealing, 1954;

*Storm over the Nile,* screenplay by Sherriff, adapted from Mason's novel *The Four Feathers,* Big Ben/London, 1955.

OTHER: *Odd Man Out,* by Sherriff and F. L. Green, in *Three British Screen Plays,* edited by Roger Manvell (London: Methuen, 1950).

R. C. Sherriff is remembered mainly for his plays, especially *Journey's End* (1929); despite the commercial success and critical acclaim enjoyed by his second novel, *The Fortnight in September* (1931), Sherriff's five works in the genre have been largely neglected since his death in 1975.

Born on 6 June 1896 at Kingston upon Thames to Herbert Hankin and Constance Winder Sherriff, Robert Cedric Sherriff graduated from Kingston Grammar School at seventeen and went to work as a clerk at the Sun Insurance Company in London, where his father was also employed. World War I began a few months later, and Sherriff served from 1914 to 1917 in the East Surrey Regiment. Severely wounded at Ypres in 1917, Sherriff, who had risen to the rank of captain, spent six months in a military hospital before returning to the insurance company as a claims adjuster. He devoted much of his free time to the rowing club in his hometown; for six years he and other members wrote the annual fund-raising plays for the club's acting troupe, The Adventurers. He learned the playwright's craft through reading and through frequent visits to London theaters; in his autobiography, *No Leading Lady* (1968), he remembered: "I joined the Times Library and read all the modern plays that were published, and once a month, on pay day, I stayed in London after the day's work was done and went to a theatre in the West End." He also studied William Archer's *Play-Making* (1912), "a wonderful book for the apprentice playwright."

In the late 1920s Sherriff decided to write a play based on his experiences in the war. Drawing on letters he had written to his parents from the front, he composed *Journey's End* and sent the manuscript to a London theatrical agent. After receiving a lukewarm endorsement from Bernard Shaw the play was staged by the Incorporated Stage Society at the Apollo Theatre on 9 December 1928; successful there, it opened at the Savoy Theatre on 1 January 1929 and ran for 594 performances. On 22 March it started a run of 485 performances at Henry Miller's Theatre in New York and went on to tour extensively in the United States. Translated into many languages, the play was performed all over Europe and in Tokyo; in 1930 it was made into a motion picture. Its enormous success enabled Sherriff to construct a luxurious home in the London suburb of Esher.

With a friend, Vernon Bartlett, Sherriff adapted the play into a novel. *Journey's End: A Novel* (1930) retains the play's plot, its setting in a dugout in the trenches before St. Quentin in March 1918, and its characters: the gentle former schoolmaster, Lieutenant Osborne; the naive, boyish Second Lieutenant Raleigh; the brave and imaginative Captain Stanhope; and Second Lieutenant Hibbert, who loses his nerve for combat. Like the play, which was lauded by critics internationally for its realistic depiction of the misery and depravity of life on the front, the novel captures the essence of the trench-

Dust jacket for the novelization of Sherriff's immensely successful play about life in the trenches in World War I (Joseph M. Bruccoli Great War Collection, The University of Virginia)

warfare experience, particularly the fear that permeates the lives of the soldiers. Near the end of the novel Sherriff and Bartlett write: "The whole thing was so damned unfair—men against machines, liquid fire, poison gas. And all these men, with childlike simplicity, looked to their officer, their sergeant, or to one of themselves, to give them the example how to die. There was heroism, all right, but what was the good of heroism in a slaughterhouse?" The *Times Literary Supplement* (20 March 1930) review concluded: "Mr. Sherriff and Mr. Bartlett have done their work well, but the play is greater than the novel."

Sherriff's next play, *Badger's Green* (1930), was a critical and commercial failure. In 1931, fulfilling a longtime ambition, he began studying history at Oxford. His second novel, *The Fortnight in September,* appeared that year. Of this work Sherriff says in his autobiography: "the down-to-earth style of writing didn't come any easier at first than the old elaborate one. It was hard to shake off the habit of looking for impressive words and clever ways of saying things.

*Claude Rains in the 1933 Universal film* The Invisible Man, *for which Sherriff and Philip Wylie wrote the screenplay based on H. G. Wells's novel*

But sooner or later a few penny plain words would break their way through a dead end, and as time went on the thing began to run so smoothly that I wrote more each night than I'd ever done before." The novel is about a middle-class London family's annual two-week vacation at Seaview, a boarding-house in the resort of Bognor. Mr. Stevens, a clerk, finds solace and optimism about the future; Mrs. Stevens attempts to conquer her fear of the ocean; and their grown-up daughter, Mary, has a brief romantic dalliance with Pat, a bit player in a nomadic acting troupe, that will forever alter her place in the family: "To-morrow she would join them in the last day of the holiday: she would join them in their conspiracy to keep back the sorrow of it: she would have her part to play like they had. She would try and forget the rest, if she could, even though nothing like it would ever happen again." In *Commonweal* (7 September 1932) M. E. Chase lauded Sherriff's "simple but exceedingly rare method of keeping himself out of the picture. His art here is representation, the 'imitation' of the ancients, not the expression of the moderns." In *The Spectator* (17 October 1932) L. A. G. Strong said that he found "more sim-

ple human goodness and understanding in this book than in anything I have read for years. . . . Once more, the author of *Journey's End* has enriched our lives."

Returning to Oxford after delivering a series of lectures in and around London, Sherriff—despite his age—joined the university rowing crew but was soon offered a job writing screenplays for Universal Studios for fifteen hundred dollars a week. In his autobiography Sherriff recalled his excitement on his departure for Hollywood: "The way was wide open for a generation of younger writers, with golden opportunities for those who could master the new technique for the talking film. If I could be one of them there'd be no more need to scrape and save to keep that fine new home of mine in Esher." Films for which he wrote the screenplays, alone or in collaboration, include *The Invisible Man* (1933), *The Road Back* (1937), and *Goodbye, Mr. Chips* (1939). During this time he returned to writing for the stage, collaborating with the actress Jeanne De Casalis on *St. Helena* (1936), a play about Napoleon Bonaparte. He commemorated his brief stay at Oxford by establishing a scholarship there in 1937.

During his time in Hollywood, Sherriff wrote two more novels. *Greengates* (1936) is a sentimental work about a fifty-eight-year-old insurance salesman, T. H. Baldwin, who is forced to retire after thirty-six years of service. On the way home after his last day at work Baldwin concocts elaborate plans for a life of leisure in which he will take up gardening and study history. Instead he purchases a new home, Greengates, and joins the membership committee of a local organization, the Welden Valley Club. In this busy, productive existence, which is far removed from the life he had planned, Baldwin finds a contentment that his tenure at the insurance company had never afforded him. At the end of the novel the narrator comments: "He will be seventy-one next year. His hair is quite white now, but his face is the color of polished oak and his eyes are clearer and keener than ever I saw them in his office days." *Greengates* received exceedingly poor critical notices. In *The New York Times* (9 August 1936) Louis Kronenberger said that "the author of *Journey's End* has swallowed his characters' viewpoint whole in an excess of sympathetic emotion, and the result is a pleasant story about as deep as a mud puddle and about as long-lived." In *The Nation* (29 August 1936) J. M. Berryman called the work a "document of despair" and a "sentimental and tedious elaboration."

In *The Hopkins Manuscript* (1939) Sherriff ventures into science fiction. In the future, archaeologists from Addis Ababa discover a manuscript in the ruins of the Notting Hill section of London. The manuscript, written nearly a century earlier by a retired schoolmaster, Edgar Hopkins, describes a lunar cataclysm that occurred on 3 May 1946: "It is hard to believe that this is Notting Hill, and the inky, silent void beneath me is London. There was a time when I could see a million lights from this window . . . but now I seem to be suspended in this broken wooden chair between unheavenly darkness and unearthly silence." In vivid and expansive detail Hopkins describes the government's preparations for the impending disaster and the frantic response of the citizens to the threat of the total destruction of humanity. After the cataclysm obliterates the existing civilization, a group of courageous and progressive individuals, including Hopkins, attempts to reestablish life on Earth in fecund "Beadle Valley"; but the greed of the other survivors defeats their efforts. Hopkins, however, maintains a refreshing optimism: "Always in the background of my thoughts lay the prayer that this tragic interlude might pass away; that reason would return, and peace would come once more to our stricken earth." Although it received a scathing notice in the *Times Literary Supplement* (1 April 1939), *The Hopkins Manuscript* also enjoyed some good reviews. In *The New Yorker* (8 July 1939) Clifton Fadiman called the novel "a modest story on a grandiose theme"; in the *Manchester Guardian* (28 March 1939) Harold Brighouse lauded its "prophetic" qualities, as well as Sherriff's skillful approach to characterization.

In the 1940s and 1950s Sherriff wrote screenplays for a series of British films, including *That Hamilton Woman* (1941), *Odd Man Out* (1947), *Quartet* (1949), *The Dam Busters* (1954), and *Storm over the Nile* (1955). In the theater he had successes with *Miss Mabel* (1948), *Home at Seven* (1950), *The Long Sunset* (1955), and *A Shred of Evidence* (1960). In his autobiography Sherriff records his satisfaction with his career at this time: "For me as a playwright it was the beginning of an Indian summer. With confidence restored all manner of ideas for plays came sailing in from the blue. Some were old ideas, bottled up and forgotten in the years of exile, but now that the theatre was open to me again I let them free."

Sherriff's final novel, *Another Year* (1948), failed to receive the critical accolades garnered by his later plays. A country parson, Roger Matthews, is transferred from his pastoral vicarage to a London parish. After succeeding in his efforts to improve the lives of his parishioners Matthews moves to California and finds success in Hollywood as an actor: "He had never hoped for anything approaching a normal life in Hollywood. At the best he had imagined an ornate, unnatural hotel garden full of sickly tropical flowers." When he learns that his London parish is suffering in his absence, Matthews returns to the city and his previous selfless existence. Critics found Sherriff's morality tale unconvincing; the *Times Literary Supplement* (21 February 1948) said: "It is clear that Mr. Sherriff has gone a long way beyond *Journey's End*. He has lost none of his benevolence or sincerity, but in this book he shows very much less than his former sense of discrimination."

As this review demonstrates, the ghost of *Journey's End* haunted Sherriff's efforts for the rest of his literary career. Although he continued to publish until the early 1970s, his works were largely neglected by critics. Sherriff, who had never married, died on 13 November 1975 in his hometown of Kingston upon Thames.

**References:**

Rosa Maria Bracco, *Merchants of Hope: British Middlebrow Writers and the First World War, 1919–1939* (Providence, R.I.: Berg, 1993), pp. 145–195;

Mark A. Graves, "R. C. Sherriff (1896–1975)," in *British Playwrights, 1880–1956: A Research and Production Sourcebook,* edited by William E. Demastes and Katherine E. Kelly (Westport, Conn.: Greenwood Press, 1996), pp. 381–394;

Steven Trout, "'Glamorous Melanchony': R. C. Sherriff's *Journey's End,*" *War, Literature and the Arts,* 5 (Fall–Winter 1993): 1–19.

# Howard Spring

*(10 February 1889 – 3 May 1965)*

John Ferns
*McMaster University*

BOOKS: *Darkie and Co.* (Oxford: Oxford University Press, 1932);

*Shabby Tiger* (London: Collins, 1934; New York: Covici, Friede, 1935);

*Rachel Rosing: A Novel* (London: Collins, 1935; New York: Hillman-Curl, 1936);

*Sampson's Circus* (London: Faber & Faber, 1936);

*O Absalom!* (London: Collins, 1938); republished as *My Son, My Son!* (New York: Viking, 1938; London: Collins, 1939);

*Book Parade* (London: Collins, 1938; New York: Viking, 1939);

*Heaven Lies about Us: A Fragment of Infancy* (London: Constable, 1939; New York: Viking, 1939);

*Tumbledown Dick: All People and No Plot* (London: Faber & Faber, 1939; New York: Viking, 1940);

*Fame Is the Spur* (London: Collins, 1940; New York: Viking, 1940);

*In the Meantime* (London: Constable, 1942);

*Hard Facts* (London: Collins, 1944; New York: Viking, 1944);

*And Another Thing . . .* (London: Constable, 1946; New York: Harper, 1946);

*Dunkerley's* (London: Collins, 1946; New York: Harper, 1946);

*There Is No Armour: A Novel* (London: Collins, 1948; New York: Harper, 1948);

*The Houses in Between: A Novel* (London: Collins, 1951; New York: Harper, 1952);

*A Sunset Touch: A Novel* (London: Collins, 1953; New York: Harper, 1953);

*Three Plays* (London: Collins, 1953)—comprises *Jinny Morgan, The Gentle Assassin, St. George at the Dragon*;

*These Lovers Fled Away* (London: Collins, 1955; New York: Harper, 1955);

*Time and the Hour: A Novel* (London: Collins, 1957; New York: Harper, 1957);

*All the Day Long* (London: Collins, 1959);

*I Met a Lady* (London: Collins, 1961; New York: Harper, 1961);

*Howard Spring (Clayton Evans)*

*Winds of the Day: A Novel* (London: Collins, 1964; New York: Harper & Row, 1965);

*The Autobiography of Howard Spring* (London: Collins, 1972)—comprises *Heaven Lies about Us, In the Meantime, And Another Thing . . .* ;

*Eleven Stories & a Beginning* (London: Collins, 1973).

Howard Spring was in the middle of a career as a successful journalist when he became a successful popular novelist. His novels deal with the strains running through British society between the world wars. Melodramatic at times, they stress the importance of love in human life and the need to endure. In his autobiography (1972) Spring says:

> In a novel called *Fame Is the Spur* [1940] I tried to bring to a crux in the relationships of one small group of people the ideas I have here been trying to express. A woman named Pen Muff, the blinded wife of a South Wales miners' leader, is told by her daughter Alice that she'll never bring children into the world "because the world is not worthy." To that Pen replies: "It's a coward's decision. Why, God love us, Alice, the world has been pretty tough on me. And if anyone said to me: 'D'you want it all over again, Pen Muff, just in the way you've had it, blindness and all?' Why, I'd say: 'Ay, and again after that, as often as you like.' It's not a perfect world for children that matters, or that you'll ever get: it's children to work for a perfect world. No, no, Alice, believe me, there's going to be no harps and wings here below. By heck there's not. But when we stop working for 'em, God help us."

Robert Howard Spring was born in Cardiff, Wales, on 10 February 1889 to William Henry Spring, a gardener who loved books, and Mary Stacey Spring. Spring's early reading included John Milton's *Paradise Lost* (1667), John Bunyan's *The Pilgrim's Progress* (1678, 1684), Daniel Defoe's *Robinson Crusoe* (1719), Henry Fielding's *Tom Jones* (1749), Charles Dickens's *The Pickwick Papers* (1836–1837), and Johann David Wyss's *The Swiss Family Robinson* (1814). Spring's mother also enjoyed Dickens's works, and a lifelong love of that author is evident in Spring's melodramatic, richly populated novels. In his youth Spring would read John Forster's *The Life of Charles Dickens* (1872–1874) with a picture of Dickens propped up in front of him.

The large Spring family—there were four girls and five boys—was quite poor, often trying to live on less than a pound a week. In his autobiography Spring says that "only the indefatigable realism of my mother kept us afloat." Spring's father died when Spring was twelve, and Spring left school—though he continued to attend technical school in the evening—and went to work first as an errand boy and then as an office boy for an accountant. After a year he became a messenger boy for *The South Wales Daily News and Echo*, working his way up to reporter. He moved to *The Yorkshire Observer* in Bradford in 1911 and to *The Manchester Guardian* in 1915. World War I had begun by then, and after a few months at the *Guardian* Spring, who was physically unfit for regular military duty, joined the Army Service Corps. He performed clerical work at General Headquarters and in France and returned to the *Guardian* after World War I ended in 1918. In 1920 he married Marion Ursula Pye; they had two sons: David, born in 1920, and Michael, born in 1922. In 1930 the newspaper magnate Lord Beaverbrook (Sir William Maxwell Aitken, first Baron Beaverbrook of Beaverbrook and of Cherkley) offered Spring a job as book reviewer for *The Evening Standard*, a position previously held by Arnold Bennett and J. B. Priestley. While he was employed by the *Standard*, Spring and his family lived in Hampstead and later in Pinner, Middlesex.

Spring's first book, *Darkie and Co.* (1932), a children's novel that he wrote for his sons, was followed by *Shabby Tiger* (1934) and its sequel, *Rachel Rosing* (1935). Both are set in Manchester in the 1920s and have as their protagonist Rachel Rosing, a selfish, ambitious Jewish woman from the Cheetham Hill district of the city. In contrast to her generous brother, Moses, "Rachel Rosing could not remember a time when she had not used people to further her own ends." But Spring's treatment of Rachel's tragedy is more complex than this dismissive judgment would indicate: near the end of the second novel the narrator says, "The bright flame that had lit her life so fiercely had been the affirmation of her woman's right to take a man without the shame of a bargain. It had been a swift revolt from the bondage that poverty had laid upon her beauty."

Spring's best-known novel, *O Absalom!* (1938), was republished in the United States in 1938 and in subsequent British editions as *My Son, My Son!* to avoid confusion with William Faulkner's *Absalom, Absalom!* (1936). It was widely popular in Britain and the United States; an American film version was made in 1940, and a British television miniseries would appear in 1979. Spring conceived the plot of the novel while sitting in a train at Keinton Mandeville station in Somerset: the station's water tank becomes the hiding place for the novel's Oliver Essex after he commits a murder. *My Son, My Son!* is narrated by the Manchester novelist and dramatist William Essex, who "had done for Manchester what Arnold Bennett had done for the Five towns." During the Irish Troubles of the 1920s his son, Capt. Oliver Essex, M.C., V.C., "scorched and twisted by war," becomes a major in the Black and Tans and kills his childhood friend Rory O'Riordon, who has become a Republican. Later, Oliver, desperate for money, murders a character named Percy Lupton and discovers the difference between killing in war and in peacetime. *My Son, My Son!* is a strong indictment of what Oliver Essex calls "a God-awful government that turns you loose to wreck and murder right and left without any rule or pity, and then slips the hounds at you because you go on being what they made you."

The success of his novels enabled Spring to leave the *Evening Standard* in 1939 and move to

*Spring's wife, the former Marion Ursula Pye, at the time of their marriage in 1920*

the beginning of World War II: "It was an age in which no good had seemed impossible, and now they accepted the age in which no evil, no bestiality, no treason or treachery seemed incredible . . . three things were immortal: good and evil and the hope in men's hearts that evil would be overcome by good." A 1946 film adaptation of the novel starred Michael Redgrave as Hamer and Rosamond John as Ann.

During World War II Spring planned a trilogy of novels to be called "So Much Glory: So Much Shame," of which he completed two: *Hard Facts* (1944) and *Dunkerley's* (1946). The third novel, "The Banner," remained unfinished, although characters from the first two novels would appear toward the end of *Time and the Hour* (1957). *Hard Facts* and *Dunkerley's* tell of Daniel Dunkerley's rise from humble Manchester beginnings to become a newspaper magnate; his success is contrasted to the tragic lives of Alec and Elsie Dilworth, a brother and sister who are victims of child abuse.

In 1947 the Springs settled in Falmouth, where Marion Spring had spent holidays as a child. There, in addition to writing novels, Howard Spring began contributing book reviews to the magazine *Country Life*. In *There is No Armour* (1948) Ted Pentecost, a successful portrait painter and member of the Royal Academy, tells the story of his life. During World War I he meets a French priest who tells him,

> *There is no armour against Fate.* You think that means that what must come must come, and that we might as well grin and bear it. I think it means that the love of God is seeking us out, and that, do what we will, it will find us in the end. It will find us when we throw ourselves unarmed and naked upon its mercy. And that will be when our first thought is to bind up one another's wounds and tell one another our names.

Cornwall. The following year he published *Fame Is the Spur,* the story of the rise to political power of Hamer Shawcross, the illegitimate son of a servant girl. Hamer inherits the saber that killed his step-grandfather's sweetheart in the Peterloo Massacre in 1819; he carries it with him throughout his life as a symbol of the oppression of the working class. Moving from Manchester to Bradford, Hamer marries Ann Artingstall. Their wedding night is movingly described: "And the roaring of their hearts and nerves died down as they slept in one another's arms, with the snow falling soundlessly upon their roof and upon the empty miles around them—falling pitilessly, remorselessly, like the obliterating years that have so much to give, that they may take all away in the end." Hamer's rise to become Viscount Shawcross is contrasted to the life of his friend Arnold Ryerson, who marries Pen Muff in Bradford and becomes a miners' leader in South Wales. Hamer and Ann's son, Charles, and Arnold and Pen's daughter, Alice, set off to fight in the Spanish Civil War, but Charles is killed when a torpedo hits their boat. The novel closes with Hamer's death at

*The Houses in Between* (1951) is narrated by Sarah Undridge, who was born three years before the opening of the Crystal Palace in 1851 and dies on New Year's Day 1948. Spring notes in his foreword: "The pathetic significance of the Crystal Palace had for long appealed to my imagination, and I wanted to make a novel out of the contrast between the fragile promise of peace and the dreadful realities of the years that followed." The novel's title comes from an old saying: "You could see the Crystal Palace if it wasn't for the houses in between." Sarah witnesses enormous changes during her long life: "I am nearing my ninetieth year as I write this. I was born in a time when my living eyes could look at the Dook who had been at Waterloo. And then I watched the great glass bubble go up and heard talk of peace on earth. . . . I had seen wooden ships with sails become ironclads with boilers, and rifles be-

*Spring at his home, the White Cottage, in Pinner*

come machine guns, and cannon-balls become explosive shells."

Much shorter than Spring's two previous novels, *A Sunset Touch* (1953) is the story of how Roger Menheniot, despite the odds, wins Kitty Littledale and regains possession of Rosemullion, the Cornish house that had once been his family's home. The last words of the novel belong to Kitty: "Then with one instinct we moved to one another, and our arms went round one another, and our bodies touched till we were one vibration of happy weeping."

*These Lovers Fled Away* (1955) was Spring's favorite among his novels. It follows the lives of Chad Boothroyd, Billy Pascoe, Greg Appleby, and Eustace Hawke through the first three decades of the twentieth century as Chad becomes a dramatist, Billy a nuclear physicist, Greg a professor of economics, and Eustace a poet. Chad tries to reveal the effects of World War I in his best play, as does Eustace in his poetry; Billy does research that leads to the development of the atomic bomb; and Greg becomes a socialist. Chad's prewar marriage to May Ingleby is destroyed by his lifelong attraction to Rose Orlop, who loves Eustace but marries Billy and, eventually, Chad.

In *Time and the Hour* Spring continues his exploration of the conflicts in English social life in the first thirty years of the century by again following the lives of four characters—Anthony Bromwich, Dick Hudson, Joanna Halliwell, and Lottie Wayland—as they move from Yorkshire to London. Anthony becomes a successful restaurateur and mar-

ries Lottie; Dick, a music-hall comedian, eventually finds happiness with Lottie's mother; Joanna, with her tragic marriage to the shell-shocked Sir William Scroop, her relationship with Rudolph Schwann, and her eventual union with Joe Morrison, who has loved her from their first meeting, is the novel's central character. The novel moves from the idyllic days before World War I through the agony of the war itself and ends with Adolf Hitler's persecution of the Jews, including Rudolph's niece, Magda. When Joanna is struck by a fascist at a London meeting, the narrator says that "all the tragedy of Europe had written itself in that red hieroglyphic on her cheek." Love, where it is permitted or possible, provides the only source of hope: "A pair of lovers was an improvement on a pair of haters. You could say that anyway."

*All the Day Long* (1959) concerns the family of a Cornish vicar. The youngest daughter, Maria Legassick, who is now an old woman living alone with her memories in the empty vicarage, narrates the story of her life and those of her siblings, Louisa, Bella, and Roger.

In *I Met a Lady* (1961) George Ledra tells of watching recruits march through the streets of Manchester at the beginning of World War I. As in many of Spring's novels, the locale shifts from Manchester to Cornwall, where George moves for health reasons. There he studies with a retired professor of Greek, Hector Chown. Sylvia Bascome, an actress who is related to Hector, is rebuilding the ruined mansion in which she lives with her daughter Janet;

the house symbolizes the world that must be rebuilt after World War I. Attracted to both Sylvia and Janet, George eventually marries Sylvia.

Spring's last completed novel, *Winds of the Day* (1964), is narrated by the orphaned Alice Openshaw, who is born in Manchester at the end of the nineteenth century. The novel concerns Alice's struggle, from her beginnings as a servant girl, to gain independence during a time when it was difficult for a working-class woman to make her way on her own. She marries a novelist, Frank Melvill, and later a playwright, Chris Harris. Human life is seen as a flow: "We were all embarked on the only life we should ever know, Flowing like the stream of Dros-Y-Mor through this and that to meet the creek at last." Alice becomes a writer herself. She observes the changes in English life from the time before World War I to the 1960s. As always, Spring, like Frank Melvill, undertakes "a searching of the heart and of manners." Spring died on 3 May 1965, following a stroke.

In *The Houses in Between* the novels of Sarah Undridge's governess, Margaret Whale, are described: "behind the well-known popular work there was a seriousness, a consistent point of view—if you care to have it that way, a philosophy of life—that would probably give this author a permanent, though hardly a notable, place in English letters." The same could be said of the novels of Howard Spring.

**Biography:**
Marion Howard Spring, *Howard* (London: Collins, 1967).

# D. E. Stevenson
## (1892 – 30 December 1973)

Sandra Hagan
*McMaster University*

BOOKS: *Meadow-Flowers* (London: Macdonald, 1915);

*Peter West* (London & Edinburgh: Chambers, 1923);

*The Starry Mantle: Poems* (London: Stockwell, 1926);

*Mrs. Tim of the Regiment; or, Leaves from the Diary of an Officer's Wife,* anonymous (London: Cape, 1932); as Stevenson (New York: Farrar & Rinehart, 1940); republished as *Mrs. Tim Christie* (New York: Holt, Rinehart & Winston, 1973);

*Golden Days: Further Leaves from Mrs. Tim's Journal* (London: Jenkins, 1934);

*Miss Buncle's Book* (London: Jenkins, 1934; New York: Farrar & Rinehart, 1937);

*Divorced from Reality* (London: Jenkins, 1935); republished as *Miss Dean's Dilemma* (New York: Farrar & Rinehart, 1938); revised as *The Young Clementina* (London: Collins, 1970; New York: Holt, Rinehart & Winston, 1970);

*Smouldering Fire: A Romance* (London: Jenkins, 1935; New York: Farrar & Rinehart, 1938);

*The Empty World: A Romance of the Future* (London: Jenkins, 1936); republished as *A World in Spell* (New York: Farrar & Rinehart, 1939);

*Miss Buncle, Married: Being the Further Adventures of the Celebrated Authoress* (London: Jenkins, 1936; New York: Farrar & Rinehart, 1937);

*The Story of Rosabelle Shaw* (London & Edinburgh: Chambers, 1937; New York: Farrar & Rinehart, 1939); republished as *Rosabelle Shaw* (London: Collins, 1967);

*The Baker's Daughter* (New York: Farrar & Rinehart, 1938); republished as *Miss Bun, The Baker's Daughter* (London: Collins, 1938);

*Green Money* (London: Collins, 1939); republished as *The Green Money* (New York: Farrar & Rinehart, 1939);

*Alister and Co.: Poems* (New York: Farrar & Rinehart, 1940);

*The English Air* (New York: Farrar & Rinehart, 1940; London: Collins, 1940);

*Rochester's Wife* (London: Collins, 1940; New York: Farrar & Rinehart, 1940);

*Spring Magic* (New York: Farrar & Rinehart, 1941; London: Collins, 1942);

*Mrs. Tim Carries On: Leaves from the Diary of an Officer's Wife in the Year 1940* (London: Collins, 1941; New York: Farrar & Rinehart, 1941);

*Crooked Adam* (New York: Farrar & Rinehart, 1942; London: Collins, 1969);

*Celia's House* (London: Collins, 1943; New York: Farrar & Rinehart, 1943);

*It's Nice to Be Me* (London: Methuen, 1943);

*The Two Mrs. Abbotts* (London: Collins, 1943; New York: Farrar & Rinehart, 1943);

*Listening Valley* (London: Collins, 1944; New York: Farrar & Rinehart, 1944);

*The Four Graces* (London: Collins, 1946; New York: Rinehart, 1946);

*Kate Hardy* (London: Collins, 1947; New York: Rinehart, 1947);

*Mrs. Tim Gets a Job* (London: Collins, 1947; New York: Rinehart, 1947);

*Young Mrs. Savage* (London: Collins, 1948); republished as *Young Mrs. Savage: Being an Account of Every-day Events in the Lives of Mrs. Savage and Her Four Children* (New York: Rinehart, 1949);

*Vittoria Cottage* (London: Collins, 1949; New York: Rinehart, 1949);

*Music in the Hills* (London: Collins, 1950; New York: Rinehart, 1950);

*Winter and Rough Weather* (London: Collins, 1951); republished as *Shoulder the Sky: A Story of Winter in the Hills* (New York: Rinehart, 1951);

*Mrs. Tim Flies Home: Leaves from the Diary of a Grass-Widow* (London: Collins, 1952; New York: Rinehart, 1952);

*Five Windows* (London: Collins, 1953; New York: Rinehart, 1953);

*Charlotte Fairlie* (London: Collins, 1954); republished as *Blow the Wind Southerly* (New York: Rinehart, 1954);

*Amberwell* (London: Collins, 1955; New York: Rinehart, 1955);

*Summerhills* (London: Collins, 1956; New York: Rinehart, 1956);

*The Tall Stranger* (London: Collins, 1957; New York: Rinehart, 1957);

*Anna and Her Daughters* (London: Collins, 1958; New York: Rinehart, 1958);

*Still Glides the Stream* (London: Collins, 1959; New York: Rinehart, 1959);

*The Musgraves* (London: Collins, 1960; New York: Holt, Rinehart & Winston, 1960);

*Bel Lamington* (London: Collins, 1961; New York: Holt, Rinehart & Winston, 1961);

*Fletchers End* (London: Collins, 1962; New York: Holt, Rinehart & Winston, 1962);

*The Blue Sapphire* (London: Collins, 1963; New York: Holt, Rinehart & Winston, 1963);

*Katherine Wentworth* (London: Collins, 1964; New York: Holt, Rinehart & Winston, 1964);

*Katherine's Marriage* (London: Collins, 1965); republished as *The Marriage of Katherine* (New York: Holt, Rinehart & Winston, 1965);

*The House on the Cliff* (London: Collins, 1966; New York: Holt, Rinehart & Winston, 1966);

*Sarah Morris Remembers* (London: Collins, 1967; New York: Holt, Rinehart & Winston, 1967);

*Sarah's Cottage* (London: Collins, 1968; New York: Holt, Rinehart & Winston, 1968);

*Gerald and Elizabeth* (London: Collins, 1969; New York: Holt, Rinehart & Winston, 1969);

*The House of the Deer* (London: Collins, 1970; New York: Holt, Rinehart & Winston, 1971).

In an unpublished "Short Biography" written in 1964, D. E. Stevenson assessed her own work: "The books of D. E. S. are essentially 'stories about people'[;] they can be read on the surface, for amusement only, but beneath the surface there is power and truth and a deep understanding of psychology." In the early part of her career critics concurred with Stevenson's estimate of her understanding of psychology: her characters "are all live people," said Margaret Wallace in a review in *The New York Times* (15 November 1942) of Stevenson's *Crooked Adam* (1942). Critics also praised Stevenson's wit and the "freshness" and "charm" of her novels. On the other hand her plots, which revolve around the details of the characters' daily lives and end happily, and her conventional style led critics to classify her work as light reading for a discerning audience. But Stevenson's repeated use of the point of view of the "wise fool" suggests a deliberate attempt to show that there is wisdom in simplicity.

From about the midpoint in Stevenson's career, the wit, freshness, and charm that impressed reviewers gradually left her work. Her later novels, while retaining her compelling characterizations, seem flatly "ladylike"—a term many reviewers used for her later works—at a time when many of the novels being published featured what Stevenson, in "The Author's Point of View," an unpublished talk she gave near the end of her career, called "depraved characters with cruel and unnatural lusts." It is unfortunate that the novels of the latter part of her career seem to have marked her for new generations of readers as a novelist of nostalgia: half of her books are out of print, and almost half of the rest are available only in large-print editions. Classics of Stevenson's style, such as the Miss Buncle and Mrs. Tim series, however, deserve to be remembered.

The two facts of her life to which Stevenson returns again and again in her works are World War II and her repeated moves as an army wife. While the war appears in many of her novels, only the Mrs. Tim series deals with the vagabond existence of a military family. Her repeated use of houses and historical tales to convey a sense of stability, however, suggests that many of her novels are concerned with a universal human need that her life of travel brought home to her: the need for a place to call one's own.

Dorothy Emily Stevenson was born in Edinburgh in 1892 to David Alan Stevenson, a civil engineer and first cousin of the writer Robert Louis Stevenson, and Anne Roberts Stevenson, a first cousin of the military hero Frederick Sleigh Roberts, Baron Roberts of Kandahar. She grew up in Edinburgh and in North Berwick. Like many middle-class girls her age, she was educated at home. She began writing at the age of eight, hiding in a storage closet because, as Stevenson says in "The Author's Point of View," "My parents were not encouraging." Probably, like many in the Victorian era, they considered the activity "unladylike." In 1916 Stevenson married Maj. James Reid Peploe. They had three children: Robert, Rosemary, and John.

Stevenson's first critical recognition came with *Mrs. Tim of the Regiment; or, Leaves from the Diary of an Officer's Wife* (1932) although she had previously published two books of poetry, *Meadow-Flowers* (1915) and *The Starry Mantle* (1926), and a novel, *Peter West* (1923). *Mrs. Tim of the Regiment* was the first installment in what became the popular Mrs. Tim series, for which, along with the Miss Buncle books, Stevenson is best known. *Mrs. Tim of the Regiment* grew out of Stevenson's diary and is written as the diary of the protagonist, Hester Christie, the wife of the army officer Tim Christie; Ruth Page, reviewing the book in the *Boston Transcript* (1 February 1940), wrote that "for the purposes of Miss Stevenson's talent and of Mrs. Tim's wit, the form is perfect." Stevenson retained the diary form throughout the series.

*D. E. Stevenson*

One reason why Stevenson's characters have such vitality is that, as Stevenson herself asserts in "The Author's Point of View," "the characters [are] real to me—and therefore real to my readers." She knows the whole history of each of her characters, she says, "all their idiosynchracies [*sic*] and their likes and dislikes," whether she actually uses this information in the novels or not. Because her characters had an existence for her beyond the bounds of the novels, Stevenson found herself reluctant to part with them; this reluctance explains why so many of her novels have sequels and why characters reappear in otherwise unrelated novels. In the foreword to *Mrs. Tim Christie,* the 1973 reprint of *Mrs. Tim of the Regiment,* she accounts for *Golden Days: Further Leaves from Mrs. Tim's Journal* (1934), the sequel to *Mrs. Tim of the Regiment,* by saying that she "had become so interested in Hester that I gave her a holiday in the Scottish Highlands."

Perhaps the most strikingly vivid of Stevenson's creations are the children, a feature of her novels for which critics are full of praise. Over the course of the five Mrs. Tim novels—her longest series—the reader follows Hester's children, Betty and Bryan, from childhood through adolescence to young adulthood. Stevenson enriches her character studies by including the children's letters as part of Hester's diary.

*Miss Buncle's Book* (1934), Stevenson's fourth novel, while well received, was considered, in the words of Charlotte Dean in *The New York Times* (1 August 1937), merely "a gentle, simple, mildly satirical tale," with none of the literary potentialities reviewers credited to the best of the Mrs. Tim series. Far from simple, however, this story of a spinster who writes a novel about the town in which she lives not only explores the relationship between fact and fiction but also comments on the creative process and the publishing industry. The events in Barbara Buncle's book, *Disturber of the Peace,* begin to take place in the real town as the inhabitants are influenced by the novel, and the writer begins to take on the personality of her heroine and to lose the ability to distinguish between her fictional village and the actual one. Mr. Abbott, the editor of *Disturber of the Peace,* is unsure how to take Miss Buncle's book: is it "a delicate satire or merely a chronicle of events seen through the innocent eyes of a simpleton?" After getting to know Barbara, he realizes that the book is not a satire—that Barbara and her book are as simple as they seem and that there is exceptional wisdom in that simplicity. Here, as in her other nvoels featuring protagonists, Stevenson opposes the integrity of the "wise fool" to the empty sophistication of many of the surrounding characters and demonstrates that this integrity allows the protagonist to see truths that the others miss. This notion is explored further in the next book in the series, *Miss Buncle, Married: Being the Further Adventures of the Celebrated Authòress* (1936), in which Barbara Buncle and Mr. Abbott become man and wife.

In *Miss Buncle, Married* Stevenson again excels in her portrayal of children. She does not romanticize childhood but captures the joys, the fears, and the innocent amorality of being young, without resorting to the usual wink and smile of the adult storyteller. Trivona Marvell, the girl who lives next door to the Abbotts, for instance, dances around in the wild joy of being alive but is tormented by a ritual, "the Nightmare Curse," which requires her to step on every rose on the carpet every night to ward off bad dreams. Trivona also makes a voodoo doll of a hated villager, Mrs. Dance, and, along with her brother, floods the Abbotts' backyard and digs an elephant pit into which Mrs. Abbott falls.

With *The Empty World: A Romance of the Future* (1936) Stevenson moved from social comedy to science fiction. The attempt was not well received; the *Times Literary Supplement* (28 March 1936) pointed out that the novel, "despite its framework, appeals more to connoisseurs of love stories than to those of scientific romances." In *Green Money* (1939) Stevenson explores the possibilities of the mystery genre, but this time she incorporates the strengths of her own style of fiction. The hero, George Ferrier, is another foolish but good and ultimately wise figure, like Miss Buncle. Much of the humor is at Ferrier's expense, but the reader learns a great deal from him. With her unique wit and warmth Stevenson proves that she can bring as much life to a male protagonist as to a female one.

Stevenson's two books of children's verse, *Alister and Co.* (1940) and *It's Nice to Be Me* (1943), again show her ability to understand children and speak their language; both collections were well received by reviewers, who compared it to Robert Louis Stevenson's *A Child's Garden of Verses* (1885) and to the poems of A. A. Milne. Once again Stevenson depicts childhood as it is. For instance, the child in "Tigers" is frustrated because the gardener is more concerned with his vegetables than with the two imaginary tigers who live in the garden. The poem ends with the child's wish: "Some day they'll make a leap at him / And tear him fiercely limb from limb— / *I hope they'll do it soon.*" Stevenson captures both the fantasy world of childhood and the delightful amorality that allows all of a child's emotions full play.

According to Stevenson's foreword to *Mrs. Tim Christie*, the third novel in the series, *Mrs. Tim Carries On: Leaves from the Diary of an Officer's Wife in the Year 1940* (1941), like the first, grew out of her diary. This time, however, she did not have to "pep it up" because in this part of her diary, covering the early part of World War II, "there was enough pep already . . . for half a dozen books." Stevenson says that writing the work helped her to get through the war: "The book was a comfort to me in those dark days; it helped me to carry on, and a sort of pattern emerged from the chaos." Stevenson wrote several books about the war while it was in progress: *Mrs. Tim Carries On* was preceded by *The English Air* (1940) and *Spring Magic* (1941) and followed by *Crooked Adam, Celia's House* (1943), and *Listening Valley* (1944). The third novel in the Miss Buncle series, *The Two Mrs. Abbotts* (1943), though published during World War II, is set during World War I. More novels about the home front during World War II, as well as some dealing with the postwar years, followed throughout the 1940s and 1950s.

It is during this period of her career that a recurring theme begins to emerge in Stevenson's work: the house as a symbol of stability and a source and embodiment of emotional and spiritual strength. Since her marriage Stevenson had moved frequently; she did not live in a home of her own until she and her husband settled in Moffat, Scotland, on her husband's retirement. Hester's relief at the end of *Mrs. Tim Carries On,* when Tim suggests that they retire to a house of their own as soon as he can get out of the army, is no doubt based on Stevenson's own feelings. In many of her works characters commune with the spirits of past inhabitants of houses, and characters' personalities are revealed through the houses in which they live or have lived. Houses can reflect both the individualities of their inhabitants and the bonds between generations. As Joanne Harack Hayne points out that in regard to Dunnian in *Celia's House,* in Stevenson's novels houses are often characters themselves; in *Celia's House* it is the people who are incidental and the house that is the center of vitality. The reader learns on the opening page that "Generations of Dunnes, born and bred at Dunnian and afterwards scattered to the four corners of the earth," return there in their imaginations, and Dunnian is introduced as if it were alive. The willing of the house to Celia causes the central conflict in the story and draws attention to the process of maintaining connections from one generation to the next and the stability and order that such connections create.

Jane Austen is the writer most frequently referred to in Stevenson's novels and is also the author who most readily comes to mind when reading Stevenson's works. Hayne says that Stevenson's "novels might best be classified as novels of manners," and Austen also wrote novels of manners.

Stevenson also resembles Austen in her careful and witty studies of individual and social character. In the fourth novel in the Mrs. Tim series, *Mrs. Tim Gets a Job* (1947), Stevenson includes a passage written in imitation of Austen and passed off by one of the characters, Erica Clutterbuck, as a passage from an Austen novel. Stevenson not only imitates Austen skillfully and amusingly but also employs the passage to reveal more about both the character who has written it and the character—Hester—who finds her out. It is Hester's mention of her love of Austen's *Emma* (1815) that breaks the ice between the two, and Erica's writing of the passage fills in for Hester "some more details in the map of Erica Clutterbuck."

Although the later Mrs. Tim books retain the witty edge of Stevenson's early novels, by the time the trilogy *Vittoria Cottage* (1949), *Music in the Hills* (1950), and *Winter and Rough Weather* (1951; republished in the United States as *Shoulder the Sky: A Story of Winter in the Hills,* 1951) appeared, her affirmation of simplicity was beginning to dominate, and her tone was beginning to lose its buoyancy. It was the rare critic who appreciated the qualities that remained; one such was Kathleen Cannell, who reviewed *Shoulder the Sky* in the *Christian Science Monitor* (25 October 1951): "Her percipience presents her characters with vitality and stature. They meet their all too human loves, griefs, mysteries, entanglements, tragedies and triumphs with a sort of clear-eyed elemental simplicity."

In addition to building a fictional world in her sequels, trilogies, and series, Stevenson often brings back characters from previous novels for guest appearances in new works. Since the village doctor is out of town, Monkey Wrench—Mr. Abbott's old war buddy and physician in *Miss Buncle, Married*—turns up in *Vittoria Cottage* to deliver Sue Widgeon's baby. What makes such crossovers possible is that Stevenson uses the same locations in many novels; Old Quinings and Wandlebury are the preferred locales in England, Ryddelton—a thinly disguised Moffat—in Scotland. The reader is tantalized by the prospect, for instance, of Hester running into an elderly Miss Buncle when Hester rents a house in Old Quinings in *Mrs. Tim Flies Home: Leaves from the Diary of a Grass-Widow* (1952). Although the meeting never takes place, wondering how the two characters would relate to one another provides interest for the reader without Stevenson actually writing such a scene. Stevenson's revisited places are full of the ghosts of characters from other novels.

Stevenson returns to a foolish-but-wise protagonist in *Five Windows* (1953). The story of David Kirke is, in many ways, Stevenson's version of

Charles Dickens's *David Copperfield* (1849–1850): the novel follows Kirke from boyhood to manhood; he becomes a writer and is entangled with the wrong girl but, as in *David Copperfield,* ends up with the right girl—one he has known from boyhood. Much of the humor in the novel is to be found in the colorful, almost Dickensian, minor characters with whom Stevenson peoples David's world. After Austen, Dickens is the writer who is mentioned most frequently in Stevenson's works.

Writing a novel about an author gives Stevenson another opportunity—as did *Miss Buncle's Book*—to comment on the craft of writing. In *Five Windows* she not only explores the process by which David creates his successful novels but also examines the unsuccessful approach of his friend Miles. David puts his finger on the "sawdust" hero of Miles's novel *Ralph's Progress* as the reason why Miles's book is so bad. This fault results from the businesslike approach to writing that Miles propounds to the incredulous David. David's assessment corresponds with Stevenson's own view of the importance of the characters in a novel, and his method of writing is closer to Stevenson's than is Miles's. In an unpublished essay, "Truth in Fiction," Stevenson says that a "novel of substance" is "a novel in which the characters are all important, and in which the play of personality is one of the underlying principles"; in contrast the characters in the typical detective story are "puppets." Although reviewers generally considered it to be cast in the mold of all of her other novels, and dismissed or approved of it accordingly, *Five Windows* is the one work in which her powers of characterization, her affirmation of simple truths, her homely warmth, and her humor all carry equal weight. While moving and memorable, however, it does not rise to the level of her classics, the Mrs. Tim and Miss Buncle novels.

With every novel Stevenson wrote, the shared knowledge between her and her audience became greater. Thus, by the time *Amberwell* (1955) was published critics were taking note of the feeling of familiarity created by her world of believable and attractive characters. Reviewing *Amberwell* in the *Saturday Review* (8 October 1955), A. F. Wolfe said: "Opening a D. E. Stevenson novel is like entering the home of a hospitable old friend." Amberwell is the house that provides a sense of continuity for the Ayrton family during World War II. The novel was followed by a sequel, *Summerhills* (1956).

Stevenson continued to draw connections between her earlier and later novels. In *Anna and Her Daughters* (1958) Anna Harcourt, newly returned to her old neighborhood, catches up on the lives of people she once knew, including Erica Clutterbuck from *Mrs. Tim Gets a Job* and Celia Dunne, who is still living in Dunnian and has married the American soldier she met at the end of *Celia's House*. Although these characters never appear directly in *Anna and Her Daughters,* the mention of their names and what they have been doing since the reader last met them helps the reader to believe that they have a reality outside the novel. The narrator, Anna's daughter Jane Harcourt, is another of Stevenson's writer protagonists. In *The Musgraves* (1960) the characters perform a stage version of Jane's novel *The Mulberry Coach.*

Throughout her career Stevenson used incidents from history in her novels, but instead of depicting sweeping historical panoramas or major figures, she concentrates on ordinary individuals who are caught up in the events. Thus, in *Katherine's Marriage* (1965) the reader hears about some of Bonnie Prince Charlie's men hiding out in a cave rather than the story of the Jacobite Rebellion or even of the prince's movements. The introduction of such tales of the past performs a function similar to that of Stevenson's treatment of houses: both the tales and the houses indicate the need for stability.

In her final novel, *The House of the Deer* (1970), Stevenson again ventures into the mystery genre. The differences between this work and *Green Money* show how her writing had changed since the early part of her career. Her sparkling wit and her gentle look at her characters' foibles made her early novels stand apart from most light fiction; while *Green Money* retains the wittiness of the most successful of the novels that preceded it, *The House of the Deer* is an earnest, unsophisticated story with neither a playful plot nor a lovably human hero such as George Ferrier. Only in her rendering of the colorful Highlanders who provide the background for the story is there a gleam of the quality that had prompted the *Saturday Review* (16 September 1939) to say of *Green Money:* "Miss Stevenson writes with freshness and energy and with a great deal of good-natured wit." Stevenson died on 30 December 1973.

**Reference:**

Joanne Harack Hayne, "D. E. Stevenson," in *Twentieth-Century Romance and Gothic Writers,* edited by James Vinson (Detroit: Gale, 1982), pp. 641–643.

**Papers:**

A collection of D. E. Stevenson's correspondence, manuscripts (including "Short Biography," "The Author's Point of View: Some notes for a talk to members of the Board of Trade and other businessmen and women in Glasgow," and "Truth in Fiction"), and photographs is housed at the Mugar Memorial Library, Boston University.

# L. A. G. Strong
*(8 March 1896 – 17 August 1958)*

Leonard R. N. Ashley
*Emeritus, Brooklyn College of the City University of New York*

BOOKS: *Dallington Rhymes* (Oxford: Privately printed for the author at the Holywell Press, 1919);

*Dublin Days* (Oxford: Blackwell, 1921; New York: Boni & Liveright, 1923);

*Twice Four* (Oxford: Privately printed at the Holywell Press, 1921);

*Says the Muse to Me, Says She* (Oxford: Privately printed at the Holywell Press, 1922);

*The Lowery Road* (Oxford: Blackwell, 1923; New York: Boni & Liveright, 1924);

*Seven: Christmas, 1924* (Oxford: Privately printed at the Holywell Press, 1924);

*Doyle's Rock, and Other Stories* (Oxford: Blackwood, 1925);

*Seven Verses: Christmas, 1925* (Oxford: Privately printed at the Holywell Press, 1925);

*Difficult Love* (Oxford: Blackwell, 1927);

*At Glenan Cross: A Sequence* (Oxford: Blackwell, 1928);

*Dewer Rides* (London: Gollancz, 1929; New York: Boni, 1929);

*The English Captain and Other Stories* (London: Gollancz, 1929; New York: Knopf, 1931);

*Patricia Comes Home* (Oxford: Blackwell, 1929);

*Christmas 1930: With Every Good Wish from L. A. G. Strong* (Oxford: Privately printed for the author at the Holywell Press, 1930);

*The Jealous Ghost* (London: Gollancz, 1930; New York: Knopf, 1930);

*Northern Light* (London: Gollancz, 1930);

*The Big Man* (London: Jackson, 1931);

*Common Sense about Poetry* (London: Gollancz, 1931; New York: Knopf, 1932);

*The Garden* (London: Gollancz, 1931; New York: Knopf, 1931);

*The Old Argo* (Oxford: Blackwell, 1931);

*Selected Poems* (London: Hamilton, 1931; New York: Knopf, 1932);

*The Brothers: A Novel* (London: Gollancz, 1932); republished as *Brothers: A Novel* (New York: Knopf, 1932);

*L. A. G. Strong in 1955 (photograph by Mark Gerson)*

*A Defence of Ignorance* (New York: House of Books, 1932);

*Don Juan and the Wheelbarrow* (London: Gollancz, 1932); republished as *Don Juan and the Wheelbarrow and Other Stories* (New York: Knopf, 1933);

*A Letter to W. B. Yeats* (London: Leonard & Virginia Woolf at the Hogarth Press, 1932; Folcroft, Pa.: Folcroft Press, 1971);

*Life in English Literature: An Introduction for Beginners,* by Strong and Monica Redlich (London: Gollancz, 1932); republished as *Life in English Literature: Being an Introduction for Beginners* (Boston: Little, Brown, 1934);

*March Evening, and Other Verses* (London: Favil, 1932);

*Sea Wall* (London: Gollancz, 1933; New York: Knopf, 1933);

*King Richard's Land: A Tale of the Peasants' Revolt* (London: Dent, 1933; New York: Knopf, 1934);

*Corporal Tune* (London: Gollancz, 1934; New York: Knopf, 1934);

*The Westward Rock* (Oxford: Blackwell, 1934);

*Fortnight South of Skye* (Oxford: Blackwell, 1934; New York: Loring & Mussey, 1935);

*The Hansom Cab and the Pigeons: Being Random Reflections upon the Silver Jubilee of King George V* (London: Printed at the Golden Cockerel Press, 1935);

*Mr. Sheridan's Umbrella* (London & New York: Nelson, 1935);

*The Seven Arms* (London: Gollancz, 1935; New York: Knopf, 1935);

*Tuesday Afternoon and Other Stories* (London: Gollancz, 1935);

*Call to the Swan* (London: Hamilton, 1936);

*The Last Enemy: A Study of Youth* (London: Gollancz, 1936; New York: Knopf, 1936);

*Two Stories* (London: Corvinus, 1936);

*Common Sense about Drama* (London: Nelson, 1937; New York: Knopf, 1937);

*The Fifth of November* (London: Dent, 1937);

*Henry of Agincourt* (London & New York: Nelson, 1937);

*Laughter in the West* (New York: Knopf, 1937);

*The Man Who Asked Questions: The Story of Socrates* (London & New York: Nelson, 1937);

*The Minstrel Boy: A Portrait of Tom Moore* (London: Hodder & Stoughton, 1937; New York: Knopf, 1937);

*The Swift Shadow* (London: Gollancz, 1937);

*Odd Man In* (London: Pitman, 1938);

*Shake Hands and Come out Fighting* (London: Chapman & Hall, 1938);

*The Nice Cup o' Tea: Christmas 1938* (London: Favil, 1938);

*The Absentee* (London: Methuen, 1939);

*Evening Piece* (London: Privately printed, 1939);

*The Open Sky* (London: Gollancz, 1939; New York: Macmillan, 1939);

*Trial and Error* (London: Methuen, 1939);

*Sun on the Water and Other Stories* (London: Gollancz, 1940);

*Wrong Foot Foremost* (London: Pitman, 1940);

*English for Pleasure* (London: Methuen, 1941);

*House in Disorder* (London: Lutterworth, 1941);

*The Bay* (London: Gollancz, 1941; Philadelphia: Lippincott, 1942);

*John McCormack: The Story of a Singer* (London: Methuen, 1941; New York: Macmillan, 1941);

*John Millington Synge* (London: Allen & Unwin, 1941; Folcroft, Pa.: Folcroft Library Editions, 1973);

*Slocum Died* (London: Published for the Crime Club by Collins, 1942);

*The Unpractised Heart* (London: Gollancz, 1942);

*All Fall Down* (London: Published for the Crime Club by Collins, 1944; Garden City, N.Y.: Published for the Crime Club by Doubleday, Doran, 1944);

*Authorship* (London: Ross, 1944);

*The Director* (London: Methuen, 1944);

*An Informal English Grammar* (London: Methuen, 1944);

*Othello's Occupation* (London: Published for the Crime Club by Collins, 1945); republished as *Murder Plays an Ugly Scene* (Garden City, N.Y.: Doubleday, Doran, 1945);

*Sink or Swim* (London & Redhill: Lutterworth, 1945);

*Travellers: Thirty-one Selected Short Stories* (London: Methuen, 1945);

*The Doll* (Leeds: Salamander Press, 1946);

*Light through the Cloud: The Story of the Retreat, York, 1796–1946* (London: Friends Book Centre, 1946);

*The Body's Imperfection: Verses* (London: Printed by A. P. Taylor, 1948);

*Trevannion* (London: Methuen, 1948);

*Maud Cherrill* (London: Parrish, 1949);

*The Sacred River: An Approach to James Joyce* (London: Methuen, 1949; New York: Pellegrini & Cudahy, 1951);

*Three Novels: The Garden, Corporal Tune, The Seven Arms* (London: Oldhams, 1950);

*Which I Never: A Police Diversion* (London: Published for the Crime Club by Collins, 1950; New York: Macmillan, 1952);

*Darling Tom, and Other Stories* (London: Methuen, 1952);

*John Masefield* (London: New York: Published for the British Council by Longmans, Green, 1952);

*The Hill of Howth* (London: Methuen, 1953);

*The Magnolia Tree* (London: Privately printed, 1953);

*Personal Remarks* (London: Nevill, 1953; New York: Liveright, 1954);

*The Writer's Trade* (London: Methuen, 1953);

*It's Not Very Nice: A Comedy in One Act for Women* (London: Deane, 1954; Boston: Baker, 1954);

*The Story of Sugar* (London: Weidenfeld & Nicolson, 1954);

*Deliverance* (London: Methuen, 1955);

*Dr. Quicksilver, 1660–1742: The Life and Times of Thomas Dover, M.D.* (London: Melrose, 1955);

*Flying Angel: The Story of the Missions to Seamen* (London: Methuen, 1956);

*The Rolling Road: The Story of Travel on the Roads of Britain and the Development of Public Passenger Transport* (London: Hutchinson, 1956);

*The Body's Imperfection: The Collected Poems of L. A. G. Strong* (London: Methuen, 1957);

*A Brewer's Progress, 1757–1957: A Survey of Charrington's Brewery on the Occasion of Its Bicentenary* (London: Privately printed, 1957);

*Courtauld Thomson: A Memoir* (London: John Murray, 1958);

*Instructions to Young Writers* (London: Museum Press, 1958);

*Light above the Lake* (London: Methuen, 1958);

*Treason in the Egg: A Further Police Diversion* (London: Published for the Crime Club by Collins, 1958);

*Green Memory* (London: Methuen, 1961).

OTHER: *The Best Poems of 1923,* edited by Strong (New York: Dodd, Mead, 1924);

*By Haunted Stream: An Anthology of Modern English Poets,* edited by Strong (New York: Appleton, 1924);

*Eighty Poems: An Anthology,* edited by Strong (Oxford: Blackwell, 1924);

*The Best Poems of 1924,* edited by Strong (New York: Dodd, Mead, 1925);

*The Best Poems of 1925,* edited by Strong (New York: Dodd, Mead, 1926);

*The Best Poems of 1926,* edited by Strong (New York: Dodd, Mead, 1927);

*The Best Poems of 1927,* edited by Strong (New York: Dodd, Mead, 1928);

Adrian Alington, L. E. O. Charlton, A. E. Coppard, and others, *Beginnings,* compiled by Strong (London & New York: Nelson, 1935);

Tobias Smollett, *The Expedition of Humphry Clinker,* introduction by Strong (London: Nelson, 1936);

*A New Anthology of Modern Verse, 1920–1940,* edited by Strong and Cecil Day Lewis (London: Methuen, 1941);

*English Domestic Life during the Last 200 Years: An Anthology Selected from the Novelists,* compiled by Strong (London: Allen & Unwin, 1942);

Walter Allen and others, *Sixteen Portraits of People Whose Houses Have Been Preserved by the National Trust,* edited by Strong (London: Published for the National Trust by Naldrett Press, 1951);

Frederick T. Bason, *Fred Bason's 2nd Diary,* edited by Strong (London: Wingate, 1952);

David Low, *Low's Company: Fifty Portraits,* verses by Strong and Helen Spalding (London: Methuen, 1952);

R. D. Blackmore, *Lorna Doone,* edited by Strong (London: Collins, 1958).

L. A. G. Strong was a leading popular writer of his time and, from 1938 until his death in 1958, a director of the important publishing house of Methuen and Company. Strong's fiction often deals with elemental passions in such rugged places as the West Country of England and the coasts of Scotland and Ireland. His lyrical verse is thoughtful, suggesting that his novels and short stories would have been deeper had he not been so prolific and had he not turned his hand to so many other kinds of writing.

Leonard Alfred George Strong was born in Plymouth on 8 March 1896, the elder of the two children and the only son of Leonard Ernest Strong, a businessman, and Marion Jane Mongan Strong. With a half-Irish father and an Irish mother, Strong would frequently write about Ireland and eminent Irishmen and would be elected a member of the Irish Academy of Letters.

Strong attended Brighton College and Wadham College, Oxford, on scholarships. He left Wadham without a degree in 1917 and became a junior master at Summer Fields School in Oxford; he returned to the university in 1919, earned a B.A. in 1920, and resumed teaching at Summer Fields. He married Dorothea Sylvia Brinton, the daughter of a teacher at Eton College, in 1926; they had one son. The success of his first novel, *Dewer Rides* (1929), and the collection *The English Captain and Other Stories* (1929) gave Strong the confidence to quit his job as a schoolmaster and try to make a living as a writer.

*Dewer Rides* is set among the mystery-shrouded wastes and peculiar people of the hard-won farms of Dartmoor. Young Dick Brandon, turning down the opportunity to acquire an education and become a gentleman, apprentices himself to a farmer. He falls in love with and becomes engaged to a local girl, Ruth Palmer, but the novel ends tragically as the engagement is broken. The characters are shrewdly conceived and deftly portrayed, but the sad conclusion seems forced; the *Saturday Review of Literature* (1 February 1930) said that Strong "seems to have been forced to end [the novel] abruptly and unsatisfactorily." The public liked the mood and the characters, however, and the critics saw promise in the

DEWER RIDES

BY
L. A. G. STRONG

LONDON
VICTOR GOLLANCZ LTD
14 Henrietta Street Covent Garden
1929

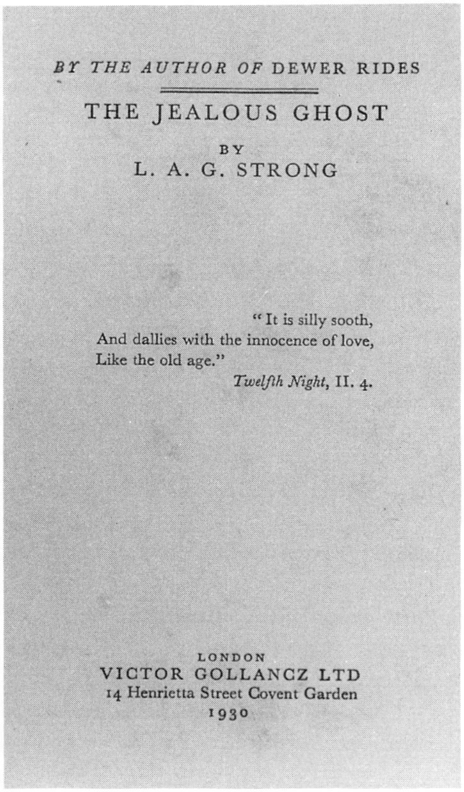

BY THE AUTHOR OF DEWER RIDES

THE JEALOUS GHOST

BY
L. A. G. STRONG

"It is silly sooth,
And dallies with the innocence of love,
Like the old age."

Twelfth Night, II. 4.

LONDON
VICTOR GOLLANCZ LTD
14 Henrietta Street Covent Garden
1930

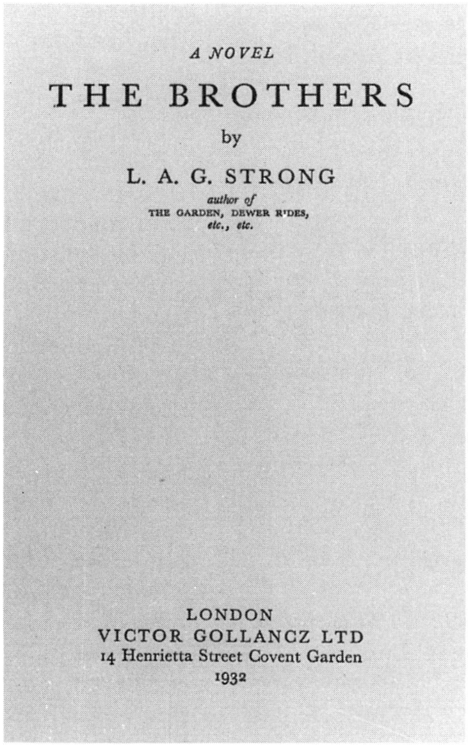

A NOVEL

THE BROTHERS

by
L. A. G. STRONG
author of
THE GARDEN, DEWER RIDES,
etc., etc.

LONDON
VICTOR GOLLANCZ LTD
14 Henrietta Street Covent Garden
1932

Title pages for three of Strong's early novels

author. The novelist L. P. Hartley, reviewing the novel in the London *Saturday Review* (1 July 1929), said that Strong's "imagination gives the impression of being endlessly fertile with untapped resources; it only remains for him to arrange them better." Gilbert Thomas caviled about the plot in the *Spectator* (22 June 1929) but admitted that Strong's "descriptive gifts are far above the average." The *Times Literary Supplement* (27 June 1929) called *Dewer Rides* "a remarkable first novel" despite some overwritten and occasionally irrelevant descriptive passages.

On 25 January 1931 *The New York Times* said that Strong, "remembered for his first novel . . . has written another book as light in touch and as appealing." The novel was *The Jealous Ghost* (1930), in which an American goes to the western Highlands of Scotland in search of his ancestors and lays to rest a ghost that is haunting the family. According to the review in *Forum* (30 April 1931), "the rather interesting group of people who drift together into a tranquil, lovely way of life, when the spell is broken, as casually drift apart." The result, said *The Nation* (24 June 1930), is a novel with charm but little "motive force," one that has "none of the vitality of 'Dewer Rides'; it remains unconvincing." Most critics did like the evocativeness of the scenery, bathed in Celtic twilight, and the memorable characterizations. The changing emotional climate is most effectively keyed to the changes in the Highland weather. The worst fault of the work, according to M. C. Davidson in *Books* (25 January 1931), is that Strong cannot make up his mind whether the novel is to be a "thoroughgoing spook thriller" or a "novel of persons and ideas." The *Times Literary Supplement* (29 May 1930) surmised that Strong was "experimenting with his subject."

The western Highlands is also the setting for *The Brothers* (1932), one of the novels for which Strong is best remembered. The title characters are Peter Macrae, the older and cleverer of the siblings, and Fergus Macrae, who is more good-hearted than intelligent. They are brought into conflict by their adopted sister, Mary. The story is told in a jumble of episodes that neither cohere nor come to a credible climax. Although *The Nation* (1 June 1932) said that *The Brothers* was "an exceptionally good novel, and should contribute considerably to the growing reputation of Mr. Strong as one of the most interesting of the younger British novelists," most reviewers found its violence unattractive and its characters flat. "There are no cliches in the climax of this novel," wrote A. R. Thompson in *Bookman* (March 1931); "there is also no credibility."

In *Sea Wall* (1933) Nicky D'Olier lives in one of two identical houses on the seawall in Kingstown,

near Dublin. His parents mysteriously disappear from time to time, and he has several other strange relatives. The Irish settings are beautifully done, but the action, according to *The Nation* (22 November 1933), is episodic and has "little movement"; the novel is crowded with portraits of odd characters that Will Holloway in *Commonweal* (8 December 1933) called "cameos." Once again, credibility is a problem. The writer William Plomer remarked in the *Spectator* (1 September 1933): "Nicky grows up to manhood without, apparently, any kind of sexual interests whatsoever. The omission must be deliberate, but I find it puzzling."

*King Richard's Land* (1933) is a juvenile historical novel in the tradition of G. A. Henty. The rousing story features the fifteen-year-old cousins Nigel and Bruce Redvers, who become involved in Wat Tyler's peasant revolt in 1381; the boy monarch Richard II, who is about their age, becomes their friend. The king and the peasants are treated more favorably here than in most histories.

When *Corporal Tune* (1934) opens, the title character has just lost his wife in childbirth, and he suspects that the child, who survives, is not his own. Nonetheless, he still loves his late wife and mourns her. His death during a futile operation enables him to rejoin his beloved wife. The final scene is marvelous, whether the medical details are accurate or not—an issue that has been debated by critics. Frank Swinnerton, one of the most perceptive critics of fiction in the period, wrote in the *Chicago Daily Tribune* (28 July 1934) that *Corporal Tune*

> is being hailed in London for its great beauty, and it is certainly one of the most sensitive and delicate of all Mr. Strong's books. Its theme is simple, the writing exquisite without affectation, the implications innumerable. At the same time the novel has both perfect detachment and a quite personal intimacy which make it unique.

E. H. Walton in *The New York Times* (12 August 1934) said that the novel was "beautifully written" but pronounced it "a little chill." T. S. Matthews wrote in *The New Republic* (29 August 1934) that "when he passes the bounds of communicable human experience," Strong's novel "becomes a fairy tale."

In 1934 Strong published another juvenile novel, *Fortnight South of Skye,* a tepid adventure story in which two English lads, Jim Russell and Walter Cronshaw, go fishing in Scotland. The *Springfield (Mass.) Republican* (1 December 1935) said that the book had a "slower-moving tempo than those written for American boys." The vividly described Scottish scenery cannot save the work.

In *The Seven Arms* (1935) Strong turns to Scotland again—this time to a remote area where Gaelic is still spoken and where a bitter rivalry between two sisters, Ellen and the incomparably nasty Jeanie, continues to the grave and beyond. Swinnerton, reviewing the novel in the *Chicago Daily Tribune* (13 July 1935), liked the work despite its violence and the loose ends that occur too frequently in Strong's headlong plot:

> Nobody [else] among living English novelists could have given this story such character. With his own quiet, sure, beautiful touch, Mr. Strong takes us into human hearts, holds us breathless, and brings us at last to his tragical culmination. A rare gift, "The Seven Arms" is equal to his best work.

*The Last Enemy: A Study of Youth* (1936) finds the author, who had been a schoolmaster for twelve years and whose father-in-law was also a schoolmaster, on more-familiar ground. Denis Boyle is a student at a school near Oxford. The time is near the end of World War I, "a period of tragic and wasteful stress," but Strong keeps death and destruction in the background and concentrates on adolescent sexuality blooming in the hothouse atmosphere of a public school. A *Tea and Sympathy*-style affair between Denis and the wife of one of the masters produces what the *Manchester Guardian* (30 June 1936) regarded as a "very unusual ending." "Mr. Strong has never written more clearly and graphically," reported the *Times Literary Supplement* (4 July 1936), "nor produced a more convincing effect of the familiar movement of life."

In *The Open Sky* (1939) David Heron, an English doctor, goes to an island off the coast of Ireland to sort out his emotional problems. He is helped by a nice young woman and by the local priest, Father Morrisey, the most colorful character in the book. He recovers and goes back to his wife. There is comedy, sentiment, and, as usual in Strong's novels, a successful evocation of place. The plot—also as usual—is somewhat unfocused and seems to have been carpentered together out of un-related incidents. Olga Owens in *The Boston Transcript* (8 July 1939) recommended *The Open Sky* as suitable for one's "summer reading list."

The mystery novel *All Fall Down* (1944) introduces the composer-detective Inspector Ellis McKay and uses the English-village setting familiar from the works of Agatha Christie. The *Times Literary Supplement* (22 January 1944) called it "admirable," and Will Cuppy in the *Weekly Book Review* (24 September 1944) considered it "required reading." The mystery genre has, however, progressed since then in the hands of such writers as P. D. James. Strong's other mystery novels are *Othello's Occupation* (1945; published in the United States the same year as *Murder Plays an Ugly Scene*), *Which I Never: A Police Diversion* (1950), and *Treason in the Egg: A Further Police Diversion* (1958). Among his other novels of all types are *Mr. Sheridan's Umbrella* (1935), *Laughter in the West* (1937), *The Swift Shadow* (1937), *The Bay* (1941), *The Director* (1944), *The Hill of Howth* (1953), *Deliverance* (1955), and the posthumous *Light above the Lake* (1958).

Strong was ready to turn his hand to virtually any kind of writing—to tell a tale; to critique William Butler Yeats, John Millington Synge, or James Joyce; to celebrate the Irish composer Tom Moore; or to commemorate the bicentenary of Charrington's Brewery. He wrote biographies, books on grammar and voice production, one-act plays for schools, and poetry. He also wrote many short stories, winning the James Tait Black Prize for the collection *Travellers* (1945). One can only guess what his career as a novelist would have been had he concentrated his talents on that genre. In addition to his prolific output as a writer, Strong was a visiting tutor at the Central School of Speech and Drama in London. He was elected a fellow of the Royal Society of Literature and received an honorary master of arts degree from Oxford. He died on 17 August 1958.

**Reference:**

Rodolpho Louis Mégroz, *Five Novelist Poets of To-Day* (London: Fenland, 1933).

# Alec Waugh

*(8 July 1898 – 3 September 1981)*

George J. Johnson

BOOKS: *The Loom of Youth* (London: Richards, 1917; New York: Doran, 1920; revised edition, London: Richards, 1955);

*Resentment: Poems* (London: Richards, 1918);

*The Prisoners of Mainz* (London: Chapman & Hall, 1919; New York: Doran, 1919);

*Pleasure* (London: Richards, 1921);

*The Lonely Unicorn: A Novel* (London: Richards, 1922); republished as *Roland Whately: A Novel* (New York: Macmillan, 1922);

*Public School Life: Boys, Parents, Masters* (London: Collins, 1922);

*Myself When Young: Confessions* (London: Richards, 1923; New York: Brentano's, 1924);

*Card Castle: A Novel* (London: Richards, 1924; New York: Boni, 1925);

*Kept: A Story of Post-War London* (London: Richards, 1925; New York: Boni, 1925);

*On Doing What One Likes* (London: Cayme Press, 1926);

*Love in These Days: A Modern Story* (London: Chapman & Hall, 1926; New York: Doran, 1927);

*The Last Chukka: Stories of East and West* (London: Chapman & Hall, 1928);

*Nor Many Waters* (London: Chapman & Hall, 1928); republished as *Portrait of a Celibate* (Garden City, N.Y.: Doubleday, Doran, 1929);

*Three Score and Ten* (London: Chapman & Hall, 1929; Garden City, N.Y.: Doubleday, Doran, 1930);

*The Coloured Countries* (London: Chapman & Hall, 1930); republished as *Hot Countries* (New York: Farrar & Rinehart, 1930); republished as *Hot Countries: A Travel Book* (London: Pan, 1948);

*". . . 'Sir,' She Said"* (London: Chapman & Hall, 1930); republished as *"Sir!" She Said* (New York: Farrar & Rinehart, 1930); republished as *Love in Conflict* (London: Hutchinson, 1977);

*So Lovers Dream* (London: Cassell, 1931); republished as *That American Woman* (New York: Farrar & Rinehart, 1932);

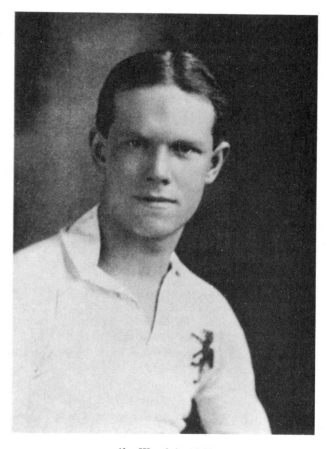

*Alec Waugh in 1919*

*"Most Women . . ."* (London: Cassell, 1931); republished as *Most Women . . .* (New York: Farrar & Rinehart, 1931);

*Leap before You Look* (London: Benn, 1932; New York: Farrar & Rinehart, 1933); revised and enlarged as *Leap before You Look; or, Such Things Spell Happiness* (London: Cassell, 1934);

*Thirteen Such Years* (London: Cassell, 1932; New York: Farrar & Rinehart, 1932);

*No Quarter* (London: Cassell, 1932); republished as *Tropic Seed* (New York: Farrar & Rinehart, 1932);

*Wheels within Wheels: A Story of the Crisis* (London: Cassell, 1933); republished as *The Golden Ripple* (New York: Farrar & Rinehart, 1933);

*Playing with Fire* (London: Benn, 1933);

*Pages in Woman's Life: A Group of Stories* (London: Cassell, 1934);

*The Balliols* (London: Cassell, 1934; New York: Farrar & Rinehart, 1934);

*Jill Somerset* (London: Cassell, 1936; New York: Farrar & Rinehart, 1936; revised and abridged edition, London: Cassell, 1953);

*Eight Short Stories* (London: Cassell, 1937);

*Going Their Own Ways: A Story of Modern Marriage* (London: Cassell, 1938); republished as *Going Their Own Ways: A Novel of Modern Marriage* (New York: Farrar & Rinehart, 1939);

*No Truce with Time* (London: Cassell, 1941; New York: Farrar & Rinehart, 1941);

*His Second War* (London: Cassell, 1944);

*Unclouded Summer: A Love Story* (London: Cassell, 1948 [i.e., 1947]; New York: Farrar, Straus, 1948);

*The Sunlit Caribbean* (London: Evans, 1948; revised, 1953); republished as *The Sugar Islands: A Caribbean Travelogue* (New York: Farrar, Straus, 1949);

*The Lipton Story: A Centennial Biography* (Garden City, N.Y.: Doubleday, 1950; London: Cassell, 1951);

*Where the Clocks Strike Twice: A Travel Book* (New York: Farrar, Straus & Young, 1951); republished as *Where the Clocks Chime Twice* (London: Cassell, 1952);

*Guy Renton: A London Story* (New York: Farrar, Straus & Young, 1952; London: Cassell, 1953; revised edition, London: Hutchinson, 1976);

*Island in the Sun: A Story of the 1950s Set in the West Indies* (New York: Farrar, Straus & Cudahy, 1955); republished as *Island in the Sun: A Novel* (London: Cassell, 1956);

*Merchants of Wine: Being a Centenary Account of the Fortunes of the House of Gilbey* (London: Cassell, 1957);

*The Sugar Islands: A Collection of Pieces Written about the West Indies between 1928 and 1953* (London: Cassell, 1958); republished as *Love and the Caribbean: Tales, Characters and Scenes of the West Indies* (New York: Farrar, Straus & Cudahy, 1959);

*In Praise of Wine* (London: Cassell, 1959); republished as *In Praise of Wine and Certain Noble Spirits* (New York: Sloane, 1959);

*Fuel for the Flame* (London: Cassell, 1960); republished as *Fuel for the Flame: A Novel Set in the Orient* (New York: Farrar, Straus & Cudahy, 1960);

*My Place in the Bazaar* (London: Cassell, 1961; New York: Farrar, Straus, 1961);

*The Early Years of Alec Waugh* (London: Cassell, 1962; New York: Farrar, Straus, 1963);

*A Family of Islands: A History of the West Indies from 1492 to 1898, with an Epilogue Sketching the Events from the Spanish-American War to the 1960's* (London: Weidenfeld & Nicolson, 1964; Garden City, N.Y.: Doubleday, 1964);

*The Mule on the Minaret: A Novel about the Middle East* (London: Cassell, 1965; New York: Farrar, Straus & Giroux, 1965);

*My Brother Evelyn, and Other Profiles* (London: Cassell, 1967); republished as *My Brother Evelyn and Other Portraits* (New York: Farrar, Straus & Giroux, 1967);

*Bangkok: The Story of a City* (London: W. H. Allen, 1970; Boston: Little, Brown, 1971);

*A Spy in the Family: An Erotic Comedy* (London: W. H. Allen, 1970; New York: Farrar, Straus & Giroux, 1970);

*The Fatal Gift: A Novel* (London: W. H. Allen, 1973; New York: Farrar, Straus & Giroux, 1973);

*Brief Encounter: A Novel* (London: W. H. Allen, 1975);

*A Year to Remember: A Reminiscence of 1931* (London: W. H. Allen, 1975);

*Married to a Spy* (London: W. H. Allen, 1976);

*The Best Wine Last: An Autobiography through the Years, 1932–1969* (London: W. H. Allen, 1978).

OTHER: *Modern Prose Literature: A Critical Survey*, edited by Waugh, *Chapbook*, 2 (February 1920); republished in book form (Folcroft, Pa.: Folcroft Library Editions, 1974);

E. S. Haynes, *A Lawyer's Notebook*, introduction by Waugh (London: Secker, 1932);

*These Would I Choose: A Personal Anthology*, compiled by Waugh (London: Low, 1948);

*Wines and Spirits*, edited by Waugh and the editors of Time-Life Books (New York: Time-Life Books, 1968).

During a sixty-year career Alec Waugh wrote twenty-nine novels and an almost equal number of books of other kinds, including travel books, short-story collections, and autobiographies. The settings for his novels, drawn from his experiences as a sportsman, soldier, gourmet, lover, world traveler, intelligence officer, and lecturer, cover the globe from England to France, the Middle East, the Far East, the Caribbean, and the United States.

Alexander Raban Waugh was born in Hampstead on 8 July 1898 to Arthur and Catherine Charlotte Raban Waugh. An Oxford graduate, Arthur Waugh had left his rural north Somerset home at twenty-three to try freelance writing in London; there, assisted by a distant cousin, Edmund Gosse, he had met the London literati and had become recognized as an important critic. Alec's brother, Evelyn, who would become a more important writer than Alec, was born in 1903. The following year Arthur Waugh became the managing director of the publishing house Chapman and Hall. In 1907 the family moved to a house called Underhill in the fashionable North End of Hampstead, and Alec enrolled in Fernden, a newly established boarding school in Haslemere. There he acquired some fluency in French and an acquaintance with French culture; the latter, he would say in his autobiography *The Early Years of Alec Waugh* (1962), produced an unpuritanical attitude to what he termed "extracurricular romance," an activity to which he would devote "a good deal of time" during his life.

In September 1911 Waugh entered a larger school, Sherborne, where he became the victim of the public-school practice "of herding together monastically children of thirteen and men of eighteen, for two thirds of the year," a situation that led to an older boy "falling in love with the nearest approach to the feminine ideal," a younger boy. At fifteen he was caned by his fellow prefects for one of these "romantic friendships," and in June 1915 he was asked to leave the school because of a similar scandal.

In September of that year Waugh joined the Inns of Court Officer Training Corps. While he was there, the minimum age for commissioned officers was raised to eighteen and one-half from seventeen, and on his graduation in January 1916 Waugh and fellow "war babies" (as the underage graduates were called) were sent to defend the coast. Waugh wrote his first novel, *The Loom of Youth* (1917), between January and March and sent it in sections to his father, who had it typed. In May, Waugh enrolled in a London "cram school" to prepare for an eight-month course at Sandhurst that would lead to a permanent commission; graduation was followed by machine-gun training. Meanwhile, to avoid charges of favoritism Waugh avoided Chapman and Hall but sent his typescript to five other publishers before Grant Richards accepted it in January 1917; Waugh saw a printed copy before he left for France in July with the Dorset Regiment. The autobiographical work follows Gordon Caruthers's four years at the public school Fernhurst, from his confusion and isolation on opening day through rebel-

*Waugh's second wife, Joan Chirnside Waugh, with their children, Veronica and Andrew, in Australia in 1943*

lious schoolboy escapades and relationships with his fellow students—including oblique references to a homosexual liaison—to his final day, when he realizes that the school has, in fact, taught him something: to rely on himself.

The novel was reprinted five times before the end of 1917, three times in 1918, and at least eight times before Waugh revised it in 1955. It received twenty-four columns of reviews in one month; was named "book of the week" by five reviewers; brought forth a deluge of letters to newspapers from anxious parents, along with reassuring responses from headmasters; and resulted in Sherborne removing Waugh's and his father's names from its list of graduates and denying admission to Evelyn. In the midst of this sudden notoriety Waugh conducted a whirlwind courtship of Barbara Jacobs, the sixteen-year-old daughter of the short-story writer W. W. Jacobs; while he was on leave in London in February 1918, they became formally engaged.

In March, Waugh and his unit were captured by the Germans near Cambrai. Waugh was imprisoned in Mainz, where he initially suffered from lice and hunger. Conditions improved somewhat by June, especially when a room was made available for him and five other imprisoned authors for discussions and writing; in *My Brother Evelyn, and Other*

*Profiles* (1967) Waugh refers to the seven-month experience as "my equivalent for a university."

After his release Waugh returned to England, where he married Barbara Jacobs in July 1919. They moved into two rooms at his parents' home, and Waugh accepted a job reading manuscripts at Chapman and Hall. He arranged to work two days in London and the rest of the week in a small bungalow, Half Acre, that he built in Ditchling, Surrey, in the spring of 1920. He was recalled to military service during the General Strike of 1921.

Waugh's marriage, whose lack of consummation Waugh attributed to his own inexperience, ended in separation after thirty months and was annulled in 1923. In the interval Waugh became involved with two women; one of them, three years older than he, he claimed, "made a man" of him.

Waugh's next novel, *The Lonely Unicorn* (1922; published in the United States as *Roland Whately,* 1922), begins with Roland Whately at Fernhurst, heavily involved with cricket and "precocious love-making." It follows his business successes as Continental agent for the Marston Varnish Company and his jilting of his childhood sweetheart, April Curtis, in favor of the boss's daughter, Muriel, and a partnership in the business. The review in *The New York Times* (12 November 1922) likened it to "a very clear and lifelike photograph of an endless train of empty freight cars moving through a desert."

Waugh, who pursued an active social life in London, is credited with inventing the cocktail party in 1924, the year in which he became literary director of Chapman and Hall. Continuing his schedule of two days a week at the publishing firm, he would spend the remaining three days in rooms at inns or hotels where he could write undisturbed.

In *Card Castle* (1924), the sequel to *The Lonely Unicorn,* Whately is happily married and successful in business. But he overturns this fragile "card castle" through an affair with a lady known as Frou-Frou that arouses the jealousy of his best friend, Gerald Marston. *The New York Times* (19 April 1925) found the novel "soundly, sympathetically written" while *The Times* of London (10 April 1924) criticized Waugh's incomplete analysis of his principal characters.

In April 1925 Waugh published *Kept: A Story of Post-War London;* originally titled "A Kept Woman," it was to have focused on the widowed Marjorie Fairfield and her middle-aged married lover, Everard Tristram. But a friend's suggestion led Waugh to enlarge the work's scope to depict a group of characters, each of whom is "kept" in a different way: Vernon Archer, who is living on the past; Eric Somerset, on capital; Lady Manon Granta, on a title; Ransom Heritage, on a reputation won during the war; and, in the background, England itself, living on the triumphs of the eighteenth and nineteenth centuries. In *The Early Years of Alec Waugh* he says that the work introduced a new technique for him, that of the symphonic novel, with "a definite plot, a theme, an action concentrated into a short space of time, with a crowded canvas, with each minor plot woven into the main plot." The novel sold well and led to a forty-year relationship with the literary agent A. D. Peters.

Peters suggested that Waugh write a serial for a newspaper; it became the novel *Love in These Days* (1926), which trebled Waugh's income in six months. It is another story of sophisticated London life, featuring Graham Moreton and his fiancée of two years, Joan Faversham, an unusually constant couple for this society until Graham is attracted to Gwen Lawrence. The resolution of the situation allows Waugh to explicate differing "codes of love." Critics castigated the novel for its boring portrayal of what *The Times* (16 September 1926) called "a dreary round of restaurant meals and nightclubs . . . perhaps this dreariness is the effect of the cocktails, which [the characters] are incessantly mixing, drinking, and talking about."

Suffering from what he calls in *The Early Years of Alec Waugh* a "sense of everything's ultimate unimportance," Waugh resigned from his job as a reader at Chapman and Hall and embarked on an around-the-world tour in June 1926. After visiting friends in Alexandria and Malaya he reached Sydney in November. He fell in love at first sight with Tahiti when he arrived there in January 1927, but he was nearly out of money. He was planning to cut his stay short, but the day before he was to leave he received payment for the American serial rights to *Love in These Days.* A romance with a native girl, Tania, would reappear in his novel *The Fatal Gift* (1973).

Eventually becoming bored, Waugh booked passage to San Francisco; aboard ship he began an affair with a married American woman named Ruth, who was rebounding from a romance with a ship's officer.

Returning to London after traveling by train across the United States, Waugh found that his English royalties for *Kept* had been lost through Grant Richards's bankruptcy, but the American royalties had been unfrozen. Resigning his directorship at Chapman and Hall, in August 1927 he returned to Tahiti for three months to rendezvous with Ruth, who was vacationing there with her husband.

After returning to England, Waugh wrote the novel *Nor Many Waters;* it was dedicated to Ruth and published on her birthday, 15 August 1928. The young lawyer James Merrick sacrifices his love for

*Waugh with his brother, Evelyn, in 1953 (Mme Yevonde)*

his beautiful client, Marion Eager, by counseling her to remain with her husband rather than face the shame to which an English divorce would subject her. *The Nation* (3 April 1929) described the hero as "dull" but the plot as "very careful"; the *Spectator* (18 August 1928) had the opposite point of view, calling Merrick "admirably drawn" and the plot "a slight story." Published in the United States as *Portrait of a Celibate* (1929), the novel was labeled by the *New York World* (17 March 1929) a "tract against the . . . divorce laws in England"; G. T. Hellman in the *New York Herald Tribune* (24 February 1929) said that it was superior to the works of "such other British sentimentalists as Warwick Deeping."

Waugh spent three weeks in February 1928 jealously quarreling with Ruth in Monterey, California. In December he left his new flat in Chelsea

for a five-month tour of the Caribbean, during which he completed the novel *Three Score and Ten* (1929). The work is the saga of three generations of the Cardew family: the father, Conway; his son, Hilary, the narrator; and Hilary's son, Godfrey. The novel concludes with the christening of Godfrey's son. Bellamy Partridge in the *New York World* (4 May 1930) averred that "I can positively guarantee that anybody who liked [Deeping's 1926 bestseller] *Sorrell and Son* will like *Three Score and Ten* much better because it is a much better book." Stanley Went in the *Saturday Review of Literature* (26 July 1930), however, judged it inferior to John Galsworthy's *The Forsyte Saga* (1922) in reproducing "the age in which each generation lived."

In the late spring of 1929 Waugh became involved with Marcella Gump, a friend of Ruth; his brother, Evelyn, even announced their engagement. Alec, however, was still enamored of Ruth and continued brooding over her during the summer in France while working on a light novel about a modern girl; he completed it at the Welcome Hotel at Margate in September. In ". . . 'Sir,' She Said," (1930) John Terance, as a result of his elder daughter Julia's transgressions, fears that his nineteen-year-old second daughter, Melanie, will also abuse the new women's freedom, but Melanie shows that she has a sense of purpose and can care for herself. *The Times* (31 July 1930) said that the conventional "happy marriage" with which the novel ends "leads one to the conclusion that [Waugh's] attitude to the modern young woman is either somewhat uncertain or decidedly Victorian."

While on a trip to East Africa in February 1930 Waugh learned that his Caribbean travel book, *The Coloured Countries* (1930; published in the United States as *Hot Countries,* 1930) had been chosen as the Literary Guild selection for May. After a three-week publicity jaunt to New York he went to Monterey to see Ruth, then returned to New York via New Orleans.

The year 1931 started for Waugh in New York, where he began an affair with the author Barbara Starke. He then went on a ten-week lecture tour of the United States. Between April and the end of the year he moved between England, where he had affairs with two married women, and France, where he had a relationship with a married Canadian he calls Mary G. Begun on 20 April, completed on 20 June, and published in November, his next novel, *So Lovers Dream* (1931; published in the United States as *That American Woman,* 1932), led Waugh to claim in his autobiography *A Year to Remember: A Reminiscence of 1931* (1975): "I have never written a book with greater confidence and greater enjoyment. . . . the enjoyment in its writing made 1931 such a happy year for me." It is a fictionalized account of his romance with Ruth, altered to protect her: in the novel the setting is Villefranche in the south of France, rather than Monterey; unlike Ruth, Faith Sweden is "elusive, indefinite, accepting situations, not creating them"; her husband is a Wall Street financier while Ruth's husband, Govie, was a writer working in motion pictures. The male protagonist, the autobiographical character Gordon Caruthers from *The Loom of Youth,* is a writer who feels imprisoned in a relationship that he recognizes as hopeless. *The Times* (10 December 1931) complained that if one subtracted Waugh's factual experiences from the novel, "it was not very highly charged with imaginative current."

Returning in August 1931 from a vacation in Cornwall, Waugh spent three weeks at the Easton Court Hotel near Chagford, Devon. There, in three weeks, he revised a serialized story he had written twenty months previously to produce the novella *Leap before You Look* (1932). It was published by Ernest Benn as one of the first of the firm's Ninepenny Novels, predecessors of the Penguin paperbacks. Faith Mailery, a London typist, is in love with a poor young man; they cannot marry until he establishes himself. Frustrated, she marries an older and wealthier man. The novel then follows all of their lives through a series of melodramatic incidents, including a revolution in a West Indian nation.

In early 1932 Waugh renewed his relationship with Barbara Starke in New Orleans. In May he met, for the third time, the thirty-year-old Joan Chirnside, an Australian. They were married on 25 October and honeymooned in Antibes. During 1932 Waugh published *No Quarter,* which appeared the same year in the United States as *Tropic Seed.* In the 1630s Roger Vaisseau, the illegitimate son of a French nobleman, becomes a buccaneer in Tortuga. His piratical tendencies are passed down through his plantation-owner descendants to the 1930s Marseille stock-swindler Doublon. Waugh blamed the novel's poor sales in England on the failure of the piracy theme to hold together the shift through the work's five main characters; reviews in the United States, however, were generally positive.

Waugh and his wife retained a London base but established their principal residence at Bishopsbourne, near Canterbury. There, in late December 1932, Waugh finished *Wheels within Wheels* (1933; published in the United States as *The Golden Ripple,* 1933). To assist the oil driller "Humper" Hempell, the oil analyst Maitland recommends that the London financier Frank Newton set up a syndicate to develop a well in Santa Marta in the French West Indies. The novel follows the impact of this advice and of the 1929 stock market crash on the business and private lives of Hempell; Maitland; Newton; the owner of the property, John Shirley of New Orleans; the New York broker Josef Bergheim, who gathers the investors; and Roy Bauer, a major American investor in the project.

Waugh's first child, Andrew, was born in July 1933. His novel *Playing with Fire,* based loosely on his 1931 affair with Mary G., appeared later that year. In the spring of 1934 Waugh's father-in-law died, making Joan a wealthy woman. Meanwhile, Waugh was working on his next novel, the family chronicle *The Balliols* (1934); he completed the work shortly before Christmas. The novel relates the history of the period from the summer of 1907 to Sep-

*Waugh at the Macdowell Colony for artists in Peterborough, New Hampshire, in 1958 with Virginia Sorensen, who would become his third wife in 1969*

tember 1930 through the lives of the various members of the Balliol family. When the work opens, the wine merchant Edward Balliol is preparing to build a home, Ilex, in Hampstead in an attempt to revive his sixteen-year marriage to Jane; at the end Ilex is being demolished to make way for a block of flats. *The Balliols* was a minor best-seller; Graham Greene in the *Spectator* (15 June 1934) said that "the novel is much more competently written than one has learnt lately to expect from Mr. Waugh, and it will certainly appeal to admirers of *The Forsyte Saga*." Veronica, the Waughs' only daughter, was born in July. Around that time they used part of Joan's inheritance to purchase an eighteenth-century house, Edrington, set in its own park near Silchester. They retained a London flat for entertaining.

In February 1935 Waugh took a seventeen-day trip to Moscow. His next novel, *Jill Somerset* (1936), was another family chronicle in the mode of *The Balliols*. Returning from her sixty-two-year-old mother's birthday party in 1934, Jill Somerset reflects on the events that have befallen her family since 1913.

For Waugh 1936 opened with a lecture tour of the United States; there he met and began an affair with Donita Ferguson. He returned to the United States in July on the zeppelin *Hindenburg* to continue the romance. Although the affair ended in Decem-

ber, Waugh traveled to New York in 1937 and from there to Cuba, returning to England for Evelyn's wedding.

In January 1938 Waugh and his wife traveled to Morocco. Waugh spent the spring and summer writing *Going Their Own Ways: A Story of Modern Marriage* (1938), which examines the consequences of the divorce and remarriage of the wealthy John Fane for his four adult children. Harold Brighouse, writing in the *Manchester Guardian* (25 October 1938), found that the number of characters was "too many for individually intensive treatment, and the effect is one more of variety than of depth."

The Waughs' third child, Peter, was born on 13 October 1938. In November Waugh left for the Windward Islands in the company of his cousin Helen Gosse; went to New York for three weeks in late December; then took a trip to Rome with Joan. Called back to active duty with the army, he was assigned to train soldiers to use a Bren gun carrier—an ironic posting for a man who knew nothing about automobiles and did not even have a driver's license. At a base party Waugh started an eighteen-month affair with a twenty-seven-year-old woman named Diana. He completed the novel *No Truce with Time* (1941) shortly before being sent to France in April 1940 as an intelligence officer; he was evacuated in May as German troops overran the country.

Joan and the children left England for the safety of Australia in July 1940; in September Waugh was posted to the Petroleum Warfare Department. In October *Redbook* bought the serial rights to *No Truce with Time,* which was published by Cassell the following February; Waugh believed that it never "caught on" because few people were concerned with a West Indies story during wartime. Set on the British West Indian island of El Santo, *No Truce with Time* traces the consequences of young Barclay Ashe's opening confession of love for his married thirty-year-old hostess, Mary Montague; among those consequences is Mary's murder of her ailing middle-aged husband, Gerald. Mary's guilt and the arrival of the insurance investigator, Hutchins, bring about the tragic and ironic ending. Waugh was criticized by J. D. Beresford in the *Manchester Guardian* (15 March 1942) for weak characterization, especially of Mary, and for using "a too familiar tale, so infinitely better done by [Somerset] Maugham in *The Painted Veil.*"

In September 1941 Waugh was posted to the Middle East. He was shuttled from Cairo to Beirut and back to Cairo as an intelligence officer before moving to Baghdad as an observer of spy rings. In the summer of 1943 he received news of his father's death. He finished his service in Public Relations, a morale-building unit that allowed him to travel extensively in the area. Having risen to the rank of major, he returned to England in June 1945. Another American trip occupied him until January 1946. On a visit to New York in the fall, Waugh started *Unclouded Summer: A Love Story;* he finished it in the spring of 1947, and it was published in December but dated 1948. In *The Best Wine Last: An Autobiography through the Years, 1932–1969* (1978) Waugh says that his intention was to write a novel in which "the characters would ask themselves in 1946 whether they had solved correctly the problems that they had been set in 1926." Sold out shortly after publication, *Unclouded Summer* is set in England and southern France and concerns the love affair of an American artist and the young wife of an elderly English diplomat; in the coda the two lovers, now middle-aged, review the affair. Briefly noticed by most reviewers, the novel was called "a conventional lightweight romance" by the *Atlantic Monthly* (April 1948) and likened to "the sound track of an indifferent Hollywood movie" by Horace Reynolds in the *Saturday Review of Literature* (28 February 1948).

In January 1948 Waugh went to New York, where he received an assignment to write *The Lipton Story: A Centennial Biography* (1950), about the tea magnate and yachtsman Sir Thomas Johnstone Lipton, and then to the West Indies to gather material for a commissioned travel book, *Where the Clocks Strike Twice* (1951; published in Britain as *Where the Clocks Chime Twice,* 1952). Because of currency-transfer problems Waugh obtained an immigrant's visa to land in New York in October 1949. In January 1951 he obtained a divorce from Joan in Nevada; nevertheless, for some years he would spend up to three months a year with her at Edrington, and most summers they would take two-week vacations together.

The title character of Waugh's novel *Guy Renton: A London Story* (1952) is a wealthy wine merchant who aids his wayward brother and unconventional sister from 1925 to 1940; there is also the usual affair with a married woman, Renee Burton. *Guy Renton* sold well in England but poorly in the United States.

In *The Best Wine Last* Waugh says that "the next sixteen years were the best years of my life": a bachelor for most of that time, he was free to travel extensively, led an active social life in London and New York, and "produced a succession of solid books." Most of his writing was done in a hotel in Nice or during one of his seven two-month visits to the Macdowell Colony for artists in Peterborough, New Hampshire.

Waugh conceived *Island in the Sun: A Story of the 1950s Set in the West Indies* (1955) while returning to England in March 1953; he worked on it for the next eighteen months but was discouraged from publishing it by his London agent. The support and persistence of his American agent, Carl Brandt, however, led to an initial run of ten thousand copies by Farrar, Straus and Cudahy in New York; serialization in the *Ladies' Home Journal;* selection by the Literary Guild; publication in abridged form in *Reader's Digest Condensed Books;* and purchase of the movie rights by 20th Century-Fox for a 1957 film. Within four weeks in April 1955 Waugh earned nearly a quarter of a million dollars, which rose to half a million before, as he puts it in *My Brother Evelyn, and Other Profiles,* "a single critic had passed judgment on it." Another enthusiastic supporter who read the manuscript was a married forty-two-year-old Mormon novelist, Virginia Sorensen, whom Waugh had met in May 1954 at the Macdowell Colony and whom he had joined in mid December for five months during her second Guggenheim Fellowship in Copenhagen.

*Island in the Sun* recounts the impact on the West Indian island of Santa Marta of Euan, the bachelor son of the recently appointed governor-general, Lord Templeton, and a jaded American reporter, Carl Bradshaw. Euan romances a local girl, Mavis Norman, and eventually marries Jocelyn

Fleury; Carl, through a series of gossipy columns, creates problems for the government with the colonial office in London. There are also interracial relationships between Denis Archer, the governor's aide-de-camp and a would-be writer, and Margot Seaton, and between Mavis and Grainger Morris, a young lawyer friend of Euan's who eventually becomes the island's attorney general. Halfway through the novel the jealous Maxwell Fleury murders the maverick planter Col. Hilary Carson; thereafter, Maxwell's conscience and the seemingly genial police chief, Colonel Whittington, plague him until he satisfies both by provoking his own death, which brings about the removal of the governor-general.

With the proceeds from the novel Waugh took a trip around the world, during which he finished his next novel, *Fuel for the Flame* (1960), in fifteen weeks in Bangkok, Fiji, and Hawaii. The novel suffered by comparison to its predecessor but still spent nine weeks on the best-seller list; its serial rights were purchased by the *Ladies' Home Journal,* and it was optioned to M-G-M. Prince Rhya, the heir apparent to the throne of the kingdom of Karak on an island in the South China Sea, brings home an English fiancée. The intended marriage becomes "fuel for the flame" for a communist plan to gain control of a British oil company on the island. The plot is foiled by the British agent Kenneth Studholme and the Criminal Investigation Division chief, Colonel Forrester.

In 1965 *The Mule on the Minaret: A Novel about the Middle East,* which Waugh thought was better than *Fuel for the Flame,* failed even to earn its advance from the publisher. The title is taken from an Iraqi folktale about a man who takes his mule to the top of a minaret to protect it from thieves while he replaces the ill muezzin in leading the villagers in prayer; afterward the villagers refuse to help him return the animal to the ground, saying, "The man who takes his mule to the top of a minaret must bring it down himself." On a flight to Baghdad to attend a conference in 1962 the historian Noel Reid recalls his years as a British intelligence officer in Lebanon during World War II. Reid's story is closely patterned after Waugh's wartime experiences in the Middle East.

During the 1960s Waugh added Virginia Sorensen's home state of Utah to his travels and embarked on a lecture tour of the United States that led to his becoming writer-in-residence at Central State University in Edmond, Oklahoma, in 1966–1967.

Following a Far East tour with Sorenson in December 1968, Waugh learned that his former wife, Joan, was dying of cancer; he spent the last ten days

*Waugh in 1965 (Berenice Perry)*

with her before her death in late February. While at Edrington, Waugh made arrangements for his son Peter to sell his extensive library and deliver his papers to the University of Texas. On his return to the United States, Waugh suggested to Sorenson, who by then was divorced from her husband, that "after a proper and appropriate interval we should get married." The marriage took place on 15 July 1969.

While Waugh considered *A Spy in the Family: An Erotic Comedy* (1970) his "best told story," it became so partly through alterations suggested by his agent, Carol Brandt. It also ended his forty-year association with the Cassell firm, which refused to publish it on moral grounds. Myra, a London housewife, is seduced by a German lesbian during a vacation in Malta; the affair is recorded and is used to blackmail Myra to act as a heroin courier and to seduce and recruit others until British counterintelligence moves in. The story ends happily as Myra employs her newly learned sexual skills on her unsuspecting civil-servant husband, Victor.

In Waugh's autobiographical 1973 novel *The Fatal Gift* the novelist-hero Raymond Peronne, the second son of a baron, possesses "the fatal gift" of beauty; he was full of promise but has failed to live up to expectations. Nevertheless, despite his confinement on his beloved island of Domenica at the end, Peronne is a happy man. The story includes adultery, male homosexuality, lesbianism, incest, and the suggestion of a ménage à trois. The reviews were generally favorable; Jay Martin in the *New Republic* (7 July 1973) said: "This volume is a litany of remembrances and enables us to see something of the being which Waugh's talents have obscured."

*Brief Encounter* (1975) received little notice. Not an original work, it was a novelization of the 1974 television remake of the 1945 David Lean film that was, in turn, based on Noel Coward's play *Still Life* (1938).

Advertised as Waugh's fiftieth book, *Married to a Spy* (1976) proved to be his last novel. In Tangier the thirty-five-year-old British intelligence agent Adrian Sims uses his younger American wife, Beryl, to help him investigate the activities of a Basque separatist group. When Beryl almost loses her life, Adrian decides that she is more important than his job.

Waugh had been visiting Tangier since 1955 and had kept a flat there since 1969. In 1980 he moved to Tampa, Florida, where he died on 3 September 1981, two weeks after suffering a stroke. His ashes were buried in the family plot in London, and a memorial service was held at Chelsea Old Church in October.

Waugh's travel writing honed his skills as a keen observer of detail who created authentic and vivid settings, described events minutely, and concentrated on action; in essence he was an accurate reporter. But he was primarily a raconteur of his own experiences rather than an imaginative creator. His style was that of a magazine writer, abounding in clichés and words drawn from the jargon of cricket and rugby. Waugh accurately categorized himself in *The Early Years of Alec Waugh* as "a very minor writer" who wrote only about what interested him.

### Reference:

Evelyn Waugh, *A Little Learning: The First Volume of an Autobiography* (London: Chapman & Hall, 1964).

### Papers:

Alec Waugh's papers are at the University of Texas and at the Boston University Library.

# Henry Williamson

### (1 December 1895 – 13 August 1977)

### J. W. Blench
*University of Durham*

BOOKS: *The Beautiful Years: A Tale of Childhood* (London: Collins, 1921; revised edition, London: Faber & Faber, 1929; New York: Dutton, 1929);

*The Lone Swallows* (London: Collins, 1922); republished as *The Lone Swallows and Other Essays of the Country Green* (New York: Dutton, 1926); enlarged as *The Lone Swallows, and Other Essays of Boyhood and Youth* (London & New York: Putnam, 1933);

*Dandelion Days* (London: Collins, 1922; revised edition, London: Faber & Faber, 1930; New York, Dutton: 1930);

*The Peregrine's Saga, and Other Stories of the Country Green* (London: Collins, 1923); revised as *Sun Brothers* (New York: Dutton, 1925); revised as *The Peregrine's Saga and Other Wild Tales* (London & New York: Putnam, 1934);

*The Dream of Fair Women: A Tale of Youth after the Great War* (London: Collins, 1924); republished as *The Dream of Fair Women* (New York: Dutton, 1924; revised edition, London: Faber & Faber, 1931; New York: Dutton, 1931);

*The Old Stag: Stories* (London & New York: Putnam, 1926; New York: Dutton, 1927); revised as *The Old Stag and Other Hunting Stories* (London: Putnam, 1933);

*Tarka the Otter: His Joyful Water-Life and Death in the Country of the Two Rivers* (London & New York: Putnam, 1927; New York: Dutton, 1928; republished with illustrations by C. F. Tunnicliffe, London & New York: Putnam, 1932);

*The Pathway* (London: Cape, 1928; New York: Dutton, 1929);

*The Linhay on the Downs* (London: Mathews & Marrot, 1929); enlarged as *The Linhay on the Downs, and Other Adventures in the Old and the New World* (London: Cape, 1934);

*The Wet Flanders Plain* (London: Beaumont, 1929; revised edition, London: Faber & Faber, 1929; New York: Dutton, 1929; enlarged edition, Norwich: Gliddon, 1987);

*Henry Williamson in 1937*

*The Patriot's Progress: Being the Vicissitudes of Pte. John Bullock* (London; Bles, 1930; New York: Dutton, 1930; revised edition, London: Macdonald, 1968);

*The Village Book* (London: Cape, 1930; New York: Dutton, 1930);

*The Wild Red Deer of Exmoor: A Digression on the Logic and Ethics and Economics of Stag-Hunting in England To-day* (London: Faber & Faber, 1931);

*The Labouring Life* (London: Cape, 1932); republished as *As the Sun Shines* (New York: Dutton, 1933);

*The Gold Falcon; or, The Haggard of Love: Being the Adventures of Manfred, Airman and Poet of the World War, and Later, Husband and Father, in Search of*

*Freedom and Personal Sunrise, in the City of New York, and of the Consummation of His Life,* anonymous (London: Faber & Faber, 1933; revised, 1947);

*On Foot in Devon; or, Guidance and Gossip: Being a Monologue in Two Reels* (London: Maclehose, 1933);

*The Star-born* (London: Faber & Faber, 1933);

*Devon Holiday* (London: Cape, 1935);

*Salar the Salmon* (London: Faber & Faber, 1935; Boston: Little, Brown, 1936);

*The Flax of Dream: A Novel in Four Books* (London: Faber & Faber, 1936)—comprises revised versions of *The Beautiful Years, Dandelion Days, The Dream of Fair Women, The Pathway;*

*Goodbye, West Country* (London: Putnam, 1937; Boston: Little, Brown, 1938);

*The Children of Shallowford* (London: Faber & Faber, 1939; revised, 1959; revised edition, London: Macdonald & Jane's, 1978);

*As the Sun Shines* (London: Faber & Faber, 1941);

*Genius of Friendship: "T. E. Lawrence"* (London: Faber & Faber, 1941);

*The Story of a Norfolk Farm* (London: Faber & Faber, 1941);

*Norfolk Life,* by Williamson and Lilias Rider Haggard (London: Faber & Faber, 1943);

*The Sun in the Sands* (London: Faber & Faber, 1945);

*Life in a Devon Village* (London: Faber & Faber, 1945);

*Tales of a Devon Village* (London: Faber & Faber, 1945);

*The Phasian Bird* (London: Faber & Faber, 1948; Boston: Little, Brown, 1950);

*Scribbling Lark* (London: Faber & Faber, 1949);

*The Dark Lantern* (London: Macdonald, 1951; revised edition, London: Hamilton, 1962);

*Donkey Boy* (London: Macdonald, 1952; revised edition, London: Hamilton, 1962);

*Young Phillip Maddison* (London: Macdonald, 1953; revised edition, London: Hamilton, 1962);

*Tales of Moorland and Estuary* (London: Macdonald, 1953);

*How Dear Is Life* (London: Macdonald, 1954; revised edition, London: Hamilton, 1963);

*A Fox under My Cloak* (London: Macdonald, 1955; revised edition, London: Hamilton, 1963);

*The Golden Virgin* (London: Macdonald, 1957; revised edition, London: Hamilton, 1963);

*Love and the Loveless: A Soldier's Tale* (London: Macdonald, 1958; revised edition, London: Hamilton, 1963);

*A Clear Water Stream* (London: Faber & Faber, 1958; New York: Washburn, 1959; revised edition, London: Macdonald & Jane's, 1975);

*A Test to Destruction* (London: Macdonald, 1960; revised edition, London: Hamilton, 1964);

*The Henry Williamson Animal Saga: Tarka the Otter, Salar the Salmon, The Epic of Brock the Badger, Chakchek the Peregrine* (London: Macdonald, 1960);

*In the Woods* (Llandeilo: St. Albert's, 1960 [i.e., 1961]);

*The Innocent Moon* (London: Macdonald, 1961; revised edition, London: Hamilton, 1965);

*It Was the Nightingale* (London: Macdonald, 1962; revised edition, London: Hamilton, 1965);

*The Power of the Dead* (London: Macdonald, 1963; revised edition, London: Hamilton, 1966);

*The Phoenix Generation* (London: Macdonald, 1965; revised edition, London: Hamilton, 1967);

*A Solitary War* (London: Macdonald, 1966; revised edition, London: Hamilton, 1969);

*Lucifer before Sunrise* (London: Macdonald, 1967);

*The Gale of the World* (London: Macdonald, 1969);

*Collected Nature Stories* (London: Macdonald, 1970);

*The Scandaroon* (London: Macdonald, 1972; New York: Saturday Review Press, 1973);

*Days of Wonder,* edited by John Gregory (Cambridge: Henry Williamson Society, 1987);

*From a Country Hilltop,* edited by Gregory (Cambridge: Henry Williamson Society, 1988);

*A Breath of Country Air,* 2 volumes, edited by Gregory (Cambridge: Henry Williamson Society, 1990, 1991);

*Spring Days in Devon and Other Broadcasts,* edited by Gregory (Cambridge: Henry Williamson Society, 1992);

*Pen and Plough: Further Broadcasts,* edited by Gregory (Cambridge: Henry Williamson Society, 1993);

*Threnos for T. E. Lawrence and Other Writings, Together with a Criticism of Henry Williamson's* Tarka the Otter *by T. E. Lawrence,* edited by Gregory (Cambridge: Henry Williamson Society, 1994);

*Green Fields and Pavements: A Norfolk Farmer in Wartime,* edited by Gregory (Cambridge: Henry Williamson Society, 1995);

*The Notebook of a Nature-Lover,* edited by Gregory (Cambridge: Henry Williamson Society, 1996).

OTHER: Douglas Herbert Bell, *A Soldier's Diary of the Great War,* introduction by Williamson (London: Faber & Faber, 1929);

"The Confessions of a Fake Merchant," in *The Book of Fleet Street,* edited by T. Michael Pope (London: Cassell, 1930), pp. 280–302;

H. A. Manhood, *Little Peter the Great,* foreword by Williamson (London: Furnival, 1931);

John Heygate, *Decent Fellows,* introduction by Williamson (New York: Cape & Smith, 1931);

Richard Jefferies, *Wild Life in a Southern County,* introduction by Williamson (London: Cape, 1934);

Victor M. Yeates, *Winged Victory,* tribute to Yeates by Williamson (London: Cape, 1935; republished, with a new preface by Williamson, London: Cape, 1961);

*An Anthology of Modern Nature Writing,* edited by Williamson (London: Nelson, 1936);

*Nature in Britain: An Illustrated Survey,* introduction by Williamson (London: Batsford, 1936);

*Richard Jefferies: Selections of His Work, with Details of His Life and Circumstance, His Death and Immortality,* edited with contributions by Williamson (London: Faber & Faber, 1937; revised, 1947);

Jefferies, *Hodge and His Masters,* revised by Williamson (London: Methuen, 1937);

A. W. Lawrence, ed., *T. E. Lawrence by His Friends,* contribution by Williamson (London: Cape, 1937);

Sir John Russell, *English Farming,* introduction by Williamson (London: Faber & Faber, 1941);

"A Devon Stream," in *Countryside Mood,* compiled by Richard Harman (London: Blandford, 1943), pp. 22–30;

"The Clodhoppers," in *Countryside Character,* compiled by Harman (London: Blandford Press, 1946), pp. 18–34;

"The Winter of 1941," in *The Pleasure Ground,* edited by Malcolm Elwin (London: Macdonald, 1947), pp. 102–120;

"The Story of a Norfolk Owl," in *Country Company,* compiled by Harman (London: Blandford, 1949), pp. 109–121;

James Farrar, *The Unreturning Spring,* edited by Williamson (London: Williams & Norgate, 1950; revised edition, London: Chatto & Windus, 1968);

George J. Gill, *A Fight against Tithes,* epigraph by Williamson (Dorking, 1952);

Walter Robson, *Letters frim a Soldier,* edited by Williamson (London: Faber & Faber, 1960);

"Some Nature Writers and Civilization," in *Essays by Divers Hands: Being the Transactions of the Royal Society of Literature,* new series, volume 30, edited by H. Hardy Wallis (London: Oxford University Press, 1960), pp. 1–18;

"Out of the Prisoning Tower," in *John Bull's Schooldays,* edited by Brian Inglis (London: Hutchinson, 1961), pp. 144–149;

"Field Garden," in *A Book of Gardens,* edited by James Turner (London: Cassell, 1963), pp. 193–204;

"Richard Aldington," in *Richard Aldington: An Intimate Portrait,* edited by Alister Kershaw and F.-J. Temple (Carbondale: Southern Illinois University Press, 1965);

*My Favourite Country Stories,* edited by Williamson (London: Lutterworth, 1966);

"A First Adventure with Francis Thompson," in *The Mistress of Vision,* by Francis Thompson (Aylesford: St. Albert's Press, 1966), pp. vi–xix;

"In Darkest England," in *The Hound of Heaven,* by Thompson, edited by G. Krishnamurti (London: Francis Thompson Society, 1967), pp. 7–15;

"Genesis of Tarka," in *The Twelfth Man,* edited by Martin Boddey (London: Cassell, 1971), pp. 71–78;

*The Wipers Times,* foreword by Williamson (London: Davies, 1973);

*The Weekly Dispatch,* contributions by Williamson, edited by John Gregory (Cambridge: Henry Williamson Society, 1983).

## SELECTED PERIODICAL PUBLICATIONS– UNCOLLECTED:

### NONFICTION

"The Tragic Spirit," *Adelphi,* 20 (October–December 1943): 17–19;

"The Sun That Shines on the Dead," *Adelphi,* 22 (January–March 1946): 72–79; (April–June 1946): 130–134;

"From a Wartime Norfolk Journal: Easter 1944," *Adelphi,* 23 (January–March 1947): 96–97;

"From *A Chronicle Writ in Darkness,*" *Adelphi,* 24 (January–March 1948): 101–108;

"The Lost Legions," *Adelphi,* 25 (October–December 1948); 1–11;

"Notes of a Prentice Hand," *Adelphi,* 25 (January–March 1949): 111–120;

"A Note on *Tarka the Otter,*" *Adelphi,* 25 (April–June 1949): 217–223;

"From *A Chronicle Writ in Darkness,*" *European,* no. 7 (September 1953): 27–33; no. 8 (October 1953): 25–34; no. 35 (January 1956): 55–62;

"Some Notes on *The Flax of Dream* and *A Chronicle of Ancient Sunlight,*" *Aylesford Review,* 2 (Winter 1957–1958): 56–61;

"Machen in Fleet Street," *Aylesford Review,* 2 (Winter 1959–1960): 321–322;

"Reflections on the Death of a Field Marshall," *Contemporary Review,* 218 (June 1971): 303–313.

Henry Williamson is best known for his wildlife stories, especially *Tarka the Otter: His Joyful Water-Life and Death in the Country of the Two Rivers*

*Williamson in 1921 holding his spaniels in the doorway of Skirr Cottage, Georgeham*

(1927) and *Salar the Salmon* (1935), in which he conveys with extraordinary immediacy the lives of various wild creatures in a finely realized natural environment in north Devon. His range is wider, however: he wrote closely observed and deeply felt nature essays, absorbing autobiographical books, and two remarkable novel sequences: the tetralogy The Flax of Dream (1921–1928) and the vast fifteen-part roman-fleuve A Chronicle of Ancient Sunlight (1951–1969). His work shows a consistent development not only in literary art but also in the presentation of social, moral, spiritual, and political themes.

Henry William Williamson was born on 1 December 1895 at 66 Braxfield Road, Brockley, in southeast London to William Leopold Williamson, a bank clerk, and Gertrude Eliza Leaver Williamson. His maternal grandmother came from a long line of yeoman farmers in Bedfordshire; from these ancestors, Williamson believed, he inherited a profound feeling for the land and its cultivation. He also thought that he had derived from his mother's side of the family an affinity for the county of Devon: in *A Clear Water Stream* (1958) he says that the family of his great-great-grandmother Sarah Shapcote Leaver had lived for many generations at Knowestone in north Devon. His writings contain many memorable descriptions of the landscape,

wildlife, and people of Devon, and the region known as "The Chains" on Exmoor became for him a place of pilgrimage whence he drew emotional and spiritual strength. From his paternal grandfather and namesake, an architect and surveyor, Williamson inherited a love of nature and an appreciation of the writings of the nineteenth-century Wiltshire nature writer and novelist Richard Jefferies. His paternal grandmother, Adela Leopoldina Williamson, née Luhn, was of German descent; this aspect of his ancestry led Williamson to regard the Germans as a cousin nation. He had an older sister, Kathleen, and a younger one, Doris Mary (Biddy).

After a brief sojourn at 165 Ladywell Road in Brockley, the Williamsons moved in 1899 or 1900 to 11 Eastern Road (now renumbered 21), Hilly Fields, in the same London district. This house features prominently in the early volumes of A Chronicle of Ancient Sunlight. (In 1984 the Henry Williamson Society and other interested parties arranged for a commemorative plaque to be placed on the house.)

Williamson attended Brockley Elementary Council School and then the prestigious Colfe's Grammar School in Lewisham, to which he won a scholarship in 1907. The headmaster of Colfe's in Williamson's day was Frank W. Lucas; he and his staff would be satirized in Williamson's fiction. Williamson was an uncooperative pupil and something of a liar; in his article "Out of the Prisoning Tower" (1961) he recalls that Lucas once told him that he was "the worst boy in the school" and that he "must raise his standard of honour." Although he did achieve some academic and athletic success and won the Bramley Prize for Divinity, his real life was lived away from school. His parents' marriage was not happy; to escape the tense atmosphere at home Williamson would frequently ride his bicycle, either alone or with one of his friends, to the fields, ponds, and woods south of Lewisham, as far as northwestern Kent, to observe wild birds. He also enjoyed watching birds and fishing for roach and rudd with his cousin Charlie Boon when he visited his relatives at Aspley Guise, near Woburn in Bedfordshire. In the spring of 1913 Williamson began keeping a nature diary; he would publish part of it in his *The Lone Swallows, and Other Essays of Boyhood and Youth* (1933). Among the books Williamson read in his boyhood were some by Jefferies that had belonged to his grandfather: *Wild Life in a Southern County* (1879), *The Amateur Poacher* (1880), and *Bevis* (1882). In these works, he says in the epigraph to his *Richard Jefferies: Selections of His Work, with Details of His Life and Circumstance, His Death and Immortality* (1937), he "lived a secret life." The vivid and detailed descriptions of nature in these books accorded with his own intuition that careful observation is a necessity for one who aspires to be a good writer.

Williamson left school in the summer of 1913 and went to work as a clerk at the Sun Insurance Company in the City of London; he would make good fictional use of this experience in *How Dear Is Life* (1954), the fourth volume of A Chronicle of Ancient Sunlight. In May 1914 he went on vacation in the village of Georgeham in north Devon. Exmoor lay to the south; Baggy Point, Saunton Sands, and Brauton Burrows to the north and west. That remote and—at the time—totally unspoiled place became for him a revelation of the beauty and appeal of the English countryside. He would portray the area vividly in many of his writings.

Williamson had joined the Territorials in January, and on 5 August his mobilization papers came. After training at Bisley and Crowborough, Sussex, he arrived on the western front in the aftermath of the First Battle of Ypres. The Christmas Truce of 1914, like his visit to Georgeham, had a profound effect on him; he refers to the experience many times in his writings. He had accepted without question the notion that the Allies were fighting for freedom and justice and the Germans for domination. As he writes in *The Story of a Norfolk Farm* (1941), however, while some of the troops "mingled and talked in no-man's land" on Christmas Day, others buried the dead, marking the shallow graves "with crosses knocked together from lengths of ration-box wood marked with indelible pencil 'For King and Country,' 'Für Vaterland und Freiheit.'" A conversation with a German soldier confirmed that each side thought that it was fighting for the same cause and had right on its side. In January 1915 Williamson was invalided home with frostbitten feet; he recovered and in April 1915 was commissioned a second lieutenant in the Bedfordshire Regiment. In the fall he was attached to the Cambridgeshire Regiment for a period of training, then transferred to the Middlesex Regiment. In late 1916 he became a transport officer with the machine gun corps and was promoted to lieutenant. In the summer of 1917 he took part in the Third Battle of Ypres. Back once more with the Bedfordshires, he was present when the Germans attacked in the Michael Offensive in March 1918. He was sent home on 18 April, probably having been gassed. After a period at Languard Fort near Felixstowe he was transferred early in 1919 to number 1 Dispersal Unit Shorncliffe; to number 3 Rest Camp Folkestone, where he had an affair with the wife of a senior officer who was away on duty in

*One of the illustrations by C. F. Tunnicliffe that first appeared in the 1932 edition of Williamson's novel* Tarka the Otter

Germany; and to Brocton Camp at Cannock Chase in Staffordshire, where he was demobilized in September 1919.

Williamson's first genuinely literary pieces are short nature essays written in the early years of the war and included in *The Lone Swallows* (1922). The best is "Winter's Eve," written during the winter of 1914–1915 and expressing Williamson's delight in tawny and barn owls. Owls fascinated him throughout his life; his drawing of a barn owl appears on his tombstone. Like many other frontline soldiers, however, Williamson found that his earlier perceptions were dulled by his experiences in the war, and for a time he lost his delight in nature. Nevertheless, he did not lose his impulse to write. He began a novel in the winter of 1917–1918 but abandoned it in October 1918, then started a second novel in November and finished it early in 1919. The novels remain unpublished; the manuscripts, in the Henry Williamson Archive at the University Library at Exeter, show them to be distinctly apprentice work and inferior to the previously written nature essays.

*Linocut by William Kermode for Williamson's novel* The Patriot's Progress

Clearly Williamson needed some new stimulus to help him develop successfully as a writer; it came in the summer of 1919 when he found a copy of Jefferies's *The Story of My Heart: My Autobiography* (1883), which he had not read before, in a secondhand bookstore in Folkestone. The blend of beautiful natural description and a sense of the past in a notable passage in chapter 3 wrought a transformation in him: suddenly, he began to relive in his imagination his happy experiences in north Devon in the summer of 1914. Reading Jefferies's account of how, stimulated by the beauties of nature that surrounded him, he felt that he could enter into the life of an ancient warrior buried in a tumulus nearby, Williamson realized that as a writer he could recreate the lives of his dead wartime comrades. He says in his essay "Some Nature Writers and Civilization" (1960) that Jefferies's book became for him "a revelation of total truth"; his purpose in life, he believed, would be "to extend Jefferies's truth of redemption through nature" to "his fellow men." His prewar delight in nature was revived, but it was richer and more mature. The result was that he was able to write some intensely beautiful and deeply

moving nature essays in which the influence of Jefferies, while strong, is absorbed into an achievement that is distinctly Williamson's own.

Some of these essays were written in London, where Williamson worked after demobilization as a salesman for the classified advertising department of *The Times* and then as motoring correspondent for the *Weekly Dispatch*. His heart, however, was not in this kind of writing, and he was discharged from the *Weekly Dispatch* in September 1920. He was then able to concentrate on truly congenial freelance work, which he placed with various magazines. An excellent example of his early nature writing is the expertly crafted and deeply moving essay "London Children and Wild Flowers," written in 1920 and included in *The Lone Swallows* (it is retitled "The Passing of the Blossom" in the enlarged edition of 1933). Dedicated to Walter de la Mare, it shows Williamson's compassion for the London poor, who are cut off for most of their lives from the beauty of the countryside. The essay depicts the sights, sounds, and inner spirit of the late spring in the countryside of northwestern Kent, then turns to recollections of woods nearer to London that have been despoiled

*Williamson on a fishing trip in Quebec in 1930 (Trustees of the Henry Williamson Estate)*

by development. Poor people from Walworth, Shoreditch, and Woolwich have taken the bluebells and the apple blossom, but Williamson's reaction when he sees the flowers in a tramcar is not one of anger but of sympathy. Recognizing that the beauty of the wildflowers has "passed into their eyes," he realizes that the ravaging has not been in vain: "For two or three days wilting flowers and stolen blossom would remind them of the sunlight and the fresh air, of the cloud-shadow that swept up and the warmth that followed when the beams of light lacquered the branches of the trees." In "Proserpine's Message," written in 1921 and also included in *The Lone Swallows,* Williamson develops a theme he learned from Jefferies: the importance of contact with nature in childhood. Such contact, he believes, will lead to a less mercenary society, for more-genuine riches are to be found in the dandelion than in gold coins: "Let us spend the golden treasure of the dandelions, now on earth while we may; so that those who follow may enjoy a more sunlit life."

The maturing influence of *The Story of My Heart* can also be seen in Williamson's development as a novelist. He wrote a third novel, "The Flax of Dream," between November 1919 and March 1920. Although it, too, remains unpublished, it is much better than the earlier two: it not only shows greater technical competence but also embodies a more profound spiritual outlook, illustrating Williamson's conviction that nature can exercise a healing power on the wounded psyche.

In 1920 Williamson began to move in literary circles: he attended meetings of Mrs. Dawson Scott's Tomorrow Club, soon to become the P.E.N. Club. In March 1921, after a quarrel with his father, he went to Georgeham to live in a cottage he had rented since 1919. Between the ceiling and the thatched roof lived a family of barn owls that entered and left by a hole in the gable end; Williamson found their presence comforting and named his home Skirr Cottage, from the sound the owls made. The swifts that nested in the thatch also delighted him. After a friend who stayed with him for a time moved out, Williamson settled down to a happy period with his owls, swifts, a spaniel, a cat, and a variety of injured wild creatures—a crow, a gull, a razorbill, and a baby otter—that he tried to heal.

Williamson's fourth novel, *The Beautiful Years: A Tale of Childhood,* shows an even greater advance. It was published in the autumn of 1921, becoming the first in the Flax of Dream series; the second novel in the series, *Dandelion Days,* appeared in 1922. That year the Stokes family—a widowed mother, two daughters, and a son—came to Georgeham, and Williamson seems to have fallen in love with the younger daughter, Mary. She appears as Annabelle in *The Sun in the Sands* (1945), part of which is a fictionalized version of Williamson's early Georgeham years. The family appears again in *The Innocent Moon* (1961), the ninth volume of A Chronicle of Ancient Sunlight. The first of Williamson's wildlife books, *The Peregrine's Saga, and Other Stories of the Country Green,* was published in 1923, followed the next year

*Williamson at a meeting of British fascists in 1939 (BBC Hulton Picture Library)*

by the third novel in the Flax of Dream series, *The Dream of Fair Women: A Tale of Youth after the Great War*. In April 1924 Williamson went on a walking vacation in the Pyrenees with two literary friends, D. B. Wyndham Lewis and J. B. Morton; he would use the episode in *The Sun in the Sands* and in *The Innocent Moon*. On 25 October 1925 Williamson married Ida Loetitia Hibbert. They moved to Vale Cottage in Georgeham, where their first two children, William and John, were born.

Another wildlife book, *The Old Stag: Stories* (1926), was followed in 1927 by Williamson's greatest success, the novel *Tarka the Otter*, which won the Hawthornden Prize for 1928 and established his literary reputation. With the prize money Williamson was able to buy a field he had long admired at Ox's Cross, on a hill above Georgeham. There he built a writing hut; in 1952 he would erect a studio there. Many of his books would be written in these buildings. Near the end of his life he would build a house at Ox's Cross, but he would never have the chance to live in it.

Williamson believed strongly in the kinship of humanity with other species. In *Tarka the Otter*, as in *The Peregrine's Saga* and *The Old Stag*, he gives his wild creatures names; but he anthropomorphizes them only to a point. He never makes them use human speech, preferring to render phonetically, as far as he can, their sounds and cries. Some of the animal characters are first encountered in the earlier vol-

umes–Chakchek the peregrine falcon, Mewliboy the buzzard, Old Nog the heron, Swagdagger the stoat, Kronk the raven, Bloody Bill Brock the Badger, and Deadlock the otter hound–but Tarka is the most memorable of them all. Williamson enables the reader to enter into Tarka's inner world and to become more truly human by realizing that he or she is not isolated from the rest of creation. This spiritual illumination is genuine, and many readers have found that *Tarka the Otter* has changed their outlook by enriching their appreciation of the natural world and their place within it.

Tarka lives in a real countryside, the area of the rivers Taw and Torridge, Exmoor, part of Dartmoor, and the coast between Bideford and Lynmouth. (The Devon County Council has arranged a "Tarka Trail" that can be followed by visitors.) This countryside is, however, presented through the eyes of a poet, so familiar things become magical. The reader is able to move easily from this heightened vision of the countryside to the less familiar reality of the lives of Tarka and the other wild creatures in the book. Williamson skillfully maintains the balance between the attractive, playful side of Tarka's nature and the darker side that comes from his being a predator. The reader reacts to Tarka, his parents, his sisters, his mates, his cubs, and the members of other species as individuals. Tarka's death in an otter hunt (now illegal in Great Britain) is both a tragedy and a triumph: the otter hound Deadlock

*Williamson, cirsa 1950, outside and inside the hut he built at Ox's Cross (photographs by Daniel Farson)*

kills him, but in his dying throes Tarka bites the hound in the throat and drags him under the water so that both die. The hunters recover Deadlock's body and look down at it "in sad wonder. . . . And while they stood there silently, a great bubble arose out of the depths and broke, and as they watched, another bubble shook to the surface and broke; and there was a third bubble in the sea-going waters and nothing more." The reader feels that Tarka has returned home: his body to the purifying sea and his spirit to the air.

In 1928 appeared *The Pathway,* the fourth and last volume in the Flax of Dream series. In the next few years all the volumes were published in revised editions, and in 1936 the final revisions appeared in a one-volume omnibus edition as *The Flax of Dream: A Novel in Four Books.* The overall title—the same as that of Williamson's third unpublished novel—is taken from a phrase in his aunt Mary Leopoldina Williamson's symbolic narrative *The Incalculable Hour* (1910), published under the pseudonym J. Quiddington West:

> Our land of heart's desire is woven of our thoughts and emotions, and no two weave alike. And it is well if, returning thence, we bring with us gifts worthy of acceptance. For many to whom the Weaver gives the Flax of Dream, weave hurriedly, and the web is spoilt.

The four novels depict significant periods in the life of the protagonist, Willie Maddison: *The Beautiful Years* takes him from age seven to nine;

*Dandelion Days* from fourteen to seventeen; *The Dream of Fair Women* from twenty-one to twenty-two; and *The Pathway* from twenty-five to his death at twenty-six. In the foreword to the one-volume edition Williamson says that he wanted to tell "the story of one human unit of Europe immediately before and after the War" and thereby to express "the vision of a new world, dreamed by many young soldiers in the trenches and shell-craters of the World War." Thus, *The Flax of Dreams* is both a bildungsroman and a thesis novel; Williamson hoped that its vision of a new order based on imaginative sympathy and understanding within families and nations and among nations "would help to alter the thought of the entire world." This vision, inspired by his experience of the Christmas Truce of 1914, owes something to the thought of Percy Bysshe Shelley; but it is also influenced by Jefferies's belief in the importance for children of contact with nature. From the difficulties of Williamson's own childhood came the conviction that families should be united in loving harmony if the children are to grow up into well-adjusted adulthood.

In *The Beautiful Years* Williamson contrasts Willie's strained relations with his real father to his happy friendship with a substitute father, Jim Holloman, a Jefferies-like nature enthusiast. The vividly described rural setting of the story carries into the reader's mind something of the healing power of nature. The affectionate relationship between Willie and his friend Jack Temperley illustrates the need of every human being, especially in childhood, for love and sympathy.

A theme introduced toward the end of *The Beautiful Years* forms a major concern of *Dandelion Days:* the contrast between the educational methods of the period and the enlightenment Williamson believes comes to young people through contact with nature. The classroom scenes in *Dandelion Days* are wildly funny; while not totally unsympathetic, the portraits of the schoolmasters–drawn from Williamson's teachers at Colfe's–show clearly the limitations of their instructional methods. Outside of school Willie delights in the beauty and wildlife of the countryside. Nature, however, is shown to be vulnerable: during a visit to Willie's country home his cousin Phillip, who will be the hero of the novel sequence A Chronicle of Ancient Sunlight, tells Willie of the destruction of the countryside by urban sprawl near the south London suburb in which Phillip lives. Nature also proves to be insufficient to assuage Willie's disappointment at the failure of his love affair with Elsie Norman, and at the end of the novel he falls back on the friendship of the faithful Jack.

Williamson skips over Willie's war years; *The Dream of Fair Women* tells of Willie's life in the summer and autumn of 1919, after his demobilization. Willie is writing a book, *The Policy of Reconstruction or True Resurrection,* the thesis of which is that a mistaken system of education helped to lead to the war by damaging the natural psychological growth of children. Attempts by revolutionary idealists to regenerate society are doomed to fail unless they cease to "neglect the secret of the woods and the fields, and how they expand man's spirit if he knows them when little." The main story concerns Willie's affair with a beautiful married woman, Eveline Fairfax, based on Williamson's relationship with the officer's wife at Folkestone. Eveline rejects him in the end, leaving Willie bitterly disappointed. But he still has nature, which, unlike women, does not betray the dreams it gives. He finishes *The Policy of Reconstruction,* recording in the last paragraph his belief in his mission to preach a new reign of love and become a "light-bringer."

*The Pathway* begins in January 1923. The reader learns in flashback that Willie, devastated by the break with Eveline, took to drink. After collapsing in the Adelphi Gardens, he reformed and, as therapy, went to France to work as a laborer with the War Graves Commission. He also visited Germany and was distressed by the deprivations suffered by the people. In a passage that Williamson added in the 1936 edition Willie recounts his encounter with "an ex-corporal with the truest eyes I have seen in any man, now rousing the young men and ex-soldiers to save the nation from disintegration; a man who doesn't smoke or drink, a vegetarian, owning no property, living for the sun to shine on the living." The "ex-corporal" is Adolf Hitler; after reading a newspaper interview with him in 1927, Williamson had come to believe that Hitler had "perceived the root causes of war in the unfulfilled human ego" and was "striving to create a new human-filled world." Willie's encounter with Hitler leads him, in a passage toward the end of the novel that was also added in 1936, to express his conviction that it is necessary to "rouse the ex-soldiers" in England to carry his own vision into actuality. In the foreword to the 1936 edition Williamson rejoices that "the vision of a new world, dreamed by many soldiers in the trenches and shell-craters of the World War, is being made real in one European nation at least"–that is, Germany. Williamson goes on to make a remark that would bring him notoriety: "I salute the great man across the Rhine whose life symbol is the happy child."

Willie's ideas in *The Pathway* are still essentially those of *The Policy of Reconstruction,* held more firmly and articulated more clearly. There is a supreme need, he believes, for a change in outlook, which can come only from better education. The old narrow ideas must be supplanted by new broader ones: "Change thought and you change the world." The central story of the book is that of Willie's love affair with Mary Ogilvie, with whom he has an affinity of spirit based partly on their shared admiration for the writings of Jefferies and Francis Thompson; the affair ends when Willie breaks off their engagement and leaves on his reforming mission. Although Williamson originally intended to allow Willie's mission to succeed, he decided that verisimilitude was better served by having Willie drown in the estuary of Taw and Torridge in September 1923. Mary sees Willie as a "light-bringer" whom she has failed, and she endorses his message. Williamson sought to convey the same message in his symbolic fable *The Star-born* (1933), which is purportedly written by Willie Maddison, but most readers consider that the novel sequence succeeds much better in doing so.

In 1929 Williamson published *The Wet Flanders Plain,* a moving account of a visit he made in 1927 to the battlefields of World War I. He deals directly with the war in *The Patriot's Progress: Being the Vicissitudes of Pte. John Bullock* (1930), which had its origin as a series of captions for linocuts of the war by William Kermode. The hero, Private John Bullock, is an "everyman" victim of the war. The battle scenes are rendered vividly, and there is a fine ironic end-

LOVE AND THE
LOVELESS

*A Soldier's Tale*

by

HENRY WILLIAMSON

Whider thou gost, i chil with the,
And whider y go, tho schalt with me—
*from the Breton lay in English called Sir Orfeo.*

MACDONALD : LONDON

A TEST TO
DESTRUCTION

by

HENRY WILLIAMSON

"He faced the spectres of the mind
And laid them: thus he came at length
To find a stronger faith his own;
And Power was with him in the night,
Which makes the darkness and the light,
And dwells not in the light alone."
*Alfred Lord Tennyson*

MACDONALD : LONDON

*Title pages for the seventh and eighth volumes of* A Chronicle of Ancient Sunlight

ing: on Armistice Day, John is back in England, having lost a leg; an old man tells him that he is a hero and that England will not forget "you fellows." Smiling, John replies, "We are England."

Williamson paints portraits of Georgeham in the 1920s in *The Village Book* (1930) and *The Labouring Life* (1932). In the preface to the American edition of *The Labouring Life*, titled *As the Sun Shines* (1933), he formulates what would thenceforth be his artistic ideal: "as a man and writer I would like to be as the sun, which divines the true or inner nature of living things. . . . The sun is entirely truthful; the sun sees no shadows." Revised selections from the two books appeared in 1945 as *Life in a Devon Village* and *Tales of a Devon Village.*

In 1929 the Williamsons moved to Shallowford, still in Devon, where they lived in a cottage rented from the Fortescue estate. Fishing rights on a stretch of the River Bray went with the tenancy, and Williamson began to fish again–an activity he had

not pursued since 1914. In August 1930 he joined his American publisher, John Macrea, and Macrea's son on a fishing trip in Quebec. He then traveled with his host to New York, where he rented an apartment overlooking Sheridan Square. He returned to England in the spring of 1931. In a novel, *The Gold Falcon; or, The Haggard of Love: Being the Adventures of Manfred, Airman and Poet of the World War, and Later, Husband and Father, in Search of Freedom and Personal Sunrise, in the City of New York, and of the Consummation of His Life,* published anonymously in 1933, he used his New York experience for some chapters dealing with the visit there of his hero, Manfred Cloudesley. Like Willie Maddison in *The Flax of Dream,* Manfred, who had been a fighter pilot in World War I, grows morally and spiritually and dies at the end. In the revised edition (1947) Williamson acknowledges his authorship and gives the real names of several of the characters. In either version the novel is one of his less-successful works.

*Williamson with his second wife, Christine Duffield Williamson, at the Rock Inn in Georgeham (photograph by Daniel Farson)*

In January 1928 T. E. Lawrence had written Edward Garnett, a reader for the publisher Jonathan Cape, how much he had enjoyed *Tarka the Otter;* Garnett had sent a copy to Lawrence in India. Garnett sent the letter on to Williamson; as a result Williamson and Lawrence began a correspondence that continued until Lawrence's death in 1935. They met twice: in 1929, when Lawrence visited Williamson in Georgeham; and in 1934, when he came to Southampton to see Williamson off on the latter's second trip to America. Williamson wrote an essay about Lawrence in 1936, quoting liberally from the letters he had received; it was published in 1941 as *Genius of Friendship: "T. E. Lawrence."* Lawrence appears as G. B. Everest in *Devon Holiday* (1935), a lighthearted account of a walking tour that Williamson uses to link together six short stories; most of the stories had appeared previously in periodicals and would reappear in *Tales of Moorland and Estuary* (1953). In a postscript to *Devon Holiday* Williamson recalls that Lawrence died as a result of a motorcycle crash on his way home from sending a telegram replying to a letter in which Williamson

had asked if he might visit Lawrence to show him a copy of the book. Later Williamson declared that he had wanted to discuss with Lawrence the possibility of organizing a peace rally of former servicemen in the Albert Hall and a meeting between Lawrence and Hitler to foster friendship between Britain and Germany; but this does not, in fact, seem to have been his intention at the time.

In 1935 Williamson's second major wildlife book, *Salar the Salmon,* appeared. Although it includes romantic and symbolic elements, it is primarily a realistic narrative of a vigorous fish's return from the sea to ascend a river to spawn and, ultimately, to die. Salar is menaced by nature and by fishermen, but he finally triumphs. The reviewer in the *Times Literary Supplement* (17 October 1935) called it "a tale which for absorbing interest leaves behind many a romance of human character." As in *Tarka the Otter* and his other wildlife books, Williamson gives his main animal characters names and seeks to convey their sensations and emotions. The style of the book is simpler than that of *Tarka the Otter,* in keeping with Williamson's starker and more realistic view of a nature in which one species preys on another and in which it is the species that counts, not the individual. But the reader can see that nature, although brutal, is ultimately good; and he or she can take an example from Salar's courage and self-sacrifice and, like Shiner, the reformed poacher, can delight in the affirmation of life shown by the salmon.

In the autumn of 1935 Williamson went on a vacation in Germany. While there he attended the Nuremberg Rally, and in *Goodbye, West Country* (1937) he recalls the favorable impression the event made on him and how life in Germany seemed happier and more purposeful than in England. The experience confirmed him in his admiration for Hitler. In the nature passages in *Goodbye, West Country* Williamson leaves a fine memorial of that aspect of his happy years at Shallowford while in *The Children of Shallowford* (1939) he gives a delightful picture of his domestic life there. The family had increased with the births of Margaret, Robert, and Richard, who, with William and John, provide the cast for many humorous and tender episodes.

By 1937 Williamson had come to believe that he had written all he could about Devon; he also felt that writing itself was too narrow a pursuit and that it needed to be supplemented by physical activity. He decided to go to another part of England and become a farmer, like some of his Bedfordshire relatives. It was a period of depression in British agriculture, but Williamson believed that an effort should be made to regenerate this basic and vital industry. Thus, on Old Michaelmas Day (11 October) 1937 he took possession of Old Hall Farm, Stiffkey, in Norfolk.

Before the end of the year Williamson, at the instigation of his neighbor Dorothy, Lady Downe, joined Sir Oswald Mosley's British Union of Fascists and National Socialists; he was attracted by Mosley's support for British agriculture and by Mosley's efforts to avoid another "cousins' war." Having believed Hitler's peace propaganda, Williamson was distressed by the German leader's territorial demands in the summer of 1939. He wanted to go to Germany and, as one former frontline soldier to another, implore Hitler not to march. Mosley forbade him to do so, declaring that "the curtain is down." With the outbreak of war in the fall of 1939, and especially with the German attacks on neutral nations in 1940, Williamson finally became disillusioned with Hitler. In June 1940 he was arrested because of his association with Mosley. He was released the next day after an interview with the chief constable of Norfolk, who realized that he was a

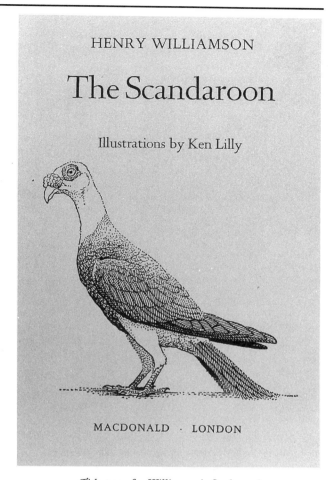

HENRY WILLIAMSON

# The Scandaroon

Illustrations by Ken Lilly

MACDONALD · LONDON

*Title page for Williamson's final novel*

British patriot and would not be a danger to national security.

Williamson's years in Norfolk up to June 1940 are chronicled in *The Story of a Norfolk Farm;* the most profound of his autobiographical books, it powerfully involves the reader in Williamson's struggle to improve his rundown farm and in the joy the family felt at the achievement of a good harvest. He continued to farm at Stiffkey until 1945, when he sold the farm and moved to Botesdale, a village in Suffolk; a daughter, Sarah, was born there.

In 1948 appeared the moving moral fable *The Phasian Bird.* Set on Williamson's Norfolk farm, it is the tragic tale of the life and death of Chee-kai, a Reeves's pheasant that symbolizes art and beauty. Wilbo, a painter, farmer, and political idealist partly based on Williamson himself, also dies, after forgiving the hunters who accidentally shoot him.

Williamson returned to Devon permanently in 1948. His *Scribbling Lark* (1949), the story of an old cart horse who wins the Derby, is a curious and not entirely successful attempt at a book for children.

*Williamson in his hut at Ox's Cross on the day before his eightieth birthday (photograph by David Steen)*

He was divorced from Loetitia in 1949 and married Christine Duffield in 1950; they had a son, Harry, in 1952 and were divorced in 1963.

After he returned to Devon, Williamson was able to achieve his long-delayed ambition of writing a second novel sequence in which he would draw on his south London childhood and his experiences in World War I. He had worked on aspects of the project since 1919, and he adapted passages from previously published works, unpublished manuscripts, and diaries and journals. The sequence as completed, however, is a genuine fictional unity and in the opinion of many readers is his greatest achievement. A Chronicle of Ancient Sunlight comprises fifteen novels: *The Dark Lantern* (1951; revised, 1962), *Donkey Boy* (1952; revised, 1962), *Young Phillip Maddison* (1953; revised, 1962), *How Dear Is Life* (1954; revised, 1963), *A Fox under My Cloak* (1955; revised, 1963), *The Golden Virgin* (1957; revised, 1963), *Love and the Loveless: A Soldier's Tale* (1958; revised, 1963), *A Test to Destruction* (1960; revised, 1964), *The Innocent Moon* (1961; revised, 1965), *It Was the Nightingale* (1962; revised, 1965), *The Power of the Dead* (1963; revised, 1966), *The Phoenix Generation* (1965; revised, 1967), *A Solitary War* (1966; revised, 1969), *Lucifer*

*before Sunrise* (1967), and *The Gale of the World* (1969). Like *The Flax of Dream,* A Chronicle of Ancient Sunlight is a bildungsroman: although it begins with the courtship and marriage of his parents in 1893, it is the story of the development of Phillip Maddison, Willie Maddison's London cousin, from his birth in 1895 through many vicissitudes and two marriages to his realization in 1947 that his true vocation, from which he must no longer swerve, is to be a writer. Williamson tries to put into practice the artistic ideal of sunlike vision he had elaborated in *As the Sun Shines* and to be less subjective than he had been in *The Flax of Dream*. His intention is to re-create the past "in ancient sunlight": that is, with objective understanding tempered by benevolence and compassion. The phrase *ancient sunlight* was probably inspired by a passage in Jefferies's *The Story of My Heart* where he recalls how he used to lie on his back in the sunshine, feeling the embrace of the earth and half closing his eyes to bear the dazzling light:

> Gradually entering into the intense life of the summer days—a life which burned around as if every grass blade and leaf were a torch—I came to feel the long drawn life of the earth back into the dimmest past, while the sun of the moment was warm on me. Sesostris on the most ancient sands of the south, in ancient, ancient days, was conscious of himself and of the sun. This sunlight linked me through the ages to that past consciousness.

Also like *The Flax of Dream,* A Chronicle of Ancient Sunlight is a "thesis novel," and to some extent its message is similar. It shows the importance of access to nature in the life of the child, and it expresses Williamson's conviction that a loving, understanding relationship between parents and children is essential for the sound development of the personality. Phillip is afraid of his irritable father and is driven into himself and out of the house to the woods. Later, when he finds himself treating his own children in a way similar to that in which his father treated him, he tries to correct this tendency. The novel sequence shows that just as love and understanding between parents and children are necessary for the healthy development of the children, so love and understanding among nations are necessary for international peace and well-being. Convinced that World War I arose out of what he calls "un-understanding," Phillip tries in the aftermath of that war to foster friendship between Britain and Germany. Then, after World War II, he supports the ideal of European union recommended by Sir Hereward Birkin, who is based on Mosley. The theme of the importance of a sound British agriculture menaced by free trade and international finance that runs throughout the sequence was modeled on Mosley's farm policy.

Influenced by Leo Tolstoy's depiction of Russia in *War and Peace* (1865–1869), which he had read during World War II, Williamson in A Chronicle of Ancient Sunlight paints a picture of many aspects of British society from the 1890s to the late 1940s. The London novels provide a rich panorama of suburban life in Wakenham–based on Brockley–before World War I, while the war novels give an accurate and compelling presentation of conditions on the western front and on the home front. The battle scenes are unforgettable, and the portraits of Phillip's fellow combatants are striking. The best of the latter are those of Spectre West, the valiant volunteer officer who hates war, and Bill Kidd, who is superficially a loud miles gloriosus but is, in fact, genuinely brave. Phillip himself attains a hard-won courage, but his final "test to destruction" comes after the war when, having quixotically taken the blame for setting a hut on fire in south London, he is imprisoned for a month and loses his Distinguished Service Order. It is then that he realizes that "no man could be destroyed, once he had discovered poetry, the spirit of life," and begins his writing career. Williamson's portrayal of life in the 1930s and during World War II is less comprehensive because it is seen through Phillip's eyes. Phillip's struggles as a farmer in Norfolk before and during the war lead to a breach in the family and the sale of the farm. At the end of the sequence Phillip begins his great literary work.

In his last book, *The Scandaroon* (1972), which he had begun in 1955 and laid aside, Williamson returns to a north Devon setting for a tale of an exotic pigeon in the 1920s. After his eightieth birthday his health began to fail, and he died on 13 August 1977. By a strange coincidence he died on the day that the death of Tarka was being shot for the highly successful film of his book.

After Williamson's death the British Treasury accepted his considerable collection of manuscripts and typescripts under the National Heritage scheme; he was the first author to have this distinction. The papers are deposited at Exeter University. In 1980 the Henry Williamson Society was founded to encourage a wider readership and deeper understanding of Williamson's work. The society publishes a journal and holds two meetings each year, one in Devon and the other in some location connected with Williamson; there are talks, discussions, displays, walks, and motorcoach excursions. A major project of the society is the collection and collation of Williamson's ephemeral writings, which previously appeared in newspapers and magazines.

Under the editorship of John Gregory, several volumes have been published under the society's imprint.

Apart from his wildlife books, Henry Williamson's work is not well known. While his fictional technique is traditional, his sensibility is distinctly of the twentieth century. Readers who deprecate his political enthusiasms will find that they are not a barrier to enjoyment of his novels. Williamson was never racist nor anti-Semitic, nor did he condone aggression. Throughout his career he showed a deep concern for wildlife and an unpolluted environment; he always placed the highest value on love.

**Letters:**

Margaret White, "Letters to Brian Busby," *Henry Williamson Society Journal* (September 1994): 43–46.

**Interview:**

"Henry Williamson Talks to Kenneth Allsop," *Listener,* 79 (8 February 1968): 170–172.

**Bibliography:**

I. Waverney Girvan, *A Bibliography and a Critical Survey of the Works of Henry Williamson* (Chipping Campden: Alcuin, 1931).

**Biographies:**

Daniel Farson, *Henry: An Appreciation of Henry Williamson* (London: M. Joseph, 1982);

Lois Lamplugh, *A Shadowed Man: Henry Williamson 1845–1977,* revised edition (Dulverton, Somerset: Exmoor Press, 1991);

Anne Williamson, *Tarka and the Last Romantic* (Phoenix Mill, Far Thrupp, Gloucestershire: Sutton, 1995).

**References:**

J. W. Blench, "The Apprenticeship of a Novelist: The Early Unpublished Fiction of Henry Williamson," *Henry Williamson Society Journal ,* no. 17 (March 1988): 5–19; no. 18 (September 1988): 39–49; no. 19 (March 1989): 31–45;

Blench, "Bedfordshire in the Writings of Henry Williamson," *Henry Williamson Society Journal,* no. 17 (March 1988): 29–43;

Blench, "Henry Williamson and the Romantic Appeal of Fascism," *Durham University Journal,* 81 (December 1988): 123–139; ( June 1989): 289–305;

Blench, "Henry Williamson: Greatness Recognized," *Durham University Journal,* 74 ( June 1982): 257–268;

Blench, "Henry Williamson's *Salar the Salmon:* An Appraisal," *Durham University Journal,* 83 (July 1991): 223–234;

Blench, "Henry Williamson's *The Flax of Dream:* A Reappraisal," *Durham University Journal,* 76 (December 1983): 81–97;

Blench, "How Good is Henry Williamson's *Tarka the Otter* as Literature?," *Durham University Journal,* 80 (December 1987): 99–110;

Blench, "The Incalculable Hour," *Henry Williamson Society Journal,* no. 8 (October 1983): 18–21;

Blench, "The Influence of Richard Jefferies upon Henry Williamson," *Durham University Journal,* 79 (December 1986): 79–89; (June 1987): 327–347;

Blench, "The Literary Qualities of Henry Williamson's Writings Set in Norfolk," *Henry Williamson Society Journal,* no. 12 (September 1985): 10–29;

Peter Brandon, "Henry Williamson: The Early *Chronicle* and the Country and the City," *Henry Williamson Society Journal,* no. 3 (May 1981): 11–20;

Peter Cole, "The London Highlanders," *Henry Williamson Society Journal,* no. 14 (September 1986): 5–17;

Cole, "The 286th Machine Gun Company," *Henry Williamson Society Journal,* no. 18 (September 1988): 30–37;

Brian Fullagar, "The Lewisham of Henry Williamson," *Henry Williamson Society Journal,* no. 31 (September 1995): 33–42;

Fullagar, "What Time in Mist Confounds," *Henry Williamson Society Journal,* no. 24 (September 1991): 5–18;

John Glanfield, "Lindenheim," *Henry Williamson Society Journal,* no. 5 (May 1982): 5–13;

John Gregory, "Henry Williamson and the BBC," *Henry Williamson Society Journal,* no. 29 (March 1994): 5–32;

David Hoyle, "In the Monkey House," *Henry Williamson Society Journal,* no. 4 (November 1981): 6–16;

Hoyle, "'Reality in War Literature': Henry Williamson's Problems in the 1920s and 1930s," *Durham University Journal,* 74 (June 1982): 251–256;

Hoyle, "Some Thoughts on Class in the Novels of Henry Williamson," *Henry Williamson Society Journal,* no. 21 (March 1990): 5–20;

Hoyle, "Why I Think Henry Williamson Is Still Worth Reading," *Henry Williamson Society Journal,* no. 11 (April 1985): 15–28;

Terence Jones, "From Manuscript to Printed Edition," *Henry Williamson Society Journal,* no. 16 (September 1987): 3–6;

Douglas Jordan, "The Perfect Stranger," *Henry Williamson Society Journal,* no. 21 (March 1990): 30–34;

T. E. Lawrence, "A Criticism of Henry Williamson's *Tarka the Otter,*" in his *Men in Print: Essays in Literary Criticism,* edited by A. W. Lawrence (London: Golden Cockerell, 1940), pp. 41–54;

Peter Lewis, "The Hawthornden Prize," *Henry Williamson Society Journal,* no. 26 (September 1992): 32–49;

Lewis, "Shedding Light on Crow Point," *Henry Williamson Society Journal,* no. 24 (September 1991): 20–31;

Mick Loates, "South Devon Days in *The Innocent Moon,*" *Henry Williamson Society Journal,* no. 24 (September 1991): 39–44;

Diana Mosley, "The Politics of Henry Williamson," *Henry Williamson Society Journal,* no. 3 (May 1981): 21–22;

John Middleton Murry, "The Novels of Henry Williamson," in his *Katherine Mansfield and Other Literary Studies* (London: Constable, 1959), pp. 97–162;

Paul Reed, "The Bond That Must Never Be Broken," *Henry Williamson Society Journal,* no. 21 (March 1990): 38–47;

Reed, "Henry Williamson and the Kaiserschlact," *Henry Williamson Society Journal,* no. 15 (March 1987): 41–46;

Brocard Sewell, "*The Aylesford Review,*" *Henry Williamson Society Journal,* no. 5 (May 1982): 23–29;

Sewell, "Henry Williamson and *The Aylesford Review,*" *Henry Williamson Society Journal,* no. 13 (March 1986): 5–9;

Sewell, ed., *Henry Williamson: The Man, the Writings. A Symposium* (Padstow, Cornwall: Tabb House, 1980);

Fred Shepherd, "From Dandelion Days," *Henry Williamson Society Journal,* no. 20 (September 1989): 46–48;

Tom and Joan Skipper, "Henry Williamson's Bedfordshire Roots," *Henry Williamson Society Journal,* no. 6 (October 1982): 26–31;

David Stokes, "Living in Georgeham," *Henry Williamson Society Journal,* no. 12 (September 1985): 41–49;

Robert Tierney, "Places and Associations in *Young Phillip Maddison,*" *Henry Williamson Society Journal,* no. 15 (March 1987): 8–17;

Steven Trout, "Terrible 'Vicissitudes': Henry Williamson, *The Patriot's Progress*," *Focus on Robert Graves and His Contemporaries,* 2 (Spring 1993): 28–32;

Ronald Walker, "The Folkestone Connection," *Henry Williamson Society Journal,* no. 28 (September 1993): 40–51;

Walker, "The Honour of Life," *Henry Williamson Society Journal,* no. 27 (March 1993): 5–17;

Walker, "A Stray Shaft of Ancient Sunlight," *Henry Williamson Society Journal,* no. 4 (November 1981): 31–36;

Walker, "The 'Victory Day' Chapters of *The Dream of Fair Women,*" *Henry Williamson Society Journal,* no. 7 (May 1983): 10–16;

Herbert Faulkner West, *The Dreamer of Devon: An Essay on Henry Williamson* (London: Ulysses, 1932);

Anne Williamson, "The Genius of Friendship–Part I: T. E. Lawrence," *Henry Williamson Society Journal,* no. 27 (March 1993): 18–25;

Williamson, "The Genius of Friendship–Part II: Richard Aldington," *Henry Williamson Society Journal,* no. 28 (September 1993): 7–21;

Williamson, "A Note on the Falcon Maps," *Henry Williamson Society Journal,* no. 16 (September 1987): 19–21;

Williamson, "Roots: An Examination of Henry Williamson's Lineage," *Henry Williamson Society Journal,* no. 31 (September 1995): 6–32;

Williamson, "Tarka's Route," *Henry Williamson Society Journal,* no. 16 (September 1987): 19–21;

Colin Wilson, "Henry Williamson," in his *Eagle and Earwig* (London: Baker, 1967), pp. 225–238;

Wilson, "Henry Williamson," *Literary Review,* no. 29 (14–27 November 1980): 16–21.

**Papers:**

An important collection of manuscripts, typescripts, and correspondence is held in the Henry Williamson Archive in the University Library, Exeter; access is available to bona fide research students. Another collection is held by the Henry Williamson Literary Estate; access is not permitted to this collection. Williamson's letters to Richard Aldington are in Special Collections, Morris Library, Southern Illinois University, Carbondale.

# Romer Wilson
*(1891 – 11 January 1930)*

Maria Aline Seabra Ferreira
*Universidade de Aveiro*

BOOKS: *Martin Schüler* (London: Methuen, 1918; New York: Holt, 1919);

*If All These Young Men* (London: Methuen, 1919);

*The Death of Society: Conte de Fée Premier* (London: Collins, 1921); republished as *The Death of Society: A Novel of Tomorrow* (New York: Doran, 1921);

*The Grand Tour* (London: Methuen, 1923); republished as *The Grand Tour of Alphonse Marichaud* (New York: Knopf, 1923);

*Dragon's Blood: Conte de Fée Deuxième* (London: Collins, 1926; New York: Knopf, 1926);

*The Social Climbers: A Russian Middle-Class Tragedy in Four Acts, Seen through Western Eyes* (London: Benn, 1927);

*Latterday Symphony* (London: Nonesuch, 1927; New York: Knopf, 1927);

*Greenlow* (London: Collins, 1927; New York: Knopf, 1927);

*All Alone: The Life and Private History of Emily Jane Brontë* (London: Chatto & Windus, 1928); republished as *The Life and Private History of Emily Jane Brontë* (New York: Boni, 1928);

*The Hill of Cloves: A Tract on True Love, with a Digression upon an Invention of the Devil* (London: Heinemann, 1929);

*Tender Advice* (London & Toronto: Heinemann, 1935).

OTHER: *Green Magic: A Collection of the World's Best Fairy Tales from All Countries,* edited by Wilson (London: Cape, 1928; New York: Harcourt, Brace, 1928);

*Silver Magic: A Collection of the World's Best Fairy Tales from All Countries,* edited by Wilson (London: Cape, 1929; New York: Harcourt, Brace, 1929);

*Red Magic: A Collection of the World's Best Fairy Tales from All Countries,* edited by Wilson (London: Cape, 1930; New York: Harcourt, Brace, 1931).

*Romer Wilson*

Romer Wilson's novels, which possess a pronounced philosophical bent, address some of the most pressing concerns of the time in which she lived. Among the issues that figure in her books are World War I and its devastating effects on civilization and personal relationships, the demise of a predominantly rural world, the harmful consequences to the countryside and to people's lives of the introduction of machinery and the substitution of automation for manual labor, the role of the artist, and the difficulties of romantic relationships thwarted by war or societal conventions.

Florence Roma Muir Wilson was born in Sheffield in 1891 to Arnold Muir Wilson, a solicitor, and Amy Letitia Dearden Wilson. When she was fifteen, she enrolled at West Heath School; after four years there she went to Girton College,

Cambridge, to study law. She left college in 1914 and did war work selling potatoes for the Board of Agriculture.

Wilson's first published work, the novel *Martin Schüler* (1918), has Faustian and Nietzschean undertones. An admirer and imitator of Richard Wagner, the ruthlessly ambitious composer Martin, who lives in Heidelberg with his parents, dreams of creating "a counter-type of Tristan and Isolde and one or two Gotterdämmerungs." His goal can only be attained at the expense of other people—especially women, whom he seduces and discards after obtaining inspiration from them: "I cannot become the father of a child nor of a masterpiece without a woman," he says. "The beauty and the voluptuousness of women are necessary to me. There is no substitute. . . . I tell you, this portfolio is a record of my *affaires de coeur.* My brain becomes clear when I am intoxicated." He tells Sophie, the latest in a string of lovers: "I forget Hella von Rosenthal . . . as easily as a fledgling forgets its mother. . . . I may forget you." His masterpiece premieres at the Berlin Opera House on 1 June 1914 and is a huge success, but its author dies in the theater on the opening night.

Wilson's next novel, *If All These Young Men* (1919), begins on Easter 1918 and is an extended meditation on the effects of World War I. The inconclusiveness of the love affair of Josephine and Sebastian is a result of the instability caused by the war. Josephine "knew not the exact nature of war, she was become war; she had exchanged her heart and soul for it; her mind, her consciousness was completely formed of it." Sebastian "felt the war swinging beneath life. Everything was thrown out of the norm by it; everything was made strange, odd, mad and terrible." Unable to go to the front, Josephine can feel a sort of catharsis by dreaming of participating in the battle like a man:

"If I could only fight," she cried to herself. "If I could only fight," and her spirit flew up. She heard the bayonet go in; phantasmagorically she went through the pantomime of conversion to human sanity. Finally, she emerged cleansed, and reinstated herself in the dull monotony of endurance.

Josephine feels as though she is in a straitjacket, her range of action severely limited: "'Neither to love, neither to fight,' she suddenly cried to herself, 'but to live in constricted anguish, not to cry aloud, not to go mad.'" She finds a measure of consolation in contemplating the English countryside although the imagery in which her feelings are described suggests defeat: "she was a dead soul gone back into the earth out of life's intricate movements, and out of the madness of war"; she is "neither man nor woman, nor boy nor girl, but only a creature contemplating to no purpose the sky and grass, and wondering at them as if they were new sights created for her amazement and joy." The novel conveys the fragmented, inchoate feelings produced by a time of instability and uncertainty.

Wilson's third novel, *The Death of Society: Conte de Fée Premier* (1921), which was awarded the Hawthornden Prize, is the story of the love affair of Rane Smith, an Englishman, and Rosa Ingman, the Norwegian wife of a philosopher who has written books on Henrik Ibsen and Friedrich Nietzsche. Rosa and Rane can never fully articulate their feelings since she does not speak English and he does not speak Norwegian. Further complicating matters, Rosa's daughter also falls in love with Rane. The novel is pervaded by nostalgia for a utopian past, a time before society exerted its pernicious influence on human beings. Rosa believes that "in the old days before men and women obeyed laws" she and Rane might have had a chance to be happy. Rosa and Rane are, however, finally unable to break free from the fetters of conventional morality, and Rosa returns to her husband.

In a letter to Sidney Waterlow dated 3 May 1921 Virginia Woolf noted: "I am reading Miss Romer Wilson's new novel, which Jack Squire [J. C. Squire, former literary editor of *The New Statesman*] says is the greatest work of genius ever written by a woman (or words to that effect)." Woolf was, however, not impressed with the work:

Well, but I assure you, when Virginia's old, no one will be talking of Romer Wilson. What a book! What a perfect example of the faux bon; every attitude, scene & word, I should say matched in the old word shop of the minor poets: never a single thing seen for herself, or dared; & yet by taking all the scenery & supplying the appropriate words she has Squire, Lynd & Turner by the heel: another proof that what people dread is being made to feel anything: a certain kind of rhapsody makes them feel wild & adventurous; & they then make out that this is passion & poetry—so thankful to be let off the genuine thing.

The review in the *Times Literary Supplement* (5 May 1921) was a mixture of praise and sarcasm:

In *Death of Society* Miss Romer Wilson has given us what we are inclined to describe as an ecstasy in five convulsions. Convulsion the first occurs when an Englishman of the name of Smith, wandering in Norway, comes by chance to the house of Karl Ingman,

# MARTIN SCHÜLER

BY

ROMER WILSON

METHUEN & CO. LTD.
36 ESSEX STREET W.C.
LONDON

*Title page for Wilson's first novel, about a ruthlessly ambitious composer*

an elderly Norwegian critic . . . and falls an immediate and abject victim to the fascination of Rosa, wife of Karl. . . . It is all so rapturous and transcendental, indeed, that a prosaic reader may easily be left boggling. . . . We have to take the author's word for all this, and this act of faith, never easy, becomes almost impossible when we realize that the lady is about seventy-one years of age. Miss Romer Wilson herself does not realize it; she thinks that Ingman himself is sixty-four, and his wife some twenty years younger. . . . Yet there it is. "During my life," says Ingman, "Carlyle, Nietzsche, Wagner . . . have all produced work, together with Grieg, Byron, Browning." . . . A slip, of course, but an unfortunate one for it introduces an element of the grotesque into a situation already sufficiently difficult of acceptance. There is, nevertheless, something that we like about this book; there is both a mind and a heart behind it, and some of the dialogue is excellent.

After the war Wilson spent three weeks in Paris; the result of the trip was *The Grand Tour* (1923), an epistolary novel in which the thirty-

year-old Parisian sculptor Alphonse Marichaud narrates the story of his cosmopolitan life and travels and expatiates on his views of love and art. Marichaud is dissatisfied with his work as a sculptor as he confesses to a friend:

> I make a terrible confession, Girrard. My art is insufficient to me. . . . After summing up existence in a block of sculptured marble, there is still so much left over, so much I have been obliged to discard, to knock off life . . . that I am left with a regret, similar to that of a hero who, in order to obtain his goal, must neglect, even destroy, a thousand wonderful and interesting objects.

He tries his hand at writing but finds this experience frustrating as well.

In 1923 Wilson married a Bostonian, the anthologist Edward J. O'Brien, whom she met in Portofino, Italy, while correcting proofs for *The Grand Tour*. After their honeymoon they settled in Rapallo, where they had one son.

In Wilson's next novel, *Dragon's Blood: Conte de Fée Deuxième* (1926), Fritz Storm, the anti-Semitic son of a German parson, dreams of creating a completely new civilization with new values:

> We shall be free. . . . No more stinking factories . . . no more smoke-blackened pastures, no more hills and rivers disfigured with concrete abortions. No more hate! Incense of wood-smoke from home dwellings; incense of pine-forests in the wood; incense of peace in men's hearts! Freedom!

He founds the New Era Club to rescue civilization from what he believes is an inexorable downward slide, but the organization is dissolved almost immediately because of rivalry between Fritz and another member. Fritz goes on to become involved in several romantic situations and political schemes, including the murder of a former ally for which a prostitute takes the blame, and ends up in an insane asylum.

*Greenlow* (1927), Wilson's next novel, is a quite different kind of work from *Dragon's Blood*. A modern pastoral, it is a romantic tale pervaded by the colors and smells of the countryside. The narrator, Jillian Holt, lives with her sister, Minnie, in Greenlow, a hamlet in a remote valley in the Derbyshire uplands with about a dozen inhabitants. She reflects: "I have lived for twenty-five years, ever since I was born, at our house in the valley, and unless I marry some worldly man, shall no doubt die there. My father is dead and the house is mine." Jillian is half in love with the "good-for-nowt" Jim Thorpe, a slothful young man who spends most of his time in pubs. Jillian, however, has romantic dreams:

> I wish some handsome young man would come and kiss me. My husband will come. I have seen his shadow in the eyes of young men who have been about. . . . As surely as the grass is doomed to grow green, I am doomed to kneel down in front of some man and say, "My Lord, beat me!"

Her fantasies materialize with the arrival of a stranger, John Wetherford, who comes to spend the summer away from the bustle of London and invites her to return there with him. *Greenlow* chronicles Jillian's turmoil as she wavers between Jim and a peaceful, uneventful existence in her native hamlet, on the one hand, and her love for John, who represents life beyond the mountains that encircle the village, on the other. Ultimately, she chooses to leave with John.

Also published in 1927 was a play, *The Social Climbers: A Russian Middle-Class Tragedy in Four Acts Seen through Western Eyes,* about the fall of a Russian family from affluence to poverty as a result of the Bolshevik Revolution, and *Latterday Symphony,* a collection of novellas set against the background of London jazz society. In 1928 Wilson and her husband moved to Locarno, Switzerland. Wilson's *All Alone: The Life and Private History of Emily Jane Brontë* appeared that year. Also in 1928 Wilson edited *Green Magic: A Collection of the World's Best Fairy Tales from All Countries;* it was followed by similar collections, *Silver Magic* (1929) and *Red Magic* (1930).

Wilson's next novel, *The Hill of Cloves: A Tract on True Love, with a Digression upon an Invention of the Devil* (1928), is a philosophical work set in Italy and consisting mainly of the conversations of Giulio Benedetto and his friend Rinaldo. Giulio speaks at great length about his impossible love for Delia, who is to be married:

> That does not make me love her the less or wish that I was eighteen instead of thirty. She often comes to my garden, and I make love to her in terms of philosophy, and shall continue to do so until one or other of us is dead and possibly thereafter. Certainly thereafter. It will be pleasant to walk with Delia upon the hills of paradise and tell her those thoughts which she has given me on earth, and which she now laughs at.

Giulio and Rinaldo also discuss salvation and other religious matters. To see the sunrise they take a symbolic walk up a hill, "through the olive groves. A cock crows." The tale is pervaded with such biblical echoes and is concerned with the Fall of humanity and how to restore as much as possible the idyllic prelapsarian harmony with nature. Giulio inveighs against industrialization, which he sees as contributing to dehumanization and alienation from the earth. He tells Rinaldo the story of the people of Cathay, who

> ploughed with the ox and with the patient ox raised water from the well. Their women spun with their hands and the young men walked upon their feet. There was peace and contentment everywhere. The slaves were as sons and daughters to their masters, and sons and daughters were content to be as slaves. I am told that then the poorest wore silk and ate honey, and if tribulation visited the land, it visited all alike. But there came some who brought with them strange machines and devices so that after a while marvellous changes were seen, changes that you and I can hardly imagine, not only spinning machines and machines to make many things that are made by hand, but carts began to go without horses and ships without sails.

Just as Adam and Eve ate from the tree of knowledge and were expelled from Paradise, so the people of Cathay succumbed to the lure of machines and city life. Then began

> the greatest and the worst slavery the world has ever seen, for the people forgot the use of their hands and were bound to the machine for the very necessaries of life. In order to be near the machine, to serve it and to live by it, they forsook the country and left the soil untilled, so that farms and good lands lay empty and idle by the score, and they so crowded upon the cities that there was no longer any room therein for each man to have his family in his own house. Then they began to build one city upon another, until six or seven cities lay one upon another as happened in Babylon, and more lately in Rome of the Caesars, until it was forbidden by law. . . . Two results came of this unnatural servitude, one of which you may almost guess for yourself. I showed you how the farms were deserted and the soil left untilled. You may easily comprehend how in time there ceased to be an abundance of every kind of food, and when I tell you that in the towns, for a reason that is not clear to me, people bred like locusts and multiplied beyond imagination, you will immediately see how in the course of two hundred years they were brought to the verge of starvation when any accident of wars or other disaster cut off their traffic with those countries from which they drew sustenance in exchange for their manufactures. . . . A man learnt to live three lives and be content with none. Women aspired to be men as well as mothers, and both men and women began to go hither and thither at great speed, seeking the old peace they had lost and never finding it. All men and all women began to have a face, a face of discontent and fear . . . a face made like a mask, handsome and unlovable, haunted with eyes of fear. Further, owing to the noise of their machines, they grew deaf to natu-

ral sounds; their sight also became dim because one among them discovered how to imitate the sun for a few pence.

Giulio's story has a happy ending, however: an emperor "in whose heart the ancient virtues and the ancient simplicity were paramount" came to the throne and ordered all the machines to be thrown into great pits dug for that purpose outside the cities, and "very soon there arose a poet who wrote a sweet ode in praise of the Emperor, and . . . suddenly thereafter everyone burst out singing."

On 11 January 1930 Wilson died in Lausanne of tuberculosis. A collection of short stories, *Tender Advice,* was published posthumously in 1935.

Romer Wilson's novels, like those of other writers of the period such as Woolf, Rebecca West, Mary Agnes Hamilton, D. H. Lawrence, Richard Aldington, and Ford Madox Ford, mourn the passing of the civilization destroyed by World War I. They dramatize the desirability of recovering the values embodied by the countryside.

**References:**

Nigel Nicolson, ed., *A Change of Perspective: The Letters of Virginia Woolf,* volume 3 (London: Hogarth Press, 1977);

Sharon Ouditt, *Fighting Forces, Writing Women: Identity and Ideology in the First World War* (London & New York: Routledge, 1994).

# Esmé Wynne-Tyson

## (29 June 1898 – 17 January 1972)

### T. J. L. Wynne-Tyson

BOOKS: *Security* (London: Collins, 1926; New York: Doran, 1927);

*Quicksand* (London: Collins, 1927);

*Momus* (London: Collins, 1928);

*Melody* (London: Collins, 1929);

*Incense and Sweet Cane: A Novel* (London: Collins, 1930);

*Prelude to Peace: The World-Brotherhood Educational Movement* (London: Daniel, 1936);

*Men in the Same Boat,* by Wynne-Tyson and J. D. Beresford (London: Hutchinson, 1943);

*The Riddle of the Tower,* by Wynne-Tyson and Beresford (London: Hutchinson, 1944);

*The Gift,* by Wynne-Tyson and Beresford (London: Hutchinson, 1947);

*The Unity of Being* (London: Dakers, 1949);

*This Is Life Eternal: The Case for Immortality* (London: Rider, 1951; New York: Dutton, 1953);

*The Best Years of Their Lives,* as Peter de Morny (London: Centaur, 1953);

*Mithras: The Fellow in the Cap* (London: Rider, 1958; revised edition, Arundel: Centaur, 1972; New York: Barnes & Noble, 1972);

*The Philosophy of Compassion: The Return of the Goddess* (London: Vincent Stuart, 1962);

*The Dialectics of Diotima,* anonymous (Fontwell, Sussex: Centaur, 1969).

PLAY PRODUCTIONS: *The Prince's Bride,* London, Savoy Theatre, 2 February 1912;

*Little Lovers,* London, Aldwych Theatre, 22 October 1922;

*Security,* New York, Maxine Elliott's Theatre, 28 March 1929; London, Savoy Theatre, 13 March 1932;

*Forty Love,* London: Grafton Theatre, 4 October 1931.

OTHER: Porphyrius, *On Abstinence from Animal Food,* translated by Thomas Taylor, edited, with an introduction, by Wynne-Tyson (London: Centaur, 1965; New York: Barnes & Noble, 1965).

Although Esmé Wynne-Tyson would later see her five early novels as the least important aspect of her literary output, they trace the formative influences on a career and personal development that showed a remarkable progression throughout her life. An only child, Dorothy Estelle Esmé Ripper was born on 29 June 1898 at 26 Stansfield Road, Stockwell, London, to Harry Innes Ripper, a stockbroker, and Minnie Maude Pitt Ripper. It was not a happy marriage, as Wynne-Tyson's semi-autobiographical novel *Incense and Sweet Cane* (1930) shows, and Dodie (as her parents called her) suffered deeply from their frequent drinking and quarreling.

The theater was in Esmé Ripper's blood. Her mother's father, William Pitt, was a member of an amateur theatrical company; her mother and her aunts, Molly and Mona Pitt, all went on the stage, and Mona owned a touring company. Esmé Ripper was placed under contract on 13 October 1910 by the theatrical agent Italia Conti; three weeks later she was engaged by Herbert Trench, director of the Theatre Royal Haymarket, to act, dance, sing, and understudy in *The Blue Bird.* Her stage name was Esmé Wynne. The following year she was engaged by the impresario Charles Hawtrey to take the part of Rosamund in the first production of *Where the Rainbow Ends* at the Savoy Theatre.

In 1912 Hawtrey, who was as enchanted by Wynne as he was repelled by her bumptious but persistent fellow child actor Noel Coward, produced Wynne's play *The Prince's Bride* at the Savoy. This production aroused such jealousy in Coward—who, despite their close friendship, had long been envious of Wynne's star stature—that, he later admitted, it was at this point that he determined that writing plays would be his main goal. He and Wynne went on to collaborate on sketches, one-act plays, songs, and curtain-raisers, although little that was published or performed appeared under their joint names.

Wynne's stage career was interrupted by her parents' decision to send her to a Belgian convent in January 1914. The separation from her parents and

*Esmé Wynne-Tyson*

friends caused her great unhappiness, but the outbreak of World War I shortened her misery to only two terms at the convent. Although her father shared Edwardian middle-class society's reservations about the acting profession, he did not forbid her to resume her career. He also encouraged her to read widely in the classics of fiction, and he praised her writing. He also implanted in her a religious awe that worked powerfully on her vivid imagination. Her childhood achievements gave her the self-confidence that would manifest itself in her ability to persuade sophisticated and intelligent people to accept her ethical and religious convictions.

Wynne's working partnership with Coward ended when she was persuaded to choose between marriage and a stage career. On 22 June 1918 she

married Lynden Charles Tyson, an officer in the Royal Flying Corps; the couple combined her stage name with his surname to form the compound Wynne-Tyson. Lynden Wynne-Tyson was good-looking, bright, and ambitious, but he was also conventional in outlook and shared none of his wife's intellectual interests. Esmé Wynne-Tyson's last appearance in the theater was as Faith, a part Coward had written for her in his *I'll Leave It to You* (1920). In 1922 she became a convert to Christian Science. The couple's only child, Timothy Jon Lynden Wynne-Tyson, was born on 6 July 1924. On 7 December 1926 Lynden Wynne-Tyson was posted to Iraq, leaving his wife and son behind; he would be away for two years.

Throughout the 1920s Esmé Wynne-Tyson increased her already prolific output of journalism, short stories, and poetry in leading national newspapers and journals, besides completing her five early novels. These novels not only mirror the mores of the post-World War I middle class but also draw on the lives and personalities of those of the period's intelligentsia she numbered among her friends. In her first novel, *Security* (1926), the Mapletons appear to be a happy and successful family. It is gradually revealed, however, that Jean Mapleton, despite her calm and gentle exterior, dominates them all. She has engineered her daughters' ambitious marriages and will do the same for her son. Beyond her control are her husband's infidelities, which started early in their married life and which she pretends to herself do not exist. James Maplestone is currently having an affair with his secretary, Aline, who becomes pregnant and commits suicide. Badgered by Aline's vengeful sister, Lillith, James, too, kills himself, with Jane's tacit encouragement. Although she does not love him, Jane marries the diplomat Sir Daniel Marchant because he can control the career of her son-in-law and, therefore, the happiness of her daughter Rosanne.

Although Wynne-Tyson later found her first novel a "rather artificial book—worldly and not really me," her portrait of the monstrous, middle-aged Jane is powerful. The period touches are excellent, revealing many details of the social life of the time. *The Daily Telegraph* (26 November 1926) said that "very few first novels show such a mastery of style. There is, indeed, nothing amateurish about it in the plot or in the telling. . . . If so promising a beginning is maintained, Miss Wynne-Tyson will soon rank high as a novelist." Wynne-Tyson adapted the novel as a stage play that was well received both in New York and in London.

An adaptation of her play *Little Lovers* (1922), Wynne-Tyson's next novel, *Quicksand* (1927), is based on an episode from her own marriage. Twenty-four-year-old Paul Myse—based on Coward—and his twenty-one-year-old sister, Pauline, live together in a studio flat in Chelsea; he writes and composes songs, and she writes poetry and short stories. After Pauline marries, Paul meets Dennis Wode, a former lover of Pauline's, and mischievously invites him to a party at which Pauline will be present. The attraction between Pauline and Dennis is rekindled, and they begin an affair. Pauline decides to leave her husband for Dennis, but he is afraid that the scandal will cost him his inheritance, and he breaks off the affair. Instead of returning home, she seeks refuge in a hotel in Sussex. Paul finds her and suggests that they live together again. She tells him that she is pregnant and that, although she does not love her husband, she must return to him; she will never, however, admit to him her affair with Dennis.

Although the first few chapters are sometimes irritatingly lightweight, the novel's purpose, as the dust-jacket blurb says, is to show that "behind the cynicism and frivolity of our much condemned younger generation there is a significant searching for a more solid happiness than that offered by the world's panaceas of friendship, marriage, love affairs, work and fame . . . their excuse is that divine discontent which always presses on often blindly—towards an anchorage which is not of quicksand." The novel was described by the *Morning Post* (14 April 1927) as providing "most entertaining pictures of the life of artists of all types in London and Paris." The reviewer for *Punch* (31 August 1927) said:

> From the first chapter you would never guess—at least I hope you would not, as I didn't—that, by the last, *Pauline* would be ready to find her happiness in "living for others—a child she had not wanted, and a husband she had never loved"—and *Paul,* not so far advanced in understanding of life as she is, beginning to suspect something more satisfying beyond the pursuit of pleasures. It is all remarkably well done, and I classed the novel as "froth," quite as Mrs. Wynne-Tyson meant me to, until very nearly the end, when the depth and sincerity of her inspiration dawned on me, just as the real meaning of life was dawning on *Paul* and *Pauline*. The frivolous pages make most amusing reading, and the "conversion" chapters, to use an old-fashioned word as a short cut, fit on to them perfectly and, for the reader of a naturally serious "turn," put the whole book into a much higher category than that to which it seems at first to belong.

The *Manchester Guardian* (29 April 1927) declared that Wynne-Tyson had written "an entertaining novel about charming people and, putting thought into it, provokes thought for others."

Wynne-Tyson's third novel, *Momus* (1928), takes its title from the god of ridicule, who was expelled from Olympus when he jeered at the creation of humanity; Wynne-Tyson described it in a letter of 3 February 1961 as "the 'imagined' love affair between Bernard Shaw and Mrs. Pat[rick] Campbell." The critic David Hest uses ridicule to destroy what he considers the false gods of his generation. One author he mocks is the beautiful, self-centered romantic novelist Alys Lesage. She meets and tries to charm Hest, but, although he is attracted to her, he spurns her advances. His review of her next work describes it as second-rate and shallow, and her reputation never recovers. Years later, in 1914, Alys is fifty, widowed, with two grown sons; Hest is fifty-nine and, in keeping with his philosophical credo, involved in a celibate marriage. His wife, Martha, attacks him for not being concerned about the war, which she believes is humanity's punishment for wickedness and blasphemy—sins to which Hest has contributed. He realizes that she is bitter about their childless and abnormal marriage and moves out of the house into his London chambers. He takes part in a debate with Alex Wiston who has written militaristic articles opposing Hest's pacifist writing in another paper. The debate is well attended, both men giving speeches that are still relevant today. Hearing that Alys has lost a son in the war, and feeling guilt for his past treatment of her, he calls to console her. He is concerned by her distress and tries to comfort her with his metaphysical beliefs; but Alys cannot accept or understand them. She is, however, helped by his sympathy. A friendship develops between them, but when the gossip columns begin to comment on their being together, he returns to Martha. When Alys's second son is killed, he again tries to comfort her and even declares his love for her; but, despite her willingness, he refuses to make love to her. Over the next several years Alys marries twice, but she nurtures a hatred of Hest both for his early treatment of her work and his more recent rejection of her love. His exposition of his philosophy of pacifism and celibacy, *The Life Beautiful,* is receiving great acclaim and has influenced the thinking of the younger generation in postwar Britain. Alys puts together extracts from the many love letters she has received during her life, including Hest's, and writes a book that makes it appear that Hest was her lover. His reputation destroyed, Hest leaves England. Alys then reads *The Life Beautiful* and finds that it brings her peace and comfort. Regretting the harm she has done to its author, she turns over to a group of Hest's disciples all of the letters and a signed confession that Hest was never her lover. She falls ill; Hest writes to thank her and ask if he might come to see her; but she dies in her sleep, clutching his letter. Perhaps the most difficult of Wynne-Tyson's early novels—its "brilliant effect" marred, in the eyes of the reviewer in the *Times Literary Supplement* (6 December 1928), by "pitiless cleverness in the execution"—*Momus* was later described by the author as her favorite of the five early novels. She was, however, conscious of their immature aspects. Her old friend Coward, in a letter written in October 1928 that he signed "Alys Lesage," said that he thought it was

> by far the best thing you've ever done and all the important parts of the book are very well written. I think your characterisations of D. H. and Alys are extremely good and the scene quite early on where Martha turns on David first rate, as are also all the later scenes between Alys and David. I think your theme and story are completely consistent and worked out to their ultimate conclusion quite splendidly. And now for the Buts.

> My only criticisms are of the superficial and comparatively unimportant side of your work (except that I consider detail vitally important to the making of a whole). You have a serene and maddening disregard for superficial details which destroys atmosphere in exactly the places where you wish by using them to create it. . . . you announce blithely on the last page that Hest had been working before the mast and having the most amazing experiences. My sweet inconsequent high-minded love, did it not strike you that a man of 70, however agile and intelligent, would be of little or no use either before or behind the mast? This was very tiresome of you as it made me laugh, at a place where I didn't want to laugh, at the thought of the poor old dear straining his aged sinews at that advanced age. . . . Apart from all this carping the real part of your book is streets ahead of anything else you've ever done, as I said before, and written without mawkishness and remarkably without bias and with the various points of view clearly and honestly defined—so therefore you ought to be proud of yourself.

Lynden Wynne-Tyson's return from the Middle East on 9 July 1928 did not close the emotional and intellectual gulf that had developed between them. The following year, when they were living in a residential hotel for the families of RAF officers serving at Henlow Aerodrome in Bedfordshire, Lynden embarked on an affair with another officer's wife.

In Wynne-Tyson's next novel, *Melody* (1929), Martyn Frome, a successful author, and his fiancée, Carol Merrin, build their dream house in a northern London suburb; they call it Melody. After a day in town buying furnishings for the house, Martyn insists that they attend a literary tea party. Carol can-

not keep up with the witty conversation, and Martyn feels that she has embarrassed him. Carol leaves the party, and Martyn renews his acquaintance with Bliss Storme, a beautiful and talented young writer and dancer. She has just been jilted by her lover, a writer named Sholto. Martyn misinterprets her mood, assuming her to be in love with him, and breaks off his engagement to Carol. He offers to let her have Melody, but she declines. Martyn and Bliss marry and move into Melody. Their marriage deteriorates, and Bliss resumes her affair with Sholto. Carol, who has been working in a Sussex home where children who have been given up by the medical fraternity are restored to health through prayer, publishes a successful book about her religious beliefs. Martyn meets her again at a literary dinner at which she is the guest of honor. When he discovers Bliss's affair with Sholto, he decides to divorce her and marry Carol; but Bliss has been rejected by Sholto and refuses to give Martyn a divorce. He decides to remain with her and give Melody to Carol for her children's home. This time, she accepts.

*Melody* is based on a period in Wynne-Tyson's life when she considered leaving her husband for an old flame, the writer E. Nils Holstius; Carol's religious beliefs are a reflection of the author's allegiance to Christian Science. The *Morning Post* (12 December 1929) found the work to be "a seriously conceived story, with some good character drawing of a set which lacks any directing power save the fulfilment of its immediate passions," but was not interested in Carol's religious ideas. Like all of Wynne-Tyson's books, *Melody* is an engrossing read but suffers from the problem of how to make an essentially good person interesting. The novel has few period touches to delight the modern reader but indicates the direction that her work was to take in later years.

Although they would not divorce until 1947, Wynne-Tyson and her husband separated in 1930. That year the last of Wynne-Tyson's early novels, *Incense and Sweet Cane*, was published. It is the story of the unhappy marriage of Clive and Betty Brade as seen through the eyes of their daughter, Mercia, who is eight years old when the novel opens. Clive is bitter because his academic career was interrupted by World War I; Betty is discontented with their quiet life and relative poverty. When Betty's nouveau riche friends introduce them to Auriol, a young writer, Clive falls in love with her. Life is made miserable for Mercia as she watches her parents quarreling without understanding the reason for their unhappiness. She and Betty vacation at a seaside guest house, where a handsome fellow guest is attracted to Betty, and a brief affair ensues. Clive's attempt at a writing career ends after he has two stories published; Betty gives him neither understanding nor encouragement, and she jeers at his lack of success. Clive begins to drink heavily and becomes physically abusive to Betty.

Finally, Clive and Betty send Mercia to a convent school, where she is homesick and frightened. After two weeks she becomes ill from the strain and dies. Clive agrees to stay with Betty, feeling that it is the least he can do to atone for Mercia's unhappiness.

Perhaps the best of Wynne-Tyson's early novels, *Incense and Sweet Cane* has strong characterizations: the selfish and silly mother and her weak but sensitive husband, though only partly based on the author's parents, are more rounded personalities than any drawn in her previous books, where her characters tend to be mouthpieces for her ideas. The *Daily News* (2 April 1930) welcomed "a sensitive and penetrating study of an only child and her suffering over the quarrels and disagreements of her parents," while Sheila Kaye-Smith in the *Sunday Express* (16 March 1930) found the novel to be "one of the most touching studies of a child that I have read—poor little Mercia suffering so sympathetically and sensitively in the quarrels of her parents, longing and praying for them to be friends, rejoicing in their reconciliations and short weeks of unity. . . . so exquisite is the author's skill, so profound her sense of pathos and her knowledge of her little heroine's mind. . . . I recommend it to those who want to think as well as to those who want to have their feelings stirred."

In 1936 Wynne-Tyson published *Prelude to Peace: The World-Brotherhood Educational Movement*, which advocated a reformed system of education. In 1939 she embarked on the most productive friendship of her life: a collaboration with the novelist J. D. Beresford. As she explained their relationship in a letter to Holstius of 3 January 1958:

> Between us, we realized that we had the essence of the highest spiritual Truth so far known to man and that the one thing we must do was to collaborate in bringing it to the notice of the world. We could both write. He had quite a considerable public, and I had all the ideas that he had been lacking for some years. But first we had to get our personal relationship right. He was deeply and absolutely in love for the first time in his life—at 65. He had no reservations at all. I had the firm reservation that, having outgrown sexuality, I was not going to be dragged back to that bondage for anything in the world. I had dedicated my life to God at the age of 24, and the work we proposed to do together could not, in my opinion, possibly be done by two people living in adultery. He to whom the physical expression of love had been a minor consideration all his life felt, at first, that I was giving it too much importance. But when he saw that our relationship must either be completely non-physical or non-existent, he agreed to come my way. And there followed eight years of the most perfect love and companionship that either of us had ever known.

*Esmé Wynne and her friend and collaborator, Noel Coward, in 1917 (courtesy of T. J. L. Wynne-Tyson)*

This intense mental and working "marriage" would continue until Beresford's death in 1947. *Men in the Same Boat* (1943), the first of the three collaborations that were published under their joint names, is the story of seven survivors—ranging from a simple seaman to a religious mystic—of a torpedoed ship. Adrift in a lifeboat with no hope of rescue, they talk of many subjects, including life after death. By the end of the first part, all have died. The second shows each of them in another existence, fulfilling his own idea of happiness without memory of his former state. The *Daily Telegraph* (13 August 1943) said that "both the authors have brought their proved powers of character-building and bold imagination" to the work. In the *Manchester Guardian* (13 August 1943) Wilfrid Gibson welcomed a novel of profound significance that "in the hands of such accomplished writers is developed to its full possibilities."

"Read this awful warning. It is a great feat of the imagination," said John Betjeman in the *Daily Herald* (25 October 1944) about Wynne-Tyson and Beresford's second work. *The Riddle of the Tower* (1944) is a novel about humanity's descent, through successful regimentation and mechanization, to the condition of insects.

Although it received a scathing review by Howard Spring in the *Sunday Graphic* (14 September 1947), *The Gift* (1947), the final collaborative novel, was praised by Joseph Taggart in *The Star* (15 September 1947) for its "striking sincerity" and by the *Western Mail* (2 October 1947) as "one of the most challenging stories published of recent years . . . a beautifully etched portrait of a young man who in thought and deed practises the Christian ethics." The book received enough enthusiastic reviews to send it through three editions, but in the postwar period few readers could respond to Beresford's insistence that "we have a fierce need of the mystic to save us from the futility of a world we understand."

In a sense, Beresford's death did not end the collaboration, as Wynne-Tyson continued to write books and articles reflecting and expanding their shared interests and convictions. Her two major works of nonfiction in her final years were *Mithras: The Fellow in the Cap* (1958) and *The Philosophy of Compassion: The Return of the Goddess* (1962). The former traces the relevance of Mithraism to the present human predicament and comes to disturbing conclusions about orthodox Christianity. The latter, though also focusing on the origins of Christianity, might be seen in today's terms as a work of "deep feminist" scholarship. According to the *Times Literary Supplement* (4 May 1962), "the author ascribes the present calamitous state of mankind to centuries of purely masculine patriarchal rule of power which superseded the once peaceable reign of the Wisdom Goddess, to whose worship, she, like [Carl] Jung,

would recall us." *The Scotsman* (23 May 1962) called the work a "scholarly study marked by a wealth of reference to and actual quotation from the literature of the classical world and of ancient Egypt and the East, which indicates a discerning as well as a weighty erudition." Not content within the confines of Christian Science orthodoxy, she developed a personal philosophy that included not only an advanced vision of feminism but also a stringent skepticism toward both religious orthodoxy and scientific "progress." Her compassionate concern for all forms of sentient life anticipated the modern animal-rights movement. As editor of the magazine *World Forum* from 1961 to 1970, she supported the ideals of nonviolence, universal brotherhood, and individual regeneration.

Wynne-Tyson spent her last twenty years in Selsey, Sussex, as a highly productive recluse. She was denied the wide recognition that many believed her contributions deserved, but this situation was in accordance with her wishes: she abhorred the cult of personality. She died on 17 January 1972.

Repudiation of two careers—acting and novel writing—when further success seemed assured might suggest a dilettantish nature. In fact, Esmé Wynne-Tyson was determined from her early years to explore the mysteries of life, to find a purpose, and to attain the highest understanding possible. This compulsion to "put off childish things" rather than take the easier route of developing talents offering more-material rewards was beyond the comprehension of some of her less perceptive friends. Nevertheless, most of them retained their affection and admiration for her.

**References:**

Clive Fisher, *Noël Coward* (London: Weidenfeld & Nicolson, 1992);

Philip Hoare, *Noël Coward* (London: Sinclair-Stevenson, 1995; New York: Simon & Schuster, 1995);

Jon Wynne-Tyson, *Marvellous Party: A Comedy in Two Acts* (London: Calder, 1989; New York: Riverrun Press, 1989);

Wynne-Tyson, "A Passionate Rationalist," *Aryan Path*, 43 (April 1972): 156–159.

# Francis Brett Young
## (29 June 1884 – 28 March 1954)

### Jacques Leclaire
*Université de Rouen*

BOOKS: *Undergrowth,* by Brett Young and Eric Brett Young (London: Secker, 1913; New York: Dutton, 1920);

*Robert Bridges: A Critical Study,* by Brett Young and Eric Brett Young (London: Secker, 1914; Folcroft, Pa.: Folcroft Press, 1970);

*Deep Sea* (London: Secker, 1914);

*The Dark Tower* (London: Secker, 1915; New York: Knopf, 1926);

*The Iron Age* (London: Secker, 1916);

*Five Degrees South* (London: Secker, 1917);

*Marching on Tanga (with General Smuts in East Africa)* (London: Collins, 1917; New York: Dutton, 1917; revised edition, London: Collins, 1919; New York: Dutton, 1927);

*The Crescent Moon* (London: Secker, 1918; New York: Dutton, 1919);

*Captain Swing: A Romantic Play of 1830,* by Young and W. Edward Stirling (London: Collins, 1919);

*Poems, 1916–1918* (London: Collins, 1919; New York: Dutton, 1920);

*The Young Physician* (London: Collins, 1919; New York: Dutton, 1920);

*The Tragic Bride* (London: Secker, 1920; New York: Dutton, 1921);

*The Black Diamond* (London: Collins, 1921; New York: Dutton, 1921);

*The Red Knight: A Romance* (London: Collins, 1921; New York: Dutton, 1922);

*Pilgrim's Rest* (London: Collins, 1922; New York: Dutton, 1923);

*Woodsmoke* (London: Collins, 1924; New York: Dutton, 1924);

*Cold Harbour* (London: Collins, 1924; New York: Knopf, 1925);

*Sea Horses* (London: Cassell, 1925; New York: Knopf, 1925);

*Portrait of Clare* (London: Heinemann, 1927); republished as *Love Is Enough* (New York: Knopf, 1927);

*The Key of Life* (London: Heinemann, 1928; New York: Knopf, 1928);

*The Furnace: A Play in Four Acts,* by Young and William Armstrong (London: Heinemann, 1928; New York: Knopf, 1929);

*My Brother Jonathan* (London: Heinemann, 1928; New York: Knopf, 1928);

*Black Roses* (London: Heinemann, 1929; New York: Harper, 1929);

*Jim Redlake* (London: Heinemann, 1930); republished as *The Redlakes* (New York: Harper, 1930);

*Mr. and Mrs. Pennington* (London: Heinemann, 1931; New York: Harper, 1931);

*The Francis Brett Young Omnibus* (London: Collins, 1932)—comprises *The Black Diamond, The Young Physician, The Red Knight;*

*The House under the Water* (London: Heinemann, 1932; New York: Harper, 1932);

*Blood Oranges* (London: White Owl Press, 1932);

*The Cage Bird and Other Stories* (London: Heinemann, 1933; New York: Harper, 1933);

*This Little World* (New York: Harper, 1934; London: Heinemann, 1934);

*White Ladies* (London: Heinemann, 1935; New York: Harper, 1935);

*Far Forest* (London: Heinemann, 1936; New York: Reynal & Hitchcock, 1936);

*They Seek a Country* (London: Heinemann, 1937; New York: Reynal & Hitchcock, 1937);

*Portrait of a Village* (London: Heinemann, 1937; New York: Reynal & Hitchcock, 1938);

*Dr. Bradley Remembers* (London: Heinemann, 1938; New York: Reynal & Hitchcock, 1938);

*The Christmas Box* (London: Heinemann, 1938);

*The City of Gold* (London: Heinemann, 1939; New York: Reynal & Hitchcock, 1939);

*Mr. Lucton's Freedom* (London: Heinemann, 1940); republished as *The Happy Highway* (New York: Reynal & Hitchcock, 1940);

*Cotswold Honey, and Other Stories* (London: Heinemann, 1940); republished as *The Ship's Surgeon's Yarn, and Other Stories* (New York: Reynal & Hitchcock, 1940);

*A Man about the House: An Old Wives' Tale* (London: Heinemann, 1942; New York: Reynal & Hitchcock, 1942);

*The Island* (London: Heinemann, 1944; New York: Farrar, Straus, 1946);

*In South Africa* (London: Heinemann, 1952).

**Collection:** *The Novels of Francis Brett Young,* Severn Edition, 26 volumes (London: Heinemann, 1934–1956)–includes *Wistanslow* (1956).

OTHER: Olive Schreiner, *The Story of an African Farm,* introduction by Brett Young (New York: Modern Library, 1927);

Edwin Cerio, *That Capri Air,* foreword by Brett Young (London: Heinemann / New York: Harper, 1929);

*A Century of Boys' Stories,* edited by Brett Young (London: Hutchinson, 1935);

"The Doctor in Literature," in *Essays by Divers Hands: Being the Transactions of the Royal Society of Literature,* third series, 15 (London, 1936), pp. 17–35.

One of the major realistic novelists in England between the world wars, Francis Brett Young became Heinemann's leading novelist after the death of John Galsworthy. An early admirer and friend of D. H. Lawrence, he consciously wrote in reaction to Lawrence's work, insisting on creating normal and balanced characters rather than neurotic ones. The practice of medicine both in peacetime and in wartime played an important part in defining Brett Young's vision of human beings as essentially courageous and noble, as well as his keen sense of the interrelation between the physical and the spiritual. In all of his work there is a tension between the idealism of the poet and musician and the matter-of-factness of the doctor. Although he was a friend of leading literary and political figures of his day, he never became part of any literary coterie. His deceptively straightforward stories were misunderstood by academic critics, who did not realize that their real structure is musical. His work, which represents the near perfection of poetic realism, has two geographic poles: the "Black Country," with North Bromwich (Birmingham) as the City of Iron, and South Africa, with Johannesburg as the City of Gold.

Francis Brett Young was born at The Laurels, Halesowen–the Halesby of his novels–on 29 June 1884, the first child of Thomas Brett Young, M.D., and Annie Elizabeth Jackson Young. He had three siblings: Doris, born in 1891; Eric, born in 1893; and Joyce, born in 1895.

Brett Young won a scholarship to Epsom College, near London; the school is evoked in his novel *The Young Physician* (1919), as is his mother's 1898 death. He enrolled as a medical student at Birmingham University in 1900. There he started writing poems and stories, set poems to music, and joined the Octette, a group of artistic medical students. He received his medical degree in 1906.

Brett Young first practiced medicine as a ship's surgeon on the S.S. *Kintuck* in 1906–1907, an experience that he would use in some of his short stories and in his novel *Sea Horses* (1925). In 1907 he became a general practitioner in Brixham, Devon. On 28 December 1908 he eloped with Jessie Hankinson, a physical-training teacher he had met at a student dance in 1904; they were married in Rowberrow Church, Somerset. Brett Young liked to call his wife Jessica, and she eventually adopted the name. She would later become a professional singer.

In collaboration with his brother, Eric, Brett Young published the novel *Undergrowth* in 1913 and a study of Robert Bridges's poetry in 1914. Francis Brett Young's knowledge of fishermen's harsh lives provided the material for his novel *Deep Sea* (1914), which was followed by *The Dark Tower* (1915). *The Iron Age* (1916) is a saga of iron manufacturers and how they benefited from World War I.

Brett Young served as medical officer during the 1916 campaign of Gen. Jan Smuts in German East Africa (now Tanzania) until he was invalided out with malaria. He decided to make his living from writing rather than medicine, which placed too much of a strain on his health. From his experience in Africa he produced a volume of poetry, *Five Degrees South* (1917), which was later included in his *Poems, 1916–1918* (1919), and *Marching on Tanga (with General Smuts in East Africa)* (1917), which Rudyard Kipling considered one of the best war books he had ever read. It is a tribute to the courage of the British soldiers, who, hacking their way on foot through virgin country and suffering from tropical diseases, had outstripped the Germans, who had the use of a railway. The book is not a mere diary; a sensitive and poetic mind renders the beauty of places and people while remaining deeply conscious of the folly of war. The novelist's African experience also forms the background of *The Crescent Moon* (1918), a romantic shocker that was the first of an intended trilogy; the second was *Sea Horses,* and the third was never written.

In 1919 Brett wrote *The Tragic Bride* (1920). The novel is set in Lapton Huish, Devon, near Totnes, between 1901 and 1903. The heroine, Gabrielle, makes the best of a depressing marriage and is visited by the decrepit and fossilized specimens of county society. At his publisher's suggestion Brett Young and his wife moved to Capri, where the cost

*Francis Brett Young in 1927*

of living was lower and the climate was better for his health. There he wrote *The Black Diamond* (1921), which introduces the reader to the life of miners and navvies in Halesby and on the Welsh Water Scheme. When life becomes unbearable for Abner Fellows at his father's home in the Black Country, he tramps into the Marches of Wales in an attempt to regenerate himself—a typical strategy of Brett Young's heroes in moments of crisis. Because Fellows lacks adequate language to deal with delicate situations, he fails in his relationships with women. After getting drunk he enrolls in the army, offering an example of how young men become "food for powder"—an alternative title Brett Young considered for the novel. Brett Young was disheartened when the novel was only a succès d'estime. The *Times Literary Supplement* (24 February 1921) said: "If there were in this country a Prix Goncourt, this is the kind of novel that should gain it; it is certainly better than many French novels that have been so rewarded. . . . The effect of elaborate realism, in which he is so accomplished, is transitory; but the undying flame of passionate simplicity is glimmering there: he has only to cherish it."

*The Red Knight* was published in the fall of 1921. It is a love story set against the background of a communist takeover in the fictitious country of Tinacria, a thinly disguised Italy. Brett Young's

main interest in the novel is in character development rather than in working out a political hypothesis. The *Times Literary Supplement* (6 October 1921) commented: "he has taken a plunge this time into high romance, with an imaginary Southern Republic for its scene. We are glad that he should be so adventurous."

In 1921 Brett Young traveled to South Africa at the invitation of relatives in Johannesburg, visiting a small mining town in the Low Veld called Pilgrim's Rest. His impressions became the germ of two novels that were originally intended as one work. *Pilgrim's Rest* (1922) is the story of John Hayman, a gold digger, and is set against the background of the great 1913 miners' strike on the Rand. The *Times Literary Supplement* (30 November 1922) said:

> This time it is the more subtly dangerous metalled roadways of the Rand, heavy with gold fever, that his hero treads. . . . The lyricism which is so marked a characteristic of the author, subdued by the tenseness of the action, springs up most brightly when the description touches trees and flowers, or the delicate beauty of womanhood. The various strands of life are woven into a bold pattern which carries with it the conviction that in the struggle to maintain his integrity of mind a man finds happiness and the reason of his existence.

*Woodsmoke* (1924) details the safari of J. D. Rawley and his wife, Janet, through the Masai steppe and along the Pangani and the Pembe Rivers under the guidance of Jimmy Antrim.

The Brett Youngs divided their time between Capri and England from 1919 until 1940. Among their friends in Capri were Edwin Cerio, Norman Douglas, F. Scott and Zelda Fitzgerald, Louis Golding, D. H. and Frieda Lawrence, Compton Mackenzie, C. K. Scott Moncrieff, Charles and Hilda Morgan, and Axel Munthe. In England they stayed at first in various places in Wales and between 1928 and 1932 at Esthwaite Lodge, near Hawkshead, in the Lake District. They were on friendly terms with John Drinkwater, Thomas Hardy, Bernard Shaw, and H. G. Wells. In 1923 Young attended his first P.E.N. Club dinner. He and his wife traveled to Cairo in 1924–1925 and to the United States in 1926–1927 for a series of sixteen lectures given in New York City, Boston, Pittsburgh, and Chicago.

*Portrait of Clare* (1927; published in the United States as *Love Is Enough,* 1927) was begun in 1924 partly as reaction against the obsessions of Lawrence and James Joyce. Brett Young declared: "I am determined to write a book about normal people with normal reactions, and if I can't make it beautiful I'll eat my hat." In his preface he calls Clare "a normal and (possibly) a rather silly woman moving quite unimportantly across the West Midland landscape which I loved and which had already established itself as my chosen scene." The novel is one of his masterpieces, not only for its variety of tone but also for its rich gallery of characters between Queen Victoria's Diamond Jubilee in 1897 and the aftermath of World War I in 1920. For the first time Brett Young makes extensive use of a symphonic construction: the novel is organized in sonata form, with methodic progression and recurrence of themes. The main theme is that of Clare, who is always associated with passages of great beauty; the contrasting theme is that of Steven, Clare's son, and goes through a series of variations, with changing keys, on his willfulness as he develops from an enticing child into a besotted bigot married to a vulgar, jealous, spoiled woman. The first three books take the reader from 1897 to March 1900; they begin as an allegro in a major key on the raptures of Clare's romantic marriage to Ralph Hingston, the son of the industrial magnate Sir Joseph Hingston, who later becomes Lord Wolverbury. Brett Young excels at describing the birth of love in young people, and their radiantly happy honeymoon in Capri is rendered with poetic echoes of the "Song of Solomon." It is accompanied by the humorously ironic counterpoints of Clare's atheist grandfather, Dr. Weir, and

Aunt Cathie, a model of Victorian propriety with county connections, judging and judged by the buzzing social activity of the newly rich Hingstons. But there is also the graver counterpoint of death: first that of Dr. Weir, then that of Ralph during the Boer War. The various characters' houses play an active part in the novel, each with its own personality: Dr. Weir's unpretentious but eminently respectable Pen House; Uffdown, the old manor house where Ralph and Clare live, which is permeated by the aura of Annabel Ombersley, its eighteenth-century lady; and Sir Joseph and Lady Hingston's Stourford Castle, with its sham stucco battlements.

The second movement carries the novel from 1908 to 1914; it is the rather sinister story of Clare's marriage of convenience with Dudley Wilburn, the family solicitor, her distress in the Victorian Gothic Tudor House, the violent antagonism of Steven and Dudley, and Clare's and Dudley's final separation. In this section death is uppermost, with the suicide of Clare's brother-in-law, "Carnation" Ernest Wilburn, an attractive and womanizing dandy who goes bankrupt; the deaths of the hundreds of miners who lose their lives in the Sedgebury Main Colliery disaster in 1908; and the decline and death of Aunt Cathie. There is also spiritual death: Clare's love for Dudley does not last; the bankruptcy of the firm of Wilburn, Wilburn and Wilburn ruins many; and the whole world founders in the maelstrom of World War I.

The third section offers a satiric picture of the training camp at Pedworth on Salisbury Plain, drawn directly from the author's memories. There Clare meets and falls in love with Colonel Hart, and his daughter, Miranda, becomes Steven's wife. Colonel Hart combines the glamour of Ralph and the culture and tact of Ernest Wilburn with something of Dudley's earnestness and reliability. The novel is saved from sentimentality by Clare's surprising but convincing questioning of the reality of her radiant love for Ralph. Above all, she reaches the modern but daring realization that her first duty is to herself: that a woman of forty is still capable of love and of starting a new life. Clare is a new type of fictional character, a middle-aged woman in full possession of her womanhood.

The novel established Brett Young's reputation as a writer. It won the James Tait Black Memorial Prize, and it sold well. The first review, by Hugh Walpole, appeared in the *New York Herald Tribune* (20 March 1927): "This new novel is a most interesting challenge to the modern manner of Mr. Joyce, Mr. Huxley, and Mrs. Virginia Woolf . . . the longest novel by an English writer since Bennett's *Old Wive's Tale.*" The *New York World* said: "There is not a clouded motive, not a forced episode, not a false note." Edward Davison in the *New York Saturday Review* (23 April 1927) commented: "A difficult book to review because of its almost perfect technique." J. C. Squire said in *The Observer:* "Nowhere since Meredith's prime has the spring of love been so lyrically and yet so truthfully painted; the translation into married life is just as beautifully done." In the *New Statesman* (7 May 1927) Naomi Royde-Smith observed: "We have to go back sixty years for any parallel in size and subject to this entirely English tale. The exquisite passages of description are both brief and lovely."

The Brett Youngs traveled again to Egypt in 1925 and in 1928. The visits to Luxor and Thebes gave the novelist the material for the Egyptian part of *The Key of Life* (1928) and for "Glamour," a short story published in *The Cage Bird and Other Stories* (1933).

*My Brother Jonathan* (1928) concerns Wednesford (that is, Wednesbury) Cottage Hospital, which had been founded by Sir Joseph Hingston—Ralph's father from *Portrait of Clare*—"in aid of his baronetcy." The hospital has become a private nursing home run by unscrupulous doctors, and Jonathan, a young physician, successfully opposes them so that the poor can once again benefit from it. Place and atmosphere play an essential part in the story, with the opposition of Higgins' Buildings—slums where destitution and disease prevail—and Wolverbury Road, where the middle class lives. The portrait of middle-class smugness and deviousness is merciless, but the lower classes are not idealized: ignorance, superstition, and stupidity often hinder Jonathan's work and result in deaths that could have been avoided. The manuscripts bear evidence of the musical construction of books 2 and 3, with two double-entry tables noting the recurrence and intensity of nine themes.

The reviewer in the *Times Literary Supplement* (18 October 1928) said that "Mr. Brett Young . . . has a fluency and a power denied to the majority of his contemporaries in the craft of fiction." The novel sold well and was made into a successful movie in 1948.

The Brett Youngs traveled to the United States in 1928 for lectures in New York and Philadelphia. Brett Young's next novel, *Black Roses* (1929), deals with a cholera epidemic in Naples. The *Times Literary Supplement* (3 October 1929) said: "It is all admirably done with a fine feeling for the atmosphere of Southern Italy."

*Jim Redlake* (1930) was originally conceived as a picaresque novel, but it is also a bildungsroman, an historical novel, and a political novel. The cen-

*Brett Young during his years as a medical student at Birmingham University*

tral theme is a quest for identity. In 1900 eleven-year-old Jim is sent from Sedgebury, near Birmingham, to Thorpe Folville in Leicestershire to be brought up by his affectionate grandfather, Doctor Weston. Cynthia Folville, a young aristocrat, becomes his first love. He is befriended by the Reverend Malthus's family, particularly Malthus's daughter Catherine. After studying medicine in London and returning to Leicestershire for his grandfather's funeral, he takes the wrong train and makes "a journey backward" to Trewern, his family's ancestral manor in Shropshire. On the way he learns of Cynthia's marriage to his friend, the gifted and wealthy Julian Hinton. In despair, he catches pneumonia and collapses on the threshold of Trewern, where he is nursed back to physical and mental health by the owner, Walter Delahay. Delahay offers him the supervision of a large farm in South Africa. Joining General Smuts's campaign in German East Africa, Jim experiences the brotherhood of arms, which seems to him to reconcile the Boers and the British and to prepare the birth of a great nation. The account of military strategy is based on Smuts's own notebooks, which he had lent to the novelist. But Young also deals with more-delicate subjects, such as the scandalous malfunctioning of the sani-

*Dust jacket for Brett Young's novel of life in the Shropshire countryside*

tary services. At the end of this section of the novel Jim has become fully mature. Delahay's death deprives him of his best friend but makes him a wealthy man. Jim makes a second journey home, where he exorcizes the phantoms of the earlier part of his life. Julian has died in the war; Cynthia is now free and still in love with Jim. Jim realizes that this brilliant woman would smother him, and he makes the wise choice to marry Catherine Malthus. With Catherine he establishes himself as a gentleman farmer in Trewern. He plans to write a book—not about the war, but "About swallows, if you like, and . . . life in general: how extraordinarily rich it is, in spite of everything." The *Times Literary Supplement* (6 November 1930) declared that the novel "is one of those spacious stories of a young man's childhood and growing up . . . which in competent hands, such as the author's, never fail to be agreeable reading."

*Mr. and Mrs. Pennington* (1931) is a story of suburban life near Birmingham. Dick and Susan Pennington live in a jerry-built semidetached house grandly named Chatsworth. Dick has been educated at a second-rate public school, and Susan has attended a university. Inspired by fashionable notions of "Living Dangerously" and "Sinning Magnificently," Susan becomes the mistress of Harry Le-

vison, a wealthy seducer. Dick, informed of the affair by anonymous letters, confronts Solly Magnus, Harry's uncle, who dies of a heart attack. After a short imprisonment, Dick moves with Susan to Chapel Green; there, in the countryside, Susan can rediscover the value of permanence.

*The House under the Water* (1932) is one of Brett Young's major novels; it is a story of failure and betrayal, on the one hand, and of development and self-realization, on the other. Griffith Tregaron, a gambler married to Lucrezia, an Italian noblewoman, inherits the ancestral manor of Nant Escob in Wales. Instead of considering Nant Escob a sacred trust, Tregaron sells it to the city of North Bromwich so that one of the big dams of the Welsh Water Scheme can be built on the Garon River, which borders the estate. Tregaron is one of those insensitive souls who feels no affinity for place. His end is a case of poetic justice: the water of the Garon, which made his fortune, takes it back when it floods the Sedgebury Main Colliery, in which he had invested most of his money. Tregaron's daughter, Philippa, is his exact opposite: she is the living image of an ancestor whose portrait hangs in the manor house, and she can feel the spirit of the place. This is one of the many instances in Young's works

*Frontispiece and title page for Brett Young's sketch of Monk's Norton, Worcestershire*

of the use of objects to connect the present with the past and thereby to establish a sense of recurrence and permanence. The reader sees the beauty of the place through Philippa's eyes. She marries the neighboring farmer, Evan Vaughan, who is ennobled by his understanding of nature. Her favorite brother, Robert, slow and mechanically minded, is opposed to her other brother, Gerald, the brilliant soldier. Gerald dies at Bloemfontein during the Boer War, and Robert becomes an automobile magnate. The novelist's notebooks bear evidence of the musical construction of the work, which is based on ten themes. The review in the *Times Literary Supplement* (29 September 1932) concludes: "It is indeed a book rich in contrast and variety, and must rank as one of his finest accomplishments. He has discovered here his full powers as a narrator of incident, a judge of character and a master in prose description of the aspects and moods of nature. He sees and feels, and we see and feel with him." The novel was reprinted three times in 1932, and as part of the Severn Edition of Brett Young's works it was reprinted six times in 1935.

In 1932 the Brett Youngs bought Craycombe House in Worcestershire, which had been built in 1791. The novelist had good business sense and made the estate pay its way. His major novels from 1932 until his death in 1954 sold between 350,000 and 500,000 copies each; many were serialized for the BBC, and several were made into movies. Some were translated into German, Danish, Spanish, Finnish, Hungarian, Italian, Dutch, Polish, Portuguese, and Swedish.

In *This Little World* (1934) Col. Miles Ombersley, a country squire, and Joe Hackett, a nouveau riche industrial magnate from North Bromwich, are at first rivals for the estate of Chaddesbourne d'Abitot. But thanks to the diplomacy of Lady Ombersley, who embodies the spirit and charm of the place, they finally learn to respect each other, and they compromise their plans for the estate. Gerald Gould wrote in *The Observer:* "Mr. Brett Young's . . . passion for the traditions of the countryside as well as for its abiding or recurring beauties—the shapes, colours, and scents of place and season—deserve the expression at once rich and austere

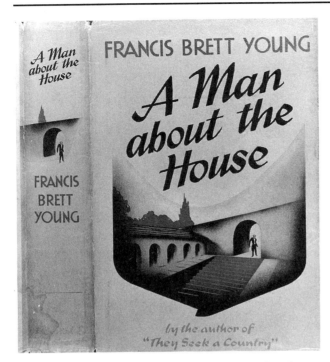

Dust jacket for the American edition of Brett Young's
melodramatic 1942 novel, expanded from an earlier
short story

that he is able to give it: moreover he can tell a
story."

*White Ladies* (1935) belongs to the English tradition of country-house novels. The title is the name
of the manor house for which Bella Tinsley, the
heiress to an industrial fortune, feels such an overwhelming passion that she marries its owner, Hugo
Pomfret. She has it rebuilt after its destruction by
fire in October 1911, sinking most of her fortune
into the project. The house is the central character
of the novel. The *Times Literary Supplement* (25 July
1935) said: "*White Ladies* is a novel that in challenging criticism disarms it . . . introduction and story together relate the whole to a century of critical development in European history."

*Far Forest* (1936) is set among farmhands, farm
maids, and chain makers of Mawne Heath. Adam
Wilden brings up his granddaughter, Jenny Hadley,
who was born in the town of Mawne and has been
rejected by her aunt, Mrs. Moule, one of Young's
great villains. Years later, when an institutional
charity attempts to take Jenny's children from her,
she goes back to the deserted ancestral cottage with
her cousin David, whose ambitions have been disappointed. Their long, silent love for each other can
now find expression, and old Adam's prophecy that
they would come back has come true. The reviewer
in the *Times Literary Supplement* (29 August 1936) sur-
rendered to the charm of the novel: "The picture of

Nineveh sunk in its dreaming forest, of the winter
and the floods there, of Gannow Green Farm and
the verdant Gothic aisles of the hops, of Mawne
Heath, ravaged by its factory settlement and yet still
retaining the 'thin and acrid' winds that used to
scrape its wastes 'like a jagged razor,' are faithful
with an intimacy that Hardy could not surpass."

In *Portrait of a Village* (1937) the village of
Monk's Norton, Worcestershire, and its crusty inhabitants are introduced in a succession of vignettes
associated with the various places and houses. The
work includes highly poetic passages that are almost
prose poems, as well as some of Young's rather dry
humor. The book is beautifully illustrated with
wood-engravings by Joan Hassall. The *Times Literary
Supplement* (4 December 1937) said: "Apart from the
portrait of their village, here is a portrait-gallery of
humans, some sketched with bold, firm lines, some
carefully etched, but all with the stamp of life on
them. . . . Mr. Brett Young is at his best."

*Dr. Bradley Remembers* (1938) is set in Sedgebury in the Black Country, where the inhabitants
have been physically stunted after generations of
working in cramped positions in the mine. Dr. John
Bradley, who is retiring from the medical profession, reminisces by the fireside on the evening of 31
October 1937, after his final surgery. His memories
retrace the development of medicine between 1880
and 1937. An aura of serenity pervades the often
cruel images that are set against the soft golden light
of a beautiful autumn evening. John was born in
1862; after his colorful father's death and his
mother's second marriage, he had been left in the
care of "Doctor" Mortimore, a one-legged bone-
setter. John's medical studies from 1881 until 1886
offer impressive descriptions of surgery before Joseph Lister introduced asepsis. John establishes himself in Sedgebury and marries Clara Medhurst.
Those are years of real happiness. Then, progres-
sively, John loses everything: Clara dies giving birth
to a daughter, who also does not survive; their son,
Matthew, fails in his medical studies, becomes a
drug addict, and commits suicide; and John loses all
his money in the Sedgebury Main Colliery disaster.
But he fights his way back to a comfortable and respected existence.

Brett Young and his wife traveled extensively
in South Africa in 1931, 1936, and 1938. Several
novels resulted from their journeys. *They Seek a
Country* (1937) begins in Worcestershire in 1836
with John Oakley's iniquitous sentence to transportation. On the convict ship *Minerva* he makes friends
with George Dicketts, a crusty one-legged veteran
of the Napoleonic Wars, and they manage to escape.
In South Africa they join the Prinsloos, a Boer fam-

ily, and with them undertake the Great Trek. The Boers see themselves as Old Testament patriarchs, and when they cross the Orange River, they believe they have reached the Promised Land. Many historical events are depicted in the novel: Boer dissensions at the ill-named United Laagers camp; the climb across the Drakensberg by Piet Retief's column; Retief's negotiations with the Zulu king Dingaan; the slaughter of Retief, Gerrit Maritz, and their companions by Dingaan's forces in February 1838; the destruction of Boer camps by the Zulus at Blauwkrans in March 1838; and the Boers' revenge at Blood River in December 1838. Oakley, who has taken the name of Grafton, and Lisbet are the only members of the Prinsloo family who escape from Blauwkrans with their lives. John and Lisbet's marriage is a symbol of the reconciliation of the Boers and the English and heralds the birth of a nation. The symbols of life multiply as they build their farm on the Witwatersrand near a spring and name it Wonderfontein. Lisbet gives birth to Adrian Grafton, whose name is half-English and half-Boer; she voices the novelist's hopes: "But he will be neither one nor the other, I think. When he grows to be a man he will call himself a South African or an Afrikander. Some day, perhaps, that will be a name to be proud of." The musical reference is explicit in the author's notebooks: the early drafts of *They Seek a Country* are titled "The Land of Promise: The African Symphony." The *Times Literary Supplement* (21 August 1937) said that the work "raises issues and interests outside the scope of the ordinary novel. . . . All that is told with that restrained eloquence characteristic of Mr. Brett Young's literary style, and illustrated by his convincing portraits of the Prinsloo family, their compatriots, John Oakley and Lisbet—altogether entertaining and sometimes piquant fare for the serious reader."

*The City of Gold* (1939) is a sequel to *They Seek a Country;* it follows the experiences of the Graftons from 1872 up to the outbreak of the Boer War. It prophesies the reconciliation of races that occurred some fifty years later. The novel includes some progressive views acknowledging the beauty and nobility of black African culture. Each member of the family symbolizes one of the possible attitudes to the race problem and participates in the musical counterpoint. The work prophesies the reconciliation of the races that would occur some fifty years later.

From 1939 to 1944 Brett Young contributed to the war effort by producing the maximum amount of food on Craycombe House's thirty-seven acres. He published his second collection of short stories, *Cotswold Honey, and Other Stories* (1940; published in

*Brett Young with his wife, Jessica, in Cape Town in 1945*

the United States as *The Ship's Surgeon's Yarn, and Other Stories,* 1940), and two light novels: *Mr. Lucton's Freedom* (1940; published in America as *The Happy Highway,* 1940), an escapist story that sends his hero from North Bromwich to the Marches of Wales on a quest for peace and regeneration, and *A Man about the House: An Old Wives' Tale* (1942), a melodramatic expansion of the short story "A Busman's Holiday" from *The Cage Bird and Other Stories.* In 1944 he published *The Island,* an epic poem of Britain from geological times to World War II. More than twenty thousand copies were sold during the first week of its publication. G. M. Trevelyan in *The Observer* (3 December 1944) noted that "Hardy's *Dynasts* started this sort of poetical history. . . . The balance and fusion of the two elements, the aid given by the history to the poetry, and by the poetry to the history, is the essence of the matter. . . . I remember that I said that Mr. Hardy's work was a new idea or form of literature and would have many successors. Here is one of them, and a good one." Excerpts from *The Island* are still often read during official ceremonies or religious services in Britain.

Heart disease, a consequence of Brett Young's 1916 bout with malaria, made running the estate too strenuous; in 1944 he sold Craycombe House and moved to South Africa. In 1947 the Board of Control of the South African Tourist Corporation commissioned him to write *In South Africa* (1952). Brett Young's health deteriorated rapidly after 1952, and he died in Cape Town on 28 March 1954. He left an unfinished novel that was published as *Wistanslow* (1956), the story of the friendship of a doctor's son and a young aristocrat.

Francis Brett Young's fictional universe forms a coherent whole in which places and characters reappear at various periods and are drawn with an almost documentary accuracy and, at the same time, a deep sense of the poetic. Worcestershire and the region around Birmingham have become Brett Young's country, just as Wessex is Hardy's. But Brett Young depicts South Africa with the same imaginative thoroughness, and biblical undertones connect Johannesburg, the City of Gold, and North Bromwich-Birmingham, the City of Iron. Many of his characters live in both places. He shows England changing over sixty years from the world's greatest power to the battered country left by World War II. His language is flexible and felicitous in finding the right word; he used to say that when a word was well chosen, it needed no adjective. His characters, male and female, are remarkably lifelike and, on the whole, attractive. There are few absolute villains in his world, but there are no complete angels either. He is fond of offering opposite and complementary views of the same situation—a method later used with success by C. P. Snow, who was one of his friends. He is a humanist for whom man is always the measure. His vision is lucid, and more ironic than indignant. He hides his craftsmanship behind a deceptive straightforwardness of narration, but his networks of imagery and counterpoint of themes, characters, and places make the reading of his works singularly rewarding.

**Interviews:**

Arnold Gyde, "Arrival of a Novelist: An Interview with Francis Brett Young," *World Today,* 53 (December 1928): 14–17;

M. J. Woddis, "Fiction and the Medical Profession: An Interview with Francis Brett Young," *Great Thoughts,* 1 (September 1931): 243;

Trevor Allen, "Interview," *John O'London's Weekly,* 62 (31 July 1953).

**Biographies:**

Jessica Brett Young, *Francis Brett Young: A Biography* (London: Heinemann, 1962);

A. S. Hill, *Francis Brett Young, Halesowen Born* (Dudley: Dudley Teachers' Centre, n.d.).

**References:**

Peter Barton, "Two Authors in East Africa," *Francis Brett Young Society Journal,* 34 (December 1995): 16–26;

David Cannadine, "Politics, Propaganda and Art: the Case of Two 'Worcestershire Lads,'" *Midland History,* 4 (Autumn 1977): 97–122;

Cannadine, "This Little World: The Value of the Novels of Francis Brett Young as a Guide to the State of Midland Society, 1870–1925," *Worcester Historical Society: Occasional Publications,* 4 (1982): 1–59;

Cannadine, "Two Worcestershire Lads: Stanley Baldwin and Francis Brett Young," *Francis Brett Young Society Newsletter,* 6 (December 1981): 1–25;

Glen Cavaliero, "Francis Brett Young's *Far Forest* and the English Rural Tradition," *Francis Brett Young Society Journal,* 9 (July 1983): 4–7;

Cavaliero, "Town and Country: Francis Brett Young, Winifred Holtby," in his *The Rural Tradition in the English Novel, 1900–1939* (London: Macmillan, 1977), pp. 81–100;

Victor Gregory, "Then and Now—The Setting of *Deep Sea,*" *Francis Brett Young Society Newsletter,* 4 (December 1980): 15–25;

H. Jack Haden, "*The House under the Water:* A Study in Fact and Fiction," *Francis Brett Young Society Journal,* 22 (December 1989): 12–30;

Haden, "*The Island* History: An Investigation," *Francis Brett Young Society Journal,* 32 (December 1994): 16–20;

Haden, "Stray Thoughts on *Portrait of Clare,*" *Francis Brett Young Society Journal,* 28 (December 1992): 10–20;

Haden, "*White Ladies* and Its Identification Puzzle," *Francis Brett Young Society Journal,* 29 (July 1993): 4–9;

Michael Hall, "After Francis Brett Young on Capri," *Francis Brett Young Society Journal,* 27 (July 1992): 6–21;

Hall, "'Indisputably Swan': An Assessment of *Mr. and Mrs. Pennington,*" *Francis Brett Young Society Journal,* 24 (December 1990): 23–44;

Hall, "*Jim Redlake:* The Education of an Artist," *Francis Brett Young Society Journal,* 32 (December 1994): 28–33;

Hall, "Tilton, Brett Young's Neglected Village," *Francis Brett Young Society Journal,* 21 (July 1989): 10–26;

Brian Harvey, "The Problem of Assessing Francis Brett Young," *Francis Brett Young Society Journal,* 12 (December 1984): 59–60;

Joe Hunt, "Francis and Hugh: A Tale of Two Writers," *Francis Brett Young Society Newsletter,* 3 (July 1980): 14–17;

Hunt, "Francis Brett Young and C. P. Snow," *Francis Brett Young Society Journal,* 10 (December 1983): 19–21;

Hunt, "Uffdown and Pen Beacon," *Francis Brett Young Society Journal,* 33 (July 1995): 29–31;

Leslie Jay, "The Importance of Place in the Midland Novels of Francis Brett Young," *Francis Brett Young Society Newsletter,* 4 (December 1980): 1–15;

Jay, "Mawne was a world in itself . . . ," *Francis Brett Young Society Journal,* 12 (December 1984): 32–46;

Liselotte Koranda, "Das Bild Englands in den Midlands Romanen von Brett Young," dissertation, University of Vienna, 1956;

Jacques Leclaire, *The Black Country* (Dudley: Dudley Teachers' Centre, 1980);

Leclaire, "The Brett Young Case," *Francis Brett Young Society Newsletter,* 2 (December 1979): 1–19;

Leclaire, "Character Creation in Francis Brett Young's Novels," *Francis Brett Young Society Journal,* 12 (December 1984): 47–58;

Leclaire, "*The City of Gold* and the Place of Africans in Francis Brett Young's Vision of the Birth of a South African Nation," *Francis Brett Young Society Newsletter,* 8 (December 1982): 6–13;

Leclaire, "Francis Brett Young's Narrative Stance in *The Young Physician,*" *Francis Brett Young Society Journal,* 38 (December 1997): 23–31;

Leclaire, *Francis Brett Young: The Black Country* (Dudley: Dudley Teachers' Centre, 1985);

Leclaire, *Francis Brett Young: The Green Country* (Dudley: Dudley Teachers' Centre, 1984);

Leclaire, "Francis Brett Young's Correspondence with His Wife During General Smuts's 1916 Campaign in German East Africa," *Francis Brett Young Society Journal,* 16 (December 1986): 9–19;

Leclaire, "Francis Brett Young's Regionalism," *Francis Brett Young Society Journal,* 20 (December 1988): 20–26;

Leclaire, "Histoire, politique et littérature dans *The City of Gold* de Francis Brett Young," *Commonwealth: Essays and Studies,* 1 (1975): 48–56;

Leclaire, "An Introduction to *Portrait of Clare* by Francis Brett Young," *Francis Brett Young Society Journal,* 28 (December 1992): 5–7;

Leclaire, "*The Island* as Francis Brett Young's Ultimate Act of Faith," *Francis Brett Young Society Journal,* 32 (December 1994): 7–15;

Leclaire, "*The Island* as the Epic of England," *Francis Brett Young Society Journal,* 10 (December 1983): 7–17;

Leclaire, "A Reassessment of Francis Brett Young: Some Questions That Need Answering," *Francis Brett Young Society Journal,* 12 (December 1984): 26–31;

Leclaire, "Slavery and Freedom in *Far Forest* by Francis Brett Young," *Francis Brett Young Society Journal,* 26 (December 1991): 4–11;

Leclaire, *Un Témon de l'Avènement de l'Angleterre Contemporaine, Francis Brett Young, 1884–1954* (Rouen: PUR / Paris: Didier, 1969); translated by Jacqueline Ivell as *Francis Brett Young: Physician, Poet, Novelist* (Kingswinford: Dulston Press, 1986);

Leclaire, "Le thème du voyage dans les romans de Francis Brett Young," in *Actes du Congrès de Nice de la SAES (1971)* (Paris: Didier, 1972), pp. 153–168;

Leclaire, "An Unpublished Brett Young Letter," *Francis Brett Young Society Newsletter,* 2 (December 1979): 8–9;

S. Soobiah, "Francis Brett Young at Epsom College," *Francis Brett Young Society Newsletter,* 1 (July 1979): 8–10;

E. G. Twitchett, *Francis Brett Young* (London: Wishart, 1935);

A. G. W. Whitfield, "Francis Brett Young: The Man, His Medicine and His Novels," *Francis Brett Young Society Journal,* 13 (July 1985): 30–38;

Muriel Brett Young, "Reminiscences of 'The Laurels,'" *Francis Brett Young Society Newsletter,* 2 (December 1979): 6–7.

## Papers:

The University of Birmingham holds the copyrights for Francis Brett Young's writings, and his manuscripts and papers are in the library there.

# Checklist of Further Readings

Aldridge, John W. *After the Lost Generation: A Critical Study of the Writers of Two Wars.* London: Vision, 1959.

Allen, Walter. *Tradition and Dream: The English and American Novel from the Twenties to Our Time.* London: Phoenix House, 1964.

Beauman, Nicola. *A Very Great Profession: The Women's Novel 1914–1939.* London: Virago, 1983.

Beddoe, Deirdre. *Back to Home and Duty: Women between the Wars 1918–39.* London: Pandora Press, 1989.

Bentley, Phyllis. *The English Regional Novel.* London: Allen & Unwin, 1941.

Bergonzi, Bernard. *Heroes' Twilight: A Study of the Literature of the Great War.* London: Constable, 1965.

Bergonzi. *Reading the Thirties: Texts and Contexts.* London: Macmillan, 1978.

Blamires, Harry. *Twentieth Century English Literature.* London: Macmillan, 1982.

Bloom, Clive. *Literature and Culture in Modern Britain. Volume One: 1900–1929.* London: Longman, 1993.

Blythe, Ronald. *The Age of Illusion: England in the Twenties and the Thirties. 1910–1940.* London: Hamish Hamilton, 1963; Oxford: Oxford University Press, 1983.

Booth, Allyson. *Postcards from the Trenches: Negotiating the Space between Modernism and the First World War.* New York: Oxford University Press, 1996.

Bracco, Rosa Maria. *Merchants of Hope: British Middlebrow Writers and the First World War, 1919–1939.* Providence, R.I.: Berg, 1993.

Branson, Noreen, and Margot Heinemann. *Britain in the Nineteen Thirties.* London: Weidenfeld & Nicolson, 1971.

Breen, Jennifer. *In Her Own Write: Twentieth-Century Women's Fiction.* London: Macmillan, 1990.

Bufkin, E. C. *The Twentieth-Century Novel in English. A Checklist,* second edition. Athens: University of Georgia Press, 1984.

Buitenhuis, Peter. *The Great War of Words: British, American, and Canadian Propaganda and Fiction, 1914–1933.* Vancouver: University of British Columbia Press, 1987.

Cadogan, Mary, and Patricia Craig. *Women and Children First: The Fiction of Two World Wars.* London: Gollancz, 1978.

Cavaliero, Glen. *The Rural Tradition in the English Novel, 1900–1939.* London: Macmillan, 1977.

Cawelti, John G. *Adventure, Mystery, and Romance: Formula Stories as Art and Popular Culture.* Chicago: University of Chicago Press, 1976.

Clark, J., M. Heinemann, D. Margolies, and C. Smee, eds. *Culture and Crisis in Britain in the '30s.* London: Lawrence & Wishart, 1979.

Cockburn, Claud, *Bestseller: The Books That Everyone Read, 1900–1939.* London: Sidgwick & Jackson, 1972.

Cole, G. D. H., and M. I. Cole. *The Condition of Britain.* London: Gollancz, 1937.

Colt, Rosemary, and Janice Rossen. *Writers of the Old School British Novelists of the 1930s.* Basingstoke: Macmillan, 1992.

Connolly, Cyril. *Enemies of Promise.* Boston: Little, Brown, 1939.

Cooper, Helen M., Adrienne Auslander Munich, and Susan Merrill Squier, eds. *Arms and the Woman: War, Gender, and Literary Representation.* Chapel Hill & London: University of North Carolina Press, 1989.

Craig, Cairns, ed. *The History of Scottish Literature,* volume 4: *The Twentieth Century.* Aberdeen: Aberdeen University Press, 1987.

Croft, Andy. *Red Letter Days: British Fiction in the 1930s.* London: Lawrence & Wishart, 1990.

Crosland, Margaret. *Beyond the Lighthouse: English Women Novelists in the Twentieth Century.* London: Constable, 1981.

Cunningham, Valentine. *British Writers of the Thirties.* Oxford: Oxford University Press, 1988.

Eksteins, Modris. "All Quiet on the Western Front and the Fate of a War," *Journal of Contemporary History,* 15 (1980): 345–366.

Eksteins. *The Great War and the Birth of the Modern Age.* Toronto: Denys, 1989.

Ellis, Geoffrey U. *Twilight on Parnassus: A Survey of Post-War Fiction and Pre-War Criticism.* London: M. Joseph, 1939.

Evans, Benjamin Ifor. *English Literature Between the Wars.* London: Methuen, 1948.

Fowler, Bridget. *The Alienated Reader: Women and Romantic Literature in the Twentieth Century.* Hemel Hempstead: Harvester Wheatsheaf, 1991.

Fox, Pamela. *Class Fictions. Shame and Resistance in the British Working-Class Novel, 1890–1945.* Durham & London: Duke University Press, 1994.

Fraser, G. S. *The Modern Writer and His World,* revised edition. London: Deutsch, 1964.

Frierson, William C. *The English Novel in Transition 1885–1940.* Norman: University of Oklahoma Press, 1942.

Fussell, Paul. *The Great War and Modern Memory.* London: Oxford University Press, 1975.

Gerber, Richard. *Utopian Fantasy: A Study of English Utopian Fiction Since the End of the Nineteenth Century.* London: Routledge & Kegan Paul, 1955.

Gilbert, Martin. *Britain and Germany between the Wars.* London: Longmans, 1964. New York: Barnes & Noble, 1967.

Gilbert, Sandra, and Susan Gubar. *No Man's Land: The Place of the Woman Writer in the Twentieth Century.* New Haven & London: Yale University Press, 1988–1994.

Gillie, Christopher. *Movements in English Literature, 1900–1940.* Cambridge: Cambridge University Press, 1975.

Gindin, James M. *British Fiction in the 1930s: The Dispiriting Decade.* New York: St. Martin's Press, 1992.

Gindin. *Postwar British Fiction: New Accents and Attitudes.* Berkeley & Los Angeles: University of California Press, 1962.

Gloversmith, Frank, ed. *Class, Culture and Social Change: A New View of the 1930s.* Brighton: Harvester, 1980.

Goldman, Dorothy, Jane Gledhill, and Judith Hattaway. *Women Writers and the Great War.* New York: Twayne, 1995.

Goldman. *Women and World War I: The Written Responses.* London: Macmillan, 1993.

Goldring, Douglas. *The Nineteen Twenties: A General Survey and Some Personal Memories.* London: Nicholson & Watson, 1945.

Green, Martin. *Children of the Sun: A Narrative of "Decadence" in England after 1918.* New York: Basic Books, 1976.

Greicus, M. S. *Prose Writers of World War One.* Harlow, Essex: Longman, 1973.

Hager, Philip E., and Taylor, Desmond. *The Novels of World War One: An Annotated Bibliography.* New York: Garland, 1981.

Harvey, Arnold D. *English Literature and the Great War with France: An Anthology and Commentary.* London: Nold Jonson, 1981.

Hawthorn, Jeremy, ed. *The British Working-Class Novel in the Twentieth Century.* London: Arnold, 1984.

Hewitt, Douglas John. *English Fiction of the Early Modern Period 1890–1940.* London: Longman, 1988.

Howarth, Patrick. *Play up and Play the Game: The Heroes of Popular Fiction.* London: Eyre Methuen, 1973.

Hughes, H. Stewart. *Consciousness and Society: The Reorientation of European Social Thought 1890–1930.* New York: Knopf, 1958.

Hynes, Samuel. *The Auden Generation: Literature and Politics in England in the 1930s.* London: Bodley Head, 1976; New York: Viking, 1977.

Hynes. *A War Imagined: The First World War and English Culture.* New York: Atheneum, 1991.

Ingram, Angela, and Daphne Patai. *Rediscovering Forgotten Radicals. British Women Writers 1889–1939.* Chapel Hill & London: University of North Carolina Press, 1993.

Jameson, Storm. *The Georgian Novel and Mr. Robinson.* London: Heinemann, 1929.

Joannou, Maroula. *"Ladies, Please Don't Smash These Windows": Women's Writing, Feminist Consciousness and Social Change 1918–1938.* Oxford: Berg, 1995.

Johnstone, Richard. *The Will to Believe: Novelists of the Nineteen-Thirties.* Oxford: Oxford University Press, 1982.

Klaus, H. Gustav, ed. *The Socialist Novel in Britain: Towards the Recovery of a Tradition.* New York: St. Martin's Press, 1982.

Klein, Holger, ed. *The First World War in Fiction: A Collection of Critical Essays.* London: Macmillan, 1976.

Light, Alison. *Forever England: Femininity, Literature and Conservatism between the Wars.* London: Routledge, 1991.

Lucas, John, ed. *The 1930s: A Challenge to Orthodoxy.* Hassocks: Harvester, 1978.

Markovic, Vida E. *The Changing Face: Disintegration of Personality in the Twentieth-Century British Novel, 1900–1950.* Carbondale: Southern Illinois University Press, 1970.

McMillan, Dougald. *Transition: The History of a Literary Era 1927–38.* London: Calder & Boyars, 1975.

Melman, Billie. *Women and the Popular Imagination in the Twenties: Flappers and Nymphs.* Basingstoke: Macmillan, 1988.

Miles, Peter, and Malcolm Smith. *Cinema, Literature and Society: Elite and Mass Culture in Interwar Britain.* London & New York: Methuen/Croom Helm, 1987.

Millett, Fred B. *Contemporary British Literature.* New York: Harcourt, Brace, 1935.

*Modernist Studies: Literature and Culture 1920–1940.* Special Supplement: "Women in the Literature and Culture of the Twenties and Thirties," 1, no. 3 (1974–1975).

Mowat, Charles Loch. *Britain between the Wars 1918–1940.* London: Methuen, 1956.

Muggeridge, Malcolm. *The Thirties, 1930–1940, in Great Britain.* London: Hamish Hamilton, 1940.

Myers, W. L. *The Later Realism: A Study of Characterization in the British Novel.* Chicago: University of Chicago Press, 1927.

O'Faolain, Sean. *The Vanishing Hero: Studies in Novelists of the Twenties.* London: Eyre & Spottiswoode, 1956.

Onions, John. *English Fiction and Drama of the Great War. 1918–1939.* New York: St. Martin's Press, 1990.

O'Rourke, Rebecca. "Where There No Women?: British Working Class Writing in the Inter-War Period," *Literature and History,* 14 (Spring 1988): 48–63.

Orwell, George. *The Lion and the Unicorn: Socialism and the English Genius.* London: Secker & Warburg, 1941.

Orwell. *The Road to Wigan Pier.* London: Gollancz, 1937.

Ouditt, Sharon. *Fighting Forces, Writing Women: Identity and Ideology in the First World War.* London & New York: Routledge, 1994.

Page, Norman. *The Thirties in Britain.* Basingstoke: Macmillan, 1990.

Parfitt, George. *Fiction of the First World War: A Study.* London: Faber & Faber, 1988.

Petter, Martin. "'Temporary Gentlemen' in the Aftermath of the Great War: Rank, Status and the Ex-Officer Problem," *Historical Journal,* 37 (1994): 127–152.

Pound, Reginald. *The Lost Generation.* London: Constable, 1964.

Priestley, J. B. *English Journey: Being a Rambling but Truthful Account of What One Man Saw and Heard and Felt and Thought during a Journey through England during the Autumn of the Year 1933.* London: Heinemann, 1934.

Pykett, Lyn. *Engendering Fictions: The English Novel in the Early Twentieth Century*. New York: St. Martin's Press, 1995.

Quinn, Patrick J., ed. *Recharting the Thirties*. Selinsgrove, Pa.: Susquehanna University Press / London: Associated University Presses, 1996.

Radford, Jean, ed. *The Progress of Romance: The Politics of Popular Fiction*. London: Routledge & Kegan Paul, 1986.

Radway, Janice. *Reading the Romance: Women, Patriarchy and Popular Literature*. Chapel Hill: University of North Carolina Press, 1984.

Raitt, Suzanne, and Trudi Tate, eds. *Women's Fiction and the Great War*. Oxford: Clarendon Press, 1997.

Rice, Thomas Jackson. *English Fiction, 1900–1950: General Bibliography and Individual Authors: A Guide to Information Sources,* 2 volumes. Detroit: Gale Research, 1979–1983.

Robbins, Bruce. *The Servant's Hand: English Fiction from Below*. New York: Columbia University Press, 1986.

Schwarz, Daniel R. *The Transformation of the English Novel 1890–1930*. Basingstoke: Macmillan, 1989.

Scott-James, Rolfe A. *Fifty Years of English Literature, 1900–1950: With a Postscript, 1951–1955*. London: Longmans, Green, 1956.

Shaw, Marion. "Feminism and Fiction between the Wars: Winifred Holtby and Virginia Woolf," in *Women's Writing: A Challenge to Theory,* edited by Moira Monteith. New York: St. Martin's Press, 1986, pp. 175–191.

Smith, David. *Socialist Propaganda in the Twentieth-Century British Novel*. London: Macmillan, 1978.

Spender, Stephen. *The Thirties and After: Party, Politics, People, 1933–75*. London: Macmillan, 1978.

Stableford, Brian. *Scientific Romance in Britain 1890–1950*. London: Fourth Estate, 1985.

Staley, Thomas. *Twentieth Century Women Novelists*. London: Macmillan, 1982.

Stevenson, John. *British Society 1914–45*. Harmondsworth: Penguin, 1984.

Stevenson and Chris Cook. *The Slump: Society and Politics during the Depression*. London: Cape, 1977.

Swinnerton, Frank. *Figures in the Foreground: Literary Reminiscences, 1917–1940*. London: Hutchinson, 1963; Garden City, N.Y.: Doubleday, 1964.

Swinnerton. *The Georgian Literary Scene 1910–1935: A Panorama*. New York: Farrar & Rinehart, 1934.

Symons, Julian. *The Thirties: A Dream Revolved*. London: Cresset, 1960.

Tindall, William York. *Forces in Modern British Literature, 1885–1956*. New York: Vintage, 1956.

Tylee, Claire M. *The Great War and Women's Consciousness: Images of Militarism and Womanhood in Women's Writing, 1914–1964*. Basingstoke: Macmillan, 1990.

Wall, Richard, and Jay Winter, eds. *The Upheaval of War: Family, Work, and Welfare in Europe, 1914–1918*. Cambridge: Cambridge University Press, 1988.

Ward, Alfred C. *The Nineteen-Twenties: Literature and Ideas in the Post-War Decade*. London: Methuen, 1930.

Ward. *Twentieth-Century English Literature, 1901–1960*. London: Methuen, 1964.

Williams, Raymond. *Culture and Society 1789–1950*. London: Chatto & Windus, 1958.

Wilson, Edmund. *Axel's Castle: A Study in the Imaginative Literature of 1870–1930*. London: Flamingo, 1984.

Wilson. *The Shores of Light: A Literary Chronicle of the Twenties and Thirties*. New York: Farrar, Straus & Young, 1952.

Wilson. *The Thirties: From Notebooks and Diaries of the Period,* edited by Leon Edel. London: Macmillan, 1980.

Winter, Jay. *Sites of Memory, Sites of Mourning: The Great War in European Cultural History*. Cambridge: Cambridge University Press, 1995.

Wohl, Robert. *The Generation of 1914*. Cambridge, Mass.: Harvard University Press, 1979.

# Contributors

Judith Adamson......................................................................Dawson College, Montreal
Leonard R. N. Ashley...............................Brooklyn College of the City University of New York
Alan Bishop.......................................................................................McMaster University
J. W. Blench.........................................................................................University of Durham
D. A. Boxwell.....................................................................................U.S. Air Force Academy
Karen M. Carney...........................................University of Illinois at Urbana-Champaign
Margaret Crosland.........................................Billingshurst, West Sussex, England
James Y. Dayananda............................................................Lock Haven University
Brian Evenson.................................................................Oklahoma State University
Diana Farr........................................................................Haslemere, Surrey, England
John Ferns.........................................................................................McMaster University
Maria Aline Seabra Ferreira.................................................Universidade de Aveiro
Lenemaja Friedman.............................................................................Columbus College
Mark A. Graves.......................................................Bowling Green State University
Sandra Hagan..................................................................................McMaster University
Allan Hepburn......................................................................................University of Toronto
Hilda Hollis........................................................................................McMaster University
Chris Hopkins...................................................................Sheffield Hallam University
Michael B. Jasper...............................................................Bilkent University, Turkey
Rosemary Erickson Johnsen...............................................Michigan State University
George J. Johnson....................................................................Waterdown, Ontario
Jacques Leclaire....................................................................Université de Rouen
Raymond N. MacKenzie.....................................................University of St. Thomas
Kathy March.................................................................................Cambridge, Ontario
Jim McWilliams....................................................................Troy State University
Sheri P. Midkiff.................................................................Williams Baptist College
Neville Newman...................................................................McMaster University
Paul W. Salmon......................................................................University of Guelph
Lisa M. Schwerdt.............................................California University of Pennsylvania
P. Joan Smith.......................................................................McMaster University
Sanford Sternlicht.................................................................Syracuse University
Wayne Templeton.....................................................Kwantlen University College
Eric Thompson.............................................Université du Québec à Chicoutimi
Kenneth Womack.....................................................................Penn State Altoona
T. J. L. Wynne-Tyson.......................................Fontwell, West Sussex, England
Teresa C. Zackodnik..........................................................University of Alberta

# Cumulative Index

*Dictionary of Literary Biography,* Volumes 1-191
*Dictionary of Literary Biography Yearbook,* 1980-1996
*Dictionary of Literary Biography Documentary Series,* Volumes 1-16

# Cumulative Index

**DLB** before number: *Dictionary of Literary Biography*, Volumes 1-191
**Y** before number: *Dictionary of Literary Biography Yearbook*, 1980-1996
**DS** before number: *Dictionary of Literary Biography Documentary Series*, Volumes 1-16

# B

# D

## E

# H

Cumulative Index

# K

ISBN 0-7876-1846-2